W9-CPZ-750

The Electrical Equipment Conspiracies

THE TREBLE DAMAGE ACTIONS

CHARLES A. BANE

The Electrical Equipment Conspiracies

THE TREBLE DAMAGE ACTIONS

FEDERAL LEGAL PUBLICATIONS, INC. / NEW YORK

Library of Congress Catalog Number 73–75126

ISBN 0–87945–023–1

Manufactured in the United States of America

Library of Congress Cataloging in Publication Data

Bane, Charles A 1913–
The electrical equipment conspiracies.

Includes bibliographical references.
1. Trusts, Industrial–United States–Law.
2. Electric machinery industry–Prices–United States.
I. Title.
KF1890.E4B3 343′.73′078 73–75126
ISBN 0–87945–023–1

For:

	EBB	
SBM	ACM	ABM
JBR		CSR Jr.
PBB	and	CAB Jr.

Contents

"People of the same trade seldom meet together even for merriment and diversion, but the conversation ends in a conspiracy against the public, or in some contrivance to raise prices."

ADAM SMITH—The Wealth of Nations

CHAPTER 1

The criminal proceedings

On February 16, 1960, after months of rumors, a federal grand jury sitting in Philadelphia returned in the United States District Court for the Eastern District of Pennsylvania six indictments, initiating criminal proceedings against the leading manufacturers of electrical equipment in the nation and certain of their individual officers and employees. Each indictment related to a conspiracy in a different product line ranging from large equipment such as oil circuit breakers to smaller items, sold almost from the shelf, such as insulators and bushings. Over the next several months, through June 1960, the same grand jury was to return twelve further indictments in twelve additional product lines, including the massive equipment of the industry, turbine generators, and other large-scale items such as power switchgear assemblies and power transformers. With the addition in September and October 1960 of two further indictments, in meters and power capacitors, the Philadelphia grand jury had returned a total of twenty indictments with respect to almost every product utilized in the generation, transmission or distribution of electricity, whether by investor-owned utilities; federal government agencies such as the TVA; public power authorities; rural electric cooperatives; municipalities engaged in the distribution of electricity; industrial enterprises engaged in the generation of electricity as a part of their manufacturing operations; and certain foreign enterprises.

General Electric Company and Westinghouse Electric Corporation, the two acknowledged leaders in the electrical equipment industry, were named in nineteen of the twenty indictments. Allis-Chalmers Manufacturing Company was indicted in eight, I-T-E Circuit Breaker Company in eight, McGraw-Edison Company in seven, and then down the list of practically every major or specialist manufacturer of electrical equipment in the industry.

The turbine generator indictment (No. 20401, filed June 29, 1960) named the three large manufacturers of turbine generators as defendants, General Electric, Westinghouse, Allis-Chalmers, and in addition indicted General Electric employees Ginn, Vice President and General Manager—Turbine Division; Saupe, General Manager—Large Steam Turbine Generator Department; and Westinghouse employees Mauntel, Sales Manager—Steam Division, and Rowland, Vice President—Steam Division. Named as co-conspirators but not indicted in turbine generators were Carrier Corporation, Worthington Corporation and DeLaval Turbine Company.

The turbine indictment charged that the defendant corporations, who accounted for 95% of all turbine generators manufactured and sold in the United States (a business according to the indictment in which sales amounted to $400 million per year during the period 1955-1959), combined and conspired beginning at least as early as November 1955 ("the exact date being to the grand jury unknown") and continuing up to the date of the indictment:

" a. To fix and maintain prices, terms and conditions for the sale of turbine-generator units; and

b. To submit noncompetitive, collusive, and rigged bids and price quotations for supplying turbine-generator units to electric utility companies, Federal, State and local governmental agencies, and other purchasers."

The indictments specified the steps and actions taken by the defendants in order to carry out the conspiracy in turbine generators:

" a. Representatives of defendant corporations have, from time to time, discussed and agreed upon changes in the prices of turbine-generator units. Included among such price agreements are the following:

1. Representatives of defendant corporations met and agreed upon adjustments in the price of certain types of turbine-generator units. Thereafter, on or about April 15, 1957, such price adjustments were put into effect.

2. Representatives of defendant corporations held a number of meetings during which prices were discussed and a 5% increase agreed upon, with the further agreement that General Electric Company would be the first to announce such price increase. Thereafter, on June 20, 1957, General Electric Company announced such price increase of approximately 5% on turbine-generator units, effective July 1, 1957. The other defendants followed with similar price increases.

3. Representatives of defendant corporations met and agreed upon a price increase of approximately 3% on turbine-generator units. Thereafter General Electric Company announced such price increase of approximately 3%, effective April 28, 1958.

b. Representatives of defendant and co-conspirator corporations frequently discussed and agreed upon bids and quotations to be made to particular prospective customers. It was agreed that one of the defendant or co-conspirator corporations would be given what was designated as 'position,' and that the other defendant and co-conspirator corporations bidding or quoting on the specific project would bid or quote a higher price than the manufacturer having 'position.'"

As an example of the position arrangements charged against the defendants, the turbine generator indictments cited the following:

" At a meeting at the Barclay Hotel in New York City in about September 1957, representatives of defendant manufacturers met and discussed invitations for bids issued by Tennessee Valley Authority for a 500,000 kilowatt turbine-generator unit. It was agreed that General Electric Company would have 'position.' Thereafter General Electric Company bid approximately $16,-112,000 and Westinghouse Electric Corporation bid approximately $16,225,000 to Tennessee Valley Authority. The contract was awarded to General Electric Company."

As to price fixing arrangements, the indictment specified a meeting in New York City:

" On or about December 2, 1958 a meeting was held in New York City and attended by representatives of all of the defendant and co-conspirator corporations. At this meeting it was agreed, among other things, that on sealed bids the manufacturers would quote no lower than approximately 3% off published book prices, and that on transactions involving price negotiations the manufacturers would quote no lower than approximately 5% off published book prices."

The indictment further charged that frequent oral communications took place between the co-conspirators and that:

> "In the course of these communications, various procedures were adopted for the purpose of avoiding detection, including telephone calls to and from residences of company officials, and the use of public telephone pay stations."

Other indictments in the major fields of equipment followed a like pattern. The power transformer indictment (No. 20361, returned May 29, 1960) charged a price fixing and market allocation conspiracy in power transformers by General Electric, Westinghouse, Allis-Chalmers, McGraw-Edison, and two smaller specialist companies, Moloney Electric Company and Wagner Electric Corporation. Named as individual conspirators were General Electric Company Transformer Division employees Ginn (in his capacity as Vice President and General Manager), Seaman and Smith; Westinghouse Electric Corporation's Transformer Division employees Chiles (in his capacity as Vice President) and McCollom; Allis-Chalmers Power Equipment Division Vice President, McMullen; and McGraw-Edison's Transformer Division Sales Manager, Swoish. This indictment charged a conspiracy in power transformers, separate from and carried out by different individuals from those engaged in the conspiracies in other product lines charged in other indictments. The charge with respect to transformers, which were stated in the indictment to represent a business of $210 million annually during the four years preceding the indictment, was that the conspiracy had begun at least as early as 1956 and that the substantial terms of the conspiracy had been action by the manufacturers

> " a. To fix and maintain prices, terms and conditions for the sale of power transformers;
>
> b. To allocate among themselves the business of selling power transformers to Federal, State and local governmental agencies;
>
> c. To submit noncompetitive, collusive, and rigged bids for power transformers to Federal, State, and local governmental agencies; and
>
> d. To submit noncompetitive, collusive, and rigged price quotations for power transformers to electric utility companies, private industrial corporations and other manufacturers of electrical equipment."

The indictment charged that sealed bid business (which is principally the business of governmental agencies) had been divided among the manufacturers by agreement so that each manufacturer would have the following percentages of the business:

General Electric Company	30 percent
Westinghouse Electric Corporation	30 percent
Allis-Chalmers Manufacturing Company	15 percent
Moloney Electric Company	10 percent
McGraw-Edison Company	8 percent
Wagner Electric Corporation	5 percent

In the indictment in power switchgear assemblies (No. 20399, filed June 22, 1960, superseding Indictment No. 20234, filed February 16, 1960), the manufacturers named as conspirators were General Electric, Westinghouse, Allis-Chalmers, I-T-E Circuit Breaker Company and Federal Pacific Electric Company. The individuals named were General Electric's Switchgear Division employees Burger, Burens, Hentschel, Houston Jones and Stehlik. This indictment also indicted as a conspirator General Electric's A. F. Vinson, Vice President and Group Executive-Apparatus and Industrial Group, the highest ranking officer of any manufacturer named in any of the indictments; Westinghouse employees Fuller, Payne and Thompson; Allis-Chalmers' Long, Nolan and Webb. This indictment (see Appendix 1) was typical of the others which had been and were yet to be filed, but alleged a method of dividing sealed bid business among the conspirators which was distinctive. After alleging a number of meetings held at various places throughout the United States attended by representatives of the defendant corporations, the indictment went on:

" e. At these periodic meetings, a scheme or formula for quoting nearly identical prices to electric utility companies, private industrial corporations and contractors was used by defendant corporations designated by their representatives as a 'phase of the moon' or 'light of the moon' formula. Through cyclic rotating positioning inherent in the formula one defendant corporation would quote the low price, others would quote intermediate prices and another would quote the high price; these positions would be periodically rotated among the defendant corporations. This formula was so calculated that in submitting prices to these customers, the price spread between defendant corporations' quotations would be sufficiently wide so as to give an appearance of competition. This formula was designed to permit each defendant corporation to know the exact price it and every other defendant corporation would quote on each prospective sale;

f. At these periodic meetings, a cumulative list of sealed bid business secured by all of the defendant corporations was also circulated and representatives present would compare the relative standing of each corporation according to its agreed upon percentage of the total sales pursuant to sealed bids. The representatives present would then discuss particular future bid invitations and designate which defendant corporation should submit the lowest bid therefor, the amount of such bid, and the amount of the bid to be submitted by others;

g. In connection with the meetings and understanding described above, precautionary measures were adopted by representatives of defendant corporations to avoid detection, such as minimizing telephone calls, avoiding leaving notepapers in hotel rooms where meetings were held and avoiding social contacts among such representatives in the hotels where meetings were being held. In addition, code numbers identifying defendant corporations were used in documents effectuating the 'phase of the moon' formula referred to above."

The effects of these activities were spelled out in the power switchgear assemblies indictment, in terms similar to like recitals in the other indictments:

" The effects of the aforesaid combination and conspiracy have been that:

a. Prices of power switchgear assemblies throughout the United States have been raised, fixed and maintained at high and artificial levels;

b. Price competition in the sale of power switchgear assemblies throughout the United States has been restrained, suppressed and eliminated;

c. Purchasers of power switchgear assemblies throughout the United States have been deprived of the benefits of free competition in the purchase of these products; and

d. Public agencies engaged in the generation, transmission or distribution of electricity have been denied the right to receive competitive sealed bids, as required by law, and have been forced to pay high, artificially-fixed prices for power switchgear assemblies."

Upon arraignment in March 1960 for pleading to the first indictments returned by the grand jury, General Electric and

Westinghouse uniformly pled not guilty, as did most of the indicted individuals. However, certain of the manufacturers, including Allis-Chalmers, Federal Pacific, I-T-E Circuit Breaker Company (with respect to some but not all of the indictments in which that company was named), and certain of the small specialist manufacturers, such as Ohio Brass Company, Lapp Insulator, Porcelain Insulator, A. B. Chance, H. K. Porter and Joslyn Manufacturing, offered pleas of *nolo contendere.*[1]

U. S. Attorney General William P. Rogers, in an affidavit[2] filed with the court, opposed the entry of the *nolo contendere* pleas upon the grounds that the violations charged were of a most serious nature; that the grand jury investigations were continuing and the acceptance of *nolo contendere* pleas in the first cases might set a pattern for other indictments that were to follow. The position of the Attorney General was accepted by the court and the *nolo* pleas were rejected. Shortly thereafter, Allis-Chalmers and its employee Long changed their pleas, in the only case in which they had been charged as defendants up to that time (oil circuit breakers), from *nolo contendere* to guilty.

No formal proceedings were thereafter had until November 1960. Further indictments, as indicated, had been entered in the meantime and the Government gave every indication of preparing for trial on the power switchgear assemblies indictment, Criminal No. 20399. But just prior to the set trial date of November 17, 1960, counsel from the Antitrust Division of the Department of Justice and counsel for the defendants appeared before Chief Judge Ganey in Philadelphia to outline an understanding arrived at with respect to the presentation of voluntary pleas of the defendants with respect to all twenty indictments.

Some of the background of the negotiations with the Government leading to the pleas in the Philadelphia criminal proceed-

---

1 *Nolo contendere* is a phrase which, literally translated, means that the pleader does not wish to contest the charges. The plea is generally regarded by the pleader as being neither an affirmance nor a denial of the charges, but the consequence is that a judgment of guilty is entered by the trial court upon a plea of *nolo contendere* just as in the case of a plea or finding of guilty.

2 Attorney General Rogers' affidavit is reprinted in CLABAULT & BURTON, SHERMAN ACT INDICTMENTS 1955-1965, at 58-62 (New York: Federal Legal Publications, Inc., 1966).

ings is given in an affidavit of Howard J. Aibel, of counsel to General Electric, dated May 11, 1962, filed with Judge Robson in the Northern District of Illinois:

> " During the month of September 1960 discussions took place between counsel for General Electric and the Government, represented by the Assistant Attorney General, Antitrust Division, Department of Justice, and other attorneys of the Antitrust Division, exploring the possibility of settlement. The Government demands were unacceptable to General Electric and to a number of other defendants who had explored settlement possibilities, including various individual defendants associated with the different defendant companies. Accordingly, General Electric reached the decision to stand trial.
>
> The Government selected *United States* v. *Westinghouse Electric Corporation, et al.*, Criminal No. 20399, as the first case for trial. A special staff of prosecutors was assigned to this matter and the trial was set to commence before a jury in Philadelphia on Monday, October 31, 1960. On Friday, October 28, a pretrial conference was called by the trial judge, Chief Judge Ganey of the United States District Court for the Eastern District of Pennsylvania. The Court invited to this pretrial counsel for all parties in No. 20399 as well as counsel for defendants in the other related cases not yet scheduled for trial. At this conference in chambers the Court suggested that the Government and the corporate and individual defendants make a further effort at settlement. The Court mentioned the risks of litigation and the Court observed that in the event that pleas were entered and trial avoided, with a saving of time and expense for the Government and the Court, the Court in sentencing might be able to give the normal special consideration which would not be possible if the defendants stood trial and were found guilty before a jury. At prior arraignments in open court the Government had taken the position that it would oppose the entry of a nolo contendere plea by any party, and the Court had in fact refused to accept such pleas after receiving an affidavit of Attorney General Rogers strongly urging such a ruling. On October 28, however, the Court suggested that the Government re-examine its position on nolo pleas in view of the additional cases filed in the interim and in view of the Court's stated intention to treat nolo pleas and guilty pleas alike in imposing sentence. The Court also said it would make its auspices available to assist the parties in reaching agreement and asked the parties to submit periodic reports on their progress. When the parties expressed a willingness further to explore settlement, the Court ordered that the trial be temporarily postponed.

There then ensued a series of conferences between various defense counsel and attorneys for the Antitrust Division. A number of conferences were also held with the Court. These discussions commenced on Monday, October 31, and continued intermittently thereafter. In the course of these negotiations the Government advised the Court that it would oppose the entry of nolo pleas in only seven cases and would accede to nolo pleas by individual and corporate defendants in all other cases. The Court then offered a hearing to parties who desired to plead nolo contendere in the seven cases known as the 'guilty' cases and decided, over Government objection, to accept some nolo pleas from particular defendants in these 'guilty' cases.

Thereafter further negotiations took place between counsel for various defendants and counsel for the Government. Ultimately a compromise agreement was reached between the defendants and counsel for the Government pursuant to which certain defendants agreed to plead guilty in certain cases and the Government agreed not to oppose pleas of nolo contendere by other defendants. Then at a further arraignment on Thursday, December 8 pleas of guilty or nolo contendere were entered in accordance with the agreed upon plan as modified and accepted by the Court and judgment entered thereon."

When proceedings opened before Judge Ganey on November 17, 1960, Baddia Rashid for the Government stated that of the twenty indictments, seven were considered by the Government to be the most important and to represent the most flagrant violations, in accordance with three criteria that had been set forth in the Attorney General's affidavit: (1) whether the violation showed persistent acts over a period of time and was of a very flagrant nature; (2) whether the measures for concealment in the particular cases were so clear and persuasive that the conclusion had to be drawn that the defendants' representatives beyond doubt realized the nature of their deeds; and (3) that there was a significant public impact which resulted particularly as respects the federal, state and local governmental agencies as substantial purchasers of the product in question.

Government's counsel stated that there seemed to be seven cases that met all three of these criteria: turbine generators, power transformers, power switchgear assemblies, oil circuit breakers, power switching equipment, condensers and industrial control equipment. He stated that the Government would require guilty pleas from the corporations and the individuals indicted in these seven product lines, and in return the Government would be willing to acquiesce and urge acceptance by the court of *nolo contendere* pleas by the corporate and individual defendants in the remaining thirteen product lines.[3]

General Electric and Westinghouse were to plead guilty to all seven of the "flagrant" conspiracies, and Allis-Chalmers was to reaffirm its plea of guilty as theretofore entered with respect to five out of the seven indictments in which that company was named. Some slight leeway was granted to some of the other corporate defendants: Joslyn Manufacturing and Schwager-Wood were permitted to file pleas of *nolo contendere* in power switching equipment as was Carrier Corporation in condensers, Federal Pacific and I-T-E Circuit Breaker in oil circuit breakers.

The Government's agreement with the individual defendants contemplated that in the case of an individual indicted in two of the cases within the seven-case group, an individual pleading guilty in one would be permitted to plead *nolo* in the other. Accordingly, Ginn, who was to plead guilty to the power transformer indictment, was to be permitted to plead *nolo contendere* in turbine generators. Showing some further leeway, three other individuals named in the turbine generator indictment, Houston Jones who was also in the power switchgear assemblies indictment, and Crawford and Long who were also in the oil circuit breaker indictment, were to be allowed to plead *nolo contendere.*

It was made clear that the arrangement was, of course, subject to the court's approval. This led to a certain stickiness, as indicated in the transcript of the proceedings of November 17, 1960, before Judge Ganey. Defendants who were to plead guilty to certain of the indictments and were to be allowed to return to plead *nolo contendere* to others, were understandably reluctant to have the cases called one by one (as they were by the court), with the "guilty" cases coming first: defendants then had to plead guilty in the early cases with no more than a hope or expectation that the court would approve their *nolo contendere*

---

[3] Distribution transformers, low voltage power circuit breakers, low voltage distribution equipment, watt-hour meters, insulators, power capacitors, lightning arresters, instrument transformers, meter transformers, bushings, isolated phase bus, navy and marine switchgear and open fuse cutouts.

pleas in the later cases. But all went according to schedule and the understanding, and the trial in No. 20399 (power switchgear assemblies) was deferred.

During the course of the November 1960 hearings Assistant Attorney General Bicks stated that the indictments had been the result of more than eighteen months' investigation and showed:

> " . . . a pattern of violations which can fairly be said to range among the most serious, the most flagrant, the most pervasive, that have ever marked any basic American industry."

Several corporate defendants, in urging the court to accept *nolo contendere* pleas even though the product line was among the "flagrant seven," made arguments that were to recur time and time again during the proceedings. Federal Pacific, with reference to oil circuit breakers, argued that it was capable of competing with Westinghouse and General Electric, the giants of that industry, but that if it was forced to plead guilty it might be subjected to damage claims so large that it would either be driven out of business or so severely injured that it could provide no competition of any kind. It was urged that the public interest required that the smaller companies be permitted to survive and to assert some measure of competition in the industry. It was also argued that in a situation where two major companies, such as General Electric and Westinghouse, do 80% of the business in an industry, the large companies must have been the prime movers in any conspiracy or action in restraint of trade that might have taken place. Attorney General Bicks, responding to these arguments, stated to the court that the question of whether any or what amount of liability for damages might be suffered by the defendants had not entered into the Government's opposition to the *nolo* pleas. Federal Pacific's plea of *nolo contendere* was accepted.

Counsel for Burke, Crawford and Schiek, employees of General Electric, in urging that the court accept their pleas of *nolo contendere* to the oil circuit breaker indictment, expounded upon the position of the individual employee in modern corporate enterprise:

> " Another element, sir, which I would urge upon you is the fact that in modern American economy I think that we are confronted with something which is in our literature, it is in the magazine

articles, it is in our motion pictures, our plays, there is the kind of thing known as the 'organization man.' And where you have the kind of situation which the Government's investigation has disclosed here, I think that it does not take any unreasonable concentration upon the problem to recognize that as to a particular individual low down in the corporate hierarchy, it becomes incumbent upon him to go along with what has become a corporate way of life or even an industry way of life, or else his own job is at stake."

The same attorney, in developing further the thought that meeting with competitors is "a corporate way of life" had this to say with respect to Burke:

" Moreover, sir, actually when I speak of a corporate way of life, the fact is in connection with Mr. Burke, that when he first was given the job as long ago as 1951 he was informed by the gentleman who indoctrinated him in his job, a gentleman, alas, now dead, that part of the job required his meeting with competitors."

It was also brought out that Burke had been disciplined by General Electric following the revelation of his activities by being reduced four levels in the company's job roster and that this represented a loss upwards of $30,000 in annual compensation.[4]

Counsel for General Electric felt that he had to respond to the "organization man" argument by pointing out that General Electric had established a policy which forbade its employees from engaging in any activity which might violate the antitrust laws:

" This corporation has had a considered, deliberate policy designed to prevent the very type of occurrence with which we are suddenly confronted here. That policy, which has been referred to here as policy 20.5, created the atmosphere and created the standard under which those loyal to the company should have conducted their affairs. They were under no compulsion to go along. They were directed, by a directive that could not be changed, to observe a wholly different course of conduct than the conduct that some of them, at least, appear now willing to say they were involved in.

---

4 Burke's plea of *nolo contendere* was not allowed and he thereupon pleaded guilty. The *nolo* pleas of Crawford and Schiek were accepted.

This policy was issued in 1954. It has been reissued and re-emphasized through the company. It states:

No employee shall enter into any understanding, agreement, plan, or scheme, expressed or implied, formal or informal, with any competitor, in regard to prices, terms, or conditions of sale, production, distribution, territories, or customers, nor exchange or discuss with a competitor prices, terms, or conditions of sale, or any other competitive information, nor engage in any other conduct which, in the opinion of company's counsel, violates any of the antitrust laws."

The court responded to General Electric's statement that what their employees were doing was contrary to the company's expressed policy:

" THE COURT: Why were they doing that? I don't know whether they got bonuses or whether they got chances for advancement or anything else. Aside from that, I don't know and I wouldn't use it as weighing the balance in the determination of the application here made, but I have been struck with this attitude all along, that if they were doing this meeting, making these arrangements, rigging prices, and having these allotments made, certainly I am not naive enough to believe that General Electric didn't know about it and it didn't meet with their hearty approbation."

Counsel for Saupe, an employee of General Electric indicted in the turbine generator case (No. 20401), argued on behalf of a *nolo contendere* plea for Saupe that, although Saupe may have talked with competitors, it was done in a "friendly and kidding manner." Rashid, responding for the Government, stated that the meetings between competitors in the turbine generators field consisted of:

" [O]ne, the high-level meetings at which they agreed upon the market price levels, percentages off book prices that they would adhere to. You have a series of price agreements. In fact, during the period covered by the indictment there were six price increases—April 1956 a 10 percent increase; September 1956 a 10 percent increase; April of 1957 price adjustments; December 1957 price adjustments; a 5 percent increase in July of 1957, and a 3 percent increase in April 1958.

In addition to those two aspects you also have the working level meetings at which specific jobs, specific turbine generator jobs, were allocated. The Grand Jury investigation disclosed, out of the many hundreds of jobs, instances of at least eighty where we have specific testimony on the allocation."

He then pointed out that Saupe had been a frequent attender at the so-called high level meetings and that one of Saupe's subordinates at General Electric had testified before the grand jury:

> " . . . that he had kept Mr. Saupe informed of his activities and on occasions discussed with him the collusive bid practices with competitors." [5]

At the conclusion of the proceedings in November 1960, the court recessed for final determination on the contested *nolo contendere* pleas and for sentencing. On the date set for sentencing, February 6, 1961, Chief Judge Ganey stated that he wanted to make certain observations concerning the indictments. He recalled that they covered some forty-eight individual defendants and thirty-two corporations, comprising virtually every large manufacturer of electrical equipment in the industry:

> " This is a shocking indictment of a vast section of our economy, for what is really at stake here is the survival of the kind of economy under which this country has grown great, the free enterprise system."

He expressed his agreement with the characterization given to the conduct of the corporate and individual defendants by Assistant Attorney General Bicks as having "flagrantly mocked the image of that economic system of free enterprise which we profess to the country," the court adding:

> " [I]t has destroyed the model, it seems to me, which we offer today, as a free world alternative to state control, to socialism, and eventual dictatorship."

The court stated that some idea of the vastness of the schemes for price fixing, bid rigging and job allocations could be gathered from the fact that the annual corporate sales covered by the indictments represented $1,750,000,000. The court then expressed its opinion as to where the blame should be placed:

> " [T]he real blame is to be laid at the doorstep of the corporate defendants and those who guide and direct their policy. While

---

5 Saupe's plea of *nolo contendere* was accepted by the court.

> the Department of Justice has acknowledged that they were unable to uncover probative evidence which would secure a conviction beyond a reasonable doubt of those in the highest echelons of the corporations here involved, in a broader sense they bear a grave responsibility; for one would be most naive indeed to believe that these violations of the law, so long persisted in, affecting so large a segment of the industry, and, finally, involving so many millions upon millions of dollars, were facts unknown to those responsible for the corporation and its conduct."

He therefore concluded that heavy fines would be imposed upon the corporate defendants.

As to the individual defendants, the court pointed out that both Attorney General Brownell and Attorney General Robert Kennedy (who had become Attorney General with the inauguration of the John F. Kennedy administration) had by letter agreed with recommendations of the Government that certain individuals serve prison sentences due to the serious nature of the violations. The court indicated that in imposing sentences it would make no distinction as between *nolo contendere* and guilty pleas, treating them as equivalents. Prison sentences would be imposed upon individuals who had ultimate responsibility for corporate conduct. In the case of individuals who had no such ultimate responsibility but rather represented the conformist, the organization man, fines and a probationary period would be the ruling:

> "[I]n the great number of these defendants' cases they were torn between conscience and an approved corporate policy, with the rewarding objectives of promotion, comfortable security and large salaries—in short, the organization or company man, the conformist, who goes along with his superiors and finds balm for his conscience in additional comforts and the security of his place in the corporate setup. That this can not in any wise be a defense to their misconduct is conceded, but long probationary periods, where a watchful eye can be kept on their activities, and fines, will suffice for these first offenses."

The first case called for sentencing was power transformers, where the Government's recommendations for sentencing were:

General Electric Company, $50,000.[6]

Westinghouse Electric Corporation, $50,000.

---

[6] Fifty thousand dollars was the maximum corporate fine established for violations of the Sherman Act. As it turned out, of the 108 corporate

Allis-Chalmers Manufacturing Company, $30,000.

McGraw-Edison Company, $25,000.

Wagner Electric Corporation, $20,000.

Moloney Electric Company, $15,000.

J. H. Chiles, Jr., $4,000, plus four months in jail.

W. S. Ginn, $5,000, plus six months in jail.

R. N. McCollom, $2,500, plus two months in jail.

J. W. McMullen, $2,500, plus four months in jail, with most, if not all, of the jail sentence suspended.

J. W. Seaman, $3,000, plus two months in jail.

W. R. Swoish, $2,000, plus three months in jail.

R. W. Smith, $2,500, plus four months in jail, with two months of the jail term suspended.

The court scaled down the fines proposed by the Government, generally by $1,000, in the case of the corporate defendants; in the case of certain individuals (Chiles and Ginn on the power transformer indictment), jail sentences actually to be served were imposed, to the surprise of the business community, but in no case in excess of thirty days. As to individual fines, in several instances, as in the case of McMullen, Smith and Swoish, the fines were increased over those recommended by the Government—McMullen and Smith to $3,000, Swoish to $5,000.

The corporate and individual defendants asserted a variety of arguments for special consideration or mitigation of sentence. General Electric, when its turn came to step to the bar of the court, argued that it could demonstrate that it had a corporate philosophy directly contrary to the illegal conduct involved in the proceeding:

---

fines imposed in the electrical equipment conspiracy cases, only one corporation (General Electric in turbine generators—see Appendix 2) received the maximum fine.

A 1969 proposal by Attorney General Mitchell to increase the maximum fine from $50,000 to $500,000 has been approved by a majority of the Committee on Criminal Practice and Procedure of the Antitrust Section of the American Bar Association, but has not been adopted by Congress.

"It simply is not a fact that there was a way of life in this company which permitted, tolerated, or winked at these violations. The men in the field who were responsible would not have been involved if they had obeyed this policy: they were out of step with the organization when they departed from the code of conduct laid down by the company."

The court responded that it believed that "20.5 was observed in its breach rather than in its enforcement," and imposed a fine of $40,000 on General Electric on this single bill of indictment.

When the turn of the individuals came, the court was adamant in adhering to its rule of imposing prison sentences where the individual had authority and responsibility, even as against pleas as to the individual's stature and reputation in the community. Counsel for Chiles stated to the court:

"Finally, your Honor, these men are not grasping, greedy, cutthroat competitors; they are men who devote a substantial time and a substantial part of their substance to their communities, to their fellow men. I give you Mr. Chiles as an example—a fellow of the American Institute of Electrical Engineers, chairman of the American Standards Association Transformer Committee, and a member of the Pennsylvania Society of Professional Engineers. Mr. Chiles has been active in his church, is a vestryman, senior warden, member of the bishop's advisory group, and a fund-raiser. He has been vice-president of his community Cancer Society, and he has been on the board of the Crippled Children's Society. In World War II he served as chairman of the Navy's Transformer Committee and led in the development of a dry type shockproof transformer for shipboard use. He received a special citation for that."

The court responded that Chiles had been a vice president of Westinghouse's Transformer Division and had participated in high level meetings throughout the period covered by the power transformer indictment. Chiles' sentence was a $2,000 fine and thirty days' imprisonment.

For Ginn, his counsel argued to the court the "business nature of the offense":

"I say again with respect to the price-fixing feature, this is a statutory business offense; it does not involve any element of moral turpitude; it does not involve any acts of coercion, any physical violence or threats—the kind of cases and the only kind of cases heretofore who have had jail sentences imposed—and even in those cases, in the most recent and the most flagrant of that type, the jail sentences, sir, had been suspended."

Counsel for Ginn added:

> " Mr. Ginn today is a vice-president of the company, and the highest-ranking individual from the General Electric Company before this Court, and also probably the youngest, that when Mr. Ginn first went to the company, and in his subsequent participation as he worked his way up through the Transformer Division, he has indicated to your Honor, and is willing to so state under oath today, that what he did was something that he inherited as a young man as a way of life that had been established within the General Electric Company even before he came to the General Electric Company. He was ordered by his superiors to go to these meetings. The whole history of Mr. Ginn's participation, dating back to his early days, starting in 1946 when he resumed his service with the General Electric Company, having served five years of honorable service in the Navy of the United States during the war, would indicate that what he did, he did as a part of an overall company policy . . .
>
> . . . [H]e started out as a young man engaged in a course of conduct which I might say in large part started, as far as the company way of life was concerned, beginning with as early as the NRA under the New Deal when this was the way the business was to be done."

The court responded that Ginn was a General Electric vice president,[7] that he was the most aggressive conspirator named in the power transformer indictment, and that he had directed his subordinates aggressively in their participation in the conspiracy. The sentence was $5,000 and imprisonment for thirty days.

On behalf of Allis-Chalmers it was argued that the company had been and still was a low profit company and that McMullen, the highest-ranking officer of Allis named in the indictments, had been cooperative and forthright with the Government in detailing his and his company's activities. The court responded that McMullen was a vice president of Allis-Chalmers, that like Chiles and Ginn, he had participated in all the high level meet-

[7] Ginn's counsel indicated that Ginn's compensation from General Electric had been as high as $135,000 per year.

ings and had actively directed his subordinates to attend. The court stated that "reluctantly," because of these circumstances, it would take the suggestion of the Government and suspend sentence because of McMullen's "complete disclosure" and "great helpfulness to the Government, in the preparation for trial of this indictment and others." The sentence was a fine of $3,000, imprisonment of thirty days, but with the execution of the prison sentence to be suspended, with probation for five years:

> " . . . it being a condition of your probation that you likewise maintain the peace, that you in no fashion whatsoever have anything to do by way of any meeting, arrangement or contact with anyone or any company which would be violative of the antitrust laws."

Counsel for Seaman said his client did what he did "to preserve some degree of price stability in the market" and that Seaman's superiors, under whose orders he had been acting, were not even before the court:

> " We have Mr. Seaman here before the Court today, and many of the superiors who were involved, and deeply involved, in the actions which he participated in, are not before this Court for sentence; and I say, sir, I can think of nothing that would bore more inward on a man's soul than to realize that he was being punished for doing something which he did upon the orders of people above him, and those people not even before the Court to get so much as a dollar fine or a minute in jail.
>
> THE COURT: I suggest you give that information to the Attorney General."

But in connection with these assertions, the record shows that on the occasion of the plea of General Electric in No. 20399, power switchgear assemblies, before General Electric entered a corporate plea of guilty the Government stated:

> " The Government has not charged and does not claim that any member of the General Electric Board of Directors, including Mr. Ralph J. Cordiner and Mr. Robert Paxton, has knowledge of the conspiracies pleaded in the indictments, nor does the Government claim that any of these men personally authorized or ordered commission of any of the acts charged in any of the indictments." [8]

---

[8] Under a proposed Federal Criminal Code, drafted by the National Commission on Reform of Federal Criminal Laws (the Brown Commission), criminal liability under federal laws would be imposed upon

Counsel for General Electric then responded: "Your Honor, with that statement General Electric pleads GUILTY in this case."

In the case of R. W. Smith, who had been in a position of responsibility with General Electric, the court took into account that he had tendered his resignation in order to avoid the necessity of attending meetings with competitors and ultimately did resign. Sentence was suspended, under conditions identical with those imposed upon McMullen.

Swoish of McGraw-Edison argued that he had attended meetings with competitors simply to find out the prices at which they were selling the product and that he also wished to prevent another "white sale" (in power transformers) similar to one that had allegedly occurred in 1954-1955. The court, unmoved by these remarks, nevertheless suspended sentence in view of the defendant's age and the relatively minor position of his company in the industry.

Following the sentencing in the power transformer indictment, the sentencing proceeded in all other product line indictments on the following day. In the end, fines aggregating $1,924,500 had been assessed against the corporate and individual defendants; seven individual defendants had been given thirty-day jail sentences which they were required to serve

---

a person who is responsible for supervising the "relevant activities of a [corporation] . . . if he manifests his assent to the commission of an offense for which the organization may be convicted by his willful default in supervision within the range of that responsibility which contributes to the occurrence of that offense". (Section 403 [4]). In an earlier draft it was proposed in Section 609 that reliance upon counsel's advice would be a defense (as a "mistake of law") but the provision was removed to avoid the possibility of a deliberately created defense. (See *Working Papers of the Brown Commission*, pp. 138-139.)

The proposed Code has been the subject of hearings before the Senate Subcommittee on Criminal Laws and Procedure, but has not been acted on by the Congress (See McClellan, *The Challenge of a Modern Federal Criminal Code*, 57 American Bar Association Journal 585 (June 1971).

In January 1963 the Supreme Court of Delaware had held that directors were not liable to shareholders of Allis-Chalmers by reason of the directors' non-discovery and non-prevention of the company's antitrust violations. Graham v. Allis-Chalmers Mfg. Co., et al., 188 A.2d 125.

(in one case, Mauntel, on a plea of *nolo contendere* rather than guilty); and an additional twenty-four suspended sentences had been imposed.[9] For a tabulation showing the pleas and sentences in what the Government characterized as the seven "flagrant" proceedings, see Appendix 2.

As a part of the arrangements between the Government and the corporate defendants to dispose of the criminal proceedings, it was also understood that the Government's civil cases in equity, in which it was seeking an injunction against any continuation by the defendants of their anti-competitive activities, would be disposed of by the entry of consent judgments without requiring an admission by the corporate defendants of liability. The judgments as entered enjoined the defendants, among other things, from allocating markets, fixing prices or pricing methods or the terms or conditions of sale, and from submitting rigged bids or price quotations. In the case of the consent judgment with General Electric, announced in September 1962, it was provided that General Electric had to issue new price lists for its eighteen products; carry out an educational program; submit affidavits with sealed bids swearing that such bids were arrived at independently; list the cost of components in bids involving certain products; and was not to refuse sales of certain component parts to less integrated manufacturers.

Customers of the manufacturers, including a number of the larger public utilities of the nation, discovered to their amazement that the form of consent decrees as proposed by the Government to the defendant manufacturers would prohibit sales by the manufacturers at "unreasonably low prices."[10] This was probably done at the urging of the smaller manufacturers, but

---

9 On December 20, 1961, Judge Ganey revoked the suspended sentences with a warning that his action was not to be regarded as mitigation of the offenses.

10 Section 3 of the Robinson-Patman Act (15 U.S.C. §13a) prohibits the sale of goods at "unreasonably low prices for the purpose of destroying competition or eliminating a competitor"; but the United States Supreme Court has held that the section is enforceable only by the imposition of criminal penalties and cannot be made the subject of a suit for damages or injunctive relief: Nashville Milk Co. v. Carnation Co., 355 U. S. 373 (1958).

it was not clear why a consent decree that was designed to break up price fixing arrangements should itself propose to establish a floor for prices. By reason of numerous objections this provision of the decree was omitted upon final entry of judgments by the court.

CHAPTER 2

Post-conviction activities

WITHIN MONTHS AFTER the sentencing in Philadelphia, hearings on "price-fixing and bid-rigging in the electrical manufacturing industry" were scheduled by the Subcommittee on Antitrust and Monopoly of the Judiciary Committee of the United States Senate. Senator Estes Kefauver, Chairman of the Subcommittee, at the opening of hearings on April 13, 1961, complained that the grand jury investigations had not resulted in "a trial which would place the full facts before the Congress and the American people." [11]

The Senator added that the Philadelphia indictments and convictions had created many more questions than they had answered and asserted that the object of the Subcommittee's hearings was to arrive at and lay the facts before the Congress and the American public. Knowledgeable witnesses were to be called, including some who had been given and served jail sentences.

Although a number of individuals who had participated in the various conspiracies were in fact called before the Subcommittee in public hearings, the amount of information developed with respect to the operation of those conspiracies was surprisingly thin. One reason no doubt lay in the Subcommittee's concern with what might be regarded as the aspects of the conspiracy with human appeal.

Much of the testimony related to the disciplinary proceedings which the corporate defendants, particularly General Elec-

---

[11] "Administered Prices," *Hearings Before the Subcommittee on Antitrust and Monopoly of the Committee on the Judiciary, United States Senate,* April 12-May 2, 1961, at 16507. These *Hearings* will hereafter be referred to as the Kefauver Subcommittee Hearings.

tric, had taken against the individual conspirators. Burke of General Electric testified, for example, that he had first been demoted two levels, from level 21 to level 19, but that he had to settle a further two levels below that since he was required to find his own position within the company after the demotion and could find only a level 17 position. Shortly thereafter he was forced to resign.

Ginn was not disciplined prior to his jail sentence, but after he had served the sentence and after a short Florida vacation, he was dismissed from the company:

> " MR. GINN: The sequence of events, sir, is that when I got out of being a guest of the Government for 30 days, I had found out that we were not going to be paid while we were there, and I got, frankly, madder than hell, and I called—I couldn't get ahold of Mr. Linder, so I called Mr. Cordiner, and he told me: 'Bill, the best thing for you to do now, you have been under stress, go down to Florida for a week, and then you come up here, and I want to talk to you.'
>
> When I came up and talked to him on the 16th of March, he said that he felt that in the best interests for myself and for the company that I should resign, and I told him in a split second that I agree." [12]

Ginn seems to have been more outraged by the refusal of General Electric to pay him during the period he was serving his jail sentence than by the sentence itself.

The Subcommittee, like certain others who were inquiring into the conspiracies,[13] seemed to be fascinated with the question of whether Arthur F. Vinson, a Group Executive of General Electric whose indictment in switchgear had been *nolle prossed* (quashed) on motion of the Government, was or was not in fact involved in the switchgear conspiracy. Charges by four switchgear executives of General Electric (Burens, Burke, Hentschel and Stehlik) were that Vinson, at a luncheon meeting in Philadelphia in the latter part of 1958, had directed them to resume meetings with competitors. The charges were denied

---

[12] Kefauver Subcommittee Hearings, pp. 17088-17089.

[13] Richard Austin Smith, *The Incredible Electrical Conspiracy* (pts. 1-2), FORTUNE (April & May 1961), reprinted in Kefauver Subcommittee Hearings, pp. 17094-17105, 17172-17182.

by Vinson before the Kefauver Subcommittee, as elsewhere. The conflict of testimony between Vinson and his four accusers, all of whom testified before the Subcommittee, was sufficient to lead Senator Kefauver to announce that the transcript of the hearings should be sent to the Department of Justice for review:

" SENATOR KEFAUVER: I think I have made it clear that I think it is our duty to send a complete transcript of the hearings to the Department of Justice. It will be examined for the possibility of perjury.

We shall point out to the Attorney General that Mr. Burens, Mr. Burke, Mr. Hentschel, and Mr. Stehlik testified under oath that there was a luncheon meeting at which Mr. Vinson was present, where price stabilization was discussed, and that Mr. Vinson, on the other hand, says that there was no meeting. Their testimony is in direct conflict, so I think we ought to let the Department of Justice review the testimony again." [14]

The hearings also brought out that the public, at least in the beginning, did not understand that the conspiracies in the electrical equipment industries did not relate to consumer appliances but were confined to heavy equipment and other items utilized in the generation and transmission of electricity. Senator Wiley called to the attention of the Subcommittee that the Assistant Attorney General of Wisconsin had been flooded with letters "asking the State to start antitrust actions on everything from fry pans to electric blankets." [15]

The hearings also made clear that the conspiracies did not relate to light bulbs. The discussion on light bulbs concluded with the following irrelevant interchange, illustrative of the manner in which Congressional hearings sometimes wander from the subject at hand:

" SENATOR KEFAUVER: Just parenthetically, I wish somebody would improve the quality of these light bulbs.

MR. BURENS: They are always being improved.

---

14 Kefauver Subcommittee Hearings, p. 16958. No further action seems to have been taken by the Department of Justice to resolve the conflict; the issue was of little importance in the treble damage actions later instituted by purchasers of electrical equipment, who brought suit only against corporate defendants and not against individuals.

15 Kefauver Subcommittee Hearings, p. 16513.

SENATOR KEFAUVER: They used to last a whole lot longer than they do now for some reason.

MR. BURENS: You just burn them longer.

SENATOR KEFAUVER: I have to do a lot of twisting to get a bulb in. It seems like I spend all my time on a chair putting in bulbs.

MR. BURENS: I am sure the life of a lamp hasn't changed for the last 25 years.

SENATOR KEFAUVER: We will talk about that later on."[16]

It became clear during the course of the hearings, from the testimony of the individual conspirators themselves, that meetings with competitors in various divisions of the electrical equipment industry had indeed taken place. Many such conspiracies were of long standing and continued uninterruptedly except for breaks during so-called "white sale" periods. "White sale" was a term used within the electrical equipment industry to refer to periods of highly competitive, even distress sales, when prices fell with no signs of bottoming out. Within the decade preceding the indictment, 1955 was the year of white sales for a number of heavy equipment items, including power transformers, turbines and switchgear.

Peters of General Electric testified before the Subcommittee that when he was in training to become a turbine salesman, he was invited by the manager of marketing for the division to attend a meeting with members of competing firms in order to discuss and explain a revised price structure for turbines. From that time on, he had met with representatives from Westinghouse and Allis-Chalmers to discuss published prices and prices for individual transactions. Furthermore, at the time meetings were held, if there was a job coming up, discussion would take place on who would have "position." The witness explained that by position he meant the determination of which supplier would quote the lowest price in order to win the order, whereupon the other suppliers would quote higher prices.[17] Peters claimed, however, that even after position had been awarded,

---

16 Kefauver Subcommittee Hearings, p. 16819.

17 Kefauver Subcommittee Hearings, pp. 16646-16649.

other manufacturers might still try to get the job, not by going back on their agreement, to quote a higher price, but by offering more efficient equipment than called for by the customer:

" MR. PETERS: But in this case, even though you had low price, in assuming in some cases the price could not be adjusted afterwards you still could obtain the order by quoting better efficiences, for example.

Just to give you one example of this, on a 300,000-kilowatt machine, 1 percent in efficiency would be worth $400,000 to $500,000. So you may have quoted a price which is $100,000 higher than your competitor, but you could easily more than make up that $100,000 in price by quoting a machine which was substantially more efficient than what your competitor quoted, and obtain the order.

SENATOR KEFAUVER: If there was still competition on efficiency and other factors, what was the purpose of these meetings?

MR. PETERS: I have asked that question to myself, sir, many times in the last 2 years."

Burke of General Electric, discussing the switchgear conspiracy, indicated that he got his job in 1950 because his predecessor was not "broad enough" to engage in meetings with competitors:

" MR. FENSTERWALD: Did they tell you why Mr. Rauber was being replaced?

MR. BURKE: Yes. Mr. Tinnerholm did. He spelled it out very clearly, that Mr. Rauber, and to use his words, as I remember it, was so religious that since he had signed this slip of paper saying that he would observe the policy of 20.5, that he would not talk with competitors, so he was not broad enough to hold down that job.

MR. FENSTERWALD: Did you sign an affidavit or piece of paper with respect to 20.5?

MR. BURKE: Yes, I think I signed a total of three or four of them up until 1960, and then I have signed two since then.

MR. FENSTERWALD: Did you consider 20.5 the real company policy or just something to stuff the files with?

MR. BURKE: I considered 20.5, because every time it reached us we had previously received instructions to cease contacting competitors, and I considered it was the truth, that we were not then doing it and we would not be asked to do it in the future.

So I was perfectly willing to sign it. After that, well, we'd get orders through the line of command that we were to sign—that we were to contact competitors." [18]

Some details concerning the switchgear conspiracy were gathered by *Fortune* magazine from a diary that had been maintained by I-T-E Circuit Breaker's sales manager for switchgear, Nye Spencer:

" There were pages on pages of notes taken during sessions of the switchgear conspiracy—incriminating entries like 'Potomac Light & Power OK. for GE' and 'Before bidding on this, check with GE'; neat copies of the ground rules for meetings of the conspirators: no breakfasting together, no registering at the hotel with company names, no calls to the office, no papers to be left in hotel room wastebaskets. . . . But the most valuable windfall from the meticulous record-keeper was a pile of copies of the 'phases of the moon' pricing formula for as far back as May 1958.

Not much to look at—just sheets of paper, each containing a half-dozen columns of figures—they immediately resolved the enigma of switchgear prices in commercial contracts. One group of columns established the bidding order of the seven switchgear manufacturers—a different company, each with its own code number, phasing into the priority position every two weeks (hence 'phasing of the moon'). A second group of columns, keyed into the company code numbers, established how much each company was to knock off the agreed-upon book price. For example, if it were No. 1's (GE's) turn to be low bidder at a certain number of dollars offbook, then all Westinghouse (No. 2), or Allis-Chalmers (No. 3) had to do was look for their code number in the second group of columns to find how many dollars they were to bid above No. 1. These bids would then be fuzzed up by having a little added to them or taken away by companies 2, 3, etc. Thus there was not even a hint that the winning bid had been collusively arrived at." [19]

In power transformers, Ginn of General Electric testified that he knew as early as 1938 or 1939, when he was a $3,000 a year employee, that meetings with competitors in power transformers were occurring:

" SENATOR HART: Mr. Ginn, as I understand it, you entered the employ of General Electric in 1936.

MR. GINN: Yes, sir.

---

[18] Kefauver Subcommittee Hearings, pp. 16736-16737.

[19] Part II, *supra* note 13, at 164, 210; reprinted in Kefauver Subcommittee Hearings, p. 17176.

SENATOR HART: At or about 1946, you were told to meet with competitors and allocate business, and so on?

MR. GINN: Yes, sir.

SENATOR HART: Had you known until 1946 that such a practice existed in General Electric?

MR. GINN: I am under oath, Senator.

Yes, I did know this. I knew this, sir, from about 1940, about 1938-39 I knew it, yes, sir.

SENATOR HART: Within——

MR. GINN: I was not directly involved, sir, but I did know it.

SENATOR HART: So that within 2 or 3 years after you went to work, you knew it?

MR. GINN: Yes, sir; and I think the reason—I think I want to be absolutely fair about this though. I was put in, directly into the stream where this was controlled. In other words, I was in power transforming engineering then I went into power transformers and I was calculating prices in those days, and I would give the prices to my boss and while he never told me what he was doing with them sometimes he'd come back with a little change on it, and at first I thought he was an awful smart man to know how close to get to the market, and by placing a few things together I found out, yes, sir.

I made a mistake once, too, Senator, and that didn't stand so good either.

SENATOR HART: Was it at that time that you were being paid $5,600?

MR. GINN: Oh, at that time, Senator, I never thought of $5,600. I was making about $3,000 then."[20]

Ginn explained the purposes and objectives of the meetings that he attended:

" SENATOR KEFAUVER: What would you do at these meetings?

MR. GINN: At these meetings what we would do is discuss list prices, prices to be quoted and jobs or recapitulation of some of the past jobs that had taken place, and in those days there was a question of allocation of certain—of governmental jobs.

SENATOR KEFAUVER: You mean who would have position?

MR. GINN: Yes, sir.

---

20 Kefauver Subcommittee Hearings, pp. 17065-17066.

SENATOR KEFAUVER: And how much the bid would be?

MR. GINN: Yes, sir.

SENATOR KEFAUVER: And depending on whoever had position, the rest of you would bid something more?

MR. GINN: That is correct, sir.

SENATOR KEFAUVER: What kind of system did you have to follow it out in those days?

MR. GINN: The only system that they had in those days, Senator, there was a question—the system that was arrived at was based on the fact that on a sealed-bid transaction, where price is the only governing feature, it was felt that those jobs should be allocated on the basis of what people had earned in the market where there was not a sealed-bid consideration.

SENATOR KEFAUVER: Do you mean what they earned, rather than percentage of market?

MR. GINN: 'Earned' would be the word we'd say. In other words, there was no allocation of private business whatsoever. It was a question if somebody had gotten 35 percent of the private business where there was no position, no allocation, that this should be more or less their percentage in the sealed bid business.

SENATOR KEFAUVER: What was General Electric's percentage during those days?

MR. GINN: Around, as I recall, Senator, somewhere around 30 percent.[21]

. . . .

SENATOR KEFAUVER: This was just part of the way of doing business?

MR. GINN: Yes, sir, at that time, yes.

SENATOR KEFAUVER: It was widespread?

MR. GINN: No, sir, this is the point. It was not widespread. This is the thing we tried to—it was confined to actually a very few individuals.

SENATOR KEFAUVER: I know. But I mean, it was confined to a few individuals in your department, a few individuals in other departments——

MR. GINN: A few in switchgear, a few in turbines, and that was——

SENATOR KEFAUVER: But it was widespread throughout the various companies?

MR. GINN: As far as the industry is concerned, you mean?

SENATOR KEFAUVER: Yes.

MR. GINN: Yes, Senator; yes.

---

21 Kefauver Subcommittee Hearings, pp. 17038-17039.

SENATOR KEFAUVER: Everybody who made transformers in any appreciable number had representatives who met with you and others?

MR. GINN: I would say only, Senator, during those days any meetings that were held were only with the major manufacturers. At that time none of the smaller concerns were ever involved in any discussions.

SENATOR KEFAUVER: They did not have any appreciable part of the market; it was General Electric, Westinghouse—

MR. GINN: Allis-Chalmers.

SENATOR KEFAUVER: Allis-Chalmers?

MR. GINN: Maloney and possibly Pennsylvania at that time.

SENATOR KEFAUVER: How much would these big transformers sell for?

MR. GINN: Well, they can sell for anywhere from—I have been out of the business now for 4 or 5 years, but, oh, I would say a large power transformer could run $150,000-$200,000. In some exceptional cases, maybe a half a million."[22]

Meetings with conspirators were sometimes stopped when outside inquiries or investigations were taking place:

" MR. GINN: . . . There was a period here at about 1949 when the company made it very clear that all contacts with competitors were to stop.

Commercial men were withdrawn from NEMA, from the National Electrical Manufacturers' Association.

SENATOR KEFAUVER: Withdrawn?

MR. GINN: Withdrawn and told they were not allowed to go; that only engineers would go in the future.

For a period of about, I would say about a year, there was an expression that the iron curtain was completely down and that none of us had any contact with competitors whatsoever.

SENATOR KEFAUVER: Who stopped the contacts?

MR. GINN: This, I don't know, sir, except it was told to me to stop it, and I believe there was an investigation of the transformer industry going on at that time, something to do with licensing or a question of cross-patents and this thing was absolutely made completely clear that it was not to continue.[23]

. . . .

---

22 Kefauver Subcommittee Hearings, pp. 17042-17043.

23 Kefauver Subcommittee Hearings, pp. 17043-17044.

SENATOR KEFAUVER: It is well understood the reason you were called out of NEMA was because that is where you met with competitors whenever you were there.

MR. GINN: This is right, I think this could be right, sir."[24]

Only a few examples of the actual workings of the conspiracy were given during the course of the hearings, some by Senator Kefauver rather than the witnesses:

" SENATOR KEFAUVER: . . . It seems to me there were 40 meetings with competitors between January of 1957 and June 1959 on turbines alone—at the Barclay Hotel in New York, the Drake Hotel in Chicago, the Carleton House in Pittsburgh, the Chase Hotel in St. Louis, the Traymore Hotel in Atlantic City, and the Homestead Hotel in Virginia, during the time when you said you were trying to stop them.

MR. GINN: Yes, sir, I was.

SENATOR KEFAUVER: This was in turbines. There were 40 meetings between January of 1957 and June 1959.

MR. GINN: Yes, sir."[25]

Burke gave testimony concerning a competitors' meeting at which an understanding was arrived at between General Electric and Westinghouse with respect to allocation of business on a large purchase for a nuclear installation:

" MR. BURKE: . . . And it was only one other occasion that I had to go to a meeting, and that was when—I think it was the latter part of 1952 when Mr. Crawford reached an impasse with Mr. Fuller of the Westinghouse Co. on how the large 345,000-volt breaker business should be allocated, that the Atomic Energy Commission was getting ready to take bids for it.

Since this was a brand-new product, and it was in a new voltage area, both the General Electric Co.—if I can call it a switchgear division of the General Electric Co.—and the Westinghouse Co. were very desirous of getting the first job for prestige purposes, because it would be the first of its kind built.

SENATOR KEFAUVER: That was Atomic Energy?

MR. BURKE: Atomic Energy Commission at Portsmouth, Ohio. They were going to buy breakers for that, and they were going to buy them in two bites. They were going to buy about half of

---

24 Kefauver Subcommittee Hearings, p. 17047.

25 Kefauver Subcommittee Hearings, p. 17074.

them one time and then later on they were going to buy the other half. So the impasse that they reached was that both of them wanted that first job.

I had to meet with Mr. Fuller, and, subsequently, Mr. Fuller and I met separately to try to argue that out, each one of us wanting the first job. We couldn't reach an agreement. We had to put it on top, and, as I recall, I reported it to Mr. Burens; Mr. Burens, in turn, reported it to Mr. Van Erben. Mr. Van Erben said leave it in his lap, he would get into it.

I next, through the line of command, received word: 'Well, you quote 3 percent below book and everything will be all right, you'll get the first job,' and that is the way it turned out." [26]

Burke also explained to the Subcommittee what was meant by the term "white sale" and how, under the pressures of competition during that period, meetings among competitors were resumed:

" MR. BURKE: Through 1954 there were no meetings, to my knowledge, of high voltage, and that is when prices began to deteriorate gradually. So, to me, the white sale began in the early part of 1954.

SENATOR KEFAUVER: What is a white sale?

MR. BURKE: Well, they referred to it as a white sale because prices were cut so drastically from book prices and the climax of it came in January, just about the time the department stores are having these linen white sales, and they just tied the name they are having a white sale, too, like all of the department stores are on linens. So it just became common talk to call it the white sale.

Anyhow, the white sale really had its beginning in the early part of 1954, because prices began to get farther and farther off book until the latter part of 1954 they were about 15 percent off book.

Then in January 1955 they really went down to the bottom, about 45 to 50 per cent off book.

Chronologically, again, if that is what you want me to——

MR. FENSTERWALD: Yes, sir.

MR. BURKE: Chronologically, that summer—and I think it was June or July 1955—Mr. Burens asked me to come over to his office, and he told me that he had to start meeting with competition again.

A meeting was arranged to meet with them at Hershey, Pa., at the Hershey Hotel, and asked if I wouldn't accompany him.

---

26 Kefauver Subcommittee Hearings, p. 16739.

There was some discussion, and there is no need of going into the details about why we should do it. We had been out of it this time, the damage has been done, and so forth. And he said something to the effect that he had no other alternative, so he guessed I didn't either. So it ended up with my being persuaded to go along with him to Hershey, Pa., for another meeting. That is when it began again." [27]

In a subsequent interview with *Fortune* magazine, Burke also referred to a white sale period from December 1957 into 1958, in switchgear and circuit breakers:

" . . . Clarence Burke got a worried report from one of his switchgear salesmen in Miami: Westinghouse had proposed to Florida Power [& Light Company] that it add all its circuit-breaker order (about a million dollars worth) to its order for Westinghouse transformers. In return, Westinghouse would take 4 percent off circuit-breaker book and hide the discount in the transformer order. Telling his man to be sure of the facts first, Burke gave him authority to meet the Westinghouse terms. A grateful Mac Smith [Chairman of the Florida Company] then decided to split the circuit-breaker order, half to Westinghouse, which had broken the price, and half to G.E., which had matched the break.

This unexpected turn of the wheel brought the Westinghouse salesman boiling into the Florida Power's executive suite. There he raised Mac Smith's hackles to a point where the latter called G.E. and asked it to do him the favor of taking the whole order. G.E. naturally obliged.

Retaliation was not long coming. 'Westinghouse went to Baltimore Gas & Electric,' says Burke, shaking his head in recollection of the chaos that ensued, 'and said they'd give them 5 percent off on switchgear and circuit breakers, and a week later Allis-Chalmers gave Potomac Electric 12 percent off. A week after that, Westinghouse gave Atlantic City Electric 20 percent off, and it went on down to much worse than the 'white sale'—in the winter of 1957-58 prices were 60 percent off book." [28]

Fortune magazine added a few details to the Government indictments in circuit breakers with respect to a November 1958 meeting of competitors at the Traymore Hotel in Atlantic City:

---

[27] Kefauver Subcommittee Hearings, p. 16740. The author's co-counsel in representation of certain plaintiffs in subsequent treble damage litigation, the late Max Swiren of the Chicago Bar, urged that plaintiffs' counsel not use the manufacturers' term "white sale" but should rather refer to "periods of competition."

[28] Part I, *supra* note 13, at 176, reprinted in Kefauver Subcommittee Hearings, pp. 17094-17105.

" Circuit-breaker prices had been dropping alarmingly ever since September, so much so that GE, Westinghouse, Allis-Chalmers, and Federal Pacific extended options to some utilities to purchase large numbers of circuit breakers at 40 to 55 percent below book. Moreover, I-T-E Circuit Breaker had got into the business via the purchase of Kelman Electric and wanted a slice of the sealed-bid market; Federal Pacific had a slice but wanted a fatter one.

Deciding what to do about prices was not particularly trying; an agreement was reached to keep them substantially identical at book. The real trouble came over changing the percentages of sealed-bid business. GE, Westinghouse, and Allis-Chalmers knew that anything done to accommodate the demands of Federal Pacific and I-T-E would have to come out of their hides. But at the end of 10 hours of angry argument they decided the only way to get the cartel going again was to submit to the knife: General Electric's percentage was sliced from 45 to 40.3, Westinghouse's from 35 to 31.3, Allis-Chalmers from 10 to 8.8. I-T-E was cut in for 4 percent and Federal Pacific got a 50 percent boost, its percentage of the market was raised from 10 to 15.6.

So began the final circuit-breaker cartel, born in recrimination and continued in mistrust. . . ." [29]

The 1955 white sale in power transformers was ascribed by Ginn to over-capacity in the industry:

" MR. GINN: The white sale, I think, was started—forces had been there ready to generate this for an awfully long time. We had gone into, during the Korean war, that we had equipment on allocation. There was more business than anybody could possibly have. Everybody expanded their facilities, and I might add that some of this was done under fast tax writeoffs and those things to get more capacity in the electrical industry, and this capacity had begun to hit in 1954, and the white sale was just pretty damn near inevitable to come in about 1955." [30]

The witnesses before the Kefauver Subcommittee uniformly admitted their attempts to cover up their activities. Burke testified that the instructions given for public consumption were to the effect that there were to be no meetings with competitors, but the instructions that he followed were those which came by word of mouth through the line of command to continue or

---

[29] Part I, *supra* note 13, at 180, reprinted in Kefauver Subcommittee Hearings, p. 17105.

[30] Kefauver Subcommittee Hearings, p. 17059.

to begin to contact competitors. He tried to avoid initiating telephone calls entirely, and when he did he would call from his home rather than his office. Expense account vouchers would avoid showing the place of actual meeting but would rather show a trip or travel to some place equidistant from Burke's home base of Philadelphia as the place of the meeting:

> " MR. BURKE: And there is one particular one I can remember that was in June; I think it was June 8, 1959—no; it was a little later than that. It was a meeting that we set up at the EEI convention in 1958 for the later part of that month, which would be June, 1958 in Chicago. My expense account shows that I went to Atlanta, Ga.
>
> SENATOR KEFAUVER: That being about the same distance from Philadelphia?
>
> MR. BURKE: About the same fare from Philadelphia, plus the fact that my home is in Atlanta, Ga.; my mother lives there, and I had that if anybody asked me, well, what was I doing in Atlanta, Ga., I could say, 'It has been so long ago I presume I went down there to see my mother,' and did some business for the General Electric Co. while I was there.
>
> SENATOR DIRKSEN: Did you do that on your own initiative, picking out a destination where you wanted to go?
>
> MR. BURKE: May I ask you to repeat that, Senator?
>
> SENATOR DIRKSEN: I say, did you do that on your own volition? You were supposed to go to Chicago. Instead of that, you made it appear you went to Atlanta, or vice versa.
>
> MR. BURKE: That particular instance was on my own initiative, but I was taught to do that by my superiors back as far as 1945, who took me to meetings with them and told me that, instead of showing Pittsburgh in your expense account, let's all show so-and-so." [31]

Ginn corroborated that in his area of power transformers, concealment was the order of the day:

> " SENATOR KEFAUVER: Why was a traveling specialist doing this? A traveling specialist is not in sales primarily, was he?
>
> MR. GINN: Yes, sir, it was sales. I don't know why I was selected for this dubious honor quite frankly, but I was in 1946.
>
> SENATOR KEFAUVER: Where would you have these meetings?

[31] Kefauver Subcommittee Hearings, p. 16772.

MR. GINN: Oh, Youngstown, Ohio; Cleveland, Pittsburgh, New York.

SENATOR KEFAUVER: Did you try to keep them quiet, on the QT?

MR. GINN: Yes, sir; this was one of the situations that was told that no one except the members of the club should know a thing about this.

SENATOR KEFAUVER: Did you call these people members of the club?

MR. GINN: I am talking about within the company, sir. But, in other words, you were never to let the manufacturing people, the engineers and especially the lawyers know anything about it." [32]

Ralph J. Cordiner, Chairman of the Board of General Electric, did not appear before the Subcommittee but testimony from other witnesses bore on the question of whether he knew of the conspiratorial activity being carried on by General Electric's employees. Burens repeated before the Subcommittee a statement, obviously hearsay, made to him by his superior Erben in 1952:

" MR. BURENS: Prices were fairly stable, and close to our book prices. But Mr. Van Erben wanted to be sure that I was indoctrinated properly, and he on several occasions gave me historical background of the business, and he never failed to mention that the only way the business could be run was to meet and cooperate with competitors. And on one occasion, I remember asking him 'Well, what about this company policy?' And he said, 'Yes, we have a company policy,' but, he says, 'I will tell you what I know.'

Now, this is Mr. Van Erben talking to me. He said, 'I went to Mr. Cordiner' and these are almost his exact words. He said, 'I asked Mr. Cordiner not to ask me not to stop doing it, and I told Mr. Cordiner that if he did not ask me to stop he would never hear anything about it.'

MR. FLURRY: Mr. Cordiner, at that time, had not been president of the company for long?

MR. BURENS: Yes, he was then president a matter of a year or so, I guess, maybe a little more. Between 1 and 2 years. I think Mr. Cordiner became president in December of 1950, and this was in 1952." [33]

---

[32] Kefauver Subcommittee Hearings, p. 17040.

[33] Kefauver Subcommittee Hearings, p. 16822.

Erben was not available to testify before the Subcommittee, having died in 1956 or 1957. Burens admitted in response to questions from Senator Hruska that following the date of the reported conversation, Cordiner had stated and restated 20.5 as controlling company policy.

Ginn testified that when he took over as General Manager of the transformer division in November 1954 he had conversations with both Cordiner and Erben with respect to compliance with General Electric's antitrust policies:

" MR. GINN: And Mr. Cordiner called me to New York before I took over the job and told me now that he wanted to make certain that I operated the division in accordance with company policy and with the antitrust laws, and that lasted about as long as I——

SENATOR KEFAUVER: Let us get when that was.

MR. GINN: That was in November of 1954, sir.

SENATOR KEFAUVER: Is that when you took over as general manager?

MR. GINN: General manager of the transformer division.

SENATOR KEFAUVER: Let us get this clear again. He called you to New York?

MR. GINN: Yes, sir.

SENATOR KEFAUVER: And what was said then?

MR. GINN: He told me that in operating this division, I should completely comply with the company policy and with the antitrust laws, and to see that my people did it. Now, this lasted about as long as it took me to get out of his office and back to Mr. Erben's office.

And Mr. Erben says:

'Now, keep on doing the way you have been doing but just use your—just be sensible about it and use your head on the subject.'

SENATOR KEFAUVER: Did you tell him Mr. Cordiner had given you other instructions?

MR. GINN: He knew that.

SENATOR KEFAUVER: That is a strange situation.

MR. GINN: It is, sir.

SENATOR KEFAUVER: Why did you follow Mr. Erben instead of Mr. Cordiner?

MR. GINN: Well, I knew Mr. Cordiner could fire me, but also I knew I was working for Mr. Erben and I will tell you quite frankly, sir, I think there had been a communication and a philosophy taught by these other gentlemen that had made more of an impression on us, and we had better communication than we had with the other groups." [34]

Ginn had another conversation with Cordiner when Ginn moved to the turbine-generator division as Vice President and General Manager in January 1957:

" MR. GINN: Now, at this time, Mr. Cordiner called me down again, and said I was now an officer of the company, he wanted to repeat what he told me in 1954, that he wanted me to operate the turbine division in accordance with the company policy and in complete compliance with the antitrust laws.

Now, this time, I was damned worried, frankly, because my air cover was gone.

SENATOR KEFAUVER: Your what was gone?

MR. GINN: My air cover was gone. I mean I had lost my air cover. Mr. Erben wasn't around any more, and all of my colleagues had gone, and I was now working directly for Mr. Paxton, knowing his feelings on the matter and what Mr. Cordiner told me, and this was the second time. And I said, and with some little soul-searching here I realized I had no alternative but to change my ways and to change them but fast.

SENATOR KEFAUVER: . . . He had told you once in 1954?

MR. GINN: That is right.

SENATOR KEFAUVER: Why did he call you in again?

MR. GINN: Because here, again, the only thing that I can figure out was I was transferring to another division. I had been made an officer of the Company.

SENATOR KEFAUVER: Did he ask you whether you had been meeting with competitors or not?

MR. GINN: No, sir; he did not." [35]

The Subcommittee gave the witnesses an opportunity to rationalize their conspiratorial activities. Senator Kefauver quoted Fred Loock of Allen-Bradley as stating:

" No one attending the gatherings [in the electrical controls industry] was so stupid that he didn't know [the meetings] . . . were

---

[34] Kefauver Subcommittee Hearings, p. 17058.

[35] Kefauver Subcommittee Hearings, p. 17062.

in violation of the law. But it is the only way a business can be run. It is free enterprise."[36]

Burke asserted that "it was not to dig the customers or anything" and added:

> " It was just to get what was a fair market value, and would produce a fair profit for the industry, and would keep the industry healthy. And I think, if you will look over the records of the industry during that period, you will see that they did not make any huge profits."[37]

He also testified that it had been suggested to him at one time that excess inventories in transportation transformers should be eliminated by achieving an agreement among competitors in the same way that competitors agreed with respect to prices.[38] But Burke claimed that from a business point of view there were both advantages and disadvantages from conspiratorial meetings: without the meetings General Electric stood to get a large share of the business, but prices would fall off to such an extent that "where you gained one place, you more than offset it another place."

> " SENATOR CARROLL: A short time ago you said that you were concerned and had some apprehension that the amount of your business would be reduced as a result of this plan—and the plan might place you in a most disadvantageous position?
>
> MR. BURKE: Yes.
>
> SENATOR CARROLL: With Westinghouse?
>
> MR. BURKE: Westinghouse and the other competitors; yes.
>
> SENATOR CARROLL: Why were you alarmed? How much business did General Electric have at the time? Why were you so apprehensive that you might lose some of that business?
>
> MR. BURKE: One of the measurements of management was percentage of the available business. I wanted to improve my percentage of the available business.
>
> SENATOR CARROLL: What percentage do you think they had at the time?
>
> MR. BURKE: I think we had in the high voltage switchgear department, I think we had around 38 percent of the available business.

36 Kefauver Subcommittee Hearings, p. 16511.

37 Kefauver Subcommittee Hearings, p. 16745.

38 Kefauver Subcommittee Hearings, pp. 16733-16734.

SENATOR CARROLL: And after reaching this so-called price stabilization agreement, how much do you think you retained?

MR. BURKE: After reaching it?

SENATOR CARROLL: Yes.

MR. BURKE: I wanted to retain at least 38 percent. I didn't want to have to give up any.

SENATOR CARROLL: Did you do that? Did you retain that much when you were through with this plan, this scheme, this conspiracy?

MR. BURKE: Well, that is hard to say, because we were on again, off again, and you never knew how it all added up, whether we improved during the conspiracy or—it was my opinion—and I strongly maintain that we did better outside of the conspiracy than we did in the conspiracy on percentage of the available, but prices went off so much. So where you gained one place, you more than offset it another place."

Burke, in his *Fortune* magazine interview, implied that the lessons of meeting with competitors might have been learned during Office of Price Administration days:

" Burke's introduction to the heavy-equipment conspiracies was easy as falling off a log. It occurred when he reported to Pittsfield, Mass., on June 1, 1945, as sales manager of distribution transformers. A month or so after Burke's arrival, H. L. 'Buster' Brown, sales manager of the whole transformer department, called the new man in and told him he'd be expected to attend a Pittsburgh meeting of the transformer section of the National Electrical Manufacturers' Association. It was a regularly scheduled affair, held during OPA days, in what is now the Penn-Sheraton Hotel, and it was attended by 30 or 40 industry people plus the NEMA secretaries from New York. But after adjournment—when the NEMA secretaries had departed—the company men reassembled within the hour for a cozier meeting. The talk this time was about prices, OPA-regulated prices, and how the industry could best argue Washington into jacking up the ceilings. Burke didn't consider this illegal, and he took part in several subsequent monthly meetings before OPA was abolished.

The convenient price klatsches following the regular NEMA meetings continued after OPA's demise. But instead of discussing pricing under Government controls, the conspirators turned to fixing prices among themselves. 'In that conspiracy,' Burke recalled this winter, 'we didn't try to divide up the market or prorate the sealed-bid business. We only quoted an agreed-upon price—to the penny.' Nor did the post-OPA agreements seem to some of the participants like Burke to put them any more outside the law than agreements under the OPA. . . ." [39]

For Ginn, just as overcapacity brought on the white sale periods, it was likewise overcapacity which came to be the rationalization for the meetings:

" MR. GINN: I think that we understand it was against the law, Senator. I don't think people considered it a serious law violation.

The moral issue didn't seem to be important at that time, because this thing has changed as it has gone down the pike.

I believe actually in the 1946-47 period it was a period of trying to obtain stability, to put an umbrella over the smaller manufacturers, to more or less give them some indication of what they should quote and which way that they should operate.

As we have gone down the line, I have seen it change, primarily due to overcapacity, to almost a situation where people thought it was a survival measure rather than a measure of stability and a price umbrella." [40]

Ginn placed some responsibility for the situation on the intense competition that develops between departments in a decentralized organization such as General Electric:

" MR. GINN: I have operated a department, I have operated a division.

Actually, operating a division, you have certain diversities in a division that you don't have in a department, that the fellow that is operating the small department is put under tremendous economic pressure.

I think this goes down in certain ways as you get further up the ladder because with a division you have six departments and you have some diversity here where you can show a fairly decent record if one department is down one year and the other one may be up, but I think decentralization has done this. It has put more pressure on the manager because he has the complete responsibility in a smaller organization.

Yes, I think decentralization has contributed, certainly, to the forces that tend to make these things a reality." [41]

Ginn claimed that though power transformer meetings were resumed after the 1955 white sale, they proved to be abortive

---

[39] Part I, *supra* note 13, at 136, reprinted in Kefauver Subcommittee Hearings, p. 17098.

[40] Kefauver Subcommittee Hearings, p. 17066.

[41] Kefauver Subcommittee Hearings, p. 17065.

because prices in the transformer market were being set by foreign competition:

"SENATOR KEFAUVER: You were general manager from 1954 to December 1956?

MR. GINN: Right, sir.

SENATOR KEFAUVER: You met with competitors during that time?

MR. GINN: On a very spasmodic basis, Senator. About this time, in 1953-54, foreign competition had entered the market.

The meetings were quite unsuccessful, and really quite unnecessary and very foolish to even have them for any purpose whatsoever.

There was enough foreign competition coming in to set the prices in the transformer market anyway, and meetings became much more spasmodic and nowhere as near orderly or conducted as they had been in the past."[42]

Peters likewise indicated that a primary reason for discontinuing meetings was not their unlawfulness but the futility of attempting to arrive at working arrangements:

"SENATOR HART: You said you concluded there would be no advantage to have it go on. In what way, that you weren't getting the business as a result of it or that you realized that there was criminal law involved or what was the motivation for this?

MR. PETERS: One reason for it was that in 1959, in this whole period of time the inability to arrive at favorable agreements—understand there was a lot of bickering going on at many of these meetings, this was reason enough to discontinue them.

Also, in 1959, we got a new element in the marketplace, foreign competition came in, and they were setting the prices and not domestic suppliers.

SENATOR HART: You have omitted reference to the law. Do I conclude that the decision was based upon the fact that it was better business to do it without these meetings than with them?

MR. PETERS: Yes, that is a good way of summarizing it.

SENATOR HART: The decision was motivated by what you thought produced the best business result. It didn't have anything to do with 20.5 or the antitrust laws?

MR. PETERS: I would say that is correct insofar as I am concerned, sir.

42 Kefauver Subcommittee Hearings, p. 17061.

SENATOR HART: The witness is very frank. Thank you."[43]

Peters claimed that he had learned his lesson:

" MR. PETERS: The way I feel about it now, sir, the way I have been, the way my company, the General Electric Co., has been damaged, the way of my associates, their personal careers have been damaged and destroyed, the way my family and myself have been suffering, if I see a competitor on one side of the street, I will walk on the other side, sir."[44]

The Kefauver Subcommittee gave its primary attention to General Electric. Out of the seventeen witnesses called, eleven were General Electric men, three from Westinghouse, and one from each of three other manufacturers. The Westinghouse witnesses, by and large, took the position either that they did not know what was going on in the way of meetings with competitors or had heard of such meetings by rumor and report but had not participated personally. However, Jenkins of Westinghouse's Medium Turbine Department testified that there had been eighteen meetings among competitors in that product line from the fall of 1956 to the early part of 1959. He also gave some information as to the circumstances under which they would take place:

" SENATOR KEFAUVER: Let us get the conventions at which they would happen. You mentioned the Electrical Manufacturers' Association?

MR. JENKINS: National Electrical Manufacturers' Association committee meetings.

SENATOR KEFAUVER: I take it you and other representatives would be at the association committee meeting and then somebody would suggest that you get together afterwards, is that correct?

MR. JENKINS: Yes; when you are walking out of the building.

---

[43] Kefauver Subcommittee Hearings, pp. 16663-16664.

[44] Kefauver Subcommittee Hearings, p. 16652. Perhaps the emotions of some of the conspirators were comparable to those revealed in an English case during cross-examination by Lord Halsbury of a witness named Newton: "Halsbury: Are you heartily ashamed of the part you played in this [conspiracy]? Newton: I am rather sorry for it, yes. Halsbury: Are you heartily ashamed of it? Newton: Naturally. Halsbury: When did this feeling of shame first come upon you? Newton: With the likelihood of exposure." DU CANN, THE ART OF THE ADVOCATE, 59 (Baltimore: Penguin Books, 1964).

SENATOR KEFAUVER: And the other one was the American Society of Mechanical Engineers?

MR. JENKINS: And the American Institute of Electrical Engineers convention.

SENATOR KEFAUVER: That is a different group from the American Society of Mechanical Engineers?

MR. JENKINS: Yes, sir.

SENATOR KEFAUVER: And then the American Power Conference?

MR. JENKINS: Yes, sir. That is another separate meeting of the power company.

SENATOR KEFAUVER: And then at what other meetings would you have these rump sessions afterward?

. . . .

MR. JENKINS: . . . there would be an occasional meeting where someone request you be present at some location.

SENATOR KEFAUVER: Will you describe one of those?

MR. JENKINS: No different than the ones that I described.

SENATOR KEFAUVER: Who would call the meeting, Mr. Jenkins?

MR. JENKINS: Usually the individual who felt that he should be the low bidder on any specific negotiation or a contract that was coming up."[45]

Apart from the testimony before the Kefauver Subcommittee, there were other indications that the manufacturers did not deny that meetings among competitors in the electrical equipment industry had indeed taken place. General Electric's Chairman of the Board, Cordiner, in a speech at a General Electric Management Conference at Hot Springs in January 1960,[46] admitted that a number of "company associates" had acknowledged that during the past several years, and in some cases continuing in 1959, "they had been a party to the discussion of prices with their competitors in violation of the company's directive policy 20.5." In its *Interim Report, The Recent Settlement of Electrical Industry Antitrust Cases,*[47] General Electric indicated that a primary reason for its agreement to plead guilty and *nolo contendere* in the criminal proceedings

45 Kefauver Subcommittee Hearings, p. 16615.

46 Reprinted in Kefauver Subcommittee Hearings as Exhibit 11, pp. 17113-17119.

47 Reprinted in Kefauver Subcommittee Hearings as Exhibit 18, pp. 17155-17165.

lay in the circumstance that "rebutting the Government's cases would be difficult to accomplish":

> " There was no blinking the hard fact that many Company employees had, contrary to instructions, engaged in activities which, if not clearly in violation of the law, might in the context of the Government's case, be held by a jury to have been part of a course of conduct violative of the law. Extended interviews with the responsible marketing personnel indicated that there was little hope of overcoming the Government's case . . ."

The *Interim Report* stated that the illegal conduct of the individuals involved had been "purposely concealed":

> " [I]t appeared that the government would attempt to make the entire industry appear in a ridiculous if not a scandalous light by emphasizing the efforts of those few involved to keep their activities secret. In an attempt to accomplish this, some had resorted to such juvenile tactics as using code names, writing anonymous letters, calling their colleagues from public phone booths, holding meetings at out of the way hotels and motels . . ."

Fortune magazine concluded its description of the criminal proceedings and the fines and punishment handed out to the twenty-nine companies by stating "So ended the incredible affair."[48] In fact, for the corporate defendants, the criminal proceedings represented only the beginning.

---

48 Part II, *supra* note 13, at 222, reprinted in Kefauver Subcommittee Hearings, p. 17181.

CHAPTER 3

Damage investigations and the Anti-trust Investigation Group

SECTION 4 OF THE Clayton Act,[49] the basic section authorizing suits for treble damages, provides:

> "Any person who shall be injured in his business or property by reason of anything forbidden in the antitrust laws may sue therefor in any district court of the United States in the district in which the defendant resides or is found or has an agent, without respect to the amount in controversy, and shall recover threefold the damages by him sustained, and the cost of suit, including a reasonable attorney's fee."

The essential elements of a treble damage claim have been summarized by the Court of Appeals for the Ninth Circuit in *Continental Ore Co.* v. *Union Carbide & Carbon Corp*:[50]

> "In a treble damage action . . . it is clear that the plaintiff, in order to make out a claim on which recovery might be had, has the burden of proof to establish the following elements of his case: (1) that the defendant has violated the antitrust laws; (2) that plaintiff has suffered an injury to his business or property susceptible of being described with some degree of certainty in terms of money damages; and (3) that a causal connection exists between defendant's wrongdoing and the plaintiff's loss . . ."

It has been clear for years that a person is injured, within the meaning of Section 4, if he as a purchaser is required to pay an excessive price for a product by reason of price fixing activities or other acts wrongful under the antitrust laws. As Justice Holmes stated in *Chattanooga Foundry & Pipe Works* v. *Atlanta*:[51]

---

[49] 15 U.S.C. §15. The statutes relevant to the matters discussed in this book are collected in Appendix 28.

[50] 289 F.2d 86, 90 (9th Cir. 1961), *aff'd,* 370 U.S. 690 (1962).

[51] 203 U.S. 390, 396 (1906).

> " [Plaintiff] was injured in its property, at least, if not in its business of furnishing water, by being led to pay more than the worth of the pipe. A person whose property is diminished by a payment of money wrongfully induced is injured in his property."

The proper measurement of the injury, or of the damage sustained, has been the subject of some discussion and of rather muddied use of certain terms by courts commenting on the matter. In general, the measure of the damage or of the injury has been regarded as the difference between the price actually paid for a product which is the subject of antitrust law violations and the price which would have been paid if the product had been sold under competitive conditions. Under this test, questions of the value or of the worth of the product or its cost to manufacture, or what would be a reasonable profit to the manufacturer, are not relevant except to the extent that they can be shown to bear on the question of what a proper price would have been under competitive conditions.

In *Story Parchment Paper Co.* v. *Paterson Parchment Paper Co.*,[52] the Supreme Court of the United States approved an instruction given by the trial court to this effect:

> " The trial court fairly instructed the jury in substance that if they were satisfied that the old prices were reasonable and that they would not have changed by reason of any economic condition, but would have been maintained except for the unlawful acts of the respondents, the jury might consider as an element of damages the difference between the prices actually received and what would have been received but for the unlawful conspiracy."

In *Straus* v. *Victor Talking Machine Co.*,[53] the Court of Appeals for the Second Circuit (in which New York is located) considered a case in which the Victor Co. had prohibited its distributors from selling records to Macy's (New York), which previously had been buying from the distributors at a dealer's discount. As a result of these prohibitions, Macy's had been compelled to buy Victor records wherever it could and was unable to secure a discount. Macy's then brought suit for the difference between what it had to pay for the records and the

---

52 282 U.S. 555, 561, 562 (1931).

53 297 F. 791, 801 (2d Cir. 1924).

prices it would have had to pay had Victor not forbidden the discount purchases. The trial court had charged the jury:

> "If a man can go out in an open and free market and buy goods at a certain price, and then, because the market is closed to him illegally . . . he is compelled to pay more, his damage is the difference between what he would have paid in an open and free market and what he actually did pay [in] . . . the illegally closed market. Now, of course, [here] there was not any free and open market. . . . There was, however, a market price in the kind of market that there was . . . [Macy's] had a legal right to go out and buy as many goods as they could or wanted to, and they are entitled to recover, as their damages, the difference between what they would have paid for such . . . goods . . . if there had been an open market, and what they actually had to pay. . . ."

In affirming this instruction, the Second Circuit stated that this instruction "was the most to which defendants were entitled."

The *Straus* and the *Chattanooga* opinions constitute examples, however, of the manner in which the expression of the principle of the "competitive price" can be confusing. The *Chattanooga* opinion refers to a plaintiff's injury if he is required to "pay more than the worth of the pipe." In *Straus,* following its approval of the quoted instruction, the court referred to the plaintiff's having been compelled to pay more than a "reasonable price," adding that the jury could probably have found that the plaintiff's deprivation (i.e., damage) was "the difference between the established reasonable price and the amount plaintiffs were compelled to pay."

One other principle of law applicable in this area of ascertaining damages from antitrust violations is the rule that if the wrongdoers by their very actions have made it difficult to determine with precision the amount of damages sustained, then estimates will be sufficient. The U. S. Supreme Court in *Bigelow v. RKO Radio Pictures, Inc.* stated:[54]

> "In such a case, even where the defendant by his own wrong has prevented a more precise computation, the jury may not render a verdict based on speculation or guesswork. But the jury may make a just and reasonable estimate of the damage based on relevant data, and render its verdict accordingly. In such circumstances 'juries are allowed to act on probable and inferential as

---

[54] 327 U.S. 251 (1946).

> well as upon direct and positive proof.' Story Parchment Co. v. Paterson Parchment Paper Co. . . . Any other rule would enable the wrongdoer to profit by his wrongdoing at the expense of his victim. It would be an inducement to make wrongdoing so effective and complete in every case as to preclude any recovery, by rendering the measure of damages uncertain. Failure to apply it would mean that the more grievous the wrong done, the less likelihood there would be of a recovery.
>
> The most elementary conceptions of justice and public policy require that the wrongdoer shall bear the risk of the uncertainty which his own wrong has created. . . ."

Applying these principles to the electrical equipment made the subject of the Philadelphia criminal proceedings, it was clear to purchasers, which would include among others practically every investor-owner public utility in the United States, and to their counsel, that the convictions in themselves, together with the information (meager though it was) developed at the Kefauver hearings, established that there had been unlawful conspiracies to fix prices and allocate markets. The first requirement for a treble damage action under Section 4 of the Clayton Act, that there should have been activity forbidden by the antitrust laws, seemed therefore to have been met. Purchasers therefore regarded themselves as required to proceed to determine whether the remaining conditions could also be met, i.e., whether they had in fact sustained injury and damage from the conspiracies.

Investor-owned utilities in the United States had been substantial purchasers of every product involved in the Philadelphia convictions, with the exception of naval and marine switchgear which is sold only to the armed forces. An inquiry into the fact of damage, and if possible the extent, the first step necessary to determine whether treble damage actions should be filed against the electrical equipment manufacturers, seemed to be entirely too large a task for any one utility or even a regional group of utilities to carry out on their own.

Through the efforts of the various counsel of the nation's investor-owned utilities, an organization was accordingly formed for the purpose of carrying through expert studies to find the answers to the damage questions that were raised by the Philadelphia convictions. The organization came to be known as the

Anti-Trust Investigation Group (ATIG), composed at the height of its activity of 164 members, all but one investor-owned utilities of the United States,[55] and doing business in every state of the United States with the exception of Alaska. Public utilities or public utility systems serving every large metropolitan area of the nation were represented in ATIG, with the exception of Consolidated Edison Company of New York.

The organization was administered through a Governing Committee, composed of a representative (usually counsel) of every member of ATIG and by a smaller Administrative Committee, composed primarily of counsel for the larger companies or systems in the membership.[56]

The Administrative Committee of ATIG, with the approval of the Governing Committee, determined that the initial requirement for damage studies would be a survey of the prices that investor-owned utilities had in fact been paying during the alleged conspiracy periods for the products in question. Somewhat surprisingly, this information was not available in any central point, partly because the manufacturers seemed deliberately to have followed policies of holding confidential prices that were actually paid by various purchasers of the same equipment. Consequently, although any given public utility would, of course, know what it had paid and was paying for any particular piece or type of equipment, it would not know what other utilities were paying. The entire responsibility for this situation cannot be placed upon the manufacturers, since a number of utilities themselves were anxious to hold confidential the prices they had paid for equipment. In any event, the result was that ATIG had to develop fairly elaborate procedures for securing information concerning prices without publishing the names of the purchasers involved in the various transactions.

---

55 One member had its principal office in Montreal, P.Q., Canada.

56 The first chairman of the Governing Committee was George D. Gibson of the Richmond, Virginia Bar, who was succeeded by the author, a member of the Illinois and New York Bars, in June 1962. The successive chairmen of the Administrative Committee were Herbert B. Cohn and David K. Kadane, both of the New York Bar, followed by Donald G. Allen of the Massachusetts Bar.

It was further determined within ATIG that the price studies, i.e., the assembly of data showing the prices paid for the various products by the purchasing utilities, should cover every one of the nineteen product lines involved in the Philadelphia criminal proceedings.[57] The information was to be acquired by questionnaire, addressed to each utility member of ATIG, and the answers would be correlated and machine-carded by Stone & Webster Service Corporation. Upon assembly of the data in useable form, the information would be turned over for analysis to two economists, Dr. Willard Thorp of Amherst College and Dr. Jerome Cohen of New York. At a somewhat later date, Professor Milton Handler, a member of the faculty of Columbia Law School and a member of the New York Bar, was retained as legal adviser or consultant to ATIG, with the primary authorization of guiding the efforts of Stone & Webster and advising the economists as to the legal principles applicable in connection with their studies.[58]

It was to be the task of the economists to organize the price data in an attempt to determine whether they showed any pattern of conspiratorial activity and if so, what the prices for the equipment might have been in a competitive, non-price fixed market. For purposes of the latter objective, utilities were asked to report their payments for the various types of equipment, not only during the alleged conspiracy periods but also for what the manufacturers claimed were white sale periods and also for periods subsequent to the convictions. Data were originally requested through June 1961 with requests eventually extending through December 31, 1961. Going back in time, it was originally contemplated that the studies would be carried back to 1954, but in view of evidence that the conspiracies might have originated earlier than the year 1956 (which was the beginning date alleged in most of the indictments in the criminal proceed-

57 Again, with the exception of naval and marine switchgear.

58 Professor Handler was not retained as litigation counsel for ATIG or its members as such. At a later date, Professor Handler was retained as co-counsel with Bethuel M. Webster of the New York Bar for the so-called "Atlantic City Group" and as counsel for the American Electric Power Company claimants. His court appearances and his pretrial and trial activities were on behalf of these claimants and not in representation of ATIG.

ings for the various conspiracies), it was eventually determined that the price studies should go back to 1948.

Although the determination was made to cover all the lines of equipment of which investor-owned utilities had been purchasers, first priority was given to ten product lines in which the most substantial purchases had been made by the utilities. These ten included, among others, turbine generators, power transformers, power switchgear assemblies, large circuit breakers, condensers, and two items commonly regarded as shelf items, meters and insulators.

The costs of the work of ATIG were to be borne by its members, and formulas were worked out whereby each member's proportion would be based upon the dollar amount of increase in its electric utility plant from 1956 to 1959, as shown on line 1 of a statistical summary prepared and published by the Federal Power Commission. This method was adopted because, in the absence at the beginning of the study of data on the volume of purchases, it was concluded by the members that growth in utility plant would afford a rough measure of the proportionate claims that might result from the studies being undertaken. Total assessments, for all the studies undertaken and completed by ATIG, amounted for a small company such as Central Illinois Electric & Gas Company to $1,576; $4,824 for a medium-sized company such as Iowa Power & Light Company; and $8,514 for a medium-large company such as Central Illinois Public Service Company.

One problem that ATIG had to face at the outset was the procurement of the manufacturers' catalogs or its prices for all the products under study. The utilities had such catalogs or list prices available in their purchasing departments, but they represented current not past prices: catalog or list prices were maintained in loose-leaf binders and as new prices were announced, the new sheets would replace the old which would then be thrown away. The ATIG studies required catalog or list price material back to 1948, and in the absence of such data in the files of the member utilities, an appeal was made to the manufacturers for cooperation in supplying the needed material. By and large the manufacturers acquiesced in supplying catalog and list price data back to 1954, but General Electric and a number of other manufacturers were unwilling to go back to 1948.

By late summer of 1961 the data on a number of the more important product lines had been delivered to the economists, and by November 1961 the material on all nineteen products under study, consisting of manufacturers' list and catalog prices and analyses of what the utilities had in fact been paying, were available to the ATIG economists. A time schedule was then established for the economists' reports.

The first report, on circuit breakers, was scheduled to be available by February 1, 1962, to be followed by written reports on meters, power transformers, insulators and turbine generators through the spring of 1962. Reports on condensers were to be completed by September 1962, and reports on all the remaining product lines by the end of the year 1962. By and large, this schedule was met.

A primary object of attention was the turbine generator study, because of the magnitude of the dollar amounts involved. The study was one of some complexity, in view of the great variety of ratings, capacities and accessories that were almost distinctive to each turbine generator. In a sense, almost every turbine generator manufactured and sold in the United States could be regarded as custom made for the individual purchaser. It was therefore necessary, if there were to be valid comparisons of prices paid for turbine generators, that all turbines purchased be put on a comparable basis by figuratively stripping them down to a basic turbine generator, with all distinctive features or accessories removed from consideration.[59] To accomplish this result, Stone & Webster within three months after the formation of ATIG circulated a questionnaire to all members, asking for detailed information concerning turbine generator purchases, including methods of negotiation, prices paid for the basic

59 If this stripping were not done, the situation would then be similar to an automobile buyer reporting the price he paid without correcting for horsepower differences or added optional equipment. The data might be correct as to payment, but would be misleading for price comparisons if the next buyer did not buy exactly the same car with the same equipment.

standard units and for modifications and accessories, distinctive features of the turbine and the like.[60]

Upon receipt of the data from the utilities, substantially accomplished through the summer of 1961, it was decided that price comparisons for a basic turbine unit could best be developed by establishing a percentage relationship between turbine prices and the manufacturers' book prices at a selected reference date. This conclusion was reinforced by the circumstance that the prices for about 30% or 170 units (564 units were covered by the turbine study) were reported by the utility purchasers as a stated percentage of the manufacturers' book prices. In choosing a particular book price for reference purposes, almost any date could have been used so long as it was used consistently for all purchases. The decision was made in favor of referring all basic turbine prices to the book price in effect during 1958-1959.

The results were shown on Chart STG-1, included in the ATIG turbine generator study and reproduced in the Appendix as Appendix 4. As Chart STG-1 indicates, each dot represents one steam turbine generator and the order price (i.e., the price paid by the purchasing utility) in terms of percentage of the 1958 book prices. Confidentiality of the information was maintained by the device of a key whereby each utility would know where its own purchases fell on the Chart, but that information would not be available to any other person. The Chart also indicates the dates of four price rises which had been made effective by all three manufacturers of turbine generators. Despite the scatter of the transactions, the pattern of turbine price behavior could be shown graphically on Chart STG-6.

The Chart clearly shows a steady rise in turbine generator prices beginning in 1948, with some fall-off in 1950-1951, then a buildup to the white sale period in 1955, and, after the white sale, a steep increase from 1956 to 1959. Then in 1959, the year in which the Philadelphia grand jury began its investigations,

---

60 See Appendix 3(a) for a copy of the instructions and the initial questionnaire. A copy of a Worksheet showing the manner in which Stone & Webster took information from the questionnaire and arrived at a basic turbine price for a turbine unit is included herein as Appendix 3(b).

STG-6
Index of Order Prices for ATIG Sample of Steam Turbine Generators and Average Monthly Order Prices Reported, 1948-1961
(Expressed as percent of 1958 peak book)

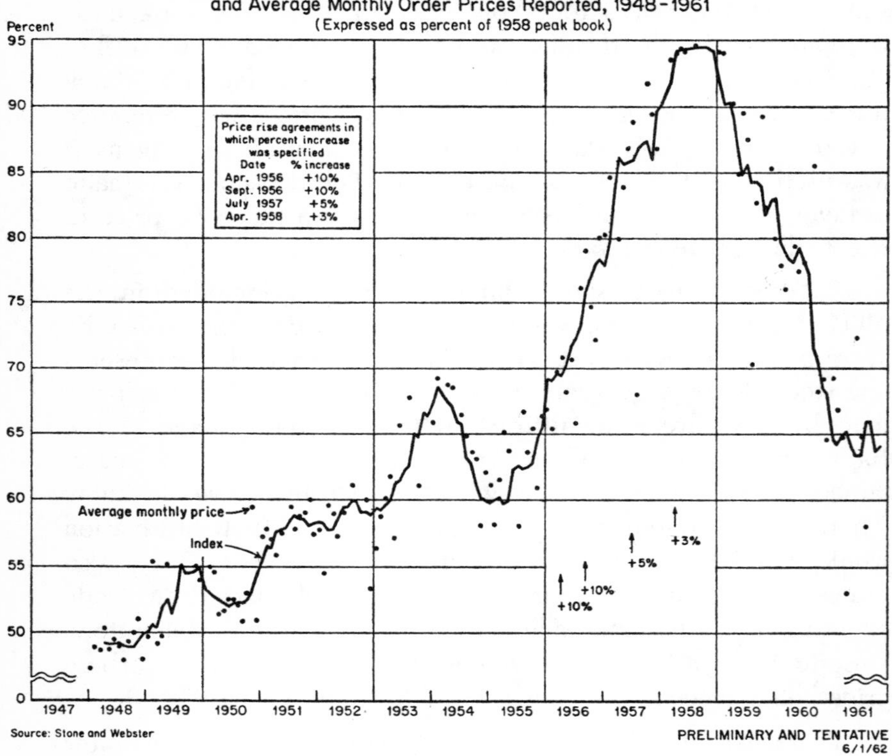

Source: Stone and Webster

PRELIMINARY AND TENTATIVE
6/1/62

there began a steep decline that continued through 1960 and 1961.

Upon the basis of data of the kind shown on Charts STG-1 and STG-6, it became the job of the ATIG economists to determine what a competitive price line would look like in relation to the charted lines showing prices paid in fact. The economists determined that they would tentatively accept four periods as representing times when turbine generator manufacturers might be considered to have been competing: 1948, 1950, 1955 (the white sale period) and 1961 (the post-conviction period). Prices charged during these periods might not have been truly competitive prices since they could still be reflecting prior conspiratorial action to some degree. Nevertheless, for purposes of the study prices during the four periods were taken as reasonably representing competitive prices.

The question then arose as to how the prices in the four periods should be connected in order to draw a continuous competitive price line. One alternative would be to connect the four periods by a straight line and accept that as the base competitive price line. This method had the possible defect of disregarding cost changes which might occur in the intervening months between the various four periods. A second alternative would take account of cost changes by connecting the four periods with a line based upon a change in cost index. If this method were to be adopted, an appropriate index had to be found or constructed.

The manufacturers themselves had utilized a kind of cost index in connection with an escalation formula provided in their contracts with purchasers of turbine generators. The ATIG economists found this formula defective, however, in a number of respects. For one thing, labor costs in the manufacturers' formula, representing 55% of the total costs, did not allow for increased productivity, with the result that the labor component did not accurately represent changes in the cost of labor. Furthermore, the materials component of the formula (set by the manufacturers at 35%) was not based upon materials actually used in the manufacture of turbines.

To overcome these defects, the ATIG economists created a cost index of their own in which the errors of the manufacturers' formula were corrected. The ATIG change in cost index was designed to measure properly changes in the cost of labor and materials going into the particular product. All other costs, as well as profits, were held constant. The ATIG economists explained that this had been done because there was no knowledge available to ATIG as to the trends of other costs nor was there knowledge available as to how such other costs were allocated to the particular product. The constant included profits but it was not known what the rate of profit was per unit of product nor the exact dollar amount of profit. Under these circumstances, it seemed to the economists that there was no satisfactory alternative but to treat all these factors other than labor and materials as constant. The difference in results was dramatic: where the manufacturers' index showed a rise in costs from 101.2 in 1948 to 171.0 in 1961, the ATIG index rose from 101.2 in 1948 to 131.8 in 1961.

The economists having developed their own cost index, it was then an easy matter to superimpose it upon Chart STG-1 so as to furnish each purchaser of a turbine with a ready comparison between the price that he paid for turbines and what he would have paid had the price been on the basic price competitive line. STG-30 is a representation of the transaction Chart STG-1 with the ATIG change in cost index utilized to connect the four periods accepted as competitive to arrive at a competitive price line continuous from 1948 through 1961.

Taking as an example the turbine, which is the subject of the Worksheet (Appendix 3[b]), the economists demonstrated an overcharge of $768,183 on a turbine whose total price was $3,844,800, approximately a 25% overcharge.[61]

In the power transformer study, techniques similar to those adopted in the turbine generator study were necessary in view of the wide variety of power transformers and accessories. It was not possible to reduce power transformers to a basic unit, and accordingly prices were found for a standard unit by utilizing the computer with linear regression analysis. The trans-

---

[61] The computation is included herein as Appendix 3(b)(1).

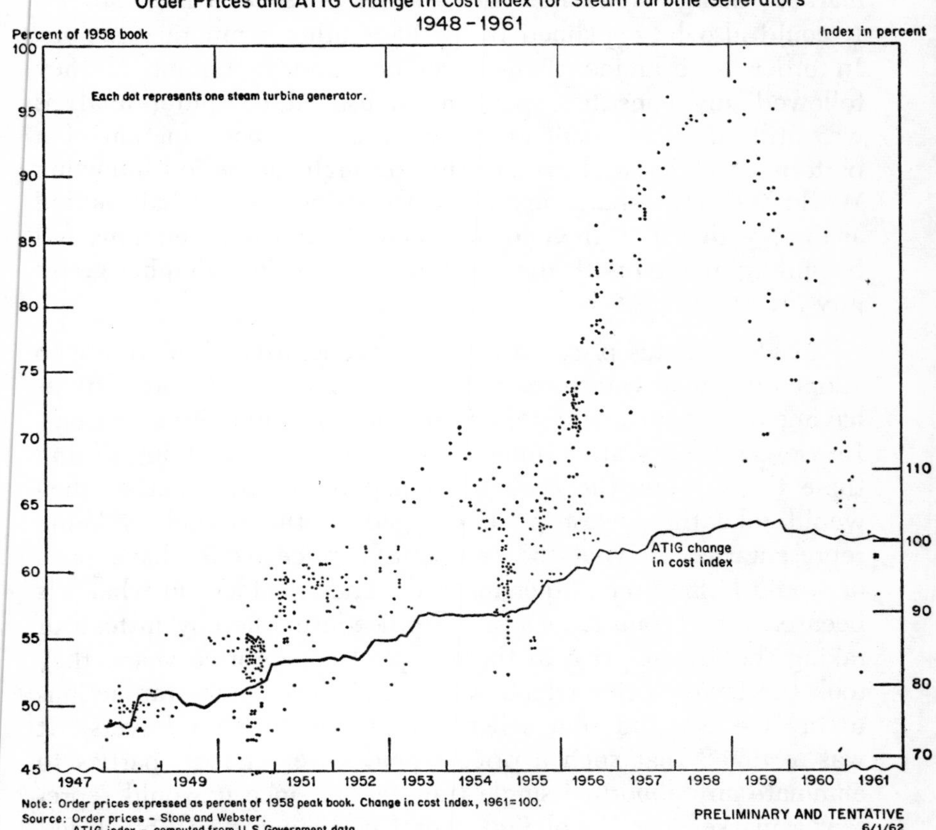
STG-30
Order Prices and ATIG Change in Cost Index for Steam Turbine Generators
1948-1961
Percent of 1958 book
Index in percent
Each dot represents one steam turbine generator.
100
95
90
85
80
75
70
65
60
55
50
45
110
100
90
80
70
ATIG change in cost index
1947
1949
1951
1952
1953
1954
1955
1956
1957
1958
1959
1960
1961
Note: Order prices expressed as percent of 1958 peak book. Change in cost index, 1961=100.
Source: Order prices - Stone and Webster.
ATIG index - computed from U. S. Government data.
PRELIMINARY AND TENTATIVE
6/1/62

action data so developed is demonstrated on Chart PT-2 for power transformers in the category of 10,000 KVA and below.[62]

The transactions for power transformers show considerable "scatter," i.e., wide variations in prices paid by the various utilities at any particular time. The economists commented that the scatter itself might be a part of the conspiracy by the market's being fragmented into a series of isolated negotiations. It could also be explained by perhaps other temporary factors. In order to examine these variations and determine if they followed any consistent pattern, highspeed computer analysis was utilized. The result of the analysis was confirmation of a pattern which showed prices rising through the period following World War II, a sharp break in early 1955 (a white sale period again), with a rise then to new heights and a precipitous fall beginning in 1959 with the institution of the Philadelphia grand jury investigations.

In view of this price pattern, the economists were willing to adopt for power transformers the years 1950, 1955 and 1961 as having an approximate representation to competitive periods. In view of the scatter among the various transactions during these three years, the economists had to decide whether they would take the lowest price charged in the period as being representative of what the competitive price would have been or would follow some other method. They decided on what has been called a "transactions price" procedure whereby instead of taking the lowest price in the accepted competitive years, they took the lowest price which would include enough transactions to involve two different sellers and three different buyers. It was assumed that such a price would cover enough parties to eliminate any abnormal single transaction, since it would represent a market level involving several participants on both sides. As in the case of turbine generators, a change in cost index for power transformers was constructed and utilized to connect the transaction price points for the three accepted competitive periods. The economists pointed out that there were three or four different methods which could be utilized for drawing competitive price lines: (1) simply drawing a straight line back-

62 Included herein as Appendix 5.

wards from the 1960-1961 transactions price level; (2) connect the 1955 and 1960-1961 levels, either by a straight line or by utilizing the ATIG change in cost index; and (3) using the 1960-1961 transaction prices as an anchor and escalate backwards or de-escalate by using the ATIG change in cost index. Hypothetical calculations showed that the range of overcharge could be determined to be a percentage range from 28.9% utilizing method (3) to 43.5% utilizing method (1). A further method which was not suggested but which would have resulted in the greatest computed overcharge of all would have been to adopt the 1960-1961 transaction price level as the anchor and then escalate backwards or de-escalate by utilizing the manufacturers' own contract formula for escalation.

In the power switchgear assemblies study, order prices were established as a discontinuous moving average of an order price index and a base price line established in accordance with techniques similar to those adopted for turbines and transformers. Chart PSA-17[63] shows the lines so drawn and demonstrates in the white areas existing between the lines the substantial range of overcharges on power switchgear assemblies, even during the white sale period of 1955.

In studying meters, which constitute a shelf item usually sold in quantity, a particular problem arose because the price data showed no white sales and no dips in prices but rather a steady price rise from the beginning point of the study in 1948. There was not even a fall-off in meter prices in 1960 and 1961, following the institution of the grand jury investigations. Further, meters were also distinctive in that manufacturers changed their quoted prices not by revising list prices but by maintaining list prices and revising a multiplier. An analysis of price data showed that the price of standard, singlephase watt-hour meters increased by 44.3% between 1948 and 1960, but an ATIG change in cost index for the same product for the same period showed an increase of only 17.7%. The difference could itself be regarded as a measure of the extent of the overcharges on this product.

---

63 Included herein as Appendix 6.

As a result of all these studies, there seemed to be no periods at any time between 1945 and 1961 which were truly competitive price periods for meters. The economists suggested that in these circumstances one method of computing overcharges would be to use mid-1948 as a base, even though there was no evidence that it was a competitive period. That base could then be escalated forward in accordance with the ATIG change in cost index. Another approach would be to attribute all multiplier increases to conspiratorial action and urge that those increases measured the overcharges. A variant would be to use the multiplier method, i.e., taking multiplier changes as presumptively representing overcharges, but adjusting for changes in cost.

The economists also pointed out, with reference to all products under study, that a further item of damage to purchasers as a result of overcharges would result from an excessive amount paid as sales or use taxes, because an excessive price would lead to an excessive tax. Their suggestion was that when a purchaser had determined on the basis of his own circumstances, utilizing ATIG material, what prices he should have paid for equipment, the amount of sales or use tax should then be calculated on the basis of the reprice and the difference between the calculation and the amount that was actually paid could be claimed from the manufacturers as additional damages.

Overall, it seemed clear to the utilities, on the basis of the ATIG studies, that they had been substantially overcharged on the products that had been made the subject of the indictments in Philadelphia. The broad outlines of the conspiracies had been established. The remaining link in the chain, i.e., to establish that the overcharges were in fact due to the conspiratorial activity, seemed at this stage of the studies to be likely but remained to be determined in detail. And for all the elements of a treble damage action—conspiracy, impact and damage—there remained the problem of developing lawful proof.

CHAPTER 4

The manufacturers' damage studies

THE MANUFACTURERS RECOGNIZED at this stage that the matter of damages was the key issue to be confronted. General Electric, in a Second Interim Report dated February 15, 1961 and entitled *Antitrust Damages: Facts in Place of Speculation,* announced its willingness to make "restitution" to any customer who could establish that it had been actually damaged. The Report went on to claim, however, that considering product improvement, customers had in fact been given "fair value" and concluded that "any extensive damage claims must be discounted in the light of the facts presently known."

In further development of the manufacturers' position that purchasers of their equipment had in fact not been hurt, various arguments were utilized. One city attorney who had followed up with General Electric on its offer to pay damages when established was told that his municipality had obviously suffered no damages because all sales had been made to the municipality at substantially below book prices.[64]

The manufacturers' position on the lack of damage suffered by investor-owned utilities was developed in greater depth. Four manufacturers, General Electric, Westinghouse, Allis-Chalmers and Ingersoll-Rand, joined in commissioning a study which was published in March 1961 under the title *Prices and Values in the Electrical Industry.*[65] The study came to be known

---

64 Report of NIMLO [National Institute of Municipal Law Officers] Task Force on Bid-Rigging Damages, 1962, p. 6.

65 There are indications that at this stage of the matter these four manufacturers and perhaps others were cooperating not only in the preparation of the Grant Report, but also had an understanding with respect to sharing expenses and perhaps liabilities that might result from any treble damage litigation. The FBI made inquiries within

as the Grant Report, by reason of the circumstances that the accounting firm of Alexander Grant & Company certified that the price indices in the Report, upon which the Report's charts were based, were presented fairly in accordance with an approved statistical program. Approval of the statistical program for the Report was given by Dr. Dorothy S. Brady of the University of Pennsylvania, who stated that the price indices produced for the study provided "accurate and reliable measures of the price behavior of six major product groups for the years reviewed," that they met standards "similar to but more exacting than those used by the U. S. Bureau of Labor Statistics and other statistical agencies in their price index construction," and concluded that the indices were to Professor Brady's knowledge "the most accurate ever produced for complex products characterized by a high degree of technical variability."[66]

The Grant Report continued the theme of General Electric's Second Interim Report that the utilities had received full value on their purchases of electrical equipment. There was a review of what were claimed to be major accomplishments of the electrical equipment industry in producing improvements in the steam heat rate for generators, drops in system losses due to improvements in transformers, and improved use of higher system voltages and improved system engineering. The consequence, according to the Report, was that without these advances total investments in generating equipment would have risen from $15 billion to $37 billion, transmission investments from $7 billion to $13 billion, and distribution investments from $15 billion to $24 billion. This portion of the Report concluded that if these advances had not been made in fuel savings, loss reductions, investment charges and decrease in manpower needs, the average price of electricity to the consumer in 1958 would have almost doubled, from 1.7 cents per kilowatt hour to 3.3 cents per kilowatt hour. If such an increase would not have been permitted by the utility regulatory commissions, the Report

---

the electrical utility industry on this subject, but of course it was an arrangement which, if it existed, would be likely to be known only to the manufacturers themselves.

66 Prices and Values in the Electrical Industry (the Grant Report), p. 24.

argued that the ratio of operating income to net plant investment would have been such in 1958 that the rate of return on investment for the Class A and Class B utilities of the nation would have been minus 3.8%.

In the price analysis section of the Report, a composite price index, based upon order price records of the four cooperating manufacturers, was prepared for four product lines: large circuit breakers, power switching equipment, power switchgear assemblies and power transformers. Separate indices were prepared for steam turbine generators and for condensers. In all cases 1954 was adopted as equaling 100. The composite order price index for electrical equipment was then presented in the Report on charts which also showed charted lines for construction and non-electrical equipment, electric labor costs, BLS [Bureau of Labor Statistics] non-electrical machinery and equipment, and for material and manpower prices. According to the Report, the charts demonstrated that trends in electrical equipment order prices for 1954-1959 were consistent with and no more than could be expected by reason of the trends in the other lines and that, indeed, in certain instances the increases in electrical equipment order prices did not match increases in other compared equipment.

The compilers of the Report had a particular problem with steam turbine generators. On the basis of the manufacturers' own data, the order price index for steam turbines showed substantial humps in the 1956-1959 period not matched by similar humps in the labor price index, BLS non-electrical machinery and equipment price index, or any other index used for comparison purposes. Figure 47 of the Report[67] demonstrates the problem. To meet this issue the Report argued that "to obtain a meaningful evaluation of turbine-generator price movements, they should be considered in relation to what the customers received for the prices they paid." It was therefore determined to work out a "price-value relationship . . . by examining the combined effects of price and heat rate only on the total cost of power generation." When this had been done, the Report produced a figure in which the charted line showed no humps

[67] See Appendix 7.

and, indeed, was practically a straight line from 1954 to 1959, varying only slightly from the line representing 100. This chart was presented as representing an index which equaled "change in turbine price minus change in turbine efficiency." [68]

The ATIG economists, after full study and review, pointed out to ATIG members what were considered deficiencies in the Grant Report and in the methods followed in its preparation. One defect was that no prices after 1959 were analyzed, so that no account was taken of the post-conviction period. Furthermore, in utilizing 1959 prices, the indices and Report utilized average prices, ignoring the fact that the drop in the latter part of 1959 was precipitous. The manpower index utilized in the Report was not adjusted for productivity and consequently did not represent a true labor cost index. The BLS index is unreliable in the case of electrical equipment since it is based on book or list prices, and it was clear from the ATIG studies that in the case of electrical equipment book or list prices did not in fact represent actual order prices.[69] Furthermore, if 1955 had

---

[68] The formula that was utilized is the following:

$$I = ABC - DEF$$

Where:

- I equals change in cost of generating electricity due to changes in turbine-generator prices and changes in efficiency,
- A equals the proportion of fixed charges accounted for by the turbine-generator unit.
- B equals the proportion total fixed charges are of total operating costs,
- C equals changes in turbine-generator prices, dollars per kilowatt, since a base period,
- D equals fuel costs as a proportion of total costs of generation,
- E equals improvements in turbine efficiency, btu/kwh, since a base period,
- F equals proportion of total steam plant efficiency attributable to improvements in the efficiency of turbine-generator units.

And where:
1954 is the base period where I equals 100. In all periods A equals 25 percent, B equals 45 percent, D equals 40 percent, and F equals 50 percent.

[69] Probably one reason that the BLS index on electrical equipment is based on book or list prices is that such prices are those that were reported to the Bureau of Labor Statistics by the electrical equipment manufacturers. However it came about, the result was that the BLS

been adopted as the beginning year of the study and taken as 100 rather than 1954, the percentage increases on the charts would have been substantially greater.

The ATIG economists also pointed out that the Grant Report dealt exclusively with heavy equipment items and presented no material on shelf items such as insulators or meters. The Grant Report, in the ATIG economists' view, threw no light on the central issue of what competitive prices would have been for the products under study.

The ATIG economists answered the argument of the Grant Report that the customers of the electrical equipment industry had received fair value:

> "The main burden of the Grant Report is that the customers of the electrical manufacturing industries received fair value for what they paid. It ignores the fact, however, that purchasers are entitled to competition in quality and service as well as price. No one will try to take away from the electrical manufacturers the credit that they deserve for their technological advances. Undoubtedly a public service has been rendered by increases in efficiency. It is no legal defense to a claim of overcharge that customers received good value for the higher prices paid, when it is clear that if there had been no conspiracy they would have received the same efficient and improved product at a lower price. In other words, absent any conspiracy, customers would have received greater value."

Following the publication of the Grant Report, in a paper prepared by manufacturers' economists Dean and DePodwin,[70] indices for various individual products were presented which seemed to have been constructed on correct principles. In certain charts included by the ATIG economists in their studies, comparisons between the ATIG order price line and the Dean and DePodwin price line showed remarkable similarity.[71]

---

index on electrical equipment did not reflect the rises and falls in actual order prices over the years under study.

70 *Product Variation and Price Indexes: A Case Study of Electrical Apparatus,* C. R. Dean and H. J. DePodwin, General Electric Co., American Statistical Assn., New York, Dec. 29, 1961, p. 34.

71 The charts showing such comparisons for power transformers and circuit breakers are included herein as Appendix 8(a) and 8(b). The BLS line shown on the circuit breaker chart is misleading in that it is based on 23 KV circuit breakers and seems to reflect the trend of book prices rather than actual order or transaction prices.

The investor-owned utilities and the manufacturers were the only groups making and presenting their own detailed economic studies to determine the extent of damages. Other groups attempted in other ways to acquire relevant information on the issue. Certain governmental bodies, including the State of California and a number of municipalities, moved before Chief Judge Ganey in Philadelphia for permission to inspect and copy the documents subpoenaed by the grand jury. It was ruled, however, that it was not in the public interest to make these documents available to the moving parties "merely to ease their proof of damage claims."

Approaches were also made to the Department of Justice, both by governmental representatives and counsel for the investor-owned utilities. Claimants were encouraged to make these approaches by reason of an announcement by Attorney General Robert F. Kennedy that the Department of Justice was ready and willing to offer all possible assistance to purchasers of electrical equipment in asserting their claims against the manufacturers. At a conference with representatives of the Antitrust Division of the Department of Justice in March 1961, the offer of assistance proved to be quite limited, at least so far as investor-owned utilities were concerned. Counsel for the utilities were seeking information relating to the prices paid by governmental agencies or instrumentalities such as Bonneville Power Administration, Tennessee Valley Authority, the Defense Department, and others for equipment of the type under study by ATIG. It was also hoped that the Government might be willing to pass on whatever information it possessed with respect to the details of the operations of the various conspiracies.

The response of the Antitrust Division was that no material could be made available if it had been presented to the grand jury, even if the documents would otherwise be public documents or consisted of materials such as copies of newspapers generally available to the public. The Government was also unwilling to make available materials with which the Government was working in connection with the preparation of its own civil suits for damages. These two categories of unavailable materials comprised almost the entirety of what the investor-owned utilities were seeking.

At the conclusion of the conference, the Antitrust Division spokesman stated that the Antitrust Division regarded its primary client as the federal agencies and that it would not do anything that would delay recovery on their behalf.[72] One member of the investor-owned utility group then asked what remained of the offer of the Attorney General to render all possible assistance to injured purchasers. The answer was that the Antitrust Division wished to be helpful but that it had to operate within the limitations which had been described.

While the damage studies were in progress, both sides, i.e., potential claimants and manufacturers, had to make known their positions and plans to various persons and agencies which had a legitimate interest. In the case of investor-owned utilities, shareholders were clamoring for information. A typical response is that which was furnished to the shareholders of Commonwealth Edison Company by its Chairman, Willis Gale, when he informed the shareholders under date of February 17, 1961, with respect to that company's position:

> " I am sure that many of you have read of the government antitrust prosecutions of some of our large suppliers of electrical equipment. You may be interested in knowing what we plan to do about claims for any damages we have suffered because of illegal price fixing with respect to equipment we have purchased. . . .
>
> The collection of all of the pertinent facts has been and is a difficult and complex task. It will, therefore, be some time before we can make a sound appraisal of the damages which we have

---

72 The spokesman for the Antitrust Division was Baddia Rashid, who was accompanied at the conference by Louis Markus, economist for the Antitrust Division. The author was in attendance among other counsel for investor-owned utilities. The Brown Commission proposal for a new Federal Criminal Code would make precise the federal government's obligation with respect to the non-disclosure of information acquired by it:

"§ 1371. Disclosure of Confidential Information Provided to Government.

A person is guilty of a Class A misdemeanor if, in knowing violation of a duty imposed on him as a federal public servant, he discloses any confidential information which he has acquired as a federal public servant. 'Confidential Information' means information made available to the United States government under a governmental assurance of confidence."

suffered. We have approximately one year within which to institute legal proceedings if that course of action proves advisable.

While we have not yet reached a decision on the precise nature of the action we will take, one thing is certain—we are determined to do whatever is necessary to protect the interests of our customers and our stockholders. . . ."

The utility's shareholder response was mixed: a number urged actions against the manufacturers, but a surprising number took the opposite position, some no doubt because they were also owners of stock in one or more of the manufacturers.

Various utility regulatory agencies were keeping a watchful eye on the situation. In February 1961, the Illinois Commerce Commission asked for a report from Illinois utilities subject to its jurisdiction on the status of their investigations. The Commission stated that it was interested because "the amounts expended by the utilities in litigation and the recovery of any sums from the electric equipment suppliers may be reflected in the income or the capital accounts of the reports to the Commission and may affect the basis for fixing future rates." The Illinois Commission was furnished in June 1961 with a full report on the ATIG studies and an announced intention on the part of a number of the Illinois utilities to bring legal actions as soon as the studies were reasonably complete. The attitude of these utilities was expressed by the author, speaking on their behalf as follows:

" The utilities for which I speak intend to pursue this matter vigorously but not vindictively. They recognize the vital role which the electrical manufacturing industry plays in service and supply of essential equipment to the electric utility industry. Nevertheless, the electric utilities which enter upon litigation will have been forced to do so by the unlawful pricing practices of the electrical manufacturing industry, but they will enter upon the litigation in the attitude that the institution of litigation will not foreclose willing cooperation on their part in a constructive solution should that become possible either upon an individual utility company or industry-wide basis."

The Florida Railroad and Public Utilities Commission on February 13, 1961 addressed a directive to all privately-owned electric utilities in Florida as follows:

> "As a result of the recent conviction of a number of electrical equipment manufacturers of violations of the Sherman Anti-Trust Act, it appears that there is a strong probability that the privately-owned electric utilities in Florida will be entitled to substantial refunds from the convicted companies from which they have purchased equipment.
>
> It follows that if these violations of the Anti-Trust Law have resulted in the over-pricing of electrical equipment sold to the electric utilities under this Commission's jurisdiction, then the investment of the utilities may also be correspondingly, albeit in good faith, overstated by them and such overstatement in investment would be reflected in the rates charged the public by these utilities.
>
> Therefore, in the public interest, the Florida Railroad and Public Utilities Commission hereby directs all electric utilities under its jurisdiction:
>
> 1. To promptly advise the Commission of the investigation they are making to ascertain the extent of overpricing by these suppliers.
>
> 2. To promptly advise the Commission of the steps which they are taking to secure any refunds to which they may be entitled.
>
> 3. To fully inform the Commission concerning purchases from these various firms during the past ten years.
>
> 4. To take all necessary steps to protect their rights to possible refunds."

Even when a public utility regulatory authority did not urge damage actions, there were early complications in administrative proceedings. Houston Lighting and Power Company, in a rate case, encountered an objection to its reproduction cost study on the basis that the prices used for the study had been conspiratorially fixed according to the company's own allegations in its treble damage complaint.

The manufacturers, although still adopting the public position that they were willing to pay damages to any purchaser who could establish that he had been in fact damaged, persisted in their view that purchasers had in fact not been hurt. They cited the Grant Report's conclusions in support of this position. Representatives of the manufacturers were dispatched to meet with the top executives of the large utilities throughout the country in an attempt to win agreement to this position and to avert if possible the filing of lawsuits. General Electric brought out of retirement its former Chairman, Charles E. Wilson, who called upon a number of leaders in the electric utility industry in an attempt to dissuade them from litigation. Westinghouse and Allis-Chalmers also had teams of management personnel in the field on similar missions.

But by the middle of 1961, the ATIG materials were beginning to become available with the showing in these studies of what seemed to be substantial overcharges, and civil actions for damages under the antitrust laws on behalf of most purchasers became inevitable.

CHAPTER 5

The complaints for damages

THE FEDERAL GOVERNMENT WAS itself the first to file for damages resulting from the electrical equipment conspiracies. In the period from March to September 1961, the United States instituted eight damage actions in the Eastern District of Pennsylvania (Philadelphia). The complaint in circuit breakers was filed in March; in power switchgear assemblies, low voltage distribution equipment, power transformers, turbine generators, distribution transformers and low voltage power circuit breakers in April; and in insulators in September 1961.

The actions were in the name of the United States of America and the Tennessee Valley Authority as plaintiffs, with the corporate manufacturers named as defendants in the respective product lines.[73] The United States, not being a private claimant, was not entitled to seek treble damages under Section 4 of the Clayton Act. But the Government attempted in its damage complaints to secure for the TVA the status of a private claimant since the TVA is a Government corporation; accordingly, treble damages were sought on behalf of that agency for its purchases.

For itself, the Government sought single damages, but also alternatively claimed double damages under the False Claim Act.[74] On purchases by U. S. Government departments, agen-

---

[73] TVA was evidently not a purchaser of low voltage distribution equipment, distribution transformers and low voltage power circuit breakers, and consequently was not joined with the United States in the complaints related to those products.

[74] 31 U.S.C. § 231-233. Under this Act any person (including a corporation, of course) seeking payment of a claim from the federal government, knowing that such claim is "false, fictitious or fraudulent" is liable to a penalty of $2,000 and "in addition, double the amount of damages which the United States may have sustained."

cies or bureaus which were not corporations, the Government's damage actions were brought only against the corporations that were convicted in the Philadelphia proceedings, not against either the convicted individuals or the corporations named as co-conspirators in the indictments. The conspiracy allegations in the complaints matched those in the respective indictments for the various product lines but added a denial that the Government had any knowledge of the conspiracy, or any facts which might have led to the discovery of the conspiracy, until 1959. The complaints alleged that the Government first became aware of the unlawful conspiracies during the course of the grand jury proceedings. The complaints also alleged that the Government could not have uncovered the conspiracy at an earlier date by exercise of due diligence, since the conspiracy had been fraudulently concealed by the defendants "through their adoption of elaborate schemes for submitting sham and collusive bids which misrepresented the independence and competitiveness thereof." The complaints recited the criminal proceedings, including allegations as to the guilty or *nolo contendere* pleas of the manufacturers and that judgment of guilty had been entered on those pleas and sentences imposed.

In its turbine generator complaint, the United States did not specify the amount of its damages, although the complaint indicated that the aggregate of purchases sued upon was approximately $50 million. The complaint simply asked for double the amount of damages suffered by the Government (treble in the case of the TVA count), together with the costs and expenses of the litigation, including attorneys' fees.

However, in its circuit breaker complaint, the United States spelled out what it regarded as the appropriate method of computing its damages. The complaint alleged that the Government had analyzed its purchases of circuit breakers for the period 1956-1960 and had found that there had been a sharp price decline from August to mid-November 1958. The complaint further alleged that during this period, referred to in the complaint as the "base period," the manufacturers' bids "most nearly approached those prices that would have prevailed under conditions of open competition." The complaint therefore claimed that the measure of damages with respect to any transaction was the difference between the amount actually paid for circuit breakers and the amount that would have been paid had the prices been computed in accordance with those in effect during the base period. On this calculation, the Government alleged that its damages on circuit breakers amounted to 40% of the purchase price of the circuit breakers purchased during the period sued upon.[75] In the case of breakers of certain types, or ratings, the Government had no base period experience and in those instances it simply calculated its damages by applying 40% to the purchase prices of circuit breakers in those other ratings. Since the complaint alleged that the aggregate purchases of circuit breakers sued upon amounted to $25 million, the Government's single damages under its computations would approximate $10 million. The data and information on the Government's purchases of circuit breakers were attached to the complaint.

During the conference with representatives of the Attorney General's office in March 1961, when the investor-owned utilities were seeking the cooperation of the Antitrust Division of the Department of Justice in supplying data and information, the question was raised by representatives of the investor-owned utilities as to how the United States would react if the investor-owned utility suits for damages were likewise filed in Philadelphia and then consolidated with the United States' suits. The Antitrust Division stated that it would probably oppose any such move by the investor-owned utilities.

Accordingly, the investor-owned utilities went forward with their plans for filing their suits, generally in their home federal districts.[76] The first major filings occurred in July 1961, in Philadelphia and Chicago. In Philadelphia, the Philadelphia Electric Company, with a group of associated plaintiffs, filed

75 The ATIG economists were convinced that the 40% figure was too high.

76 Generally no problems involving service of process were present in the various jurisdictions in which the suits were filed, although a venue question was raised in Ohio and Illinois by one of the small defendants, Schwager-Wood. Venue questions in individual districts proved to be of small importance in the litigation in view of the national character which developed for the entire litigation.

initially nine complaints in nine different product lines, including, among others, turbines, power transformers, switchgear and circuit breakers. In Chicago, Commonwealth Edison Company together with a group of midwestern public utilities likewise filed in nine product lines. As to seven of the nine product lines, the Philadelphia and Chicago filings were the same. However, in Chicago filings were also made in condensers and meters which were not at that time sued upon in Philadelphia, and Philadelphia sued on industrial control equipment and low voltage distribution equipment which were not then sued upon in Chicago. The Philadelphia actions were set up as class actions, alleging that they were filed on behalf of all electric utilities in Pennsylvania. The Chicago actions were brought only on behalf of those specifically named as plaintiffs.[77]

The Philadelphia and Chicago complaints established the pattern for those which were yet to come. Under this pattern, as in the case of the United States' actions, no attempt was made to join the individual conspirators as defendants in the damage actions, nor was there in the usual case a joinder as defendants of those manufacturers who had been named in the indictments only as co-conspirators.[78]

In the utilities' complaints, the definition of the product and the broad allegations as to what the conspiracy consisted of were generally adopted from the information given in the Philadelphia indictments. The Chicago complaints were set forth in two counts. The first count alleged a conspiracy beginning as far back as the claimants considered that they could reasonably

---

77 The Chicago complaint in turbine generators is included herein as Appendix 9.

78 The Department of Water & Power of the City of Los Angeles in its complaint originally named all corporate conspirators as parties, but later amended to leave only the major manufacturers as parties and to drop all others as defendants, placing them in the category of co-conspirators. In the latter category were Federal Pacific, Cornell-Dubilier, I-T-E Circuit Breaker, Kuhlman Electric Company, Moloney Electric Company, Wagner Electric Corporation, Sangamo Electric Company, A. B. Chance, H. K. Porter and Porcelain Insulator. Arizona Public Service Company on the other hand, in its power switching equipment complaint, named the corporate co-conspirators as defendants.

expect to prove a conspiracy: for most product lines this was taken to be January 1, 1948, although in the case of circuit breakers the year 1951 was adopted. In all cases the conspiracy was alleged to have continued "at least until sometime in 1960." The complaints alleged that the exact dates of the beginning and the termination of the conspiracies were unknown to the plaintiffs.

The circumstances of the criminal proceedings were set out in detail, including specification of the pleas and allegations that judgments of guilty were entered on the pleas and sentences imposed. The effects of the conspiracy were set forth, in the following language in the case of turbine generators:

" 19. The effects of the aforesaid combination and conspiracy were that:

a. Prices of turbine-generator units throughout the United States, including the prices charged plaintiffs, were raised to, fixed and maintained at high and artificial levels;

b. Price competition in the sale of turbine-generator units throughout the United States, including sales to plaintiffs, was restrained, suppressed and eliminated;

c. Purchasers of turbine-generator units throughout the United States, including plaintiffs, were deprived of the benefits of free competition in the purchase of these products;

d. Purchasers of turbine-generator units throughout the United States, including plaintiffs, did not receive competitive bids and quotations; and

e. Purchasers of turbine-generator units throughout the United States, including plaintiffs, were forced to pay artificially fixed prices for turbine-generator units which were higher than the prices they would have paid had no such combination and conspiracy existed."

The complaint alleged, in order to anticipate a motion to strike based upon the four-year statute of limitations, that various subterfuges had been adopted by the conspirators to conceal their activities. In the case of turbine generators, the Chicago complaint alleged:

" 17. The aforesaid combination and conspiracy necessitated frequent communication among representatives of the defendant and co-conspirator companies. In the course of this communication various procedures were adopted by the defendants for the purpose of avoiding detection. These included telephone calls to and from residences rather than offices of company representatives, the use of public telephone pay stations instead of company telephones and concealment and destruction of written records. Defendants and the co-conspirator companies further actively conspired to rig bids and quotations in such a way as to create the illusion that bids and quotations were competitive. As a result of these and other acts done by defendants and the co-conspirator companies for the purpose of actively and fraudulently concealing the existence of the aforesaid combination and conspiracy, plaintiffs neither had knowledge, nor by the exercise of reasonable diligence could they have learned, of the existence of such combination and conspiracy until they first became aware of the grand jury proceedings which resulted in the indictment of the defendants in June, 1960."

The amounts of damages were not specified but were claimed in language which suggested the standards by which the damages could be determined. The Chicago turbine-generator complaint was typical:

" 21. By reason of the aforesaid combination and conspiracy, each plaintiff has been injured in its business and property, sustaining damages in an amount equal to the difference between the prices charged each plaintiff for turbine-generator units and the prices which would have been established by the operation of free and open competition had no such combination and conspiracy existed, plus the difference between the use taxes, if any, paid and for which plaintiffs will become liable and the use taxes they would have paid and for which they would become liable had prices been established by the operation of free and open competition.

" 22. Pursuant to Section 4 of the Clayton Act (15 U.S.C. § 15), each plaintiff is entitled to recover from the defendants threefold the damages sustained by it and its costs of suit, including reasonable attorneys' fees."

The complaints were possibly defective in not specifying the dollar amounts of damages. However, the defendants indicated early in the proceedings that they would waive in writing any objection to the complaints on the grounds of non-specificity of damages. The manufacturers must have concluded that it was in their best interests that the plaintiffs not be forced to specify damages in the complaint. Their reasoning, perhaps, was that if the plaintiffs were so forced, they would specify as damages dollar amounts so large that manufacturers' shareholders, investment analysts and others would be alarmed as to the extent of the potential liability. Further, the specifying of high damages might also make it impossible for the parties later to agree on settlements substantially below the suggested amounts.

In a second count, the same cause of action was repeated but was confined to the period 1955 to 1960. Such a period would be within a statute of limitations period, and the claim would be allowable even if it could not be established that the conspiracy had been fraudulently concealed. If the defendants filed a motion to strike on the statute of limitations ground, there would remain a second count not susceptible to any such motion.

Plaintiffs asked that any judgment be joint and several, as they were entitled to do, in order that they might enforce any judgment obtained against any one or all of the corporate defendants.

The Philadelphia complaints asked for a jury trial. The Chicago complaints did not: there was a substantial debate on the point among the attorneys representing the Chicago claimants. In favor of a jury request, it was argued that a jury would be likely to have little sympathy with large national corporations accused of engaging in substantial and shocking price fixing conspiracies; it was therefore urged that a jury would be likely to be plaintiff-minded in an action of this kind even though the plaintiffs themselves were large and substantial corporations. On the other hand, it was argued that a jury might be unwilling to award damages in the incredibly large sums that would be requested. Some attorneys believed that the object of the actions ought not to be to secure the largest possible amounts of damages but that rather the judgment ought to be only for such amount as would be determined to be properly owed under the legal standards for computing damages: proponents of this view argued that a court rather than a jury would be better able to perform this function.

The issue did not have to be decided upon the filing of the complaints, since under the Federal Rules of Civil Procedure a jury can be requested by either party until the time of filing the last responsive pleading. The Chicago plaintiffs determined that they could postpone the decision on a jury request until the defendants had answered the complaints. As it turned out, on those complaints that approached trial in Chicago, the defendants themselves requested a jury trial.[79]

In December 1961 the Chicago plaintiffs filed in ten additional product lines, with complaints being practically identical with those filed earlier except for a minor change: plaintiffs earlier had alleged that in furtherance of the conspiracy and combination the defendants had done certain things, followed by a description of various meetings and agreements. In the later complaints, plaintiffs alleged that there were meetings and outlined the meetings, agreements and acts, and then stated that the meetings, agreements and acts alleged were in furtherance of the combination and conspiracies alleged. The reason for the change was to make it more difficult for the defendants to enter a general denial of the meetings, agreements and acts, which they might have done in the case of the earlier complaints, not on the ground that they had not occurred but with the rationalization that they were not in furtherance of the conspiracy and combination.

In the several months following the July 1961 filings in Philadelphia and Chicago, substantial numbers of additional complaints were filed throughout the country. In December 1961 the so-called Atlantic City Group, consisting of forty-four investor-owned utilities, filed complaints in twelve product lines in the Southern District of New York, with a jury demand.

Electric utilities were not the only claimants: El Paso Natural Gas Company and three associated natural gas pipeline companies filed in ten product lines; American Sugar Refining Company sued in three product lines; AT&T and related Bell companies filed in industrial control equipment, low voltage distribution equipment and power switchgear assemblies. Several

---

79 This surprised the plaintiffs somewhat since it was assumed that the defendants had analyzed the situation in much the same manner as the plaintiffs and would have concluded that a jury would be likely to be plaintiff-minded. However, the defendants perhaps reasoned that a jury would be unwilling to return verdicts in the large amounts that would be sought as damages by the plaintiffs.

foreign purchasers brought actions: the Israel Electric Corporation filed in the Southern District of New York.

The Metropolitan Sanitary District of Chicago filed a complaint, alleging not only separate conspiracies by product lines but also a so-called "basket conspiracy," which was an allegation that there was a single overall conspiracy involving all the product lines. Counsel for the Sanitary District later stated that this allegation had been included in the complaint because it seemed more likely than not that there had been a single overall conspiracy. The City of Chicago filed a class action on behalf of itself and all other municipalities in Illinois and in other States which might be similarly stituated.[80] The City also included a basket count in its complaint. Suits were filed in various federal districts throughout the country by hundreds of other municipalities, power authorities and districts.

Consolidated Edison Company of New York decided to work out specific damage figures before it filed. Its complaints included these specific percentages of purchase prices as representing its damages: 10% for circuit breakers, 10% for power switchgear assemblies, 6% for power transformers and 11% for turbines.

Several complainants filed in hydroelectric-generators, a product that had not been the subject of criminal proceedings in Philadelphia. These complainants included Puget Sound Power & Light, the City of San Francisco and the Chelan Public Power District (State of Washington).

Toward the end of 1961 the filings for treble damages had swollen to a torrent. In part this was because the ATIG ma-

80 By later decision, the City of Chicago was permitted to maintain its class action. The class was held to be proper in that: "(1) the group is composed of municipal corporations performing essentially similar public functions; and (2) the group generally utilizes a like method in awarding contracts, the sealed bid." The court was satisfied on the requirement that the plaintiff give adequate representation to the class by a showing that plaintiff itself had a substantial interest in the litigation; other members of the class were similarly interested; and plaintiff would energetically maintain the action with experienced counsel. In addition, the court emphasized the "impelling need" to "minimize possible duplication." City of Chicago v. Allen Bradley Co., 1963 Trade Cases ¶70,729 (N.D. Ill. 1963).

terial with respect to the probability of damages having been suffered was becoming available to the investor-owned utilities for all product lines. Furthermore, under one interpretation of the suspension provision of the Clayton Act (a provision which suspends the running of the statute of limitations for one year following the termination of Government proceedings),[81] the suspension period might have been calculated from the date of judgments entered in the criminal proceedings in Philadelphia beginning in February 1961, so as to cause the suspension period for some products to end in early February 1962.

In a last desperate attempt to avert the filing of damage claims, Westinghouse announced to the electric utility industry that in order to prevent further suits, it would stipulate to a suspension of the statute of limitations until one year after the closing of the Government's equity antitrust suits, or whenever the customer wanted further time to study the question of filing damage claims. General Electric offered to agree with any utility which refrained from suing for a period of twelve months that General Electric would not assert the statute of limitations by reason of such deferral if the utility ultimately decided, after such twelve months, to bring its lawsuit. General Electric also expressed a willingness, in the event that such differences could not be ironed out before the expiration of twelve months, to extend its agreement not to assert the statute of limitations by reason of such further deferral. These offers had no substantial acceptance.

When the smoke had cleared and the 1961 and early 1962 filings had been made, the manufacturers of electrical equipment found themselves defendants in 1,912 separate treble damage proceedings,[82] filed in thirty-five districts of the United States.[83] Most

---

81 Section 5(b), 15 U.S.C. § 16(b), of the Clayton Act provided: "Whenever any civil or criminal proceeding is instituted by the United States to prevent, restrain, or punish violations of any of the antitrust laws . . . the running of the statute of limitations . . . shall be suspended during the pendency thereof and for one year thereafter . . ."

82 Address by Chief Justice Warren at the 44th Annual Meeting of the American Law Institute, May 16, 1967.

83 A chart, included herein as Appendix 10, gives the data on 1,880 damage suits filed.

of the complaints related to separate product lines, on the theory that there were separate conspiracies for each product line. By reason of the action of a number of plaintiffs in joining together in a single complaint, of which the Chicago complaints are perhaps typical, the 1,912 separate cases in fact represented over 25,000 separate antitrust claims. No one can be precise as to the amounts of damages that were sought in view of the plaintiffs' practice and inability at this stage to specify damages. However, in the light of the total sales that seemed to have been involved in the claims, estimated to range from $6 to $7 billion, and applying the percentages of damages developed by the ATIG studies and from other sources, it is clear that the claims for damages, after trebling, were in the hundreds of millions of dollars. The claims covered every product line involved in the Philadelphia criminal proceedings.[84]

84 With the exception of naval and marine switchgear.

CHAPTER 6

Motions on matters of law–fraudulent concealment and passing on

As the plaintiffs had anticipated on the filing of their complaints for treble damages, almost the first motions of the defendants were addressed to the claims in the complaints for damages going beyond the four-year statute of limitations period and the related allegations of the plaintiffs that fraudulent concealment served to toll or lift the curtain of the statute.

The statutory provision, Section 4B of the Clayton Act,[85] reads:

> " Any action to enforce any cause of action under sections 15 or 15a of this title shall be forever barred unless commenced within four years after the cause of action accrued."

On February 1, 1962 the defendants named in the Chicago complaints jointly filed a two-part motion, one part of which asked the District Court[86] to strike from the complaints all allegations of damages for any time prior to the four-year period allowed by Section 4B of the Clayton Act and all allegations relating to the claimed fraudulent concealment. On May 9, 1962, by order of the court, this motion was made applicable to all 226 electrical cases pending in the United States District Court for the Northern District of Illinois.

The defendants contended that Section 4B constituted an absolute bar against any action commenced more than four years

---

85 15 U.S.C. § 15(b).

86 United States District Court for the Northern District of Illinois, Judge Edwin A. Robson, to whom all electrical equipment antitrust cases filed in the Northern District of Illinois had been assigned for pretrial and discovery.

after the cause of action accrued and that the statute is not subject to tolling on the ground of fraudulent concealment unless the plaintiffs could point to a specific exception in the limitations statute relating to fraudulent concealment. The defendants relied upon the simple, absolute language of the statute itself.

The plaintiffs argued, on the other hand, that a long line of decisions of the United States Supreme Court supported their position that fraudulent concealment would toll the statute of limitations as a matter of common law, without express statutory provision; and in support of this proposition the plaintiffs cited the statement of Mr. Justice Frankfurter in *Holmberg* v. *Armbrecht*:[87]

> "And so this Court long ago adopted as its own the old chancery rule that where a plaintiff has been injured by fraud and 'remains in ignorance of it without any fault or want of diligence or care on his part, the bar of the statute does not begin to run until the fraud is discovered, though there be no special circumstances or efforts on the part of the party committing the fraud to conceal it from the knowledge of the other party.' *Bailey* v. *Glover,* 21 Wall. 342, 348; and see *Exploration Co.* v. *United States,* 247 U.S. 435; *Sherwood* v. *Sutton,* 5 Mason 143.
>
> This equitable doctrine is read into every federal statute of limitation."

The legislative history of Section 4B, which both sides examined and attempted to utilize, was inconclusive. The plaintiffs cited a "colloquy"[88] between Congressmen Celler and Patman:[89]

> "MR. PATMAN: Mr. Chairman, after the word 'accrued' in line 7, page 2, I have an amendment prepared to include the phrase 'and become known' so as to make it clear that the cause of action or that limitation would not commence to run against a cause of action until it is discovered, until it became known, and, therefore, I would like to ask the chairman of the committee this question: Is it your understanding, Mr. Chairman, that the

87 327 U.S. 392, 397 (1946).

88 This is the term applied to an exchange of questions and answers or statements on the floor of a legislative body. A colloquy sometimes blurs rather than clarifies the meaning of the language in the bill under discussion.

89 Reported in 101 CONG. REC. 5129-30, 5132-33 (1955).

cause of action will not commence to run, the limitation will not commence to run on the cause of action until after it is discovered, 4, 6 or 10 years hence?

MR. CELLER: The statute of limitations will start running from the time the action accrues, not from the time of discovery. If you make it time of discovery, then you practically have no statute of limitations at all. An action could have accrued and the person aggrieved might not have heard of it for 20 years. Under the suggested amendment he would have a right to bring an action after 20 years, after the evidence will have been lost, and the defendant would be put in a rather deplorable situation in that regard. We provide that the 4-year statute shall start to run from the time of the accrual of damage, from the time the wrong was done, not from the time of discovery.

MR. PATMAN: Even in the case of fraud or conspiracy?

MR. CELLER: No. In the case of fraud or conspiracy the statute of limitation only runs from the time of discovery.

MR. PATMAN: That is the point I wanted to make sure of. You are not attempting to change that particular part of it?

MR. CELLER: Not at all."

The plaintiffs contended that Congressman Celler's answer to Congressman Patman was simply a restatement of a view he had expressed five years earlier when he was urging the passage of a nearly identical bill, except that it proposed a six-year limitation period rather than the four ultimately adopted. This earlier statement was prompted by a question from Congressman Hale:[90]

" MR. HALE: Mr. Speaker, I am in favor of this legislation. I think that the Committee on the Judiciary is to be congratulated on bringing it out. The particular provision of the bill which interests me and on which I want to make a few observations, is section 4(c) which provides that–

Any action (including an action brought by or on behalf of the United States) to enforce any cause of action under this section shall be forever barred unless commenced within 6 years after the cause of action accrued.

I think it is altogether desirable that there should be a uniform period of limitations applicable throughout the Nation, and that we should not be remitted to the various limitation periods prescribed by the several State statutes. It seems to me regrettable, however, that there is no provision in the bill that the statutory

[90] Reported in 96 CONG. REC. 10442 (1950).

period of limitation shall not commence to run until a conspiracy brought about by fraud or concealment shall become known to the plaintiff. I should like to inquire, if I may, of the gentleman from New York (Mr. Celler), whether I am correct in apprehending that this bill would not affect any State statute concerning the effect of fraud or concealment on the period of limitation.

MR. CELLER: Mr. Speaker, if the gentleman will yield, may I be permitted to read a note I made in reference thereto?—

Several States by statute or judicial decree provide for the tolling of the limitation period during the time the defendant fraudulently conceals the cause of action from the plaintiff or is otherwise guilty of fraudulent conduct. I am informed that frequently the statutory period does not begin to run until the plaintiff has discovered the facts of his cause of action which have been fraudulently concealed by the defendant. This bill is not intended to change those rules of the various States insofar as they presently apply to triple-damage actions under the antitrust laws. The period of 6 years, under this bill, will be uniform throughout the United States but the State rules benefiting a plaintiff in a case where the defendant has been guilty of fraud or of some other proscribed conduct will remain in effect.[91]

I would say that the answer to the inquiry would be that you need have no concern on that score.

MR. HALE: I thank the gentleman for his answer. I am very pleased with the situation as he describes it."

The defendants in response concentrated upon the statement by Congressman Celler, in the 1955 colloquy, to the effect that "the statute of limitations will start running from the time the action accrues, not from the time of discovery. If you make it time of discovery, then you practically have no statute of limitations at all." Defendants argued that the attempt by the plaintiffs to establish fraudulent concealment as an exception to the absolute running of the statute of limitations was an attempt to sell to the court the provision which had been expressly rejected by Congressman Celler, that the statute of limitations should run from the time of discovery. The defendants in their arguments continued an attempt to equate fraudulent concealment

---

91 By the time of the electrical equipment litigation, it had been determined that the applicability of fraudulent concealment to the limitation period was to be determined by federal rule and not by state statute or decisions: Moviecolor Limited v. Eastman Kodak Co., 288 F.2d 80 (2d Cir. 1961), *cert. denied,* 368 U.S. 821 (1962).

and discovery and then utilized statements made by one of plaintiffs' counsel, Professor Milton Handler, in opposition to "discovery" provisions in a statute of limitations:[92]

> " The bill not only suspends the statute until discovery of the violation, but conditions the operation of the new statute of limitations upon the discovery of 'the facts relied upon for proof of the conspiracy.' Such a statutory standard is clearly open to the criticism that it is indefinite, vague and uncertain."[93]

In August 1962, Judge Robson denied the motion of the defendants, affirming that fraudulent concealment would serve to toll the running of the statute of limitations. He then certified the question of law as one proper for interlocutory review by the court of appeals pursuant to the Interlocutory Appeals Act.[94] The Court of Appeals for the Seventh Circuit granted interlocutory review and on March 29, 1963 affirmed, in a unanimous decision, Judge Robson's denial of the defendants' motion to strike.[95] The court found "the legislative history interesting but not decisive of the issue." It rejected, as had other courts, attempts by the defendants to equate the doctrine of fraudulent concealment and the doctrine of "discovery," i.e., the argument

---

92 *Hearings on H. R. 7905 Before the Subcomm. on Study of Monopoly Power,* 81st Cong., 2d Sess., ser. 14, pt. 1, at 21-22 (1950).

93 Joint Brief of Appellants, United States Court of Appeals for the Seventh Circuit in No. 13903, Allis-Chalmers Mfg. Co., et al., Appellants v. Commonwealth Edison Co., et al., Appellees.

94 28 U.S.C. § 1292(b). Generally speaking, in the federal system only final orders or decisions are appealable. However, the Interlocutory Appeals Act, in § 1292(b) provides:

"When a district judge, in making in a civil action an order not otherwise appealable under this section, shall be of the opinion that such order involves a controlling question of law as to which there is substantial ground for difference of opinion and that an immediate appeal from the order may materially advance the ultimate termination of the litigation, he shall so state in writing in such order. The Court of Appeals may thereupon, in its discretion, permit an appeal to be taken from such order, if application is made to it within ten days after the entry of the order: Provided, however, That application for an appeal hereunder shall not stay proceedings in the district court unless the district judge or the Court of Appeals or a judge thereof shall so order."

95 Allis-Chalmers Mfg. Co. v. Commonwealth Edison Co., 315 F.2d 558 (7th Cir. 1963).

that a statute of limitations runs only from the time that a cause of action is discovered. The court quoted with approval the observation of the Court of Appeals for the Eighth Circuit which had previously ruled, in the context of the electrical equipment antitrust litigation, that the statute of limitations was tolled by fraudulent concealment:

> " While lack of uniformity in the state statutes of limitations was undeniably a prime factor which motivated Congress to enact § 4B, our careful consideration of all phases of the instant controversy drives us irresistibly to the conclusion that Congress was equally concerned with efficient enforcement of the Clayton Act which certainly cannot be accomplished if the statute is given a literal construction. We are not persuaded to believe that Congress meant to proscribe and outlaw conspiracies and combinations in restraint of trade, only to reverse itself by enacting a statute of limitations that would reward successful conspirators. When the antitrust laws are violated, the wrongdoers who are successful in cloaking their unlawful activities with secrecy through cunning, deceptive and clandestine practices should not, when their machinations are discovered, be permitted to use the shield of the statute of limitations to bar redress by those whom they have victimized." [96]

Substantial reliance was placed by the Court of Appeals of both the Seventh and Eighth Circuits on Justice Frankfurter's comment in *Holmberg*.

The defendants raised the identical question in a number of other districts in which the treble damage actions had been filed. A divergence of view resulted among the nine district courts that passed upon the question, but in the ultimate outcome, eight courts of appeals out of a total of eleven passed on the question and all reached the same conclusion, that fraudulent concealment would toll the statute of limitations.[97] The

---

96 Kansas City, Missouri v. Federal Pacific Electric Co., 310 F.2d 271, at 284 (1962), *cert. denied,* 371 U.S. 912 (1962). The decision of the Court of Appeals for the Eighth Circuit was an affirmance of a similar holding by the Western District of Missouri (Judge Becker), 210 F. Supp. 545 (1962).

97 Second Circuit: Atlantic City Electric Co. v. General Electric Co., 312 F.2d 236 (1962), *cert. denied,* 373 U.S. 903. Third Circuit: United States v. General Electric Co., 209 F. Supp. 197 (E.D. Pa. 1962), *lv. to appeal denied* by the Court of Appeals for the 3d Cir.,

defendants petitioned for certiorari to the United States Supreme Court from three of the decisions (the Courts of Appeals of the Second, Eighth and Tenth Circuits), and in all instances the petitions were denied.[98] It was admitted by defendants[99] that they had delayed their application for certiorari to the United States Supreme Court on the statute of limitations in the hope, which proved to be vain, that a conflict between circuits might develop. In the case of the decision of the Seventh Circuit, the defendants requested a rehearing before the Court sitting *en banc* (i.e., before the full Court) but the petition was denied.

A further legal question that the treble damage claimants had to face at the outset of their litigation was the so-called "passing on" doctrine.

Concentrating on the requirement of Section 4 of the Clayton Act that a claimant must demonstrate that it had "sustained" damages, the Court of Appeals for the Seventh Circuit in 1943 in the so-called "oil jobber cases"[100] had held that a claimant

---

Sept. 21, 1962. Fifth Circuit: General Electric Co. v. City of San Antonio, Texas, 334 F.2d 480 (1964). Seventh Circuit: Allis-Chalmers Mfg. Co. v. Commonwealth Edison Co., 315 F.2d 558 (1963). Eighth Circuit: City of Kansas, Mo. v. Federal Pacific Electric Co., 310 F.2d 271 (1962), *cert. denied,* 371 U.S. 912 (1962). Ninth Circuit: Westinghouse Electric Corp. v. Pacific Gas & Electric Co., 326 F.2d 575 (1964). Tenth Circuit: Public Service Co. of New Mexico v. General Electric Co., 315 F.2d 306 (1963), *cert. denied,* 374 U.S. 809. Dist. of Columbia Circuit: Westinghouse Electric Corp. v. City of Burlington, Vt., 326 F.2d 691 (1964).

98 In the case of the Eighth Circuit decision a petition for certiorari to the United States Supreme Court was filed by plaintiffs, the parties who prevailed. This unique and unusual procedure was justified by the petitioners on the ground that the issue was pending in over 1,700 actions in the federal courts and needed determination by the highest court. This petition was denied (U.S. Supreme Court, Nov. 19, 1962). A later petition was filed by the defendants as unsuccessful parties and was likewise denied.

99 At a San Antonio pretrial conference later described.

100 Northwestern Oil Co. v. Socony-Vacuum Oil Co., 138 F.2d 967 (7th Cir. 1943), *cert. denied,* 321 U.S. 792 (1944). Other cases in the category of the oil jobber cases are: Leonard v. Socony-Vacuum Oil Co., Inc., et al., 42 F. Supp. 369 (W.D. Wisc. 1942), *appeal dismissed,* 130 F.2d 535 (7th Cir. 1942); Twin Ports Oil Co. v. Pure Oil Co., 119 F.2d 747 (8th Cir. 1941), *cert. denied,* 314 U.S.

has not sustained damages if it has shifted or passed on the burden of excessive prices to its customers. In the oil jobber cases a jobber had sued defendant oil companies for fixing the "spot tank car" prices of gasoline. The court of appeals affirmed the action of the district court in directing a verdict for defendants when the evidence showed that the claimant's margin of profit had not been affected by the conspiracy: the plaintiff jobber had geared its retail prices to its costs and its service station prices had followed up and down increases and decreases in the tank car market.[101]

Defendants in the electrical equipment cases attempted to assert the passing on doctrine against public utility claimants by arguing that the rates of a public utility represent a collection from customers of the cost of the utility service (plus a return on the plant), that these rates are based upon what the utility pays for its equipment and supplies and that, accordingly, public utilities could be said to "pass on" any price increase to customers. Under these circumstances, the defendants urged, public utility claimants had not "sustained" damages within the requirement of Section 4 of the Clayton Act.

The question was raised initially in the Chicago cases, probably because the defendants wished to have the issue determined in the Seventh Circuit (in which Chicago is located), where the oil jobber decisions were controlling. Defendants posed the issue by serving upon the plaintiffs written interrogatories, pursuant to Rule 33 of the Federal Rules of Civil Procedure, designed to elicit facts concerning the extent to which the plaintiff utilities may have passed on to their customers the alleged excessive costs for electrical equipment. The interrogatories, twenty-three in number, and addressed to each of the Chicago claimants, covered the following subjects:

---

644 (1941); Farmers Co-Op. Oil Co. v. Socony-Vacuum Oil Co., Inc., et al., 133 F.2d 101 (8th Cir. 1942); Clark Oil Co., et al., v. Phillips Petroleum Co., et al., 148 F.2d 580 (8th Cir. 1945); H. E. Miller Oil Co. v. Socony-Vacuum Oil Co., Inc., et al., 37 F. Supp. 831 (E.D. Mo. 1941); McCain v. Socony-Vacuum Oil Co., Inc., et al., 64 F. Supp. 12 (W.C. Mo. 1945).

101 The claimant's formula for establishing its retail prices was tank car cost, plus freight, plus 5½ cents per gallon (138 F.2d 967, 969).

1. Plaintiff's corporate status;

2. predecessors of plaintiff;

3. states and counties in which plaintiff sells electric energy;

4. contracts for interchange of electric energy and for rates based on cost of service;

5. contributions in aid of construction;

6. changes in rates, tariffs, service classifications, changes in gross revenues;

7. recording of cost of work in progress, retirements, depreciation and amortization, allocation thereof among states, lease by plaintiff;

8. all individual amortization and depreciation rates, allocations among functional classifications and among plant accounts, tax depreciation, retirements;

9. The title, date, author (with present address and occupation) of each document respecting each allocation, determination and study referred to in (8);

10. regulatory agencies, franchises, rate orders;

11. all regulatory agency proceedings;

12. reports of electric utility operations to regulatory agencies and trustees;

13. negotiations with regulatory agencies;

14. reports to agencies of measures of value of property for rate bases, including cost new, accumulated depreciation, rates of annual depreciation, and adjustments;

15. as to all formal and informal rate proceedings, all price indexes, accounts to which applied, classification given equipment in price index, percentage changes therein, dollar changes therein, for trended original cost measure and for reproduction cost measure, adjustments by regulatory agency;

16. documents reflecting these rate bases;

17. itemizations from these documents;

18. interest during construction;

19. amortization under Internal Revenue Code;

20. rate of return and detailed computations relating thereto;

21. communications from regulatory agencies regarding antitrust recoveries;

22. persons assisting in answers; and

23. author, date, addressee and title of all documents referred to.[102]

Upon plaintiffs' objections to the interrogatories as irrelevant and immaterial, the issue was joined as to the applicability of the passing on doctrine to the electrical equipment cases. The claimants argued that the oil jobber cases constituted a narrow exception to the general trend of the law in providing reimbursement for damages to the person who suffers the immediate loss. They argued that this principle had been recognized by the Supreme Court of the United States in the *Darnell-Taenzer* case:[103]

> "The general tendency of the law, in regard to damages, at least, is not to go beyond the first step. As it does not attribute remote consequences to a defendant so it holds him liable if proximately the plaintiff has suffered a loss."

Furthermore, Justice Holmes, speaking for the Supreme Court in the *Chattanooga Foundry* case,[104] had held in effect that the law does not look beyond the first sufferer:

> "It was injured in its property, at least, if not in its business of furnishing water, by being led to pay more than the worth of the pipe. A person whose property is diminished by a payment of money wrongfully induced is *injured* in his property. . . . But when a man is made poorer by an extravagant bill we do not regard his wealth as a unity, or the tort, if there is one, as directed against that unity as an object. We do not go behind the person of the sufferer. We say that he has been defrauded or subjected to duress, or whatever it may be, and stop there . . ."

The claimants also had the advantage of a three-judge court decision by Judge Goodrich, a member of the Third Circuit

---

102 The full interrogatories are set forth in Appendix 11.

103 Southern Pacific Company, et al. v. Darnell-Taenzer Lumber Co., et al., 245 U.S. 531, 533-34 (1917).

104 Chattanooga Foundry v. City of Atlanta, 203 U.S. 390 (1906).

Court of Appeals, which in effect confined the passing on doctrine to situations which represented a true "middle man" transaction.[105] Judge Goodrich had held:

> " Where the plaintiff is a consumer of the product, rather than a middle man who resells it, he may recover the excess paid whether or not he ultimately passed the excess along to his customers."[106]

Defendants attempted to bring themselves within this principle by asserting that they believed that they could show that in numerous instances the plaintiff utilities resold to their customers electrical equipment purchased from the defendants, rather than consuming or using the product in generation, transmission or distribution of electricity. However, the examples cited were so insignificant in terms of the total purchases that the decision on passing on did not turn on any such circumstances of asserted resale. The defendants also claimed that the utilities' "excess facilities contracts" with customers are in effect contracts for the resale of equipment. Under these agreements, certain customers are required to contribute to the utility the cost of electrical equipment, if it is beyond what is usually furnished by the utility, although title is retained by the utility.

Finally, the plaintiffs argued that there is a principle of law which, in the words of the United States Supreme Court, is "older than the country itself" and "deeply rooted in our jurisprudence": namely, that "no man may take advantage of his own wrong."[107]

On December 27, 1963, Judge Robson sustained the plaintiffs' objections to the defendants' passing on interrogatories. He distinguished the oil jobber cases as being true "middle men" cases and found that the passing on defense was limited to such situations. He relied upon *Darnell-Taenzer* and *Chattanooga* as expressing the correct principle in the supplier-consumer situation. Further, Judge Robson found that sustaining the passing

---

105 Hanover Shoe, Inc. v. United Shoe Machinery Corp., 185 F. Supp. 826 (M.D. Pa. 1960), *aff'd* 281 F.2d 481 (3d Cir. 1960), *cert. denied,* 364 U.S. 90 (1960).

106 185 F. Supp. at 831.

107 Glus v. Brooklyn Eastern District Terminal, 359 U.S. 231, 232-34 (1959).

on doctrine would mean that the "defendants would be left with the profits of their wrongdoing," a result which "is directly contrary to the general equitable principle that no man should be allowed to profit by his wrongdoing." [108]

Judge Robson certified[109] to the Court of Appeals for the Seventh Circuit that his ruling involved a question of importance as to which an immediate appeal would advance the ultimate termination of the actions. An interlocutory appeal was therefore allowed by the court of appeals. That court affirmed Judge Robson's denial of the passing on interrogatories and ruled that the passing on defense had no place in the electrical equipment cases,[110] relying primarily on *Darnell-Taenzer*. In distinguishing the oil jobber cases the court of appeals did not agree with Judge Robson's and Judge Goodrich's distinguishing of those cases as applying only when there is a middle man relationship. The court of appeals stated that the applicability of the passing on defense should not depend entirely on whether claimants are classified as middle men or consumers; the court of appeals rather distinguished the oil jobber cases on the ground that there the ultimate consumers had independent rights under the antitrust laws to recover damages, and permitting the jobbers to recover under those circumstances would have subjected defendants to multiple liability. In the electrical equipment cases, on the other hand, the court found non-existent the possibility that present or future customers of the public utility claimants could recover against the defendant manufacturers. The court referred to its prior decision in the electrical equipment cases in which it had denied intervention in the utilities' suits by the State of Illinois claiming to represent the utilities' consumers.[111] There the court of appeals had said:

---

108 Memorandum on Plaintiffs' Objections to Defendants' "Passing On" Interrogatories, Appellants' Appendix, U.S. Court of Appeals for the Seventh Circuit, No. 14459, Commonwealth Edison Co., et al., Plaintiffs-Appellees, v. Allis-Chalmers Mfg. Co., et al., Defendants-Appellants.

109 Pursuant to 28 U.S.C. §1292(b).

110 Commonwealth Edison Co. v. Allis-Chalmers Manufacturing Co., et al., 335 F.2d 203 (7th Cir. 1964).

111 Commonwealth Edison Co. v. Allis-Chalmers Mfg. Co., 315 F.2d 564 (7th Cir. 1963), *cert. denied,* 375 U.S. 834 (1963).

" The alleged conspiracies spent themselves on these purchasers [plaintiffs]. The aftereffects of the hurt on the consumers are consequential and too remote for the consumers to gain rights against the conspirators. . . . The consumers' rights do not penetrate through to the antitrust conspiracies."[112]

In arguing for passing on in the court of appeals, the defendants had attempted to counter Judge Robson's "windfall" argument by stating that if the plaintiffs were permitted to recover treble damages for the amounts passed on to their customers then it would be plaintiffs who would receive the windfall. To this the court of appeals responded:

" Defendants argue that, if plaintiffs are permitted to recover treble damages to the extent of the amount passed on to their customers, plaintiffs will receive a windfall. As the judge in *Atlantic City Elec. Co.* v. *General Elec. Co.,* 226 F. Supp. 59 (S.D. N.Y. 1964), observed, if there is to be a windfall, plaintiffs as innocent purchasers should receive it rather than defendants."

Some time after Judge Robson's decision, the identical question arose in the Southern District of New York.[113] Judge Feinberg similarly sustained the objections of the plaintiffs in that District to the passing on interrogatories of defendants. He rejected the defendants' contentions because he found that in the Second Circuit (where New York is located), the court of appeals had ruled that when damages are sought under an overcharge theory, it is irrelevant whether the plaintiff's profit margin increased or decreased during the period of the defendant's

---

112 Judge Kirkpatrick of the Eastern District of Pennsylvania had reached the same conclusion in denying the Pennsylvania Public Utility Commission's petition to intervene in the Pennsylvania cases and was affirmed by the Court of Appeals for the Third Circuit: Philadelphia Electric Co. v. Westinghouse Electric Corp., et al., 308 F.2d 856, *cert. denied,* 372 U.S. 936. Apart from governmental agencies, other persons claiming an interest in the litigation attempted to intervene. In Missouri a shareholder of a public utility plaintiff sought but was refused the right to intervene: Stadin v. Union Electric Co. (oral opinion) (E.D. Mo. 1962), 309 F.2d 912 (8th Cir. 1962), *cert. denied,* 373 U.S. 915 (1963).

113 Atlantic City Electric Co., et al. v. General Electric Co., et al., 226 F. Supp. 59 (S.D. N.Y. 1964), *interlocutory appeal refused,* 337 F.2d 844 (2d Cir. 1964).

unlawful activity.[114] Judge Feinberg reasoned that recognition of the passing on doctrine would be tantamount to a repudiation of the "increased costs" measure of damages and would limit a claimant's recovery of damages primarily to lost profits, in the face of the traditional determination that there are three theories of recovery: loss of profits, increased costs and decrease in value of investment. Judge Feinberg also cited in support of his decision "the strong policy in favor of private treble damage actions, which are intended not only to compensate those injured by violations of the antitrust laws, but also to function as an independent method of enforcing antitrust policy."

In the *OVEC* decision[115] defendants argued any overcharge by the manufacturers had been passed on by the utilities through their demand charge, the court (Judge Feinberg again) explaining the defendants' argument:

> " . . . Rate calculation is based upon two components: an energy charge based upon the cost of fuel, and a demand charge representing fixed charges and operating expenses. These charges are designed to provide OVEC (and therefore IKEC) with sufficient revenue to cover costs, amortize OVEC's outstanding debt over a twenty-five year period and return eight per cent on its common stock. Defendants focus upon the demand charge elements of the rate which includes fixed charges covering, among other things, interest and debt amortization. Since the units in suit were originally paid for by a portion of OVEC's debt capital, defendants' argument is that these elements of the rate, in paying off OVEC's debt, enable it to pass on the costs of all eleven units to its customers, the AEC and the sponsoring companies."

Furthermore, the defendants argued that the *OVEC* case represented a different factual situation from that involved in previous decisions which rejected the passing on doctrine, the difference being, as the court stated,

> " . . . principally that recoupment of costs by OVEC and IKEC is guaranteed by the agreements referred to above. This would not appear to be a sufficient reason for distinguishing Atlantic City, if that decision is otherwise sound. Most utilities, while not legally guaranteed a return by their customers, are, in effect, practically assured of a return on investment so that sooner or later costs are recouped."

---

114 Straus v. Victor Talking Machine Co., 297 F. 791 (2d Cir. 1924).

115 Ohio Valley Electric Corp., et al., v. General Electric Co., et al., 244 F. Supp. 914, 928 (S.D. N.Y. 1965).

The court rejected the arguments for passing on, relying upon preceding decisions rejecting the doctrine but also upon a new circumstance:

> " There is, however, one significant new fact present here that, if anything, suggests that Atlantic City should be followed. Plaintiff utilities here have only one large customer (the AEC) or a narrowly defined and easily identified group of customers (if the sponsoring companies are added by hypothesis), to whom all of their product (electricity) is sold. In such a case—where a utility's entire output is sold to one customer and the customer has paid rates which include a component based upon an illegal overcharge to the utility—that one customer may also have a right to bring suit for the antitrust violation and, equally important, may be in a practical position allowing it vigorously to assert such claims. This, of course, would contrast sharply with the usual situation of an electrical utility selling its product (electricity) to many thousands of consumers, none of whom has the incentive or economic strength to sue. Where there is such a customer, or group of customers, with the ability to sue the turbine manufacturers, it may be necessary to protect the manufacturers from the possibility of multiple liability. But such is not the case here. Neither the United States nor the sponsoring companies threatens defendants on the claims asserted by OVEC and IKEC; in fact, they have settled all outstanding civil claims against defendants and at no time in the settlement negotiations did any party ever take the position that the OVEC and IKEC claims properly belonged to the AEC or the sponsoring companies. Therefore, allowing passing-on as a defense on this record would, without question, eliminate defendants' liability to anyone for a serious antitrust violation."

In the United States District Court for the Western District of Washington (Northern Division), Judge George H. Boldt reached the same conclusion. He refused to take the steps that would have authorized an interlocutory appeal from his decision because

> " . . . in good conscience I cannot certify to having the opinion 'an immediate appeal from the order may materially advance the ultimate determination of the litigation' as required for interlocutory appeal under 28 U.S.C. 1292(b)." [116]

---

[116] Appellants' Appendix, U. S. Court of Appeals for the 7th Cir., No. 14459, Commonwealth Edison Co., et al., v. Allis-Chalmers Mfg. Co., et al., pp. 79-80.

Judge Boldt added, in a memorandum opinion dated March 9, 1964, with respect to defendants' position that plaintiffs passed on their damages and thus were not in a position to sue:

> " It is incredible that such subversion of the purpose and intent of the antitrust laws will ever be permitted in this or any circuit or be sanctioned by the Supreme Court of the United States."

The decisions in the electrical equipment cases did not bring to an end attempts by defendants to assert the defense in antitrust cases. In 1968 the United States Supreme Court reviewed the validity of the passing on doctrine in a treble damage case against a manufacturer and distributor of shoe machinery.[117] United claimed that Hanover, the claimant and lessee of United's shoe machinery (United insisting upon leasing rather than selling its shoe machinery), during the damage period had reflected any illegal overcharge by United in the price charged by Hanover for shoes sold to its customers. The Supreme Court rejected what it referred to as "the so-called 'passing on' defense," saying:

> " We think it sound to hold that when a buyer shows that the price paid by him for materials purchased for use in his business is illegally high and also shows the amount of the overcharge, he has made out a prima facie case of injury and damage within the meaning of § 4.
>
> If in the face of the overcharge the buyer does nothing and absorbs the loss, he is entitled to treble damages. This much seems conceded. The reason is that he has paid more than he should and his property has been illegally diminished, for had the price paid been lower his profits would have been higher. It is also clear that if the buyer, responding to the illegal price, maintains his own price but takes steps to increase his volume or to decrease other costs, his right to damages is not destroyed. Though he may manage to maintain his profit level, he would have made more if his purchases from the defendant had cost him less. We hold that the buyer is equally entitled to damages if he raises the price for his own product. As long as the seller continues to charge the illegal price, he takes from the buyer more than the law allows. At whatever price the buyer sells, the price he pays the seller remains illegally high, and his profits would be greater were his costs lower.

[117] Hanover Shoe, Inc. v. United Shoe Machinery Corp., 392 U.S. 481 (1968).

Fundamentally, this is the view stated by Mr. Justice Holmes in *Chattanooga Foundry & Pipe Works* v. *City of Atlanta,* 203 U.S. 390 (1906), where Atlanta sued the defendants for treble damages for antitrust violations in connection with the city's purchases of pipe for its waterworks system."

The Court in a footnote recognized the statement in the Court's decision in *Darnell-Taenzer* that "the general tendency of the law, in regard to damages at least, is not to go beyond the first step."

In the *Hanover* case the Supreme Court rejected an argument that sound principles of economics require recognition of the defense:

" The rule, United argues, should be subject to the defense that economic circumstances were such that the overcharged buyer could only charge his customers a higher price *because* the price to him was higher. It is argued that in such circumstances the buyer suffers no loss from the overcharge. This situation might be present, it is said, where the overcharge is imposed equally on all of a buyer's competitors and where the demand for the buyer's product is so inelastic that the buyer and his competitors could all increase their prices by the amount of the cost increase without suffering a consequent decline in sales.

We are not impressed with the argument that sound laws of economics require recognizing this defense. A wide range of factors influence a company's pricing policies. Normally the impact of a single change in the relevant conditions cannot be measured after the fact; indeed a businessman may be unable to state whether, had one fact been different (a single supply less expensive, general economic conditions more buoyant, or the labor market tighter, for example), he would have chosen a different price. Equally difficult to determine, in the real economic world rather than an economist's hypothetical model, is what effect a change in a company's price will have on its total sales. Finally, costs per unit for a different volume of total sales are hard to estimate. Even if it could be shown that the buyer raised his price in response to, and in the amount of, the overcharge and that his margin of profit and total sales had not thereafter declined, there would remain the nearly insuperable difficulty of demonstrating that the particular plaintiff could not or would not have raised his prices absent the overcharge or maintained the higher price had the overcharge been discontinued. Since establishing the applicability of the passing on defense would require a convincing showing of each of these virtually unascertainable figures, the task would normally prove insurmountable.[118] On the other hand, it is not unlikely that if the existence of the defense is generally confirmed, antitrust defendants will frequently seek to establish its applicability. Treble damage actions would often require additional long and complicated proceedings involving massive evidence and complicated theories.

In addition, if the buyers are subject to the passing on defense, those who buy from them would also have to meet the challenge that they passed on the higher price to *their* customers. These ultimate consumers, in today's case the buyers of single pairs of shoes, would have only a tiny stake in a lawsuit and little interest in attempting a class action. In consequence, those who violate the antitrust laws by price fixing or monopolizing would retain the fruits of their illegality because no one was available who would bring suit against them. Treble damage actions, the importance of which the Court has many times emphasized, would be substantially reduced in effectiveness."

The Supreme Court did not rule out the passing on defense in all circumstances:

" We recognize that there might be situations—for instance, when an overcharged buyer has a pre-existing 'cost-plus' contract, thus making it easy to prove that he has not been damaged—where the considerations requiring that the passing on defense not be permitted in this case would not be present."

Not all of the considerations pertinent to an industrial manufacturer such as United Shoe Machinery Corporation would be equally applicable to a regulated public utility. Nevertheless, the Supreme Court in a footnote to its *Hanover Shoe* decision commented without approval or disapproval that the passing on defense had been rejected in the electrical equipment cases brought "by local utilities who purchased equipment at unlaw-

---

118 Court's Footnote: "The mere fact that a price rise followed an unlawful cost increase does not show that the sufferer of the cost increase was undamaged. His customers may have been ripe for his price rise earlier; if a cost rise is merely the occasion for a price increase a businessman could have imposed absent the rise in his costs, the fact that he was earlier not enjoying the benefits of the higher price should not permit the supplier who charges an unlawful price to take those benefits from him without being liable for damages. This statement merely recognizes the usual principle that the possessor of a right can recover for its unlawful deprivation whether or not he was previously exercising it."

fully inflated prices and used it to produce electricity sold to the ultimate consumer."

Actually, if plaintiffs had not prevailed on the passing on issue as a matter of law, the defendants would have faced a difficult practical problem in establishing that the utilities had indeed passed on to their customers the excess costs by recoupment in their rates of charge for utility service. Almost without exception the equipment purchased by the utilities from the manufacturers was not "expensed" in the utilities' accounts but rather was entered in the plant accounts as a capital investment. If plant investments were to be regarded as having been recovered from utility customers, it could only be through the mechanism of the annual depreciation charge, with the consequence that the utility would not be made whole until the expiration of the life of the property in question; and utility plant property, particularly the heavy equipment which was the subject of many of the complaints, is long-lived.

CHAPTER 7

Further motions on matters of law

THE MOTION OF THE defendants in Chicago to strike certain portions of the complaints (the second part of which raised the issue of fraudulent concealment) contained in its Part I a motion to strike all references in the complaints to the prior criminal indictments and judgments against the defendants and the alleged co-conspirators, on the principal ground that the prior criminal judgments did not constitute prima facie evidence in the treble damage actions.

The effect to be given in treble damage actions of prior criminal judgments is governed by Section 5(a) of the Clayton Act[119] which reads:

> " a. A final judgment or decree heretofore or hereafter rendered in any civil or criminal proceeding brought by or on behalf of the United States under the antitrust laws to the effect that a defendant has violated said laws shall be prima facie evidence against such defendant in any action or proceeding brought by any other party against such defendant under said laws or by the United States under Section 15a of this title, as to all matters respecting which said judgment or decree would be an estoppel as between the parties thereto: *Provided, That this section shall not apply to consent judgments or decrees entered before any testimony has been taken* or to judgments or decrees entered in actions under Section 15a of this title." (Emphasis supplied.)

The defendants' motion raised the question of whether the judgments entered in the criminal actions constituted "consent judgments or decrees." Since the judgments had been entered upon both *nolo contendere* and guilty pleas (although the judgment was one of guilty in either case), the defendants' motion raised separately the issues of whether judgments entered on

[119] 15 U.S.C. §16(a).

nolo contendere pleas were consent judgments and whether judgments entered on guilty pleas were likewise consent judgments, within the meaning of Section 5(a).

The plaintiffs argued in opposition to the motion that the statutory phrase "consent judgments or decrees" had no applicability to criminal proceedings and that, on the contrary, the well-established meaning of "consent decree" refers to civil decrees entered with the consent of the parties upon approval by a court. In asserting this point the plaintiffs cited the statement of Judge Nordbye in *Twin Ports Oil Co.*[120] where he held that a judgment based upon a *nolo contendere* plea could be regarded as a consent judgment, and added:

> " Strictly speaking, it may be that there is no such thing as a consent judgment in criminal proceedings. One who enters a plea of guilty does not necessarily consent to the judgment that the court imposes."

This attitude had been adopted in an early consideration of the issue in the electrical equipment cases. In *Sacramento Municipal Utility District (SMUD)* v. *Westinghouse Electric Corp.*[121] the court had said: "A plea of guilty cannot be construed as being a consent decree, any more than a crime can be consented to."

The defendants countered this argument by pointing out that Judge Nordbye in *Twin Ports* had in fact found that a *nolo contendere* plea could be construed as a "consent judgment"; and they argued further that judgments on guilty pleas could likewise be so considered since Section 5(a) at the time of its original enactment in 1914 had a proviso which referred to "consent judgments or decrees rendered in criminal proceedings or suits." [122]

As is customary in these situations, each side attempted to find something in the legislative history of Section 5(a) that would support its position. The plaintiffs pointed to an explanation made by Senator Chilton, the main spokesman for the

---

120 Twin Ports Oil Co. v. Pure Oil Co., 26 F. Supp. 366 (D. Minn. 1939).

121 1962 CCH Trade Cases ¶70552 at 77225 (N.D. Cal. 1962).

122 38 Stat. 731 (1914).

United States Senate Conferees in explaining Section 5 during the debates in 1914 on the Clayton Act:

> " It may be said, in conclusion of this matter, that section 5 is an effort at justice and fairness, and is intended to give a remedy to suitors who may not be as able as the Government to secure evidence. The provision takes no unfair advantage of anyone, but it does encourage those corporations who want to conform to the ideas of the Government and who desire to adjust their business and dissolve the combination in accordance with the demands of the Government. There is even an inducement that they should do so. It is new matter and grants a privilege and a right to those injured by monopoly. The fact that we could not get all that the Senate may have wanted is no reason for defeating the bill and depriving the litigants of a substantial benefit." [123]

Plaintiffs argued that Senator Chilton's explanation of the rationale of the proviso was limited to consent judgments in equity cases since dissolution of combinations and adjustments "to conform to the ideas of the Government" were remedies available only in equity proceedings.

Senator Reed, on the other hand, made certain remarks indicating that the phrase "consent decrees or judgments" could include judgments in criminal proceedings, although the Senator seemed to have confused guilty and *nolo contendere* pleas:

> " MR. REED: . . . 36 defendants entered pleas of *nolo contendere*. . . . Now, a citizen wronged by this combination, robbed by these criminals, can not under this report of the conferees, if it becomes a law, introduce in evidence the record showing their plea of guilty . . .
>
> MR. WALSH: Let me inquire of the Senator if he understands the purport of the bill as it is recommended by the conference committee to reach the case of a judgment entered on a plea of guilty.
>
> MR. REED: I do, a judgment by consent, in my opinion, covers a judgment entered upon a plea of *nolo contendere* . . .
>
> MR. WALSH: That is what I wanted to inquire of the Senator. He thinks the term 'consent judgment' would reach to a judgment entered on a plea of guilty?

---

123 51 CONG. REC. 16004 (1914).

MR. REED: I think it would. It is a judgment *nolo contendere*. It is really a judgment by consent. . . . It is my opinion, from that language, that the deduction must be drawn that the exception applies to criminal as well as civil consents. The only way you can consent in a criminal case is by an absolute plea of guilty or the plea of *nolo contendere* . . .

MR. WALSH: I scarcely think the Senator will care to say that judgments hereinafter entered upon a plea of guilty would fall under the discrimination of consent judgments or decrees, because I take it that no criminal would ever consent that a judgment be entered against him when he pleads guilty. The judgment goes as a matter of course against him . . ." [124]

In view of the confusion, plaintiffs cited Justice Peckham on the general unreliability of legislative history:

" Those who did not speak may not have agreed with those who did; and those who spoke might differ from each other; the result being that the only proper way to construe a legislative act is from the language used in the act, and, upon occasion, by a resort to the history of the times when it was passed." [125]

The plaintiffs argued that, even if a court were inclined to believe that judgments in criminal proceedings could be considered to be "consent decrees or judgments," a distinction ought to be made between *nolo contendere* pleas on the one hand and guilty pleas on the other. Plaintiffs maintained that this distinction had indeed been drawn by defendants' counsel in the criminal proceedings when the pleas were being proffered to Chief Judge Ganey. Thus, counsel for Federal Pacific at that time had said:

" If Your Honor, by refusal to accept nolo pleas, places a smaller company like this in great jeopardy as a result of litigation which might result from these indictments by forcing a plea of guilty, Your Honor may put Federal Pacific Electric Company in the position where it will be either driven out of business or so severely injured that it could provide no competition of any kind. . . ." [126]

---

[124] 51 CONG. REC. pt. 16, pp. 15823, 15824 (1914).

[125] United States v. Trans-Missouri Freight Ass'n, 166 U.S. 290, 318-19 (1897).

[126] Hearings before Judge Ganey, Nov. 21, 1960, p. 214.

Similarly, counsel for General Electric had stated:

> "I hope Your Honor realizes that if corporations are permitted to plead nolo contendere and G.E. and Westinghouse are not, it is not just a question of relieving those corporations of a treble damage liability, but it is a determination by Your Honor that a great proportion of that damage must be assessed against General Electric and Westinghouse. I suggest that the pleas are not to be used as the basis for bargaining among corporate defendants on the question of subsequent liability in litigation not yet brought." [127]

Judge Robson in October 1962 ruled that judgments in criminal proceedings, whether entered upon pleas of guilty or *nolo contendere* could be regarded as "consent judgments" within the proviso of Section 5(a), and he therefore granted the defendants' motion to strike from the complaints the references to the criminal proceedings and judgments. Judge Robson concluded his decision by stating:

> "[i]n view of the contrariety of decisions interpreting Congressional intent in enacting the proviso and the great importance to the orderly conduct of this multiple litigation for a definitive ruling, this Court respectfully recommends an immediate appeal for determination of the issue." [128]

An interlocutory appeal was granted on the petition of Commonwealth Edison Company and its associate plaintiffs by the Court of Appeals for the Seventh Circuit.

Prior to Judge Robson's ruling, Judge Kirkpatrick of Philadelphia had granted the motions of defendants to strike all portions of the treble damages complaints filed in that district in their reference to the *nolo contendere* pleas; the defendants maintained that such references were "impertinent, scandalous and immaterial." Judge Kirkpatrick ruled that under the *Twin Ports* case he would grant the motions but observed:

---

[127] Hearings before Judge Ganey, Nov. 21, 1960, p. 262.

[128] Appendix to Appellants' Brief, United States Court of Appeals for the 7th Circuit, No. 14024, Commonwealth Edison Co., et al., Appellants, v. Allis-Chalmers Mfg. Co., et al., Appellees, p. 73.

> "The allegations objected to certainly can't be called impertinent or scandalous, but I think they must be called immaterial, and I can see possibilities of prejudice." [129]

The Court of Appeals for the Seventh Circuit affirmed[130] Judge Robson's holding that a judgment entered upon a *nolo contendere* plea constituted a consent judgment but reversed his holding (one judge dissenting) that the same was true of judgments entered on guilty pleas. The court relied on the temporary proviso which in 1914 had referred to consent judgments in criminal proceedings. Further, as to *nolo contendere* pleas, the court found that the record of the Philadelphia criminal proceedings bore out the element of consent, in that the record showed that the pleas had not been entered except with the approval of the Government and after compromise negotiations with the Government.

The court of appeals found support for its position that judgments entered on guilty pleas should not be regarded as within the exclusionary proviso, i.e., that guilty plea judgments should constitute prima facie evidence within the meaning of Section 5(a), by referring to President Woodrow Wilson's Special Message to the Congress, January 20, 1914, urging the enactment of provisions to facilitate the bringing of treble damage suits by private antitrust litigants. In that Message President Wilson had stated:

> "I hope that we shall agree in giving private individuals who claim to have been injured by these processes the right to found their suits for redress upon the facts and judgments proved and entered in suits by the Government. . . . It is not fair that the private litigant should be obliged to set up and establish again the facts which the Government has proved. He can not afford, he has not the power, to make use of such processes of inquiry as the Government has command of. Thus shall individual justice be done while the processes of business are rectified and squared with the general conscience." [131]

---

129 Philadelphia v. Westinghouse Electric Corp., 1961 CCH Trade Cases ¶7143 at 78553 (E.D. Pa. 1961). See discussion in Seamans, Winson & McCartney, *Use of Criminal Pleas in Aid of Private Antitrust Actions,* 10 Antitrust Bulletin 795, 804 (1966).

130 Commonwealth Edison Co., et al., v. Allis-Chalmers Mfg. Co., et al., 323 F.2d 412 (7th Cir. 1963).

131 51 Cong. Rec., p. 1964 (1914).

The court stated that by giving private antitrust litigants the prima facie benefit of judgments obtained by the Government, Congress intended to save private litigants great time and expense. On the other hand, by enacting the exclusionary proviso, Congress sought to aid antitrust enforcements by encouraging defendants to capitulate, at a saving of time and expense to the Government. Both purposes of Section 5(a) served the broad objective of antitrust enforcement and, the court stated, "Although the two purposes are distinct, an accommodation must be made to preserve the essence of both." [132] But the court concluded that a guilty plea is not really a consent plea resulting in a consent judgment; and further, if guilty pleas were held to be consent judgments and therefore within the exclusionary proviso, along with *nolo contendere* pleas, the private litigant would thereby be denied the total benefit of Section 5(a) since pleas leading to a judgment of guilty can be only *nolo contendere* or guilty pleas. The result then would be that the section "would help antitrust violators at the direct expense of the victims of those violators." The court concluded that its construction of Section 5(a), by including *nolo* pleas within the proviso but not guilty pleas, struck the balance which it believed that Congress had contemplated between the two specific purposes of Section 5(a):

> " Congress intended a choice be made as to the respective values of these purposes by the exercise of the District Court's discretion in a criminal antitrust proceeding. The Court can in a suitable case accept a plea of nolo contendere and save the Government both time and expense; in another case—perhaps where the Government's proof is more than adequate, and the offense of a more serious nature—the court may choose, on Government objection to reject a defendant's capitulation by the nolo plea, thereby serving the specific objective of aiding and promoting the treble damage actions of injured parties. In either case, more effective enforcement of the antitrust laws is achieved, and the choice between the specific objectives of § 5(a) is vested in the District Court, not the antitrust violator."

Judge Knoch dissented from the court's finding that guilty pleas were outside the scope of "consent judgments" because,

---

132 Here the court was quoting Mr. Justice Harlan, dissenting in Wood v. Georgia, 370 U.S. 375, 396 (1962).

in his view, the accused by a plea of guilty agrees "to the government's allegations of fact and consents to whatever judgment the court may impose." Judge Knoch interpreted the Congressional history as showing a primary Congressional purpose of inducing capitulation by defendants to avoid protracted litigation and to give the benefit of prima facie evidence only to judgments against those convicted after trial.

The defendants attempted to secure review by the U. S. Supreme Court of the decision of the court of appeals that judgments on guilty pleas did not constitute "consent judgments" by petition for a writ of certiorari filed in January 1964. Plaintiffs did not file a cross-petition for a review of the court of appeals decision with respect to *nolo contendere* pleas. Defendants' petition for certiorari was denied.[133]

Initially certain plaintiffs' counsel regarded the holding respecting guilty pleas as one of the most important of the legal issues decided in favor of the plaintiffs. Such counsel at the outset of the litigation were inclined to believe that all that was required to prove the treble damage case would be (1) evidence of the guilty pleas, and (2) damage evidence as to excess prices paid; and that thereupon judgment for the plaintiffs would automatically follow. None of the plaintiffs' counsel held this simplified view for long.

These same questions respecting the effect of guilty and *nolo contendere* pleas received varying answers in other circuits. In Missouri, judgments based on pleas of guilty were found by a district court to be consent judgments, and no appeal was taken to the Eighth Circuit.[134] District judges in the Fifth and Ninth Circuits concluded, as had Judge Robson, that both *nolo contendere* and guilty pleas were to be regarded as consent judgments and accordingly to be denied prima facie effects. On appeal, the Fifth and Ninth Circuit Courts of Appeals reached the same conclusion as had the Seventh Circuit, that *nolo con-*

---

[133] 376 U.S. 939 (1964).

[134] N. W. Power Co-op, Inc. v. General Electric Co., 30 F.R.D. 557 (W.D. Mo. 1961, Judge Duncan), 1963 CCH Trade Cases ¶70691.

tendere pleas led to consent judgments but guilty pleas did not.[135]

An attempt was made in the 1966 session of Congress to secure a legislative reversal of the holding that judgments on *nolo contendere* pleas were to be regarded as consent judgments. Senate Bill 2512, introduced by Senator Phillip A. Hart of Michigan, received strong support in hearings before the Senate Antitrust Subcommittee from attorneys who had been active in representation of plaintiffs in the electrical equipment cases, but the bill failed to pass.[136] Senate Subcommittee hearings were held on May 11, 1966. Witnesses in favor of the legislation included Harold E. Kohn, antitrust counsel for Philadelphia Electric Company; Richard E. Cullen (speaking for the National Association of County Civil Attorneys); and the late Thomas C. McConnell, antitrust counsel for the Metropolitan Sanitary District of Chicago.

By reason of the holding with respect to the *nolo contendere* pleas, there were stricken from the complaints relating to *nolo contendere* product lines the paragraphs which recited the return of the indictment covering the particular product line, the summary of the charges contained in the indictment, the pleas entered by the defendants and alleged co-conspirators, and allegations that on a specified date judgments of guilty were entered on *nolo contendere* pleas and that sentences were imposed. In order that the complaint would not be without any reference of any kind to the criminal proceedings, Judge Robson in the Northern District of Illinois, after ordering the striking of the foregoing matter, granted leave to plaintiffs to amend the complaint by inserting the following paragraph, simply to identify the proceedings and indicate that they had been terminated:

" The United States of America instituted criminal proceedings on ...., ... in Cause No. .... in the Eastern Dis-

---

135 Dept. of Water and Power v. Allis-Chalmers Mfg. Co., 1963 CCH Trade Cases ¶70656 (S.D. Cal. 1963, Judge Byrne), *aff'd*, Burbank v. General Electric Co., 329 F.2d 825 (9th Cir. 1964); City of San Antonio v. General Electric Co., Civ. No. 3063 (W.D. Texas 1963, Judge Spears), *aff'd*, General Electric Co. v. City of San Antonio, 334 F.2d 480 (5th Cir. 1964).

136 See also S. 1538, 90th Cong., 1st Sess. (1967).

trict of Pennsylvania and civil proceedings on ...., ... in Cause No. .... in said district against among others the defendants named herein charging unlawful combination and conspiracy under the antitrust laws of the United States. The aforesaid criminal proceedings terminated on ...., ... and the civil proceedings on ...., ..."[137]

In Utah Judge Christensen refused to strike the allegations of the complaint relating to the *nolo contendere* product lines but indicated that at the trial he would not permit the plea to go to the jury.

At the conclusion of the arguments and decisions on the legal questions raised by defendants' attacks on the plaintiffs' complaints, plaintiffs were in a position where it had been established: (1) they were not to be confined to the statutory four-year period in proving their damages but could go as far back as the beginning of the conspiracies, provided that they could prove that the conspiratorial action in the pre-limitation period had been fraudulently concealed; (2) plaintiffs were not to be required to prove as a condition of establishing their damages that they had not passed on the excess costs to their customers; and (3) in respect of those product lines in which the defendants or some of them had pleaded guilty, the plaintiffs were to have the prima facie benefit of the judgments of guilty entered upon those pleas;[138] with respect to those product lines where the defendants pleaded *nolo contendere,* there would be no benefit in the civil cases from the judgments in the criminal proceedings.

The plaintiffs, having prevailed on substantially all legal issues, were still confronted with a gigantic task of establishing, through a pretrial discovery program which would have to be applicable and relate to the more than 1,900 cases on file, that there had in fact been conspiracies of the defendants which

---

137 Order dated December 14, 1962, of Judge Edwin A. Robson, reprinted in Appellants' Appendix in the United States Court of Appeals for the Seventh Circuit, No. 14024, Commonwealth Edison Co., et al., Appellants, v. Allis-Chalmers Mfg. Co., et al., Appellees.

138 Of course, in the cases involving hydroelectric generators, where no criminal proceedings had been instituted, there could be no benefit from any judgments of guilty in criminal proceedings.

had fixed unlawful prices, that the plaintiffs had paid such prices for equipment in the various product lines in suit, that such conspiracies had been fraudulently concealed, that plaintiffs did not know and would not reasonably have been expected to know of such conspiracies (which knowledge would have negatived fraudulent concealment), and finally, that the plaintiffs had indeed suffered damages by paying for the equipment prices greater than would have prevailed in a free, open, competitive and non-conspiratorial market.

The benefit of having as prima facie evidence the judgments of guilty entered on guilty pleas would be of small assistance in this task, since such pleas would be evidence only, in the language of Section 5(a), "as to all matters respecting which said judgment or decree would be an estoppel as between the parties thereto"; and such "matters," it was clear from prior authority,[139] would show only that there had been in fact a price fixing conspiracy. As to the details of the conspiracy; its operation in fixing specific prices for equipment purchased by the plaintiffs; the techniques of fraudulent concealment; and the specific damages suffered by the plaintiffs—all these were essential elements of the plaintiffs' case which remained to be established by the plaintiffs' own efforts. These constituted essential matters as to which the guilty judgments would be of no assistance.

---

[139] Emich Motors Corporation v. General Motors Corporation, 340 U.S. 558 (1951).

CHAPTER 8

Pretrial discovery

UNDER THE FEDERAL RULES of Civil Procedure parties to civil litigation in the federal courts are entitled to "discover," by a variety of methods, facts that may be relevant at the trial or which may lead to facts relevant at the trial. These methods include oral examination (depositions) of persons who for good reason are thought to have such information; they may include written interrogatories addressed to and requiring answer by the parties; motions for the production of documents; and requests addressed from one party to another for the admission of facts and genuineness of documents.[140]

For plaintiffs, discovery was the basic tool with which they hoped to establish the basic facts of the conspiracies. Little assistance could be derived from the criminal judgments of conviction since the judgments simply established that there had been a conspiracy to fix prices in the various product lines at some time during the period alleged. What the plaintiffs needed to establish was that there had been specific meetings and agreements to fix the specific prices which the plaintiffs had paid for the products in suit; and plaintiffs further had to demonstrate that such specific conspiracies had been fraudulently concealed. None of these issues was present in the Government's criminal proceedings.

In the early days of the civil litigation counsel for plaintiffs in several of the cases set out on discovery programs of their own. Counsel for Chelan County, whose suit was pending in the State of Washington, took depositions in New York City of thirteen General Electric employees and one employee of

---

140 These matters are covered in Part V, Rules 26-37 of the FEDERAL RULES OF CIVIL PROCEDURE.

Allis-Chalmers. These depositions were placed under seal and were not available to other counsel, nor to the general public, by order of the Washington trial judge, Judge George H. Boldt. The Philadelphia plaintiffs gave notice of depositions respecting the product line of power switchgear assemblies: the individuals whose depositions were sought included high-ranking officers of General Electric, Cordiner, Vinson and Burke, and of Westinghouse, Cresap and Price. I-T-E Circuit Breaker requested the court to seal the Philadelphia depositions because publication thereof would result in "harmful public relations." Judge Kirkpatrick denied the motion, indicating that all discovery in the Philadelphia action would be made available nationally as a matter of policy.

In Chicago counsel for the utility plaintiffs proposed to defendants' counsel to take the depositions of sixteen named officers or employees of the defendants in depositions to begin in January 1962. The names proposed included Ginn, Lilly, Neblett, Burens, Burke and Raymond Smith of General Electric; Mauntel, Fuller, J. T. Thompson, Pyle and Chiles of Westinghouse; McMullen and Long of Allis-Chalmers; Spencer and Wilcox of I-T-E Circuit Breaker; and Romano of H. K. Porter; and, in addition, plaintiffs' counsel proposed to depose one person each in charge of meter pricing, names unknown to them, from General Electric, Westinghouse and Sangamo.

In the Northern District of California (San Francisco), the Sacramento Municipal Utility District (SMUD) filed a motion to produce documents falling into two categories: (1) documents concerning the holding of meetings and showing specifically what was done in furtherance of the alleged conspiracies, and (2) documents relevant to what prices would have been had there been no such conspiracy. In a Memorandum and Order dated June 6, 1962, Judge Halbert granted most of the SMUD requests, but limited to the products involved in the SMUD cases and to the period from four years prior to the filing of the complaints up to December 31, 1961. The products involved in the SMUD suits were power switchgear assemblies, power transformers, circuit breakers, distribution transformers, meters and hydro-generators. Among the items granted were defendants' annual reports to their stockholders; reports to stockholders relating to the Government criminal proceedings; writings relating to company antitrust policy and investigation of possible antitrust violations; writings relating to meetings with competitors at which prices were fixed or discussed; writings relating to allocation of customers or markets as among the defendant companies; and writings showing corporate structure, including divisions or departments, and directors, officers and divisional or departmental heads and subheads. SMUD also proposed to take the depositions of General Electric officials Cordiner, Paxton and LaPierre, which General Electric moved to stop, citing discussions looking toward a nationwide discovery plan. Judge Halbert denied the General Electric motion and the depositions proceeded as scheduled on August 2 and 3, 1962, at the Waldorf-Astoria Hotel in New York City, with attendance and access to the depositions limited to the parties to the Sacramento actions. Judge Halbert, on August 9, 1962, had also ordered the defendants to produce documents which had been made the subject of motion to produce by SMUD. Later, on October 8, 1962, Judge Halbert stayed all discovery in his court.

It had become clear to the judges and to practically all parties concerned that discovery in the individual cases was not the answer. If the individual attempts to take depositions, submit interrogatories and move for the production of documents were multiplied by a number representing all the cases pending in the federal courts, the result would be intolerable. Judge Robson stated in this connection:

> "It has become clear to the judges, and I am sure to the lawyers, that we are either going to proceed in a systematic, logical way, or, if we do not, there will be chaos in this litigation." [141]

The situation called for a centralized, unified method of pretrial discovery.

The first attempts of the judiciary along these lines consisted of steps to consolidate all cases within a single district before

141 Transcript of proceedings, San Francisco, Aug. 17, 1962, p. 8.

a single judge, at least for pretrial and discovery purposes. In Philadelphia all civil cases were assigned to Judge Kirkpatrick, with the Government's damage cases going to Judge Van Dusen. In the Western District of Missouri Judge Becker on his own motion consolidated all cases for pretrial procedures. In the Northern District of Illinois the Executive Committee denominated Judge Robson as the pretrial and discovery judge for all cases pending in that district.[142]

But even district by district procedures would have resulted in tremendous duplication of discovery efforts. A group of counsel for plaintiffs from various parts of the country accordingly explored methods of unified action early in the proceedings. In December 1961, Bane and Swiren, counsel for a group of plaintiffs in the Northern District of Illinois, had a meeting in New York with Messrs. Webster, Handler, LeBoeuf, Lamb and Clark, counsel for various investor-owned utility plaintiffs in the Southern District of New York, including the Atlantic City group, to explore the possibilities for concerted action among counsel for plaintiffs in the districts in which the largest numbers of cases were pending.

Within the ATIG organization there were discussions whether that group should be utilized for a unified and cooperative approach to the litigation, particularly for the discovery phase. Members of ATIG were almost evenly divided on the proposition, and eventually it was determined that whatever cooperative efforts were worked out should be entirely independent of the ATIG organization.

The federal judiciary took the initiative in the matter. In January 1962, in the Northern District of Illinois, Judge Robson informed counsel in the cases pending before him that it was his intention to raise, at the March 1962 meeting of the Judicial Conference of the United States, the question of whether the Judicial Conference should formulate a plan for the handling of all treble damage cases arising out of the Philadelphia indictments on a nationwide basis. At his request counsel for the plaintiffs, on January 18, 1962, submitted a memorandum which

142 See Bane, *Pretrial Discovery in Multiple Litigation from the Plaintiffs' Standpoint,* 32 ANTITRUST LAW JOURNAL 117, 118 (1966).

recommended such handling of the cases. Shortly thereafter, on February 6, Chief Justice Warren established a panel of federal judges to examine techniques for handling the damage suits, the panel being established as a Subcommittee of the Committee on Pretrial Procedure of the Judicial Conference of the United States (the "Coordinating Committee"). Chief Judge Alfred P. Murrah (Tenth Circuit) was appointed Chairman of the Subcommittee, and the members were: Chief Judge Sylvester J. Ryan (Southern District of New York), Chief Judge Thomas J. Clary (Eastern District, Pennsylvania), Chief Judge Joe E. Estes (Northern District, Texas), Chief Judge Roszel C. Thompsen (Maryland), Judge Edwin A. Robson (Northern District of Illinois), Judge George H. Boldt (Western District, Washington), Judge William M. Byrne (Southern District of California), and Judge William H. Becker (Western District of Missouri). The charge to the Coordinating Committee by the Chief Justice was to consider "discovery problems arising in multiple litigation with common witnesses and exhibits." [143]

There was no question that the electrical equipment litigation constituted such a situation because the issues in the cases were common. Although the suits numbered more than 1,800 and the claims more than 25,000, the complaints in each product line, wherever filed, alleged the same conspiracy against the same manufacturers and involving the same participants. For example, the conspiracy that was alleged in turbo-generators

---

143 Letter from Chief Justice Warren to Judge Edwin A. Robson, Jan. 26, 1962, quoted in Neal and Goldberg, *The Electrical Equipment Antitrust Cases: Novel Judicial Administration,* 50 American Bar Association Journal 621, 623 (1964).

Judge George H. Boldt told the author of an incident relating to the formation of the Coordinating Committee. He recalled that shortly after he had gotten under way in the Chelan County suit, with depositions which proved to be abortive, he wrote to Chief Justice Warren asking for an appointment to discuss the necessity for national coordination of the electrical equipment cases. Judge Boldt did see the Chief Justice and urged this course upon him, although the Chief Justice was somewhat reluctant and made a counter-suggestion for coordination on a circuit basis. One week later, according to Judge Boldt, Judge Robson called on the Chief Justice (with Judge Prettyman of the District of Columbia) to urge national coordination. This latter visit was followed by the Chief Justice's appointment of the Coordinating Committee.

in the suits filed in the Southern District of New York was the same conspiracy alleged in the complaints filed in turbo-generators in the Northern District of Illinois or in the Eastern District of Pennsylvania or elsewhere throughout the country. And the same situation was true with respect to all products under consideration, whether power switchgear assemblies, power transformers, meters or whatever. This is not to say that the same conspiracy was alleged in meters as was alleged in turbo-generators, but all allegations of conspiracy in a given product line related to the same conspiracy.[144]

Under these circumstances, it was clear that if discovery was to be conducted district by district, even with consolidation for pretrial purposes within the district, there could be as many as thirty-five calls on the same witness for a deposition, with the problem multiplied then by the hundreds or even the thousands in view of the number of individuals alleged to have been involved in the various conspiracies. Furthermore, there could have been thirty-five calls for the production in thirty-five different districts of the same documents, which could and did eventually number more than a million, produced by the various defendants. The defendants could have found themselves confronted with thirty-five varying sets of comprehensive interrogatories in each of the nineteen different product lines, and with answers required to be filed in all thirty-five courts in which the suits were pending.

The consolidation in each district of all claims in a product line would still have meant more than 400 cases pending. And this type of consolidation procedure would have complicated the remaining suits by increasing the number of plaintiffs involved in each case: in certain instances several hundred plaintiffs with varying interests would have been joined in a single suit.[145]

---

144 Even the complaints which alleged a so-called "basket" conspiracy, charging an overall conspiracy that embraced all product lines, went on to allege individual conspiracies by product line. The course of the discovery and the trials indicated that the conspiracies were indeed of the product line rather than the "basket" variety.

145 Neal and Goldberg, *supra* note 143 at 621-622 n. 6.

At its first general meeting held in Philadelphia on March 22, 1962, the Coordinating Committee invited all judges before whom electrical equipment cases were pending. Some twenty-five district judges were there, many of them skeptical that a program of coordination could be carried out successfully. However, the group encouraged the Coordinating Committee to make the attempt by adopting the following resolution:

> "RESOLVED that a Committee composed of the present members of the Sub-Committee, and such others as may be desired, be appointed by the chair to suggest ways and means of handling the electrical antitrust cases, from discovery through pre-trial, and that it be the sense of this meeting that a plan for co-ordinating discovery procedures and expediting rulings on key legal questions, as well as a means for disseminating information, be devised and submitted to the trial judges involved at the earliest practicable time; and that, in the meantime, procedures leading toward the securing of information needed for ultimate disposition of the litigation be followed, as nearly as practicable, by each individual judge."

Following further meetings in Norfolk, Virginia, in April and in Chicago in June 1962, the Coordinating Committee took its first important step by recommending that all judges before whom electrical equipment cases were pending enter seven pretrial orders based on those already entered by Chief Judge Ryan in the cases pending before him in the Southern District of New York.

This initial set of pretrial orders, which came to have the designation of National Pretrial Orders Nos. 1 to 7,[146] accomplished several objectives. First, they took control of discovery from counsel in the various cases and placed that control in the judges. Accordingly, it was ordered that interrogatories previously served by any party were to be vacated; depositions previously noticed were stayed; and all further interrogatories and depositions were made subject to further orders of the court.[147]

---

146 A number of national pretrial orders are reproduced in II BORDEN'S FEDERAL PRACTICE FORMS, 440.35 et seq.

147 National Pretrial Orders Nos. 1 and 3.

Second, these initial pretrial orders initiated coordinated discovery by prescribing two important sets of uniform interrogatories appropriate for all cases. The defendants had been insisting that they could not prepare for litigation unless they were informed by the plaintiffs as to what purchase transactions the plaintiffs were suing on. Defendants claimed that they could not identify such transactions from their own records. Accordingly, uniform interrogatories[148] addressed to the plaintiffs were allowed the defendants, requiring that plaintiffs furnish so-called "purchase identification data" to provide the defendants with full information about the transactions to which the plaintiffs claimed damages. Set No. 2 of interrogatories propounded by certain of the defendants required plaintiffs to provide each defendant from whom they had made any purchases during the period 1956 to 1960 with certain data concerning preferred or qualified bidders lists.[149]

Plaintiffs also had prepared a set of interrogatories addressed to the defendants that had been approved in the Southern District of New York. These interrogatories sought comprehensive information about meetings and communications among competitors, the personnel of the defendants who had been involved in these activities and the pricing practices of each defendant. Although other varying interrogatories had been submitted in other districts and approved, as in the Northern District of Illinois, ultimately the set submitted and approved in the Southern District of New York was adopted for nationwide use.[150]

The first national pretrial order encouraged early determination of the issues of law by setting up a schedule for filing and

---

148 See Appendix 12.

149 A copy of this Set No. 2 is included herein as Appendix 13.

150 This set of interrogatories is included herein as Appendix 14. In the Eastern District of Pennsylvania the court determined to allow the interrogatories that had been submitted by Philadelphia plaintiffs' counsel to stand and accordingly did not enter Judge Ryan's pretrial order on plaintiffs' interrogatories. It is Judge Boldt's recollection that the proposal to adopt the New York interrogatories for standard use in all the electrical equipment cases was put to the twenty-five judges meeting in Philadelphia in March 1962, and was adopted by a margin of one vote.

hearing motions raising objections to the complaints. These procedures related primarily to the issues concerning the statute of limitations and fraudulent concealment and the effect of the *nolo contendere* and guilty pleas. One commentator has complained about the action of the Coordinating Committee in expediting rulings on key legal questions. He claimed that in normal litigation, decisions on some law issues are best deferred until all the facts are in while others may be disposed of in earlier stages; but he stated, "no such cautions accompanied the resolution of the Coordinating Committee." [151]

A procedure was established in the initial pretrial orders[152] whereby, with consent of the parties, cases could be placed in an inactive status, the so-called "back burner" cases, which could stand by while national discovery was going forward. At a very early date more than 104 cases had been agreed to be placed on the back burner by the plaintiffs and defendants involved, and in some districts all cases pending in the district were placed in such a status. Indeed, as matters developed, the active prosecution of discovery was carried on primarily by counsel for plaintiffs whose suits had been filed in the large metropolitan centers of New York, Philadelphia, Chicago, Washington, D. C., Los Angeles, San Francisco and Seattle.

Following the entry of pretrial orders dealing with housekeeping details and preliminary interrogatories for each side, the Coordinating Committee turned its attention to the problem of depositions, which go to the very heart of a discovery program. The Coordinating Committee could turn to no statute nor to any rules of civil procedure for guidance. The Judicial Conference had adopted a *Handbook of Recommended Procedures for Trial of Protracted Cases* (March 1960),[153] but the *Handbook* related to litigation within a single district. Therefore, new procedures and new ground rules had to be worked out and an order of priority as among product lines established.

---

151 McAllister, *Judicial Administration of Multiple-District Treble Damage Litigation*, 1966, N. Y. State Bar Assn. Antitrust Law Symposium, CCH ed. at p. 76.

152 National Pretrial Order No. 2.

153 Reprinted in 25 F.R.D. 351.

In July 1962 Judge Robson indicated that the Coordinating Committee, in its consideration of the possibilities for national depositions, might decide to proceed simultaneously in all nineteen product categories. In that event there might be appointed a panel of traveling judges to hear all depositions or, as an alternative, the country would be divided into geographic areas with certain judges sitting in those areas designated to hear depositions. At the suggestion of the respective judges, plaintiffs in New York and Chicago submitted a proposed set of ground rules to Judges Ryan and Robson respectively in August 1962. The suggestions, worked out beforehand by consultation among plaintiffs' counsel in the two districts, were practically identical. One plaintiff in the Northern District of Illinois not agreeing with the proposals was the Metropolitan Sanitary District of Greater Chicago.

In August 1962 the Coordinating Committee met in Palo Alto, with invitations extended to all judges before whom electrical cases were pending. The meeting was attended by twenty-six judges from twenty-one states.[154] Assurances had been given that at the conference the judges would not discuss possible rulings on legal questions but rather, would discuss principles and procedures under which the national discovery program should be carried out. At Palo Alto approval was given to the idea of national depositions and to the use of national pretrial orders to implement the national discovery program.

Immediately thereafter the Committee met with counsel for the plaintiffs and defendants in San Francisco.[155] There presentations were requested from counsel for both sides as to suggested ground rules and as to the priorities to be established among the product lines for depositions. Judge Robson informed the meeting that its purpose was to work out "a unified program in what is probably the heaviest load of multiple litigation throughout the country." He added that the program was to be

154 Transcript of proceedings, San Francisco, Aug. 17, 1962, p. 7.

155 The judges present were Murrah, Ryan, Robson, Boldt and Becker. In addition, Dean Phil Neal of the University of Chicago Law School, Executive Secretary of the Committee, was present, and Messrs. Shafroth and Olney from the Administrative Office of the United States.

voluntary, if possible, and Judge Murrah remarked that if there were plaintiffs' or defendants' counsel who did not wish to cooperate, he was confident that authority could be found within the federal judicial system for carrying out a national deposition program.

During the course of the San Francisco meeting, counsel for both the plaintiffs and the defendants submitted drafts looking toward a pretrial order which would cover the subject matter of the meeting. The pattern established, at this and at subsequent meetings, called for submittal of such proposals from each side in advance of the meetings, followed then by argument at the meetings before all the judges in attendance on the points disputed between counsel. The judges then retired and, after reviewing the arguments, announced (still during the course of the meeting) their conclusions, whereupon representatives of the Committee and of counsel for both sides sat down and worked out a pretrial order which would embody the decisions and agreements arrived at. These meetings and conferences have been characterized, particularly by defense counsel, in various ways. One defendants' counsel has stated that the proceedings resembled "a diplomatic conference more than typical judicial proceedings."[156] Another commentator has characterized these hearings as "one simultaneous pretrial hearing in virtually all of the cases."[157]

The pretrial order so drafted had no intrinsic force and effect except that it constituted a recommendation from the Coordinating Committee to the individual judges before whom the cases were pending; accordingly, the form of pretrial order was sent to the individual districts for entry following notice to all parties. Theoretically the parties were free to reargue the terms and provisions of the proposed pretrial order at the district level but in practice the judges, who almost uniformly cooperated with the Coordinating Committee by accepting the Committee's recommendations, were intolerant of any extended argument on matters that had already been covered at the meetings of the

---

[156] O'Donnell, *Pretrial Discovery in Multiple Litigation from the Defendants' Standpoint,* 32 ANTITRUST LAW JOURNAL 137 (1966).

[157] McAllister, *supra* note 151, at 61 n. 15.

Coordinating Committee. At the San Antonio conference it was suggested by a defense counsel that the record of objections made at the national meetings should be incorporated as a part of the record in the local hearings when they were scheduled and held on the question of entering the national pretrial order locally. Plaintiffs' counsel agreed and the procedure was adopted. In Los Angeles, counsel for H. K. Porter argued that National Pretrial Order No. 8 ought not to be entered there because it was "an unwarranted intrusion into the historic rights of parties . . . to conduct their own lawsuits." He was overruled.

Throughout this whole process the Coordinating Committee urged defendants' and plaintiffs' counsel to get together prior to the submittal of their proposals to define the areas of agreement to the greatest possible extent. So intent were the judges to emphasize the voluntary nature of these procedures that Judge Murrah characterized the San Francisco meeting as a voluntary meeting among counsel at which the judges were the guests of the lawyers. Evidently the judges were prepared, in the event that the parties could or would not submit a workable plan, to prepare a plan of their own and adopt it. Certain counsel, particularly counsel for SMUD, argued for permission to pursue a deposition program in his own way, but ultimately all plaintiffs' and defendants' counsel agreed to cooperate in a national discovery program.

Another concern, not apparent at the San Francisco meeting but surfacing in later proceedings, was the fear among plaintiffs' counsel from the Western States that the entire national discovery program might be dominated by New York. In San Antonio counsel for certain plaintiff municipalities had addressed a letter to his district judge, which in turn was made available to the Coordinating Committee, protesting any New York domination. He was assured by Judge Spears, following a San Antonio meeting of the Coordinating Committee, that there would be no such domination.[158] The court added that there was a belief that the effective and orderly disposition of the cases was affected with such a public interest that judicial action to approve a national

158 Transcript of proceedings, Aug. 30, 1962, San Antonio, Texas, United States District Court, Western District, Electrical Equipment Antitrust Cases, pp. 6-7.

discovery program was justified. As Judge Spears put it, when a lawsuit is in the lawyer's office it is his business, but when filed in court it is the "public's business." [159]

National Pretrial Order No. 8, which came out of San Francisco, authorized the oral deposition of six employees or former employees of the defendants (or more as might be added by further order), to be selected by the plaintiffs; and the plaintiffs throughout the country were prohibited from taking any other depositions except upon further order of the court. The ground rules for the depositions, based upon the views of Dean Neal and the suggestions of plaintiffs' and defendants' counsel, provided that each of the depositions could be used in accordance with Federal Rule 26(d) by or against any party who was present or represented at the deposition or who had notice of it. Matters relating exclusively to the amount of particular damage suffered by any individual plaintiff were not to be gone into on the deposition. This left available for examination the entire areas of liability including the manner of operation of the conspiracy, the agreements or understandings arrived at, the effect of such agreements on prices paid by the plaintiffs (the "impact of the conspiracy") and matters relating to the extent of the injury to plaintiffs generally. The reference to Rule 26(d) made clear that subject to limitations and the rules of evidence, the deposition material could be used as evidence at the trial if (1) the deposition was that of an officer, director or managing agent of a defendant corporation, or (2) the witness in any event is dead at the time of trial, or unable to attend because of age, sickness, infirmity or imprisonment, or (3) if the witness is at a greater distance than 100 miles from the place of trial, or (4) if the party offering the deposition has been unable to procure the attendance of the witness at the trial by subpoena. Any deposition could be used to contradict or impeach the testimony of the deponent as a witness.

It was required under the pretrial order that plaintiffs and defendants should agree as to the various counsel who would conduct the deposition examination or cross-examination, but "no counsel shall be excluded from participating in the examina-

---

[159] *Id.* at 17.

tion or prevented from exploring more fully lines of questions previously pursued provided that counsel shall not engage in unnecessary repetition." Copies of the transcript were to be made available to all plaintiffs and defendants and were to be corrected and signed by the witness within thirty days of availability of the transcript to him, and filed in all the districts where cases were pending.

One of the objections to a national deposition program that had been made by counsel for certain of the smaller defendants was that they would be required to bear the expense of attendance of counsel at every deposition merely out of fear that something might be developed that would affect that particular defendant, even though it might be a different product line from the one in which the particular defendant was interested. In order to obviate this objection, the pretrial order provided that upon the completion of a deposition the hearing would be adjourned for approximately forty days, during which time all parties could examine the transcript and determine whether their interests had been so affected that further interrogation was required. Any counsel desiring further interrogation was required to make written application to the deposition judge within thirty days following adjournment, showing good cause and specifying the subject matter and necessity for additional inquiry. In the absence of any such application no further interrogation would be permitted.

Important decisions were made at San Francisco that the product lines to be given priority for the deposition program would be turbo-generators, hydroelectric generators and power transformers. This was in line with the plaintiffs' recommendations, although plaintiffs had argued for the inclusion of a fourth product, large oil circuit breakers, in the first priority products; but the Coordinating Committee determined to limit the number of products in the first priority lines to three. Defendants evidently could not agree on the product lines which they would recommend for priority.[160] It was also determined that the depositions would be taken, not simply before a reporter as in the usual case, but before a judge presiding over the deposition in

[160] O'Donnell, *supra* note 156, at 136.

the various districts (not necessarily his own) where the depositions were to be taken.

In view of the numbers and a certain disparity of interest on the plaintiff side, an organization among plaintiffs' counsel to carry out the plaintiffs' obligations under the deposition program was called for. Approximately eighty attorneys representing plaintiffs met in Chicago on September 4, 1962 and organized the plaintiffs' counsel Steering Committee.[161]

Defendants' counsel at San Francisco had acquiesced in the proposed national discovery program, including national depositions. Later commentary has indicated, however, that there was considerable dissatisfaction. For one thing, there were complaints that under a national program defendants' counsel would be unable to "control the tempo and influence the course of events in terms of his own client's interests and problems."[162] The same commentator also complained that under a national discovery program defendants' counsel could find that its opposition consisted of experienced members of the antitrust bar rather than being opposed "in a relatively remote section of the country by a lawyer not experienced in the field."[163] It was also argued that a national program was unfair because plaintiffs could pool their resources and thereby lessen their costs, the author frankly stating that:

> " Like it or not, from the defendant's standpoint the potential cost to be incurred by plaintiffs in prosecuting a treble damage case is a factor which may lead to a favorable, reasonable and satisfactory settlement under ordinary circumstances."[164]

---

[161] The author was designated chairman of the Steering Committee which, in addition, consisted of Joseph L. Alioto, San Francisco; Robert W. Bergstrom, Chicago; Thomas C. McConnell, Chicago; Northcutt Ely, Washington, D. C.; William H. Ferguson, Seattle; Harold H. Fisher, Newark; Milton Handler, New York; Harold E. Kohn, Philadelphia; Horace R. Lamb, New York; Marcus Mattson, Los Angeles; Brice W. Rhyne, Washington, D. C.; Robert E. Sher, Washington, D. C.; Seymour F. Simon, Chicago; Gilmore Tillman, Los Angeles; and Bethuel M. Webster, New York.

[162] O'Donnell, *supra* note 156, at 133, 136.

[163] *Id.* at 138.

[164] *Id.* at 139.

Finally, the defendants complained that under a national program "each plaintiff is handed a ready-made case to the extent that expert lead counsel can establish it, and, in any event, a far better case than most plaintiffs could ever establish without a coordinated program." [165]

The plaintiffs' counsel Steering Committee at its meeting early in September 1962 in Chicago was able to agree readily on the witnesses whose depositions were to be taken in the first round, the place of deposition and lead counsel. In lieu of the six proposed by National Pretrial Order No. 8, the Steering Committee recommended twelve witnesses: Fink, Peters, Saupe, Burke and Ginn of General Electric; Fuller and Mauntel of Westinghouse; W. G. Lewis, Nairn and McMullen of Allis-Chalmers; Allen of Wagner Electric; and Sellers of Carrier. The depositions were scheduled to begin October 1 and to carry through until the first week in December. Five were scheduled to be taken in Philadelphia, three in New York, three in Chicago and one in Seattle.[166] The October 1 date was chosen for the beginning of the depositions despite the fact that the order authorizing the depositions, National Pretrial Order No. 10, was not worked out and entered until September 27, 1962.

Another necessary step preceding the taking of depositions was not worked out until shortly before the depositions were due to begin. In view of the allegations in the complaints that the activities of the conspirators had been fraudulently concealed, it was important to plaintiffs to secure for each witness who was to be deposed copies of his expense accounts, vouchers and other supporting documents relating to his travels. The production of each witness' diary, appointment book, calendar pad, letter book and telephone call memoranda prior to taking his deposition was also necessary. It was also important to have copies of any document taken to or received or prepared at any meeting relating to prices or allocation of markets, and any memoranda, reports, notes of telephone conversations, instructions, orders to subordinates, or other documents concerning

165 *Id.* at 139.

166 The Seattle deposition, that of W. E. Saupe, was later changed to New York City.

such meetings. In view of the public knowledge, and indeed in many instances the public announcement, that the defendants had conducted investigations among their employees as to possible antitrust violations, it would be helpful for plaintiffs' counsel conducting the depositions to have all documents relating to such investigations and copies of the companies' statements of policy with respect to employees meeting with competitors. Further, organization charts and other documents for the defendant corporations would be helpful in assessing the degree of responsibility of the particular individual involved.

Shortly before the beginning of the depositions, the production of documents such as the foregoing was ordered by National Pretrial Order No. 9. Under the order, documents were required to be produced not only with respect to the twelve witnesses to be deposed but also, in anticipation of further depositions, from an additional sixty-four individuals, employees or former employees of the various defendants in the three designated priority product lines.

In addition to documents of the kind specifically required for the depositions, National Pretrial Order No. 9 ordered the defendants to produce a copy of each of the documents in the possession of or obtainable by any defendant which was (1) produced by such defendant before any grand jury in the Eastern District of Pennsylvania in the course of investigations leading to the return of the indictments in that court in 1960; (2) documents previously marked on depositions or produced by the defendants in any pending electrical equipment proceedings; (3) any reports, statements or other documents transmitted to any member of the board of directors of any defendant or to any management executive with respect to the involvement or lack of involvement of any officer or employee of that defendant in the conspiracy relating to the particular product line; (4) lists of any documents furnished to any officer or agency of the United States or any state or municipal government in connection with any legislative, administrative or judicial investigation or proceeding involving the pricing or marketing of the particular product; (5) all circular letters and market letters, reports or bulletins concerning explanation for changes in prices or price adjustment clauses with respect to the particular product;

and (6) such other specific documents as might be reasonably necessary for the taking of depositions as may be ordered by the court on application of a plaintiff. Somewhat surprisingly to the plaintiffs, the larger defendants offered no argument against the production of grand jury documents, although General Electric mentioned that in its case more than 100,000 documents were involved.[167] Smaller defendants did not acquiesce voluntarily in this requirement and made an appeal in general terms, which was to be repeated at practically every meeting and conference with the Coordinating Committee, that the burden on small defendants of the nationwide discovery ought to be borne in mind by the judges.

National Pretrial Order No. 9 was worked out at a meeting of the Coordinating Committee and conferences with lawyers held in Washington, D. C. on September 21, 1962 and was entered on September 27, 1962. The period of time for which documents had to be produced was from January 1, 1948 through April 1, 1961. During the conference in Washington the proposed terms of the production order, which were generally along the lines suggested by the plaintiffs, were strenuously opposed by the defendants. Nevertheless, certain areas of concern to the defendants were recognized in the order. To the extent that the defendants produced and deposited documents pursuant to the order they were not to be subject to any further motions to produce in any pending action, except that plaintiffs were entitled to have the originals produced at the trial (copies being sufficient for the purposes of the pretrial order). The stay on production was not to apply in favor of any defendant who failed substantially to comply with National Pretrial Order No. 9. Defendants asserted that they would expect to claim privilege with respect to certain of the documents, and as to those the pretrial order provided that they could be deposited under seal and were not to be inspected except upon order of the district court for the district in which the deposit had been made or upon order of the judge before whom depositions were taken.

---

167 Transcript, Coordinating Committee Conference, Washington, D. C., Sept. 21, 1962, pp. 30, 32.

The documents to be produced by defendants were not simply to be handed over to plaintiffs or their representatives. The pretrial order established "national document depositories" initially contemplated to be located in the Northern District of Illinois, the Northern District of California, the Southern District of New York and the Western District of Texas, at addresses proposed by the defendants. The depositories were to be maintained at the expense of the defendants and were to be under their control and supervision. Counsel for a plaintiff was to have reasonable access to each document in any national document depository and could obtain a copy thereof at the plaintiff's expense. The initial depository was located in Chicago, in the Northern District of Illinois. As the proceedings developed the establishment of depositories in other locations proved not to be necessary: with that decision extensive arguments between the plaintiffs and defendants as to who would bear the cost of copying documents for the additional depositories became moot.

After a certain amount of experience under National Pretrial Order No. 9, it developed that further provisions were required to be made for documents which defendants wished to have treated as confidential, whether for reasons of protecting business secrets or otherwise. Accordingly, under National Pretrial Order No. 14 the defendants were permitted, with respect to documents containing information of a financial nature or relating to engineering and technological developments, or dealing with marketing techniques and programs or containing information relating to future development plans, to stamp the documents as "confidential" upon their being placed in the national depository. Documents so designated could be inspected by attorneys for the plaintiffs, but they were not to permit disclosure of the documents' contents to anyone except persons assisting them in the prosecution of the claims. The same rule was to be applicable to any copies of the documents that attorneys for the plaintiffs might make. Plaintiffs were entitled to use such documents in the taking of depositions, and in that event confidentiality was to be protected in such manner as would be determined by the judge presiding at the deposition.

Before the first round of depositions got under way, a motion was made in the Northern District of California by A. B. Chance and H. K. Porter to vacate or modify the pretrial orders (Nos. 8, 9 and 10) ordering the first round of depositions and the production of documents in connection therewith. On December 28, 1962 Judge Zirpoli denied the motion concluding that in view of the extraordinary nature of the cases, the liberality of the federal rules and defendants' opportunity to be heard both before the Coordinating Committee and in the Northern District of Illinois, defendants had not demonstrated that they were unduly prejudiced by the national program so as to warrant special treatment.

The national deposition program began on schedule with the taking of the deposition of A. C. Allen of Wagner Electric on October 1, 1962 in Philadelphia. Senior Judge William H. Kirkpatrick of the Eastern District of Pennsylvania presided, and in addition, there were in attendance Judges Clary, Robson and Boldt. There had been dire predictions that so many lawyers would be in attendance that a structure the size of Radio City Music Hall would be required for the holding of the depositions. In fact, on the first day of the depositions an ordinary courtroom was sufficient—although crowded because of the widespread interest on the part of the judiciary and of lawyers in the proceedings. One lay commentator stated of this deposition that "150 lawyers showed up to question one officer of General Electric." [168] It is correct that a number of lawyers were in attendance at the deposition (the witness was an officer of Wagner Electric, not General Electric), but the interrogation was in the hands of a single lead counsel who had been designated by the plaintiffs' counsel Steering Committee, Aaron Fine of Philadelphia. There was minimal questioning of the witness by other plaintiffs' counsel and by defendants' counsel following the completion of Mr. Fine's examination.

The technique of having the deposition presided over by a judge led to prompt rulings on several important questions of privilege and other matters, thus obviating delays which might otherwise have occurred. The examination, pursuant to the ground rules, covered all classes of equipment with which the witness had any familiarity. In Allen's case this meant power

[168] MAYER, THE LAWYERS 323 (New York: Harper & Row, 1967).

transformers, distribution transformers and network transformers. In the case of two witnesses, their poor health required some deviation from the regular deposition procedures. For Watkins, written interrogatories were substituted for an oral deposition; in the case of Neblett, an oral deposition was taken in Judge Feinberg's chambers rather than in the courtroom and attendance was kept to an absolute minimum.

After the first deposition, the numbers in attendance rapidly dwindled; lead counsel as designated by the plaintiffs' counsel Steering Committee proceeded with the examination of assigned witnesses, and by early December the twelve initial witnesses had been examined.

Before the first round of depositions had been completed, counsel and the judges were considering the witnesses and the product lines to be covered in a second round. It was determined that in the second round three product lines in addition to the three covered in the first round would be the subject of the depositions. The three added products were power switching equipment, distribution transformers and large oil circuit breakers.

Plaintiffs had proposed for the second round that two or perhaps even three witnesses might be deposed simultaneously; the defendants resisted the suggestion and urged that only one witness at a time be deposed. General Electric, Westinghouse and Wagner Electric filed their objections in writing, maintaining that simultaneous depositions would deny them due process of law "by preventing assertion of a uniform defense." The plaintiffs' suggestions were adopted and the second round schedule was established in National Pretrial Order No. 11: the number of witnesses for the second round would be greatly expanded; a total number of forty-three witnesses were to be deposed. For the period from March 4 to July 15, 1963, two, three and even four witnesses were scheduled each week, often in more than one city. For example, for the week of March 18, Cordell and Romano, power switching equipment witnesses, were scheduled for New York City, and Clothier, a hydro-generator witness, was scheduled for Seattle. In the week of June 3, Beard and Watkins, distribution transformer witnesses, were scheduled for

Chicago, and Matthes and Johnson, hydro-generator witnesses, were scheduled for New York City.

The terms and conditions for the second round, set forth in Schedule B of National Pretrial Order No. 11, were substantially identical with those established for the first round depositions. With respect to documents to be produced in connection with the second round, National Pretrial Order No. 12 ordered production of expense account and travel data covering a period from January 1, 1948 through April 1, 1961 for 150 individuals. Experience in the first round of depositions indicated that the documentary request for that round relating to transportation records needed to be and was expanded in National Pretrial Order No. 12 to include logs of company planes and records of the use of company cars.

The documentary order for the second round dealt specifically, as the order for the first round did not, with documents with respect to which defendants claimed the attorney-client privilege or non-availability of documents under the work product doctrine. As to documents where the privilege was claimed, the order provided that they should be deposited under seal, adequately described, and the basis for the claim of privilege stated on the cover or in the paper of transmittal. Thereafter they were not to be inspected except upon order of the district court for the district in which the depository was located (i.e., the Northern District of Illinois) or except upon order of a judge before whom the related deposition was being taken. As to work product documents, they were to be adequately described by affidavit and were declared by the order to be prima facie within the work product doctrine, solely for purposes of the order, and protected from discovery and production until, upon a proper showing of relevance to the issues and good cause for production, it should be determined by the appropriate court that the documents were not entitled to work product protection. In describing and listing the documents as to which privilege or work product protection was asserted, the defendant depositing the documents was required to give, among other things, information as to the name and corporate position of each person, other than attorneys representing defendants in the civil or criminal proceedings, to whom the contents of the documents had theretofore been communicated by copy, exhibition, reading or substantial summarization.

National Pretrial Orders 11 and 12 were worked out at a Coordinating Committee conference and meeting with lawyers in San Antonio on February 6 and 7, 1963. During the course of those discussions Judge Becker defined "privilege" as meaning "not subject to compulsory discovery under federal rules." The justification for permitting work product documents to be retained in the possession of the party (subject to an order to disclose if the work product doctrine was found not be applicable) was because of the bulk and number of documents the defendants claimed that they were constantly being burdened with in connection with the litigation.

In Philadelphia, Judge Lord ruled for the plaintiffs on their request for data given by defendants to their "national analysts." Defendants' position was that the material included work done in trial preparation and also in developing their theory of damages. The material in question consisted of lists for each transaction from 1955 to 1962 for all defendants, and from 1946 to 1962 for Westinghouse, comprising the name of the purchaser, the type of customer, the actual price less escalation, the date of commitment, the date of shipment, the book price, the commitment date book price, a recalculation of the price to a 1954 price, and information on backlogs and capacities.

The defendants' performance with respect to the production of documents for the first round of depositions had been tardy and unsatisfactory, in the plaintiffs' view. In a number of instances in the case of the first round of depositions the documents relating to a particular witness were coming in right up to the time and even during the course of his deposition. Plaintiffs requested entry for the second round of a special order requiring defendants to demonstrate by a set time the status of their compliance with the document production requirements for the second round. This requirement was set forth by an order of Judge Robson dated April 15, 1963.

The second round of depositions proceeded on schedule. Larger numbers of plaintiffs' counsel were involved, although the major portion of the work, as in the case of the first round, was performed by counsel in New York, Philadelphia, Chicago, Washington, D. C. and Seattle. The Coordinating Committee also had to furnish a substantial number of judges for presiding, with heavy burdens being carried by Judges Robson and Boldt. Judge Boldt traveled to various parts of the country, in some instances (as in the Southern District of New York) sitting as a "special master." Chief Judge Ryan of the Southern District of New York had considered making a request to Chief Justice Warren to designate out-of-state deposition judges (Boldt, Robson and Becker principally) for temporary assignment in the Southern District of New York. But the special master technique was utilized instead.

At the national depositions of John T. Peters and David Morgan in New York plaintiffs moved for the production of a large number of documents not called for in the pretrial orders. On December 15, 1962 Judge Boldt ruled that such broad requests for production were inappropriate for decision by the deposition judge and could more usefully be decided by the Court for the Northern District of Illinois where the principal national depository was located. Judge Boldt therefore denied plaintiffs' motions without prejudice to similar motions being presented in the Northern District of Illinois. Since Judge Boldt was sitting as special master, his order was presented to and approved and confirmed by Chief Judge Ryan of the Southern District of New York.

A third round of depositions, the final round for plaintiffs, was established by National Pretrial Order No. 16. Twenty-three witnesses were to be deposed in the period from the latter part of July to the middle of October 1963 in the product lines previously designated or, in the case of some witnesses, in all categories. Included among the witnesses to whom the latter designation was applied were Cordiner, the chief executive officer of General Electric, and Cresap, the chief executive officer of Westinghouse.

Whenever possible during the course of the depositions, use was made of depositions that had been taken prior to the beginning of the national deposition program. For example, both sides agreed to use the depositions of Schoenig and Schmalz which had been taken by the Government in the TVA damage action in March 1963. Defendant Westinghouse agreed to supplement Schmalz' depositions to show his presence at various locations on specific dates and to incorporate this information into the national discovery program (Schedule C to National Pretrial Order No. 16). Plaintiffs also requested that provision be made so that the judge who would have presided over Schmalz' deposition would compare his grand jury and deposition testimony for inconsistencies and entertain any application for re-examination.

At the conclusion of the three rounds of depositions, seventy-five witnesses had been examined by plaintiffs' counsel in six cities and before twelve separate deposition judges. There were 25,000 pages of transcript and tens of thousands of documents had been produced and examined.

One housekeeping matter that was troublesome to the plaintiffs and which was discussed at San Antonio arose from the circumstance that the plaintiffs were not being compensated for the cost of the transcripts of the depositions which were furnished to districts in which the cases were on the back burner. The judges were sympathetic with the problem and ultimately through their efforts substantially all required payments were made.

So great had the responsibilities of the Coordinating Committee become that it had established its own headquarters and staff in Chicago. The Committee maintained its own looseleaf service to provide the relevant information on all cases pending throughout the country and the various activities under the national discovery program.

Although the federal government was not a participant in the national discovery program, advantages would have accrued to it had it gone to trial in its own damage actions. In January 1963, Judge Kraft in Philadelphia entered a pretrial order (No. 2) which approved a stipulation in all eleven damage actions filed by the federal government for the use in those actions of the national depositions and the answers to the national interrogatories.

CHAPTER 9

Testimony by deposition

THE PLAINTIFFS' DEPOSITION program was directed primarily toward those officers and employees of the defendant manufacturers who the plaintiffs had reason to believe had participated in meetings with competitors at which price and market arrangements were agreed upon. The plaintiffs' principal purpose in the deposition program was to establish that there had indeed been such meetings, that prices were discussed and agreed upon, that customers were allocated and markets divided by agreement among competitors and that positive steps had been taken to conceal the facts of such meetings and such agreements.

The depositions were clearly productive in all these respects. One of the principal and most forthright witnesses was William S. Ginn, whose deposition as a part of the electrical equipment antitrust actions was first taken in Philadelphia on November 29 and 30, 1962 before Judges Kirkpatrick and Boldt. Mr. Ginn had held responsible positions within General Electric in two major fields of electrical equipment—power transformers from 1945 until 1956 (in the latter five years of the period as General Manager of Power Transformers), and in turbines, from 1957 to 1961 as Vice President and General Manager of the Turbine Division. At the time of his deposition he had been dismissed by General Electric Company and had served a prison term resulting from his conviction on a plea of guilty in the electrical equipment criminal proceedings in Philadelphia.

Early in his deposition Mr. Ginn, in discussing his early days in the Transformer Division of General Electric, was asked to describe his responsibility as to pricing transformers:

" Q. Did it also involve computing the price from your price books?
A. Yes, sir; it did; and at that time, sir, there was also, which was not the job description, there was the, the duty, too, of—of heading the competitive relations, sir.

Q. I am sorry. I didn't hear that.
A. It was of handling the competitive relations.

Q. What does that mean?
A. Well, to put it bluntly, sir, to—the one who was to discuss any matters with competitors.

Q. That was one of your duties?
A. Yes, sir."

As to topics discussed with competitors:

" A. One subject would be deviation from standards, discussion of past jobs, comparison of price calculations, allocations, discussion of change in price rules and formula.
I think that about does it sir. That's all I can remember."

It became clear that the conspiracy encompassed also allocations of sealed bid business (which occurred primarily in the areas of governmental and public authority purchasing):

" I think that—I don't like the word 'conspiracy,' and I will agree that there were attempts made to establish list prices, pricing rules and market level for prices, and secondly to allocate sealed bid business among the defendants according to fixed percentages, and thirdly to attempt to fix prices and quotations on non-sealed business."

The frequency of meetings among competitors was illustrated by a chart (Exhibit NX247) compiled from the expense accounts of persons who had been in attendance at some or all of the meetings. The chart[169] shows during the year 1956 alone a total of eighteen meetings among competitors in power transformers, a number of them of several days' duration. Mr. Ginn stated that in other years meetings had been held as often as once a month. The witness explained that it was routine at such meetings for competitors to engage in price discussions:

" Q. Now, this Atlantic City meeting—I don't want you to be impatient with me, but sometimes when you have a recess you don't remember every detail that took place before the recess. In this Atlantic City meeting in June 1956 there were price discussions then also?
A. I expect there were, sir. I can't remember, but that was the way that things usually happened, and I would expect that that is what took place."

---

[169] See Appendix 19.

For a proper understanding of the manner in which price discussions were held it was important, according to him, to understand the meaning of "list price," "multiplier" and "book price." He explained these terms in this manner:

" Q. Would you explain for the record what is the meaning of list price as used in the transformer division?
A. Well, a list price would be the—you would have a size of a transformer that gets different voltage classes which would give you the so-called base. To this, depending upon the characteristics of the transformer, you would make certain percentage additions. In addition to that you would have, as I recall, then you apply the multiplier and the accessories I believe were in net dollars. You would add the accessories to the developed price of the transformer. That resulted in what is known as the book price.

Q. Could you explain for the record what is meant by multiplier?
A. A multiplier is a reciprocal of a discount.

Q. I think that I am not the only one in the room that could be helped by a further explanation.
A. Well, all right. If you got—suppose that you have a list price—to make it simple. If you keep a list, you had a list price and you had your prices way up here, but to get the true price you had a 50 per cent discount. In that case you multiply it by .5 or take 50 per cent off and come up with the answer. It's the multiplier. It is really—it's the relation to the discount.

Q. This is one of the ways and this is the principal way in which you determine the price you are going to quote?
A. Right.

Q. Now, is it correct to say that you follow the pricing rules set out in the price book to develop the list price and then you have a multiplier which is also set out in the book which is applicable during the period of time?
A. Right.

Q. And you multiply that list price by the multiplier?
A. Right.

Q. And you come out then with the net book price?
A. Right.

Q. Now, you have used multiplier and discount as synonymous but actually you have, and your competitors have given a reduction from the net book price; have they not?
A. Oh, yes.

JUDGE KIRKPATRICK: *Does your multiplier have a decimal point in front of it?*
THE WITNESS: *Yes, sir.*

MR. HANDLER: *A decimal point, yes. I will have an exhibit to show that.*

JUDGE KIRKPATRICK: *That makes it clear. I was wondering how you got a discount by multiplying.*

THE WITNESS: *If your discount was 66⅔, Your Honor, you multiply by .33 and get the same thing.*

JUDGE KIRKPATRICK: *Yes.*

Q. When you gave a reduction from net list price wasn't this generally described in the industry as selling at a discount off net book price?
A. That's right.

Q. That discount is not to be confused with the multiplier?
A. That is correct.

Q. So that in this testimony can we use multiplier to indicate this figure that you have indicated to apply to the list price and discount will be the reduction from the net book price?
A. All right.

Q. While you were with General Electric in the power transformer division it had a printed book containing list prices; did it not?
A. Right.

Q. What?
A. Right, yes, sir.

Q. What was that book called?
A. As far as I know it was the power transformer handbook.

Q. And this handbook contained the rules for determining the price?
A. Right.

Q. And it also contained the multipliers which were in effect at the particular time?
A. That's correct. Normally the multiplier, as I remember it, was on a separate sheet because the theory of the multiplier was that your list prices didn't change very often but your multipliers might.

Q. Was there one book which applied to all different ratings, sizes and characteristics of power transformers?
A. I think there was—as I recall the complete handbook, yes it did.

Q. To your knowledge did Westinghouse, Allis-Chalmers and your other competitors have printed price books for power transformers?
A. Yes."

Exhibit NX248,[170] listing multipliers in effect from 1948 to 1957 for large transformers, demonstrates the identity of multipliers used throughout the period by all three principal manufacturers, General Electric, Westinghouse and Allis-Chalmers. There was no doubt that changes in the multiplier were the subject of price meetings among competitors:

" Q. Now these changes in the multiplier were the equivalent of price increases, weren't they?
A. Right.

Q. Do you know whether the list price remained constant during this entire period or were there changes in GE's list price also?
A. I don't really know. There could have been some changes in list prices over the time to change relationships or something.

Q. But basically the list price remained the same, did it not?
A. Well, as long as—I gather it did looking at this, because you stayed within a range of .7 to 1.19. I wouldn't suspect that the list price had been changed a great deal.

Q. Describe the procedure by which a change in a multiplier was initiated and then effected in the transformer division.
A. Well, it wasn't—you can't point out any universal thing that happened every time. In some cases the changes in the multiplier were discussed with the competition and I think on a few occasions that unilaterally we moved and they followed or unilaterally they moved and we followed."

The witness testified that in the beginning in 1949, for a brief period of time, meetings and discussions among competitors in transformers ceased ("the Iron Curtain descended"). The witness proceeded to relate that in the middle months of 1950 he was called to Schenectady by a Mr. Erben:

" Q. From Pittsfield?
A. From Pittsfield by Mr. Erben. In his office with Mr. Fairman present he told me that he felt that, to put it in his words as I remember them, that things were not going as well as he would like to see them in the market place. He felt that I should go, with his backing, back to meeting with competitors but to leave it to myself and not to involve anyone else."

And the witness was clear that prices did rise in the years subsequent to the resumption of meetings in 1950:

---

170 See Appendix 20.

" Q. In fact, you did resume meetings in 1950, as you testified yesterday;——
A. Yes.

Q. ——is that not so?
A. Yes.

Q. And you discussed at these meetings market-price levels and discounts from book prices?
A. Yes.

Q. The level of order prices rose during 1951, 1952, and 1953 following the resumption of meetings, did they not?
A. Following–yes."

The first resumed meeting was held in Chicago:

" Q. Could you tell us what was discussed in terms of topics at this resumed meeting?
A. No. I can't recall any topics that were discussed. I told them that they had known the policy that General Electric had had of taking the commercial people out of NEMA and that we were not to resume meetings, but that now we thought it was the best interest that maybe we should go back to having at least some top-level meetings occasionally.

. . . .

Q. Had there been discounts from the net-book prices during the iron-curtain period?
A. My recollection is at that time there had been a gradual deterioration of the price level.

Q. And would it be fair to say that the purpose of the meeting was to correct what you have called the deteriorated-market condition?
A. I would say that was one of the causes, yes, sir, one of the reasons.

Q. Would it be fair to say that the purpose of the meeting was to bring the actual market prices up to the net-book prices or as close thereto as you could get?
A. I think that would be the attempt, yes, sir.

Q. That was the purpose?
A. That was the–or the attempt, yes, sir.

Q. I am asking you, was that the purpose of the meeting?
A. I think so, yes."

In the following years there were not only so-called "top level" meetings but also "working" or lower level meetings:

" Q. Now taking the period from '50 to '54, how would you characterize the meetings that you attended, as high level, low level, or both?
A. Well, I would characterize the meetings from in the '50-'51 period as more of a combination of working level and top level. I would say after 1952 anything that I was involved in would be purely and simply top level.
Q. Now you have given us the people that attended the top-level meetings from '52 to '54. Were there low-level meetings during that period to your knowledge?
A. Yes, I believe there were low-level meetings at that time."

The witness did not mention it, but the men who attended working level meetings referred to the top level personnel, sardonically, as the "heroes."

From 1954 to 1956 a new element—foreign competition—entered the market place to complicate the lives of the domestic competitors who had heretofore allocated the markets among themselves and determined the prices that customers were to pay:

" Q. Now, let's—let's move to the period from 1954 to 1956 when you were general manager of the transformer division; you attended meetings during that period?
A. On a decreasing scale, yes.
Q. And these were high-level meetings?
A. Yes.

. . . .

Q. And would it have been fair to say that the subjects discussed at this—these meetings were the same as the discussions—the subjects discussed during the earlier periods——
A. No; I——
Q. ——when you——
A. No; I wouldn't say it would be fair to say the same things were discussed, because here we—we enter into a new phase of where foreign competition was coming into the market, and the allocation system was beginning to completely fall apart, and the meetings began to become very futile at about that time.
Q. All right. Now, you tell us what subjects were discussed at the meetings during this period.
A. Well, as I say, there weren't very many meetings held, and, in general, I think that the main question was what effect the foreign competition was going to have, the question of whether or not we should—not to panic on the thing, to try to keep some sense of balance, and the usual re—the usual recriminations of what took place on other jobs."

Mr. Ginn was precise that the manufacturers had met and agreed upon an allocation of sealed bid business with a specified percentage of the total business for each company:

" Q. Now, all the questions that I am going to put to you, sir, relate to the period when you were working with and on power transformers, is that correct, 1946 until the end of 1956?
A. I would like to make it October, 1956, but it is all right.

Q. Whatever that date is; is it a fact that you attended meetings for the purpose of allocating among the defendant manufacturers sales of power transformers to governmental agencies pursuant to sealed bid invitations?
A. Yes.

. . . .

Q. And the purpose of the meetings that you so attended was to provide each defendant manufacturer with an agreed-upon approximate percentage of the total sealed bid business?
A. Yes.

Q. And the percentages were 30 per cent for Westinghouse?
A. My best recollection is that is correct.

Q. 15 per cent for Allis-Chalmers?
A. Same answer.

Q. 30 per cent for General Electric?
A. Same answer.

Q. McGraw-Edison, 8 per cent?
A. Same answer.

Q. Moloney Electric Company, 10 per cent?
A. Same answer.

Q. Wagner Electric Corporation, 5 per cent?
A. Same answer.

Q. Now, by 'same answer' you mean 'yes'?
A. That is correct, to the best of my knowledge.

Q. Now, is it a fact that at many of these meetings which you attended cumulative lists of sealed bid business secured by each defendant manufacturer was circulated and the representatives present compared the relative standing of each company according to its agreed-upon percentage of the total sales made pursuant to sealed bids?
A. Yes.

Q. And is it a fact that the representatives at these meetings then discussed future sealed bid invitations?
A. Yes.

Q. And designated which manufacturer should submit the lowest bid——
A. Yes.

Q. —therefor?
A. Yes.
Q. Now, is it a fact that these meetings were also conducted for the additional purpose of agreeing upon a price designated by the defendants as the book price to be used in computing future sealed bids to governmental agencies?

. . . .

Q. You heard me say that, did you Mr. Witness?
A. Yes.
Q. Now, would you answer my question.
A. Yes."

The allocations were worked out in accordance with specific procedures:

" Q. Now before you go into the mechanics—and I am going to ask you that, sir—I have a very narrow question. Would you define for the record what the word 'position' means in this context.
A. 'Position' in this context means the man who is given the opportunity to submit the bid below the floor. It in no way connotated a guarantee that he would receive the job.
Q. But it did connote that he was the one who was to submit the lowest bid?
A. The lowest bid initially, yes.
Q. Now on what basis was each company given or denied position?
A. Well, you had—I previously pointed out that there was a schedule. Now there was no method of definitely saying who would be given position. There several things were taken into consideration: The percentage off of this allocation that the man was. Obviously if someone was getting 35 per cent they weren't in a very favorable position to be given position. Yet if someone was below this they could put up an argument to get the low position.

There was no definite system of flipping coins or anything else to do it. It was just finally tried to argue out until somebody—the modus operandi was worked out.
Q. You referred in your answer to a schedule. Could you tell us what you meant by that?
A. This was the schedule that you mentioned over here in Paragraph (b), the percentage that each manufacturer was going to receive of the sealed bid business.
Q. Well, now, would you explain the mechanics of how a company got position. Was this a matter of discussion among the representatives present?
A. Discussion sometimes very amiable but mostly heated as it could be.

Q. Would it take the form of a company saying, 'I want this job'?
A. That would be a very poor argument. You would have to find a better one than that.

Q. Well, then, perhaps I ought not to speculate and it might be well if you would tell us exactly what happened.
A. Well, there is lots of arguments were advanced. Number 1 is, 'My poor boy out in Portland hasn't sold a job out there in years.' That would be one of them.
'I am way behind, my factory needs the work.'
'I am a good fellow.'
'You guys are getting too much of the business.'
Oh, you could just dream up millions of them.

. . . .

Q. Did you have a list of the customers with you when you went to a meeting?
A. Yes.

Q. That was in writing?
A. In writing of one form or another.

Q. What would you do with the writing after the meeting?
A. Generally I would tear it up.

Q. Now after you had this discussion and position was assigned to one of the companies, did the group set the price that that company was to quote?
A. The only price that was set was the floor. And I am pointing out here that where I take exception to this, that in all cases the floor was not the book, the net book price. It was the price that was existing in the marketplace at the time.

Q. It was a price, however, that was agreed to by the participants as the floor below which the preferred bidder was not to go?
A. No, the preferred bidder was to go.

Q. Slightly below?
A. That's right.

Q. And the others——
A. He could go as low as he wanted. Nobody would care. He would just go below it.

Q. And the others would stay around the floor or above it.
A. Nobody went too high, for obvious reasons didn't want to go too high above the floor."

The witness described the spirit in which the competitors left their meetings after "position" had been determined:

" Q. After discussions so that everybody agreed on the interpretation.
A. That's right. Then you get the price calculated which was a mathematical problem. Then you get into the world of, all right, boys. You have got it calculated. What are you going to do about it? The last time out here you took this and went 15 per cent off and the other guy went 20 off, and this is where the fun began because you get the vows of chastity and the vows that they are going to behave themselves from here on in, and then you take your courage and go out into the night and hope you are going to come out all right."

With the onset of the white sale in 1954-1955 the manufacturers were unable to stem the tide of declining prices. Mr. Ginn testified:

" Q. Was there any discussion at meetings with competitors about stopping the white sale?
A. I went to a meeting right after it started and tried to stop it and got nowhere.

Q. Would you tell us what you said and what was said at that meeting by those who attended it?
A. As I remember attending it, this was right after it started. I didn't report this to anybody because it was probably not in accordance with over-all strategy. But when price had gotten down to about I think 15 per cent, I went and tried to talk to the guys to see if we couldn't get it stopped, that this was going to be chaotic, the way, the acceleration at which it was going. But there was no confidence. Everybody lost complete confidence in each other, and the snowball had begun to roll and we gave up. And as I remember, I never talked to them again until several months later."

The witness was asked whether price cutting during the white sale had a punitive purpose:

" Q. There was no punitive purpose; was there?
A. No, not to my knowledge. There was no punitive purpose. It was mighty expensive punitivity if it had been."

Actually, during the white sale prices fell to a point 50% off the book price:

" Q. But you kept on booking business at these low levels?
A. Until we got to 50 per cent, then we quit.

Q. Why?
A. Well, below 50 per cent you are getting a little bit rough. You don't start giving them away.

Q. Well, now, the 50 per cent, you mentioned you got 50 per cent of the total market.
A. No, 50 per cent discount off of the net book price calculated by the list price multiplied by the multiplier.

Q. At that point you cried quits?
A. We cried."

The transformer business was not a profitable business during the white sale:

" Q. Did they endeavor to develop any averages on a weekly or monthly basis for you?
A. No. I think we looked at particular jobs to get the trend. We didn't know how to average it. We weren't that smart.

Q. You didn't have any statisticians?
A. I didn't have any economists around.

Q. You had no statisticians?
A. We couldn't afford ourselves in those days."

Eventually the manufacturers were able, by discussions among themselves, to bring the chaos of the white sale to an end:

" Q. Was the termination of the white sale discussed at meetings before the white sale in fact ended?
A. Yes.

Q. What was the nature of the discussions?
A. Well, the nature of the discussions, can't we put a stop to this? Can't we get the market back up to some value that we can live?

Q. Was a target date set for the end of the white sale?
A. When you have no confidence, when people have been through this kind of experience, you couldn't set a target date for anything.

Q. I am asking you as a point of fact.
A. No target date was set, no.

Q. No target date was discussed?
A. No target date was discussed.

Q. Now, you had meetings after the white sale; didn't you?
A. Yes.

Q. And at these meetings you discussed market price levels?
A. Yes.

Q. Reductions from net book prices?
A. Yes.

Q. Multipliers?
A. Yes.

Q. Net book prices?
A. Yes.

Q. Terms and conditions of sale?
A. Yes.

Q. Was there any discussion of meetings subsequent to the white sale with regard to preventing any future white sales?
A. No.

Q. At these meetings subsequent to the white sale you discussed with competitors, did you not, ways and means of stabilizing and bringing order prices as close as possible to the net book prices again?
A. Subsequent to the white?

Q. Subsequent.
A. I think we discussed the desirability of doing so, yes.

Q. And in fact prices did recover; didn't they?
A. From the 50 per cent low, yes.

Q. And they recovered and went up beyond their highest level of 1954; did they not?
A. I don't know that for a fact."

When the decisions arrived at during the meetings were to be carried out the negotiators were careful not to disclose to the pricing personnel within their companies the manner in which the price to be quoted had been arrived at:

" Q. Would you direct the person conducting—would you give instructions to the person conducting the negotiations regarding the price to be charged?
A. Yes.

Q. That would take the form of either your specifying the net book price or a percentage discount?
A. Actually from the practical operation you would—you could do it either way. Actually what you would give him was a price, not the per cent off on the book price because it was too complicated.

Q. But you took care not to disclose to him what had happened at the meeting?
A. Absolutely.

Q. You saw to it that those who implemented your instructions did not know that position had been given to another company in a sealed bid transaction?
A. Well, yes, that's right.

Q. And you also saw to it that they didn't know that you had position.
A. That's correct.

Q. And you saw to it that the negotiators did not know that there had been discussions concerning price at any of these meetings?
A. That's correct."

Various other procedures were followed to disguise or prevent disclosure of meetings with competitors. Mr. Ginn testified:

" Q. Would you tell us what procedures you and your associates adopted to avoid disclosure of your meetings and other discussions with competitors?
A. Yes. I am speaking for myself personally. To the best of my recollection in the matter of expense accounts I always put in the town to which I was going. I did use the telephone from places other than the office to make telephone calls. I didn't believe in written communications and so I sent very few of those, but in general that's about it.

Q. Can we retrace the steps? You say that in your expense account you merely stated the city at which the meeting was to be held?
A. If I were going to a meeting in New York I would say 'Company business in New York,' but I would put in that I had been to New York.

Q. But you would describe the purpose as company business?
A. That's correct. I wouldn't put down meeting with competitors on the top of it.

Q. Did you ever falsify the city?
A. No, not to my recollection have I ever falsified the city.

Q. Did you ever hear of any of the members of the club falsifying the city in which they indicated they were visiting on their expense accounts?
A. I understand that some people have done that, yes.

Q. Now, with respect to the making of telephone calls you say you made them out of the office?
A. Made them out of the office, yes.

Q. Pay telephone booths?
A. Telephone booths.

Q. Did you make them from your home?
A. Nope, not very often.

Q. Did you receive calls from your home?
A. I have received them, yes.

Q. From the tone of your voice in which you said 'Nope' am I correct in assuming that the reason you didn't make them, telephone calls from your home was to avoid detection?
A. That was one of the reasons, yes.

Q. Am I correct that whatever documents, writings, scraps of paper you brought to the meetings, and whatever you took from the meetings you saw that they were destroyed?
A. I did.

Q. And the purpose of that was to conceal what you were doing?
A. Yes.

Q. The answer is yes?
A. Yes."

Ginn's deposition as t his turbine generator activities came several months later than the power transformer testimony. After a long period of responsibility for power transformers, Ginn had come to the turbine division of General Electric as Vice President and General Manager in January 1957, continuing in that position until his dismissal from General Electric in March 1961. Ginn was less informative in his deposition on turbines about meetings with competitors. In testifying concerning a meeting on December 2, 1958 in New York City (the witness could not recall whether it was the Lexington, the Biltmore or the Roosevelt Hotel), he maintained that he was invited by McMullen of Allis-Chalmers for a continuation of a discussion on patents. This was in the face of testimony from a previous deposition witness, Sellers of the Elliott Company division of Carrier Corporation, that the members of the working level group urged the "heroes," members of the higher level group, to come together to discuss a number of problems that were developing at the working level. Ginn was truculent in discussing his meeting with McMullen:

" Q. I believe you testified and the record will show that he invited you to meet him in the hospitality room.
A. Obviously we had to meet somewhere. He is not going to say 'Meet me in New York.' It is a big place, you know. You ought to know that, you live there.

Q. That is right. And you walked into a hospitality room——
A. Right.

. . . .

Q. Didn't you tell him when you walked into the room and you saw a lot of people there, 'Bill, why don't we go to some private and quiet place where we can have a private discussion?'
A. As a matter of fact, I think we did go into the bedroom for a little while and discussed this.

Q. You mean the hospitality room had bedrooms on the side?
A. It was really a suite, if you look at my testimony. I said it was not a hospitality room of the same type, but it was a big suite.

Q. Well, now, this is the first time that I recall your mentioning a big suite.
A. Well, read the Kefauver testimony over carefully. Your boy forgot to read it.

Q. Didn't you testify within the past ten minutes that you met him in a hospitality room?
A. A hospitality room. What is your definition of a hospitality room?

Q. Well, not having been in one——
A. Oh, now, come.

Q. Not having been in one I don't know what you mean. We use different language in our professions.
A. We certainly do. That I will agree to."

Ginn denied that the objective of the meeting of December 2, 1958, was that which had been set forth in the turbine generator indictment:

" Q. I show you the indictment and I direct your attention to paragraph 12(c), which reads as follows:

On or about December 2, 1958, a meeting was held in New York City attended by representatives of all of the defendant and co-conspirator corporations. At this meeting it was agreed, among other things, that on sealed bids the manufacturers would quote no more than approximately 3% off published book prices and that on transactions involving price negotiations the manufacturers would quote no more than approximately 5% off published book prices.

Was the objective of the meeting which you attended in New York on December 2, 1958, that on sealed bids the manufacturers would quote no lower than approximately 3% off published book prices?
A. No, sir, that was not my objective.

Q. Was it the objective of the meeting as you determined it after you walked into the hospitality room?
A. I couldn't say that was the objective.

Q. And you couldn't say that it was not the objective?
A. Well, if you say, you don't think it was the objective, it certainly goes around the other way, doesn't it?

Q. The answer is yes?
A. The answer is yes to what?

Q. To my previous question. Is it yes or is it no?
A. I repeat what I said.

MR. KIERNAN: *May we have the question read, if Your Honor pleases.*
THE COURT: *Surely.*

(The reporter read the record as follows:

'Q. *And you couldn't say that it was not the objective?*
A. *Well, if you say, you don't think it was the objective, it certainly goes around the other way, doesn't it?*

Q. *The answer is yes?*
A. *The answer is yes to what?')*

THE WITNESS: My answer to that is no."

Sellers had testified that there was a meeting of minds among the competitors that prices ought to be stabilized at 2 or 3% off book; Ginn stated that he thought Sellers was wrong:

" Q. I read to you further from the testimony of Mr. Sellers at page 3966 to 67.
Would you show the witness where that is.
A. I see that.
[Reading from Sellers' testimony]
'Q. *Were there promises made on behalf of any of the manufacturers at these meetings, rather, this meeting, that if other manufacturers would adhere to a certain level with relation to book prices that they would do the same?*
A. *Well, I think in general always everybody made these statements. Now, this is surrounded with an 'if'.*

Q. *Can you recall who it was, if anyone, who proposed that the prices might be stabilized or ought to be stabilized at 3% off book on sealed bids and 5% off book on negotiated bids?*
A. *My recollection is that the numbers were 2 or 3%, and I will not quarrel with whether it was 3 or 2 or 3.*

Q. *2 or 3 on sealed?*
A. *Sealed bids, yes.*

Q. *Is it your recollection that it was 5% on negotiated?*
A. *I don't have a recollection that that was so. My recollection is that it was 2 or 3 on all of them. I don't attempt to distinguish.*

Q. *Now, do recall* [sic] *who suggested that?*
A. *I believe Mr. Ginn made the statement.*

Q. *Did Mr. Ginn make that statement as an announcement of what General Electric was going to do?*
A. *Well, I would call this a meeting of minds in the sense that if everybody would quote 3% of the book, yes.*

Q. *And there was a meeting of minds to that effect?*
A. *Yes.'*

Q. Did you make a statement to the effect that everyone ought to quote no more than 3% off book prices?
A. I don't recall that I did.

Q. Are you willing to deny that you did?
A. I am willing to deny that I did.

Q. And are you willing to state that Mr. Sellers' testimony that you did is erroneous?
A. Mr. Sellers does not make a definite statement. Mr. Sellers says, 'I believe Mr. Ginn made the statement.'
I believe Mr. Sellers is wrong.

Q. Do you understand that there was a meeting of the minds to the effect that 3% ought to be the maximum reduction from book prices and sales of turbine generators?
A. It was my opinion there was not meeting of the minds on anything."

Ginn maintained that when he learned, following the December 1958 meeting, of his subordinates' meeting with competitors, he instructed his subordinates that meetings were to be discontinued, that they were to compete aggressively and "that they were not even to speak to competitors," all of which Ginn characterized as his "leprosy policy." In a conference with McMullen Ginn admitted that he had discussed certain improvements which General Electric had made in its turbine generators and the effect that these improvements had had on its prices. Ginn was asked why this was a subject for discussion between competitors:

" Q. Why did you feel it was important to tell a competitor that the improvements that you made, not knowing whether he had made like improvements, were a justification for the level of your prices?
A. Well, the fellow was sitting there in my office. I wanted to be nice to him. I had to have something to talk about. I couldn't talk about the things that you think I talked about, so I got him in to talk about this.

Q. Of course, you didn't talk about golf or the World Series?
A. I don't like to talk to McMullen about golf; I like to play golf with McMullen. That is a source of non-taxable income."

Ginn gave this explanation for having lunch with his counterpart, Rowland of Westinghouse, in Philadelphia:

" Q. Did you have lunch with Mr. Rowland while you were in Philadelphia?
A. I recall that I did that day.

Q. You did have such a luncheon?
A. Yes.

Q. What was the subject matter of your discussion at lunch?
A. General discussion about how the world looked.

Q. Was the word 'price' ever mentioned?
A. Not that I can recall.

Q. Are you prepared to deny it?
A. Yes, I am prepared to deny it.

Q. What was the reason for the luncheon with a competitor?
A. What is wrong with having lunch with a competitor?

Q. That is not an answer to my question.
A. I wanted to go down to Bookbinders and get a good lunch. I was hungry.

Q. That was the purpose of the luncheon?
A. Yes, I was hungry.

Q. Was Mr. Rowland hungry?
A. Mr. Rowland is always hungry."

The following is Ginn's explanation of a golf game that he played with Mauntel of Westinghouse:

" Q. Are there any golfers in the Westinghouse family that you played with?
A. I don't know. I might have played with Monty once down in Hot Springs. I can't remember anybody else.

Q. Monty is Mauntel?
A. Mauntel.

Q. And when you played with Mauntel did you ever ask him how is business or did he ever ask you how is business?
A. Only when you wanted to upset a putt or something."

Ginn was questioned, as he had been before the Kefauver Committee, with respect to two instances, in 1955 and 1957, when he had been called before Mr. Ralph J. Cordiner, then Chairman and chief executive officer of General Electric, and warned that he must operate within the General Electric policies on the antitrust laws. The first instance occurred when Ginn took over as General Manager of the transformer division and the second when he became General Manager in turbines. The witness affirmed his belief that Mr. Cordiner did not know that discussions had been held by General Electric personnel with competitors in transformers and turbines:

" Q. What occasioned the second discussion with Mr. Cordiner?
A. The fact that I had been made an officer of the company. I had taken on my new division. It was my understanding it was Mr. Cordiner's policy to talk to all new division managers.

Q. Did he indicate that he had reason to believe that during the three years since he had last discussed this directive with you you had not effectively administered in the Transformer Division?
A. No, sir.

Q. Did you suspect that Mr. Cordiner was aware of the violations of this directive while you were general manager of the Transformer Division?
A. No, sir.

Q. Did Mr. Cordiner indicate that he was aware of meetings with competitors in the Turbine Division?
A. No, sir.

Q. Did you indicate that meetings with competitors had been going on according to rumor among Turbine Division personnel?
A. No, sir.

Q. In fact, again you concealed from Mr. Cordiner your price discussions with competitors prior to 1957?
A. Yes, sir."

On redirect examination by counsel for General Electric the witness gave his analysis of the price or market factors which affect prices in the heavy electrical industry:

" And in 1950-51 the Korean War broke out and at the urging of the Government additional capacity was put in, which I think resulted a great deal in the white sale, because of all the overcapacity that had been put in and the demand wasn't there.

It is the overcapacity problem coupled with I think we have a situation now, too, that makes this doubly effective, is the question of labor in the shops. Back in the old days if your business fell off you laid people off, reduced your costs, pulled in your horns, and were still able to operate in a fairly respectable manner. Now you have got a situation where labor is no longer a variable commodity such as it was at one time and not only do you incur the expenses of unemployment compensation, training expenses, but we have this very real problem of bumping, that under most union contracts you lay off the junior man first and then bump the people down. Now, it takes normally, if you relieve one man from the payroll, it normally means you make about six moves to compensate for that one man being laid off, and each move involves a considerable amount of expense not only in training but arbitrating to get them in the right position, and as business begins to pick up you might begin to repeat this same process, six down and six up.

I think people have felt that it was absolutely necessary to keep business in their shops to avoid this kind of situation, and when you get overcapacity there is no question that people go out to obtain business at whatever price is necessary to fill their shops.

I think another one that has come into the picture, that some smart college boy wrote a little paper on incremental pricing, that you are better to go out and take a job at direct labor and direct material if you just absorb a little overhead than not to take the job at all. Well, you don't have to have but one or two of these incremental pricing jobs and people take a look at them and think that is where the market is and you have nothing but chaos.

Q. Did GE ever succumb to that idea?
A. Well, you know how they are. They would be the first one to think of some damn-fool new idea. Sure, they would be the first one to want to do that.

I think that this in itself is for my money, and based on my experience, and with no axes to grind or a damn thing, that I can't help but feel, and feel very strongly, that capacity, overcapacity, and factory load is the real determinant of prices in the market place."

The witness discussed the problems of conspiring to fix prices when foreign competition is substantial:

" Q. What is the significance of the entry into a market of a new seller able to control and enjoy as much as 10, 12, or 13 per cent of the market?
A. Well, it would be pretty hard to carry on an alleged conspiracy with nobody, with half of the conspiracy not there.

Q. Can you do it if 12 per cent of the conspiracy isn't there?
A. Well, 12 per cent could cause an awful lot of trouble, and my personal opinion, looking back in retrospect, is that it couldn't be done, and wasn't done."

There were intimations that meetings with competitors were necessary as a matter of self-protection and in order to acquire information that would enable a manufacturer to compete effectively:

" Q. What would be your situation as the department manager if your particular company was not attending meetings and you had reason to believe that your competitors might be?
A. Well, you would be in kind of a bad spot if the boys had a pretty good deal going. They could saw you up pretty bad. One could be low on you one time and one low on the next, and you would be pretty bloody by the time the thing finished.

You got to have really what you are striving to do, and it is pretty hard. We have had these erudite discussions the last three days here walking the tightrope between antitrust laws, 20.5's, industrial espionage, golf games, and social contacts. They are pretty hard to define sometimes, and it gets to be quite a problem, because, with the leprosy policy, how do you know that the other fellows have not at least got enough contacts with one another? They may be not even discussing prices. They may not even be trying to make any market stabilization, but they know each other, and human nature is such that you trust most people that you know a lot better than folks you don't know.

Third, it is really a nice little fat problem, and as I sometimes say, it is easy to sit where you gentlemen sit as lawyers and have all the answers, but it is pretty hard sometimes in the cold realistic outside world to put some of these things together.

Q. When you say industrial espionage, Mr. Ginn, do you mean the acquisition of information for competitive purposes?
A. Certainly. I would like to find out everything in the world I can about my competitors. I love to know what kind of shop they got. I love to know what their costs are. I love to know what kind of people they are. Good heavens, yes.

Q. For the purpose of competing with them more successfully?
A. That's right, for competing with them more successfully and more profitably.

Q. Did you acquire such competitive information as a result of any kind of communication of one kind or another, however they are characterized, with competitors?
A. Sure. As far as I know, there is nothing against the law in going through a competitor's plant, but you can learn an awful lot, some of it good and some of it bad. He may be doing some things you are not doing. You may be doing some things he is not doing. I think you can learn an awful lot from such visits. You can learn an awful lot from playing golf with a fellow, what kind of fellow he is. Is he a gambler? Is he conservative? It is like everything else."

There was an explanation of the phrase "Iron Curtain" in response to a question from the court:

" Q. By the way, I don't remember that the Iron Curtain period has been referred to? What do you mean by it, exactly?
A. That was the period, Your Honor, when General Electric took their commercial people out of the National Electrical Manufacturers Association and didn't allow them to attend meetings at all, and this got one of those names like the Iron Curtain.

Q. Yes.
A. It was a little tighter than the Iron Curtain we are talking about.

Q. Yes, I know. White sale, iron curtain, leprosy.
A. A bunch of fun-loving lads, Your Honor."

And finally the witness cited the following circumstance as showing that there could not have been conspiracy or collusion in turbines:

" I keep repeating that our principal competitor did not receive a job in 1958, the whole year, and based on my experience I never heard of anybody colluding to go out of business."

Peters gave details as to the steps that were taken to conceal defendants' calls to competitors and in the process rebutted any argument by defendants that concealment was directed only toward officers of General Electric:

" Q. These calls were made from where by you?
A. I called—whenever I did call an individual, I called from a pay station.

Q. And where is that pay station?
A. Within a few miles from my home in Schenectady.

Q. You had to take the car to go there?
A. I usually did, sir.

Q. And you did that outside of business hours?
A. Yes, sir.

Q. At night?
A. Yes, sir.

. . . .

Q. Did you ever make any of these telephone calls from your home?
A. I don't remember making any calls from my home, sir.

Q. Why not?

. . . .

A. I made them from the pay station because I wanted to make sure that there was no record on my telephone bill that I had called Milwaukee or Philadelphia.

Q. Why was it that you did not want any record?
A. It wasn't legal.
Q. What is that?
A. Because it was my opinion that calling on a telephone was not legal under the circumstances.
Q. And you wanted to conceal that fact from others in your company?
A. Yes, sir.
Q. And you wanted to conceal that fact from your customers?
A. Yes, sir.
Q. And from the United States Government?
A. Yes, sir."

When plaintiffs took the deposition of Ralph J. Cordiner, Chairman and chief executive officer of General Electric during the period of the conspiracies, there was intense interest on the part of the plaintiffs and numerous others in the electrical and public utility industries in the question of whether Mr. Cordiner knew of the conspiratorial acts and attendance at meetings with competitors on the part of General Electric personnel. There was some belief that Mr. Cordiner was faced with a dilemma: he must either admit knowledge of what his subordinates were doing, in which event he would be virtually a participant in the conspiracies, or, if he denied knowledge, then he would confess shortcomings as chief executive officer of the General Electric enterprises in not knowing of such widespread activity among his personnel.

From a narrow point of view, it might have been in the plaintiffs' interest not to have questioned Mr. Cordiner closely on the question of his knowledge and allowed to stand undenied his representations that he did not know of any of the conspiratorial activities of his employees and that those activities had been concealed from him. With Mr. Cordiner taking such a position, General Electric could then hardly have argued that though their chief executive officer did not know and could not be expected to have known of the conspiratorial activities, the plaintiffs on their side either knew or should have known of those same activities. Nevertheless, the plaintiffs questioned Mr. Cordiner closely with respect to a number of allegations that either he participated in conversations with competitors or was informed that others in his organization were doing so. All such questions were met with firm denials by the witness.

The witness' attention was called to a statement made during the course of the deposition of Mr. J. W. Seaman of General Electric that he, Seaman, had secondhand information that Cordiner and Paxton of General Electric had talked with their Westinghouse counterparts about Westinghouse's discount policy:

" Q. I direct your attention to printed page 309 of the deposition of Mr. Seaman, where he testified that Mr. Ginn told him upon returning from a management meeting in 1955 or 1956 that you and Mr. Paxton talked with your Westinghouse counterparts about Westinghouse's excessive discounts.

Does that testimony refresh your recollection of any conversations with Westinghouse representatives?

A. There was never any such discussion where I was present.

Q. You flatly deny there was any such conversation?

A. I flatly deny there was any such discussion where I was present."

It was called to Mr. Cordiner's attention that in the original memorandum of interview with Mr. Seaman, conducted by Howard J. Aibel, of the staff of counsel to General Electric, the report about Paxton's and Cordiner's conversations with Westinghouse had been included but that it was omitted from the copy of the memorandum that was submitted to Mr. Cordiner. The witness was asked if he had an explanation and furnished none:

" Do you have any idea or was it ever reported to you, Mr. Cordiner, why it was that this specific part of Mr. Seaman's interview was omitted from the original interview report?

A. Which one are you talking about now, NX1058?

Q. NX1060.

A. I never saw this document before, but let me say before we go any further that there never was any discussion by Cordiner in this or any other period about Westinghouse counterparts.

Q. Was it ever reported to you that Mr. Seaman had made this charge against you?

A. It never was.

Q. Was it ever reported to you why this part of the interview was omitted from the original interview report?

A. No. As I said to you a moment ago, that I never saw this report previous to a few minutes ago when it was given to me.

Q. Do you have any explanation to give us why this was not called to the attention of the board of directors when the confidential report on Mr. Seaman was submitted to the board? And I am now referring to NX1058.
A. No.

Q. If you had been given an opportunity before the board to deny Mr. Seaman's charges, I presume from your testimony today that you unqualifiedly would have denied them?
A. I would have denied it just like I denied it now because it is not true."

Mr. Cordiner was asked about an incident involving a speech by the manager of General Electric's general purpose control department:

" Q. Now, do you recall Mr. Oswalt, formerly general manager of the general purpose control department?
A. I do.

Q. Do you recall being present during the speech by Mr. Oswalt at a General Electric management conference in January or February, 1956?
A. I might have been present. I don't recall his particular speech.

Q. Do you recall any particular incident in connection with that speech?
A. I don't remember the speech. Where was the speech given, under what auspices?

Q. It was a General Electric management conference.
A. Well, I probably was one of those present.

Q. Do you recall an incident where Mr. Oswalt was asked how he had such stable prices and yet made so much profit, to which he replied, 'By continuing the practices that were established in the past'?
A. I do not.

Q. Do you recall that this caused Mr. Luebbe to become very agitated and jump to his feet to try and smooth over the matter?
A. I do not.

Q. Do you recall discussing an incident of this nature with Mr. Luebbe?
A. I do not.

. . . .

Q. Do you flatly deny that any such incident occurred?
A. I flatly deny that any such instance as far as Cordiner is concerned occurred.

Q. That is, you were not present at any such incident?
A. I remember no such incident."

The witness also denied a secondhand report that General Electric personnel had been led to believe that it would be all right to contact competitors so long as Mr. Cordiner heard nothing about it:

" Q. Are you aware of the testimony of Mr. Burke that Mr. Erben told Mr. Burens in the presence of Mr. Burke that it was all right to contact competitors, and Erben said that he, Erben, had told you, Cordiner, not to ask him whether he was contacting competitors or not, and you will never hear anything about it?
A. That is not true. Mr. Erben and I never had such a discussion or such an understanding.

Q. So that Mr. Burke's testimony in this regard also was false.
A. It is very false.

. . . .

Q. I show you NX1615, Aibel's report to the board of directors on Burke. Can you tell us why the reference to your alleged conversation with Erben is omitted from that report?
A. I would not know the answer to that question, but let me read you something from this report, since you wish to refer to it. The very first one under 'Candor', it says, 'Burke gave at least two false statements to the company.' "

Mr. Cordiner denied a report that he had met with a representative of Moloney Electric Company to discuss changes in terms of sale to utilities:

" Q. Do you know Mr. Charles D. Auringer, vice-president of Moloney Electric Company?
A. I do not.

Q. Do you know Mr. Mullins of Moloney Electric Company?
A. What is the first name?

Q. Jim Mullins.
A. I think I have met Jim Mullins.

Q. Did you meet with Mr. Mullins in 1957 to discuss changing the escalation clause used in selling to utilities?
A. I did not.

Q. According to the testimony of J. D. Hogg——
A. Who?

Q. J. D. Hogg.
A. Who is he?

Q. Purchasing agent of Cleveland Electric Illuminating Company at N23578-79 of his National deposition, Mr. Auringer advised Mr. Hogg in 1957, '58 or '59 that you had met with Mr. Mullins and discussed the possibility of changing the escalation clause then in use by all the electrical equipment manufacturers.

Mr. Hogg testified that he did not believe you would meet with someone from Moloney and he was not able to reach a firm conclusion as to whether you had done so.

. . . .

Q. Was what Mr. Auringer told Mr. Hogg about the conversation, alleged conversation between you and Mr. Mullins, correct or incorrect?

A. It is completely untrue."

An attempt, in connection with this latter series of questions, to ascertain whether Mr. Cordiner thought that Hogg, if he had been duly diligent, would have reported to the Department of Justice the alleged meeting between Cordiner and Mullins, was met by an objection from defendants' counsel which the court sustained.

Plaintiffs' counsel could not secure an admission from Mr. Cordiner that his own lack of knowledge about conspiratorial activities could reasonably be matched by the utilities' lack of knowledge:

" Q. Referring to 1614, your 1961 Chicago speech, and I quote, Page 5, first full paragraph, 'The members of this conspiracy went to great lengths to conceal their activities from those charged with assuring compliance with the company's directive policies. The concealment was highly effective, much more so than would be supposed from the comic opera descriptions in some publications. It took 18 months of government investigation, including access to competitive information and more than 500 witnesses appearing before four separate grand juries to uncover the facts.'

That represents at least in part, does it not, a basis for your view of why neither you nor any other executive officer of GE learned of these conspiracies?

. . . .

A. That is a direct quote from my remarks, March 1, 1961, and I obviously believed this or I would not have stated it.

Q. The facts to which you refer in your 1961 Chicago speech and those which are described in the interim report would have tended to prevent the utilities and anyone else not a party to the conspiracies from learning about them; isn't that so?

. . . .

A. I would say that utility customers, if they were exchanging information among themselves as to prices paid and were unfamiliar with the economic conditions that went on in the market nationally, might well have wonderment, as I said earlier today, as to whether there was conspiracy or not. I don't know personally because I have not been attending these depositions, except this one of my own, what the position is with regard to information being exchanged by the investor-owned utilities, purchasing agents, one with another, so I don't know how to answer your question.

Q. You used the word 'wonderment' and I ask you the question, did you ever have any wonderment about what was going on?
A. No, I did not."

Even after he had been informed of the conspiratorial activities of General Electric personnel, violative of the antitrust laws and of General Electric Policy 20.5, Mr. Cordiner showed a disinterest in any details or specifics of such activity:

" Q. Very good. At some point of time after October, 1959, you learned that certain employees in the steam turbine division were involved in conduct inconsistent with 20.5?
A. That's right.

Q. Power Transformers?
A. That's true.

. . . .

Q. In any event, there is no doubt that the major products, like the two I mentioned, and circuitbreakers, were reported to you?
A. Reported to me that General Electric gentlemen acknowledged that they had violated company policy 20.5.

Q. When this was reported to you, in what respect were you told they had violated 20.5?
A. I don't remember that I was told the details. General counsel would come and report to me verbally, in my office.

Q. You are not suggesting that he failed to tell you that they had discussed prices with competitors?
A. I don't remember that he told me that. I think that their conversation usually went this way, that he regretted to advise me that Joe Silz, whoever the new name was, had admitted that he had acted contrary to company policy, and that they had another case of where we had to exercise or implement the disciplinary procedure that we had established.

Q. And you did not ask him in what respect did they violate 20.5?
A. I did not.

Q. You did not feel that it was important for you to know the nature and extent of their violation of 20.5 in exercise of the responsibility invested in you by the board to impose discipline?
A. I did not.

Q. Were you aware that G.E. employees who appeared before the grand jury dictated summaries of their testimony after their appearance?

A. I don't remember having that information ever submitted to me.

Q. Were you advised of the substance of any of these summaries of grand jury testimony?

A. I do not remember receiving such advice."

So far as any personal involvement or knowledge was concerned, the witness maintained that he had in effect been exonerated by the Philadelphia grand jury:

" There was another very exhaustive investigation that was reported by Mr. Bicks and Mr. Rogers, at that time attorney general, and it is a matter of record in the Philadelphia court, that mentions my name, Cordiner, and that after 18 months and four grand juries and five witnesses, that there was no evidence that Cordiner participated or knew anything about this situation. That probably was the most thorough investigation." [171]

The witness also indicated that all his correspondence prior to the year 1959 had been destroyed (which meant all correspondence throughout the entire conspiracy period) in accordance with a General Electric policy of destroying all correspondence at the end of two years throughout the whole company; a policy which the witness stated he himself had insisted upon.

In relating his testimony Mr. Cordiner attempted to minimize the importance to utilities of the cost of electrical equipment and to stress that in the more important area of utility operating costs, the manufacturers had taken the lead in bringing about economies for the utility industry:

" Q. A little bit further on in that paragraph you told the Senate Committee, 'One reason that the price of electricity would be down 21 per cent is the contribution of electrical manufacturers in concentrating great effort on the design of ever more expensive

[171] It will be recalled that during the criminal proceedings it was stated by an Assistant Attorney General on behalf of the Department of Justice that the Government had not charged and did not claim that any member of the Board of Directors of the General Electric Company, including Ralph J. Cordiner, Chairman, and Robert Paxton, President, had knowledge of the conspiracy pleaded in the indictments, nor did the Government claim that any of these men personally authorized or ordered the commission of any of the acts charged in any indictment.

but more efficient and automatic power generating equipment that burns less fuel per kilowatt hour. You see, the main cost in making electricity is not the machinery, such as turbine generators, but the cost of fuel, year after year.'

That is correct, is it not, Mr. Cordiner?

A. That is right.

Q. Then you went on to say, 'In two years a modern turbine generator will consume its original ost in fossil fuels. In fact, an electric utility could not afford a urbine as a gift if it were as little as 10 per cent less efficient than the best produced today.'

That statement was correct, was it not?

A. Not only correct, but it is my opinion."

Overall the deposition program established incontrovertibly that meetings among competitors had been held to discuss and fix prices and allocate markets. Like information came from other sources. When General Electric was required to answer the so-called "proxy interrogatories" in Philadelphia, it identified a meeting in May or June 1957 among Lilly and Peters of General Electric and "employee or employees" of Westinghouse and Allis-Chalmers, and then stated: "A price increase of 5 per cent was agreed upon." In the answer to the same proxy interrogatories General Electric identified a meeting "subsequent to the adoption of the BLS escalation clause by General Electric in 1955" between Peters (of General Electric) and "an employee" of Westinghouse and stated: "Westinghouse agreed to use the BLS escalation provision that General Electric used." On job allocations General Electric in its answer to the proxy interrogatories, with reference to a Commonwealth Edison turbine order, gave the content of a telephone call in the middle or latter part of March 1959, from Peters of General Electric to Eikner of Westinghouse as follows: "Peters told Westinghouse the price Westinghouse was to quote and that General Electric would quote a higher price."

Certain non-General Electric personnel were as explicit as General Electric personnel. Sellers of Carrier (Elliott Division) in his national deposition testified that he participated in the "nudging" by the working-level people to bring about a meeting with the policy-level group. At the time, prices were 10% to 15% off book and "everyone" at the meeting (all the manufacturers were represented) spoke out in favor of getting order prices closer to book. (Ginn had proposed that all quote 2%

or 3% off book.) Sellers thought the same percentage applied to sealed and non-sealed business. Sellers stated that the meeting closed "with a meeting of the minds" that all would quote at 2% (or 3%) off book if everyone else did.

Eikner of Westinghouse testified that, following a 10% increase in book prices in April 1953 announced by General Electric, Westinghouse was anxious for a meeting with General Electric because Westinghouse was confused "about computing book prices correctly" and "wanted to determine the same book prices that General Electric would determine."

Neblett of General Electric gave a vivid description of the reaction of competitors when Warren of General Electric announced to representatives of competitors that General Electric was going to maintain prices in turbine generators close to the book prices:

" Q. Could you place that meeting?
A. Could I place it?

Q. Yes, where did it take place?
A. In New York.

Q. In a hotel?
A. Yes, sir.

Q. Do you recall who else was present?
A. Mr. Warren, Mr. Saupe, myself, Mr. Mauntel, and I believe Mr. Miers.

Q. Was Peters there?
A. No, sir.

Q. Can you tell us what happened at this meeting?
A. It was very simple. The meeting was arranged, and Mr. Warren made the statement to Mr. Mauntel and everybody present that we were going, or rather we had gone and were going to maintain prices very close to the handbook.

Q. What did the representatives of the other companies say in response to this observation of Mr. Warren?
A. To the best of my knowledge, Professor Handler, they said 'Thank God'."

CHAPTER 10

Privilege and the proceedings before the grand jury

When a grand jury is sitting, those called as witnesses come before it unaccompanied by counsel or any other assistant. When the witness leaves the grand jury room he is free, if he wishes, to reveal what he observed of the proceedings, the questions he was asked and the answers that he gave.

In the case of the electrical equipment grand jury, uniformly as the employees of the defendant manufacturers emerged from the grand jury room, they were interviewed as to the testimony they had given. Usually the interview was conducted by counsel for the witness' employer, who was house counsel in some cases, and in others outside counsel retained by the employer for antitrust defense purposes. In some instances the conference with respect to testimony before the grand jury was with the witness' personal counsel. The deposition testimony of Ginn describes the circumstances under which his testimony before the grand jury was reviewed by him with his personal counsel:

" Q. Now, sir, taking the first of the three documents that you referred to, which was a memorandum of the testimony that you gave before the Grand Jury, would you describe for us the circumstances under which that document was prepared.
A. I went before the Grand Jury on Thursday, April the 13th of 1961. After leaving the Grand Jury I returned to my private counsel's office and——

Q. Who was that counsel?
A. Mr. Henry Reath—and dictated—well, I used a tape-recording thing and stated what had taken place at the Grand Jury, from which this memorandum was made.

Q. You dictated it without any questioning on his part?
A. There was some reminders, sir, not questions as such but he asked a few questions, 'Was this asked; was that asked?'

Q. Mr. Reath at that time was acting as your personal counsel?
A. That is correct, sir.

Q. And not as counsel for General Electric?
A. That is correct, sir.

Q. And was anybody else present?
A. No, sir.

Q. No representative of General Electric?
A. No, sir.

Q. Would you turn to the second of the three documents that you referred to?
A. Yes, sir.

Q. Who supplied the basic information from which this document was prepared?

JUDGE KIRKPATRICK: *Before you get to that, let me get this straight. The first document was prepared by Mr. Reath, was it, or was it you yourself?*
THE WITNESS: *I dictated it, sir, with one of those——*
JUDGE KIRKPATRICK: *Oh, this was the thing you dictated that you talk about?*
THE WITNESS: *Yes, sir.*"

In other circumstances, and this was true particularly of General Electric, employees who appeared before the grand jury were later interviewed by company counsel, not with the primary purpose, evidently, of determining what went on before the grand jury but to inquire whether there had been violations of company policies with respect to the antitrust laws. Ginn's testimony again indicates the circumstances under which interviews of this kind took place:

" Q. Now, would you turn to the third of these documents, sir?
A. Yes, sir.

Q. And tell us what that is and the circumstances surrounding its preparation.
A. This is a memorandum of the meetings held with General Electric counsel in discussion of any of my dealings or actions in connection with the company's directive, policy on 20—of the antitrust laws.

Q. This was an investigation which counsel made once it became known that the Government was investigating these violations to determine what part had been played by various employees of the company?
A. Yes, sir.

Q. Is this the investigation that was conducted by Gerard Swope, Jr.?
A. Well, not my particular one, sir. These were—I was never interviewed by Mr. Swope; it was other company counsel. I never talked to Mr. Swope."

Counsel for plaintiffs were interested in securing the production of memoranda of this kind since it was the obvious route to information concerning the operation of the conspiracies as revealed to the grand jury or to the witness' employer.[172] Defendants countered by claiming that all such documents were subject to an attorney-client privilege, or, in the alternative, constituted a "lawyer's work product" which could not be required to be produced.

The attorney-client privilege has been defined in classic terms by Wigmore as follows:

> "(1) Where legal advice of any kind is sought, (2) from a professional legal advisor in his capacity as such, (3) the communications relating to that purpose, (4) made in confidence, (5) by the client, (6) are at his instance permanently protected, (7) from disclosure by himself or by the legal advisor, (8) except the protection be waived."[173]

When a memorandum of testimony before the grand jury was prepared by a witness in consultation with his personal attorney, there was no question that the attorney-client privilege applied. Judge Sirica in Washington ruled that this was likewise the case if the witness' personal attorney were simply present, even though the questioning and the conferring were carried on by the witness' employer's counsel.

---

172 A technique developed after the electrical equipment cases permitted treble damage plaintiffs who bring suit following an antitrust criminal case to have access to the presentence memoranda filed by the Government in the criminal case: U. S. Industries, Inc. v. U. S. District Court, 84 345 F.2d 18 (9th Cir. 1965), *cert. denied,* 382 U. S. 814 (1965); Washington v. American Pipe and Construction Co., 41 F.R.D. 59 (S.D. Cal. 1966). But in Hancock Bros., Inc. v. Jones, 293 F. Supp. 1229 (N.D. Cal. 1968) doubt was expressed as to the ruling in United States Industries by reason of an amendment to Federal Criminal Rule 32 which permitted disclosure of presentence reports to defendants. Hancock Bros., Inc. held that plaintiffs would be permitted equal access only upon a showing that denial would result in "unfair advantage" to the defendant.

173 8 WIGMORE, EVIDENCE § 2292 (McNaughton rev. 1961).

But when a personal counsel was not present and the questioning and the conferring with the witness were carried out by counsel for the witness' employer, there was a serious question whether the attorney-client privilege existed. The witness could not claim the privilege because this would not be a situation in which Wigmore's conditions (1) and (2) could be met, that is, legal advice is sought by the witness from a professional legal advisor in his capacity as such. And if the corporation, the employer, claimed privilege, the question then became whether the witness was such a duly authorized representative of the corporation that it could be said that the corporation was seeking legal advice in the course of the conference between the corporation's counsel and the witness.

Judge Kirkpatrick of the Eastern District of Pennsylvania rendered an opinion which came to be regarded as the definitive ruling on these questions in *City of Philadelphia* v. *Westinghouse Electric Corporation*.[174] In considering whether the attorney-client privilege applied to a memorandum which reflected information acquired by counsel for General Electric Company in the course of his interrogation of employees, Judge Kirkpatrick first ruled that there was no privilege as between attorney and the employee:

> " It is clear in this case (as it was in the other) that the claim of a privilege personal to the employee, claimed in his behalf, is without merit. He was definitely advised by the lawyer that, although his disclosures were 'privileged,' if it should turn out that they revealed a violation of written policy directives, the lawyer would 'report that fact to management.' This disposes of any possible claim that the communications were confidential."

On the question of whether there was an attorney-client privilege that could be asserted by General Electric, the court first stated that in its view the attorney-client privilege was available to corporations.[175]

---

[174] 210 F. Supp. 483 (E.D. Pa. 1962), *petition for writ of prohibition and mandamus denied,* 312 F.2d 742 (3d Cir. 1962); *cert. denied,* 372 U.S. 943 (1963). For a criticism of Judge Kirkpatrick's holding see 56 Illinois Bar Journal 542, 544-545 (March 1968).

[175] Chief Judge Campbell of the United States District Court for the Northern District of Illinois had ruled in Radiant Burners, Inc. v. American Gas Association, 207 F. Supp. 771 (N.D. Ill. 1962), that

Judge Kirkpatrick stated that the question that was to be asked and the answer to be given were the following:

"Now, in cases where an employee of a corporation in an executive or managerial position communicates a fact relative to pending litigation to a lawyer retained or employed by the corporation, the question frequently arises: When he does so, is the corporation seeking the advice of the attorney? In other words, was he at the time, in contemplation of law, the corporation seeking advice? If not, then he was giving the lawyer information in order that the latter could advise a client other than himself. In such case the employee is merely a witness. . . .

Keeping in mind that the question is, Is it the corporation which is seeking the lawyer's advice when the asserted privileged communication is made? the most satisfactory solution, I think is that if the employee making the communication, of whatever rank he may be, is in a position to control or even to take a substantial part in a decision about any action which the corporation may take upon the advice of the attorney, or if he is an authorized member of a body or group which has that authority, then, in effect, he is (or personifies) the corporation when he makes his disclosure to the lawyer and the privilege would apply. In all other cases the employee would be merely giving information to the lawyer to enable the latter to advise those in the corporation having the authority to act or refrain from acting on the advice."

Judge Kirkpatrick accordingly held that there was no privilege either in the witness or in General Electric with respect to the memorandum that was before him.[176]

---

the attorney-client privilege was not available to corporations. This ruling, still in force in Illinois at the time of Judge Kirkpatrick's opinion, was later reversed by the United States Court of Appeals for the Seventh Circuit in Radiant Burners, Inc. v. American Gas Association, 320 F.2d 314 (1963).

176 In a later decided case, Harper & Row Publishers, Inc. v. Decker, 423 F.2d 487 (7th Cir. 1970), affirmed without opinion by an equally divided Supreme Court of the U. S. (400 U. S. 348 [1970]) the Court of Appeals for the Seventh Circuit considered a request for according the attorney-client privilege to memoranda of interviews between employees of the publishing company and the company's attorney.

The court pointed out that each employee had made his disclosure to the attorney at the direction of his corporate employer and on its behalf and that the subject matter of the employee's grand jury testimony and of the debriefing interview was germane to the duties of his employment. On the other hand it was not demonstrated that any of the employees was in a position to control or take a substantial

Another argument used by plaintiffs against the existence of an attorney-client privilege in the corporate employer related to Wigmore's condition number (8), that the privilege not be waived. In the case of the General Electric statements, it was argued by plaintiffs that when General Electric published a General Proxy Statement dated March 17, 1961, in which it had outlined what had been discovered as to the activities of its employees as a result of the investigations that were made and then gave even more details in a published document entitled *Interim Report—The Recent Settlement of Electrical Industry Antitrust Cases,* dated December 14, 1960, it had published the results of its investigation to such an extent that privilege should be regarded as waived. The author of the Interim Report, Howard J. Aibel, filed a "supplemental affidavit" in the electrical equipment cases, denying that the statements in the Interim Report constituted a "summary" of the interviews conducted by General Electric counsel. A definitive ruling on this point was not made.[177]

---

part in a decision about action which the corporation may take upon the advice of the attorney nor that he was a member of a group having that authority.

The Court of Appeals pointed out that District Judge Decker had substantially followed the "control group" test as enunciated by Judge Kirkpatrick in City of Philadelphia v. Westinghouse Electric Corp., 210 F. Supp. 483. The court noted that a similar test appears in Rule 5-03(a)(3), Preliminary Draft of Proposed Rules of Evidence for the United States District Courts and Magistrates, March 1969.

The Court of Appeals in Harper & Row Publishers rejected the "control group" test:

"We conclude that the control group test is not wholly adequate, that the corporation's attorney-client privilege protects communications of some corporate agents who are not within the control group, and that in those instances where the order here under attack must rest entirely upon the control group test, the order is unlawful.

. . . .

We conclude that an employee of a corporation, though not a member of its control group, is sufficiently identified with the corporation so that his communication to the corporation's attorney is privileged where the employee makes the communication at the direction of his superiors in the corporation and where the subject matter upon which the attorney's advice is sought by the corporation and dealt with in the communication is the performance by the employee of the duties of his employment."

177 The Interim Report contains statements indicating that the interviews with employees were not always productive of a truthful account of

The defendants attempted to assert an attorney-client privilege in another situation. Plaintiffs had addressed interrogatories to the defendants asking for details of meetings of competitors in which prices, territories and terms of sale of electrical equipment were discussed. The answers filed by defendants refused to give most of the information, invoking the attorney-client privilege. Typical answers stated that the only information relevant to the interrogatories was in the possession of counsel and was obtained by counsel in interviews conducted by him with employees of the company in order to give the company (or, in some cases, the employees interviewed) legal advice and to prepare for the defense of criminal prosecutions. In denying the applicability of the attorney-client privilege in this situation, Judge Kirkpatrick said:

> " In these cases it is the client, a corporation and a party to the suit, who is being interrogated. Wigmore's classic statement of the rule relating to the privilege may be accepted as law, and it is not questioned that the attorney-client privilege protects the client as well as the attorney. However, it is evident that the objections are based upon a fundamental misconception of just what it is the disclosure of which is forbidden by the rule. The point which the defendants appear to have missed is that the protection of the privilege extends only to *communications* and not to facts. A fact is one thing and a communication concerning that fact is an entirely different thing. The client cannot be compelled to answer the question, 'What did you say or write to the attorney?,' but may not refuse to disclose any relevant fact within his knowledge merely because he incorporated a statement of such fact into his communication to his attorney.
>
> The principles stated in this memorandum are practically hornbook law and require no elaboration or citation of authorities." [178]

As an alternative argument used by the manufacturers to resist production of the memoranda of interviews, the point was attempted to be made that they constituted a lawyer's "work product" which ought not to be required to be produced.

---

their activities. A group of General Electric employees prior to the first interviews by company counsel decided, according to the Interim Report, that "so long as we've lied to our lawyers up to now, we'd better continue to do so."

[178] City of Philadelphia v. Westinghouse Electric Corp., 205 F. Supp. 830, 831 (E.D. Pa. 1962).

The so-called "work product" doctrine, not to be confused with the attorney-client privilege, was defined by a decision of the Supreme Court of the United States in *Hickman* v. *Taylor.*[179] In that case the Court had to consider whether oral and written statements of witnesses secured by counsel for one party in the course of preparation for possible litigation would have to be submitted and made available to the other party. The Court ruled that to the extent that the memoranda and statements reflect the work and mental impressions of an attorney, they do not have to be made available to his adversary:

> " Here is simply an attempt, without purported necessity or justification, to secure written statements, private memoranda and personal recollections prepared or formed by an adverse party's counsel in the course of his legal duties. As such, it falls outside the arena of discovery and contravenes the public policy underlying the orderly prosecution and defense of legal claims. Not even the most liberal of discovery theories can justify unwarranted inquiries into the files and the mental impressions of an attorney."

The Supreme Court added that unusual circumstances might justify a production order:

> " Where relevant and non-privileged facts remain hidden in an attorney's file and where production of those facts is essential to the preparation of one's case, discovery may properly be had. Such written statements and documents might, under certain circumstances, be admissible in evidence or give clues as to the existence or location of relevant facts. Or they might be useful for purpose of impeachment or corroboration. And production might be justified where the witnesses are no longer available or can be reached only with difficulty."

The Court was particularly disturbed by the argument that oral statements made to counsel might be ordered to be produced:

> " But as to oral statements made by witnesses to Fortenbaugh, whether presently in the form of his mental impressions or memoranda, we do not believe that any showing of necessity can be made under the circumstances of this case so as to justify production. Under ordinary conditions, forcing an attorney to repeat or write out all that witnesses have told him and to deliver the account to his adversary gives rise to grave dangers of inaccuracy and untrustworthiness. No legitimate purpose is served by such production. The practice forces the attorney to testify as to what

---

[179] 329 U.S. 495 (1947).

he remembers or what he saw fit to write down regarding witnesses' remarks. Such testimony could not qualify as evidence; and to use it for impeachment or corroborative purposes would make the attorney much less an officer of the court and much more an ordinary witness. The standards of the profession would thereby suffer."

The defendants had some success in asserting the work product defense. Judge Robson in *Commonwealth Edison Company* v. *Allis-Chalmers Manufacturing Company*[180] ruled that memoranda of interviews were protected as work products and would be produced only upon good cause shown; he rejected the argument that the unique character of the litigation was in itself a sufficient showing of good cause for production within the rules stated in *Hickman* v. *Taylor.* The court therefore entered orders of protection for the documents, adding that if there were a valid showing of good cause for their production, an *in camera* inspection of the documents by the court would then be appropriate.

In Philadelphia,[181] Judge Clary came to the same conclusion where a witness tape recorded a lengthy account of his testimony before the grand jury which, when transcribed, constituted the document that the plaintiffs were attempting to secure. By agreement of the parties, the court was asked to review the statement and determine whether there was good cause for its production and disclosure to the plaintiff. The court ruled that there was not such good cause:

" I have read the statements. They were delivered to me under an agreement by the parties that I should take them temporarily and, before announcing my ruling as to whether or not good cause appeared in the case, would redeliver them to defendant's attorney in order that he might have an opportunity to take whatever measures he desired in order to resist their being delivered to the plaintiff. I am not sure that the procedure adopted, namely, having the judge read the statements and compare them with the testimony on deposition in order to determine what, if any, discrepancies exist, is a wise one. In the present case, it was a considerable burden and I can easily envision cases in which

---

180 211 F. Supp. 736 (N.D. Ill. 1962).

181 City of Philadelphia v. Westinghouse Electric Corporation, 32 F.R.D. 350 (E.D. Pa. 1962).

> it would be practically an impossible one. Moreover, it, in effect, transfers the burden of showing good cause from the plaintiff to the judge, requiring him, if he orders disclosure, to justify his action, at least to himself. Therefore, I should say that I do not wish to endorse this procedure as desirable or make its use in this case stand as a precedent where production is sought under Rule 34.
>
> I am of the opinion that sufficient cause for the production of these statements does not appear in the present case. Under the procedure adopted here any discussion at this point would constitute an invasion of the privacy which the ruling is intended to protect. The motion to compel production of them is denied and they will be redelivered to the defendant's attorney."

In the case of the witness Burke, Judge Kirkpatrick ruled that there was good cause shown for the production of a memorandum statement by the witness, primarily because there were indications from the witness himself that his oral testimony would be unreliable because he was deliberately attempting to forget his conspiratorial activities. Judge Kirkpatrick found good cause for production of the Burke statement in the "inconsistencies of his testimony and prior deposition and his fading recollection" and in the circumstance that "in this particular case the witness aided the process by active effort on his part to suppress and eradicate from his mind anything that might be helpful in the case." [182] Judge Kirkpatrick also held: "I do not order the production of memoranda of counsel, and what they were told by him (Burke), which were not in any way authenticated or assented to by Burke and proof of which would depend entirely upon the testimony of counsel. Insufficient cause for this action appears." General Electric dragged its feet in producing the Burke statements and finally was ordered on April 1 to produce the documents by April 3 or suffer a default judgment. The statements were produced on April 3.

In the course of passing on a request for the production of another memorandum, relating to the witness Rissinger, Judge Kirkpatrick ruled that the document, to be within the work product doctrine, had to be something more than a mechanical transcription of the witness' statement: "I just can't see why it

---

[182] Transcript of hearing, Philadelphia, Nov. 20-21, 1962, pp. 45-46.

is work product merely because a lawyer calls a witness before him and presses a button or turns a knob on a machine and sits there and what the witness says is mechanically taken down and the lawyer has his secretary transcribe it." As the plaintiffs argued, in such a case the work product was that of the witness, not of the lawyer. Judge Boldt agreed in requiring production of a statement of Burens: "I conclude, after examining the paper, that its essential nature in all substantially important particulars is not actually work product but is merely a memorandum of a witness' statement." [183]

The defendants were in a dilemma on the question of whether the memoranda of interviews should be made available to the interviewed witness before that witness was called for his deposition. In the case of Sellers, Judge Boldt stated that he found it astonishing that counsel did not, before the deposition, show to Sellers the memoranda summarizing Sellers' recollection of his grand jury testimony: Judge Boldt thought that a reading of the memoranda might have helped the witness' lagging memory during his deposition. On the other hand, in the course of the deposition of James W. Seaman in Philadelphia, Judge Stanley ruled, with reference to a statement that Seaman had given to counsel for General Electric, that the claim of work product had been waived when General Electric gave a copy of the statement to Seaman.

In all of this the question of who had actual possession of the statement sought to be produced made a difference. Witness Metzler, following his grand jury testimony, had given a statement to outside counsel for Westinghouse: the statement was mostly narrative, with no questioning by counsel. At the time of his deposition the statement was not in the possession of that

---

[183] In Harper & Row Publishers, Inc. v. Decker, the court of appeals said, on the question of whether a debriefing memorandum could be characterized as work product:

". . . Where an attorney personally prepares a memorandum of an interview of a witness with an eye toward litigation such memorandum qualifies as work product even though the lawyer functioned primarily as an investigator. . . . Indeed, the qualified privilege might even attach to a document prepared under the supervision of the attorney even though not drafted by the attorney himself. . . . Of course, the less the lawyer's 'mental processes' are involved, the less will be the burden to show good cause."

counsel nor of Westinghouse but in the possession of a member of the firm that was general counsel for Westinghouse. Judge Lord ruled that since the statement was not in the possession of Metzler nor of Westinghouse, it could not be reached by a Rule 34[184] motion addressed to Westinghouse or by subpoena to Metzler, citing *Hickman* v. *Taylor* as authority. But Judge Lord added that if the statement had been in the possession of house counsel it could be obtained by a Rule 34 motion directed to the corporation.

When the plaintiffs began to encounter difficulties in securing the production of the memoranda of interviews of witnesses who had appeared before the grand jury, they began to take steps to determine whether as a shortcut and a more direct route to the information sought they could require the production of the actual minutes of the grand jury proceedings.

Several attempts had been made, prior to the plaintiffs' deposition program, to secure grand jury transcripts and had been denied. In March 1961 the Attorney General of California had applied in Philadelphia for the release of names of the grand jury witnesses and for documents that had been subpoenaed by the grand jury; this motion was denied.[185] The Federal Trade Commission had made application to Judge Harold H. Wood for permission to see the Philadelphia grand jury transcript in order to determine whether certain orders of the Commission relating to turbine generators and condensers had been violated; the request was denied.[186]

But the United States as a claimant had been placed in an especially favored position in this regard. In August 1962, in the Eastern District of Pennsylvania, Judge Kraft had ruled that the attorneys for the United States could use the grand jury transcripts in prosecuting damage actions on behalf of the United

---

184 A federal rule which permits a party to litigation to require, for good cause shown, that any other party produce documents and tangible things for inspection, copying or photographing. A party is a plaintiff or defendant. A witness is not a party as such.

185 Application of California to Inspect Grand Jury Subpoenas, 195 F. Supp. 37 (E.D. Pa. 1961).

186 *In re* grand jury proceedings, 29 F.R.D. 151 (E.D. Pa. 1961), *aff'd*, 309 F.2d 440 (3d Cir. 1962).

States, although he ruled that the attorneys for TVA could not do so.[187] The ruling was based on the language of Rule 6(3) of the Federal Rules of Criminal Procedure,[188] which sets forth the terms and conditions for the disclosure of matters occurring before the grand jury:

> " (e) Secrecy of Proceedings and Disclosure.
> Disclosure of matters occurring before the grand jury other than its deliberations and the vote of any juror may be made to the attorneys for the government for use in the performance of their duties. Otherwise a juror, attorney, interpreter, stenographer, operator of a recording device, or any typist who transcribes recorded testimony may disclose matters occurring before the grand jury only when so directed by the court preliminarily to or in connection with a judicial proceeding or when permitted by the court at the request of the defendant upon a showing that grounds may exist for a motion to dismiss the indictment because of matters occurring before the grand jury. No obligation of secrecy may be imposed upon any person except in accordance with this rule. The court may direct that an indictment shall be kept secret until the defendant is in custody or has given bail, and in that event the clerk shall seal the indictment and no person shall disclose the finding of the indictment except when necessary for the issuance and execution of a warrant or summons."

In interpreting the rule and the policy against disclosure of grand jury proceedings, the United States Supreme Court and other federal courts[189] had cited five reasons as compelling the rule of secrecy:

" 1. To prevent the escape of those whose indictment may be contemplated;
2. To insure the utmost freedom to the Grand Jury in its deliberations, and to prevent persons subject to indictment or their friends from importuning the Grand Jurors;

---

187 United States v. General Electric Company, 209 F. Supp. 197 (E.D. Pa. 1962).

188 There seems to be no question that Rule 6(e), although a part of the Federal Rules of Criminal Procedure, is applicable in both civil and criminal cases: See note, 112 U. of Pennsylvania Law Rev. 1133, 1142.

189 United States v. Procter & Gamble Company, 357 U.S. 677, 681-682, n. 6 (1958); United States v. Rose, 215 F.2d 617 (3d Cir. 1954); United States v. Amazon Industrial Chemical Corporation, 55 F.2d 254, 261 (D.C. Md. 1931).

3. To prevent subornation of perjury or tampering with the witnesses who may testify before the Grand Jury and later appear at the trial of those indicted by it;
4. To encourage free and untrammeled disclosures by persons who have information with respect to the commission of crimes;
5. To protect innocent accused who is exonerated from disclosure of the fact that he has been under investigation, and from the expense of standing trial where there was no probability of guilt."

In their attempts to secure the production of the grand jury minutes as a part of the deposition program in the electrical equipment proceedings, plaintiffs argued that reasons (1), (2) and (3) were inapplicable at that time, the grand jury having met and been discharged and the criminal proceedings resulting from the grand jury deliberations having been completed. Reason number (5) was argued to be inapplicable in the circumstances of the electrical equipment proceedings, leaving number (4) as the principal policy reason for grand jury secrecy to be met.

Nevertheless the plaintiffs were encouraged by the provision of Federal Criminal Rule 6(e) which permitted the disclosure of matters occurring before the grand jury "when so directed by the court preliminarily to or in connection with a judicial proceeding." Accordingly, in connection with the very first deposition taken as a part of the plaintiffs' deposition program, that of A. C. Allen of Wagner Electric Corporation, a motion was made before the District Court in Philadelphia, where the grand jury had sat, for the production of the transcript of Allen's testimony before the grand jury. A memorandum of Allen's testimony had been made available to the plaintiffs, having been held not to be privileged, but the plaintiffs, believing that details of testimony before the grand jury may have been omitted from the memorandum, petitioned the court for the right to review the testimony itself.

Chief Judge Clary concluded that the court had power, by reason of the provision of Rule 6(e), to order disclosure to non-Government litigants of testimony given by a witness to a federal grand jury. He concluded, however, that the secrecy of the grand jury proceedings must be maintained except in the face of a particular compelling need; and he found in the case of the

Allen testimony that there was not such a compelling need since a memorandum of Allen's testimony before the grand jury had already been made available to the plaintiffs.

But Judge Clary went on, "because of the importance of the question involved," to discuss the circumstances under which transcripts of grand jury proceedings might be made available as a part of the electrical equipment deposition program. On this question, the court had requested a statement of the position of the Department of Justice and Donald G. Balthis, head of the Philadelphia office of the Antitrust Section of the Department of Justice, had stated the position of the Government as follows:

" 1. That such power exists in this Court.
2. That such power should be exercised only if and when the Court makes the same kind of determination as to the need for such disclosure that a trial court would usually make.
3. That such a determination requires an in camera examination of the transcript of this Court for the purpose of deciding whether or not the rule of justice will be better served by such disclosure than by non-disclosure, that is, whether the public interest in maintaining secrecy of the Grand Jury process is outweighed by a particularized showing that disclosure is needed to achieve a just result in this litigation.
4. That where such a determination is made only so much of the transcript shall be disclosed as is needed to achieve this result.
5. That before any particular transcript is turned over, the Justice Department be given a reasonable opportunity to express its view as to the propriety of the contemplated turnover of the testimony in question."

The court found that the position of the Government was fair and reasonable but added that a grand jury transcript should never be opened solely for discovery purposes. However, the court pointed out that the depositions in the electrical equipment proceedings were trial depositions which might be utilized in any section of the country since the depositions were being taken pursuant to Rule 26(d) of the Federal Rules of Civil Procedure.

Concentrating on the traditional reasons for secrecy in grand jury proceedings, the court said with respect to number (4) that it was a factor which could not be ignored by any court, but added its belief that production should be ordered

> " . . . where in camera examination by a deposition Judge uncovers material discrepancy or significant facts which the witness concealed, or failed to remember, at his deposition. Such disclosure as is necessary to uncover full and complete facts must be allowed. If, at the completion of any deposition taken in the national program, a motion is made for the production of that witness' Grand Jury testimony, and if the deposition Judge requests it from this Court for examination in camera, the testimony will be immediately made available to him. The deposition Judge may then contrast the Grand Jury testimony with the deposition and determine, in his own discretion, whether in the interest of justice there is a compelling need for disclosure." [190]

Judge Clary also spelled out the procedures that would be followed in making the transcripts available to the deposition judge:

> " Not all situations that may confront a deposition Judge can be foretold or foreseen, but some workable program in this connection must be devised which will insure the production of Grand Jury testimony under proper safeguards. Therefore, upon the request of any deposition Judge to this Court, a single copy of the witness' testimony will be made and sent by the Clerk of this Court, by registered mail, and under the seal of the Court, to the deposition Judge for his examination and action, and thereafter when it has served its purpose, it shall be returned to the Clerk of this Court who will impound it. Should a deposition Judge, prior to the taking of the deposition of a witness, request such a copy, his request will be honored, and a copy of the transcript forwarded, again under the seal of the Court. If no motion is made with respect to the testimony of the particular witness, the transcript will be returned to the Clerk of this Court unopened. This action is being taken solely for the purpose of expediting the national discovery program."

---

190 The United States Supreme Court has recently expressed disapproval of the technique of *in camera* inspection by a trial judge to be followed by production of grand jury testimony in the event the judge found inconsistencies between trial testimony and that before the grand jury. In Dennis v. United States, 384 U.S. 855 (1966), Justice Fortas expressed a distinct preference for the production of grand jury testimony to counsel rather than the preliminary examination of it by the trial judge, saying: "In our adversary system, it is enough for judges to judge. The determination of what may be useful to the defense can properly and effectively be made only by an advocate. The trial judge's function in this respect is limited to deciding whether a case has been made for production, and to supervise the process . . . " Even the dissenters joined with the majority in this portion of the opinion.

An appeal from Judge Clary's order pursuant to Section 1291 of the Federal Judicial Code was dismissed without opinion on the grounds that the order was interlocutory and that the defendants lacked standing to appeal.[191]

As a result of Judge Clary's opinion and order the plaintiffs made a series of motions during the depositions to obtain the grand jury minutes of various deponents. Four of these motions were decided in favor of release by Judge Boldt, all on the same day: Peters, Sellers, Nairn and McMullen.[192] Judge Kirkpatrick denied release of the W. G. Lewis transcript and Judge Boldt denied the release of the C. E. Burke transcript.

Judge Feinberg in New York, in releasing the transcripts of testimony of W. G. Swoish and Joseph D. Hoffman, outlined the procedures which he followed in arriving at his decision:

---

191 Order, City of Philadelphia, No. 14296, 3d Cir., Feb. 21, 1963.

192 See Order on Motion for Release of Deponent's Grand Jury Testimony, In the Matter of the National Deposition of John T. Peters, Civ. No. 61-4264 and related cases, S.D. N.Y., Dec. 18, 1962 (Boldt, Special Master), *approved and conf'd,* Dec. 20, 1962, S.D. N.Y. (Ryan, C.J.), *petition for leave to appeal or in the alternative for a writ of mandamus denied sub nom.* Atlantic City Elec. Co. v. A. B. Chance Co., 313 F.2d 431 (2d Cir. 1963) (per curiam) (Appeal under 28 U.S.C. § 1292[b] [1958]), appl. for stay denied, 372 U.S. 699 (Apr. 10, 1963) (Harlan, J., in chambers); In the Matter of the National Deposition of Brenan R. Sellers, 32 F.R.D. 473, 475 (N.D. Ill. 1963) (Boldt, J., sitting by assignment), *pet. for leave to appeal or in the alternative for a writ of mandamus denied,* No. 14027, 7th Cir., Feb. 5, 1963 (appeal under 28 U.S.C. § 1292[b] [1958]), *appeal dismissed,* 7th Cir., Apr. 19, 1963 (appeal under 28 U.S.C. § 1291 [1958]); Order on Motion for Release of Deponent's Grand Jury Testimony, In the Matter of the National Deposition of Donald J. Nairn, Civil No. 29810 and related cases, E.D. Pa., Dec. 18, 1962 (Boldt, J., sitting by assignment in the Northern District of Ill.), *approved and conf'd,* Dec. 20, 1962, E.D. Pa. (Clary, C.J.), *pet. for writs of prohibition and mandamus denied sub nom.* Nairn v. Clary, 312 F.2d 748 (3d Cir. 1963) (per curiam), *pet. for rehearing denied on other grounds, id.* (Mar. 13, 1963), *appeal dismissed,* No. 14319, 3d Cir. Feb. 21, 1963 (appeal under 28 U.S.C. § 1291 [1958]); Order on Motion for Release of Deponent's Grand Jury Testimony, In the Matter of the National Deposition of J. W. McMullen, Civ. No. 1135M, S.D. Fla., Dec. 18, 1962 (Boldt, Special Master), *approved and conf'd,* S.D. Fla., Dec. 20, 1962 (Dyer, C.J.), *aff'd sub nom.* Allis-Chalmers Mfg. Co. v. City of Fort Pierce, 323 F.2d 233 (5th Cir. 1963).

> "I have carefully reviewed the grand jury testimony of these two witnesses and compared it with their testimony in the depositions conducted in New York. Moreover, in accordance with Chief Judge Clary's opinion, the Department of Justice has been given an opportunity to object to the release of any portion of this grand jury testimony and has not done so. I find that in the case of each witness, there are either material discrepancies or important factual issues between grand jury testimony and deposition testimony or significant facts that the witnesses failed to reveal at the deposition. I find that in the interest of justice there is a compelling need for a disclosure of portions of the grand jury transcript of these witnesses and accordingly these portions will be released. I have also kept in mind and so find—that some portions of the released testimony are so interwoven with other portions thereof that they should not be segregated from each other. Moreover, it does not appear that any portion of the released testimony should be withheld on the ground that such release would be for discovery purposes only or would be prejudicial to grand jury security."

Despite the defendants' rather desperate attempts to secure review of the orders of Judges Clary and Boldt, only the Fifth Circuit did in fact review an order, that which related to McMullen. In *Allis-Chalmers Mfg. Co.* v. *City of Fort Pierce, Florida,*[193] Judge Hays stated for a divided court that disclosure of grand jury minutes could be ordered when there is a showing of a set of compelling circumstances sufficient to overcome the policies against disclosure and that disclosure should not be barred simply because it would be in aid of recovery by a civil plaintiff rather than to defend against recovery or a criminal conviction. The court also relied upon the statement by Mr. Justice Harlan in denying an application for a stay with respect to the Peters minutes that "there is no reasonable expectation that certiorari will be granted by this Court with respect to the underlying question."

In ordering certain portions of the grand jury testimony of McMullen delivered to lead counsel for plaintiffs Judge Boldt had said:

> "The transcript will be so provided solely for the personal perusal of counsel attending the taking of the deposition and will be used only for such futher interrogation of deponent as may be author-

[193] 323 F.2d 233 (5th Cir. 1963).

ized. No part of the transcript shall be copied or reproduced in any form and the whole thereof shall be returned to the undersigned Judge when its use for the purpose stated has been completed."

This had been preceded by an *in camera* examination of the grand jury testimony by Judge Boldt after which he found that "in several particulars obviously of utmost importance in this litigation, particular and compelling need has been shown." The court of appeals found that this was a determination which was within the discretion of Judge Boldt to make. Circuit Judge Cameron dissented, primarily on the ground that the depositions in the electrical equipment proceedings were for discovery purposes; that they might never be used as evidence; and that, accordingly, McMullen's deposition was not properly to be regarded as a trial deposition.

The procedures followed after the release of grand jury minutes to plaintiffs' counsel for examination are typified by the provisions with respect to Richard V. Schmalz, contained in Schedule C of National Pretrial Order No. 16. Under that provision, plaintiffs' counsel, following the private examination of the minutes of Schmalz' grand jury testimony, were permitted to make application for the recall of Schmalz for further interrogation based upon the additional information derived from the grand jury transcript. Plaintiffs' counsel had to show good cause for the additional interrogation and had to specify the subject matter and the necessity for additional inquiry.

Grand jury minutes were released in a number of instances in which memoranda of interviews could not or were not made available to the plaintiffs. In the case of witness J. R. Mann, a subpoena had been served on Allis-Chalmers counsel for the production of a statement made by Mann to his attorneys following his grand jury appearance. The defendants' motion to quash the subpoena was granted, but at the same time plaintiffs' application for the release of Mann's grand jury testimony was also granted. In the case of Rissinger, a motion for the production of a memorandum of interview was dismissed as moot after the grand jury minutes had been produced. In argument on Kastner, the argument was made that a turnover of the interview memorandum would take the place of an attempt to secure the grand jury minutes.

Nairn was one of the witnesses recalled for deposition after his grand jury testimony had been made available to plaintiffs' counsel.[194] Upon re-examination of the witness his grand jury testimony was initially used in an attempt to refresh his recollection. Counsel taking the deposition would request the court to show the witness designated portions of his grand jury testimony and, following the witness' reading of it, counsel would then ask whether his recollection had been refreshed. In some instances it proved to have been refreshed and in others not. In the latter case, the court was asked to read the designated portion of the grand jury transcript into the deposition as past recollection recorded and the court (Judge Boldt) did so. The witness was then asked whether he recalled the answers as read, whether they were true at the time they were given before the grand jury, and whether the witness had any reason to doubt the accuracy of the answers. The witness' reply to this last question was consistently negative. On eight occasions during the re-examination Nairn stated that the grand jury minutes did refresh his recollection. However, when he failed to recall certain relevant details, and on twenty-nine additional occasions when the minutes did not refresh his recollection, the relevant portions of the grand jury minutes were read into the record.

Certain matters in the grand jury testimony were valuable in going beyond or contradicting information given on deposition. For example, Saupe in his deposition testimony had denied all participation in any meetings with competitors; but the transcript of McMullen's testimony before the grand jury contained this question and answer with reference to a May 1958 meeting among representatives of Allis-Chalmers, Westinghouse and General Electric:

" Q. Do you recall whether or not Mr. Saupe said anything during this discussion?

A. Mr. Saupe was criticizing Mr. Rowland for their activities on both the Commonwealth Edison and Union Electric jobs. He again was criticizing about the fact that they had eliminated

[194] The author.

progress payments based on reports that the General Electric Company had on this loss of their business. Mr. Rowland did not deny or affirm that these statements were correct. Mr. Saupe continued to accuse Mr. Rowland of disregarding his previous commitments made by his company to insist on progress payments."

Furthermore, when McMullen was unable to recall whether there had been a discussion among competitors of a condenser purchase by Commonwealth Edison and the method by which it was determined who among the manufacturers would have the preferred position, Judge Boldt read into the record this excerpt from the transcript of McMullen's grand jury testimony:

" Q. Mr. McMullen, when we recessed we were discussing, I believe, the meeting at the Biltmore Hotel about the middle of 1956, the purpose of which, as you mentioned, was to discuss pricing practices in the condenser field. Now, just at the close you mentioned something about drawing lots, and I wonder if I could direct your attention to that particular portion of that testimony and ask you whether or not there was any discussion on this matter of drawing lots.

A. There was no discussion in my presence, but there was discussion in the room. As I say, Mr. Feldman and Mr. Rowland and myself were at one side of the room, but the so-called working boys in the area of Haas and Goodrich and some of these other boys that were sitting in the other part of the room, they were doing a lot of conversing, and I understood from Mr. Haas that there was some question as to who was the closest on the Commonwealth job, and I think that the consensus of opinion was that everybody felt as though they had a good chance of getting it or were in a position to get it, and I don't think that any lots were drawn at that particular meeting, but I do think that probably at the subsequent meeting there were some lots drawn on the thing, and I understood from this meeting, which was the first one I was at in a discussion of this kind, that when it was debatable who was closest to the customer, that they would put slips in a hat and would draw to see who would be the low bidder. What they would do, based on my understanding, is that if there were five people there, they would draw out five slips. The number one slip got the job, number two slip would be one per cent above number one, and number three would be two per cent above number one, and so on."

Entirely apart from the value of specific information revealed by the grand jury transcript, the principal benefit to the plaintiffs in having the procedures available for securing the grand jury minutes was that it served to sharpen considerably the memory and recollection of the deposition witnesses who had appeared before the grand jury. If the witnesses' testimony could not have been checked against the grand jury testimony, their answers on the depositions might well have been vague and ambiguous. As Judge Clary said with reference to Allen's deposition testimony:

> " It is quite apparent, after the Court had held the written record of his testimony not privileged, that his memory became sharper and keener than it had been up to that time."

CHAPTER 11

Defendants' depositions and the further course of discovery

UPON COMPLETION OF THE plaintiffs' depositions of defendants' witnesses in the first three priority product lines (steam turbine generators, hydro-generators and power transformers), the Coordinating Committee insisted that the defendants embark upon their own deposition program in those product lines.

The plaintiffs opposed a national program for defendants' depositions. They argued that in the case of their depositions of defendants' witnesses, the issues of liability and conspiratorial activity which they were exploring were common to all the plaintiffs. On the other hand, plaintiffs argued, the issues which the defendants would intend to explore were not common to all the plaintiffs but would represent matters related to particular defenses against the individual plaintiffs. The plaintiffs cited as an example the defendants' assertions, in order to counter the fraudulent concealment allegations, that the plaintiffs knew or ought to have known of the existence of the conspiracy. The plaintiffs argued that this would be a matter of exploration with each plaintiff individually and it would not be an issue that related to the plaintiffs as a group or in association with each other.[195]

---

[195] In a later writing, one of the counsel for defendants agreed that in cases such as the electrical equipment cases, only a few subjects were common to all the plaintiffs, or a substantial number of them, and that by and large defendants' discovery is local as distinguished from national. O'Donnell, *Pretrial Discovery in Multiple Litigation from the Defendants' Standpoint,* 32 ANTITRUST LAW JOURNAL 142 (1966).

The formal distinction between national and local discovery was argued by the parties before the Coordinating Committee and the Committee's distinction was set forth in National Pretrial Order No. 15:

> " 'National discovery' (as herein used) includes all pre-trial discovery and preservation of information and evidence which may be necessary or useful in a substantial number of the cases pending in the several districts, and the pre-trial discovery of evidence or information as to which economy of effort in providing or using such information and evidence will be promoted by uniformity of form in interrogatories, requests for admissions, requests for production, stipulations and the like, or by the use of a National Document Depository provided for by pre-trial orders heretofore or hereinafter entered in these cases.
>
> 'Local discovery' (as herein used) includes all other appropriate pre-trial discovery and preservation of information and evidence permitted under the Federal Rules of Civil Procedure."

Plaintiffs argued against the inclusion in the definition of national discovery of the consideration of "uniformity of form," urging that it was the usefulness of information in a substantial number of cases in the several districts which should be the test. But the Committee decided otherwise, and national discovery was taken to be that discovery which related to the issues of "(i) the existence of the alleged conspiracy or conspiracies and (ii) the existence of alleged injury in business or property as a result thereof," and local discovery was considered to be discovery "solely on the amount of damages alleged to have been sustained by any particular plaintiff or plaintiffs." [196]

Pursuant to these definitions, and following what it announced as the principle of "sauce for the goose, sauce for the gander," the Coordinating Committee, meeting in New York, not only permitted but ordered an extensive national oral deposition program to be conducted by the defendants. On the same "sauce for the goose" principle, plaintiffs' personnel who were to be examined on deposition by defendants were required, as had been the witnesses examined by the plaintiffs, to produce expense accounts, travel data, diaries and the like, although at no time was there any indication that plaintiffs had traveled to

[196] National Pretrial Order No. 15, par. (8).

gather at meetings and had attempted to disguise their activities with false accounts and memoranda, as the plaintiffs alleged was the case with defendants' officers and employees. An example of the extensive requests for documents made by defendants and complied with is contained in Paragraph 7(c) of National Pretrial Order No. 31, where for each witness to be deposed by the defendants the plaintiffs were required to produce:

> " All correspondence, circular and market letters, bulletins, memoranda, analyses, speeches, studies and reports contained in any personal file of any present or former officer, employee or agent of plaintiff listed in Schedule A to National Pre-Trial Order No. 30 or in any file maintained by plaintiff for such person, which relate in whole or in part to prices, price rules, terms or conditions of sale (including, but not limited to, progress payments, price adjustment policies and escalation), purchasers' purchasing practices, standards, standardization and quality of one or more of the products upon which the plaintiff seeks to recover damages."

Under National Pretrial Order No. 15, to carry out the defendants' deposition program, defendants were given the opportunity to file written interrogatories addressed to the plaintiffs designed to disclose the names of all prospective deponents on oral examination. Thereafter the defendants were to file their list of those whose depositions they wished to take and were to begin such depositions no later than November 4, 1963. Defendants' initial submittal called for the deposition of thirty-one witnesses, to be deposed during the period from November 6 to December 23, 1963. Included in the list were six representatives from Stone & Webster Engineering Corporation, including R. D. Stone who had been in charge of the ATIG studies. Also included were representatives of *Electrical World,* purchasing agents of utilities such as J. Daniel Hogg of Cleveland and Oliver D. Butler of Commonwealth Edison Company. Also included was an unnamed "representative of the Department of Justice," from whom the defendants indicated they wished to secure information as to whether any plaintiffs had ever complained to the Department concerning defendants' activities with respect to prices of electrical equipment.[197]

---

[197] O'Donnell, *supra* note 195, at 142 n. 28. The Department of Justice resisted the production of a witness for deposition for this purpose

Under a revised list of deponents and approved by National Pretrial Order No. 30, defendants' list was expanded to eighty-eight witnesses and the period extended to January 31, 1964. The terms and conditions established for defendants' depositions were practically identical with those in effect for plaintiffs' depositions.[198] An addition was made to the previous requirement that a copy of each deposition be filed in each district in which cases were pending: there was express provision that such filing should be "without prejudice to the right of a party to object to admissibility of such deposition." As in the case of plaintiffs' depositions, provision was made for ten days' notice of the taking of each deposition; although in fact, the defendants took several depositions, such as those of representatives of *Electrical World* and *Purchasing Magazine,* without giving the required notice. The defendants' first deposition of plaintiffs' witnesses began with Cole on November 6 to 8, 1963, in New York City, Judge Feinberg of the Southern District of New York presiding.

During the course of the defendants' depositions, discovery in other forms in the first priority product lines was going forward, both for plaintiffs and defendants. By National Pretrial Order No. 17 a broad motion of plaintiffs for production of defendants' documents pursuant to Rule 34 of the Federal Rules of Civil Procedure was granted. The documents to be produced were to be protected by a confidentiality provision of the same kind that was placed into effect for documents produced in connection with the deposition program. As in the case of such documents, the Rule 34 documents were to be deposited in defendants' document depository in Chicago, and defendants were required within sixty days to file an affidavit of full com-

---

and resisted also the production of documents for a similar purpose. The United States District Court for the District of Columbia ruled with the Department of Justice in this respect, quashing defendants' *subpoena duces tecum.* Judge Sirica's grounds were that the information was protected by the informer privilege and that the request was unduly burdensome. This action was reversed by the Court of Appeals for the District of Columbia, Westinghouse Electric Corporation v. The City of Burlington, Vermont, 351 F.2d 762 (1965), but the decision came too late in the cases to have any practical consequences.

198 Schedule B, National Pretrial Order No. 30.

pliance with the Order or setting forth the reasons why compliance was not possible. Documents with respect to which privilege or "work product" doctrine were claimed were to be treated in the same manner as documents for deposition purposes. The list of documents so ordered to be produced was contained in Exhibit A of National Pretrial Order No. 17.[199]

Plaintiffs and defendants were able to agree to a substantial degree on the documents to be produced by the defendants pursuant to the plaintiffs' Rule 34 motion. Counsel for plaintiffs in New York, Chicago and Philadelphia conferred with defense counsel in June 1963 in New York City and substantial progress was made. The documents called for comprised defendants' price lists and catalogs, information as to how price changes took place, information as to how each manufacturer learned of price changes of his competitors, any document relating to the manner in which the market was shared by the various manufacturers, the manner of operation of the manufacturers' price adjustment clauses, profit and loss and cost data, and copies of all work papers behind the Grant study. There was some debate among plaintiffs' counsel whether data concerning manufacturers' cost, profits and profit goals ought to be requested, certain counsel believing that a request for such data might admit the relevance of such information in the computation of plaintiffs' damages.

Plaintiffs in Chicago also took advantage of the availability of the technique of requesting admissions by requesting defendants to admit the ATIG data on steam turbine generators and power transformers. A like request was filed by plaintiffs in the Southern District of New York. In order to further this request, representatives of Stone & Webster Service Corporation outlined to representatives of General Electric, Westinghouse and Allis-Chalmers, at a meeting held in New York City in December 1963, the nature of the ATIG assignment to Stone & Webster and the procedures used for comparing prices of turbine generators.

With reference to defendants' interrogatories, except for transaction interrogatories (1 a to h of Set No. 1), the Coor-

---

199 See Appendix 15.

dinating Committee had not acted upon the remaining interrogatories in defendants' Set No. 1 nor on any of those contained in defendants' Set No. 2. Following argument before the Coordinating Committee in New York, National Pretrial Order No. 19 approved broad interrogatories, twelve in number. A final form of such interrogatories[200] was approved in National Pretrial Order No. 37. As part of the ground rules for defendants' interrogatories, it was provided that plaintiffs were under no obligation to interview past employees to obtain information not otherwise available. It was also provided, as in the case of plaintiffs' interrogatories, that if a plaintiff in lieu of identifying documents preferred to produce the documents for inspection and copying by the defendants, he could do so. The time period covered by the interrogatories was to begin with the earliest date of a purchase on which a plaintiff sought to recover damages, running then to April 1, 1961.

A number of interrogatories went to the question of whether plaintiffs had any knowledge or information (whether actual knowledge, rumor, hearsay, assumption or surmise) that representatives of the manufacturers were meeting with respect to prices and the allocation of markets. Further questions inquired whether the plaintiffs had taken any action when they received identical bids, whether the plaintiffs as purchasers had exchanged information with respect to the manufacturers' products (price, performance or terms of sale) and finally, whether the plaintiffs had communicated with any state or federal agency charged with enforcing antitrust laws or with any legislative committee or subcommittee concerned with such laws with respect to prices of the products involved.

In accordance with plaintiffs' practice, the defendants also moved for the production of any documents which would be identified by the plaintiffs in the course of responding to the interrogatories ordered by National Pretrial Order No. 19. By National Pretrial Order No. 20 the plaintiffs were required to produce such documents at a depository to be established by the plaintiffs in the Southern District of New York, the counterpart of defendants' depository in Chicago.

---

200 See Appendix 16(a).

Prior to the establishment of a depository for court-ordered documents, the plaintiffs for their own purposes had established in New York City a "Library of Electrical Antitrust Documents" (LEAD) with a lawyer serving as attendant librarian.

LEAD maintained complete records of pretrial orders and all documents filed pursuant thereto, transcripts of the meetings of the Coordinating Committee, transcripts of all depositions, copies of all answers to interrogatories, and the like. When the depository was established it was staffed by the personnel of LEAD, and except for the maintenance of separation of documents for depository purposes, the operation of the two agencies was fully integrated.

With respect to document production, plaintiffs claimed two items were unduly burdensome, one category being documents relating to utilities' projected or estimated requirements for the first priority line products. It was provided that such documents need not be produced if their production would be burdensome unless later required upon demand of the defendants and order of the court. No plaintiff was to be required to produce documents duplicative of those produced by any other plaintiff. The pretrial order contained the customary provisions respecting an affidavit of compliance and protection for documents as to which confidentiality was claimed. The provisions with respect to privilege and work product doctrine documents were similar to those put into effect for the protection of defendants' deposition documents.

An example of the manner in which the interrogatories and document production ordered were keyed is illustrated by paragraph 1 of each request. In the interrogatory order paragraph 1 required each plaintiff to state whether it had acquired or had any information that any officer, agent or employee of a manufacturer had communicated in any way at any time with any officer, agent or employee of another manufacturer with respect to prices, pricing rules, or terms or conditions of sale. Paragraph 1 of the production order then required plaintiffs to produce each document that contained any reference to or reflected the acquisition or possession by the plaintiff of any information that any officer, agent or employee of any manufacturer communicated in any way at any time with any officer, agent or employee of any other manufacturer with respect to prices, pricing rules, or terms or conditions of sale.

The defendants submitted an additional thirty interrogatories for response by plaintiffs in the three priority product lines. By National Pretrial Order No. 22, an additional sixteen[201] were permitted. Included in this second set of interrogatories were questions whether plaintiffs selected their suppliers on the basis of any criteria other than prices or terms and conditions of sale and whether they maintained any preferred bidders lists; whether the plaintiffs systematically rotated, divided, spread or allocated their purchases of electrical equipment among any suppliers or contractors; and a question, the relevance of which to an antitrust action was difficult to see, whether plaintiffs had any policy "concerning the solicitation or acceptance by your employees of gratuities, entertainment or the like from representatives of suppliers."

As in the case of the first set of interrogatories approved by National Pretrial Order No. 19, defendants submitted an order for the production of documents identified in the answers to the Set No. 2 interrogatories; such request was approved in National Pretrial Order No. 23. Although this production did not relate to witnesses to be deposed, the defendants submitted a request that among the documents to be produced would be expense accounts, travel vouchers and supporting documents for any officer, employee, agent or consultant of plaintiff identified in the answers to the interrogatories, as well as any diary, appointment note, appointment book, calendar pad, letter book and telephone call memorandum of each officer of plaintiff so identified. Plaintiffs were also required to produce each document "in the possession of or obtainable by any plaintiff which was produced by such plaintiff before any Grand Jury in the Eastern District of Pennsylvania in the course of investigations leading to the return of indictments involving these products in that Court in 1960," although it was the defendants' activities and not the plaintiffs' that were being investigated by that grand jury.

During the course of the discussions on defendants' interrogatories, plaintiffs complained that, though they had hurried

201 See Appendix 17(a).

to answer defendants' transaction interrogatories (1, a to h) upon the defendants' insistence they needed such information at the outset of the proceedings, nothing further had been heard from the defendants as to whether they accepted or disagreed with the plaintiffs' answers to the transaction interrogatories. Accordingly, by National Pretrial Order No. 24 the defendants were taken to have admitted the correctness of plaintiffs' answers to the transaction interrogatories unless any defendant should take exception to a specific answer with a written objection filed with the court.

The original set of defendants' interrogatories which contained the transaction interrogatories had contained certain further questions (1 i to o and Question 2). These additional questions were designed to elicit further information with respect to the plaintiffs' purchases, such as the place of installation of the equipment; Question 2 asked the interesting question whether plaintiffs had made any purchases from defendants on which they were not suing and claiming damages. By National Pretrial Order No. 28 the plaintiffs were permitted to defer answering these interrogatories until the cases had been set for trial.

The plaintiffs also served a second set of interrogatories on the defendants which were approved by National Pretrial Order No. 29.[202] These interrogatories sought information from the manufacturers as to the quantity of orders placed with them by domestic and foreign purchasers; information as to any factors which had brought about a change in manufacturing capacity, methods and techniques whereby the manufacturers measure their productivity; descriptions of each significant technique, technology or quality change applied by the manufacturer to each of its products; whether the manufacturer had knowledge as to whether any officer, agent or employee of a purchaser had any information concerning meetings among officers, agents or employees of the manufacturers; whether the manufacturer had communicated with any purchaser with respect to the identical bids which that purchaser had received; whether the manufac-

[202] For the latest version of such interrogatories, appearing as Schedule G to National Pretrial Order No. 37, see Appendix 18(a).

turer had instructed its personnel to withdraw from membership in the National Electrical Manufacturers Association (NEMA) and if so, the reasons; and information as to each officer, agent or employee who had been served with a grand jury subpoena.

In the first stages of the national discovery program the defendants attempted to argue that all discovery ought to be completed in one product line, for example turbine generators, before any discovery beyond depositions was begun in a second product line (for example, power transformers), even though both product lines were assigned first priority. The judges resisted these suggestions on the basis that, as explained by Judge Robson, the judges wanted discovery in power transformers to go forward so that if the turbine generator cases were settled, power transformers would be in the wings and an early trial date could then be set for them.

Throughout the discovery program, at any given stage, the judges were pressing the parties to go forward with remaining discovery in the priority product lines and in turn, while discovery in one set of priority product lines was going forward, the parties were being pressed to make known their wishes as to the products to be included in the next set of priorities and to suggest a schedule for discovery for those products. For example, in February 1963, just after the parties and the Coordinating Committee had worked out a schedule for the second round of plaintiffs' national depositions, the Coordinating Committee, in National Pretrial Order No. 13, required each side to set forth in writing within approximately six weeks their proposals for any additional national discovery in the first priority product lines, including specifically additional discovery of documents, requests for admission, written interrogatories, and any other discovery desired under a national program. If any party was proposing discovery outside the United States, there was to be furnished the subject matter of the discovery desired, the names, addresses and connections of the witnesses, and the manner in which the discovery was to be taken. Thereafter, in National Pretrial Order No. 15 entered in the latter part of May 1963, specific due dates were established for plaintiffs and defendants on the additional discovery that each side had proposed. By the same order plaintiffs and defendants were to file proposed schedules for national discovery in four products which were to constitute the second priority product lines: large circuit breakers, distribution transformers, power switching equipment and power switchgear assemblies. Throughout this period the plaintiffs were going forward with their third round of national depositions and defendants with their first round of depositions.

At this point the defendants yelled "Uncle." On November 1, 1963 the defendants filed a petition "for relief from the current pre-trial schedule imposed under the national discovery program and orders relating to local discovery." The defendants listed fourteen "matters" with which they were confronted:

" 1. Analyzing and preparing objections to plaintiffs' requests for admissions.
2. Analyzing plaintiffs' answers to interrogatories now on file and those due to be filed on November 1, 1963.
3. Reviewing plaintiffs' documents now deposited and due to be deposited on November 1, 1963.
4. Completing verification of the plaintiffs' answers to the Priority Product Line transaction interrogatories.
5. Taking defendants' first round of depositions which commence November 4, 1963.
6. Completing by November 4, 1963, the deposit of defendants' documents called for by National Pre-Trial Order No. 17.
7. Preparing a schedule of supplemental witnesses for national depositions, due November 18, 1963.
8. Answering plaintiffs' national interrogatories, Set No. 2, to be argued on November 20, 1963.
9. Preparing defendants' requests for admission, due December 2, 1963.
10. Preparing defendants' requests for further answers to discovery, due December 2, 1963.
11. Preparing legal briefs relating to 'passing on' and other matters.
12. Preparing briefs setting forth the legal and factual issues involved in the turbine and power transformer cases, due under certain local pre-trial orders.
13. Preparing for and commencing local discovery as required in certain jurisdictions by local pre-trial orders.
14. Possible commencement of discovery in Secondary Product Lines."

Specifically, they pointed with respect to their obligations under the national deposition program that, commencing in the latter part of November 1963, they would have to depose no fewer than eight witnesses a week employing two teams of interrogatory counsel, and they argued that such a schedule does not permit complete and orderly preparation. The defendants stated that, unlike the plaintiffs, the defendants did not have a "road map" for their discovery and that theirs would be a "discovery" program in the literal sense of the word. The defendants therefore urged the postponement of discovery in the second priority lines so long as discovery or trials proceeded in the first priority lines.

In an appendix to the petition the defendants set forth the schedule of pretrial dates that had been established for the latter part of 1963 and early 1964 and showed, for example, the following with respect to November 1, 1963:

" 1963 November 1

NATIONAL PROGRAM—Pursuant to National Pretrial Order No. 24 plaintiffs and defendants are to file in all districts their respective proposals for national discovery in the product lines known as Large Circuit Breakers, Distribution Transformers, Power Switching Equipment and Power Switchgear Assemblies.

NEW YORK—1. Plaintiffs' objections to defendants' 'pass-on' interrogatories are due.

2. Plaintiffs' compliance with defendants' Rule 34 motion (National Pre-trial Order No. 23) is due this date.

3. Plaintiffs are to file and serve answers to defendants' interrogatories 12 through 27, Set No. 2, in the priority product lines.

4. Defendants' objections to plaintiffs' requests for admission of facts in the steam turbine generator cases due.

CHICAGO—1. Defendants are to file petition for relief from the Pre-trial Schedule in the National Discovery Program.

2. Informal pre-trial conference before Judge Robson set for this date at 11:00 a.m. to discuss:

a. Minimal and no sale defendant program;

b. Closing of the City of Chicago Class Action;

c. Handling of the recently filed municipal law suits.

3. Plaintiffs' objections to defendants' transaction interrogatories, para. 1 (i)-(o) and 2, are due this date pursuant to para. 6 of National Pre-Trial Order No. 24.

SAN FRANCISCO—The last day in which General Electric may plead to the amended complaints filed by the City of Alameda, California, City of Palo Alto, California, Modesta Irrigation District and Turlock Irrigation District.

SEATTLE—1. Pre-trial conference set to hear the State of Washington's motion to strike the Statute of Limitations and other procedural defenses from defendants' answers to the complaints.

2. The following matters are proposed for the pre-trial conference scheduled for this date:

a. Propriety of consolidating for trial claims in various product lines.

b. Motion to show cause why answers of plaintiffs to interrogatories Nos. 1 through 11 under Pre-Trial Order No. 19 should not be stricken as non-responsive.

c. Schedule for responses to defendants' interrogatories Nos. 12 through 27 of Set No. 2.

d. Motion of Chelan PUD for an extension of time within which to object or respond to 'pass-on' interrogatories.

e. Response by Chelan to defendants' interrogatories, Sets Nos. 1 and 2.

f. Schedule for local discovery in the Chelan case.

g. Status of claimants who have not as yet identified purchase transactions.

h. Allis-Chalmers' request for an extension of time in which to verify transaction interrogatory answers previously filed by plaintiffs in this district in priority product lines.

PHILADELPHIA—Last day in which the defendants may file papers in opposition to plaintiffs' motion for summary judgment in the power transformer case.

KANSAS CITY, MO.—Defendants are required to verify plaintiffs' answers to the transaction interrogatories in the priority product lines."

Of course, the schedule shows, although defendants did not remark on this, that the burdens imposed upon the defendants were matched by those imposed upon the plaintiffs.

The defendants' petition for relief was denied, and the schedules remained unchanged. In early January 1964, defendants filed a second petition for relief, maintaining that the eight weeks that had elapsed between the rejection of their first petition and the filing of the second petition had demonstrated that it was not humanly possible for the defendants to keep up with the present schedule or to conclude their discovery or prepare for trial in the time allotted. In connection with their deposition program they pointed out that they had activated six deposition teams since the depositions were to be taken in six cities, and that they had found it necessary to take as many as seventeen depositions a week, although the judges had thought that eight depositions a week would be sufficient. They predicted that under these circumstances they might have to recall witnesses by reason of the premature termination of the initial examinations. The defendants concluded with a statement which implied that the national discovery program as it was being applied to them was unconstitutional as violative of the procedural requirements of due process of law.

The two petitions for relief had been signed on behalf of the six defendants in the first priority product lines: General Electric Company, Westinghouse Electric Corporation, Allis-Chalmers Manufacturing Company, McGraw-Edison Company, Moloney Electric Company and Wagner Electric Corporation.

The only response of the judges to the second petition for relief was to postpone the beginning of the depositions in defendants' second and final round (first priority products) until February 10, 1964 and to shorten the period in which a party could petition for leave to re-examine any deponent. All other requested relief was denied.

The defendants sought also to avoid the force of the national discovery program by urging upon the judges a procedure whereby all due dates for defendants' action would be keyed to the time that the plaintiffs had answered an initial set of defendants' interrogatories; and then, upon the filing of such answers by a substantial majority of plaintiffs, defendants suggested they would file motions for the production of documents. Thereafter, when a large majority of plaintiffs had complied with the document production orders, the defendants would then file a deposition list. Defendants suggested that compliance by approximately three-fourths of the plaintiffs should be required before they should be expected to proceed with the next step in the discovery program. This suggested procedure of defendants was not adopted, the Coordinating Committee instead fixing specific dates for compliance by both plaintiffs and defendants with the various required steps in national discovery.

After defendants' second round of depositions was under way, fourteen witnesses were added, including a number of representatives of the Rural Electrification Administration and two secretaries to J. D. Hogg of Cleveland Electric Illuminating Company. A final addition added seven more witnesses, including two representatives of the Philadelphia Electric Company. Counsel were requested to make maximum use of the relevant portions of the previously taken local depositions of the latter two witnesses.

True to their prediction, defendants did attempt to recall certain deposition witnesses for a second examination. Judge Caffrey, District of Massachusetts, on January 2, 1964 denied the defendants' petition to recall T. F. Fearnside and C. A. Maloney of Stone & Webster Engineering Corporation on the ground that the absence of documents complained of "was the direct product of defendants' serving the voluminous subpoena, which was quashed as unreasonable, and of defendants' persisting in refusing to modify the subpoena, until after it was quashed." On March 6, 1964 Judge Becker, acting as Special Master in the Northern District of Illinois, refused to recall C. F. Ogden of Detroit Edison Company on similar grounds. During the course of the deposition of Philip Sporn, counsel for defendants protested against the indication by the presiding judge that the deposition had to be finished during the course of one day even if it meant sitting until midnight; counsel contending that the plaintiffs had not been subjected to any such deadlines during the course of their depositions. Defense counsel was given another day to complete the deposing of Mr. Sporn.

It was during the course of the deposition of Philip Sporn that Judge Feinberg made a succinct explanation of the purpose and effect, to his mind, of objections frequently made as to "form" during the course of both the plaintiffs' and defendants' deposition program:

" It has been some time since I have presided at a deposition where the lawyers have turned out in force and there has been an at-

> mosphere of hammer and tong, but I just want to make clear again what my attitude is on these depositions so that we can save time today.
>
> My attitude is that objections to form can be noted. There is no need for any extensive discussion on it. Examining counsel knows well that he is taking a chance, that the answer may not be admissible. If he wants to, he can rephrase the question after you point out to him what the problem is."

Upon completion of the second and final round of depositions in the first priority product lines, the defendants had deposed 150 witnesses over a period of four months, with 15,000 pages of transcript.

At the conclusion of their three rounds by plaintiffs, seventy-five witnesses had been examined, with 25,000 pages of transcript, the depositions having been taken in six cities with a total of twelve judges used as presiding judges. Third round depositions had been taken outside the presence of a judge, although one was readily available in the courthouse in the event he was needed. Experience had shown by this time that depositions could be taken in an effective and orderly manner without a judge being present during every minute of the deposition.

The provisions for discovery in the second priority product lines were contained in a wrap-up order, National Pretrial Order No. 37, which dealt with all aspects of discovery in a single order. The second priority product lines were defined to include large circuit breakers, power switching equipment and power switchgear assemblies (an originally proposed fourth product, distribution transformers, was excluded over plaintiffs' objections). The order established schedules, running from April to August, 1964 for plaintiffs' depositions and approved interrogatories along the lines of those approved for the first priority product lines. For oral depositions by plaintiffs, seven witnesses were scheduled in power switching equipment, nine in power switchgear assemblies and twelve in large circuit breakers. Discovery in the second priority product lines brought into the act a number of defendants beyond the six involved in the first priority product lines, including for the first time, I-T-E Circuit Breaker.

A number of the witnesses proposed to be deposed in the second priority lines had had their depositions taken in Philadelphia prior to the institution of the national deposition program: the order provided that those depositions were to be deemed to have been taken pursuant to the national pretrial order and that printed transcripts of those depositions were to be filed pursuant to the requirements of the national pretrial order. With respect to certain other witnesses whose depositions had been taken before the institution of the national discovery program, counsel were simply urged to make maximum use of the depositions in deposing under the national program.

Certain defendants pointed out in connection with the depositions in the second priority product lines that some witnesses might be unwilling to come into a jurisdiction for fear that service of process in other cases might be made upon them during their visit. Accordingly, the pretrial order provided:

> "No legal process issued out of the Court in which this order is entered may be served upon any witness or lawyer during his attendance at any deposition provided for by this Schedule E or during the three days preceding and three days following such deposition, except in the case of such witness or lawyer who would be present in this county or district regardless of the scheduling of the deposition."

National Pretrial Order No. 37 also outlined an oral deposition program for the defendants, with the depositions of twenty-five witnesses to be taken in the five-week period from June 9 to July 14, 1964. The interesting feature of the provisions ordering document production by the parties was the exception that documents need not be produced if they had been previously furnished in the national discovery program or to the Kefauver Committee. Even so, the statistics with respect to document production in connection with the national discovery program were almost staggering. Nearly 1,000,000 documents were produced by the defendants and placed in the depository in Chicago. The plaintiffs produced approximately 200,000 documents in the New York depository.

Discovery in the second priority product lines was followed by the designation of a set of third priority products and a delineation of the discovery requirements for them. Six products were designated for inclusion in the third priority lines—distribution transformers, network transformers, condensers, low voltage distribution equipment, insulators and meters. Completion of discovery in the third priority lines was to be accomplished by March 1965. The plaintiffs scheduled for deposition ten witnesses in distribution transformers, six in network transformers, twenty-two in condensers, fourteen in low voltage distribution equipment, eighteen in insulators and eight in meters, the depositions to be taken from November 9, 1964 to February 26, 1965. Defendants' lists of witnesses for depositions in the third priority product lines were unusually foreshortened with only seven witnesses scheduled, principally in distribution transformers and condensers. Only two teams were to be utilized. With the advent of the third priority product lines, the cases moved for the first time into products which were classifiable as "shelf items," with condensers, insulators and meters falling into this category; and this inclusion of "shelf items" served also to bring actively into the national discovery program for the first time a number of smaller or specialist defendant manufacturers.

While scheduling was going on for the third priority product lines, the Coordinating Committee, true to the pattern that had been previously established, called in National Pretrial Order No. 38 for suggestions for national discovery in all the remaining product lines. Defendants responded that nothing beyond the first and second priority lines ought to go forward until the situation could be reviewed in early 1965. They pointed out at the time of filing their response that they had still more than 200 depositions to take in the first and second priority lines. The Coordinating Committee, rejecting these suggestions, in National Pretrial Order No. 40 established a schedule beginning January 1965 for plaintiffs and defendants to submit their specific requirements for discovery in the remaining product lines. This order was the last of the operational pretrial orders and was succeeded only by National Pretrial Order No. 41, which prescribed a questionnaire in which the Coordinating Committee requested information as to which cases were settled and dismissed and which were still pending.

CHAPTER 12

Settlement—preliminary negotiations

As early as December 1962, at a hearing in Philadelphia before Judges Clary and Kirkpatrick, Judge Clary requested the parties to the Philadelphia actions to open settlement negotiations. He reviewed the situation in the context of the national program and referred to the tremendous expense of the litigation for all parties. Judge Kirkpatrick concurred in Judge Clary's statements and asked the defendants to agree on a small committee to confer with the plaintiffs and report back to all defendants. Both judges requested the parties to remain and discuss their suggestions, but counsel for Westinghouse demurred, stating the need to go through channels. Nothing further developed in the Eastern District of Pennsylvania from these requests.

In the early part of 1963 certain plaintiffs had begun to think about the basis on which a settlement offer might be made to the defendants. The Atlantic City group took the lead at this time and, working with the economists who had assisted in the preparation of the ATIG material, devised formulas to determine so-called "overcharge ratios."

These studies were embodied in a Blue Book entitled, *Procedures for Calculating Overcharges in Eleven Product Lines,* dated June 25, 1963. The Blue Book was furnished to defendants' counsel in June 1963 in justification of a settlement offer made by the Atlantic City group at that time.

Under the Blue Book, overcharge ratios were computed by taking the average order price (from an order price index) in a given period in relation to the competitive price determined for the same period. Accordingly:

$$\text{Overcharge Ratio} = \frac{\text{Average Order Price Minus Competitive Price}}{\text{Average Order Price}}$$

To illustrate, if 90 is the average order price and 75 is the competitive price, then

$$\text{Overcharge Ratio} = \frac{90-75}{90} = \frac{15}{90} = \frac{1}{6} = 16.66$$

The overcharge ratio in this illustration is 16.66%.

So far as the competitive price base line was concerned, for certain products—steam turbine generators, circuit breakers and power transformers, among others—there were selected for reference certain periods in which there seemed to have been some aspect of competitive pricing. Average order prices were computed for those periods and were then linked by a change in cost index computed for the particular product (these changes in cost indices were those derived by the economists from their ATIG studies).

The use of average order prices was regarded as conservative since there was economic support for utilizing lower, or even the lowest, prices in the so-called "competitive periods." The studies were also regarded as conservative because the reference periods chosen as being "competitive" were not necessarily periods when the conspiracy could be said to have had no effect on prices; rather they were periods when there seemed to be some approach, however limited, to competitive pricing.

For shelf items, such as distribution transformers, meters and condensers, the overcharge ratio technique was used, but the competitive price base line had to be developed by other means because of the absence of a workable number of "competitive" reference periods. In the case of distribution transformers, the December 1961 price was taken as a competitive base, and the competitive price base line was then developed by running a line back from December 1961. For meters, the base multiplier set in 1952 by the manufacturers was adjusted to allow for subsequent changes in cost, and the extent of the overcharge was then estimated on the basis of the relationship of the actual multipliers to the adjusted multipliers. The study noted that the overcharge ratio, developed as it was by using an average order price index, did not differentiate in any given period between a purchase above the average and one below the average: it reflected only the average purchase in the period.

For steam turbine generators the reference periods "deemed to be competitive" to some extent were (a) 1948, (b) April-October 1950, (c) November 1954-March 1955, and (d) October 1960-August 1961. The November 1954-March 1955 reference is the so-called white sale period, and the October 1960-August 1961 period follows the break-up of the conspiracy in turbine generators.

Overcharge ratios were then developed for each quarter of each year from 1948 to 1960 inclusive as follows:

STEAM TURBINE GENERATORS OVERCHARGE RATIOS

1948-1960

	QUARTER				ANNUAL
YEAR	1ST Q	2ND Q	3RD Q	4TH Q	AVERAGE
1948	0	0	0	0	0
1949	0	2.3	6.2	7.0	3.9
1950	2.8	0	0	0.1	0.7
1951	2.8	5.0	6.2	5.3	4.8
1952	4.7	5.5	5.6	3.6	4.8
1953	3.5	4.6	5.8	9.8	5.9
1954	12.4	11.1	6.8	1.1	7.9
1955	0	1.2	1.8	3.2	1.6
1956	9.8	10.2	13.0	16.3	12.3
1957	19.1	24.3	24.1	24.2	22.9
1958	27.4	30.0	29.9	29.2	28.1
1959	26.5	23.1	21.4	19.8	22.7
1960	18.2	16.2	—	—	—

The calculation shows, of course, no overcharge ratios for the reference periods. Further, the overcharge ratio did not take account of escalation overcharges, which involved an additional calculation to determine what the appropriate escalation should have been and then adding this percentage to the base competitive price.[203]

For circuit breakers the four reference periods chosen were the pre-conspiracy period (supposedly) of January 1948-September 1950, the white sale period from January to March 1955, a period when circuit breaker prices broke from September to December 1958, and the post-conspiracy period of September 1960 to October 1961. The overcharge ratios developed in the Blue Book for circuit breakers for each quarter of the years 1956 to 1959 were:

	QUARTER				ANNUAL
YEAR	1ST Q	2ND Q	3RD Q	4TH Q	AVERAGE
1956	18.3	22.6	30.1	28.1	24.8
1957	35.1	36.1	31.9	32.5	33.9
1958	34.4	35.4	13.8	0	20.9
1959	20.2	31.4	39.4	36.8	32.0

For large power transformers the study adopts for reference periods simply the white sale period from January 21 to February 28, 1955, and the post-conspiracy period from July 1960 to June 1961. The results were overcharge ratios for the 1956 to 1959 period as follows:

---

203 The Blue Book suggested that in the case of steam turbine generators an appropriate escalation charge could have been determined as follows:

"(a) Determine the average change-in-cost index value for steam turbine generators for the three months period centered on the order price date. (The change-in-cost index is adapted from the manufacturer's index escalation formula. It utilizes weights derived from the 1958 Census of Manufacturers and adjusts the labor factor for changes in productivity.)

(b) Determine the average change-in-cost index value for the 18 months prior to largest lump sum payment date (this is usually six months prior to final payment).

(c) Derive the percentage escalation by the following formula:

$$\text{ESC.} = \frac{(b)}{(a)} - 1$$

(d) This escalation percentage is applied to the previously determined base competitive price to obtain the dollar amount of appropriate escalation."

	QUARTER				ANNUAL
YEAR	1ST Q	2ND Q	3RD Q	4TH Q	AVERAGE
1956	34.9	36.6	37.3	41.4	37.6
1957	43.1	38.2	40.8	42.0	41.0
1958	36.3	42.4	37.9	38.5	38.6
1959	37.3	36.2	35.0	20.9	32.3

To compute overcharge ratios back to 1948, the average charges for the January to February 1955 reference period were extended back by a straight line. For power transformers, the Blue Book contained a chart showing the order price index, the competitive price line and overcharge ratios illustrated by a bar chart.[204]

For watt-hour meters, the overcharge ratios were computed by the multiplier technique previously described and produced overcharge ratios for the 1956 to 1959 period as follows:

	QUARTER				ANNUAL
YEAR	1ST Q	2ND Q	3RD Q	4TH Q	AVERAGE
1956	8.9	8.9	10.1	10.7	9.6
1957	10.7	11.7	13.2	13.2	12.2
1958	14.5	14.5	14.5	15.0	14.6
1959	16.4	16.4	16.4	16.4	16.4

The Blue Book chart showed for watt-hour meters the order price index, the competitive price line and the overcharge ratios.[205]

In transmitting the Blue Book to counsel for the defendants, the Atlantic City group stated that in making their settlement proposal they had applied the overcharge ratios only with respect to:

1. Purchases of steam turbine generators and hydroelectric generators ordered or paid for between January 1, 1956 and June 30, 1960;
2. Purchases of power transformers, large circuit breakers, power switchgear assemblies, condensers, and power switching equipment ordered or paid for between January 1, 1956 and December 31, 1959; and

[204] See Appendix 21.
[205] See Appendix 22.

3. Purchases of distribution transformers, instrument transformers, meters and insulators made between January 1, 1956 and December 31, 1959.

In this instance, and in subsequent settlement discussions, plaintiffs were to concentrate on the 1956 to 1959 period, a period during which the overcharges seemed to be greatest and likewise a period which was within the statute of limitations so that liability was not dependent upon establishing fraudulent concealment.

The Atlantic City group pointed out in their settlement offer that they had not computed overcharges based on escalation except for steam turbine and hydroelectric generators. It was also understood that the proposal was limited to claims for single damages only. Furthermore, no amount was added for reimbursement of fees and expenses of litigation incurred by plaintiffs.

To arrive at a dollar amount for settlement, each plaintiff in the Atlantic City group computed his damages in accordance with the Blue Book formulas, the amounts were then totaled and a lump sum offer made to the defendants for settlement by all Atlantic City plaintiffs with all defendants. The settlement offer was approximately $85,000,000, representing 16% to 17% of purchases by the Atlantic City group for the 1956 to 1959 period. It was estimated at the time that settlement on this basis, projected for the entire investor-owned segment of the public utility industry, would produce on the order of $500,000,000, of which about half would be paid by General Electric, 28% by Westinghouse, 9% by Allis-Chalmers, 5% by McGraw-Edison, and smaller percentages by the other defendants.

The Blue Book computations seem conservative by comparison with the ATIG studies. The latter had suggested a series of methods of referring to appropriate "competitive prices" using a variety of base periods. The Blue Book adopted one of the ATIG methods and multiple base period selections for each product; in general, the base periods and method selected by the Blue Book were on the conservative side, that is, not calculated to produce maximum damages. For example, the Blue Book used four base periods to establish the competitive price line for turbine generators. One of the ATIG methods suggested the possibility of using a single base period, 1955, which would have yielded about 25% more in damages than the Blue Book. Furthermore, ATIG studies suggested that for any given base period the competitive price might be regarded as that price at or below which there had been transactions between two sellers and three buyers. A competitive price so computed is ordinarily substantially below the average price in a selected base period. Nevertheless, the Blue Book used the average price during a base period as the competitive price for overcharge determinations.

One aspect of the Blue Book computations would not affect overall results for the industry but could have an important effect on a particular plaintiff. The Blue Book form of settlement called for the determination of an average overcharge percentage for purchases in all relevant periods and the application of that percentage to the dollar amount of each company's purchases. This meant that a plaintiff utility which bought at prices better (i.e., lower) than the average would have done just as well under the settlement formula as a utility which paid more than the average.

The Atlantic City group, in arriving at its proposed offer, had attempted to take account of the ability or capacity of defendants to pay. The plaintiffs had devised for this purpose a table showing the average rate of return on net worth for twenty-four of the defendants for three periods—1956 to 1959, 1957 to 1961 and 1959 to 1961.[206] These rates of return ranged in the indictment years 1956-1959 from 5.3% for Moloney Electric Company to 6.4% for Allis-Chalmers, 7% for Westinghouse, 19.4% for General Electric, and a high of 21.2% for Ingersoll-Rand. Percentages for the other two periods shown on the table (the five years from 1957-1961 and the three years 1959-1961) were comparable, although down practically all along the line in the three years 1959-1961 from the indictment years 1956-1959. Indeed, in the later period, when the conspiracies had ended, Moloney Electric and Cornell-Dubilier showed negative returns.

---

206 See Appendix 23.

Another table converted the average rate of return on net worth for the twenty-four defendants into an "Index of Relative Profitability" with General Electric representing 100. In this table Westinghouse showed profitability of 36% to 45.8% (in the three periods on which the tabulation was based), indicating that Westinghouse would be able to pay 36% to 45% of what General Electric would be able to pay in settlement. Allis-Chalmers rated from 23.8% to 33.2% in the index; McGraw-Edison from 55.5% to 62%. Moloney Electric showed a negative ability to pay for the most recent period and only 7.5% of General Electric's ability to pay for the five-year period 1957 to 1961. I-T-E Circuit Breaker showed a wide band, ranging from 14.9% based on the three years 1959 to 1961, to 52.6% based on the indictment years 1956 to 1959.

An alternative approach to ability to pay was to determine the amounts that defendants could pay if settlements were to specify that 50% of their net income before taxes, for one year, were to be paid as damages. This calculation was based upon the assumption that the payments would be treated as allowable deductions for income tax purposes. The data so developed[207] showed that based on 1961 performance, General Electric in accordance with this formula could pay damages of $242 million, leaving General Electric $121 million of net income after taxes and after damages. For the remaining twenty-three defendant companies, total damage payments, comparable to General Electric's $242 million, would amount to $146 million, leaving the twenty-three companies with $73 million of net income after taxes and after damages, compared with General Electric's $121 million.

A number of utilities in the Middle West and on the Pacific Coast were engaged in consideration of whether they would likewise make a proposal to defendants in conjunction with the Atlantic City group and based upon the Blue Book formulas. Commonwealth Edison of Chicago had made computations as to what it would be entitled to receive from its largest suppliers. These computations showed, that under the strict Blue Book formulas, General Electric alone would be required to make a

207 See Appendix 24.

payment as a price adjustment of $10,985,633, representing on either an ordered or delivered basis, 18.3% of related purchases.

The offer of the Atlantic City group was summarily rejected by the defendants.

Throughout the latter part of 1962 and 1963, the federal government had been achieving settlement of its damage claims against the defendants. In July 1962 the federal government settled with General Electric, represented by Clark Clifford, upon the payment by General Electric of $7,470,000, of which all but $1,000,000 was because of purchases by the Tennessee Valley Authority. Upon a purchase base of $70 million, this represented a percentage settlement of 10.7%. The Department of Justice announced that the settlement figure was "a lump sum figure" and made no reference to a computation in accordance with any formula. General Electric's announcement, on the other hand, stated that the offer of settlement "reflected the application of various formulas designed by the Company to calculate compromise price adjustments in each product line."

General Electric also announced its intention to offer settlement to other complainants on the basis of the same formulas as utilized for the Government settlement, estimating that the cost of settlements under such formulas to General Electric would be $45 to $50 million. General Electric Chairman Cordiner stated that General Electric had charged $50 million against 1962 sales as price adjustments and as a reserve for settlement of antitrust claims against General Electric.[208] Plaintiffs estimated that this amount would represent a figure of not more than 2% of purchases overall.

As a condition of the settlement, the Government entered into a "covenant not to sue." It was expressly provided in the covenant that it was not to be considered as a release of General Electric or anyone else and that the Government was not relinquishing its rights to proceed against any other person in respect of claims arising out of its purchases of the products in suit other than purchases from General Electric.

The reason for making clear that the covenant not to sue did not constitute a release arose because the law was uncertain at

[208] Wall Street Journal, Feb. 19, 1963, at 1.

the time as to whether a release of one joint tort feasor might not constitute a release of all others, even though the document stated to the contrary.[209] The pattern of negotiating a covenant not to sue rather than an outright release continued throughout all the settlement procedures, whether negotiated by the federal government or by private parties.

On August 31, 1962, Judge Kraft accepted the settlement agreed upon between General Electric and the United States and the Tennessee Valley Authority, dismissing the actions against General Electric in accordance with the terms of the settlement agreement.

Settlement by the federal government with other defendants followed early in 1963. Settlement with Westinghouse called for the payment by Westinghouse of $800,000 which, upon a purchase base of $15,700,000, amounted to a 5.1% settlement. The settlement agreement between Westinghouse and the federal government recited that Westinghouse had furnished the United States with detailed financial information designed to show that payment by Westinghouse of an amount greater than the total amount settled for, together with payments which Westinghouse anticipated it would have to make in disposing of private damage suits, "could have seriously impaired the effectiveness of Westinghouse as a competitive factor in those branches of the electrical equipment industry in which it is engaged."

In April 1963 the federal government settled with McGraw-Edison and a number of smaller defendants—Wagner Electric, Moloney Electric, Joslyn Mfg. & Supply, Southern States, Lapp Insulator and Ohio Brass. The settlement with McGraw-Edison amounted to 4.2% of the purchase base (for an unspecified period), and the other settlements seemed to represent amounts ranging downward from 3.5% for Wagner to 2.1% for Moloney and 2% for Southern States. Allis-Chalmers settled for an amount representing approximately 3.1%.

---

[209] See Twentieth Century-Fox Film Corp. v. Winchester Drive-In Theatre, 351 F.2d 925 (9th Cir. 1965); Miami Parts & Spring, Inc. v. Champion Spark Plug Co. (5th Cir. Oct. 24, 1968), CCH Trade Regulation Reports, 1968 Trade Cases ¶72,606.

The press release of the Department of Justice (April 26, 1963) announcing the settlements quoted Attorney General Robert F. Kennedy as stating:

> " These settlements take into account the overall financial condition and competitive position of these defendants as well as their positions in each of the equipment fields in which Government purchases were made.
>
> There are 1,800 private damage suits stemming from the same criminal cases now burdening the federal courts. The Department of Justice has a responsibility to help clear up this congestion if that is at all reasonably possible. Thus, we are hopeful that the fact the Government and TVA have entered into settlements in these cases may help encourage equitable settlement of the private damage suits."

In the settlement papers with Moloney it was recited that Moloney had represented to the United States that during the period 1960 through 1962 it had incurred heavy losses and that Moloney had represented and had furnished supporting financial statements that settlement of the treble damage actions against it "would impose a serious drain on the financial resources of Moloney and could seriously impair the effectiveness of Moloney as a factor in those branches of the electrical equipment industry in which it is engaged."

None of the settlements with the federal government went beyond single damages, not even in the case of the TVA where the Government had asserted a standing to claim treble damages.[210]

No provision was made for any reimbursement of the Government's fees or expenses, and none of the federal government's settlements contained a so-called "most favored nations clause" whereby the Government would be given the advantage of any later, more favorable settlements with other complainants.

---

210 Judge Kraft had upheld this position in the Government's action for damages in Philadelphia, by opinion dated Aug. 22, 1962. The court concluded that the TVA is a "person" and that its business and property, except for real property, is separate and distinct from that of the United States; and that accordingly injury to the TVA may properly be the subject of treble damage claims.

In several instances the United States dismissed defendants without the payment of any damages. In November 1962, A. B. Chance was dismissed from the insulator action, and Kuhlman Electric likewise, the Government consenting to such dismissals because there were practically no purchases from these two defendants and, accordingly, claimed damages were nominal. In April 1963, Cutler-Hammer and Square-D were dismissed from the low voltage distribution equipment action because of the minimal nature of the Government's claim.

Throughout the period in which settlements were being negotiated with the federal government, certain defendants were exerting pressure on utility plaintiffs for dismissal from the antitrust actions without the payment of any amounts in settlement. Generally these defendants fell into the category of so-called "no sale" or "minimal" defendants, those in the former category being defendants who had made no sale to particular plaintiffs and therefore urged those plaintiffs to dismiss them from their actions. This was not and could not be urged on the ground that there was no liability, since the law was clear that a manufacturer participating in a conspiracy in violation of the antitrust laws is liable jointly and severally with the other conspirators to those who were damaged, whether or not the particular manufacturer made any sale to a particular plaintiff.[211] Nevertheless, certain plaintiffs agreed to a dismissal of defendants under these circumstances. In New York, Appalachian Power Company, Indiana and Michigan Electric Company, Connecticut Power Company and Ohio Power Company dismissed Carrier Corporation, defendant in an action on condensers. This was upon the condition, as expressed in the order entered May 2, 1963, by Judge Sylvester J. Ryan, that:

> " Carrier Corporation will remain available for depositions and other necessary discovery with respect to the product line condensers as part of the national discovery program, upon the same terms and with the same rights as if it remained a party to this action, and will remain available for local discovery with respect to the transactions involved in this action if it appears that the information sought cannot be obtained from defendants remaining in this action."

211 City of Atlanta v. Chattanooga Foundry & Pipe Works, 127 Fed. 23 (6th Cir. 1903), *affm'd,* 203 U.S. 390 (1906).

The minimal defendants were those whose sales to particular plaintiffs were small enough that they urged, in effect, that they should be categorized with "no sale" defendants and dismissed. In this instance, the interests of the plaintiffs and of the judiciary were diverse. Plaintiffs' counsel were not willing to acquiesce in any dismissals of the minimal defendants, not because they were interested in the relatively minor amounts of money that might be recovered, but because they believed that only by keeping all the defendants in all the cases could they exert pressure for meaningful settlement negotiations. Pursuant to this attitude, plaintiffs' counsel announced at the San Antonio meeting of the Coordinating Committee that plaintiffs were opposed to any dismissal of minimal defendants.

The judges, on the other hand, were anxious to show some disposition of claims in advance of full scale trial so that progress could be demonstrated as to disposition of claims. Chief Judge Ryan has been quoted as stating at one of his co-called "good and welfare" conferences in the Southern District of New York on May 15, 1963:

> " When you come to consider the defendants you have to group them and take the smaller defendants and get them out of these cases as quickly as possible. If you only had the smaller defendants out you would have only about one-tenth of the cases filed. Otherwise you will put them out of business." [212]

Chief Judge Ryan had previously granted motions for the dismissal from damage actions of certain companies who were named as co-conspirators but not as defendants in the Government indictments; these motions were not opposed by the plaintiffs.

In National Pretrial Order No. 13, which resulted from the San Antonio meeting, Paragraph I provided:

> " Plaintiffs and defendants shall file proposals for the time, manner and means of effecting dismissals against defendants in the separate cases from whom (1) the plaintiffs made minimal purchases or (2) the plaintiffs made no purchases. This proposal should

---

212 Quoted in McAllister, *Judicial Administration of Multi-District Treble Damage Litigation,* 1966 New York State Bar Association Antitrust Law Symposium (CCH) at 55, 86, fn. 95.

contain a specification of the specific dollar amount or amounts which would be considered a minimal purchase."

When Chicago plaintiffs submitted their proposal as required by National Pretrial Order No. 13, they took the position that the "smaller defendants" had in effect been granted substantial relief in the Northern District of Illinois when the court had determined that turbine generators would be the priority line initially to be prepared for trial in that District, since no small defendant was named as a defendant in any case involving turbine generators. Plaintiffs resisted any suggestion of dismissal of "no sale" defendants, arguing that this would not in fact produce relief for such defendants:

" 1. Unless each such defendant were dismissed from all cases throughout the country involving a given product line, that defendant would be relieved of no part of the burden of the national discovery programs of plaintiffs or of defendants.
2. Unless each such defendant were dismissed from all cases in the Northern District of Illinois involving a given product line, that defendant would be relieved of no substantial part of the burden of either the local discovery of plaintiffs and of defendants or of their pretrial and trial preparation.
3. Unless each such defendant were dismissed by all of the plaintiffs in any case where there are multiple plaintiffs, dismissal by some of such plaintiffs would be meaningless."

Plaintiffs therefore concluded that the defendants were asking for a dismissal for no reason other than a desire "to reduce their total potential liability whether or not they were involved in the conspiracies alleged." Plaintiffs also pointed out that in certain actions, the minimal or "no sale" defendants might include such major manufacturers as General Electric, Westinghouse, Allis-Chalmers and McGraw-Edison, and plaintiffs indicated that they would not be willing, under any circumstances, to dismiss a major defendant.

Defendants, in their National Pretrial Order No. 13 program, suggested an outright dismissal of "no sale" or minimal defendants but stated that such defendants would agree to a condition similar to that on which Carrier Corporation had been dismissed in New York. There was an intimation that "no sale" defendants might have a valid defense in that they might be able to establish "that they were foreclosed, by plaintiffs' own conduct, from bidding on certain jobs or selling to certain plaintiffs"; there was a suggestion that if the "no sale" defendants had to continue in the cases, they would have to explore this issue. Defendants pointed out that in the Northern District of Illinois, in the 226 cases, the defendants had been named a total of 1,116 times. According to defendants, dismissal of all "no sale" defendants would reduce this number by 325 or approximately 29%.

In their reply plaintiffs pointed out just how small some of the so-called "smaller" companies were:

	TOTAL ASSETS	SALES	NET INCOME
Carrier Corporation (as of 10/31/62)	$235,688,059	$270,665,257	$7,796,760
Federal Pacific Electric Co. (as of 6/30/62)	78,059,837	97,285,125	1,504,688
Wagner Electric Corporation (as of 12/31/62)	71,540,008	106,745,683	3,451,303
I-T-E Circuit Breaker Co. (as of 12/31/62)	70,400,533	111,753,408	1,462,196
Joslyn Mfg. & Supply Co. (as of 12/31/62)	52,790,560	82,886,931	3,195,360

Plaintiffs also argued, taking Carrier Corporation as an example, that the deposition of Sellers of Carrier had disclosed "that this company was inextricably intertwined in the devising and implementing of the steam turbine generator conspiracy; and this massive industrial giant ought not receive a shelter from its own actions." Plaintiffs also repeated their argument that dismissal would not simplify the cases or facilitate their disposition because:

> " In a major center of litigation, such as Chicago, such a program would not release any defendants from the burden of litigating in any product line. They would still have to appear in court for every hearing involving such a product line because they would still be defendants in that product line in that court as to some plaintiff or plaintiffs."

While this issue was under consideration by the courts, certain of the smaller defendants made offers of settlement to the plaintiffs. Manufacturers such as Joslyn, Lapp Insulator, Southern States, Wagner Electric, McGraw-Edison, Moloney Electric and Ohio Brass had been required as a condition of their settlement with the federal government to make a comparable offer of settlement of private claims. Pursuant to this undertaking, Joslyn offered to settle for 2½% of purchases in the period 1956 to 1959 for insulators and the period from mid-year 1958 to 1959 in the case of power switching equipment, lightning arresters and open fuse cut-outs, an offer which was represented to be in line with the basis on which settlement was achieved with the federal government. Joslyn's undertaking with the Government was to offer an amount not less than 2% to plaintiffs other than the federal government; and accordingly, in its view, its offer of 2½% was better than that required to be made by the terms of its federal government settlement.[213]

Moloney, producing financial statements to demonstrate its poor financial condition, offered 1% on power transformer sales, ½% on distribution transformer sales and ½% on network transformer sales, in each case for the period 1956 through 1959. Furthermore, Moloney stated that it would have to be given five years to discharge by equal annual payments any single settlement exceeding $10,000. Moloney represented that on these formulas the total amount that it would be required to pay would be about $700,000, and that was the maximum financial strain that it could carry.

Lapp Insulator made an offer of 2¼% and was so anxious to achieve settlement that at the end of 1963 it delivered to Commonwealth Edison Company a check for $767,000, representing 2¼% of that company's purchases from Lapp. Edison accepted, not as a settlement and without prejudice to any of its claims, upon the understanding that in the event of a later settlement the check so delivered would be a set-off.

In order to assist the smaller defendants in working out some settlement program, the courts stepped in. In the Northern District of Illinois, Judge Robson requested the smaller defendants to formulate a suggested settlement program and then to discuss that program with the plaintiffs. In their submittal defendants

---

213 Plaintiffs had information that Joslyn had settled the federal government claims at a percentage which was approximately 3% of sales for the designated periods.

complained that plaintiffs generally were unwilling to settle with smaller defendants before settling with the major suppliers. Defendants suggested that counsel for each side be bypassed and that a conference be held between executives of the smaller defendants who were interested in settling their cases and executives of a representative group of major utilities from various parts of the country. Counsel would be present in an advisory capacity only. This proposal was submitted on behalf of ten defendants: Foster Wheeler, Hubbard, Joslyn, Lapp Insulator, Moloney, Ohio Brass, Sangamo, Southern States and Wagner Electric.

Plaintiffs did not react favorably to this suggestion. In fact, plaintiffs had been concerned by a predilection of executives of defendants for approaching executives of the plaintiffs without plaintiffs' counsel being present and had considered a complaint to the courts based upon Canon 9 of the Canons of Legal Ethics. This canon provided:

> " A lawyer should not in any way communicate upon the subject of controversy with a party represented by counsel; much less should he undertake to negotiate or compromise the matter with him, but should deal only with his counsel."

In Opinion 75 of the Committee on Professional Ethics and Grievances of the American Bar Association (August 27, 1932), the Committee applied this canon to a situation where the defendant's attorney, without the consent of the plaintiff's attorney, advised or sanctioned an effort by his client to procure a compromise adjustment of the suit through a personal interview with the plaintiff. The Committee stated:

> " The attorney should not advise or sanction acts by his client which he himself should not do.
>
> Even should the client suggest a personal interview for the purpose of compromise without the consent of the adversary's attorney, it would be the duty of his attorney to endeavor to dissuade him from so doing, as Canon 16 provides 'A lawyer should use his best efforts to restrain and prevent his clients from doing those things which the lawyer himself ought not to do.' Again, candor and fairness to his brother attorney should restrain the defendant's attorney from giving any such advice or sanction, as Canon 22 states that 'The conduct of the lawyer before the Court and with other lawyers should be characterized by candor and fairness.' "

In the Eastern District of Pennsylvania on September 17, 1963, before Judges Clary and Lord, plaintiffs' counsel suggested to the court that the defendants refrain from direct settlement offers to the plaintiffs and that in the event that they did not do so, the problem would be referred to the Pennsylvania Board of Censors or to the Bar Association's Committee on Unauthorized Practice. Defendants argued that it was not inappropriate for a non-lawyer employee of a defendant to contact an officer or an employee of a plaintiff. The court stated that it considered the question a serious one but took no action.

As the parties came into the latter part of 1963, it was obvious that the key to settlement lay with the larger manufacturers and, above all others, with General Electric.

CHAPTER 13

Settlement—General Electric

IN LATE SUMMER 1962 plaintiffs' counsel learned that General Electric was preparing formulas pursuant to which it would make what it termed "price adjustments" with respect to certain equipment purchased during the period 1956 through 1959. Some of the methods employed to secure acceptance lacked subtlety. Ralph J. Cordiner, in a speech before the New York Society of Security Analysts, warned that private utility customers who sued General Electric and recovered damages might bring on themselves "one of the most penetrating rate investigations they ever experienced." [214]

Counsel for General Electric were unwilling to discuss the formulas with plaintiffs' counsel, saying that non-lawyer employees of General Electric would discuss them with the individual companies. Shortly thereafter a company executive to company executive approach began. In the case of Commonwealth Edison Company, Hoyt P. Steele, Manager-Antitrust Settlement and Litigation Operation, addressed a letter dated October 10, 1962 to J. Harris Ward, Chairman and President of Commonwealth Edison Company, transmitting an offer for settlement. The letter stated that formulas worked out by General Electric had been applied to Commonwealth Edison's purchases from General Electric during the calendar years 1956 through 1959 and produced a total of price adjustments of $1,428,645 on purchases computed by General Electric to aggregate $36,381,853. This was a percentage offer of 3.1% on the purchases under consideration; although in the case of turbines where a price adjustment of $1,032,031 was proposed for purchases of

[214] HERLING, THE GREAT PRICE CONSPIRACY 295 (Washington: Robert B. Luce, Inc., 1962).

$24,809,686, it amounted to 4.16%. The Steele letter stated that acceptance of the offer would require dismissal of General Electric from all suits Commonwealth Edison Company had filed for damages on purchases in any of the nineteen product lines named in the Philadelphia proceedings, and further, would require execution by Commonwealth Edison Company of "covenants not to sue (a) General Electric on claims pertaining to purchases of those products named in the Philadelphia Electrical Equipment Cases and (b) any other electrical equipment manufacturer named in the Philadelphia Electrical Equipment Cases on damages arising out of purchases of products of General Electric origin."

The reason the covenant required elimination of sales by General Electric from claims against other defendants lay in the provision of the defendants' sharing agreement whereby among themselves each defendant took responsibility for its own sales but not for those of any other defendant. The effect of the covenant was summarized by counsel for one client as:

> " (a) to assure that no claims will be asserted against General Electric for alleged violations of antitrust laws in connection with the products involved in the actions listed above; and (b) to assure that no such claims will be asserted against anyone else insofar as they relate to any such products manufactured or sold by General Electric or any of their respective subsidiary or affiliated companies or agents or to any such products sold under their respective trade names or trade marks."[215]

The Steele letter further recited, without further explanation, that the offer was subject to the condition that the "sharing agreement" which General Electric had entered into with certain other manufacturers to share certain costs arising out of the litigation be amended within 180 days, the letter stating that only if the arrangement were to be amended would it be practicable for General Electric to make payment of the "voluntary price adjustments."[216]

---

215 Opinion of Isham, Lincoln & Beale, dated April 28, 1964, to the Boards of Directors of Commonwealth Edison Company and Commonwealth Edison Company of Indiana, Inc.

216 Several months later, Mr. Steele advised Mr. Ward that the sharing agreement had been amended and that, accordingly, the condition referred to in the letter of October 10, 1962 had been satisfied.

General Electric effected few settlements as a result of this type of offer. One, achieved under the auspices of Chief Judge Ryan of New York, was with the Power Authority of the State of New York. Chairman Robert Moses of the Power Authority announced in August 1962 a settlement with General Electric for the lump sum of $307,000. Chairman Moses stated that in coming to agreement with the Power Authority, General Electric had made use of a formula for determining liability and damages which was unsatisfactory to the Authority. General Electric had agreed, however, "that the Authority's acceptance of the lump sum agreed upon did not imply acceptance by the Authority of the formula. Conversely, since the Authority's willingness to settle for $307,000 on a lump sum basis is predicated upon the exercise by the Trustees of their best business judgment, the Authority has no concern with how General Electric on its part justifies the settlement." As an overall justification for the settlement, the statement added that the Trustees of the Power Authority "have no desire to attempt through long litigation to collect punitive damages from companies whose products have contributed to the success of the Authority's projects."

The statement added:

> " In making the settlement which does not contain any element of punitive damage the Trustees of the Authority exercised their best business judgment, taking into consideration all factors including the importance of General Electric to the welfare of the State and the nation, the fact that damage to the Authority was minimized by its acceptance of foreign bids, the fact that there is uncertainty as to result in all litigation, the fact that carrying on litigation is time consuming and expensive, the fact that this anti-trust litigation is placing an intolerable burden on the Courts, and the fact that energies and talents of engineers and others should be engaged in productive activities for the benefit of the country rather than in preparing ammunition for legal jousting."

About eight months later General Electric had made such small progress in its settlement program that it recited, in a memorandum dated May 7, 1963, of its Antitrust Settlement and Litigation Operation, that of 184 investor-owned utility plaintiffs in approximately 1,000 cases, it had achieved settlement with eleven plaintiffs, accounting for eighty-three lawsuits. Of 250 public agency plaintiffs where the total number of cases approximated 500, settlement had been achieved with seven agencies which, in the aggregate, were parties to thirty-eight lawsuits.

By September 1963, with no substantial progress made in settlement, General Electric (as well as the other major manufacturers) found itself in this position in the proceedings: Plaintiffs had conducted and practically completed a national deposition program in the major product lines (including turbine generators and power transformers, both "high-damage" lines); and these depositions had established that meetings had taken place among competitors, that there had been understandings on the "proper" level of book and order prices, discussions of position on various jobs, and that elaborate steps had been taken to conceal these activities. Furthermore, with reference to certain key witnesses, the deposition judge had made available to the plaintiffs the transcripts of the grand jury proceedings and testimony of these witnesses, and plaintiffs' counsel were preparing to reexamine witnesses in the light of their testimony before the grand jury. Documentary production by the manufacturers was being ordered by judges so extensively as to require that manufacturers give to the plaintiffs full information concerning the revenues, expenses and rate of earnings for their various divisions or product lines.[217]

General Electric had been forced to admit, in its answers to the complaints, with respect to just one price increase:

> " . . . that at some time prior to June, 1957, an employe or employes of General Electric discussed with an employe or employes of one or more co-defendants, a price increase, and further admits that on or about June 20, 1957, it announced a price increase of approximately 5% for certain types of turbine generator units effective July 1, 1957."

General Electric's answer also contained admissions with respect to earlier and later price increases on turbine generators, and with respect to "position" had admitted:

---

217 Data on rate of return by product line were not being required, but data that were made available would enable anyone to make an arithmetical computation of the rate of return.

> " . . . that one or more employes of General Electric, met on occasion with one or more employes of one or more co-defendants or alleged co-conspirator companies and that occasionally one of the defendants or alleged co-conspirator companies was given what was designated as 'position' and that on occasion the bids or quotations submitted by the defendants or co-conspirator companies were higher than the bid or quotation submitted by the defendants or co-conspirator companies with position . . ."

While the manufacturers had been forced into the position of virtually admitting liability, their defenses were tenuous. In their deposition program defendants' efforts had been directed toward establishing that there was certain information on hand or available to plaintiffs concerning the defendant manufacturers' meetings and activities, designed to counter the fraudulent concealment assertions of the plaintiffs. This did not seem to be a defense that would affect any large number of plaintiffs. Furthermore, from the plaintiffs' view, the defense was likely to ring hollowly with a jury, the defense coming as it would from manufacturers whose chief executive officers had maintained that they did not know and could not have been expected to know what was going on.

Furthermore, at this point in time, trials seemed imminent in two important product lines—power transformers in Philadelphia and turbine generators in Chicago and New York—all scheduled for the early part of 1964. Such trials would inevitably bring out in the greatest detail the manufacturers' activities during the so-called "conspiracy period." When the manufacturers had been confronted with the possibility of these activities being publicized as a result of the Philadelphia criminal proceedings, they had decided then that that possibility must be averted even though the cost was that of pleading guilty or *nolo contendere* to the criminal indictments. In plaintiffs' view, the alternative in the civil suits of realistically working out a settlement would require a much less difficult decision than that which had led to the guilty and *nolo contendere* pleas in the criminal proceedings.

On September 10, 1963, General Electric made arrangements for a conference to be held in the Federal Courthouse in the Southern District of New York between the senior executives of General Electric Company and the senior executives of certain selected public utilities: Consolidated Edison Company of New York, Commonwealth Edison Company, Pacific Gas and Electric Company, Southern California Edison, the Southern Company, Middle South Utilities, Inc., Consumers Power Company and Niagara Mohawk Power Corporation. At least two of the companies present, Niagara Mohawk and Consolidated Edison, in addition to being customers of General Electric also had General Electric as customers of themselves, Niagara Mohawk to a substantial degree. Counsel for each of the participants were also invited. Invitations were not issued to any representative of the Atlantic City group, the American Electric Power system or the Philadelphia Electric Company. The latter company was preparing strenuously for trial in power transformers and had shown a disinclination toward settlement discussions. It was a surprise that representatives of the Atlantic City group and American Electric Power were not invited to participate, in view of the magnitude of their claims and the fact that their cases had been filed in the Southern District of New York. Other companies whose cases had been filed in other Districts, such as Commonwealth Edison Company and the two West Coast companies (Pacific Gas and Electric and Southern California Edison) were invited.

Presiding at the meeting was Chief Judge Ryan of the Southern District of New York, with Judge Feinberg of the Southern District of New York and Judge Robson of the Northern District of Illinois also in attendance.

Judge Ryan made an opening statement in which he indicated that General Electric had initiated and called the conference, listed the names of the private utilities, their executives and counsel who were in attendance, and stated that the purpose of the conference was "to have a discussion between the executives of the various corporations here represented, in which the possibility of adjusting and settling these suits will be discussed by them." He stated that the judges were present so that "they may be informed as to the contentions of General Electric Company and the various utility companies here present concerning adjustment and settlement of their differences."

Chairman Cordiner of General Electric opened the session by stating that though some settlements had been achieved, only one large company (Detroit Edison, which had not brought suit) had settled (the basis for settlement with Detroit Edison was not revealed).[218] Mr. Steele stated for General Electric that General Electric was willing to add to its previous offer by bearing a share of the litigation expenses provided that they would be confined to attorneys' fees and outside disbursements, not "in-house expenses," and that the reimbursements would have to be based on some proportion of claims against General Electric to total claims.

The utility executives responded that it was primarily a matter of dollars and cents and that General Electric's offer, which for most utilities present represented about 2½%, was not acceptable. Chief Judge Ryan interposed at that point and asked General Electric whether it was not the case that its formula produced more like 4% than 2½%. One utility executive remarked that his accountants had informed him that his company had suffered 15% to 20% in damages and that they would be subject to trebling. He stated that on $20,000,000 in purchases from General Electric, he had been offered $300,000 in settlement. Judge Ryan interposed to state that the $20,000,000 figure was not correct and was, rather, $11,000,000. The executive replied that the figure that the Judge had was General Electric's figure. Judge Ryan remarked that what the utility executive was asking for would break General Electric and put it out of business.

With reference to the Blue Book computations, Steele stated that the problem with that approach was that it did not consider the effect on prices of order backlogs and plant utilization. On questions of why the federal government settlement had produced such a higher percentage for the federal government than was being offered to the private utilities, if the formulas were the same, General Electric replied that a large portion of the federal government settlement related to the Widow's Creek unit purchased by the TVA at a particularly high price, and this required an adjustment unique to the TVA. Mr. Cordiner stated

218 The Detroit Edison settlement was reported in ELECTRICAL WORLD, Nov. 26, 1962, where a spokesman for Detroit Edison was quoted as saying that dollar amounts were not disclosed at the request of the manufacturers.

that this unit, of 500 megawatts, was the first unit of its size and that General Electric always charged more for the first unit of a new class "unless we made a mistake." The utility executives protested that they were not tied to the Blue Book, although it should not be dismissed summarily; and General Electric replied through Cordiner that General Electric simply would not consider a percentage like 16%: that was the point "at which we litigate."

At the close of the first day's session, General Electric announced that it would return the next day with revisions of its settlement offer which would increase their offer by 30%, resulting in a total increase for the electric utility industry of $15,000,000. Judge Ryan remarked that that seemed to him to be a significant increase in General Electric's offer.

On the following day General Electric presented a revised basis of settlement which they explained as follows:

" 1. The inclusion in price adjustment calculations of all turbine-generators ordered prior to 1956 but shipped in the 1956-1959 period and the calculation of a price adjustment on such turbines at a rate of 2½% of the final selling price.

2. A revision of the original turbine-generator formula to provide for payment on a turbine-by-turbine basis ordered during the 1956-1959 period. The revision provides a price adjustment which is the higher of the difference between the final price paid and (a) a reconstructed price calculated by the method formerly used, or (b) a reconstructed price based upon drawing a straight line between the September 1955 and March 1961 handbook prices for such a turbine. In addition, as an alternative to the modification of the formulas previously used, it is proposed that on a turbine-by-turbine basis a minimum price adjustment of 2½% on the final price paid would be offered.

3. For power transformers, power circuit breakers, and power switchgear assemblies, the following changes are proposed:
   a. Inclusion of all orders received during the second half of 1955 at a price adjustment rate of 2½% of final billing prices.
   b. For equipment ordered in the 1956-1959 period, calculation of price adjustments on a final selling price basis which results in a higher refund on any escalation which may have been paid.

4. It is also proposed that the original power transformer formula which was based upon comparing prices with the 1954 hand-

book plus 5% be revised to eliminate the 5% factor and, therefore, the comparison price used is only the 1954 handbook.

5. The original formula offered a price adjustment based upon the higher of the aggregate of formulas applied to nine lines or 2½% applied to fifteen lines. It is proposed that the 2½% minimum be applied on a product line-by-product line basis, except that, as described above, turbine-generators would be on a turbine-by-turbine basis. Therefore, for each product line the customer would be offered the higher of the amount produced by application of the original formulas as amended or 2½%.
6. It is proposed to include price adjustments on certain 'borderline' products such as network protectors which formerly had been excluded from price adjustment calculations in the belief that such products were non-indicted.
7. In addition to the changes described above, it is proposed that reimbursement be made for General Electric's share of substantiated legal fees and other out-of-pocket expenses incurred in connection with matters arising out of the Philadelphia Electrical Equipment Cases up to a maximum payment of 10% of the aggregate of price adjustments produced under the formulas."

For one utility, Commonwealth Edison Company, these revisions resulted in an increase in the amount offered in settlement from $1,428,645 to $2,720,000, an increase of approximately 90%. Of this figure, $2,147,873 represented price adjustments, amounting to 3.5% of the purchases to which the adjustments related.

General Electric stated in proposing this revision that its new proposals would pay to the utilities present a total of $18.1 million, compared with $8.5 million required by the previous offer, or an increase of 113% over its prior offer. General Electric added that it was a condition of the new proposals that at least five out of the eight utilities present, or 60% of the aggregate of the transactions between General Electric and those utilities, would have to find the proposals acceptable. Chairman Cordiner stated that the revised proposal represented the maximum settlement that General Electric was willing to offer. A statement was furnished by General Electric with its proposal, containing a specific discussion of the formulas and the other terms and conditions relating to the settlement.[219] There were also presented

219 See Appendix 25.

forms of a proposed Agreement of Compromise and Settlement, together with proposed form of Covenant Not To Sue.[220] A further meeting was then scheduled for late September 1963.

Prior to the resumed meeting scheduled for September 27, General Electric made further upward revisions in its offer of September 10-11. In a conference with Commonwealth Edison Company, Mr. Steele stated that General Electric had decided that there had been considerable damages on certain large new machines delivered in 1959 and later. He stated that they had decided to make a "commercial adjustment" which would apply on all turbines ordered in the 1956 to 1959 period which were shipped after July 1959 and up through 1962. For turbines in the 500 megawatt class, they were going to adjust to 82% of the March 27, 1961 handbook price. He said this would be about the same and maybe a little lower than the 1963 price level. For turbines in the 200 to 300 megawatt class they would adjust to 90% of the 1961 handbook price, and for 75 to 200 megawatt turbines to 95% of such price. He said that this would change their offer on Commonwealth Edison's Will County #4 from $1,032,000 to $3,851,000 and would bring their offer to Commonwealth Edison on all turbines to $4,445,000 and the total offer to $5,139,000 plus legal fees.

Mr. Steele left a book dated September 27, 1963 with Commonwealth Edison Company outlining the new proposal. It was inferred from this circumstance that General Electric would present the revised proposals at the September 27 meeting to be held in New York and that, in fact, was done. Certain further minor adjustments were made at this meeting. Pacific Gas and Electric Company argued that it wished to have its inside legal and company expenses included in the total for reimbursement; this proposal was rejected by General Electric, but it increased the maximum on outside legal and out-of-pocket cost from 10% of price adjustments to ¾ of 1% of purchases.

In the course of one calendar month, therefore, General Electric had increased its offer in the case of one utility, Commonwealth Edison Company, from $1,426,645 to $5,448,130 ($5,139,575 commercial and price adjustments—about 8.3% on 1956-1959

[220] See Appendix 26.

purchases—plus $308,555 of reimbursement), a trebling of the offer. Most of the increase took place by reason of the so-called "commercial" adjustment for large turbines which, of course, are purchased only by large utilities. The formulas for commercial adjustment, therefore, seemed clearly to be designed to effect substantial increases in the settlement offers for large utilities, leaving the offers to smaller utilities where they were prior to the September revisions.

The point of this strategy was obviously to achieve settlement with the major utilities which were the strong litigating companies in each of the major litigating groups (the Atlantic City group excepted), in the expectation by General Electric that if the litigation leaders settled, the litigation would thereupon collapse because the remaining smaller companies would not be able or strong enough to go forward on their own.

This strategy of favoring the larger utility was effective to a limited extent. As a result of the September conferences Consolidated Edison, Niagara Mohawk, the Middle South Companies, Southern California Edison and Pacific Gas and Electric accepted the General Electric offers. The percentages represented by settlements for the various companies varied widely. In the case of Niagara Mohawk, the settlement amounted to 5.2% of purchases; in the case of Consolidated Edison, 7.4%; in the case of Pacific Gas and Electric, 10.9%; and for Southern California Edison, the highest percentage of all, 11.5%, but attributable in large measure to the circumstance that Southern California Edison had received a "commercial adjustment" from General Electric prior to starting suit of $5,200,000.

Among the companies which refused the September revised offer were the Southern Company, Consumers Power, the Atlantic City group, Philadelphia Electric, American Electric Power and Commonwealth Edison.

Following the main meeting on September 27, Commonwealth Edison's representatives found themselves in a small meeting with Judges Ryan and Robson, and Cordiner, Phillipe and Steele of General Electric. Judge Ryan told the Commonwealth Edison representatives that he thought that they would throw their arms around General Electric in accepting the September

27 offer and asked whether Commonwealth Edison expected to get more money than Consolidated Edison. Chairman Cordiner indicated that the whole meeting had been called at Commonwealth Edison's suggestion, and that General Electric had hoped that Commonwealth Edison would be aboard. Judge Ryan stated that he was still unable to understand why Commonwealth Edison did not accept the revised offer and added that certain of the utility executives were complaining that the settlement favored Commonwealth Edison.

Commonwealth Edison had worked out the computations of its single damages on 1956-1959 purchases from General Electric on a variety of bases. This information showed:

BASIS	PRICE ADJUSTMENT	% OF PURCHASES
Blue Book	$10,985,633.	18.3
ATIG	13,536,858.	22.6
1961 Prices	9,619,869.	15.6
1963 Prices	8,961,794.	14.6

On the basis of this data, the Commonwealth Edison representatives informed General Electric and Judge Ryan that they could not settle with General Electric for any amount less than $9 million.

The small conference ended with a suggestion from the Commonwealth Edison representatives that they would be pleased to meet the following week in Chicago with representatives of General Electric before Judge Robson.

A private meeting similar to that with the Commonwealth Edison representatives was likewise held late in the afternoon between executives of Consumers Power and the Southern Company, representatives of General Electric, and Judge Ryan.

At a hearing held December 18, 1963, before Judge Ryan in the proceedings pending in the Southern District of New York, counsel for the Atlantic City group protested that the General Electric formulas had been weighted heavily in favor of the purchasers of the largest sizes of steam turbine generators. Judge Ryan responded that it was not within counsel's province to make this general statement, in view of the fact that counsel was in ignorance of the details of purchases made by the numerous plaintiffs throughout the country and that counsel's statement was rash. Counsel, by letter to Judge Ryan of December 23, 1963, protested that the transcript of the proceedings did not reflect counsel's further comment: "Your Honor, I make the statement because I am familiar with the formulas." The letter went on to protest that the formula was heavily weighted against the Atlantic City group, the great majority of whose steam turbine generator purchases during the period in suit were smaller than 200 mw. The available data showed that the September settlement offers would produce in the Atlantic City group 4.2% on purchases compared with more than 10% for Pacific Gas and Electric and Southern California Edison.

At a meeting in Judge Robson's chambers in January 1964 Commonwealth Edison protested to General Electric in the presence of the court as to the arbitrary nature of the General Electric formulas. Commonwealth Edison pointed out that the formulas provided no adjustment for Commonwealth Edison's unit Joliet 6 while Mercer No. 1, a unit of Public Service Electric and Gas of New Jersey, a unit of the same type and ordered in the same month as Joliet 6, provided an adjustment of about $1,900,000 simply because it was delivered after July 1959. Commonwealth Edison suggested that the formula made no provision for the fact that there may have been an overcharge on cross-compound units, a type purchased by very few purchasers; General Electric did not respond favorably to the implied suggestion that special consideration might be given to such units.

Three months later, in April 1964, General Electric revised its offer to Commonwealth Edison substantially upward by further revisions in its turbine generator "commercial" adjustments. No economic justification was presented for this further revision, just as no economic justification had been presented for the original commercial adjustment on turbines. The revisions, in effect, extended the commercial adjustment to include turbines purchased between January 1, 1956 and March 31, 1960, and the adjustment basis was revised to 82% of the handbook price for machines in the 300,000 kilowatt class; and for machines below this level but above 200,000 kilowatts, the adjustment would be based on 86% of the handbook price.

With respect to other product lines, further adjustments were also proposed. On large circuit breakers, power transformers, isolated phase bus, power switchgear, and power switching equipment, General Electric proposed price adjustments equal to the greater of the amount produced by the formulas previously offered, or 2½% on purchases made in the last half of 1955 and 10% on purchases made in the period 1956-1959. As in the case of turbines, these revisions seemed designed to favor the large utility customer.

On distribution transformers, meters and insulators, General Electric proposed price adjustments equal to the greater of the amount produced by the formulas previously offered (slightly modified in the case of distribution transformers), or 5% on all purchases made in the period 1956-1959.

General Electric proposed an adjustment equal to 5% on all purchases of indictment items in the period 1956 through 1959, excluding industrial control equipment, low voltage circuit breakers, low voltage distribution equipment, and navy and marine switchgear.

These adjustments produced a proposed settlement figure for Commonwealth Edison of $8,210,412, representing 13.3% of purchases to which the adjustments were applicable, plus $233,593 as reimbursement of out-of-pocket expenses, making a total of $8,444,005,[221] subject to further minor revisions as the data were developed. On April 30, 1964 it was announced that Commonwealth Edison had accepted the General Electric offer.[222] General Electric stated that its total cost of settlement with all claimants on the basis of the new formulas would be more than $150,000,000.

In the settlement General Electric drew one check to Commonwealth Edison for the "commercial" adjustment portion of the settlement payment, and another for the so-called "price adjustments" and reimbursement.

The pattern of settlement toward which General Electric seemed to be striving, that is, settlement with the large claimant

---

221 In the final revisions, the total offer of General Electric to Commonwealth Edison was $8,457,455.

222 Chicago Tribune, April 30, 1964, §3, at 9.

in a litigating group in the expectation that thereafter settlements could be achieved with the smaller claimants, worked. In the case of the Commonwealth Edison group, for example, following the Commonwealth Edison settlement, the remaining companies in the group accepted General Electric's settlement offers. In terms of percentages, the smaller companies found, by reason of the weighting by General Electric of its settlement formulas in favor of the larger purchasers, that their percentages realized on settlements were somewhat smaller than that of Commonwealth Edison. For example, whereas Commonwealth Edison's settlement produced 13.3% of applicable purchases in settlement, the percentages for other members of the group were in the 5% to 6% range for three utilities, in the 6% to 7% range for two utilities, in the 7% to 8% range for two utilities, and for one was at 8½%.

An issue of some contention during the settlement negotiations with General Electric related to the terms of a so-called "most favored nations" clause. Under this provision, which all plaintiffs were insisting upon, General Electric was called upon to agree that if after a given settlement General Electric made a later settlement which was more favorable than that which had been provided to the earlier settling party, then the benefits of the subsequent settlement would be accorded to the earlier settler. The wording of the clause as it appeared in the General Electric settlement agreements was:

> " In the event that prior to July 1, 1965, GE enters into any agreement with any other electric utility pursuant to which GE is or shall become obligated to make price adjustments or reimbursement for litigation expenses, or if GE makes such price adjustments or reimbursement for litigation expenses, on account of claims arising out of the indictments referred to in Preamble B hereto to any other electric utility, more favorable than as provided in Appendix 1.A. annexed hereto, and, when applied to purchases by Customer, would produce a larger price adjustment on any products listed in Preamble B hereof, or would reimburse out-of-pocket expenses in amounts greater than GE has agreed to pay to Customer hereunder, or if GE adopts any other program of adjustment, no matter how constituted or denominated, which when applied to purchases of products within the scope of Appendix 1.A. would produce a larger adjustment on such products

purchased by Customer prior to December 31, 1960, then, in any of such events, GE agrees (a) to notify Customer promptly in writing of such fact; (b) to grant Customer the benefits of such more favorable basis if Customer so requests in writing within 30 days after receiving such notice from GE; and (c) to pay to Customer promptly thereafter an amount equal to the difference between the amount agreed to be paid to Customer hereunder and the more favorable amount that would have been paid to Customer if the more favorable basis had been applied to Customer's purchases from GE." [223]

The issue arose on the question of what exceptions were to be provided. In the earlier phases of its negotiations, following the September 1963 conference, General Electric was proposing that the most favored nations clause would not be applicable to (a) payments made in satisfaction of judgments, (b) payments made in settlement of a case within sixty days of the trial date for that case, and (c) nuisance settlements, involving less than $200,000 worth of purchases. The first two exceptions were designed to provide that the favored nations clause would not apply to settlements made as a result of a trial, during the course of a trial or within a reasonable period prior to trial (a so-called "courthouse steps" settlement). The third exception was designed to allow General Electric to achieve small settlements on the basis of whatever would be required to get the claimant out of the way, without regard to formulas.

Most claimants had no problems with respect to the first and the third exceptions but did resist the "courthouse steps" exception. Finally, during the course of the Commonwealth Edison negotiations, General Electric agreed to drop this exception so that the exception paragraph in the settlement agreement read as follows:

" The foregoing provisions shall not be construed to obligate GE to make any additional payments to Customer arising from price adjustments similar to those provided for in Paragraph 2 hereof or reimbursement of out-of-pocket expenses similar to those provided for in Paragraph 3 hereof which are accorded to an electric

---

223 Although the clause speaks of "price adjustments," it was clear from the context that so-called "commercial adjustments" were also included in the clause's operation.

utility which purchased any of the products treated within Appendix 1.A. hereto from GE during the period from January 1, 1956 to December 31, 1959 for which the aggregate purchase price paid to GE was less than $200,000 nor shall the foregoing provisions be construed to obligate GE to make any additional payments to Customer arising out of the compromise or satisfaction of any judgment."

As it turned out, General Electric was required to make substantial additional payments under the favored nations clause. The turbine generator commercial adjustment under which a substantial number of settlements had been achieved provided as follows:

" For each steam turbine-generator ordered or shipped during the continuous period January 1, 1956 through March 31, 1960, the General Electric Company has calculated as a commercial adjustment, a reduction in the final price paid for each such turbine to the extent that the final price paid was higher than the amount produced by applying the following ratios of the March 27, 1961 Handbook price for a turbine-generator of comparable size and design:

86% of the Handbook price of machine less than 150,000 kilowatts,
82% of the Handbook price of machines 150,000 kilowatts up to 499,000 kilowatts,
80% of the Handbook price of machines 500,000 kilowatts and over."

In order to effect a settlement with the American Electric Power system, General Electric had to reduce the 80% for large machines to 72% and change the minimum size for that classification from 500,000 kw. to 400,000 kw. This called for substantial payments under the favored nations clause to earlier large settlers.

A second revision in the formula for settlement with American Electric Power was designed to be peculiar to the American Electric Power system and, accordingly, had little effect on other prior achieved settlements. This was a provision that:

" [W]here a customer committed two or more turbine-generators of like size and design within any three month period between January 1, 1956 and March 31, 1960, such transactions shall be considered for adjustment separately from other turbine-generators purchased by such a customer."

As a result of the former revision Commonwealth Edison received an additional amount of $1,164,241, which meant that the final settlement percentage for Commonwealth Edison was increased from 13.3% to approximately 15.25%.

Upon the expiration of the favored nations period, on July 1, 1965, certain utilities were careful to inquire whether any further payments under the General Electric favored nations clause were due. In response to the Commonwealth Edison inquiry General Electric answered that no further payments were due to the company.

As a result of the progress made in settlement with General Electric, the turbine generator trial which had been set in the Northern District of Illinois for October 12, 1964 was deferred, Judge Robson declaring a "moratorium" so that the settling and non-settling plaintiffs and defendants could re-assess their positions. Ultimately, settlements were achieved so that there was no necessity for a turbine generator trial in the Northern District of Illinois.

General Electric pursued its settlement program vigorously. Settlement was achieved with the Atlantic City group for an aggregate amount of $26,500,000.[224] Since the Atlantic City group was an aggregation of electric utilities companies smaller than the giant of the industry, settlement with them required General Electric to extend its "commercial adjustment" to all turbines of whatever size, although the adjustment for smaller turbines was proportionately less than the adjustment for larger sizes. This betterment in the formula in turn redounded, under the most favored nations clause, to the benefit of all smaller utility claimants.

By April 30, 1964, General Electric was able to announce that it had settled 90% of its damage suits for a total of $160 million.[225] And by the end of 1964 substantially all General Electric claims had been settled. From the information furnished in General Electric's 1964 Annual Report (inside cover page), it appears that price adjustments for the years 1963 and 1964 had

[224] New York Times, May 1, 1964, at 58, col. 3.

[225] New York Times, April 30, 1964.

amounted to $148 million, to which there should be added a $50 million reserve created by General Electric in 1962 for settlement payments. Thus, the total amount of price adjustments made by General Electric came to $198 million. This would represent about 8% of the purchases to which the price adjustments were applicable[226] and is exclusive of payments made to claimants for remibursement of fees and expenses and, of course, exclusive of General Electric's own costs, fees and expenses. In an undoubted reference to General Electric, it has been estimated that the total cost of the treble damage actions against it was more than $300,000,000,[227] but this seems high on the basis of the published figures.

General Electric was able to take in its stride the amounts that it was required to pay in settlement. It was a company with tremendous strength and financial resources, and furthermore, as it was to turn out, the United States Treasury would agree to bear one-half of General Electric's burden by allowing deduction of the entire amounts paid in settlement. The after-tax consequences were that General Electric's earnings in 1964 were reduced from $312 million to $237.3 million, or, on a per share basis, from $3.44 to $2.62 a share. Price adjustments for 1963 had reduced General Electric's earnings from $283.1 million to $270.6 million, or a reduction from $3.14 per share to $3.00 per share. Nevertheless, earnings remained substantial enough for General Electric to cover its dividend in each year and, in fact, to increase its dividend from $2.00 per share in 1963 to $2.20 per share in 1964.

---

226 This is based upon General Electric's computation that price adjustments of $45 to $50 million would equal 2% of purchases to which the settlements were applicable.

227 *House of Delegates Proceedings*, 55 AMERICAN BAR ASSOCIATION JOURNAL 381 (April 1969).

CHAPTER 14

Settlements after General Electric

Settlement with Westinghouse and other major manufacturers followed hard on the heels of the General Electric settlements. In fact, for a few plaintiffs, such as Commonwealth Edison Company, the Westinghouse settlement preceded settlement with General Electric.

Commonwealth Edison settled with Westinghouse for a lump sum of $5,000,000, with no separate allowance for reimbursement of fees and expenses. On a purchase base of $50 million, this was accordingly a settlement for 10%, a figure which compares with Commonwealth Edison's computations of these percentages based on various alternative calculations:

Blue Book	11.6
ATIG	14.6
1961 prices	12.7
1963 prices	11.7

The 10% settlement compared with a 5.1% settlement for the federal government.

Although General Electric made payment of its settlements in cash as a lump sum, Westinghouse requested and received authority to make payment of its settlement in five equal installments. As was the case with General Electric, the settlement agreement called for the execution of a covenant not to sue and recited that the settlement arrangement was not to be construed as a release.

The lesser percentage for Westinghouse as compared with General Electric was justified upon the basis of Westinghouse's lesser ability to pay. Westinghouse represented to Commonwealth Edison Company that its formula of settlement, if applied to all of Westinghouse's utility customers, would result in Westinghouse giving back more than the total net income on its turbine generator sales to customers for 1956 through 1959 (before deducting losses in some years).

After the earlier settlements, Westinghouse was required to make a further payment pursuant to its most favored nations clause. The percentages to be paid on various products were adjusted upward in later settlement, and in its revision Westinghouse also undertook to reimburse for out-of-pocket expenditures, which were defined as including "payments to lawyers (and those costs incurred in dismissal of these cases), economists, statisticians and other specialists and their assistants retained especially for work performed in connection with matters arising out of the Philadelphia Electrical Equipment cases." The latter reference included ATIG expenses of the settling utilities. As a result of these adjustments, the settling amount for Commonwealth Edison was increased from $5,000,000 to $5,617,130.

No information is available on the aggregate cost to Westinghouse of settlement, but it announced in its 1964 Annual Report that:

> " [T]he amount earmarked for purposes of settlement was increased in 1964 from $50 million to $110 million. Provisions for price adjustments were made in the accounts of the Corporation by charging income reinvested in business in the amount of $55 million, which is net of estimated taxes based on income."

Just as the Westinghouse settlements were scaled down from those of General Electric, so was Allis-Chalmers on a still smaller scale. In the case of Commonwealth Edison Company, the Allis-Chalmers settlement was at a 3.1% rate. Allis-Chalmers' levels of earnings and ability to pay were so unsatisfactory that Allis-Chalmers in fact offered, in the early days of settlement negotiations, to settle by making a price adjustment or refund which would be equal to either 25% of its profits before taxes on a particular product or 1¼% of the invoice price of each sale, whether or not profitable. Counsel for Commonwealth Edison Company justified the lower settlement percentage for Allis-Chalmers on the basis of the less favorable financial position of Allis-Chalmers in comparison with General Electric and Westinghouse and "the importance of financially healthy competitors in the electrical equipment industry." This latter consideration was important in the case of Allis-Chalmers which had announced during the course of the electrical equipment antitrust proceedings that it was withdrawing from the turbine generator business.

Not all claimants with whom Allis-Chalmers subsequently settled were as understanding, with the result that in order to achieve later settlements Allis-Chalmers had to increase its price adjustment offers substantially. This resulted in payments under the favored nations clause to those who had previously settled; in the case of Commonwealth Edison Company, the original settlement amount of $763,290 was increased by $571,816, equivalent to a 75% increase.

McGraw-Edison justified its settlement offer, which ultimately worked out to 5% in the case of Commonwealth Edison Company, on the ground that it was in the best interests of the utility industry to have McGraw-Edison continue to function as an effective competitor of the larger suppliers. It was argued that if the utility supply business came to consist of only one or two giant suppliers, the utilities themselves would be the eventual losers and the purpose of the antitrust laws would be defeated. McGraw-Edison also cited its low profits on products sold to electric utilities, claiming that in 1963 its net profit on utility products was 2% on their related capital investment. McGraw-Edison also recited that in order to secure a stronger position in the utility field, it had had to devote large sums of money to research engineering and development.

Following settlements with the big three (General Electric, Westinghouse and Allis-Chalmers) and McGraw-Edison, the plaintiffs turned to the offers of the smaller or minimal defendants. Settlement was achieved with Moloney at the nominal rate of 1% on power transformers and ½% on distribution and network transformers. This was justified by counsel for Commonwealth Edison Company in his opinion to the Board of Directors on the ground that it was important that Moloney continue as a supplier of transformers and that it was important to settle because, in view of Moloney's poor financial condition, there was substantial doubt that Moloney could survive extensive litigation; counsel therefore recommended a settlement which was at levels below those achieved with other transformer manufacturers. Certain plaintiffs proposed to Moloney that the minimal settlement be supplemented by additional payments of "one-half of excess profits earned in any one of the four years following the year of settlement." Moloney protested that on this basis there would be no finality in their settlement arrangements until 1970 and the proposal was accordingly unacceptable.

Kuhlman presented a settlement formula based upon their computations of excess profits earned during the four years of the conspiracy period, 1956 to 1959. In their computations this worked out to ½ of 1%, an offer which was ultimately accepted by some claimants, including Commonwealth Edison, because they did not wish to bear the expense of further litigation, particularly in the light of the circumstance that the federal courts were taking steps to transfer cases between circuits so that the litigation might have had to be prosecuted in a federal district other than the home district of the plaintiff.

Ohio Brass, for purposes of its settlement offer, attempted to determine what would have been the fair selling prices for insulators in the 1956-1959 period. This was done by taking insulator prices during World War II as the base period and then applying BLS Wholesale Price Indexes (Durable Manufacturers) to the base period prices. The study then purported to conclude that except for two minor instances Ohio Brass' published insulator prices during the indictment period fell below the "fair price" level so determined.

Foster Wheeler justified its low offer on the ground that in the product line with which it was concerned, condensers, meetings between competitors were not effective; and furthermore, "the existence of the conspiracy in condensers was rather well known to the purchasing departments of most utilities and was regarded as something of a joke in those circles both because of the existence of the outside group of manufacturers and because of the individual conspirator's general willingness to cut prices on each other." [228]

Sangamo Electric justified its settlement offer of 2½% on meters on the ground that payment at such a rate would mean

[228] Letter dated May 13, 1964, from Harold E. Kennedy, General Attorney, Foster Wheeler Corporation, to Gordon Corey, Executive Vice President, Commonwealth Edison Company.

that Sangamo would pay in settlement approximately its entire pre-tax profit realized for the preceding 3½ years.

Some settlements, though negotiated pursuant to formula, in fact resulted in a nominal dollar settlement: Commonwealth Edison settled all of its antitrust litigation with Southern States for the sum of $837.

Throughout 1964 and the early part of 1965, settlements were achieved at such an effective rate that by the spring of 1965 one large utility, Commonwealth Edison Company, had settled with all defendants except I-T-E Circuit Breaker. The total amounts achieved in settlement by this one company amounted to $17,791,745, representing amounts paid in initial settlement, additional payments under favored nations clauses, and reimbursement of fees and expenses. The latter amount, reimbursement of fees and expenses, totaled $588,868, about 3½% of the amounts achieved in settlement.

On the subject of how much the lawyers realized from the plaintiffs' recoveries, an expert antitrust lawyer for plaintiffs has explained the financial arrangements which ordinarily exist between lawyer and client in antitrust matters:

> "The usual agreement, with variations, involves a retainer within range of $5,000 to $25,000, a percentage arrangement on damage recovery, and some understanding on the attorney's fee which is ordered by the Court to be paid by the defendant. All clients should be given the opportunity to take an arrangement which provides for a straight hourly rate in lieu of the contingency. Costs must always be paid by the client on regular monthly billings. The plaintiff who accepts an hourly rate should still pay the retainer since, more often than not, the plaintiff is accepting the benefits of a good deal of work already done in the same industry by the particular lawyer involved." [229]

---

[229] Alioto, *The Economics of a Treble Damage Case,* 32 ANTITRUST LAW JOURNAL, 87, 93 (1966).

Mr. Joseph L. Alioto, later elected Mayor of San Francisco, had represented the State of Washington, and several municipal utilities or utility districts in the State, among other clients, in the electrical equipment treble damage actions. Settlements in the amount of $16.2 million were achieved for the Washington claimants for which Mr. Alioto received $2.3 million in fees. The fee contract signed in August 1962, had provided that Mr. Alioto was to get 15% of the amounts recovered, with a maximum fee of $1 million. After the

Many of the utility claimants in the electrical equipment cases were represented by their regular counsel, and in most such instances the fees payable were based, not upon contingency arrangements, but upon straight time charge computations.

The Commonwealth Edison settlements did not include any amount for special damages arising from the escalation clause used by a number of manufacturers, despite plaintiffs' position that there were three major defects in the manufacturers' escalation formula: (1) it embraced a greater portion of the purchase price than was in fact affected by price increases; (2) the escalation clause raised the entire purchase price to cost levels existing on the date of delivery, whereas the cost of materials and labor was actually spread over the entire period between the contract date and the delivery date; and (3) the weighting of material, labor and fixed costs was in incorrect proportions.

All settlements involved a favored nations clause, although there were variations as among the various plaintiffs and the various defendants. In the Atlantic City group settlement with Allis-Chalmers the favored nations clause excluded settlement of any case in which trial had commenced prior to the date of the settlement. It also excluded settlements necessary to clear up the tail-end of Allis-Chalmers litigation, the exception referring to price adjustments "made at a time when the remaining electric utilities which have antitrust litigation pending against

---

initial settlements, the then Washington State Attorney General, John O'Connell, removed the $1 million limitation with the result that the Alioto fees rose to $2.3 million. It later developed in 1969 that Mayor Alioto had shared these fees with two Washington State officials (about $530,000 going to Mr. O'Connell and $272,000 to George K. Faler, a member of Mr. O'Connell's staff). (New York Times, December 28, 1969.)

Messrs. Alioto, O'Connell and Faler were sued by the State of Washington and the utilities involved, claiming a return of the $2.3 million paid in fees. The suit contended that Mr. Alioto improperly shared fees with O'Connell and Faler after O'Connell had lifted the $1 million fee limitation without informing the clients. On March 26, 1972, a Superior Court jury in Vancouver, Washington, returned verdicts in favor of the three defendants on all counts (*Chicago Tribune,* March 27, 1972). The federal government indicted the same three defendants in 1971, in connection with the same set of circumstances, for bribery, conspiracy and mail fraud. On June 19, 1972 these charges were dismissed by U. S. District Judge Ray McNichols in Tacoma, Washington.

A-C with respect to purchases by them of any of the products defined in the foregoing indictments account for less than 25 per cent of the aggregate purchases from A-C by all electric utilities during the years 1956 through 1959 of such products." This latter provision varied considerably, particularly in the percentage that was specified: in the case of A. B. Chance, the 25% was negotiated to 15%.

All settlements were made subject to court approval. Approval was preceded by a hearing in open court during which counsel for the claimant enumerated for the court the various studies and other financial data that formed the basis for the settlement. Counsel for Commonwealth Edison Company phrased it this way in seeking approval of the United States District Court for the Northern District of Illinois (Judge Robson) for Commonwealth Edison's Westinghouse settlement:

> " We have reviewed with the Court various studies relating to the potential damages and other financial data relating to the claims of the companies against Westinghouse, including studies which have been based upon a re-pricing of the purchases made from Westinghouse in accordance with 1961 prices, and also studies relating to a re-pricing based upon the use of 1963 prices; also we have presented data relating to the computations that might be made on the basis of a so-called Blue Book, which is a series of computations prepared by the so-called Atlantic City group, who are plaintiffs in the Southern District of New York, and we have reviewed with your Honor certain data that would result or have a bearing, perhaps, with respect to these claims relating to studies that have been made by the anti-trust investigation group.
>
> Upon the basis of all of these studies, your Honor, bearing in mind the fact that this settlement is being achieved in the pre-trial stage, we as counsel for Edison and Edison of Indiana would like to urge upon your Honor that your Honor approve the agreement and the understanding as fair and reasonable, and we respectfully urge you to do so.
>
> The only other statement that I would make, sir, is that although this settlement arrangement was achieved outside of your Honor's presence, I am sure that I speak for counsel for Westinghouse as well as for myself in stating that we do not believe it would have been possible for us to have arrived at the understanding had it not been for the attitude, the impartial and objective attitude that your Honor has taken with respect to all of these matters and that in fact this settlement satisfactory to both sides as it is, is one which we believe we can honestly attribute

to your Honor and your Honor's efforts, and we wish to thank you for it."

The Court thereupon noted that the price adjustments were being made on a uniform basis and pointed out other circumstances which justified the settlement:

" The defendant has adopted a price adjustment program in an attempt to dispose of a substantial part of this unprecedented mass of litigation prior to trial of the issues on the merits. In connection with the present motion, defendant has represented that the price adjustments are on the same basis as those currently being offered by such defendant to other utility claimants whose claims involve the same classes of products.

. . . .

The actions in which the motion is made involve claims based upon thousands of transactions with respect to many different types of electrical equipment. Pre-trial proceedings have already taken many months, and completion of preparation for trial and litigation to final judgment could take many more months, involving a very substantial cost to all parties and the expenditure of a vast amount of the time of their executive and engineering personnel that could be devoted to more constructive activities. Moreover, because of the interdependence of plaintiffs and defendants in the domestic market for electrical equipment for use by utilities, the continuance of this litigation poses a threat to the health and well-being of an essential member of an essential industry.

. . . .

The parties have made disclosure and the Court has been fully informed in detail of all relevant facts required to evaluate the price adjustment. Although the Court has examined various studies pertaining to the claims of damages in amounts which are higher than the price adjustment, the Court, after reviewing all facts, is of the opinion that the price adjustment is fair and reasonable to the parties and to their stockholders and the consumers of plaintiff.

Accordingly, the Court approves the proposed disposition of these claims, and, upon the presentation of an appropriate motion to dismiss, the Court will enter an order dismissing Westinghouse Electric Corporation." [230]

Judge Boldt, in the Western District of Washington, in approving certain plaintiffs' settlements with General Electric Company, said:

---

[230] Transcript of proceedings before Judge Edwin A. Robson, Dec. 11, 1963, pp. 1-17.

> "Soon it will be forty years I have spent as advocate and judge in the conduct of litigation. While I learned the adage as a young man, more than ever I recognize the truth of it now: 'A fair settlement is better than the best lawsuit.' That is true of lawsuits generally, but it is more particularly true of these lawsuits than any I have had any experience with."

There was some question as to the precise effect of the approval of the settlements by the courts. Such approvals were not required by federal rules in any of the cases which were not true class actions. It was the general opinion of plaintiffs' counsel that the approval amounted to an expression of opinion of the court that the settlement was fair and reasonable but did not amount to a binding adjudication. At the same time, plaintiffs' counsel felt that the court approval would be one of the factors which would be considered in determining whether officers and directors of plaintiffs had acted properly in approving a particular settlement.

Public utilities, although subject to regulation by state authority, ordinarily were not required to seek regulatory approval of the settlements, but they were required to seek regulatory commission approval of the method proposed to account for the settlements. The position of many utilities was illustrated by the petition of Illinois Power Company to the Illinois Commerce Commission seeking authority to credit the amounts received in settlement, less the aggregate of cost and expense of suit, to utility plant accounts. Illinois Power proposed to adjust depreciation charges prospectively in recognition of the reduced carrying value of the equipment but not to attempt to adjust the existing depreciation reserve in view of the *de minimis* nature of the amounts involved in relation to the totals in the plant accounts. The Illinois Commerce Commission approved the Illinois Power proposals, except that it required that the total amount received in settlement should be credited to the plant accounts and the costs and expenses of the suit should be charged to operating expenses.

In advance of and throughout the settlement negotiations all parties were intensely conscious of the possible tax consequences of their settlement agreements. Plaintiffs' analysis early in the cases had led to the conclusion that so far as the recipients of amounts paid in settlement or on judgment were concerned, the compensatory portion would be treated as a return of capital and not taxable, except possibly to the extent of previous tax benefits claimed. In an award by a court, one-third would be taken as compensatory and the remaining two-thirds of the recovery would represent punitive damages and would be likely to be taxed at ordinary income tax rates. In the case of a settlement, the portion of the recovery which would be regarded as representing compensatory damages (as contrasted to punitive damages) would depend upon the nature of the claim, the pleadings, the intention of the parties and the terms of the settlement expressing such intention. In all cases where the compensatory portion would be treated as a return of capital, the amount of such recovery would reduce the basis of the capital items to which the recovery related. The plaintiffs' analysis recognized, in the case of the manufacturers, that if the full amounts paid by them on the claims were to be deductible, then the cost to the manufacturers of amounts paid in settlement or upon judgment would be 48% (the corporate income tax rate at the time being 52% on net income in excess of $25,000).

In advance of a definitive ruling, the manufacturers feared that the Internal Revenue Service would disallow as deductions any damage payments, on the ground that such allowance might frustrate the public policy underlying the antitrust laws. Furthermore, it was not clear whether the frustration of public policy doctrine, if applied, would differentiate between settlement and treble damage judgments or would distinguish between the single and trebled portions of any award or settlement reflecting trebling.

Several hundred millions of dollars were at stake in the answers to these questions.[231] It was computed in September 1964 that on the General Electric settlement payments negotiated as of that date, in the amount of $162 million, a tax reduction of approximately $81 million would be afforded to General Electric. On the basis of the ultimate settlement figures of approximately $200 million, about one-half would be borne by

231 Halper, *The Unsettling Problems of Settlement in Antitrust Damage Cases,* 32 Antitrust Law Journal 98, 101 (1966).

the taxpayers of the country in view of the deductibility ruling. It was reported that some experts estimated the eventual tax loss from the electrical equipment cases at $250 million.[232]

In the event, the manufacturers' fears of non-deductibility proved to be groundless. They were able to procure a ruling from the Internal Revenue Service[233] that amounts paid or incurred in satisfaction of claims for treble damages under the antitrust laws, as the result of a conspiracy to fix prices, are deductible as "ordinary and necessary" business expenses. The ruling was applicable both to claims reduced to judgment in civil suits and claims settled prior to the institution of suit or prior to judgment. The public policy doctrine was held not to be applicable since treble damage actions under the antitrust laws are remedial in nature, designed "to provide the victim with a means of recovering damages inflicted, and not to punish the wrongdoer." The Internal Revenue Service held otherwise with respect to amounts paid to the United States as damages under Section 4A of the Clayton Act or under the Federal False Claims Act, finding that those statutory provisions, although resembling restitution, were in effect punishment for injury to the public.

With respect to attorney's fees and legal expenses, it was found by the Internal Revenue Service that no public policy would be frustrated by permitting their allowance; and, accordingly, it was held that amounts paid or incurred for attorney's fees and directly related expenses were deductible except in cases in which the United States Government was the injured party.

---

232 Chicago Daily News, Sept. 18, 1964, §3, at 29.

233 Rev. Rul. 64-224 dated July 24, 1964. For a discussion doubting the wisdom of Revenue Ruling 64-224, see Arthur John Keeffe, ed., *Reactions to Current Legal Literature,* 54 AMERICAN BAR ASSOCIATION JOURNAL 1227-1229 (Dec. 1968), commenting in turn on an article entitled *The Deductibility of Antitrust Treble Damage Payments,* MINNESOTA LAW REVIEW (June 1968).

The manufacturers were represented before the Internal Revenue Service by counsel highly knowledgeable in Washington affairs. It was reported at the time that General Electric was represented by Clark Clifford, but this has been denied by Mr. Clifford: JOSEPH C. GOULDEN, THE SUPERLAWYERS, 97-98 (New York: Weybright & Talley, 1972).

The ruling produced an immediate adverse reaction in Congress. Senator Hart and Congressman Celler introduced legislation in the 89th Congress (1965) to overturn the ruling. Upon failure of this legislation, Senator Hart renewed his attack in the 90th Congress in S.2804 introduced December 15, 1967. Under this latter proposal "no deductions shall be allowed under subsection (a) for two-thirds of any amount paid or incurred on any judgment entered against the taxpayer or in settlement of any action brought against the taxpayer . . . by reason of anything forbidden in the antitrust laws."[234] Revision was finally effected by the Tax Reform Act of 1969, which denies a deduction for two-thirds of a post-1969 treble damage payment where the payor is convicted of a related criminal antitrust violation or pleads guilty or *nolo contendere.* (*Internal Revenue Code,* Sec. 162.)

Plaintiffs in their settlements were happy to acquiesce in the defendants' characterization of the settlement payments as "price" or "commercial" adjustments, in order to remove any implication that any part of the settlement payments could be attributed to the trebling factor and therefore possibly regarded as a penalty. Furthermore, judicial approval of the settlements, in language which spoke of the settlements as "price adjustments," was also regarded as helpful.

The tax position of the plaintiffs as recipients of payments in settlement was ultimately clarified by Internal Revenue Service Rev. Proc. 67-33, dated July 31, 1967. Under the ruling amounts received in settlement, excluding recovery of legal expenses, which are less than the actual damages sustained and less than the basis of the assets involved, were not to be treated as income to the recipient but would serve to reduce the basis of such assets. On the other hand, settlement amounts which are greater than the actual damages sustained or greater than the basis of the assets involved would be income in the year of receipt. Legal fees paid by the plaintiffs were held to be deductible when incurred or accrued; a recovery of legal fees would be treated as income in the year of receipt. In effect, then,

234 The staff of the Joint Committee on Internal Revenue Taxation, in a study released Nov. 1, 1965, took a similar position.

the Internal Revenue Service ruled that any amount presented in a settlement which would represent the trebling factor over and above single damages would constitute income but that the single or compensatory damages would be regarded as a return of capital.[235]

When the Commonwealth Edison settlement was announced, an attempt was made by a customer to secure a distribution of the amounts paid in settlement directly to the consumers rather than permitting their retention by the utility. Opal Cummings, a customer of Commonwealth Edison, filed a class suit in the Circuit Court of Cook County on behalf of all customers of Commonwealth Edison, asking the refund to such customers of all monies paid to Commonwealth Edison as the result of the antitrust litigation and for a declaratory judgment that Edison's customers were entitled to such monies. The circuit court sustained Commonwealth Edison's motion to dismiss. On appeal the Illinois Appellate Court found that the plaintiff's claim, properly regarded, was that she and other customers were charged excessive rates for which she was, in effect, seeking reparations. The court ruled that granting the plaintiff's request would be a usurpation of the functions of the Illinois Commerce Commission, the State regulatory body, since a ruling in the customer's favor would require a determination of what would have been a reasonable rate for Commonwealth Edison to have charged during the period in question and the specific class or classes of customers entitled to a refund by reason of the company's charges in excess of such a reasonable rate. The court also rejected the argument that the monies received by Commonwealth Edison in settlement constituted a trust fund, the court pointing out that the monies collected by Edison were never in

---

235 Tax treatment by the recipient of amounts paid on treble damage antitrust claims is now governed by Section 186 of the Internal Revenue Code, added by the Tax Reform Act of 1969. Under this complex provision, the portion of the recovery which is not punitive in nature is not required to be included in income to the extent that the losses to which such portion relates did not give rise to a tax benefit. The remaining portion of the award or amount paid in settlement (e.g., the two-thirds of the recovery which does not represent economic injury but which is punitive in nature) remains taxable as income as before. See proposed Internal Revenue Service Regulations, Secs. 1.186 and 1.186-1 (Federal Register, April 29, 1972).

the possession of or under the control of the circuit court so as to support a theory of an equitable trust fund or constructive trust existing on behalf of the customers of Commonwealth Edison.[236]

The progress in settling cases throughout 1964 was remarkable. The Coordinating Committee for Multiple Litigation, in its report of March 2, 1965, presented statistics showing that of 1,910 cases filed in various Districts in the United States, 861 had been dismissed entirely, with 1,049 remaining pending. Of the claims, numbering 25,600, represented by the cases filed, 13,638 had been dismissed, leaving 11,962 claims pending.

The Coordinating Committee did not expressly claim credit for the number of settlements that had been achieved, but doubtless the pressures of the national discovery program contributed greatly to the defendants' desire to be relieved of the burden of the electrical equipment cases. Accordingly, to the extent that court procedures are designed to dispose of cases, whether by settlement or trial and judgment, the national discovery program must be regarded as a success. But one commentator takes an entirely different view: that the national discovery program did not produce the settlements but was indeed saved by the settlements:

> " The program (even limited as it was to priority product lines) seemed to be headed for disaster when it was saved by the rash of settlements that removed at least a thousand cases from the dockets in the spring and summer of 1964." [237]

The same commentator accordingly concluded, with respect to the national discovery program, that "there is little in its makeup or procedures to commend it as an example to be followed in the future." [238]

---

236 Cummings v. Commonwealth Edison Co., 64 Ill. App. 2d 320 (1965). Leave to appeal denied, Supreme Court of Illinois, 1966.

237 McAllister, *Judicial Administration of Multiple-District Treble Damage Litigation,* 1966 N.Y. State Bar Association Antitrust Law Symposium (CCH 1966) at 55, 86.

238 *Id.* at 85.

CHAPTER 15

The Philadelphia trial

At Philadelphia, Philadelphia Electric Company and other plaintiffs in the Eastern District of Pennsylvania proceeded as if their cases were going to be tried and not settled.

In the beginning stage of the Philadelphia proceedings, early in 1962, Philadelphia Electric Company had come close to securing a judgment by default. The court granted the Company judgment after General Electric Company failed to answer its turbine generator complaint, but shortly thereafter the judgment was stricken and defendants were given further answering time for all complaints. When defendants' answers did come, the Philadelphia plaintiffs moved to strike the Westinghouse and Allis-Chalmers answers in the power transformer cases as "sham." Plaintiffs argued that the depositions of Westinghouse and Allis-Chalmers employees taken during the national discovery program had established most of the complaint's allegations of conspiracy and that even in the light of this deposition testimony, Westinghouse and Allis-Chalmers in their answers had chosen to deny the conspiracy and the overt acts charged in the complaint. Plaintiffs' counsel pointed out that because of the statements concerning grand jury testimony made by employees in 1960 to counsel for these two defendants, who had a responsibility for the answers, they had known the true facts since at least that time. The court deferred ruling on the plaintiffs' motion to strike the two defendants' answers and gave leave to all defendants to file amended answers within thirty days.

The amended answers when filed were considerably more realistic. For example, General Electric, in responding to the allegation of the power transformer complaint that representatives of defendants had held numerous meetings in various cities throughout the United States since at least 1956, answered:

> " It is admitted that at some of the aforesaid meetings allocations of sealed bid business to certain governmental agencies was dis-

cussed and that efforts were made by some of the persons present at said meetings to allocate sales in accordance with some percentage.

It is admitted that during part of the period designated meetings were held at some of which there were discussions of list prices and price rules. It is admitted that there were instances during some periods of telephone communications to homes and mail communication in plain envelopes."

Westinghouse's answer to the same allegations was:

" Westinghouse admits on information and belief based on statements made by employees of Westinghouse that at various times during the period from June, 1956 through sometime in 1959 one or more employees of Westinghouse met with employees of one or more other defendant corporations at various places in the United States including those set forth in subparagraph (a).

Admits on information and belief based on statements made by employees of Westinghouse that at one or more of the meetings referred to in subparagraph (a) one or more of the following took place: Discussions with respect to defendants' approximate percentages of the sealed bid market; discussions with respect to some future sealed bid invitations; discussions with respect to the approximate published price value of equipment represented by some of such invitations; and circulation of cumulative lists showing the amount of sealed bid business secured by each defendant.

Admits, on information and belief, based on statements made by employees of Westinghouse, that on some occasions in late 1956 and early 1957, employees of Westinghouse communicated orally and in writing with employees of one or more other defendants with respect to published prices on the published rules used to compute prices for power transformers.

Admits that during the period from about July, 1957 through October, 1957 Westinghouse announced changes in its published prices on price rules for power transformers.

Admits, on information and belief, based on statements made by employees of Westinghouse, that on some occasions employees of Westinghouse discussed with employees of one or more other defendant corporations approximate levels of market prices of power transformers, including levels of approximately 15 per cent or 10 per cent below the published prices.

Admits, on information and belief, based on statements made by employees of Westinghouse, that employees of Westinghouse on some occasions communicated orally and in writing with employees of one or more other defendants and that such communications included telephone communications to home telephones and written communications in plain envelopes addressed to home addresses."

The other defendants answered in a similar vein.

These answers to the Philadelphia complaint established the pattern for defendants' answers in the litigation throughout the United States.[239] Compare, for example, the following answers of General Electric and Westinghouse, respectively, filed in the turbine generator action (No. 61 C 1284) in the United States District Court for the Northern District of Illinois, *Commonwealth Edison Company, et al.* v. *Allis-Chalmers Mfg. Co., et al.:*

" 13. With respect to Paragraph 13(a) of the Complaint, admits that at some time prior to April 1957 an employee or employees of General Electric discussed with an employee or employees of one or more co-defendants, adjustment of the price of certain types of turbine-generator units, and further avers that it put into effect on or about April 15, 1957 certain price adjustments different from those which were the subject of such discussions.

With respect to Paragraph 13(b) of the Complaint, admits that at some time prior to June 1957 an employee or employees of General Electric discussed with an employee or employees of one or more co-defendants a price increase and further admits that on or about June 20, 1957 it announced a price increase of approximately 5% for certain types of turbine-generator units, effective July 1, 1957.

With respect to Paragraph 13(c) of the Complaint, admits that at some time prior to April 28, 1958 an employee or employees of General Electric discussed a price increase with an employee or employees of one or more co-defendants and further admits that it announced a price increase of approximately 3% effective April 28, 1958."

And from Westinghouse:

" Westinghouse admits, based upon information and belief, on the basis of statements made by employees of Westinghouse that at various times during the period alleged in paragraph 8 of the

---

[239] The Coordinating Committee, in Pretrial Order No. 13, had raised the question whether uniform answers would be appropriate for all cases pending throughout the country. Both plaintiffs and defendants opposed the suggestion, and in Pretrial Order No. 15 the Committee recommended against standard national answers and in favor of individual answers to the complaints.

> complaint, employees of Westinghouse attended meetings and had communications with employees of other defendants and of the alleged co-conspirator companies in which price of or position as to turbine-generator units were discussed, and admits that it raised or changed its prices of turbine-generator units at various times during such period, but it denies each and every other allegation of those paragraphs as they relate to it and is presently without knowledge or information sufficient to form a belief as to the truth of such allegations as to other defendants and co-conspirators. Westinghouse denies that, as a result of the aforesaid meetings and communications, plaintiffs suffered any injury whatsoever and, further, specifically denies that its employees were authorized by Westinghouse to attend such meetings or participate in such discussions."

The entire answer of General Electric is contained herein as Appendix 27.

While the amended answers were being filed, the Philadelphia plaintiffs renewed their motion for a default judgment against General Electric on the issue of liability on the grounds of improper answers to so-called "Proxy Statement Interrogatories," in which plaintiffs had asked for detailed information concerning statements made by General Electric in its 1961 Proxy Statement. Ultimately this motion of plaintiffs was denied.[240]

In mid-1963 the Philadelphia court established February 17, 1964 as the trial date for power transformers on the issues of both liability and damages, Judge Joseph S. Lord, III to preside. Plaintiffs offered to waive a jury but defendants General Electric and Westinghouse indicated that they would not waive. The court thereupon proceeded on the assumption that the trial would be a trial by jury.

In October 1963 plaintiffs filed a pretrial brief and moved for summary judgment in the power transformer cases on all

240 In Philadelphia the plaintiffs had served comprehensive interrogatories on the defendants prior to the institution of the national program. So dilatory were the defendants in answering that plaintiffs had moved for summary judgment against General Electric, Westinghouse, Allis-Chalmers and Carrier Corporation for failure to comply with court orders requiring answers to the interrogatories. This was denied, as was the later motion based upon the contention that the answers, when they did come, were improper.

issues except the amount of damages. In November 1963 defendants filed their pretrial brief. In it they readily admitted that the defendants had met to discuss the prices and pricing of power transformers but stressed that a private claimant, unlike the Government in a criminal antitrust proceeding, must show not only a violation of the antitrust laws by the defendants but also "the impact of the violations upon him and damage to him resulting from the violations of the antitrust laws," quoting *Simpson* v. *Union Oil Company of California:* [241]

> " It is clear that the private litigant in a suit charging violation of the antitrust laws stands in a different position than the government in an antitrust action. In a government action, there need be present only a violation of the laws and damage to individuals need not be shown. The private litigant must not only show the violation of the antitrust laws, but show also the impact of the violations upon him and damage to him resulting from the violations of the antitrust laws."

Defendants argued in their pretrial brief that throughout the period of the alleged conspiracy, power transformer prices had risen and fallen, not as the result of conspiratorial action, but as the result of economic forces, primarily orders received (demand) and the existence and extent of a backlog of orders, compared with capacity of the transformer industry at the time.

They gave examples:

> " In other words, the defendants' shops were half as full in the spring of 1954 as they had been in the fall of 1953. When orders for the ensuing six months from the spring to the fall of 1954 fell to the level of but 7 million KVA, it is hardly surprising that a desperate scramble for orders ensued. This was the white sale—a classic price war. There is an absolute correlation between the curve of prices in this period and the curve of supply and demand.
>
> By the same token, in the six months' period from October, 1954 to April, 1955, the volume of orders placed jumped from 7 million to 24 million KVA (see NX 1050); prices responded accordingly. Demand and back-log continued to rise until 1957; so did prices. Thereafter orders and back-log steadily declined, with some slight recovery in 1959."

Defendants also claimed in their pretrial brief that for some participants the objective of the meetings was not to fix prices

[241] 311 F.2d 764, 767 (9th Cir. 1963).

but "to carry on a commercial intelligence or espionage operation." For this point they quoted the deposition testimony of Rissinger of Westinghouse:

" A. I was desirous of finding out what competitors were quoting; any intelligence I could obtain from them at any time.

Q. You were simply engaged in industrial espionage?
A. This was a pretty good place to get some information. This was a very important aspect."

And Seaman of General Electric: "All I got at these meetings was perhaps a little industrial espionage."

And Plank of Pennsylvania Transformer:

" A. I would say that the principal reason that Pennsylvania Transformer attended such meetings was, A, primarily sales leads, and secondly, trying to find out where the market might be."

In their pretrial brief defendants also cited a so-called "black box" program as bearing on the prices established for transformers. They cited the deposition testimony of J. W. Seaman on this subject:

" Q. Now, Mr. Seaman, it has been said previously at these depositions, specifically, the deposition of Mr. Kastner, that you were the central figure in the concept and planning of that which has come to be known as the black box program.

Would you have time and just tell us the origins and the course of the development and the objectives of that program?
A. Well, shortly after I became associated with this particular business and after I had attended one or two of these meetings with competitors and had observed the reaction pricewise in the market, I came to what I think was a rather obvious conclusion. These gentlemen meeting together were rather silly in thinking that they could solve an excess capacity problem simply by getting together. Regardless of what they tried to do, the economics of the situation would be the only thing that would do anything for them as time progressed.

. . . [A]nybody who has cost leadership can obviously survive a sort of an economic decline better than those who don't; and if you are the cost leader, then you presumably set your prices where you make a reasonable profit and if you do set your prices where you make a reasonable profit this tends to limit the flexibility of your less effective producers to oscillate their prices in this kind of a period. In other words, if you have a good cost leader, a price leader in an industry, it tends to stabilize the market through periods of stress and strain.

So we looked our situation over and to make a long story short it was obvious that we had a very high overhead operation. We were no different than anybody else in this industry in that this was where a good deal of our costs were coming from.

We finally decided that we had to, in effect, automate our overhead and I think that we were the first in the country to devise a way of applying a computer to our complete over-all business system. This had been done before this time. Inventories had been put on computers, payrolls had been put on computers. Some engineering problems had been solved with computers but nobody had, so far as I know, even investigated a way of having a computer handle your order from the time it comes in the front door through all the various processing and paper work and engineering to the time when the product is finally shipped.

This we set out to do and we knew that if we could successfully consummate this we would have to be the cost leader and hence the market stabilizer and the price leader.

Our computer program got under way in early 1956 and by 1957 we had established that it was feasible on a small band of our power transformers.

. . . .

We then had to find a way to try to cross the whole spectrum of our production. In power transformers at this time we were designing power transformers three different ways. We were designing by hand.

. . . .

Well, we came up with the black box approach, which meant that we had one basic design concept, which could be computerized. This meant that we had to standardize certain dimensions. We had to have an X and a Y, like you have to have a zero on a six-foot rule, for the computer to start from.

We had, of course, three dimensions in transformers. We had length, height, and width. We eliminated the third variable by saying that that will be the railroad clearance and which left them with an X and a Y and once we did that we could then tell the computer how to design, produce production papers, price operations, and so on.

By the beginning of 1958 we had progressed to the point where we could see a 20 per cent cost reduction potential in this but it meant that our customers, who historically had always had special requirements for their individual transformers had to accept a transformer which would do their job magnificently from a technical standpoint but might not have the bushings in the exact location that Bill Smith, their engineer, had historically used them, or it might not have the corners rounded which they might have liked to put in a particular space.

. . . .

. . . [T]his approach meant that we could mechanize our shop and turn it from a blacksmith shop into a production flow shop."

Defendants also argued that plaintiffs could not have been damaged by any activity of the defendants because the plaintiffs at all times had available alternate sources of supply, foreign and domestic, comprising manufacturers not involved in any of the meetings.[242]

Defendants also argued that the plaintiffs had not been overcharged and that the prices paid by them for power transformers were fair and reasonable. The defendants stressed that research and development in the power transformer industry, as in the heavy electrical industry as a whole, has been almost entirely in the hands of the defendants. They argued:

" The significant technological improvements in the product over the last 50 years have been developed by one or another of the defendant companies, the utility industry having relegated this function to the manufacturers. Indeed, the utilities recognized that it was desirable and necessary for the manufacturers to enjoy a fair margin of profit so that they could continue the vital work of research and development.

---

242 Philip Sporn, in the course of a deposition taken by defendants, explained the unwillingness of his large utility system (American Electric Power Company) to purchase foreign-made turbines:

"Q. But insofar as the turbine generators were concerned, up to that time you did not consider that the technology of the foreign manufacturers were sufficiently advanced for you to consider the purchase of one of their— A. They were behind our technology and we were operating in the forefront of American technology—'our' in this case being American. The Europeans I think were behind in some areas, behind American technology, and we in AEP were in the forefront of American technology.

Q. You, in the course of this letter, in referring to your not being willing to buy a turbine generator from a foreign manufacturer make the rather colorful statement: 'In this case we would definitely not want to furnish the beard on which the foreign manufacturers would practice the art of barbering.' Has AEP continued, since that time, to refuse to furnish the beard? A. Oh, no. We have been a beard for many of our manufacturers, domestic, and had it cut to pieces many times, I assure you. We didn't want to do it for the foreigners specifically."

> Over these years the cost per kilowatt hours of electricity in the United States has steadily declined, as the plaintiffs regularly point out to the public in newspaper and magazine advertisements.
>
> Prices must be commensurate with the responsibility to continue research and development."

And finally, defendants argued that plaintiffs could not recover damages for activities which "they knew about, condoned, and encouraged." The defendants cited the so-called Hogg questionnaire:

> " Also, in 1957 34 utilities responded to a questionnaire sent out by Mr. Hogg, a top executive of the Cleveland Electric Illuminating Company, in which response the overwhelming majority indicated a belief that the electrical manufacturers were meeting to attempt to fix prices, terms and conditions of sale and, further, that the manufacturers used the occasion of NEMA meetings to carry on such discussions."

Plaintiffs in a pretrial reply brief responded to the defendants' position that foreign manufacturers were available as an alternate source of supply by citing a General Electric document[243] which stated:

> " Foreign competitive entrance into the domestic transformer market began to increase noticeably in 1952. The steady rise of business secured by foreign manufacturers, attaining a peak of 12% [in 1955] of the total U. S. business, is shown in Table IX. Since 1955 this percentage has steadily decreased to 1.6% of the total U. S. market in 1960. The price instability in the domestic market during 1960 resulted in a price level [to] which most foreign competitors are not willing to go."

In response to the defendants' argument about the operation of economic forces, the plaintiffs argued:

> " [T]he witnesses called by the defendants for national depositions have to date been of the view that during periods of heavy orders and backlogs, prices should go down, not up, because defendants' plants are running at higher capacity and therefore at a higher rate of efficiency and lower cost. To state, as defendants do, that in periods of high backlogs and orders, prices went up, is merely to emphasize the extent of the overcharge maintained by the conspiracy."

---

243 No. 300841 in the National Depository.

On the black box, plaintiffs argued that the "mass production-automation" revolution visualized by General Electric in 1959 through the medium of the black box design "does not withstand even the most cursory analysis." Seaman of General Electric, characterized as "the father of the concept," was held to have admitted that it contemplated a 20% price reduction "at the end of 1963," four years after the conspiracy had come to an end, and then only if accepted by the utility industry and only to the extent that inflation could be held in check. As against this proposed reduction plaintiffs cited the circumstance that by April 1961 prices were down 40% to 45%, much lower than the maximum of 20% projected for the end of 1963.

As a further part of the pretrial proceedings, defendants were directed to supply the name of their expert economist who had been working on power transformer prices. A pretrial conference was scheduled for January 7 and the trial itself was postponed until March 16, 1964.

At the pretrial conference the defendants successfully resisted the establishment of a procedure whereby the plaintiffs would cite every fact deemed to be relevant to the trial and the defendants would then be called upon to specifically answer or admit the facts one by one, as if they were answering to a pleading. Indeed, the parties, to the distress of Judge Lord, were not even able to agree outside the courtroom on the issues to be tried:

> " JUDGE LORD: I am sure that you are all aware that in other districts courts habitually require counsel to sit down, before they come into a pretrial conference, and themselves frame the issues that are to be tried, and come in with a pretrial order.
>
> . . . .
>
> JUDGE LORD: I think it is outrageous to insist that the Court sit here and go through it paragraph by paragraph.
>
> . . . .
>
> When you people know much more about the case than I do, when it is your case, and you are grown men—I think it is perfectly outrageous."

At one point during the argument defense counsel laughed at a suggestion being made by counsel for plaintiffs:

> "MR. KOHN: Why, sir, shouldn't we cover the thing in detail and say that unless within a week they specify what specifically is incorrect, and what the evidence is upon which they base their answer to every one of the paragraphs in that proposed motion for summary judgment—they are all of the same type——
>
> MR. KOHN: I don't know what is funny, and I have a good sense of humor—better than most of the defendants.
>
> JUDGE LORD: One thing I think that will not advance us very far is comparing senses of humor."

The trial opened on March 16, 1964, as scheduled, before Judge Lord and a jury.[244] The plaintiffs were Philadelphia Electric Company, The United Gas Improvement Company and Conowingo Power Company. Defendants were General Electric Company, Westinghouse Electric Corporation, Allis-Chalmers Manufacturing Company, McGraw-Edison Company (as successor to Pennsylvania Transformer Company), Moloney Electric Company and Wagner Electric Corporation. The conspiracy being tried was the one alleged to have existed in power transformers, and it was an agreed fact that 90% to 95% of the power transformers manufactured in the United States were manufactured by the six defendants in the case. The plaintiffs presented their case from March 16 to April 7. The defendants began on April 13, and the trial concluded with a jury verdict on June 2, 1964.

As the trial opened, the courtroom was jammed. In addition to the parties and their counsel, there were as many as fifty attentive visiting lawyers sent by their various clients to observe the first civil treble damage trial arising out of the electrical equipment conspiracies.[245] Plaintiffs, going forward after their opening statement, read to the jury a mass of material in the pleadings and related documents. Parts of the complaint and

---

244 Judge Edwin A. Robson of the United States District Court for the Northern District of Illinois estimated that it might have taken seven years for the Philadelphia trial to get under way if normal procedures had been followed rather than the thirty-four months it did take with a national discovery program (BUSINESS WEEK, April 18, 1964, at 178).

245 BUSINESS WEEK, April 18, 1964, at 176.

answers were read, including the admissions in the defendants' answers as to the meetings. Portions of the defendants' pretrial brief were read. A striking statement on the subject of meetings was read from the defendants' pretrial brief:

> " Defendants admit that at various times during the period 1946 to September, 1959, some of their employees held meetings to discuss prices and the pricing of power transformers. There is evidence that meetings continued with GE present at least until March or April of 1957 and probably until May, and without GE until August. There is also evidence that although General Electric announced its withdrawal from the meetings there were some telephone communications between Rissinger and Kastner of General Electric and Mann of Allis-Chalmers and Kastner. These communications were in the early part of the year."

Plaintiffs' counsel read to the jury Paragraph 10 of the power transformer indictment to which, it was pointed out, the defendants had pleaded guilty:

> " 10. Beginning at least as early as 1956, the exact date being to the grand jurors unknown, and continuing thereafter up to and including the date of the return of this indictment, the defendants, together with other persons to the grand jurors unknown, have engaged in a combination and conspiracy in unreasonable restraint of the aforesaid interstate trade and commerce in power transformers, in violation of Section 1 of the Act of Congress of July 2, 1890, entitled 'An Act to protect trade and commerce against unlawful restraints and monopolies,' as amended, commonly known as the Sherman Act."

Thereupon the court, at the request of defendants, explained to the jury the implications of the indictment and the guilty pleas:

> " Members of the jury, you have heard read to you a portion of the Indictment to which these defendants pleaded guilty. The effect of that plea of guilty is that the Indictment and plea are prima facie evidence of the facts contained therein; namely, prima facie evidence that the defendants did conspire to violate the Sherman Act, which is the Antitrust Act.
>
> Prima facie evidence means that kind of evidence which establishes at first glance, or which establishes of itself a given set of facts, and which remains in the case throughout the trial and would be sufficient in itself to prove those facts without other evidence.

It may, however, be rebutted by the defendants by evidence which would rebut it if believed by you. It is not proof of any means by which the conspiracy, which has been admitted, was carried out, and it is proof only of the existence of the conspiracy during the period charged in the Indictment; namely, from 1956 to 1960; nor is it any proof that the plaintiffs have been damaged by the conspiracy which has been admitted by the plea of guilt."

Ralph Cordiner was called by plaintiffs as the first witness. The witness affirmed his prior position that he knew nothing of the meetings or the price fixing activities in power transformers until General Electric's counsel had investigated after the grand jury inquiry had begun, but he did concede that responsible employees of General Electric ultimately had admitted price fixing with competitors:

" Q. So, in October or November, 1959, Seaman, Smith, the other people did come in and admit they had been fixing prices in power transformers with your competitors?

MR. SAWYER: Objected to, Your Honor. That is a legal conclusion.

THE COURT: No. I don't think that is a legal conclusion.

THE WITNESS: Mr. Luebbe—"

By Mr. Kohn:

" Q. Could you answer yes or no and then explain.
A. The answer is yes, but then I have to qualify my reply because they did not come in to me. The general counsel reported to me that they had admitted their violation of company policy.

Q. Despite the fact this was your exclusive responsibility you delegated it to Mr. Luebbe. They went in and told Mr. Luebbe they had been doing these things and then he told you?
A. Well, he told me; that's right."

The court clashed with Mr. Cordiner in the course of a redirect examination by plaintiff's counsel:

" Q. How about the Turbine Division?
A. Am I supposed to be talking about things other than power transformers here? I don't know how to be responsive to this.

THE COURT: Mr. Cordiner, you don't make the rules in this Court. Your counsel will object if they think the question is objectionable and I will rule on it. If the question was not objected to, you answer the question."

A bizarre incident occurred about a week after the trial opened. For the period of the trial plaintiffs' counsel had taken a room in the Benjamin Franklin Hotel almost across the street from the Federal Courthouse. On March 24 three men were surprised in the act of tampering with or photographing evidence compiled by the plaintiffs. They were discovered when plaintiffs' counsel, having carefully locked the door, left the room shortly after 10:00 P.M. on March 24. When he reached the street an early spring shower came on and counsel turned back for an umbrella. As he walked down the thirteenth floor corridor on which his room was located he saw a strange man emerge from counsel's room followed by two other men who fled, evidently in panic, stumbling over each other down a fire tower to the street. The police were called. Nothing had been taken, but detectives noticed that the files had been disturbed and concluded that the men had been photographing them.

The entire incident was reported to the court, which ordered a full investigation. All parties and the court were concerned at the publicity given to the incident, most of which assumed or implied that the defendants were responsible. The *Philadelphia Inquirer* for April 17, 1964 carried this headline: "D. A. Hunting 3 Spies Who Rifled Data in Vast Price-Fixing Suit." Defendants made no counteraccusation, but they pointed out that both of the newspapers which carried the full story on the incident—the *Inquirer* and the *Philadelphia Daily News*—were clients of plaintiffs' law firm.

The newspaper articles also, in attempting to put the whole incident in context, outlined the issues in the litigation, in some instances presupposing decision of matters that were at issue. Thus the *Philadelphia Daily News* stated that the defendants had "fixed prices for $36 million worth of transformers."

Defendants moved for a mistrial. The jury was called in, and in response to the court's question a majority of the jurors indicated that they had read the newspaper articles or had heard radio broadcasts concerning the hotel incident. The court denied the motion for a mistrial but did issue to the jury cautionary instructions that they were to disregard and put out of their minds all that they had read or heard about the incident. The court indicated to the jury that the newspaper stories had contained "gross misstatements of fact" and that it was convinced that no party to the case and no counsel trying the case "had anything to do with it." After the cautionary instructions the court asked the jurors as a body to indicate whether they "had any lingering doubt that the defendants or the parties or the lawyers are not concerned in this matter." There was no response. Next the court asked the jurors to indicate whether any of them believed that "there is any question as to whether they could render fair, impartial justice based on the evidence produced, the summations of the lawyers and the charge of the Court." Again there was no response. The court thereupon permitted the trial to proceed.

William S. Ginn followed Mr. Cordiner on the stand. An attempt was made by plaintiffs to secure a ruling that he was being called as an adverse witness, but the request was overruled. Ginn was as frank in his testimony at the Philadelphia trial as he had been in his deposition on power transformers. He admitted that from 1945 or 1946 up to 1956 he had been an active and frequent participant with competitors in price meetings relating to power transformers. He named the individuals at General Electric, Westinghouse, Allis-Chalmers, Moloney, Wagner and McGraw-Edison who had participated in the meetings and added that his meetings with McMullen of Allis-Chalmers had been quite frequent over an extended period of at least ten years. He balked only at admitting that the meetings had resulted in formal "agreements":

" Q. As you spoke to these people at the meeting it was your understanding from what they said that the intent was that that was the price that was to be charged?

. . . .

THE WITNESS: Yes, I would say that's what their intention was at the time.

By the court:

Q. And how did you gain knowledge of that intention?
A. By simply—I would say primarily by after the calculations were completed, Your Honor, it was said, 'Now, does anybody have any different ideas on how this price was calculated? Is it not everybody's understanding that is the right way to calculate the price?'

Now, maybe very childishly, Your Honor, we always tried to avoid trying to use the word 'agreement' for whatever it might stand up for. It was a very childish thing, but nobody ever left there with the idea that they had an agreement."

Ginn readily admitted that steps were taken to conceal what was going on:

" Q. To get back to where we were, when you made telephone calls did you make them from your office?
A. Very seldom.

Q. As a matter of fact, you very seldom even made them from your home?
A. That's right.

Q. You made them from pay stations?
A. That's right.

Q. Why?
A. Well, I simply didn't want the—the problem was I didn't care about the world knowing what I was doing.

Q. And whatever papers or scraps of paper you had at these meetings or documents of any kind you got rid of?
A. Yes, sir.

Q. Destroyed?
A. Yes.

Q. And when you used paper you didn't use paper that had GE's name printed on it or your own name printed on it?
A. I don't know whether I ever got quite that elaborate.

Q. Well, don't you recall that you did testify to that effect?
A. I don't recall that I did, but the chances are that I wouldn't have used the company stationery, yes.

Q. For the same purpose?
A. Yes, sir.

. . . .

By Mr. Kohn:

Q. Now, you endeavored to conceal these activities from everyone, didn't you, except those, of course, who were meeting with you?
A. Yes. Those that didn't need to know didn't get to know; that's right."

At the court's request Ginn gave an explanation of the term white sale:

" Q. Now you used the expression, I think, 'white sale' equating it to the sales of linens and pillows and sheets and counterpanes and things like that that the ladies attend in department stores; is that the genesis of this expression?

MR. KOHN: Objection.

THE COURT: Overruled. I have often wanted to know what the term meant.

THE WITNESS: That is how the phrase was coined. I just hope—

By the court:

Q. Who coined it, do you know, Mr. Ginn?
A. I don't know who that gentleman who is going to live in infamy who did it, but I hope the department stores did better than we did.

MR. KOHN: I ask that the last remark be stricken.

THE COURT: Yes, I will strike that remark."

It was during the course of Ginn's cross-examination that the court commented on Mr. Cordiner's capacity as a witness:

" MR. KOHN: I also think that he has not qualified this man [Ginn], who was neither in manufacturing nor accounting, as a person qualified to state what the costs of this company were.

We had Mr. Cordiner's testimony yesterday that there were no separate figures for transformers so far as he knew at any time during the time that he was the chief executive officer.

THE COURT: There were a lot of things that Mr. Cordiner didn't know about."

Following the live testimony of Cordiner and Ginn, plaintiffs' counsel began the utilization of deposition testimony. In the beginning plaintiffs' counsel read to the court and the jury both the questions and the answers, the court explaining the matter to the jury in the following terms:

" In the meantime, members of the jury, you have heard reference to depositions. I sort of think you know by now what they are but I am going to explain them to you again for the record.

For a number of months—well, for a long time before this trial many of the witnesses who were essential witnesses were brought into court or came into court and testified without a jury present at all but with a judge present, and they were examined by counsel for both sides. There was a reporter present just as there is now and their testimony was taken down and transcribed and later reproduced in different ways, either printed or typed, and some of those witnesses who previously testified in advance of the trial are now unable or cannot be brought into court.

Consequently the attorneys are going to read what they previously testified to. Now, this is a procedure that is provided for

> by the rules of the Federal Courts; that is, for the taking of these depositions. These were depositions when they came in and testified and this is provided for by the rules of Courts so that the testimony will be available in case a witness cannot come into court or for some reason or other cannot be subpoenaed into court, and when this testimony is read to you it has exactly the same force and effect as if the witness himself were here on the witness stand today testifying before you."

It was also ruled by the court that if defendants' counsel wished to supplement portions of the deposition not being read by plaintiffs' counsel, defense counsel could at the appropriate place take over from plaintiffs' counsel and read to the jury those portions of the deposition which the defendants wished to have in the record. So far as objections were concerned, the court stated that it would proceed as if the deponent were a live witness, so that in the event of an objection when a question was read from a deposition, the court would rule on the objection before the answer was read. If the objection was sustained, the answer would not be read at all. If it was overruled, the deposition answer would then be read. No attempt was made to read any comments made by the deposition judge on the deposition's questions or answers.

It proved to be difficult to keep the jurors' attention while the deposition materials were being read in this fashion. Sensing this, plaintiffs' counsel, on the sixth day, changed his technique and placed upon the stand a young lady, an associate lawyer in his office, who thereafter read the answers while counsel read the questions. Since the young lady read with precision and expression the technique was considerably more satisfactory from the plaintiffs' point of view. The defendants continued with the technique of having counsel read both the questions and the answers. One commentator on this technique compared the proceeding to the casting of a play rather than a trial:

> " Both sides present the bulk of their evidence by reading the documents aloud in court. The effect is more like watching a play being cast than a trial. One lawyer sits in the witness chair, reads the answers of a deposition from a distant witness while another lawyer reads the questions. Opposing lawyers challenge the 'remote-control' testimony as if it were happening 'live.'"[246]

[246] BUSINESS WEEK, April 18, 1964, at 178.

Plaintiffs' counsel's method of reading the questions raised an objection from defendants' counsel:

" MR. WARD: If Your Honor please, I cannot restrain myself any longer from making a protest concerning the inflection with which these questions are read. I hardly recognize this as the coloration of the tone and the tenor of the original deposition. I really think that in fairness it ought not be put argumentatively as if this information were being torn from the witness, as it was not, as I think is implicit in these responses. I can't restrain myself from making that protest.

THE COURT: Overruled. I think he has a right to ask the questions any way he chooses. I don't know how the questions were asked at the time of the deposition, and I doubt if anybody does. I think he has a right to ask the question any way he chooses, so long as he conforms to the question that was asked at the deposition."

The deposition material bore strongly on the issue of liability and served to buttress Ginn's testimonial admissions of meetings and agreements. For example, the following excerpts from the deposition of Mann were read to the jury:

" Q. Well, would you say that there were occasions where you had meetings with your power transformer competitors where you left the meetings with the understanding, from the sentiments voiced by the people there, that certain price rule changes would be put into effect, so that you reasonably expected that they would be put into effect?
A. Yes.

Q. And would you say in that sense that you agreed to the price rule changes with your power transformer competitors?
A. Yes.

Q. Now, after you had had your 15 per cent discussions with your competitors was there a meeting at the end of 1958 or early 1959 where it was agreed to raise the market level to about 10 per cent off net book prices?

. . . .

A. There was discussion of changing it from 15 to 10, yes.

Q. And was it so agreed?
A. Well, in the broad sense of the word 'agreement' I would say that the operating level did expect that each person at the

meeting would try to get 10 per cent. There was a reasonable expectation.

Q. And after that set of expectations was set up at the operating level, did all the power transformer defendants quote on certain specific jobs at the 10 per cent level pursuant to their expectations?
A. Approximately, yes.

Q. And did that continue until the fall of 1959?
A. I don't recall now, but in my Grand Jury testimony I said yes to that.

Q. Now, were you able, before the Grand Jury, to identify some specific meeting dates?
A. Yes.

Q. And was one of the dates on which you recalled definitely meeting with your power transformer competitors October 3, 1958, in Chicago?
A. Yes.

Q. And was another such date October 16, 1959, in Chicago?
A. Yes.

Q. And would you say that was the last working level meeting that you were familiar with?
A. Yes, sir."

All in all, on the issues of the case other than the damages, plaintiffs presented only three witnesses live (Cordiner, Ginn and Monk) and nineteen by deposition: Butler, Kastner, Seaman, Raymond Smith, Rissinger, McMullen, Clothier, Knox, McKinley, McCullom, Warsaw, Beard, Castner, Long, Plank, Tindall, Best, Swoish and Mann. Defendants, when their turn came, used on the liability issue only four deposition witnesses (Snow, Wolfe, Hoff and Coveli) and some further material from plaintiffs' depositions of Seaman and Kastner.

Grand jury testimony was permitted to be liberally used by the plaintiffs during the course of their presentation. It was accorded its traditional use for the impeachment of witnesses—that is, when there seems to be a contradiction or inconsistency on material points between grand jury testimony and the witness' deposition or trial testimony; but further, Judge Lord took the position that if grand jury testimony did not refresh a witness' recollection, but if he nevertheless stated that he was telling the truth for the grand jury (as every witness would), then the grand jury statement could stand as confirmatory evidence in the case. Furthermore, in the case of one deposition witness (Seaman), his and counsel's notes of his interview with General Electric counsel following his appearance before the grand jury were admitted as plaintiffs' exhibits in the case. A similar summary made by deposition witness Knox was admitted, and in the case of Kastner the 22-page statement made to the grand jury was likewise admitted.

The court explained to the jury, in connection with the admission of the grand jury testimony of Rissinger, the circumstances under which his grand jury testimony had become available:

> " Members of the jury, after the witness Rissinger testified on depositions as you have just heard, a motion was made to the court for the release of that testimony that he had previously given before the Grand Jury. Upon examination of the Grand Jury testimony of Mr. Rissinger and a comparison of that testimony with the testimony that he gave on depositions, the Court was of the opinion that sufficient good cause had been shown to release the Grand Jury testimony in that there were contradictions between his testimony previously given before the Grand Jury and the testimony that he gave on depositions.
>
> When the testimony before the Grand Jury was released the witness was then recalled, that is Rissinger was then recalled, and questioned as to those inconsistencies based upon his testimony previously given before the Grand Jury. It is that deposition on the recall of the witness that you are now about to hear."

On the issue of computation of damages plaintiffs presented no experts. Instead they called as a witness Philadelphia Electric's purchasing agent for power transformers (Mayson), whose technique for measuring damages was simple.

Taking a quarterly index of average prices paid by all purchasers for power transformers between 1946 and 1962, as stipulated by the parties, Mayson charted the index. He then averaged the index price for the ten quarters following May 1960, the month in which the defendants were indicted for the power transformer conspiracy; a horizontal line representing this average (57.8 on the index scale) was extended backward on the index chart through the earlier period covered by the index, that is, to 1946.[247] This showed that the index of prices for every quarter prior to the third quarter of 1960 was higher than the post-indictment average (except for the first three-fourths of 1946). Mayson then ascertained the numerical difference between the price index for a given quarter and 57.8, then converted that numerical difference into a percentage of the price index value. This percentage difference for a particular quarter was then multiplied by the dollars of purchases by plaintiff Philadelphia Electric Company in that quarter to reflect the dollar "difference" for each such purchase. Finally, these dollar differences were totaled, and the totals were claimed as the amount of damage suffered by Philadelphia Electric Company. In essence, plaintiffs' theory of damages was that the average index of prices for the ten quarters beginning in the second half of the year 1960 was a measure of the price that would have prevailed, absent a conspiracy, for the preceding 14½ years. The method assumed that Philadelphia Electric paid, as to any purchase in a given quarter, a price at the same level as the average price paid by all purchasers of power transformers in that quarter as shown on the price index.

Plaintiffs adopted a different method with respect to single-circuit unit substations, although the method still represented, in effect, a comparison theory. For purchases made after 1956, comparisons were made between some pre-indictment and some post-indictment prices and the differences claimed as damage. Prices of purchases made prior to 1957 were compared to the price paid for twenty-eight substations purchased at the depth of the white sale, and again the differences were claimed as damages. Plaintiffs' counsel made no attempt to utilize ATIG calculations in proof of damages.

As a result of these calculations Philadelphia Electric Company, on purchases of $36,445,642 claimed damages of $12,499,-409, or about 34% of the purchase price; United Gas Improvement Company on purchases of $584,126 claimed damages of $210,853, or about 36%; and Conowingo Power Company, on

[247] In his deposition, Cordiner had virtually admitted that 1961, 1962 and 1963 prices for heavy electric equipment were competitive prices (Tr. p. 267, Deposition of Ralph J. Cordiner, New York, N. Y., March 1964).

purchases of $433,008 claimed damages of $166,279, or about 38% of the purchase price.

When defendants' turn came, they made no effort, on the issue of liability, to deny the fact of meetings and indeed practically admitted in the course of their case that the conspiracies had resulted in unlawful price fixing agreements. Defendants presented an expert witness on damages, Dr. John J. Corson, who testified:

> " Your Honor, I started off with the assumption that there was collusion, that there were meetings, that there were agreements. I realized that throughout this period."

And further:

> " They agreed on various floors at different times and in testifying on it yesterday several of those were pointed out; 10%, 15%, plus or minus 2 or 3% at different times. There were different floors agreed upon."

And counsel for General Electric, in a side bar conference (the term utilized in Philadelphia to designate a conference between the court and counsel conducted at the side of the bench out of hearing of the jury), admitted:

> " [W]e come in as guilty defendants. We come in with the pleas. All that is part of the law. I recognize that. You come in with this blood on your hands."

Defendants attempted to counter the fraudulent concealment evidence of plaintiffs with evidence that the plaintiffs knew of the defendants' price fixing activities.

Snow of Cleveland Illuminating had testified on deposition on the issue of knowledge in the utility industry of the manufacturers' price fixing activities:

> " A. There was certainly the feeling that our people shared with many others that there was an artificial level being maintained by the manufacturers.
>
> Q. Now, when you say 'artificial level' would you, again, be more concrete?
> A. I mean by getting together, and you are very familiar with what I'm talking about.
>
> Q. You say that was shared by many others?
> A. Yes.

Q. Would you, to the best of your recollection, help us by indicating who the many others were that you believe shared that view?
A. No, I'll not pinpoint that specifically by name. It was shared by so many among the better utilities that it was almost universally felt, I would say.

Q. You believe that it was almost universally felt, do I understand you correctly by the—I think you said 'better utilities'?
A. Yes."

In the Philadelphia trial, defendants had to establish Philadelphia plaintiffs' knowledge of the conspiracy (and not just the industry's generally). For this purpose they presented a series of memoranda that had been produced by plaintiffs for the national depository. In one, H. M. Ramsey, an employee of Philadelphia Electric with purchasing responsibilities, indicated to his chief executive officer that he believed that defendants in 1952 had an agreement on the subject of progress payments. Defendants also attempted to present the results of the so-called Hogg questionnaire. In November 1957, J. Donald Hogg, Manager of the Purchasing Department of the Cleveland Electric Illuminating Company, had addressed to "Members of the Public Utility Buyers' Group" a questionnaire on which the recipients were asked to designate a yes or no answer to various questions relating to "Manufacturing Industries Contributing to Inflation." Four of the questions were the following:

" Do you believe manufacturers have price agreements with one another on material and equipment sold to utilities?

If your answer to number three was yes, do you believe that as a result utilities pay higher prices than would be necessary if real competition existed?

Do you feel that there is usually real price competition between electrical equipment manufacturers?

Do you believe that meetings of manufacturers' trade associations are used to discuss and agree upon prices, terms and conditions of sale?"

The results of the questionnaire, allegedly showing that 82% of the thirty-four utility buyers who responded had answered yes to the questions on whether they believed there was collusion, was excluded by the court, as was testimony from the depositions of Hogg and other purchasing agents who had testified on depositions to holding such convictions. The ground for exclusion was that none of this material was tied in to the plaintiffs in the Philadelphia proceedings.

There was admitted a memorandum of October 6, 1954,[248] which had been identified during the national discovery deposition of George H. Cole. The memorandum had noted that at a meeting of the Edison Electric Institute Committee on Purchasing and Stores, the question was asked, "Do you believe that electrical manufacturers engage in the collusive setting of prices, terms and conditions?" The memorandum asserted, "The answer was unanimously given as 'yes.'" The memorandum recited the presence of a representative of Philadelphia Electric Company at the meeting, and it was indicated that he was one of those who believed there was price fixing.

When defendants presented local sales representatives and other employees of the defendants, plaintiffs' counsel asked on cross-examination whether they knew of the conspiracy prior to the time it was uncovered in 1959. The uniform answer was that they did not. This testimony permitted the plaintiffs to argue, at a later point, that the defendants were putting forward one set of employees who were ignorant of the conspiracy to deal with the plaintiffs, while another set of employees, who had the real pricing authority, were secretly fixing prices.

One defendant, Wagner Electric Company, attempted to escape liability by presenting evidence that it was not an approved supplier of Philadelphia Electric. Wagner argued that since Philadelphia itself had restricted competition to four suppliers, "the jury could draw an inference that such conduct caused such plaintiff to pay more than it otherwise would if it had purchased on a seller's market open to all the defendants, without exclusion of bidders by the act of the buyer"; and accordingly, that plaintiff had contributed to its injury by its own practice of restricting competition. This was consistent

[248] National Discovery Program, Exhibit NX 1180.

with the position that a number of defendants had taken during the course of the discovery proceedings that plaintiffs had adopted purchasing practices in many instances which "effectively precluded them from taking advantage of a wholly competitive market." [249]

[249] In Defendants' Second Petition for Relief, dated Jan. 16, 1964, at 6, footnote 9, defendants stated: "The depositions taken thus far reveal that a large majority of plaintiffs adopted purchasing practices which effectively precluded them from taking advantage of a wholly competitive market. Many utilities preferred a particular manufacturer's product and thus would not seriously consider proposals received by other manufacturers (Sheehan–Tr. 3N73; Hampshire–Tr. N25736-37; Fearnside–Tr. 2N3636-40). Purchasers of smaller equipment, such as distribution apparatus, were by and large allocated according to percentages established by plaintiffs to various manufacturers (Stevens –Tr. N24975; Carmichael–Tr. N25509-10), so that, again, the manufacturers were effectively precluded from participating in an unrestricted market. Thus, by plaintiffs' own activities, in the market in which defendants competed the low bidder was not necessarily successful (Sheehan–Tr. 3N71; Elzi–Tr. 5N378)."

CHAPTER 16

The Philadelphia trial—continued and concluded

THE DEFENDANTS' PRINCIPAL DEFENSE went to the issue of impact. An attempt was made to establish that whatever the defendants may have done in the way of meetings and attempting to fix prices, the fact was that prices were established by forces operating in the market place. Counsel for General Electric, demonstrating a chart designed to show that prices had responded more to demand and capacity than to meetings, stated that some conspirators might have thought they were affecting prices but they really were not. But defendants' attempts to introduce testimony of Ginn, Seaman and Butler as to forces which they believed controlled the market prices of transformers, and testimony from expert witness Corson as to whether any agreement to bring prices to book price levels or other levels was effective, was excluded as calling for an opinion which the witnesses were not competent to give. Defendants were allowed to introduce exhibits designed to show that the periods of high prices for transformers were periods of high demand, scarcity of materials, heavy backlogs, high utilization of available capacity and rising costs; and that periods of price declines in transformers were characterized by declining demand, falling backlogs and the development of increased amounts of idle capacity.

Defendants also attempted to introduce evidence as to their costs, profits and losses on power transformers.

Defendants explained their basic purpose in offering such evidence as being an intention "to demonstrate to the jury that the prices plaintiffs argued should have prevailed prior to 1960 were prices that would have been substantially below defendants' costs of production during that period, with the result that defendants would have suffered tremendous losses had they sold transformers at these prices during the period 1946-1960. From this evidence, the jury could reasonably have found that the prices which plaintiffs argued should have prevailed during the period 1946-1960 could not have prevailed during that period." Defendants argued that if they had been permitted to present their cost testimony, they could have demonstrated that if the four defendants who sold power transformers and substations to Philadelphia Electric had sold them at the prices which Philadelphia Electric claimed in its testimony they should have paid, they would have suffered substantial losses on transactions with Philadelphia Electric: e.g.

Manufacturer	Period Covered	Loss
Allis-Chalmers	1955-1959	$1,766,000
General Electric	1951-1959	2,038,000

The court excluded this evidence. The court expressed the view that only "variable costs" had any validity and went on to rule that full costs could be admitted only if certain "underlying proofs" were first furnished by the defendants to plaintiffs' counsel. According to the court, "variable costs" meant "principally material and labor costs, as opposed to fixed costs, which would be more in the nature of overhead," and included "labor directly attributable to the manufacture of the transformer, material directly attributable to it, selling expenses directly attributable to that transaction, and any other variable costs that would not be in the nature of a fixed cost such as overhead."

The court explained during the course of the trial the reasons for the difficulty that it had in admitting cost and profits evidence that went beyond variable costs:

> " The difficulty that I have in my mind with this evidence of cost and profits is that they are both such fluctuating and malleable figures in the sense that as a perfectly proper legitimate corporate bookkeeping method certain things could be charged up to transformers. There may be a choice between charging them up to the transformer division or to the turbine division, or something of that sort, and it would be perfectly legitimate but it would give really a false picture as to what the cost and profits were. . . .
>
> . . . I think I gave you or somebody the example of the Reading Railroad that has its lines between Philadelphia and Bethlehem, and they could charge up all of the signal towers and all of the right of way to the Passenger Department and show a loss in the Passenger Department."

The "underlying data" or "underlying proofs" required from the defendants by the court's order were:

" 1. Proof of a corporate policy on the part of any defendant to discontinue the manufacture and sale of 'a substantial product' selling below the combination of fixed and variable costs.
2. Proof that the discontinuance of the manufacture and sale of any such product was directly caused by the loss on that product."

The court subsequently defined "a substantial product" as "products akin to the products with which we are dealing here [power transformers]. I am sure that I don't have enough knowledge to say precisely what they are. I don't mean toasters, I don't mean coffee pots or items like that, I mean heavy equipment such as this." Ultimately, the court defined "substantial products" as all items of heavy electrical equipment manufactured by any defendant, including, but not limited to, all indictment products.

The court explained the reasons for its requirement of "underlying proofs":

" As I see it the difficulty with the defendants' argument is that there has not yet in this case been presented sufficient underlying data to make evidence of cost and profit relevant at this time. I cannot take judicial notice of the fact that these or any of these defendants would discontinue the manufacture and sale of power transformers even in a loss situation, defining loss as a price received below the combination of fixed and variable costs.

We have been told, for example, although these facts are not actually in evidence as yet, that Wagner Electric has suffered a loss since at least 1959 and yet has continued the manufacture and sale of power transformers.

We have also been told that since 1959 Allis-Chalmers suffered a loss of 50 percent on all transformers sold to Philadelphia Electric Company but nevertheless continues to sell.

There are or can be many factors entering into the probative value of evidence of costs and profits. All of the defendants sell products other than those presently in issue on the price-fixing charges. Within this context of corporations with more than one product, is it an undoubted fact that such diversified corporations will stop selling one of its products if that product's sale price is below the combination of fixed and variable costs?

Certainly this nexus must be established as to what a corporation producing more than one product would do in the event that a specific product was being sold below its fixed and variable costs. Until this nexus is established, the admissibility of such cost data becomes questionable.

If the corporation has no alternative use for the facilities and if it can thereby recapture part of their fixed costs, a corporation may or may not continue the practice of selling below costs for the long run.

But here again, what is in this industry 'the long run'?

I do not know nor can I know whether it is at least the five years apparently envisaged by Wagner and Allis-Chalmers or whether it is ten years or fifteen years or twenty years. Again, this record in no way establishes any corporate policy on the part of any defendant to discontinue the manufacture and sale of a substantial product which it sells at a loss or at marginal profit.

In the absence of such evidence the proof of full cost and profits is totally devoid of probative value. Furthermore, even the discontinuance of a product is of no value unless the loss factor was the direct proximate cause of the discontinuance.

I can recognize that a given manufacturer may not sell below variable costs, for selling below variable costs would result in no recapture of any part of fixed costs and would result in a true loss on their product manufactured and sold at such level.

But here again, there is no proof of this as to these defendants, and the matter is not so certain that I can notice it judicially. Thus, absent the necessary underlying proofs, the relevance of the proffered proof is so speculative as to require its exclusion."

To meet the court's underlying proofs requirement, defendants offered to prove:

" a. the existence of corporate policy to discontinue the manufacture and sale of any product line selling below total cost where that condition continued beyond a reasonable period of time;

b. specific examples where product lines had actually been discontinued under these circumstances as a direct and proximate result of such losses;

c. that they would have discontinued the manufacture and sale of power transformers if price levels for power transformers during the period 1946-1960 had been as much below costs as the prices which plaintiffs said should have then prevailed."

Thereupon plaintiffs made an oral motion for the production of

" 1. profit and loss data on every department of each defendant broken down as to appropriate products over the period 1946 to date;

2. company instructions, memoranda, reports, executive committee minutes, board of director minutes and other documents of that kind which show what factors did enter into this or that decision [to discontinue a particular product line] and who the persons were who actually made the decision [to discontinue a particular product line] and what factors those persons took into account."

The court entered a production order along the lines demanded by the plaintiffs.

General Electric advised the court that it was unable to comply with the production order within the required two-day period, explaining its failure in a letter to the court from its counsel, stating:

" The second reason was that as the material began to be gathered to be furnished to Mr. Kohn this afternoon, the vastness of the quantity and the great variety of the nature of documents 'commenting upon, explaining or referring to' profits or losses in the whole gamut of heavy electrical equipment involving offices at plants stretching from Northern New England to Southern Alabama and from Philadelphia to California became more and more apparent. This was not only compounded but geometrically multiplied by the fact that the data was to cover all such references over a seventeen and a half year period, stretching from the end of World War II to presumably the date of the order, May 6, 1964. . . . In short, as we got into the problem we concluded that this would not be possible in two days' time."

Upon General Electric's failure to meet the two-day deadline, the court precluded all defendants from offering evidence of their costs, profits and losses. Additional testimony which the defendants wished to offer was refused by the court because the prospective witnesses had not been listed in the defendants' pretrial list of witnesses to be called; certain other witnesses were excluded because their names had not been furnished in answer to the plaintiffs' interrogatories as individuals having pricing authority; and certain testimony was excluded on the ground that it would be in conflict with previously filed answers to interrogatories. Certain cost reduction evidence (relating to the "black box") was excluded because of defendants' failure to answer interrogatories on the subject.

At the close of the defendants' case the court rendered its charge to the jury.[250] The court stressed that the jury is the sole judge of the facts, even as against the court's own comments:

> " If I should refer to the evidence, and I will, in a way that does not agree with your recollection, disregard what I say about the evidence, because again I am not the finder of the facts. You are the finders of the facts, so that if I should refer to the evidence in a way that you think is wrong, disregard it.
>
> During the course of the trial I asked certain questions of witnesses and made certain comments from time to time. You should attach no significance whatsoever to those comments or to those references or to those questions. Those comments or questions do not in any way indicate any belief that I may have and indeed, any belief that I might have, if I did have one, is unimportant and totally unimportant."

The court explained to the jury the false swearing principle:

> " Finally, there is one other thing on which I should charge you, and that is a legal principle, that if you find that any witness willfully swore falsely to a material fact, then you may disregard the entire testimony of that witness.
>
> Now, there are two important elements of what I have just told you. First of all, it must be a willful false swearing, not inadvertent or accidental, and secondly that you may, not must, disregard that witness's testimony."

and the principle that the acts and declarations of a conspirator are admissible against all co-conspirators:

> " Of course, there has been alleged here a conspiracy and if you find that a conspiracy did exist, then the acts and declarations of every other co-conspirator are admissible against a co-conspirator if they were done during the continuance of the conspiracy and in furtherance of it.
>
> In explanation of that, if you find that a conspiracy existed, then for example and for example alone, the acts of any employee of Westinghouse or Moloney, or of Allis-Chalmers, would be admissible against General Electric, Wagner and McGraw-Edison."

The court also explained the "missing witness" rule:

> " [I]f a witness was under the peculiar control of a party, that is in this case as an employee, and if he was not examined on a subject that would have been logically part of the claim or defense of the

---

250 Judge Lord's charge to the jury in the Philadelphia case appears (with deletions) in 1964 Trade Cases ¶71123 at ¶79435 (Civ. No. 30015, June 1, 1964, E.D. Pa.).

party who employed him, and if it is likely that the witness would have had knowledge on that subject, and if in addition to the failure to examine him on depositions he was not called, and he still remained an employee up until the time of the trial, if all of these are taken together, then you may draw the inference that that witness's testimony would have been unfavorable to the party in whose peculiar control he was."

The court explained the standard of proof in civil cases as distinguished from criminal proceedings:

" Now, you may have heard in connection with criminal cases, 'proof beyond a reasonable doubt.' That is not the standard that is employed in civil cases. It need not be proof beyond a reasonable doubt.

It need only be proof by a preponderance of the evidence, and by that we mean evidence of the greater convincing force. It is not necessarily the number of witnesses nor the number of exhibits, but rather the quality of the evidence which would lead you to conclude that the burden had been sustained by a preponderance of the evidence.

Perhaps the best way I can describe what we mean by a preponderance of the evidence is to give you a simple illustration. I am sure you are all familiar with the old-fashioned grocer's scales with two pans on it. When one pan tips, then that pan, that side preponderates. When the other side tips, then that side preponderates. If they remain equally balanced, then neither side preponderates.

It is up to the plaintiffs and it is the plaintiffs' burden simply to tip that scale in their favor. If the scale tips in favor of the defendants on any element of the plaintiffs' case, then the plaintiffs have not sustained their burden of proof and your verdict must be for the defendants.

If the scales remain equally balanced, the plaintiffs have not sustained their burden of proof and your verdict must be for the defendants. If, on the other hand, the scales tip ever so slightly in favor of the plaintiffs, then the plaintiffs have sustained their burden of proof and your verdict must be for the plaintiffs."

The court summarized the three requirements of proof by the plaintiffs if they were to recover:

" There are three essential elements which the plaintiffs must prove in order to establish their claims:

First, that there was a conspiracy among some or all of the defendants to fix the prices of transformers; namely, that they did conspire, that they did agree, that they did combine to fix, maintain or stabilize the prices of the electrical equipment here involved;

Secondly, that having so conspired, having so agreed, that they took action which affected the prices paid by the plaintiffs; that is, that the plaintiffs sustained injury to their business or property by reason of a higher price paid for transformers, brought about by a conspiracy and by the actions taken under the conspiracy;

Thirdly, the plaintiffs must prove to you that they sustained damages which are capable of computation on a rational basis from the evidence which is presented.

Now, the plaintiffs must prove each of these elements by a preponderance of the evidence as I have described it to you. If they do not prove each of these elements, then your verdict must be for the defendants. If, on the other hand, the plaintiffs have shown you each of these elements by a preponderance of the evidence, then your verdict must be for the plaintiffs."

In explaining to the jury the legal requirement that a "conspiracy" had to exist, the court stated:

" In determining whether a conspiracy existed mere similarity of conduct, mere association to discuss common aims and interests, if innocent, is not in itself evidence of a conspiracy. However, you would be entitled in this respect to consider the fact that at least certain of the employees of the defendants admitted that they knew that they were violating the law. It will be for you to say whether or not such an admission or such a statement would be consistent with a meeting whose purpose was wholly innocent.

You need find no formal agreement, no particular form of words to establish a conspiracy. It need not be in writing. It is enough that the defendants who are charged with conspiracy either positively or tacitly, that is impliedly, agreed to act in concert, agreed to act together in fixing prices or maintaining prices, or stabilizing prices at a certain level."

The court explained the purpose of the antitrust laws:

" In considering the charges that are made here or the complaints that are made here you should recognize that the antitrust laws are designed to preserve and foster our system of free competitive enterprise. They are designed to preserve the fullest competition in the marketplace, including competitions as to prices, and that any agreement which eliminates that form of competition is, per se, in itself a violation of the antitrust laws.

It does not matter that there may be business justification on the part of the defendants for so doing. It does not matter that the prices charged were reasonable. . . ."

In explaining the effect of the guilty pleas, the court repeated but elaborated somewhat on the instructions to the jury given during the course of the plaintiffs' case:

" Now, the defendants pleaded guilty to that indictment and I charge you that that plea of guilty is prima facie evidence that the defendants did at some time at least between 1956 and 1960 conspire to violate the Antitrust Act in respect to power transformers.

Prima facie evidence is that evidence which in and of itself is sufficient to establish the facts alleged. It may be rebutted by other evidence but it remains throughout the case and would be sufficient in itself without other evidence to prove the facts alleged in that indictment; namely, that the defendants did at some time at least between 1956 and 1960 conspire to violate the antitrust laws.

It is not evidence of the fact that the plaintiffs have been damaged. It is not evidence of the amount of any damage. It is not evidence that the conspiracy had any effect on prices. It is not evidence of any conspiracy before 1956. As to that, the plaintiffs will have to and do rely on other proof which they say is direct proof of the conspiracy, quite aside from the indictment.

. . . .

The plaintiffs have brought out evidence of meetings that began at least as early as 1946 at which prices [were] discussed. It will be for you to determine whether at those meetings prices were discussed and agreements were reached. If you so find, and there certainly is evidence of that fact, then the plaintiffs would have direct proof in addition to the prima facie effect of the plea of guilty for the years involved in that plea; namely, at least from 1956 to 1960.

As to that period the plaintiffs would have the prima facie effect of the plea and also direct proof of a conspiracy, if you so find. As to the products not involved in the guilty plea and as to the years before 1956, plaintiffs point to these continued meetings attended by various representatives of the defendants."

The court instructed the jury that General Electric's Policy 20.5 was no defense:

" You have heard some mention of General Electric's Policy 20.5, which was a policy against violation of the antitrust laws; that is to say, there was a policy that their employees would not violate the law. This is no defense. The mere fact that General Electric had a policy to that effect is no defense to General Electric if their employees did in fact violate the law, because there is no question here about the authority of those employees to act for and to bind General Electric by their actions."

The court also commented on the evidence that competitors' meetings had been suspended from time to time:

> " There is also some evidence that from some time in 1948 or '49, and I leave the date to you, until some time in 1950 there were no meetings. I leave it to you to determine whether that was an interruption of the conspiracy or whether the conspiracy simply continued but was hung in suspension without meetings."

The court enunciated the rule as to those who may have joined the conspiracy late:

> " There is also some evidence that some of the defendants were not in a conspiracy from 1946 on but joined it later. That is evidence as to Wagner, Moloney, and McGraw-Edison's predecessor, the Pennsylvania Transformer Company.
>
> There is also evidence to the contrary, that they were in from the beginning. I leave that to you, but I charge you that if they joined the conspiracy during the period of its existence, if one existed, with knowledge of the prior existence of the conspiracy and in order to promote the object for which it was organized, then they are equally liable for all of the acts of the other co-conspirators, if there was a conspiracy, and I also charge you that McGraw-Edison is liable for the acts of its predecessor, Pennsylvania Transformer Company, if Pennsylvania Transformer Company was a member of the conspiracy."

The court summarized the plaintiffs' impact and damage testimony:

> " Coming now to the proof of the effect of the conspiracy, which is the second element of the plaintiffs' proof, the plaintiffs have pointed to the industry price curve showing the trend of prices of power transformers from 1946 to 1962. This is the now famous or infamous, depending upon what side you take, I suppose, P-49, you will remember, the chart with the green line on it. I am certain that you will not forget P-49. I am certain I will not, at all events, and the plaintiffs point to that chart showing that the average post-indictment prices were less than the average prices or the price trend before 1959.
>
> The plaintiffs argue to you that you should infer, and you are free to do so, that this change in price is not purely coincidental, that the uncovering, they say, the plaintiffs, of the conspiracy, the Government investigation, the indictment, have brought about now

a free market untainted by a conspiracy and that these are the prices, and you can fairly look at them and say we are now in a free market and have been since 1960 for here are the prices, and they point to the prices before that happened and the plaintiffs argue that this shows that the conspiracy did in fact have an effect on prices. You would be free to make that inference if you so chose."

The court commented on the defendants' position:

" The defendants also point and argue vigorously that—and I think it is fair to say that the biggest factor in determining prices and in causing the changes in price levels was the law of supply and demand. You have heard evidence of the backlogs, capacity and utilization of that capacity.

The defendants say that these economic factors were what caused the variations in prices and not the cessation of the conspiracy, if it existed, and that the conspiracy, if it existed, did not have an effect on the prices but rather that it was the law of supply and demand.

The defendants say, I think to boil it down to its utmost simplicity, that in periods of high demand and low capacity prices will be high. In periods of low demand and high capacity the prices will tend to be lower. They have pointed out to you the evidence on this.

The plaintiffs, on the other hand, have pointed out to you periods where the demand was low and the capacity was high but nevertheless prices remained high, and vice versa, and the plaintiffs argue that you can really put no faith in the operation of a normal economic law in the face of an agreement to fix prices, and if you find that there was an agreement to fix prices you are also free to find that the normal operation of the laws of economics do not apply. On the other hand, you would be free to find to the contrary."

The court also commented on the defendants' cost reduction evidence:

" You have also heard evidence of cost reduction. The defendants argue that when a manufacturer can produce an article for less money, that is, at less cost to himself, that he can afford to sell that article for a lower price, and the cost reduction programs resulted in a lessening of the cost to the manufacturers with a consequent lowering of the price to the consumer.

The plaintiffs, on the other hand, point out that cost reduction programs had been going on for a long period of time. I think if I remember one of the things they point to is the fact that the breakthrough in silicon steel came in the 1930's. Well, that will be for you to consider and it will be for you also to determine whether the reduction in prices that apparently began somewhere around 1959 was a purely coincidental effect of the cost reduction program or rather whether the Government investigation and indictment were purely coincidental with any effect of the cost reduction programs."

The court explained the rules with respect to expert testimony:

" Now, I have mentioned Dr. Corson to you. This is as good a place as any to tell you about an expert witness. He properly qualified as an expert economist, and ordinarily a witness is not permitted to express an opinion because that would be invading the province of the jury. The expert witness is one exception, and he testified as to his opinion on the movement of prices and the reasons for that movement based on statistical studies, prices actually paid, and various negotiations.

However, you are not bound to accept his opinion. You have the right to use your own common sense, and if the opinion that he expressed does not agree with your opinion as derived from the evidence that you have heard here for the past two and a half months, then you are completely free to disregard the opinion expressed by Dr. Corson, or you are free to accept it."

The court instructed the jury that the plaintiffs were not required to show that the price as to each transaction had been conspiratorially fixed:

" I have told you that one of the elements of the plaintiffs' burden is to show by a preponderance of the evidence, having shown a conspiracy, if they have, that the conspiracy and its operation and the actions taken had an effect on the prices. The plaintiffs must show that as to each transaction for which they seek recovery; however, the plaintiffs need not show that the defendants sat down, met, conspired, and agreed on the price of each separate transaction. It would be enough for the plaintiffs to show that there was an all-pervasive conspiracy which affected all prices and thus necessarily affected the price of each transaction. If the plaintiffs have shown a conspiracy and if you find that it was such an all-pervasive conspiracy, then you may find that each transaction of which the plaintiffs complain was so affected."

The court also explained the situation where a combination of factors might be operating to determine prices:

" As to the effect of the conspiracy then, you may find that prices were affected and that the movement of prices was caused solely by economic factors separated from the conspiracy, and in which event you should award the plaintiffs no damages for that effect.

You may find that it was affected in part by the conspiracy and in part by economic factors, in which event the plaintiffs would be entitled to recover that portion of their damage which was the result of the conspiracy and not that portion of their damage which was the result of economic factors.

Finally, you may find that the movement of prices was the result of the conspiracy alone and in that event the plaintiffs would be entitled to recover the full amount by which prices were affected by the conspiracy."

In connection with the fraudulent concealment issue, the court told the jury that it could take into account the circumstance that Mr. Cordiner and investigators of General Electric had not discovered the conspiracy:

" On the other hand, the plaintiffs point out to you in connection with whether they could have discovered any collusive activity in the exercise of reasonable diligence that Mr. Cordiner could not find it out in the exercise of reasonable diligence in his own company and that investigations were conducted by General Electric and they could find and uncover no evidence of wrongdoing. You would be entitled to consider that in determining whether or not the plaintiffs could have discovered their cause of action in the exercise of reasonable diligence."

The court admonished the jury not to be influenced by the high claims for damages:

" Mr. Sawyer mentioned to you that 12,499,000 dollar bills laid end to end would bring you to a point 117 miles west of Sioux Falls, South Dakota, and he said to you that that is a lot of money, and it is a lot of mileage too, I suppose, and he is right. It is a lot of money, but if the plaintiff suffered that damage, if you so find, you would be doing less than your oaths required you to do if you did not bring in that sum."

The court referred to the circumstance that it could not cover in its charge of one hour and twenty-five minutes the entire testimony in the two and one-half months of the trial. The court urged upon the jury that those who might find themselves in a minority re-examine their opinion:

" Your verdict, of course, must be unanimous. I urge you to try to reach a verdict. I urge you to consider that if you find yourself in a minority to examine closely whether the majority might not be right. I urge you to listen carefully, conscientiously, and with an open mind and open ears to the arguments, the opinions, the reasoning of your fellow jurors.

No one could ask you, no one could ask any of you to give up a fixed principle simply for the sake of expediency, but we can and do ask you if you have such principles, examine them closely, examine into their validity. Don't adhere to them merely for the sake of adhering to a principle. Listen, as I say, to the persuasions, to the reasoning of your fellow jurors."

At the conclusion of the charge, the court expanded its comments, at the request of counsel for General Electric, on the defendants' theory of economic factors operating to determine prices:

" Mr. Sawyer says that I did not correctly state his theory on the economic factors, that I have limited it—or rather on the question of supply and demand. He says, and I believe I state it correctly, that there was a threefold interaction of supply, demand and backlog acting through cost reduction. Does that state it correctly, Mr. Sawyer?

MR. SAWYER: Yes, Your Honor. Thank you."

On one point the court did not instruct the jury—that if the verdict were for the plaintiffs, the damages found would be trebled under the provisions of Section 4 of the Clayton Act. Ordinarily in antitrust cases plaintiffs are anxious that the fact of trebling shall not be made known to the jury in anticipation that if it were so known, the jury might discount its verdict accordingly.[251]

---

251 There have been many decisions by trial courts on this subject, on both sides of the matter; but the only appellate court decision is Bordonaro Bros. Theatres v. Paramount Pictures, 203 F.2d 676 (2d Cir. 1953), where the court said: "The final two assignments of error are of perhaps more general interest. They concern the references by court and counsel to (a) the treble damages claimed and allowable under the statute. . . . It is to be noted that in its complaint plaintiff . . . pleaded the appropriate sections of the Sherman and Clayton Antitrust Acts, and specifically claimed the treble damages provided by statute. . . . Surely reference either to the pleadings or to the governing statute is so usual a course in jury trials as to occasion no comment. . . ."

After slightly more than ten hours of deliberation the jury returned a verdict for all three plaintiffs against all six defendants. Damages were awarded to Philadelphia Electric Company in the amount of $9,374,556; to Conowingo Power Company in the amount of $124,709; and to United Gas Improvement Company in the amount of $158,139. Judge Lord thereupon entered judgment for treble the damages found on the verdict—$28,123,670 for Philadelphia Electric, $374,127 for Conowingo and $474,419 for United Gas Improvement. The total amount of the judgment entered against the defendants aggregated $28,972,216.

Before dismissing the jury Judge Lord commented:

> " I have never in all of those years seen a jury like this one. Your verdict reflects it. It is an intelligent verdict. It is obvious that you did not give it scant consideration. You have our thanks . . . "

He also read the following note which was addressed to "His Honor, Judge Lord, lawyers and members of the court" and signed individually by all the jurors:

> " Dear Sirs: On the second day of June, 1964, after long, careful and prayerful deliberation we submit our verdict with the hope that we have done our task well. It was not easy and far above our poor power to add or detract.
>
> Kindly accept our sincere thanks for your many kindnesses to us through this long space of time."

As is customary in civil cases, following the entry of judgment, defendants moved for judgment notwithstanding the verdict (n.o.v.) or in the alternative for a new trial. In August 1964 they filed a brief in support of the motion.

In their brief, defendants maintained that plaintiffs had not submitted valid testimony on the measure of damages. According to defendants, plaintiffs' evidence as to the average of prices prevailing after the indictment of defendants in May 1960 was no evidence of the price that would have prevailed in the earlier fourteen and one-half year period unless plaintiffs established, which they did not do, that the economic forces affecting prices were the same in the two periods. Furthermore, said defendants, plaintiffs' theory of damages rested upon the proposition that the price of power transformers would have remained constant from 1946 through mid-1960, a period which included such varied market conditions as those that existed during the immediate post-World War II period, the recession of 1949-1950, the Korean War and the recession of 1957-1958. Defendants maintained that the use of average prices in plaintiffs' calculations was a grave error since a number of defendants' exhibits, the so-called "measles" charts, showed that prices in any given quarter varied widely above and below the average level for the quarter and varied widely from week to week within a quarter; a given purchase may have been made at as many as 20 or 30 index points or more above or below the quarterly average. Furthermore, defendants maintained that the plaintiffs themselves had been inconsistent in calculating the price for substations where plaintiffs adopted white sale prices rather than post-indictment prices; defendants maintained that if plaintiffs had relied upon the post-indictment level of prices for substations, the differences (and hence damages) on pre-1957 purchases would have been minimal and for most of the years, non-existent.

Defendants maintained that the "pristine simplicity" of the calculations and their arithmetical accuracy must have weighed heavily on the jurors' minds and that each step in plaintiffs' damage presentation had compounded the prejudice to defendants since the jury would be misled into an assumption of reliability on the figures themselves, whereas, in fact, there was no foundation for the calculations.

Defendants complained of the exclusion of their testimony relating to costs, profits and losses and stated that without that testimony the jury was left free to find that defendants would have sold power transformers below cost for the better part of fourteen and a half years, "an economically nonsensical, suicidal result that would have destroyed in short order the very competition which the statutes under which this action was brought attempt to foster." Defendants also complained of the exclusion of evidence relating to the values conferred on plaintiffs, defendants maintaining that a buyer is willing to buy at a higher price if he receives greater value for his money and that, therefore, evidence as to such design improvements which resulted in increased reliability, better service characteristics, lower noise level, lighter weight and lower load losses was relevant to assist the jury in determining what the price of transformers would have been in a competitive market.

Defendants maintained that the jury's approach to damages was simplicity itself, that the jury simply took plaintiffs' summarized claims of damages and discounted them by precisely 25%; in defendants' view, a 25% discount was no more supportable, predictable or rational than a 5% or 75% discount would have been. Defendants maintained:

> " The weight of the evidence was that virtually all of the significant price changes between 1946 and 1962 coincided with changes in economic conditions that would, in a free market, prompt those changes. For example, prices rose after World War II when price controls were abandoned, the utilities tried to catch up with the pent-up demand caused by a cessation of transformer production during the War, capacity was strained, costs went up, and critical materials were in short supply. Prices began to level and then declined slightly in 1949 and early 1950; however, the Korean War ensued, demand spurted, materials were allocated, capacity was fully utilized, delivery became a problem and prices rose. Demand slackened by 1954 and fell off sharply in late 1954, more capacity came on line through the Rome plant of General Electric and prices fell to the White Sale levels. Heavy buying during the White Sale filled the plants again, deliveries were strung out, Westinghouse had a long strike, and full production followed. Prices rose. But more capacity began appearing (first Terre Haute, then the Pittsfield modifications, then Muncie), demand again slackened, technological advances were made and prices fell. When demand failed thereafter to come up to expectations and something like forty per cent excess capacity continued to exist, prices stayed down." [252]

Defendants argued that the verdict and judgment were excessive. The trebled judgment, by their calculations, would mean that the plaintiffs were paying for the equipment sued upon only one-fourth of the agreed-upon purchase price and less than one-third of what it cost the manufacturers to build

---

[252] It was the observation of one public utility purchaser of electrical equipment that the price structure in the electrical equipment industry "was not responsive to recessions or similar phenomena in the national economy." SPORN NATIONAL DEPOSITION, Vol. 2, p. 3N1615.

the equipment. At the most, defendants argued, they should have been deprived of any profits, and the extraction of any further sum was claimed to be unconstitutional.

Defendants maintained that in treating the damages the jury's task was

> " to reconstruct what should have been the prevailing price for power transformers during the period 1946-1960 under normal competitive conditions. To do this the jury was required, in a sense, to place itself in the shoes of a marketing manager in a normal competitive market who was deciding at what price level he was going to sell his product. There can be no question but that an important criterion upon which a marketing manager would base such a decision would be the cost of production."

Defendants claimed that plaintiffs themselves had recognized the relevance of defendants' cost and profit data, since in the plaintiffs' first set of local interrogatories a number of questions sought information as to defendants' costs, profits and losses. Plaintiffs' counsel was quoted as saying during the course of an argument before Judge Kirkpatrick:

> " I think that is a very pertinent question, their annual profits during the period from the very products in which the conspiracy is charged. It goes to damages; it goes to a variety of things."

Defendants complained of the timing of the court's "variable costs" ruling entered just before defendants' counsel opened to the jury. Since the court had admonished the defendants that any claims they might make to the jury with respect to costs, if subsequently excluded by the court pursuant to its ruling, could be commented upon adversely by the plaintiffs, defendants claimed to have been effectively deprived of one of their most telling and important arguments to the jury in their opening addresses—that defendants' total costs substantially exceeded the prices which plaintiffs said should have been charged.

Defendants claimed that the court had committed error in its "underlying proofs" order. They maintained that the two days allowed to General Electric to comply with that order should be compared with National Pretrial Order No. 17 where defendants were given more than a month's time to assemble and produce what was in many ways less detailed profit and loss data, for a shorter period of time, and for three products only. The defendants other than General Electric also claimed that if a sanction were to be imposed, it should be against General Electric only because the other defendants were not the "disobedient" parties and were indeed ready to comply with the production order. Finally, the defendants claimed that plaintiffs' counsel took advantage of the situation in his closing address to the jury when he told the jury that the defendants had not followed up on their promises to show the jury their profits and to open up their books completely, and that the reason they had not done so was because they had refused to give plaintiffs complete and accurate information. In the defendants' view they were accordingly not only precluded from offering evidence which would have been damaging to plaintiffs but "they were damned in the eyes of the jury for not offering the very evidence which they were precluded from offering."

Defendants claimed that it was error for the court not to have granted their motion for a mistrial following the newspaper publicity on the hotel room incident involving the plaintiffs' counsel's papers. Among other objections to the publicity, the defendants maintained that they had been hurt by reference in the newspapers to General Electric's settlement with the federal government. Defendants also pointed to the circumstance that the newspaper articles had referred to the actions as treble damage actions as justification for their request that the court instruct the jury on this subject, and in this connection defendants argued:

> " The propensity of jurors to assume responsibilities not assigned to them by the trial judge is well known to every experienced judge and lawyer. The risks involved in failing to disclose the trebling feature to the jury are too prejudicial to the interests of the defendants to justify a ruling that reference thereto may not be made by counsel. Experience teaches that a little knowledge on a subject can be dangerous and produce unfair and unjust determinations, results and conclusions. The jury in this case should have had a full and perfect knowledge of all the provisions of the Act, under appropriate instructions from the Court, and it was reversible error to deny the defendants the right to have the jury so instructed."

With reference to fraudulent concealment, defendants maintained that plaintiffs' testimony should have been interpreted as indicating that defendants' employees, in falsifying expense accounts, communicating with each other at home rather than in the office, were simply attempting to hide their activities from house counsel and their employing companies; and that the concealment was not directed at the plaintiffs or at purchasers in general. Defendants quarreled with the plaintiffs' evidence and the court's instructions to the jury on the ground that plaintiffs were required actually to show due diligence and not simply to introduce evidence tending to demonstrate that they could not have discovered defendants' activities even if they had exercised due diligence.

Defendants maintained that since the individuals who had been indicted and pled guilty were not defendants in the present treble damage action, it was error for the court to permit plaintiffs to refer to the individual defendants as having been indicted and found guilty. On the admittance of grand jury testimony defendants claimed that even if it were proper to base such admission upon the exception to the hearsay rule for "past recollection recorded," one requirement for such an exception is that the recording take place soon after the events described, a condition not met by the grand jury testimony. Grand jury testimony was claimed by the defendants to be particularly prejudicial "in light of the fact that leading questions were asked during the grand jury hearings and there was no opportunity then to cross-examine the witness."

Defendants quarreled with the "missing witness" instruction on the ground that the doctrine is applicable only where a particular witness is peculiarly available to one party and is not available by subpoena or otherwise to the other party. Defendants argued that inasmuch as "the national discovery program provided a method by which any witness available to any of the defendants could be made equally available to the plaintiffs, the missing witness charge had no place in this case."

Defendants claimed that they were seriously prejudiced by an unreasonably speeded-up schedule for pretrial activity and by the setting of an early date for the trial itself:

" Defendants were naturally quite concerned with the impression their case made on the jury, as well as with the substance of the testimony. The continued difficulty of getting their witnesses on the stand, the continued objections of the plaintiffs because of the non-compliance with the witness list requirement and the general appearance of ineptitude (which plaintiffs invariably implied was not ineptitude but trickery on defendants' part) which was created by this constant wrangling seriously prejudiced the defendants before the jury. That prejudice was directly attributable to the time pressure which resulted in the incomplete witness list and other pretrial problems which led to exclusions at trial."

Plaintiffs filed a response to the defendants' brief in September 1964. On the point of the non-comparability of the post-indictment and pre-indictment periods, plaintiffs maintained that the leading case on measuring damages in antitrust cases, *Bigelow* v. *RKO Pictures, Inc.*,[253] upheld as one method of proving damage a comparison of periods when there was a conspiracy with periods when the conspiracy was no longer in effect. In response to defendants' contention that plaintiffs' calculations were simplistic, plaintiffs responded that they had presented all the essential material facts on damages to the jury, and it was not incumbent on the plaintiffs to offer expert testimony to interpret them.

In response to defendants' contention that plaintiffs had originally favored the introduction of cost and profit data, plaintiffs responded that defendants had likewise changed their position by originally opposing cost and profit data, plaintiffs quoting General Electric in a brief filed June 7, 1963 to the following effect:

" On any issue,—existence of a conspiracy, fact of damage, or damages, cost and profit information has rarely been deemed relevant. Even the issue of damages is not a function of profit or loss. The measure of damages in a price-fixing conspiracy case is the difference between what the plaintiff actually paid and what it would have paid absent the conspiracy. Amount of, or existence or absence of profit does not enter this formula.

The relationship between costs and profits and price rises is an exceedingly complicated economic question. So many considerations enter into the determination of price that it is impossible to say that because a particular defendant made a profit,

[253] 327 U.S. 251 (1946).

> there was a price conspiracy. Profits depend not only on the price of an individual item, but on its volume, the product mix sold by the seller, the seller's efficiency, its skill or management, or even on such fortuitous circumstances as whether its competitor has a strike in its plant. The price charged for an individual item is determined by what buyers are willing to pay and may be completely unrelated to the seller's cost of the product. . . ."

Plaintiffs maintained that the court's refusal to receive testimony on the subject of profit and loss was shown to be proper in the light of subsequent testimony of defendants' own economic expert, Dr. Corson, who had testified as to the three sole causes for price declines in 1955 and subsequently from 1957 to 1961:

> " . . . one, the decline in demand for power transformers. Secondly, the excess of capacity to produce power transformers, and thirdly, the buyers' and sellers' knowledge of what was going on in this market."

In response to the defendants' citation of the *Bordonaro Bros.* case as justifying the mention of trebling damages to the jury, plaintiffs pointed out that in that case the jury apparently did what is to be feared from such mention—namely, they divided the plaintiffs' actual damages by three.

In connection with the Hogg memorandum, plaintiffs pointed out that Hogg had not only questioned utility buyers but also had asked an employee of Westinghouse whether it was engaged in collusion and was told that it was not.

Before the defendants' motion for judgment n.o.v. or in the alternative for a new trial could be disposed of, the Philadelphia plaintiffs and defendants settled the case for a lump sum payment of $18,000,000. How this was divided among the individual defendants is not known, although there is an indication that the Philadelphia defendants (Moloney Electric Company excepted) entered into a sharing arrangement to share liabilities on the basis of their respective sales of products to the plaintiffs. As one antitrust defense lawyer has remarked:[254]

---

[254] O'Donnell, *Pretrial Discovery in Multiple Litigation From the Defendants' Standpoint*, 32 ANTITRUST LAW JOURNAL 133, 135 (1966).

" Although 'every person who participates in a conspiracy is liable for everything done during the period of its existence regardless of the exact time at which he became a member or the extent of his participation' (*Dextone Co.* v. *Building Trades Council,* 60 F.2d 47 (2d Cir. 1932)), defendants in multiple litigation frequently are able to work out an arrangement whereby each defendant assumes responsibility for its own sales and thus virtually eliminates the possibility of a defendant having to pay that part of any judgment founded upon a codefendant's sales."

CHAPTER 17

Other trials, other places

By THE MIDDLE OF 1964 four additional suits were well on their way toward trial: (1) *N W Electric Power Cooperative, Inc.* v. *Moloney Electric Co., et al.*, Civil Action No. 13290-3, in the Western District of Missouri before Judge William H. Becker, a jury trial involving power transformers with a rural electric cooperative as plaintiff against the six defendants named in the Philadelphia trial; (2) the *City of Burlington, Vermont* v. *Westinghouse Electric Corporation, et al.*, Civil Action No. 348-62, in the District of Columbia before Judge John J. Sirica, a jury trial involving one plaintiff's purchase of steam turbine generators; (3) *The City of San Antonio* v. *Westinghouse Electric Corporation, et al.*, Civil Action No. 3064, in the Western District of Texas before Judge Adrian A. Spears, a jury trial involving purchase by the City of San Antonio of steam turbine generators, with General Electric, Westinghouse and Allis-Chalmers as defendants; and (4) *Public Utility District No. 1 of Chelan County* v. *General Electric Company, et al.*, Civil Action No. 5271, in the Western District of Washington before Judge George H. Boldt, a bench (non-jury) trial involving power transformers.

Not quite ready but scheduled and proceeding toward trial was *Ohio Valley Electric Corp., et al.* v. *General Electric Company, et al.*, Civil Action No. 62 C 695, in the Southern District of New York, a bench trial before Judge Wilfred Feinberg involving steam turbine generators.

In advance of the trial of these and related cases, the Coordinating Committee had attempted to determine whether national guidelines for trial procedures could be laid down. As early as National Pretrial Order No. 13 (February 15, 1963) plaintiffs and defendants had been asked to submit "their suggestions and proposals on the separation of issues for the purpose of trial, including, but not by way of limitation, the separation of the issue of liability from the determination of damage."

The trial judges themselves raised questions whether all cases in a given district in the same product line ought not to be consolidated for trial. Judge Robson, in the Northern District of Illinois, requested plaintiffs to submit a memorandum on this subject. In response, counsel for the Commonwealth Edison group proposed (prior to the settlement of their turbine cases) that three turbine generator cases be consolidated, thereby disposing of ten plaintiffs' claims and about 70% of the total dollar amount of turbine generator purchases by plaintiffs in that District: counsel asserted that if more cases were consolidated, the case to be tried would become unduly burdensome and there would be introduced complicated issues common only to a few cases.

The trial judges also expressed views on the utilization of a special master. Judge Sirica in the District of Columbia announced his decision not to have a special master supervise the conduct of local discovery. In the Northern District of Illinois Judge Robson tentatively indicated that if plaintiffs were going to use, as part of their theory of damages, purchases by utilities outside that District, and if defendants requested additional discovery as to such purchases, Judge Robson might appoint a master to travel around the country and take such depositions.

In the Southern District of New York the Atlantic City plaintiffs proposed a single consolidated trial of all turbine generator cases in that District, arguing that the issues of law and fact were common and that by means of a consolidated trial the questions of violation, general impact and the proper measure of damages could be authoritatively settled with the judgment binding on all parties. Thereafter, it was suggested, the remaining questions of specific dollar computation of damages and the defenses peculiar to particular plaintiffs could be tried separately, either in separate trials or by reference to masters. The Atlantic City plaintiffs rejected a suggestion that an initial trial of one company's purchases might serve as a test case, the results of which might be accepted by all parties. The plaintiffs argued that this suggestion was not realistic because neither the plaintiffs nor the defendants would be likely to accept an unfavorable result in the trial of a single plaintiff's claims, and the verdict could not be made legally binding.[255]

Some consideration had been given to the question whether there could or should be a national trial, but at the San Antonio hearing and meeting of the Coordinating Committee on February 6-7, 1963, it was made clear that a national trial was not contemplated and that each District would have its own trial and would set up its own trial ground rules.

The Coordinating Committee attempted, on a national basis, to bring the factual issues in the cases into manageable form. Accordingly it required, in National Pretrial Order No. 13, that plaintiffs and defendants file a statement of "the relevant factual areas which at this time are uncontroverted" and to file "a statement of the remaining factual areas which they consider to be the proper subject of a stipulation or agreed statement of fact proposing the time, manner and means by which such agreed statement should be consummated." Plaintiffs and defendants also were to file the traditional type of pretrial memorandum setting out "(1) the factual issues and (2) the legal issues which they deem to be involved in these cases." The order also required the parties to submit "proposals concerning the manner and means for use of the depositions on oral interrogatories and the documents which may be offered in evidence at trial with a view toward organizing this material, reducing its volume and presenting it in a useful form at trial and for use in pretrial proceedings, including, but not by way of limitation, proposals for agreeing upon narrative summary of depositions on oral interrogatories."

In the Western District of Missouri, Judge Becker was concerned to find a technique which would alleviate the problem raised by National Pretrial Order No. 13 of bringing the amounts

---

255 Memorandum on the Nature of the Steam Turbine Generator Trial, January 24, 1964, filed in Atlantic City Electric Co., et al., plaintiffs v. General Electric Company, et al., defendants, United States District Court, Southern District of New York, 61 Civ. 4258, and related cases.

of material into manageable form and reducing the factual issues to a minimum.

Early in 1964, Judge Becker rejected plaintiffs' pretrial brief which had been patterned on the brief filed by plaintiffs in Philadelphia. He stated that the kind of brief he wanted would be a detailed statement of plaintiffs' fact allegations with each sentence numbered so that the defendants could and would be required to confirm or deny each statement. He held to his determination and eventually a pretrial brief of the kind that he had outlined, which has come to be known in antitrust circles as a "Becker Brief" was filed.

Counsel for Allis-Chalmers indicated to Judge Becker that he was without authority and did not intend to answer or admit the detailed allegations in plaintiffs' pretrial brief; he stated that such admissions would be tantamount to an admission of liability. Judge Becker's response was that if the truth means liability, then the time has come to stipulate liability and added that if Allis-Chalmers did not answer plaintiffs' pretrial brief he would enter a default judgment against Allis-Chalmers.

Then, using the Becker Brief as a base, Judge Becker required the parties to draft, comment upon and finally agree upon a sixty-nine-page document entitled "Pretrial Report for Use of Jurors, Counsel and Court." The document recited at some length details concerning conspiratorial meetings and other evidentiary matters. It was read to the jury at the outset of the trial.[256]

---

256 In a later trial in Seattle (Grant County PUD), Judge Boldt read to the jury the stipulated facts in the case which had been embodied in a final pretrial order. In this trial, involving ten hydroelectric generators, a movie was shown to the jury explaining the various parts of a hydro-generator. In the Northern District of Illinois, plaintiffs Commonwealth Edison and the City of Chicago filed a pretrial brief dealing with the steam turbine generator cases. The brief, in traditional fashion, described the product, the conspiracy and the damages suffered by plaintiffs because of the conspiracy. A number of proposed jury instructions also were set forth. The appendix contained a summary of the pleadings; a list of main conspiracies; competitors' meetings; the units discussed by two or more competitors; and an index of deposition witnesses. These Illinois cases were settled before trial.

An issue that loomed large in a number of post-Philadelphia trials, as it had in Philadelphia, was the admissibility of evidence on defendants' costs, profits and losses. In Missouri Judge Becker drafted and filed a "Draft Memorandum on Admissibility of Evidence of Actual Costs During and After Period of Conspiracy." The memorandum recited that each defendant was proposing to offer evidence of its actual costs to show:

> " (1) that if it had sold at the prices claimed by the plaintiff (to be prices which would have prevailed in the absence of a conspiracy), defendants would have sustained losses or earned profits inadequate to remain in business. The actual cost experience evidence is also offered for use as one of the bases for expert testimony of the defendants' expert, who proposes to testify that the market level in the absence of a conspiracy would have been no lower than the level of actual prices charged to the plaintiffs and to others."

Judge Becker stated that the court had at least three alternatives:

> " *First,* the Court can admit the actual costs (incurred during the conspiracy) upon the theory that the jury can, without the aid of expert testimony on the subject, determine whether the actual costs are the costs which would have been incurred in the absence of a conspiracy, and consider only those costs which they find would have been incurred in the absence of a conspiracy.
>
> *Second,* the Court can assume that the actual costs are tainted by the conspiracy and reject the evidence unconditionally.
>
> *Third,* the Court may assume that the actual costs may or may not have been tainted by the conspiracy. The Court may take notice of elementary economic authorities, and reason therefrom that the actual costs may be affected by the conspiracy. It may also assume that in this particular case there may be substantial expert opinion based upon a recognized authority or authorities, that the particular costs in question were not tainted or affected by the conspiracy. Then the Court may rule that the actual costs are admissible only if they are shown to have been no higher than the costs which would have been incurred in the absence of the conspiracy."

The court proposed to follow the third alternative, and accordingly ruled that before there could be any admission of evidence of actual costs, defendants would have to submit the opinion of a qualified expert, supported by substantial economic authority, that the actual costs were no higher than the costs which would have been incurred in the absence of a conspiracy. Even with such an expert opinion the court still reserved on the question whether evidence of actual costs is of relevant significance or conjectural or has too remote a connection with the issues of the case.

Judge Becker indicated that a number of questions which he had not considered in the memorandum would bear upon the issue of admissibility:

> " This draft memorandum does not undertake to discuss the propriety of requiring a division of the costs into direct and indirect costs (fixed or variable); does not undertake to discuss the cost accounting problems involved; does not undertake to discuss the requirements to be satisfied in authenticating the data and cost accounting methods involved; does not undertake to discuss whether admission of general overhead costs in a multi-product industry should be denied on the grounds that unmanageable collateral inquiries into the effect of other conspiracies and into complicated cost records of other products would be confusing and impractical; does not undertake to discuss the propriety of rejection of this evidence by a preclusion order for failure to make discovery; and does not undertake to discuss whether the evidence of costs of some suppliers should be rejected because of the absence of evidence of costs from substantially all of the suppliers who would have been in the market in the absence of conspiracy."

In explaining the court's doubts whether costs during a conspiracy had validity, the court quoted Judge Learned Hand in *United States* v. *Aluminum Co. of America*:[257]

> " Many people believe that possession of unchallenged economic power deadens initiative, discourages thrift and depresses energy; that immunity from competition is a narcotic, and rivalry is a stimulant, to industrial progress; that the spur of constant stress is necessary to counteract an inevitable disposition to let well enough alone. Such people believe that competitors, versed in the craft as no consumer can be, will be quick to detect opportunities for saving and new shifts in production, and be eager to profit by them. . . ."

In working out the ground rules for the Kansas City trial, Judge Becker ruled that if defendants in their opening to the jury were going to refer to costs, they should conform to Judge

---

[257] 148 F.2d 416, 427 (2d Cir. 1945).

Lord's ruling in Philadelphia and distinguish between fixed and variable costs. He also stated that it was his tentative ruling that plaintiffs would be entitled to cross-examine on the effect of the other nineteen conspiracies if there were no showing that the costs in question were not affected by the conspiracies.

Prior to the settlement of the turbine cases in Chicago, defendant manufacturers took an approach in those cases different from the cost and profits argument. They indicated that they expected to prove that the prices, terms and conditions of sale of the turbines in suit in Chicago had been affected by plaintiffs' own actions:

a. The size, knowledge of the market and competitive strength of turbine buyers conditioned competition and, in turn, prices, terms and conditions of sale.

b. Turbine buyers also influenced prices and terms and conditions of sale by actions such as:

1. restricting the number of bidders;
2. dividing business among manufacturers;
3. preferring manufacturers for reasons other than price or quality;
4. writing specifications to exclude certain manufacturers;
5. purchasing electrical equipment in package deals;
6. awarding letters of intent without soliciting competitive proposals;
7. requesting uniform terms and conditions of sales; and
8. discussions and contacts with other buyers.[258]

On the question of mentioning to the jury that any damages the jury awarded in its verdict would be trebled by the court, the trial judges reached varying answers. In Missouri, Judge Becker ruled that the jury would be told that the suit was a treble damage action. In the District of Columbia, Judge Sirica ruled that trebling of damages was not to be mentioned in the opening statements and ultimately ruled that he would give no

---

258 Commonwealth Edison Co., et al. v. Allis-Chalmers Mfg. Co., et al., No. 61 C 1284, U. S. District Court for the Northern District of Illinois, Eastern Div., Defendants' Supplemental Memorandum Relating to the Further Definition of Factual and Legal Issues for Trial, dated April 24, 1964.

instruction that mentioned treble damages. In San Antonio, Judge Spears instructed the jury, at the time of its selection, that damages would be trebled, but the instruction was coupled with a strong admonition that this was actually none of the jury's business since its only function was to decide actual damages. In Seattle, Judge Boldt ruled that there should be no mention of trebling in opening statements or in interrogation of witnesses without permission from the court; and he added that he believed that an instruction on the subject should be given, phrased in such a way that the jury would not be concerned about the matter in its own fact finding.

On the matter of handling the guilty pleas and the criminal convictions, in the District of Columbia Judge Sirica accepted an instruction agreed upon by plaintiffs and defendants which omitted any reference to the guilty pleas as being prima facie evidence but did consider them as admissions against interest. In Missouri, Judge Becker recalled to the jury that in the "Pretrial Report" the defendants had admitted a conspiracy in the years 1951 to 1959 and had denied a conspiracy prior to 1951.

In the District of Columbia, Judge Sirica laid down ground rules for trial which were more or less typical of all. Document authenticity was presumed unless counsel questioning the authenticity made his point within a short period of time. Each side was to have a single spokesman. Grand jury testimony was allowed in to test credibility, an example of which was given by plaintiffs in a memorandum in which they indicated their intention to utilize testimony from the recall deposition of Whitescarver, an employee of General Electric in its turbine-generator division:

" Q. Mr. Whitescarver, did you attend a competitor's meeting of which there was a discussion of a turbine job for the City of Jacksonville, Florida?
A. I have no recollection.

MR. HANDLER: With the Court's permission, I will ask the witness to read Pages 124 to 126 of the minutes of his grand jury testimony.

(Witness reads.) . . .

THE WITNESS: I have read it.

Q. Having read Pages 124 to 126 of the transcript of your testimony before the grand jury, does that refresh your recollection

that you attended a competitor's meeting at which there was a discussion of a job for the City of Jacksonville?
A. According to that record, I stated at the grand jury that I did. I did not recall that until I was shown this. If I testified to that extent, which I obviously did, that must be the case."

In San Antonio, Judge Spears allowed portions of the testimony of Paxton before the Kefauver Committee to be read to the jury.

In Missouri, Judge Becker took care to assure an efficient selection of a jury. In advance of the trial, the court sent out a questionnaire to each of the 125 jurors to be impanelled, the questionnaire including some general *voir dire* questions: copies of the answers were then made available to counsel prior to their examination of the jurors. The judge also instructed counsel that no private detectives or other methods of investigation of the jurors or their backgrounds were to be used, and the attorneys were to grant no newspaper interviews.

In Missouri an attempt was made to sever from the trial defendants from whom plaintiff had made no purchases or minimal purchases. Plaintiffs and the two large defendants, General Electric and Westinghouse, objected and the severance was denied.

In Missouri, following Judge Becker's instructions to the jury, he commented on the evidence. He discounted any application of the statute of limitations and expressed his belief that fraudulent concealment had been proven. He also stated his belief that the conspiracy had existed prior to 1946. Further, he expressed a belief that defendants' figure on damages was too small and that the plaintiffs' estimate was too large.

The methods for computing damages in the various cases differed. In the District of Columbia, a turbine generator action, plaintiffs worked out an average order price per kilowatt for turbine generators during the post-indictment period of July 1, 1960 through December 31, 1963, in the size range for the turbines in suit (7,500 to 15,000 kilowatts). In estimating what the competitive kilowatt price would have been on the purchase dates for the turbines in suit, the plaintiff deflated the post-conspiracy price by means of a composite materials and labor cost index. By computing the ratio of prices at the respective order dates of plaintiff's five units to the average prices in the post-conspiracy period, and then applying this ratio to the average price per kilowatt in the post-conspiracy period, plaintiff determined what the estimated competitive price per kilowatt would have been at the order dates. With respect to a portion of their damage claim, plaintiff submitted an alternative theory. Under this approach, the plaintiff, City of Burlington, claimed that the handbook price increases by General Electric on December 12, 1951 and March 30, 1953 were the result of a conspiracy and accordingly had been illegally and collusively made and put into effect. Since plaintiff had paid the amount of $98,515 for these two increases under its escalation clause, it claimed this amount as obviously representing partial damages.

An alternative method of computing damages for turbine generators was presented by Consumers Power Company in a brief presented in the Southern District of New York.[259] Consumers planned to use as one benchmark the average price at which comparable steam turbine generators were sold in the years 1962 and 1963. This average price was assumed to be a non-conspiratorial price reflecting the various natural and competitive forces present in a free market over a substantial period of time. In order to have a beginning point for the period in suit, Consumers planned to compute the average price at which comparable steam turbine generators were sold in 1948, thereby assuming that prices charged in 1948 were competitive even though the evidence showed that they were not. Then, to calculate the level of prices which would have existed between 1948 and 1963 in the absence of a conspiracy, Consumers planned to join the benchmarks with a straight line. Conceding that it was unlikely that prices would move over a straight line during a period of fifteen years, Consumers argued:

" It is not possible, however, to state at a given moment whether any fluctuation would have been up or down or to estimate the

[259] Brief of Plaintiff Consumers Power Company Pursuant to Paragraph 3 of Local Pretrial Order No. 11, United States District Court, Southern District of New York, Consumers Power Company, plaintiff v. Allis-Chalmers Manufacturing Company, General Electric Company, Westinghouse Electric Corporation, defendants, 62 Civ. 4285. The Consumers Power case was settled before trial.

magnitude of the increase or decrease. The reason for this impossibility, of course, is that the conspiracy prevented the market from finding its natural level. In the absence of specific knowledge, we believe that a straight line is most likely to average the fluctuations which would have taken place."

In none of the cases on trial was an attempt made to separate the issues of liability and damages. In Seattle there had been preliminary discussion between counsel and the court on the advisability of appointing a master for the determination of the damage issues. In a later case involving hydroelectric generators purchased by the Grant County Public Utility District, a special master was utilized to ascertain facts which bore on the subject of damages.

In each of the trials the outcome was highly favorable to the plaintiffs. In Kansas City, after one hour's deliberation, the jury, on December 15, 1964, returned a verdict of $688,581 which was then trebled to $2,065,743. In the District of Columbia, after one day's deliberation, the jury entered a verdict on December 16, 1964, for $168,000 on purchases of $1,086,000, trebled to $504,000. The plaintiff's request had been for $279,000 single damages. In San Antonio, settlement was reached on December 17, 1964, the ninety-ninth day of trial, before the case went to the jury, with a lump sum of $2,650,000 (including costs and attorney's fees).

In Seattle the plaintiffs won on summary judgment after General Electric had submitted a statement that it would not contest that it had violated the antitrust laws or that there had been price discussions in 1957 prior to the award of bids for the Chelan Generating Station and that minimum bids and prices had been discussed and agreed upon at those meetings. General Electric did deny that the meetings had any effect on the price of the power transformers at issue. Judge Boldt found that the only remaining issues were impact and damages, and after a bench trial, judgment was entered on November 24, 1964, for $1,275,000 against General Electric.

The suit of Ohio Valley Electric Corporation (OVEC) against General Electric and Westinghouse, a non-jury trial before Judge Feinberg in the Southern District of New York, commenced on

February 16, 1965 and ended approximately two months later. Thirty-five trial days were utilized, plus an adjournment of five trial days to allow the court to read approximately 2,100 pages of national deposition testimony. Since the trial was a bench trial, the Philadelphia technique of reading the deposition material in open court was deemed unnecessary.

Eleven steam turbine generators had been purchased in 1952 by plaintiffs OVEC and Indiana-Kentucky Electric Corporation (IKEC) at prices that were admittedly the result of hard bargaining by the principal executive officer of the plaintiffs, Philip Sporn. The bargaining was so effective that the data developed in preparation for trial indicated that plaintiffs had paid less for the turbines than the average price of comparable turbines in the post-indictment year of 1962.

Plaintiffs were therefore confronted with the problem of establishing damages. To meet the issue, they determined to demonstrate that the conspiracy in turbine generators was a conspiracy not to establish a dollar level of order prices or of book prices, but was a conspiracy to assure that the discount off book would be as minimal as possible. Plaintiffs reasoned that if this could be established as the object of the conspiracy, they could then base their damage claim by taking the percentage representing discount off book which existed in the post-indictment period, apply that percentage to the book prices for turbines in 1952 and arrive at the price that would have been charged in 1952 had there been no conspiracy.

The evidence at the trial showed by stipulation that the General Electric units were purchased in 1952 at 11.1% discount off then existing book and the Westinghouse units at 11.97% discount off book. Plaintiffs used a witness, not an economics expert, to present data showing that the post-conspiracy non-conspiratorial discount off book (as existing from 1961 to 1963) averaged 25.33%. The difference between these two ranges of discounts, approximating 14%, was applied to book prices for turbines existing in 1952 and resulted in an amount of $8,167,773 claimed as damages.

The court had no difficulty, on the basis of the national deposition testimony, in finding that the purpose of the competitors' meeting was "to stabilize prices as close as feasible to the published book price." [260] The court cited as an example the testimony of witnesses representing all three manufacturers of turbines—Jenkins of Westinghouse:

> " That was what I went to every meeting for . . . to try to bring order prices closer to book prices. I tried to sell turbines the best I could."

And Peters of General Electric:

> " Q. [I]n substance, in principle, your objective was to keep order prices as close to book prices as you could?
> A. That's true.
>
> Q. That was Westinghouse's position also?
> A. What do you mean that was Westinghouse's position?
>
> Q. That you should quote your order prices as close to book prices as possible.
> A. Yes, we all believed that we should quote as close to book.
>
> THE COURT: That idea was discussed and expressed at your meeting?
> THE WITNESS: That's correct."

And McMullen of Allis-Chalmers:

> " Q. Wasn't your purpose in participating in these competitors' meetings to stabilize prices and to try to get market prices up to book?
> A. I would say that practically all of the meetings that I ever attended, so-called competitors' meetings, were along those lines."

The defendants argued that the very circumstance that there were negotiations leading up to the transactions refuted the existence of conspiracy relating to the turbines in suit. They argued that if there had been an effective conspiracy, Sporn, despite his skill as a negotiator, would not have been able to obtain price concessions by playing one company off against the other. The court answered this contention:

> " However, Sporn's ability to obtain concessions off a list price is in no way inconsistent with a conclusion that the list prices were conspiratorially established. . . . The spirit of *United States* v.

---

[260] Ohio Valley Electric Corp., et al. v. General Electric Co., et al., 244 F. Supp. 914, 928 (S.D. N.Y. 1965).

Socony-Vacuum Oil Co., 310 U.S. 150, 222 60 S. Ct. 811, 844, 84 L.Ed. 1129 (1940) is in accord, for, as the Supreme Court stated, 'prices are fixed . . . if the range within which . . . sales will be made is agreed upon. . . .' "

On the issue of fraudulent concealment there were no factual disputes. In the pretrial national deposition of Sporn defendants had made several passes in an attempt to determine whether he had knowledge of the price fixing activities of the manufacturers:

" Q. Do you recall whether you told Mr. Neblett [of General Electric] in the course of these negotiations that he ought to talk to Westinghouse and tell them that they were very foolish in holding out for five turbines when you were giving them an offer for four against your past practice and your better judgment?
A. I recall no such thing and I am quite sure I never said it, and I can't imagine my saying it then or at any other time. I just wasn't in the habit of using intermediaries, particularly the intermediary aid of a competitor, to talk to a manufacturer with whom we were negotiating. I didn't operate on that basis."

And again, a little later:

" Q. Do you recall whether at either of these meetings you made the inquiry as to whether the price that General Electric was quoting was the NEMA price and asked whether you would get your 10 per cent off of that price?
A. Well, I am sure that I never referred to the NEMA price because I discovered the NEMA price for the first time in reading this testimony and it struck no responsive chord in my memory, and my memory is at least roughly as good as the average, and it is not too bad. I don't recall any such thing and I don't recall ever discussing NEMA prices with anyone, either at General Electric or with any other manufacturer of circuit breakers, or manufacturer of anything else, for that matter." [261]

At the trial it was the defendants who objected when plaintiffs attempted to question Sporn on his knowledge of the manufacturers' meetings. The objection was sustained, the court ruling that defendants would likewise be precluded from going

---

261 Although the questioner did not explain, the implication was that a "NEMA" price was a price agreed upon by manufacturers during the course of a NEMA (National Electric Manufacturers Association) meeting.

into the subject on cross-examination. The defendants stated at that point that their position was that they denied there was a conspiracy, and they therefore did not propose to assert as a defense that the witness Sporn knew of a non-existent conspiracy. They did propose to contest whether there was fraudulent concealment, but in this respect their argument was that the acts of fraudulent concealment must have been related to or directed to the plaintiffs. The court rejected this argument:

> " In some of the cases cited by defendants, there is language that something akin to direct misrepresentation to a plaintiff is necessary to toll the statute, and it may be that defendants are urging that position as well. However, such restrictive interpretations of the doctrine of fraudulent concealment are hardly required by the cases, and negate the policy behind the doctrine."

On the issues of impact and damages the court took the position that the two issues were essentially the same in a price fixing case:

> " [T]he question is to what extent, if any, has a purchaser paid more for a product than he would have paid had there been no conspiracy.
>
> . . . In other words, in a price fixing case, impact and damages are coextensive; the overcharge constitutes the plaintiff's injury (impact) as well as the measure of his damage (damages) and is the difference between the price actually paid and the price he would have paid absent the conspiracy."

Furthermore, the court sustained plaintiffs' contention that their burden on damages was not to prove the extent of a monetary loss to a certainty but only "to introduce evidence permitting the trier of fact to estimate the damages as a matter of just and reasonable inference." The court cited two decisions of the United States Supreme Court: in one, *Story Parchment Co.* v. *Paterson Parchment Paper Co.*, 282 U.S. 555 (1931), the Supreme Court stated:

> " In such a case, while the damages may not be determined by mere speculation or guess, it will be enough if the evidence show the extent of the damages as a matter of just and reasonable inference, although the result be only approximate. The wrongdoer is not entitled to complain that they cannot be measured with the exactness and precision that would be possible if the case, which he alone is responsible for making, were otherwise.

> . . . And the adoption of any arbitrary rule in such a case, which will relieve the wrongdoer from any part of the damages, and throw the loss upon the injured party, would be little less than legalized robbery."

And in *Bigelow* v. *RKO Radio Pictures, Inc.*, 327 U.S. 251 (1946), the Supreme Court elaborated on the rule:

> " In such a case, even where the defendant by his own wrong has prevented a more precise computation, the jury may not render a verdict based on speculation or guesswork. But the jury may make a just and reasonable estimate of the damage based on relevant data, and render its verdict accordingly. In such circumstances 'juries are allowed to act upon probable and inferential, as well as direct and positive proof,' . . . Any other rule would enable the wrongdoer to profit by his wrongdoing at the expense of his victim. It would be an inducement to make wrongdoing so effective and complete in every case as to preclude any recovery, by rendering the measure of damages uncertain. Failure to apply it would mean that the more grievous the wrong done, the less likelihood there would be of a recovery."

Defendants made a number of arguments against the plaintiffs' "discount off book" damage theory. They argued that the relationship of order price to book, or discount off book, was meaningless as a means of reconstructing an assumed competitive price. They asserted that sales of turbines were made in the trade not in terms of discount off book but with reference to dollars charged per kilowatt. But plaintiffs responded that one of General Electric's pricing personnel had stated of discount off book: "That is how we sold most jobs. They were negotiated that way." [262]

The defendants also urged that it was meaningless to compare discounts off book in periods when different levels of book price prevailed, as was the case between 1952, on the one hand, and 1961-1963 on the other. Their economic expert, Dr. M. A. Adelman, stated that a comparison between discounts off book in different periods is "useless" as a measure of price change. Adelman said, in reference to a comparison of discounts, "It would be just like the drunk who lost his wallet across the street on the dark side but comes over to look for it under the lamp

---

[262] Ohio Valley Electric Corp., et al., supra, note 260, at 938.

on this side." In further explanation of his position Dr. Adelman, in response to questions from Judge Feinberg, maintained that unless price is set at one level, as in the oil tanker business where all bargaining is centered around percentages off the one set level, differences in discount are merely numbers which do not permit you to ascertain whether prices are moving up or down.

Furthermore, defendants argued that plaintiffs' comparison of the two periods was objectionable because different economic forces were at work in each period. According to defendants the post-indictment period of 1961-1963 was marked by "the presence of effective foreign competition for the first time, an increase in the manufacturers' capacity to produce steam turbine generators which caused an oversupply, a lessening of ordinary growth in demand, and a drop in manufacturing cost which allowed defendants to offer their products at a lower price." But plaintiffs argued that the difference between discounts off book in the pre-1959 period and the much larger discounts in the years immediately after was explained simply by the termination of the conspiracy.

The court ruled with the plaintiffs, finding that there was factual and economic validity for the use of a discount off book theory to prove damages and that there was ample legal precedent for proving damage by comparing economic conditions during a conspiratorial period with those before or after.

The court gave scant attention to the argument that plaintiffs were not damaged because prices were higher in the post-conspiracy period than they were in 1952:

> " It is true that actual turbine generator prices in plaintiffs' post-conspiratorial reference period were appreciably higher than when plaintiffs bought in 1952. But it hardly follows from this observation that prices in 1952 would not have been lower with full competition. A decade had intervened with many economic forces at work, increased costs of labor and materials not the least among them. The real issue is not whether the units purchased by plaintiffs would have cost more in 1962; it is whether they should have cost less in 1952."

For the defendants Dr. Adelman had reconstructed a competitive price for the period of 1952 and came out at a figure which, if accepted, would show that plaintiffs were not overcharged in the 1952 order price but actually received a substantial bargain. But Dr. Adelman's use of actual costs in 1952 as a method of reconstructing the 1952 price was rejected on the same ground that had bothered other courts with respect to cost data—that is, that costs in a conspiracy period were unreliable because, to quote Judge Feinberg in the OVEC case, "collusion inhibits the usual competitive desire to lower costs in order to increase profit." The court quoted a General Electric document that had been deposited in the National Depository which stated of the years in question that "manufacturers raised prices instead of improving productivity to recover their own cost increases."

The second fault that the court found in Dr. Adelman's reconstruction was an adjustment that he had made based upon the degree of utilization of capacity:

> " . . . on the premise that a high percentage of capacity produces an increase in incremental cost and, therefore, of prices, as compared to a low utilization of capacity."

The relevance of utilization of capacity, according to Dr. Adelman, is that when a facility is being worked at a high percentage of capacity, incremental costs are high and there is upward pressure on prices. The converse is also true. Incremental costs were defined by the witness as being what it takes to produce a given addition to an output or what would be saved by a given contraction of output and is essentially that which ties demand and supply together. Dr. Adelman stated that backlog figures are an excellent predictor of industry percent utilization of capacity two years later. Adelman would not agree with plaintiffs' counsel's assertion that since the defendants allowed customers to buy at the existing price for a period after a new price increase, a situation was created in effect whereby price increases affected backlog rather than backlog affecting prices.[263]

Plaintiffs made no attempt on their own to introduce cost and profit data despite the circumstance that there were indi-

---

263 The facts with respect to industry capacity and utilization had been testified to by another witness and found faulty and unreliable by the court.

cations in documents filed in the National Depository that General Electric's Large Steam Turbine Generator Department had been highly profitable. One General Electric document (No. 359856) stated that that Department's "profitability is among the highest in the Company," and further, "To a large extent, the profitability of the Large Steam Turbine Generator Department in the last ten years has been maintained through pricing." In terms of total income to sales billed, another General Electric document (No. 357190) showed how much better the performance of the Large Steam Turbine Generator Department was by comparison with the Company overall:

	RATIO OF TOTAL INCOME TO SALES BILLED	
YEAR	COMPANY	LST-G
1948	13.3	13.9
1949	12.6	7.9
1950	18.9	20.5
1951	17.9	23.8
1952	15.8	24.7
1953	15.2	26.9
1954	13.2	27.1
1955 (Budget)	13.5	27.2

In another document (GE 356823) Peters wrote in 1956:

> " We have deliberately increased the prices for the larger ratings substantially more than the smaller ratings in order to increase the gross margins. Inasmuch as we are selling more of the larger units, our prices have been advanced substantially more than the indices and our costs. I believe that this deliberate method of increasing prices has contributed more than anything else to raising the normal gross margin from 13.7% in 1949 to 28.7% in 1955 or a 110% increase."

In another document (No. 356829) return on investment figures for the Large Steam Turbine Generator Department were given and showed, from 1951 to 1957, a range of return from 29.1% to 84% (the latter in 1955). By combining the information shown on a number of General Electric documents (Nos. 357073, 357990 and 370251) it could be determined that even taking net income after taxes, the return on investment for the Large Steam Turbine Generator Department in the period 1950 to 1961 ranged from 27.9% to 97.7% (in 1959). During the same period the rate of return on investment for all United States manufacturing corporations ranged from 8.6% to 15.4%, and for manufacturers of electrical machinery, equipment and supplies, from 8.9% to 20.8%.[264] Another comparison, based on the same data, showed that from 1953 through 1961 General Electric's Large Steam Turbine Generator Department's percentage was approximately double that for all United States manufacturing corporations, and for the years 1959 to 1961 was approximately three times as large.

The court rejected a defense by Westinghouse based upon an attempted showing that it lost a substantial amount on the four units sold by it to OVEC:

> " However, at the time Westinghouse expected not to suffer a loss but to make a profit, albeit in a lesser percentage than that predicted by GE. Moreover, apart from the fact that Westinghouse costs would have been lower absent the conspiracy, it is the GE, not the Westinghouse, prediction of profit at the time which is more significant because GE was the low-cost producer. GE budgeted a gross margin of thirty-two per cent on the Clifty Creek units, which margin it regarded as 'very profitable,' so that the room for downward movement in price, if competition had been effective was substantial."

The court rejected plaintiffs' arguments that evidence should not have been admitted with respect to what a reconstructed competitive price might have been:

> " Rather, they [defendants] urge, even assuming conspiracy, that plaintiffs were charged no more than they would have been under competitive conditions and that the evidence they offer is relevant to that proposition. The latter contention is correct. Plaintiffs would acknowledge, as indeed they must, that the concept of reconstructed competitive price is a vital part of the damage equation in this case. Yet, in insisting that defendants' economic evidence be deemed inadmissible, plaintiffs are, in effect, seeking to preclude defendants from contradicting plaintiffs' computation of an assumed competitive price. Reconstruction of a competitive price based on supply, demand, costs and other economic indicators is a logical and judicially recognized technique."

---

264 Source: FEDERAL TRADE COMMISSION, PROFIT RATES OF MANUFACTURING CORPORATIONS, 1947-1962 (Washington, D.C., 1963).

On evidentiary matters, the court accepted grand jury testimony. The court stated that it was clearly admissible to impeach a deposition witness or refresh his recollection since "under familiar rubric, these statements are not offered for the truth of the facts they contain"; the court approved the admission of certain statements from grand jury testimony offered as substantive evidence, but added overall that in any event "no grand jury testimony was necessary to any finding in this case."

General Electric also objected to the admission or the use in the OVEC trial of answers to interrogatories filed by General Electric in the Philadelphia power transformer case. The court replied that answers to interrogatories "formally filed by a party in a judicial proceeding would appear to be an admission by it, admissible as evidence against the party in some other proceeding."

The court, in reaching its final judgment, accepted defendants' economic case in part:

> " Despite plaintiffs' arguments to the contrary, much of it was persuasive of a finding that economic factors did contribute to the psychology of a buyer's, rather than a seller's, market and account for some of the greater discount off book in the post-1959 measuring period. For example, while backlogs in 1952 were not much higher than in 1962, industry capacity in the latter year was greater, and there are indications that per cent utilization of capacity was higher in the earlier period. Foreign competition became a real threat in the later period; while earlier it was not. Korean War price control was in effect in 1952 and ended in 1953; after 1959, there was no comparable artificial depressant on price levels which might narrow the gap between book and order prices.
>
> Plaintiffs minimize the significance of these circumstances and claim that the conspiracy itself tainted the forces of demand and supply so that they cannot be used for comparison purposes; e.g., the defendants created short-run demand by announcing price increases and then allowing sales at the old prices for a short while. While this practice was followed from time to time during the conspiracy, its effect in the fourth quarter of 1952 would not seem to be marked. . . . I am persuaded that a portion of the increase in discount is due to the economic characteristics of the 1961-1963 period.
>
> . . . The vital question remains to what extent the economic changes from the 1950's to the 1960's account for the radical

> change in relationship between book and order prices. . . . In other circumstances, it might be considered rash indeed to attempt to isolate the force of economic determinants on price; even those most learned in the field will agree that such judgments are at best inexact. It is, however, the duty of this court to make just such a determination, and the difficulty of the task does not eliminate the necessity for making it.
>
> . . . I conclude that the difference in economic factors between 1952 and 1961-1963 accounts for a substantial portion of the discounts off book in the post-1959 era—a figure equal to between four and five per cent as compared to the full 25.33 per cent average discount in the later period. In other words, instead of applying the full 25.33 per cent average discount to arrive at what plaintiffs call the non-conspiratorial price, I would apply only twenty-one per cent, on the theory that the remaining 4.33 per cent of the average discount in the early 1960's was due to economic conditions prevalent in that period. It should be noted that this is a significant reduction from the damages asserted by plaintiffs since their claim is only for the difference between the discount off book actually achieved by plaintiffs in 1952, which was 11.1 per cent (GE) or 11.97 per cent (Westinghouse), and 25.33 per cent, the discount off book plaintiffs say competition would have brought them. This is a total claim of only 14.23 or 13.36 per cent of the book price of the units sold. My finding as to damage eliminates about thirty per cent of the damage claimed."

The court accordingly found overcharges aggregating $5,624,-401, slightly under 11% of the total final order price for all units and slightly under 10% of the total final billed price, including escalation.

CHAPTER 18

I-T-E Circuit Breaker

AT THIS STAGE PRACTICALLY all claims of plaintiffs against practically all defendants had been either tried or settled or were on their way to settlement—with the major exception of defendant I-T-E Circuit Breaker Company. As of October 7, 1965, I-T-E had pending against it some 365 cases involving about 1,090 claims originally brought in sixteen districts throughout the country.[265] I-T-E, named as a defendant in complaints relating to power switchgear assemblies, circuit breakers, power switching equipment, among others,[266] had refused to discuss settlement, even as a part of the plaintiffs' program for settling with the so-called "smaller" defendants at levels substantially below those at which settlements had been reached with the major manufacturers. I-T-E had also consistently resisted all steps looking toward trial of the cases in which it was a party defendant.

The Coordinating Committee, frustrated by this situation and attempting also to solve the problem of discovery in the seven product lines in which national discovery had not been conducted,[267] determined upon a course of action whereby cases involving the remaining product lines, together with those in which trials had not been had or complete settlements effected, were to be made the subject of inter-circuit transfers for trial, if the transfer were approved and ordered by the district judges

---

[265] Atlantic City Electric Co. v. I-T-E Circuit Breaker Co., 247 F. Supp. 950, 953 (1965).

[266] The others were open-fuse cutouts, insulators, low-voltage distribution equipment and isolated phase buses.

[267] In National Pretrial Order No. 40 the Coordinating Committee had called upon the parties to the electrical equipment litigation for suggestions as to the carrying out of a national discovery program in these remaining product lines.

before whom the cases were pending. One product line, in which I-T-E had been named a defendant in a number of cases throughout the country, power switchgear assemblies, was determined to be a product line as to which all cases were to be transferred to the Northern District of Illinois. I-T-E strenuously resisted these transfers.

In the Western District of Missouri Judge Becker, initially acting almost on his own motion but ultimately on the basis of plaintiffs' motion, ordered the transfer of five cases involving power switchgear assemblies, power switching equipment and insulators pending before him.[268] He recited that all defendants in the actions other than I-T-E had compromised and settled the plaintiffs' claims for damages against them and had in fact secured formal orders of dismissal. I-T-E, he said, had been sued in thirty districts, had made no offers of any sum to any plaintiff, and was not seeking trial of any cases in which it was defendant, in Missouri or elsewhere. He pointed out that the cases had been pending more than three years.

Judge Becker stated that some of the facts considered to be of importance in considering the transfer to Chicago were:

" 1. The convenience of witnesses, on the national issues of alleged conspiracy and its effect on prices charged by I-T-E, will be served by a central location for trial. . . .

2. The convenience of the parties will be served by reducing the cost of separate preparation of Power Switchgear Assembly cases by separate counsel in both Kansas City and in Chicago; and by accessibility of documents in defendants' National Document Depository located in Chicago for use in preparation and in trial.

3. The interest of justice will be served by an early trial in Chicago permitted by the condition of its docket, and illustrated by the orders setting similar cases for trial in March, 1965; and by concentrating these cases of national aspect in one jurisdiction, on the basis of product lines involved, so as to avoid endless repetitive trials in many jurisdictions. In fact only by doing so is there a hope of processing this unprecedented mass of litigation."

---

268 Kansas City Power & Light Co. v. I-T-E Circuit Breaker Co., 240 F. Supp. 121 (W.D. Mo. 1965).

I-T-E appealed from Judge Becker's decision to the United States Court of Appeals for the Eighth Circuit: *I-T-E Circuit Breaker Company* v. *Honorable William H. Becker, United States District Judge.*[269] The court of appeals, in an opinion *per curiam* (i.e., by the court without designation of any specific judge as the author of the opinion), confirmed Judge Becker's action. The court of appeals summarized I-T-E's attitude toward the electrical equipment cases:

> " Petitioner admitted before the district court, as it had before the Co-ordinating Committee, and as it does here, that it has not formulated any program, and indeed that it is without even a suggestion of any plan, for effecting termination of the litigation thus pending against it, either by way of desire to engage in trials, of intention to attempt settlements, or of basis to seek dismissals. What it seemingly wants done is simply to have all of the suits against it left alone."

I-T-E complained that Judge Becker lacked authority to order the transfer because he had, in effect, acted on his own motion rather than the motion of the parties. The court of appeals analyzed the language of § 1404(a) of the Judicial Code which provides:

> " For the convenience of parties and witnesses, in the interest of justice, a district court may transfer any civil action to any other district or division where it might have been brought. . . ."

The court of appeals concluded that Judge Becker probably had such authority but added that it did not need to decide the question since in fact there had been a motion by the plaintiffs for the transfer. The court concluded in approving the transfer of the cases to the Northern District of Illinois:

> " Needless to say, petitioner will be afforded the opportunity for a fair trial. It cannot ask, however, to continue to have its cases stand still."

The Eighth Circuit looked at the matter again upon an appeal by I-T-E from an order of transfer entered by the United States District Court in St. Louis. In this latter case the court of appeals said that it was unnecessary for the district judge, prior

---

[269] 343 F.2d 361 (8th Cir. 1965).

to ordering the transfer, to require the plaintiff to answer such written interrogatories as to how much nearer to Chicago certain witnesses lived than to St. Louis. The court said that in the final analysis the question of the convenience of parties and witnesses under § 1404(a) is one "which must be measured in terms of 'the interest of justice' in relation to the situation which is involved and on the basis of proper judicial discretion exercised as to its whole."

In the Third Circuit, the court of appeals approved a transfer on the court's own motion of the Philadelphia Electric cases involving power switchgear assemblies, among others, to the Northern District of Illinois and certiorari was denied by the United States Supreme Court.[270] A switchgear claim of the Puerto Rico Water Resources Authority was transferred from the District of Columbia to the Northern District of Illinois.

In the Southern District of New York,[271] Judge Feinberg approved major transfers of cases from that district to other districts:

> " Two motions have been brought in this court, pursuant to 28 U.S.C. § 1404, which are in accord with these recommendations. One seeks an order to transfer cases in the circuit breaker and power switchgear assembly product lines to the Northern District of Illinois. As of November 15, 1965, there were pending in this district nine cases in the former product line and twenty-two in the latter. The other motion seeks an order transferring cases in seven other product lines to various transferee courts, as follows: insulators (nine), power transformers (four) and network transformers (one) to the Northern District of California; hydroelectric generators (two) to the Western District of Washington; power switching equipment (sixteen) to the Eastern District of Missouri; distribution transformers (four) to the Eastern District of Pennsylvania; and low voltage distribution equipment (nine) to the Western District of Missouri."

Judge Feinberg also summarized the status of transfers as of the time of his decision:

---

270 381 U.S. 936 (1965).

271 Atlantic City Electric Co. v. I-T-E Circuit Breaker Co., 247 F. Supp. 950 (1965).

> "As of November 10, 1965, orders transferring sixty-five cases had been entered in the Southern District of California, the District of Columbia, the Western District of Kentucky, the Eastern and Western Districts of Missouri, the Northern District of Illinois, the Eastern District of Pennsylvania, and the Southern and Western Districts of Texas, coinciding with recommendations of the Co-ordinating Committee."

Judge Feinberg summarized the advantages of transfer in terms similar to those used by previous courts:

> "There are obvious advantages to having the remaining cases in a particular product line centered in one locale before one judge. Final pretrial and trial preparation can be done with a minimum of duplication of expense and effort before a court which has acquired, or will rapidly do so, detailed knowledge of all the problems raised in the litigation affecting that product line. Witnesses and parties with knowledge of the particular product line will not be required to undergo the demands of repetitive trials in various localities involving the same product. Consolidation of cases in the same product line for final pre-trial preparation (including local discovery) and for trial will be facilitated because all will be in the same court. Such consolidation is not at all unlikely since evidence of conspiracy and even of injury may well be similar in most, and perhaps all, of the remaining cases in any product line. In any event, concentration of cases in a product line will confine to one district the multitude of procedural and substantive problems that might otherwise be posed in various districts.
>
> . . . .
>
> If each transferring court, and particularly this transferring court, had to try cases in each of the nine product lines affected by the transfers out, as well as the two product lines scheduled for trial here, it is obvious that in cases of this magnitude, trials in all the product lines could not be completed with the same convenience and speed."

In noting that I-T-E was the principal objector to the transfer proposals, the court pointed out that I-T-E was involved in all fifty-six cases in the nine product lines pending in the Southern District of New York; and that of these, thirty-one appeared to be pending against I-T-E alone, since other defendants in the suits had settled with the respective plaintiffs.

One commentator quarreled with the transfer program on the grounds that it had not taken place at the beginning of the litigation rather than toward the end.[272] In the House, Congressman Celler proposed statutory authorization for inter-circuit transfers with a bill[273] which by its title provided "for the temporary transfer to a single district for coordinated or consolidated pretrial proceedings of civil actions pending in different districts which involve one or more common questions of fact, and for other purposes." The substance of this bill was enacted into law in 1968[274] by adding a new § 1407 to the Judicial Code with the following provisions:

" a. When civil actions involving one or more common questions of fact are pending in different districts, such actions may be transferred to any district for coordinated or consolidated pretrial proceedings. Such transfers shall be made by the judicial panel on multidistrict litigation authorized by this section upon its determination that transfers for such proceedings will be for the convenience of parties and witnesses and will promote the just and efficient conduct of such actions. Each action so transferred shall be remanded by the panel at or before the conclusion of such pretrial proceedings to the district from which it was transferred unless it shall have been previously terminated. . . .

b. Such coordinated or consolidated pretrial proceedings shall be conducted by a judge or judges to whom such actions are assigned by the judicial panel on multidistrict litigation. For this purpose, upon request of the panel, a circuit judge or a district judge may be designated and assigned temporarily for service in the transferee district by the Chief Justice of the United States or the chief judge of the circuit, as may be required, in accordance with the provisions of chapter 13 of this title. With the consent of the transferee district court, such actions may be assigned by the panel to a judge or judges of such district. The judge or judges to whom such actions are assigned, the members of the judicial panel on multidistrict litigation, and other circuit and district judges designated when needed by the panel may exercise the powers of a district judge in any district for the purpose of conducting pretrial depositions in such coordinated or consolidated pretrial proceedings.

---

272 McAllister, *Judicial Administration of Multiple-District Treble Damage Litigation*, 1966 N. Y. State Bar Association Antitrust Law Symposium (Commerce Clearing House, 1966) at 55, 87.

273 H. R. 8276, 89th Cong., 1st Sess. (introduced May 19, 1965).

274 Public Law 90-296, 90th Congress, approved April 29, 1968, under the title of Multidistrict Litigation Act.

c. Proceedings for the transfer of an action under this section may be initiated by—

1. the judicial panel on multidistrict litigation upon its own initiative, or

2. motion filed with the panel by a party in any action in which transfer for coordinated or consolidated pretrial proceedings under this section may be appropriate. A copy of such motion shall be filed in the district court in which the moving party's action is pending.

. . . .

. . . The panel's order of transfer shall be based upon a record of such hearing at which material evidence may be offered by any party to an action pending in any district that would be affected by the proceedings under this section, and shall be supported by findings of fact and conclusions of law based upon such record.

. . . .

d. The judicial panel on multidistrict litigation shall consist of seven circuit and district judges designated from time to time by the Chief Justice of the United States, no two of whom shall be from the same circuit.

. . . .

g. Nothing in this section shall apply to any action in which the United States is a complainant arising under the antitrust laws."

It should be noted that the purpose of the Act is primarily to provide for inter-circuit transfers for pretrial purposes, whereas the inter-circuit transfers in the electrical equipment cases were for the purposes of completing pretrial and for trial. It is also notable that in subsection (b) there is provided statutory authority for what was done uniformly in the course of the electrical equipment cases—that is, assigning district judges outside their home districts to preside at pretrial depositions; by giving the assigned judge the powers of a district judge in the assigned district, the statute avoided the awkwardness of appointing the assigned judge a "special master."

Upon the transfer of the power switchgear cases against I-T-E to the Northern District of Illinois, that court first required filing by the parties of trial briefs. In the trial brief filed on behalf of the Commonwealth Edison group of plaintiffs, together with plaintiffs such as Southern California Edison Company whose cases had been transferred to the Northern District of Illinois, there were identified by date and place the number of "working level" meetings among the switchgear manufacturers in the post-white sale period. The data showed that in the twenty-month period between May 1955 and December 1958 there were forty-one such meetings. In the twelve-month period between November 1958 and October 1959 there were twenty-eight working level meetings.

Plaintiffs' trial brief traced, with respect to low voltage and metal-clad switchgear, the price increases that had taken place between 1946 and 1957. The data showed an aggregate increase, taking the book price in effect on December 21, 1945 as a base, of 136½% for low voltage switchgear and 248% for metal-clad switchgear through 1957. Even after 1957, the switchgear manufacturers achieved a 10% book price increase through the uniform adoption of a .55 multiplier to obtain net book prices in lieu of a previously agreed-upon .50 multiplier to be applied to 1958 book prices to obtain net book. This use of a multiplier had been agreed upon in November 1958 at a meeting at the Commodore Hotel in New York and had been proposed by General Electric. The advantage of a multiplier was deemed to be that it would make future changes in price sheets easier and less expensive, since future price changes could be effected by changing the multiplier, and complete reprinting of price books would be avoided.

Switchgear was the product line in which position among the various manufacturers was determined by the operation of the "phase of the moon" formula. An exhibit identified during the deposition of Nye Spencer of I-T-E showed that position was rotated among the five companies every two weeks; for the two-week period January 3 to January 16, 1969, I-T-E (identified as No. 6) had low position on switchgear assembly jobs with a book price over $25,000. The formulas at the bottom of the exhibit showed precisely what quotation was to be made by each company: I-T-E, having low position, was to quote $200 below the book price; Westinghouse (identified as No. 2) would quote $100 below the book price; Federal Pacific (identified as B1) would quote $50 below the book price; General Electric (identified as B2) would quote .1% below book price; and Allis-

Chalmers (identified as B3) would quote the full book price. And a further detail with respect to the phase of the moon operation, from Nye Spencer's deposition:

> " Q. Mr. Spencer, in telling us about the meeting on November 21, which you testified to in regard to NX-1791, you discussed the 'light of the moon' arrangement and I would like to know how the rotation order among the companies represented at that meeting was determined?
>
> A. We flipped a coin."

W. M. Scott of I-T-E, in his deposition had related an incident, occurring prior to World War II, where a General Electric man, participating in a phase of the moon operation, inadvertently mailed to the customer a memorandum showing the prices that all of the companies were to quote to that customer.

The conspirators had problems with secretarial assistance. It was agreed at the Commodore Hotel meeting in November 1958 that telephoning to offices would be kept to a minimum but would be done when necessary; thereafter competitors complained to Nye Spencer that when they called him a typist in his office always asked "Who is calling?" Spencer wrote a note to himself to take steps to stop this practice and thereafter made an entry "O. K.," indicating that the matter had been taken care of with the erring typist.

To demonstrate I-T-E's interest in the switchgear meetings, the plaintiffs' trial brief cited the circumstance that Spencer sent his associate Day to Atlanta, Georgia to attend a meeting which had been scheduled for October 14, 1959, even though Day had been told by someone from Federal Pacific that the meeting was called off. Day nevertheless showed up with his price make-up sheets in his hand, but no one else came.

The trial brief, although not setting forth specific amounts of damages, outlined the steps that would be taken to analyze I-T-E's shop order files to secure relevant information. All I-T-E shop order files involving the domestic sale of power switchgear assemblies during the period 1946 through 1964 were being reviewed. The analysis would extract all price data reflecting the level at which sales were made both during and after the conspiratorial period. The study would establish for each sale made by I-T-E the book price of the equipment ordered, the actual order price, the purchaser, the type of equipment, the date of the book and the discount from book at which the sale was made. The trial brief promised that the effectiveness of the conspiracy could be demonstrated from the analysis of actual I-T-E order prices. According to the trial brief, during the periods of intense conspiratorial activity (particularly the 1940's, the period 1950 to mid-1958, with the exception of the white sale, and in 1959), this effectiveness was shown in the narrow margin of discount from book prices. In contrast, following the exposure of the conspiracy in late 1959 and early 1960, order prices fell, with the discounts from book ranging from 30% to 50% or more.

The post-conspiracy order price index was to be taken as representative of a non-conspiratorial price and would be used in plotting the level at which the plaintiffs' purchases during the conspiracy should, in their view, have been made. On this basis plaintiffs presented a tentative figure of total overcharges on the products in suit of $2,473,734 on purchases (actual order price basis) of $8,879,721, a percentage overcharge of approximately 27%.

I-T-E's response as contained in its formal answers to the complaints was to the effect that:

> " [I]t was an unwilling victim of the major defendants (General Electric, Westinghouse and, from time to time, Allis-Chalmers) who not only wrongfully threatened I-T-E with imminent and substantial loss and with its elimination as a competitor but who also subjected I-T-E to wrongful acts of coercion, duress and compulsion which have resulted in substantial losses to I-T-E and have impaired its ability to effectively compete with them and others. More specifically, the coercion, duress and compulsion have consisted of, among other things:
>
> a. An ability and willingness of the major defendants, acting together and individually, to use their enormous wealth and gigantic size, measured by assets, sales and income, and their highly diversified business activities to dominate and control the competition of the smaller independent electrical equipment manufacturers, including I-T-E.
>
> b. The employment as business methods, particularly by General Electric, of price uniformity, the elimination over the long run of price competition in each segment of the electrical equipment business, and the preservation of the shares of the market enjoyed

by the major defendants. This has included insistence by the major defendants that smaller manufacturers, including I-T-E, meet with the major defendants and do as they are told or suffer retaliatory action. Such retaliatory action was frequently the uniform application to the products sold by such recalcitrant independent manufacturers of an abnormally and unreasonably low price which often approached and sometimes was below such independent manufacturer's cost for such products.

c. The adoption and implementation by the major defendants, particularly General Electric, of discriminatory pricing practices which had the effect of squeezing their smaller competitors, including I-T-E, by reducing or eliminating their profit margins (e.g., extreme reductions of the prices charged by the major defendants for equipment sold by them in competition with high-quality equipment of such smaller manufacturers; and the lowering of prices of assembled equipment in relation to the cost of components of such equipment sold to independent assemblers by I-T-E and others)."

I-T-E's admission of attendance by its employees at meetings with competitors was phrased this way:

" c. I-T-E admits that one of its employees met five times between January and June, 1958 with employees of some or all of the other defendants in cities of the United States at which there was discussion of the abnormally and unreasonably low price levels of sales of some power switchgear assemblies in 1957 and 1958, and I-T-E's position at these meetings that the prices of power switchgear assemblies should not be increased by agreement and that I-T-E would not be forced into agreeing to any such increases which might be made by others. . . ."

And its answer with respect to the phase of the moon operation:

" h. I-T-E admits that at some of the meetings referred to in subparagraph 13(g) of this answer there was discussion of a formula (sometimes referred to as 'phase of the moon' or 'light of the moon') for rotating low, high and intermediate prices for some types of power switchgear assemblies to some electrical utility companies, private industrial corporations, and contractors. I-T-E denies that such a formula was used by all or any defendants in pricing all sales of power switchgear assemblies to electric utility companies, private industrial corporations and contractors, that price competition was eliminated among the defendants, and that each defendant knew the exact price it and every other defendant would quote on any prospective sale. . . ."

In summary, I-T-E answered:

" Any acts done by I-T-E which may have been consistent with the purposes of any conspiracy or combination as alleged by the plaintiffs were done solely as a result of such threats and acts."

Upon the filing of the trial briefs and I-T-E's answer, the principal plaintiffs in switchgear moved for summary judgment on all issues except the amount of damages. They argued that the records in the proceedings, including pleadings, depositions, answers to interrogatories and the parties' trial briefs, showed that there was no genuine issue as to any material fact and that each plaintiff was therefore entitled to judgment as a matter of law, except as to the matter of damages suffered by each plaintiff. The brief in support of the motion for summary judgment recited that there was no doubt that I-T-E's officers and employees had participated in the conspiratorial meetings and such activity was concealed to such an extent that directors of I-T-E, a number of whom were deeply involved in the affairs of the company, testified that they had no knowledge of the conspiratorial activities until the time of the grand jury investigations or later. Plaintiffs argued that summary judgment was appropriate in price fixing cases, citing the decision of the United States Supreme Court in *White Motor Co.* v. *United States*:[275]

" If competitors agree to divide markets, they run afoul of the antitrust laws. . . . Price fixing, both vertical . . . and horizontal . . . have also been held to be *per se* violations of the antitrust laws; and a trial to show its nature, extent and degree is no longer necessary."

The deposition material cited by plaintiffs in support of their motion for summary judgment was rich in admissions that price fixing by competitors was a way of life in the switchgear industry. Burens of General Electric gave deposition testimony:

" Q. Did you have any conversations with Mr. Van Erben about how the switchgear industry had to be run?
A. Well, again, I would say on many occasions.

Q. You have not answered my question. You did have some conversations, so your answer would be yes?
A. How the switchgear had to be run, yes.

---

[275] 372 U.S. 253 (1963).

Q. Would you tell us what Mr. Van Erben told you on these occasions?
A. Well, concerning what?

Q. Concerning competitors.
A. He told me that the switchgear business had always been run, as far as prices were concerned, by meeting with competitors to stabilize prices."

And Scott, the president of I-T-E:

" Q. In what words did Mr. Burens express his solution to the problem?
A. He said the only solution lies in all competitors going back to book immediately, or words substantially like that.

Q. Did you tell Mr. Burens, did you question the legality of the book price?
A. I did.

Q. Did you tell Mr. Burens the reason you questioned the legality of the book price?
A. I think I did.

Q. What was the reason you told Mr. Burens?
A. That those book prices had been arrived at in meetings in concert."

And McGuire of Allis-Chalmers:

" Q. Can you tell me, from August 15, 1955, when you became manager of the switchgear department, until you switched to the Pittsburgh Works on January 1, 1958, what kind of meetings you attended with competitors on the subject of prices?
A. There was the hero group meetings.

Q. What was the hero group?
A. These were the, in general, the managers of the operations as compared to the sales managers.

Q. Did those meetings, then, take place from time to time from August 15, 1955 until January 1, 1958?

. . . .

BY THE WITNESS: A. Yes, sir.

. . . .

Q. Were proposed changes in published prices discussed?
A. Yes.

Q. And following those discussions were the changes sometimes made?
A. Yes.

Q. Would the discussion include a discussion of how much the price should be raised?

. . . .

BY THE WITNESS: A. Yes.

Q. And that applies both to power circuit breakers and power switchgear assemblies, does it not?
A. Yes.

Q. What was your object in attending these hero level meetings?
A. To try to make the lower level meetings work."

And Nolan of Allis-Chalmers explained the purpose of the phase of the moon operation:

" Q. Is it true that this formula was so calculated that in submitting prices to electric utility companies, private industrial corporations, and contractors the price spread between the manufacturers' quotations would be sufficiently narrow so as to eliminate actual price competition among them, but sufficiently wide so as to give an appearance of competition?

. . . .

A. Yes."

Burke of General Electric outlined a meeting which seemed to be a lesson in futility:

" Q. Now, did you attend a meeting at the Hershey Hotel in Hershey, Pennsylvania, in about June of 1955?
A. Somewhere along there, in the summer of 1955, yes, sir.

Q. Would it be June or July of 1955, to the best of your recollection?
A. To the best of my recollection it would be June or July.

Q. Who asked you to attend that meeting?
A. Mr. Burens.

. . . .

Q. When you got to Hershey did you meet someone?
A. Yes. After registering in and getting in our room, well, Mr. Burens sometime later called me on the telephone and told me to come over to his room and we would go down to Room So-And-So to meet with two of the Westinghouse representatives.

Q. Who were those two representatives?
A. Mr. McCully and Mr. McNeil, I think his name is.

. . . .

Q. Can you tell us how long this meeting lasted?
A. Well, the meeting itself was quite short and sweet in that everybody mutually agreed that prices were so stinking low that they should do something about it, but both Mr. McNeil and Mr.

McCully said that they know so little about switchgear prices that they would have to get Mr. Fuller to discuss the details with Mr. Burens. So then we went and had dinner together in the Hershey Hotel, and the next morning we played golf, as I remember it, together. And then we broke up and went back to our respective places."

There were some interesting details concerning the Traymore meeting. Buck of I-T-E testified:

" Q. Was the Atlantic City meeting in the Traymore Hotel?
A. Yes.

Q. And was it about November 9, 1958?
A. About then.

Q. Was it on a Sunday?
A. It was a Sunday.

Q. Was it the first day of the NEMA convention?
A. I don't know whether they convened on Monday or Sunday, but it was the Sunday either coincident with or just before.

Q. Was it in Mr. Roby's hotel room?
A. Yes, it was in Mr. Roby's room in the Traymore Hotel.

. . . .

Q. How long did it last?
A. Well, we convened at noon as being most convenient for those arriving from out of town, and being a Sunday it was thought that many might want to attend church services in the mornmg and they would meet at noon. We met at noon and in the eyes of some people it probably ended at 5:00 o'clock, but in the eyes of others I don't think it ended until 10:30.

. . . .

Q. Mr. Burens says, that at Traymore we agreed to go to book prices.

. . . .

Q. Was it agreed to go to book prices?
A. It was agreed toward the end of the meeting that the pricing of the equipment should be based upon the published price levels."

Nye Spencer's notes contain this entry with respect to the "hero" meeting at the Traymore: "Mgmt. people agreed to go to book overnight—no tapering."

Buck confirmed the percentage allocations for sealed bid business agreed upon at the Traymore:

" Q. Now look at that portion of the paper for Tuesday the 28th. These dates I realize are just to identify the part of the paper. Are the final figures on the far right which go 'GE 39, Westinghouse 35, Allis-Chalmers 8, ITE 11, and Federal Pacific 7,' are they the final percentages that were agreed upon at the Traymore meeting for allocation of sealed bid business?

. . . .

THE WITNESS: They were the final percentages that were read out to apply to the several companies in the sealed bid business in the near future."

Scott added a detail inconsistent with Buck's testimony on percentages:

" I do recall one thing, yes, that on the subject of business to be taken, that Westinghouse and General Electric were quite adamant that whatever else happened, that they were to get between them 72 and some percent, some fraction, of the business and they would not disclose to the other competitors present the proposed division between General Electric and Westinghouse. . . ."

Buck also gave some details on how the meetings among competitors terminated in 1959:

" Q. Did the meetings just terminate for lack of anyone inviting you to another or convening another?
A. I don't know how they terminated or failed to reconvene except in my own case and that is Mr. Burger telephoned me that a meeting that had been set for some time subsequent to September, say early or mid October, would not be held.

Q. And did you ask why?
A. I certainly did.

Q. And did he say?
A. He said there would be no further meetings until in their judgment they could be held. That there were industry investigations or others going on, that it was deemed advisable on their part to hold no further meetings."

Hentschel of General Electric testified that Buck even then was anxious for a continuation of the meetings:

" Q. Did you attend any more meetings with the competitors following this September, 1959 meeting?
A. I attended no further meetings. I did receive one or two telephone calls from Harry Buck, of ITE, trying to get us to again have some further meetings. Burger, at the time was, I believe,

at Croatenville in school, he could not be contacted, and we refused.

Q. Can you fix the approximate time of these phone calls from Mr. Buck?

A. I would say within a month after the September meeting."

In their motion for summary judgment plaintiffs were subject to the protective orders entered by the court with respect to material produced by I-T-E which was stated to be confidential: accordingly, two appendices, one relative to plaintiffs' purchases from I-T-E after June 30, 1960, and the other comprising I-T-E order price data, were printed separately and filed with the court under seal.

Judge Robson denied the motion for summary judgment, holding that there seemed to be no disputable question so far as the existence of a conspiracy was concerned, but finding that there were issues of fact respecting the impact of the conspiracy on the plaintiffs. He therefore ordered the case to proceed to trial.

During the course of proceeding to trial, a series of local pretrial orders numbered from 1 to 17 were issued by the court. They established schedules for depositions and interrogatories on local (i.e., damage) issues, made provision for a trial brief which was to contain separately numbered paragraphs setting forth:

" a. The facts which plaintiff expects to prove in support of each claim for relief, distinguishing between those facts which plaintiff contends on the basis of the answers or otherwise are admitted and those which are contested;

b. The legal issues, contentions and supporting authorities related to each claim for relief including plaintiff's contentions as to the measure of damages pertaining to each claim and the party bearing the burden of proof on each issue."

And similarly for defendant:

" a. The facts which defendant expects to prove in defense of each claim for relief, distinguishing betwen those facts which defendant contends, on the basis of the complaint, plaintiffs' briefs or otherwise, are admitted and those which are contested;

b. The legal issues, contentions and supporting authorities related to the defense of each claim for relief including defendant's

> contentions as to the measure of damages pertaining to each claim and the party bearing the burden of proof on each issue."

A schedule was established for the designation by plaintiffs and defendant of the portions of the national and local depositions which each party expected to read into testimony at the trial; and each party was to designate all documents on which it intended to rely or introduce into evidence at the trial. Plaintiffs and defendant alike were given opportunity in advance of the trial to object to the designations of testimony and documents by the other side. It was provided that "any fact, legal issue, contention, claim or defense" which was not set forth in detail as required by local pretrial order should be deemed "abandoned, uncontroverted or withdrawn," with the exception of testimony of expert witnesses. Similarly, any portion of deposition testimony or documents not designated or filed would be deemed abandoned and withdrawn, again with the exception for the evidence to be introduced by an expert witness.

The court scheduled a pretrial conference at which final trial plans were to be developed and at which the following matters were to be considered:

" a. The then undetermined issues of fact and law will be delineated and, to the extent feasible, simplified;

b. The reception in evidence of documentary matters not precluded by stipulation of fact, subject to such objections, if any, as may be reserved for the trial;

c. The identity and scope of testimony of witnesses to be called at time of trial will be considered and possible limitation with respect thereto;

d. An agreement upon a trial schedule;

e. The handling of documentary evidence;

f. Authentication of documents;

g. Witness lists;

h. Spokesmen;

i. Examination of witnesses;

j. Use of written narrative statements of expert witnesses;

k. Use of depositions, including the possible use of narrative summaries or verbatim extracts;

l. Trial briefs filed pursuant to Local Pretrial Order No. 1A;

m. Limitation of opening statements;

n. Current index of the record;

o. Daily transcripts;

p. Instructions;

q. Separation of issues;

r. Use of and mechanics for special jury verdict, or general verdict with interrogatories;

s. Possibility of settlement."

I-T-E was required to verify the 1(a) to (h) answers by plaintiffs to defendant's interrogatories and the answers were to be deemed admitted unless objections were filed.

I-T-E was further required by Local Pretrial Order No. 4 to file with the court a detailed written statement setting forth all facts and contentions relating to its defense of "coercion, duress and compulsion" and I-T-E's alleged inability to refrain from participating in the alleged conspiracy in switchgear; I-T-E was also to set forth any facts concerning any attempts which it had made to withdraw from the switchgear conspiracy.

After I-T-E made a filing purporting to comply with these requirements of Local Pretrial Order No. 4, Judge Robson granted plaintiffs' motion to strike all portions of I-T-E's defense of economic coercion, stating that the defense was without foundation and was dilatory, and that in view of the time and effort that had been required to reach that conclusion, the court would consider a motion to assess against I-T-E attorneys' fees and costs reasonably expended by the plaintiffs.[276] In Judge Robson's opinion he found that economic coercion was not a defense in treble damage actions, citing the decision of the United States Supreme Court in *United States* v. *Paramount Pictures, Inc., et al.*:[277]

" There is some suggestion on this as well as on other phases of the cases that large exhibitors with whom defendants dealt fathered the illegal practices and forced them onto the defendants.

---

[276] Commonwealth Edison Co. v. Allis-Chalmers Mfg. Co., et al., 245 F. Supp. 889, 901 (N.D. Ill. 1965).

[277] 334 U.S. 131, 161 (1948).

> But as the District Court observed, that circumstance if true does not help the defendants. For acquiescence in an illegal scheme is as much a violation of the Sherman Act as the creation and promotion of one."

Analyzing the factual background, Judge Robson found that I-T-E had failed to show any instance where it was deprived of free will in its dealings with its large competitors, and indeed, I-T-E's statement pursuant to Local Pretrial Order No. 4 related instances of I-T-E's independent action. The court cited paragraph 67 of the response where I-T-E had stated:

> " 67. Notwithstanding discussions among competitors at the Traymore meeting referred to in paragraph 57 and at other meetings, I-T-E personnel were instructed to run I-T-E's business their own way. For example, when Buck reported to Scott the proposed 4% allocation of sealed-bid business, Scott told him to forget it and Buck gave similar instructions to his subordinates."

The court further cited I-T-E's failure "to cite a single instance in the 1940's or 1950's where its independent actions resulted in prompt retaliation against it by the major producers."

Furthermore, the court found that I-T-E had to demonstrate for the validity of the defense that it did not have an adequate remedy in law; and the court found that there were two legal remedies available to I-T-E which it had failed to pursue to fruition. The first would have been to bring suit for injunctive or treble damage relief under the Clayton Act. The second was to report the illegal activities to the Justice Department. The court recited I-T-E's course of action in this latter respect:

> " In 1940 I-T-E, through Mr. Scott, its President, took the initial step in this direction, and reported to the Justice Department that antitrust violations were occurring in the circuit breaker industry. Thurman Arnold, then Assistant Attorney General, responded requesting that Mr. Scott '. . . communicate with me [Arnold] concerning this matter.' Mr. Scott did not communicate further. His present explanation is that he '. . . rather expected they [the Justice Department] would approach me further, which they never did.' He decided 'with the changed circumstances accompanying the war . . . not to risk the competitor retaliation which he expected might follow from pursuing such a complaint.' "

The court responded to I-T-E's contention that General Electric had engaged in coercion by meeting the lowest price quoted by a competitor by pointing out:

> "The meeting of competitors' prices may be completely legal. A major aim of the antitrust laws is an open economy in which the meeting of competitors' prices is the rule rather than the exception. I-T-E has not established that General Electric would have violated any law by carrying out its threats."

CHAPTER 19

I-T-E and the electrical equipment litigation concluded

CONTINUING IN CHICAGO TO prepare for trial against I-T-E in switchgear, plaintiffs were required to produce for defendant their materials relating to their study of I-T-E transaction or order files (referred to as "Corplan" material because the study had been carried out for the plaintiffs by Corplan Associates, an affiliate of IIT Research Institute). The Corplan study required the analysis of 6,700 files covering the sales of three major categories of I-T-E power switchgear assemblies for the period 1946 through 1959.

The specific material required to be produced by plaintiffs included the following:

" a. All data analysis sheets. . . .

b. All keypunch cards prepared from above data analysis sheets.

c. Final printouts prepared from above keypunch cards. . . .

d. List of transaction files produced by I-T-E which were not included in this Corplan study.

e. The keys and other information necessary to interpret the Corplan material.

f. Instructional sheet or sheets reflecting the procedure used by Corplan to extract information from I-T-E files."

In turn, I-T-E was then to furnish to the plaintiffs all its documents containing any comment, analysis, report or note regarding the Corplan material, including but not limited to any notations of errors, corrections, and agreement or disagreement with any of the material; and at the same time I-T-E was to submit in writing to the plaintiffs "what approach it will take at the trial with respect to the validity of the 'Corplan' material." To the extent that I-T-E did not controvert any data contained in the Corplan material, such data were to be deemed admitted or admissible in evidence as the court would determine.

Dates were established by which each party was to identify each witness that it intended to call in its case in chief and to indicate whether such witness would appear in person or by deposition. Initial points for charge to the jury and questions on *voir dire* (i.e., to be asked of prospective jurors) were to be furnished in advance of the trial which was set for May 2, 1966. The parties were also required to confer and attempt to agree upon a joint statement of the material facts relating to the conspiracy which were without substantial controversy. Throughout the course of local discovery and pretrial proceedings, cases transferred from other districts, such as those of the Philadelphia Electric Company, were integrated into the local program.

Plaintiffs, in their suggested questions for *voir dire,* showed a concern that a juror would not have his judgment affected by the large sums of money involved. Their proposed question 17 was:

> " Plaintiffs are seeking to recover substantial sums of money, contending that the damages they have incurred total millions of dollars. Is there any reason why, if the evidence shows that plaintiffs are entitled to such sums, you would not or could not render a verdict for the plaintiffs in such amounts? Would you set any ceiling on the amount that you could award?"

Defendant, on its side, showed concern for various aspects of the case that might result in a juror's prejudice against I-T-E. They submitted this question 19:

> " If it should develop that the outcome of this lawsuit could possibly have an effect on whether your or your close relatives' electric rates would continue as they are now or would be reduced, can you honestly say that that would not make you favor the plaintiffs, either consciously or subconsciously?"

And a final broadside question 39:

> " Do you believe that the plaintiffs here are more likely than I-T-E Circuit Breaker Company to be right about the dispute between them?"

On the suggested request for instructions to the jury I-T-E attempted to get the court to indicate, when the time came for charging the jury, that I-T-E could opt out of the conspiracy. This was an I-T-E suggested instruction:

> "Even if you find that there was a conspiracy on the part of the other manufacturers and that I-T-E went to their conspiratorial meetings, had the same book prices, and obtained the same order prices, you are not required to find that I-T-E thereby became a member of any such conspiracy. You might conclude, for example, after you have considered all the evidence, that this defendant followed such a course of conduct for its own reasons and in its own interest, and not because it had agreed with the others."

I-T-E also submitted an instruction attempting to distinguish between a treble damage civil action and a federal criminal proceeding under the Sherman Act:

> "The position of the plaintiffs in this trial, which is, as you know, a trial for money damages, is different from the position of the federal government in a criminal proceeding brought under the Sherman Act. In a criminal case brought by the federal government, proof of a single unlawful agreement in restraint of trade is sufficient to convict the defendant. In such a criminal case it does not matter whether or not the agreement was actually followed or adhered to, or carried out by any of the conspirators. Nor does it matter whether the conspiracy was a failure or a success. Nor does it matter whether or not the agreement was effective. Nor does it matter whether or not the prices agreed upon were high or low, reasonable or unreasonable, increased or decreased, or whether or not the agreement resulted in any damage to any particular person or corporation."

I-T-E also raised a number of what plaintiffs referred to as "sandstorm issues." One of these was that plaintiffs' own purchasing practices or procedures contained variations or characteristics which led to the plaintiffs' problems: for example, that some plaintiffs used negotiation rather than bidding procedures; further, I-T-E argued that some plaintiffs did not buy "on price." Plaintiffs responded that variations in purchasing practices among plaintiffs and variations by one plaintiff in various transactions do not give manufacturers a license to engage in illegal price fixing.

I-T-E attempted also to defend itself on the ground that its prices were reasonable and were so considered by purchasing agents of the plaintiffs. Plaintiffs responded that it has long been established that price fixing is illegal per se under the Sherman Act and that the Supreme Court of the United States has held that it is immaterial whether "the prices actually agreed upon are reasonable or unreasonable."[278] The Supreme Court elaborated its holding in *United States* v. *McKesson & Robbins, Inc.,* 351 U.S. 305, 309-10 (1956):

> " It has been held too often to require elaboration now that price fixing is contrary to the policy of competition underlying the Sherman Act and that its illegality does not depend on a showing of its unreasonableness, since it is conclusively presumed to be unreasonable. It makes no difference whether the motives of the participants are good or evil; whether the price fixing is accomplished by express contract or by some more subtle means; whether the participants possess market control; whether the amount of interstate commerce affected is large or small; or whether the effect of the agreement is to raise or to decrease prices."

Plaintiffs pointed out that Judge Sirica in his instructions to the jury in the District of Columbia trial had specifically followed these principles when he instructed the jury:

> " Thus, any interference by contract, or combination or conspiracy, with the ordinary and usual competitive-pricing system of the open market constitutes an unreasonable restraint of trade, and is in itself unlawful. The mere fact that there may be business justifications for the fixing of prices, or the fact that the wholly or partially fixed prices may be reasonable, will not relieve the members of the price-fixing combination or conspiracy from liability under the antitrust laws."[279]

I-T-E even attempted to quarrel with an assertion by Commonwealth Edison Company of a claim on behalf of a predecessor company, I-T-E maintaining that the Commonwealth Edison complaint did not even "hint" that Edison might be claiming on this transaction. Plaintiffs' response was to recall that defendant had signed a stipulation, long before the statute of limitations expired, that complaints would not be attacked on the basis that they did not specify damages.

In the pretrial stage of the switchgear cases, the issue of the admissibility of I-T-E's costs, profits and losses was extensively debated. The court, by Order of February 21, 1966,

---

[278] United States v. Trenton Potteries Co., 273 U.S. 392, 401 (1927).

[279] City of Burlington v. Westinghouse Elec. Corp. (D. D.C. 1965), Civ. Act. No. 348-62, printed instr., p. 12.

directed I-T-E to file an offer of proof and supporting memorandum to permit determination of whether I-T-E could satisfy the court's ruling that "evidence of actual costs, profits and losses will be admitted at the trial only if I-T-E (1) can establish that actual costs are the costs which would have been incurred absent a conspiracy, and (2) offers costs, profit and loss data for all significant market factors." I-T-E made a presentation of what it contended were the actual costs which it would have incurred had there been no conspiracy. Plaintiffs responded that the presentation could not represent costs absent the conspiracy because no attempt had been made either to deduct or adjust for costs which were directly attributable to conspiratorial activity, such as expenses incurred in traveling to and from competitors' meetings and the related hotel bills. No adjustment was made, plaintiffs argued, for costs incurred by I-T-E in printing and distributing conspiratorially established price books or the cost for time consumed by I-T-E's employees in attending price fixing meetings.

Plaintiffs argued generally that I-T-E's costs and profits were not relevant to any determination of what prices would have been during the conspiracy period because by I-T-E's own contention General Electric was the price leader, and, therefore, I-T-E's cost data would have no effect on establishment of prices. I-T-E contended that its cost data were relevant because it would show that if prices had been established during the conspiracy period at the levels plaintiffs claimed would have prevailed, I-T-E would have been forced out of the switchgear business. Plaintiffs responded that it is no answer to a charge of price fixing that a firm might not have remained in business:

> " The Sherman Act demands that prices be set without collusion. It does not guarantee anyone license to remain in business." [280]

The plaintiffs also referred to Judge Lord's rejection of this argument in the course of the Philadelphia trial, where the court stated:

---

[280] Plaintiffs' Brief dated January 14, 1966, on Paragraphs 1.B through 1.F of Local Pretrial Order No. 13, No. 61 C 1278 and related power switchgear assembly cases, United States District Court, Northern District of Illinois.

" Defendants argue, quoting from the charge in the Chattanooga Foundry & Pipe Works versus City of Atlanta, 203 U. S. 390, appearing in the record of the Supreme Court at Page 76:

. . . it is presumed that people dealing in the market, according to the usual course of business, will not do so without a profit; that they will not as a regular thing do so at a loss.

From here the defendants' argument runs that any price which is within a reasonable profit margin over the combination of fixed and variable costs represents the price that would be paid in a free market; that is, the 'but for' price.

As I see it the difficulty with the defendants' argument is that there has not yet in this case been presented sufficient underlying data to make evidence of cost and profit relevant at this time. I can not take judicial notice of the fact that these or any of these defendants would discontinue the manufacture and sale of power transformers even in a loss situation, defining loss as a price received below the combination of fixed and variable costs.

There are or can be many factors entering into the probative value of evidence of costs and profits. All of the defendants sell products other than those presently in issue on the price-fixing charges. Within this context of corporations with more than one product, is it an undoubted fact that such diversified corporations will stop selling one of its products if that product's sale price is below the combination of fixed and variable costs?

"Certainly this nexus must be established as to what a corporation producing more than one product would do in the event that a specific product was being sold below its fixed and variable costs. Until this nexus is established, the admissibility of such cost data becomes questionable." [281]

I-T-E had stated that it included in its concept of cost direct labor and materials, manufacturing overhead, administrative overhead and sales costs including sales commissions. Plaintiffs responded that if any cost data were offered, it would be necessary to ascertain what portion was fixed and what portion was variable. Furthermore, it would be necessary to know whether I-T-E's definition was all-inclusive; how much of the total cost was attributable to each category; what items were included under "manufacturing" and "administrative" overhead; whether the two items of overhead were determined by allo-

---

281 Philadelphia Elec. Co. v. Westinghouse Elec. Corp. (E.D. Pa. 1964), Civ. Act. No. 30015, Tr. p. 5000.

cating departmental, divisional or company overhead and, if so, the basis of the allocation; and, if allocations of costs applicable to other products were involved, what total costs were attributable to such other products and whether such other products were also affected by illegal price fixing conspiracies.

Judge Robson ruled that defendants were precluded from offering cost data at the trial. He recalled his oral ruling that evidence of I-T-E's actual costs, profits and losses would be admitted only if I-T-E (1) could establish "that actual costs are the costs which would have been incurred absent a conspiracy," and (2) offered costs, profit and loss data for all significant market factors. He found that prior decisions in the electrical equipment litigation supported his imposition of these two conditions, and he distinguished the OVEC decision, where Judge Feinberg admitted the cost evidence, on the ground that that was a bench trial where the court could proceed "under a more relaxed standard of admissibility" than would be the case in a trial by jury.

Judge Robson referred to the absence of cost data with respect to General Electric by quoting Judge Becker:

> " In other words, how can you determine what a man could buy a good automobile for if you had the going prices of everybody but General Motors, the low-cost producer in the field. I don't think a rational determination could be made." [282]

Judge Robson referred to a number of economic studies indicating that monopolistic costs are not likely to be representative of the costs that would be achieved in an efficient competitive industry. He cited Judge Wyzanski's reference to "the danger of a business becoming slothful, routinized, sleepy or wanting in alertness, initiative, and progressiveness, as a result of the quiet life sought and usually achieved by a monopolist." [283] Judge Robson also quoted with approval Pribam on *Cartel Problems* (C.C.H., 1935), p. 29:

---

[282] N. W. Electric Power Coop., Inc. v. Moloney Electric Co., et al., Civ. A. No. 13290-3 (W.D. Mo., Becker, J.), trial transcript pp. 2489-2495.

[283] U. S. v. Grinnell Corp., et al., CCH TRADE REG. REP. ¶ 71,298 at 80,255 (Nov. 27, 1964).

> " Since the members of price associations are expected to secure prices which will at least cover costs and some profit, the minimum prices fixed, which are likely to become uniform prices, tend to be adjusted to the costs of marginal or high-cost producers."

In holding that the cost data proposed to be presented by I-T-E would not be typical of competitive costs, the court adopted plaintiffs' argument that I-T-E had not even eliminated the expenses of conspiratorial activity from its cost figures.

Finally, the court concluded that it was fatal to I-T-E's position that I-T-E had not attempted to meet the problem of what their fellow conspirators' costs, profits or losses would have been in the absence of a conspiracy. The court said that it had no basis for assuming that I-T-E's costs would have set the market competitive price even if such costs had not been affected by the conspiracy, and, in fact, "I-T-E's position that it was a small, inefficient producer 'which frequently found itself in a loss position and never achieved a reasonable profit on power switchgear assemblies in the period 1946-1960,' argues to the contrary." [284]

---

[284] Memorandum and Order dated April 21, 1966 on I-T-E's Proffered Evidence of Actual Costs, Profits or Losses, No. 61 C 1278 and related power switchgear assembly cases, United States District Court for the Northern District of Illinois, CCH 1966 TRADE CASES ¶ 71756.

In an article in THE ANTITRUST BULLETIN, Vol. XII, Winter 1967, *The Use of Cost Data in Private Antitrust Cases,* Professor Leonard B. White suggests the following procedures to establish the validity of costs in a treble damage action:

"An industry which has been involved in a price fixing conspiracy cannot use cost in defending itself in a treble damage suit unless it can establish what its costs would have been in the absence of the conspiracy. The actual costs of the firms involved are not valid in this instance; however, these costs can be compared to and adjusted by: 1) Costs of firms in the industry but not in the conspiracy. 2) Costs of firms not in the industry or conspiracy but using similar techniques of production. 3) Costs of foreign firms (using adjustments for wages and productivity). 4) Costs of firms in the industry and in the conspiracy for time periods before and after the conspiracy.

"Using these adjustments, an index of direct costs for the industry can be produced. Although this index cannot be used to establish price, it can be used as an argument that price in the industry would not have been below a certain level. Calculation of this form of cost

Plaintiffs presented their damage calculations in a supplemental trial brief. They recited that on the basis of the Corplan analysis of shop order files (which had been coded on IBM tabulating cards and run through a computer which printed the relevant information, including tabulations of monthly and quarterly average percent discounts off book price), they had computed damages on two alternative methods of calculation. The first was the discount off book approach, similar to that adopted for turbine generators in the OVEC trial. The Corplan study was regarded as establishing that the average post-conspiracy discount off book price was 33.10%, but the average percentage discounts for book were also computed separately for the post-conspiracy period for the five major categories of power switchgear assemblies: low voltage switchgear, 5 kv metal-clad switchgear, 15 kv metal-clad switchgear, secondary unit substations and primary unit substations. The Corplan study indicated that the competitive average percent discounts for these categories were, respectively, 30.15%, 34.96%, 27.61%, 38.51% and 34.21%. Damages on individual transactions during the conspiracy period were then computed by calculating the difference between the discount actually received at the time of the transaction and the post-conspiracy discounts off book price. The resulting percentage figure was then applied to projected book price figures which were established from the final price paid by the plaintiff for each transaction. When the average post-conspiracy off book percentage was utilized, the calculations showed an aggregate damage amount for the Commonwealth Edison Company group of plaintiffs of $2,165,980. Applying the post-conspiracy discount off book percentages derived for the five major categories produced a remarkably similar figure for aggregate damages for the same group of $2,285,503.

Plaintiffs also computed damages for the individual transactions on an "order price index" basis, submitting these calculations primarily to confirm, as they claimed, the validity of the discount off book analysis, but also as an alternative method of computing damages. The average post-conspiracy order price indices were

index which would represent costs in the absence of a conspiracy is rather cumbersome. However, its value to either plaintiff or defendant could prove to be not insubstantial."

constructed on two bases: (1) on the basis of plaintiffs' purchases of power switchgear assemblies from I-T-E, and (2) the I-T-E order book summaries which showed I-T-E's total sales of power switchgear assemblies during the post-conspiracy period. The average post-conspiracy indices were then compared with the order price of each transaction, in order to secure a figure representing the difference between the price paid under competitive conditions, as represented by the post-conspiracy period. On the basis of the order price indices the total damages for the Commonwealth Edison Company group of plaintiffs were computed at $1,707,254.

To determine the correlation among the price behavior of plaintiffs' purchases, Corplan data and I-T-E order books, correlation coefficients were calculated on the basis of quarterly average percent discounts off book. The correlations were calculated on the basis of the following standard statistical formula:

$$r = \frac{\Sigma X Y - N \bar{X} \bar{Y}}{\sqrt{\Sigma X^2 - N(\bar{X})^2} \sqrt{\Sigma Y^2 - N(\bar{Y})^2}}$$

The correlation coefficients are set forth in the following table:

CORRELATION COEFFICIENTS

LOW VOLTAGE SWITCHGEAR

	Plaintiffs	Corplan	I-T-E
Plaintiffs	1.000	.8553	*
Corplan	.8553	1.000	.9282
I-T-E	*	.9282	1.000

5 KV METAL-CLAD SWITCHGEAR

	Plaintiffs	Corplan	I-T-E
Plaintiffs	1.000	.8768	.8721
Corplan	.8768	1.000	.9679
I-T-E	.8721	.9679	1.000

15 KV METAL-CLAD SWITCHGEAR

	Plaintiffs	Corplan	I-T-E
Plaintiffs	1.000	.9306	.8261
Corplan	.9306	1.000	.9194
I-T-E	.8261	.9194	1.000

* No correlation calculated.

For impact evidence, plaintiffs cited the events at the November 1958 Traymore meeting and the subsequent behavior of order prices for switchgear. It had been established through the testimony of Buck, I-T-E's Executive Vice President, that the "heroes" agreed at the Traymore to return to book prices. Shortly thereafter prices in fact rose from in excess of 40% off book price discounts, on the average, to within 10% of book price. Further, to demonstrate the effect of the conspiracy on prices, plaintiffs cited the testimony of Getz, a participant in the conspiracy:

> " I cannot name you the year [of competitors' meetings], but it can be determined by checking the record of price level versus book price. When there was no meetings there was price cutting. And the so-called white sale is a typical example."

Further with respect to damages, plaintiffs argued that if there was any inexactitude in their calculations, which they did not admit, the inability to be exact was the result of the price fixing activities of the defendants with the resultant frustration of the operation of normal supply and demand factors. Plaintiffs quoted the United States Supreme Court in *Bigelow* v. *R.K.O. Pictures*:

> " The most elementary conceptions of justice and public policy require that the wrongdoer shall bear the risk of uncertainty which his own wrong has created. . . . [T]he wrongdoer may not object to the plaintiff's reasonable estimate of the cause of injury and of its amount, supported by the evidence, because not based on more accurate data which the wrongdoer's misconduct has rendered unavailable." [285]

Plaintiffs argued for the validity of the discount off book method of calculating damages by urging that it was consistent with what the conspiracy was intended to do and what it in fact did: as described by numerous participants, the conspiracy was designed to and did keep order prices at or near the book price level and, absent the conspiracy, discounts substantially increased. Furthermore, it was argued, the discount off book analysis was consistent with the manner in which the manufacturers themselves approached and maintained records of prices: I-T-E documents were cited to show that the manu-

---

[285] 327 U.S. 251, 265 (1946).

facturers themselves found it necessary to compare transaction order prices by use of discounts off book prices even over substantial periods of time.

To demonstrate that I-T-E was at times a leader in the conspiratorial activity, plaintiffs cited the Commodore Hotel meeting on November 14, 1958, where I-T-E complained violently that the new General Electric metal-clad price sheets were not sufficiently high, with the result that I-T-E's complaints led ultimately to a 10% book price increase for metal-clad switchgear by the adoption of a .55 multiplier in lieu of the .50 multiplier previously agreed upon.

Plaintiffs responded to I-T-E's contention that whatever agreements were arrived at were not fully effective because participants cheated on each other by putting prices below the level agreed upon at the meetings. Plaintiffs pointed out that any effect which conspiratorial activity has on prices, even if it be only 10% effective, results in damages which may be recovered under Section 4 of the Clayton Act. Plaintiffs cited a decision of the Court of Appeals for the Ninth Circuit, *Plymouth Dealers' Ass'n* v. *United States*:[286]

> " When the term 'fix prices' is used, that term is used in its larger sense. . . . The test is not what the actual effect is on prices, but whether such agreements interfere with 'the freedom of traders and thereby restrain their ability to sell in accordance with their own judgment.' Kiefer-Stewart Co. v. Joseph E. Seagram & Sons, supra, 340 U.S. at page 213, 71 S. Ct. at page 260. The competition between the Plymouth dealers and the fact that the dealers used the fixed uniform list price in most instances only as a starting point is of no consequence. It was an agreed starting point; it had been agreed upon between competitors; it was in some instances in the record respected and followed; it had to do with, and had its effect upon, price.
>
> The fact that there existed competition of other kinds between the various Plymouth dealers, or that they cut prices in bidding against each other is irrelevant."

To support their position and their calculations plaintiffs filed an affidavit of Morris Hamburg, Professor of Statistics and Operations Research at the Wharton School of the University

[286] 279 F.2d 128, 132 (1960).

of Pennsylvania. Dr. Hamburg found a strong correlation between the conspiratorial activity and price behavior:

" Turning to the conspiratorial objective of maintaining order prices close to book prices, there is a strong correlation between the time pattern of the operation of collusive activity and the price behavior of power switchgear assemblies. In general, this behavior may be characterized in terms of the existence of substantially increased discounts from book prices during the 'white sale' period, the period prior to the November, 1958 Traymore meeting and the post-conspiracy period, in contrast to the reduced discounts at other time periods since 1946.

. . . .

For example, the Corplan data on 5 kv metal-clad switchgear shows that in 26 of the 36 quarters preceding the white sale (from 1946 through 1954), the quarterly average discount off book was less than 3%. In only 5 of the other quarters was the discount off book more than 4%. The deposition testimony shows that meetings among the manufacturers ceased in late 1954 and Table II shows a dramatic decrease in the level of order prices in relation to book. Thus, in the first quarter of 1955 the average discount off book, in contrast to the small discounts theretofore, was 25.1%. Relatively substantial discounts off book, compared to the earlier period, existed in the rest of 1955; however, the lowering of the discounts in 1955, in successive quarters of 18.0%, 12.8% and 13.0% trace the resumption of the manufacturers' joint activities. By 1956, quarterly discounts off book ranged from only 4.7% to 7.4%. Similar patterns are shown in the low voltage metal-enclosed and 15 kv metal-clad switchgear."

Dr. Hamburg also testified in his affidavit that the coefficients between the three sets of datà utilized (I-T-E's, Corplan and plaintiffs'), ranging from .8261 to .9679, represented strong correlations, and added that by standard tests it was highly unlikely that these correlations could be ascribed to chance factors. Dr. Hamburg also expressed a preference, in choosing a competitive period, for the post-conspiracy period rather than the white sale period. His reason was that, while some competition existed during the white sale, prices even then could not be regarded as untainted by previous periods of collusive agreement.

He also expressed an opinion that the discount off book analysis was valid. It is necessary, he stated, to find a common denominator by means of which price behavior could be examined over a lengthy period of time; in the case of switchgear, average discounts from book prices provide a reasonable common denominator for an appropriate measure of price behavior on dissimilar pieces of equipment.

I-T-E countered the Hamburg affidavit with that of Morton S. Baratz, Professor of Economics, Chairman of the Department of Economics at Bryn Mawr College. Professor Baratz utilized three basic indicators of economic activity: quarterly figures on Gross National Product (GNP); quarterly figures on total expenditures on producers' durable equipment; and quarterly figures, available only to 1947, on the implicit price deflator for producers' durable equipment (an average of prices for producers' durables alone). He argued that the general trend of economic conditions explained the deep fall-off in prices in the post-conspiracy period:

> " A new period of expansion began in mid-1958 and continued till the late summer of 1960. During this boom GNP increased about 16 per cent, expenditures on producers' durables grew 28 per cent, and the price deflator for producers' durables rose about 3 per cent. In the early stages of the recovery in 1959, I-T-E's average percentage discounts narrowed substantially from the levels hit in 1958. But as the impetus of the recovery began to weaken with the beginning of 1960, so did discounts become larger; by 1960-61 they ranged between 25.5 per cent and 31.5 per cent."

I-T-E buttressed its position with an affidavit of its President, Scott, that I-T-E could not have survived if it had charged during the conspiracy period the prices which the plaintiffs claimed as the proper competitive prices:

> " 3. If, beginning with 1946, I-T-E were to have received prices for its power switchgear assemblies about 30% lower than they in fact were, I-T-E would not have lasted more than about a year as a manufacturer of such equipment.
>
> 4. If I-T-E were to have received for its power switchgear assemblies the prices plaintiffs say they should have paid under their order price index theory, I-T-E would not have lasted through the early 1950's and the 'white sale' as a manufacturer of power switchgear assemblies."

Judge Robson, faced with this mass of contradictory material on damages, took an unusual step. As early in the proceedings as August 1963 when he was considering the entry of National Pretrial Order No. 19, he had stated that if the parties did not agree on separation of the issues of liability and damages, he would consider appointing a special master to report to the jury on each company's damages. Consistent with this early-expressed attitude the court in the switchgear cases, by Local Pretrial Order No. 16, after reciting that the parties, although requested by the court to do so, had been unable to agree on an impartial economic expert, went on to appoint such an expert for the court: Reuben A. Kessel, Professor of Business Economics at the University of Chicago. Dr. Kessel was authorized to request from the parties such materials as he might wish, was authorized to consult with the court and its representatives, and, subject to objection by the parties, with the employees, representatives and experts of both the plaintiffs and the defendant. After the filing of his report he was to meet with the court and the parties for the purpose of reviewing it, and in the event of trial he could be called as a witness for or on behalf of any of the parties, or the court might call him as its own witness. His charges and expenses were to be shared by the parties, and at the conclusion of the proceedings the charges and expenses paid to the expert were to be assessed as costs.

Dr. Kessel filed his report in late April 1966. He took the position that post-conspiracy prices were abnormally low:

> " When an industry which has been engaged in an economically effective price conspiracy over a protracted period of time suddenly becomes competitive, profits and prices typically fall below the level that would have existed had there been no conspiracy. The abnormally low level of profits and prices is caused by a larger capacity than would have existed in the absence of price conspiracy. After the dissolution of a price conspiracy, the firms in the newly competitive industry find themselves with uneconomically large capital investments given the new and much lower prices for their products. Consequently, there is a period of time when prices are below the levels that would have existed if there had been no conspiracy, and capital investment is above what it would have otherwise been. . . ."

He found that price behavior could not be rationalized on any basis related to backlogs or demand conditions in the switchgear industry:

" It appears that it is difficult to rationalize price cutting of switchgear and business conditions in the industry. The sharp price declines that occurred during the latter years of conspiracy and afterwards ought not to be attributed to a fall in the demand conditions for switchgear. My examination shows that at no time after 1955 was I-T-E's backlog as low as it was during that year. If backlogs were adjusted for the decline in switchgear prices, backlogs from 1960 through 1964 would rise relative to earlier years. Clearly the bulk of the responsibility for the fall in prices and the low level of prices during the years 1959, 1960, 1961, 1962 and 1963 is to be attributed to the dissolution of the conspiracy and a restoration of more usual methods of product pricing.

The fact that prices fell so dramatically in the last years of the conspiracy and the post-conspiracy period is powerful evidence against the thesis that the fall in prices can be accounted for by a decrease in demand conditions. . . ."

By reason of his conclusion that prices were artificially low during the early post-conspiracy period, Dr. Kessel determined that he would not use 1960-1963 prices but would instead adopt 1964 prices as the benchmark for determining what prices would have been during the conspiratorial period under competitive conditions. As Dr. Kessel put it:

" On theoretical grounds, one can say that the further in time one gets away from the period of the conspiracy, the more likely it is that prices resembling non-conspiracy prices will be observed. Whether 1964 is far enough away, or too far, depends upon what has been the rate of capital formation in this industry during the pre- and post-conspiracy years. I have not seen this data."

He did not quarrel with the use of discounts from book as a method of converting switchgear prices to a common denominator, but he was not convinced that discount off book analysis was appropriate for the determination of the amounts of damage:

" Plaintiffs seem to place too great reliance upon the 'discount from book theory.' Professor Hamburg states that the objective of the conspiracy is to maintain order prices at or near book prices. Surely this is wrong. Presumably, the objective of the conspiracy is to extract monopoly profits. Maintenance of book prices could be and probably was one vehicle for achieving this goal. It is not unreasonable to argue that it was a particularly important vehicle for price collusion, given the fact that the members of the price conspiracy were selling a product that was so lacking in homogeneity. However, for the post-conspiracy period, it is difficult to assign a very important role to book prices and discount from book. Presumably, there exist various combinations of book prices and discounts that yield identical order prices, the relevant consideration from the point of view of buyers and sellers. Hence, after the conspiracy disintegrated, revision of book prices was purely an administrative matter that could have varied from company to company in its timing. Those companies with higher book prices could give larger discounts than companies with lower book prices. What is relevant under these circumstances is the behavior of order prices over time. This is what an order price index would provide. . . ."

The plaintiffs' order price indices were accepted; and Dr. Kessel proceeded to compute damages by taking each transaction, comparing its order price with a weighted average of comparable prices in 1964; in making the comparison he adjusted the transaction price for changes in the purchasing power of money. The comparison of the order price of the specific transaction with the 1964 base revealed to him whether damages occurred. If damages did occur, the difference between the adjusted order price and the base was used to determine the relationship between actual and competitive prices, and the difference taken as a ratio to the base yielded the overcharge percentage. This overcharge percentage was then applied to actual sales prices (not order prices) to determine the estimate of damages. Changes in the purchasing power of money were computed by utilizing the Consumer Price Index.

His report presented his analysis of I-T-E's backlog as reported in the monthly statements of backlog provided by I-T-E. The data itself served to disprove to Dr. Kessel that price variations could be accounted for by variations in demand:

" These data played an important role in rejecting the view that the variation in prices of switchgear from 1946 through 1964 can be accounted for by variations in demand. In my view, when backlogs are large, the incentive to cut prices is small and conversely. Consequently, it is difficult, if not impossible, to rationalize the observed variation in prices during these years as a consequence of variations in demand."

As examples of the findings of Dr. Kessel, for Gulf State Utilities Company, which made purchases of switchgear from 1949 to 1956 in the aggregate amount of $378,289, he found overcharges of $91,237, or 24%. In the case of Kansas City

Power & Light, on purchases of switchgear in the period 1952 to 1959 aggregating $580,205, the overcharge finding was $123,224, or 21%.

I-T-E argued against the release of Dr. Kessel's report but Judge Robson ordered the release of the report and of all material furnished to or utilized by Professor Kessel in its preparation.[287] The court cited the opinion of the Court of Appeals for the Ninth Circuit in *Olympic Refining Co.* v. *The Honorable James M. Carter, Judge of the United States District Court of the Southern District of California*:[288]

> " In the federal judicial system trial and pretrial proceedings are ordinarily to be conducted in public. Rule 43(a), Federal Rules of Civil Procedure, provides that in all trials the testimony of witnesses shall be taken orally in open court unless otherwise provided in the rules. The purpose of the federal discovery rules, as pointed out in Hickman v. Taylor, 329 U.S. 495, 501, 67 S. Ct. 385, 91 L.Ed. 451, is to force a full disclosure." (p. 264)

The trial got underway on May 2 as scheduled. But at the end of the first day, after the jury had been chosen, it became clear that I-T-E, perhaps shaken by the Kessel recommendations, was ready to discuss settlement. Settlement was quickly achieved, a true courthouse steps settlement, and the trial never proceeded beyond the jury selection stage.

The settlement amounts, aggregating two and one-half million dollars for the Commonwealth Edison group of plaintiffs, covered not only switchgear but all other products that were the subject of claims against I-T-E: open fuse cutouts, insulators, power switching equipment, low voltage distribution equipment circuit breakers and isolated phase buses. Commonwealth Edison alone was paid $700,000. Kessel had recommended for Commonwealth Edison damages for switchgear only in the amount of $401,773, or 10.1%. Gulf State settled for $79,000, whereas Kessel had recommended $46,180, or 12.2%; Kansas City Power & Light settled for $100,000, whereas Kessel had recommended $77,713, or 15.3%; and Southern California Edison settled for $550,000, whereas Kessel had recommended $123,704, or 9.7%. The amounts of settlement in excess over those

287 By order dated May 26, 1966.

288 332 F.2d 260 (1964), *cert. denied,* 379 U.S. 900 (1964).

recommended by Dr. Kessel were generally, of course, attributable to the claims in the other product lines.

The court approved the settlements, reciting as a basis for its approval that it had examined the various studies pertaining to damage claims, including Kessel's findings for power switchgear assemblies.

In recommending the settlement to the Board of Directors of the Commonwealth Edison Company, that company's counsel pointed to the Kessel recommendation, recited that a six-weeks trial would be required and that additional time and expense would undoubtedly be involved in post-trial motions or appeals or both. Furthermore, counsel stated, I-T-E was an important supplier of a number of products, and its continuation in business should improve future competition in the industry, with concomitant benefits to purchasers. Counsel stated that while I-T-E's financial situation had improved considerably in 1964 and 1965, there was a serious question whether I-T-E could survive if all of the claims pending against it were prosecuted to judgments. The Commonwealth Edison settlement of $700,000 represented 15% of 1956 to 1959 purchases of all products made the subject of claims against I-T-E, plus an allowance for fees and expenses.

This settlement resulted in a complete disposition of the electrical equipment treble damage claims of Commonwealth Edison, as illustrated by a memorandum from the Statistical Research Department of the company dated September 1, 1966: "We have settled all our electrical equipment cases and are now in a position to dispose of the files."

This settlement with I-T-E broke the logjam, and settlements by I-T-E with other complainants throughout the nation came rapidly. According to the Coordinating Committee's statistics, by September 27, 1966, out of a total of 1,912 electrical equipment cases filed, 1,815 had been determined or dismissed, leaving 97 pending, of which 61 were I-T-E cases. In terms of claims, out of 26,118, 25,027 had been dismissed, leaving 1,091 pending, of which 420 were I-T-E's. By the end of 1966 practically all of the remaining pending cases had been disposed of, and the electrical equipment treble damage litigation had come to an end.

CHAPTER 20

L'envoi

THE FEDERAL JUDICIARY took satisfaction in the part which it had played in the disposition of the electrical equipment cases. Addressing the American Law Institute at its 44th Annual Meeting on May 16, 1967, Chief Justice Earl Warren said:

" And now I turn to some highly dramatic developments in administration in the federal courts. When I addressed the American Law Institute in 1962, I called to your attention the appearance the year before of unprecedented multi-district litigation arising out of antitrust suits in the electrical equipment industry. Beginning in 1961, there were filed in 35 district courts 25,623 separate civil antitrust claims for relief—1,912 civil actions, in many of which multiple plaintiffs joined their separate claims in a single action and in many of which there were multiple counts each based on a separate claim. Each claim for relief was a potentially protracted case and, as I reported, this unprecedented multi-district litigation was imposed upon the ever-increased burden of the ordinary civil and criminal dockets. Our alarm was understandably great and makes equally understandable the measure of my satisfaction in being able to report to the Institute at this meeting that every single one of these cases has been terminated. Not a single one remains pending. Whatever backlog problems the federal courts may have, they do not include any of these cases.

Now, this is history—stimulating and useful history. This remarkable result was achieved by the foresight and organizing ability of a committee of the Judicial Conference of the United States, with Chief Judge Alfred P. Murrah of the Tenth Circuit as its chairman and with Judge Edwin A. Robson of the Northern District of Illinois and Chief Judge William H. Becker of the Western District of Missouri as successive chairmen of its principal subcommittee. These judges, without a chart and without the power to change the rules of procedure created for less demanding tasks, secured the full cooperation of all the district judges to whom these cases were assigned. They were assisted by a small, temporary staff, provided by the Administrative Office on an emergency basis, and now have succeeded in terminating these 1,912 antitrust cases in a period of six years and two months, which would not be regarded as an unusual length of time for the processing of a single complex antitrust case.[289] If it had not been for the monumental effort of the nine judges on this committee of the Judicial Conference and the remarkable cooperation of the 35 district judges before whom these cases were pending, the district court calendars throughout the country could well have broken down."

The Coordinating Committee did not stop work upon the settlement and disposition of the electrical equipment litigation. Coordination of cases was worked out, on the pattern established in the electrical equipment cases, e.g., in aluminum cable, rock salt and pipe antitrust litigation. The Committee published, for the guidance of the bench and bar, an *Outline of Suggested Procedures and Materials for Pre-Trial and Trial of Complex and Multiple Litigation,* which formed the basis for and was followed by a *Manual for Complex and Multidistrict Litigation* published in 1968 under the motto: "There are no inherently protracted cases, only cases which are unnecessarily protracted by inefficient procedures and management." The manual was prepared by a subcommittee of the Coordinating Committee composed of the following members: Judge George H. Boldt, Chief Judge Thomas A. Clary, Chief Judge Joe Ewing Estes, Chief Judge Edwin A. Robson, and Chief Judge William H. Becker, Chairman, Drafting Subcommittee.

The efforts of the lawyers on the plaintiffs' side would seem to bear out the expectation of the Congress in enacting Section 4

---

[289] Supporting the Chief Justice's view is the circumstance that United States v. Procter & Gamble Co., CIV 1196-52 (N.J.) involved more than nine years of pretrial. But this did not set a pretrial record. According to Malcolm A. Hoffman, *Proof of Damages in Private Litigation,* 36 A.B.A. ANTITRUST L. J. 151 (1967):

> "There is pending in England a dispute between the Prior and the Convent of Durham Cathedral as to which has the jurisdiction to administer the spiritualities of the diocese during the absence of the Bishop. The complaint and answer were filed and the matter fiercely argued in 1283, according to the Guinness *Book of World Records.* It smoldered until 1939, having flared up again in 1672, 1890 and 1920. In 1939 the Archbishop of Canterbury appointed the Dean as the guardian of the spirituality of Durham Cathedral, 'without prejudice to the general issue.' That issue had been formulated 656 years before. . . . [T]he matter is still pending with no trial on the merits having taken place. It is still at pre-trial."

of the Clayton Act that it would create "a nation of attorneys general . . . ready to enforce the free enterprise system." [290] The result of the prosecution of the electrical equipment cases was a substantial increase in the number of treble damage suits filed:

> " The treble damage suits at one time were filed at the rate of four or five a year but after the movie industry was put on the spit in 1949 and after the electrical equipment industry was wrestled to the mat by powerful plaintiffs all over the United States, the number of antitrust private suits exceeded by far the number of prosecutions instituted by the United States. To some extent, Congress' desire for a host of private avengers became realized. The small police force, which is the Department of Justice, has become augmented by numerous worthy counsel. . . ." [291]

For the individual lawyer there was the satisfaction which comes to a successful trial lawyer, summarized by an experienced Chicago trial lawyer:

> " The architect of the continuing American revolution is the trial lawyer—the product and the instrument of the adversary system. The trial lawyer tends to be an individualist. He is generally not as dependent on retainers as others and therefore is freer than most. For this he pays a price. His income is variable; he leaves part of his body in every courtroom; he is constantly subjected to grave temptations and frequently accused falsely of succumbing to them. He risks the obloquy of contempt citations; he is tortured by mistakes which hindsight points up after every day of trial. The trial lawyer in short lives dangerously, *but he lives.*" [292]

The electrical equipment litigation became a case history in the Harvard Business School where Professor C. Roland Christensen has led discussions on "The Electrical Industry and Price Fixing" before a blackboard containing the commandment:

---

290 Adair, *Disproof of Damages in Private Litigation,* 36 A.B.A. ANTITRUST L. J. 168 (1967).

291 Hoffman, *supra* note 289, at 167. The efforts of plaintiffs' counsel were also assisted by recourse to one of the world's great poets. In commenting at one point in the proceedings on defendants' inability or unwillingness to recognize a point of law which seemed obvious to plaintiffs, Milton was quoted: "Oh, dark, dark, dark amid the blaze of noon."

292 Abram, *The Challenge of the Courtroom: Reflections on the Adversary System,* THE LAW SCHOOL RECORD, U. OF CHICAGO 7 (Autumn 1963).

"Thou shalt not price fix."[293] And the litigation led the *Harvard Business Review* to publish in March-April 1963, a tongue-in-cheek article, *How to Conspire to Fix Prices,* which contained such suggested general and operating rules as:

" RULE 1. Do not overlook the fact that the purpose of a price-fixing conspiracy is to make more money than you would have made if you had not conspired in the first place.

. . . .

OPERATING RULE 2A. Get your economists and market analysts busy. Do not continue a profitless conspiracy. And, if you are not now conspiring, do not overlook this potentially profitable marketing technique.

. . . .

RULE 4. Before conspiring, be sure that follow-the-leaderism and conscious parallelism are not in the cards. They are much less dangerous and work every bit as well.
OPERATING RULE 4B. Conscious parallelism may be illegal, but it is certainly not as illegal as conspiring. Moreover, it is hard to prove.

. . . .

OPERATING RULE 6A. If it cannot be done without writing it down, do not do it.
OPERATING RULE 6B. If you feel you must have something in writing, you are temperamentally unsuited to conspiring.
OPERATING RULE 6C. Learn to take pride in a scratch pad well-burned or an alias well-rendered.

. . . .

OPERATING RULE 15B. If you are getting more than you would have gotten, stay in; if you are not, get out.

. . . .

IMPORTANT OPERATING RULE 17A. Avoid giving the appearance of selling below cost. It antagonizes the Federal Trade Commission.

. . . .

PHILOSOPHICAL RULE 18. Conspiracies work best on shelf items, but are least necessary. They work worst on special-order items, but are most needed in these areas.

. . . .

RULE 19. When the heat is on, get out.

. . . .

MORAL: Even price-fixers who do not get caught may not benefit by conspiring."

Of course, the prospect of a substantial fee is a stimulant for a trial lawyer. An ancient writer, Holyday, is reported to have said: "A man may as well open an oyster without a knife as a lawyer's mouth without a fee." CHICAGO TRIBUNE MAGAZINE, THE MODERN ALMANAC, April 30, 1972.

293 New York Times, Nov. 10, 1968, §6 (Magazine), at 27.

An important question to be answered is whether the electrical equipment antitrust litigation succeeded in bringing to an end the maintenance of artificially high price levels in the electrical equipment industry. During the course of the proceedings there were numerous predictions that this would not be accomplished: that manufacturers either by more subtle forms of conspiracy or by price leadership or conscious parallelism, or otherwise, would find ways of restoring prices to levels comparable to those in existence during the conspiratorial period. Furthermore, there were some predictions that prices would rise to even higher levels in that the manufacturers would add on to their post-conspiracy prices amounts sufficient to recover from purchasers the vast sums that the manufacturers had expended in settlement or payment of damages in the electrical equipment litigation. This was a cynical prediction that the very consumers who recovered damages from the conspiracy would ultimately repay those damages in the form of higher prices to the manufacturers.

A comparison to determine the correctness of these prophecies is available. Oil circuit breakers, of the 138 kv type, constitute an item of equipment that has been reasonably standard from 1950 to the present time. The chart on page 386 shows the course of prices for this type of circuit breaker from 1951 to 1968.

This is a dramatic demonstration that electrical equipment prices have not been restored to anything like their conspiratorial period peaks from 1956 through 1959. Indeed, what increase has been shown in prices since the bottom was reached in 1961 (immediately following the convictions) can be attributed to the general forces of inflation which have produced for industrial goods an increase in wholesale prices of 10.2%, at December 1968, over the 1957-1959 levels.[294]

An analysis of the oil circuit breaker chart demonstrates that 1968 prices for oil circuit breakers, despite inflation, did not reach even the depths of the white sale prices in 1955-1956 and were little more than half of the prices existing at the peak of the conspiracy in early 1959.

---

294 U. S. NEWS AND WORLD REPORT, Jan. 13, 1969, at 68.

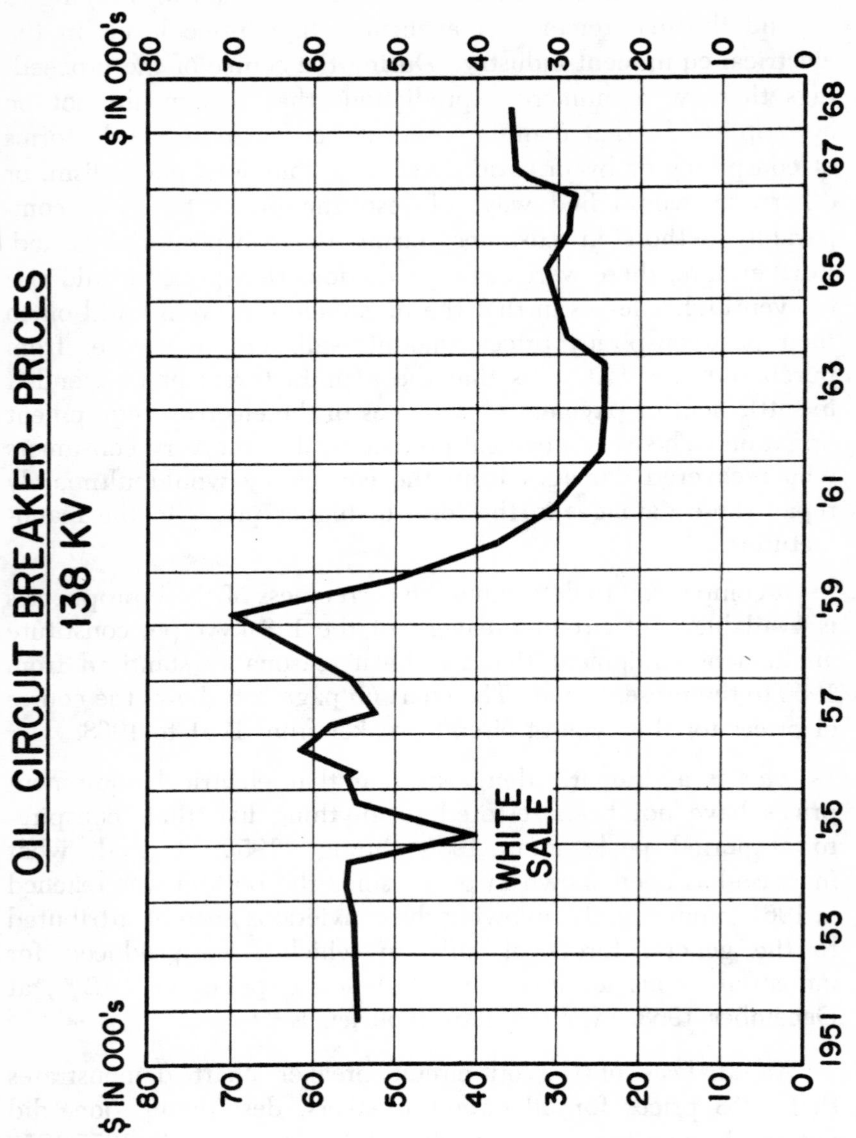
OIL CIRCUIT BREAKER - PRICES
138 KV
$ IN 000's
80
70
60
50
40
30
20
10
0
1951
'53
'55
'57
'59
'61
'63
'65
'67
'68
WHITE SALE

In the case of other products, one utility's records show that distribution transformer prices reached an all-time low in January 1969 and that power transformer prices in recent years have been steadily moving downward. The electrical equipment litigation achieved its purpose in breaking up price fixing conspiracies and the maintenance of artificial price levels.[295]

Nor is there any evidence that electrical equipment manufacturers have been unable to remain in existence and even prosper at competitive price levels. None has gone out of business except Moloney Electric Company, which was in financially straitened circumstances even before the break-up of the price fixing conspiracies.

This case history began with a quotation from Adam Smith:

> " People of the same trade seldom meet together, even for merriment and diversion, but the conversation ends in a conspiracy against the public, or in some contrivance to raise prices."

But that is not the entire quotation. Adam Smith added this sentence, as to which the entire electrical equipment litigation stands in rebuttal:

> " It is impossible indeed to prevent such meetings, by any law which either could be executed, or would be consistent with liberty and justice." [296]

---

295 However, in turbine-generators, General Electric and Westinghouse were charged, in a suit filed in December 1971 by a subsidiary of American Electric Power Company, with a continuing agreement to establish book prices "which were and continue to be essentially the same" and to have established a "pricing method consisting of the application of a single uniform discount or multiplier to the book price." (Complaint filed in Appalachian Power Company v. General Electric Company, et al.; see Antitrust and Trade Regulation Report No. 544 January 4, 1972, pp. A-7-8. In their answers General Electric and Westinghouse contend that plaintiff is estopped from claiming, as it does in the complaint, that General Electric's pricing policy in May 1963 and Westinghouse's pricing policy in December 1963 represented a combination or conspiracy in restraint of trade. The basis for the estoppel, according to the defendants, is that in the OVEC proceeding (see Chapter 17) plaintiff's privies had taken the position that the defendants' pricing policies in 1963 were competitive and that the turbine-generator market at that time was a competitive market.

296 ADAM SMITH, THE WEALTH OF NATIONS (New York: Modern Library, 1937), at 128.

Guide to appendices

APPENDIX

UNITED STATES DISTRICT COURT

FOR THE EASTERN DISTRICT OF PENNSYLVANIA

Criminal No. 20399

Filed: June 22, 1960

UNITED STATES OF AMERICA

—v.—

WESTINGHOUSE ELECTRIC CORPORATION, ALLIS-CHALMERS MANUFACTURING COMPANY, FEDERAL PACIFIC ELECTRIC COMPANY, GENERAL ELECTRIC COMPANY, I-T-E CIRCUIT BREAKER COMPANY, LEWIS J. BURGER, GEORGE E. BURENS, LANDON FULLER, H. F. HENTSCHEL, HOUSTON JONES, L. W. LONG, FRANK M. NOLAN, A. W. PAYNE, FRANK E. STEHLIK, J. T. THOMPSON, A. F. VINSON and DAVID W. WEBB,

Defendants.

INDICTMENT

The grand jury charges:

I.

DEFINITIONS

1. As used herein, the term "power switchgear assemblies" means metal-clad switchgear assemblies in the general rating class of 5 and 15 kilovolts, drawout low voltage metal-enclosed switchgear assemblies in the general rating class of 600 volts and below, and primary and secondary unit substations. It does not include such assemblies constructed for use aboard ships.

II.

DEFENDANTS

2. The corporations named below are hereby indicted and made defendants herein. Each of said corporations is organized and exists under the laws of the State indicated, has its principal place of business in the city indicated, and manufactures power switchgear assemblies in plants at the locations indicated. Within the period of time covered by this indictment, said corporations engaged in the business of manufacturing and selling power switchgear assemblies throughout the United States:

Name of Company	*State of Incorporation*	*Principal Place of Business*	*Location of Plants*
Westinghouse Electric Corporation	Pennsylvania	Pittsburgh, Pennsylvania	Atlanta, Georgia Chicago, Ill. East Pittsburgh, Pa. Hillside, N. J. Houston, Texas Philadelphia, Pa. Sunnyvale, Calif.
Allis-Chalmers Manufacturing Company	Delaware	West Allis, Wisconsin	West Allis, Wisconsin
Federal Pacific Electric Company	Delaware	Newark, New Jersey	Newark, N. J. Chamblee, Ga. Cleveland, Ohio Dallas, Texas Long Island City, New York Los Angeles, Calif. St. Louis, Mo.
General Electric Company	New York	New York, New York	Philadelphia, Pa.
I-T-E Circuit Breaker Company	Pennsylvania	Philadelphia, Pennsylvania	Philadelphia, Pa.

3. Each of the individuals listed below is hereby indicted and made a defendant herein. Within the period of time covered by this indictment, each was associated with one of the defendant corporations in the capacity indicated:

Name of Individual	*Capacity*	*Defendant Corporation*
Lewis J. Burger	General Manager, Switchgear and Control Division	General Electric Company
George E. Burens	Vice-President and General Manager, Switchgear and Control Division	General Electric Company
Landon Fuller	Assistant General Manager, East Pittsburgh Division	Westinghouse Electric Corporation
H. F. Hentschel	General Manager, Medium Voltage Switchgear Department	General Electric Company
Houston Jones	Manager, Draw-out and Load Center Sales Subsection, Low Voltage Switchgear Department	General Electric Company

Name of Individual	Capacity	Defendant Corporation
L. W. Long	Assistant General Manager, Power Equipment Division	Allis-Chalmers Manufacturing Company
Frank M. Nolan	Manages of Sales, Switchgear Assemblies and Unit Substations, Power Equipment Division	Allis-Chalmers Manufacturing Company
A. W. Payne	Sales Manager, Assembled Switchgear and Unit Equipment Section, Assembled Switchgear and Devices Department	Westinghouse Electric Corporation
Frank E. Stehlik	General Manager, Low Voltage Switchgear Department	General Electric Company
J. T. Thompson	Sales Manager, Assembled Switchgear and Devices Department	Westinghouse Electric Corporation
A. F. Vinson	Vice President and Group Executive, Apparatus and Industrial Group	General Electric Company
David W. Webb	Manager, Switchgear Department, Power Equipment Division	Allis-Chalmers Manufacturing Company

4. The acts charged in this indictment to have been done by each of the defendant corporations were authorized, ordered, or done by the officers, agents, employees, or representatives of each defendant corporation, while actively engaged in the management, direction or control of its affairs, including the individuals named as defendants herein.

III.

Co-Conspirators

5. The corporations listed below are hereby named as co-conspirators herein. Each has participated in the combination and conspiracy hereinafter charged and has performed acts and made statements in furtherance thereof. Each is in the business of manufacturing and selling unit substations comprised in part of metal-clad switchgear assemblies and low voltage metal-enclosed switchgear assemblies purchased from defendant corporations:

Company	State of Incorporation	Principal Place of Business
McGraw-Edison Company	Delaware	Elgin, Illinois
Moloney Electric Company	Delaware	St. Louis, Missouri
Wagner Electric Corporation	Delaware	St. Louis, Missouri

IV.

Nature of Trade and Commerce

6. Defendants Westinghouse Electric Corporation, Allis-Chalmers Manufacturing Company, Federal Pacific Electric Company, General Electric Company, and I-T-E Circuit Breaker Company are the five principal manufacturers of power switchgear assemblies in the United States.

7. "Power switchgear assemblies" is a class of equipment which controls and protects electric apparatus used in the generation, conversion, transmission, and distribution of electric energy throughout the United States. Such assemblies consist of switching and interrupting devices in combination with control, metering, protection and regulating equipment, their associated interconnections and supporting structures.

8. There are three principal kinds of power switchgear assemblies: metal-clad, drawout low voltage metal-enclosed, and primary and secondary unit substations.

9. Metal-clad switchgear assemblies are manufactured for use indoors and outdoors, and include as component elements power circuit breakers rated from 2.5 to 13.8 kv. This type of power switchgear assembly is commonly referred to in the industry as the "5 and 15 kv metal-clad switchgear".

10. Drawout low voltage metal-enclosed switchgear assemblies are manufactured for use indoors or outdoors and include as component elements air circuit breakers, rated at 600 volts or below.

11. A unit substation, as used herein, consists primarily of one or more transformers connected and coordinated in design with one or more metal-clad or low voltage metal-enclosed switchgear assemblies or combinations thereof. A primary unit substation has a low voltage rating of 601 volts and above, while a secondary unit substation has a low voltage rating of 600 volts or below.

12. Practically all power switchgear assemblies sold in the United States by defendant and co-conspirator corporations are sold to the following classes of customers:

(a) Electric utility companies located throughout the United States;

(b) Various Federal, State, and local governmental agencies engaged in the generation, transmission, or distribution of electricity which by the laws of the United States, a State or subdivision thereof, are required to purchase items from the lowest bidder after sealed bids have been requested by the agency. Such agencies include, among others, Tennessee Valley Authority, United States Department of Interior, Atomic Energy Commission, United States Army Corps of Engineers, United States Navy, and United States Air Force;

(c) Private industrial corporations; and

(d) Contractors engaged in the building and construction trades.

13. Power switchgear assemblies are manufactured by defendant and co-conspirator corporations in plants located in California, Georgia, Illinois, Missouri, New Jersey, New York, Ohio, Pennsylvania, Texas and Wisconsin, and are sold and shipped by them in interstate commerce to electric utility companies, to Federal, State, and local governmental agencies, to private industrial corporations and to contractors located throughout the United States. Such customers purchase power switchgear assemblies valued at approximately $125,000,000 annually from the defendant corporations.

V.

Offense Charged

14. Beginning at least as early as 1958 and continuing thereafter at least to September 23, 1959, the defendants, together with the co-conspirators and other persons to the grand jurors unknown, engaged in a combination and conspiracy in unreasonable restraint of the aforesaid interstate trade and commerce in power switchgear assemblies, in violation of Section 1 of the Act of Congress of July 2, 1890, entitled "An act to protect trade and commerce against unlawful restraints and monopolies" as amended (c. 647, 26 Stat. 209, 15 U.S.C. Sec. 1) commonly known as the Sherman Act.

15. The aforesaid combination and conspiracy consisted of a continuing agreement, understanding, and concert of action among the defendants, the co-conspirators and other persons to the grand jurors unknown the substantial terms of which were:

(a) To fix and maintain prices, terms, and conditions for the sale of power switchgear assemblies;

(b) To allocate among themselves the business of supplying power switchgear assemblies to Federal, State, and local governmental agencies;

(c) To submit noncompetitive, collusive and rigged bids for supplying power switchgear assemblies to electric utility companies, Federal, State, and local governmental agencies, private industrial corporations and contractors throughout the United States; and

(d) To refrain from selling certain types of power switchgear assemblies or components thereof to other manufacturers of electrical equipment.

16. During the period of time covered by this indictment, the defendants, co-conspirators and other persons to the grand jurors unknown, for the purpose of forming and effectuating the aforesaid combination and conspiracy, did among other things, the following:

(a) On or about October 8, 1958, following previous discussions, representatives of defendant corporations (other than defendant Allis-Chalmers Manufacturing Company) met at the Hotel Astor in New York City to discuss increasing the price levels for power switchgear assemblies;

(b) On or about November 9, 1958, a meeting was held at the Traymore Hotel, Atlantic City, New Jersey, at which representatives of all of the defendant corporations agreed, among other things, that:

(1) In the sale of power switchgear assemblies to electric utility companies, private industrial corporations, and contractors, all of the defendant corporations, except Federal Pacific Electric Company, would sell power switchgear assemblies at "list" or "book" price levels;

(2) In the sale of power switchgear assemblies to electric utility companies, private industrial corporations, and contractors (except low voltage drawout metal-enclosed switchgear assemblies sold to private industrial corporations) defendant Federal Pacific Electric Company would be permitted to quote prices at a specified differential below the prices quoted by the other defendant corporations;

(3) Representatives of all of the defendant corporations would meet periodically and allocate bids to Federal, State, and local governmental agencies according to the following approximate percentage shares:

General Electric Company	39 per cent
Westinghouse Electric Company	35 per cent
I-T-E Circuit Breaker Company	11 per cent
Allis-Chalmers Manufacturing Company	8 per cent
Federal Pacific Electric Company	7 per cent

(c) On or about November 14, 1958, at New York, New York, another meeting was held for the purpose of establishing a systematic procedure for carrying out the agreements reached at the November 9, 1958 meeting. At this and subsequent meetings, the defendant corporations agreed that the General Electric Company price lists would be the "book" or "list" prices for power switchgear assemblies. At this meeting they also agreed that metal-clad switchgear assemblies would not be sold to switchboard assemblers;

(d) Following the November 14, 1958 meeting, a series of periodic meetings were held throughout the United States attended by representatives of all of the defendant corporations. At least 25 such meetings were held between the middle of November 1958 and October 1959 at various cities, including:

Philadelphia, Pennsylvania
New York, New York
Chicago, Illinois
Pittsburgh, Pennsylvania
Detroit, Michigan
Newark, New Jersey
Louisville, Kentucky
Milwaukee, Wisconsin
Cherry Hill, New Jersey

(e) At these periodic meetings, a scheme or formula for quoting nearly identical prices to electric utility companies, private industrial corporations and contractors was used by defendant corporations, designated by their representatives as a "phase of the moon" or "light of the moon" formula. Through cyclic rotating positioning inherent in the formula, one defendant corporation would quote the low price, others would quote intermediate prices and another would quote the high price; these positions would be periodically rotated among the defendant corporations. This formula was so calculated that in submitting prices to these customers, the price spread between defendant corporations' quotations would be sufficiently narrow so as to eliminate actual price competition among them, but sufficiently wide so as to give an appearance of competition. This formula was designed to permit each defendant corporation to know the exact price it and every other defendant corporation would quote on each prospective sale;

(f) At these periodic meetings, a cumulative list of sealed bid business secured by all of the defendant corporations was also circulated and the representatives present would compare the relative standing of each corporation according to its agreed upon percentage of the total sales pursuant to sealed bids. The representatives present would then discuss particular future bid invitations and designate which defendant corporation should submit the lowest bid therefor, the amount of such bid, and the amount of the bid to be submitted by others;

(g) In connection with the meetings and understandings described above, precautionary measures were adopted by representatives of defendant corporations to avoid detection, such as minimizing telephone calls, avoiding leaving notepapers in hotel rooms where meetings were held and avoiding social contacts among such representatives in the hotels where meetings were being held. In addition, code numbers identifying defendant corporations were used in documents effectuating the "phase of the moon" formula referred to above.

(h) Pursuant to these agreements, the defendant corporations submitted bids in 1958 and 1959 to various Federal, State and local governmental agencies and other awarding authorities throughout the United States.

VI.

Effects

17. The effects of the aforesaid combination and conspiracy have been that:

(a) Prices of power switchgear assemblies throughout the United States have been raised, fixed, and maintained at high and artificial levels;

(b) Price competition in the sale of power switchgear assemblies throughout the United States has been restrained, suppressed and eliminated;

(c) Purchasers of power switchgear assemblies throughout the United States have been deprived of the benefits of free competition in the purchase of these products; and

(d) Public agencies engaged in the generation, transmission or distribution of electricity have been denied the right to receive competitive sealed bids, as required by law, and have been forced to pay high, artificially-fixed prices for power switchgear assemblies.

VII.

Jurisdiction and Venue

18. The combination and conspiracy charged in this indictment was carried out in part within the Eastern District of Pennsylvania, and within the jurisdiction of this court. During the period of time covered by this indictment and within the five years next preceding the return thereof, the defendants performed within the Eastern District of Pennsylvania many of the acts hereinbefore charged.

Dated: June 22, 1960

A TRUE BILL

JANE DE LONG
Foreman

/s/ WILLIAM L. MAHER
William L. Maher

/s/ ROBERT A. BICKS
Robert A. Bicks
Acting Assistant Attorney General

/s/ DONALD G. BALTHIS
Donald G. Balthis

/s/ CHARLES L. WHITTINGHILL
Charles L. Whittinghill
Attorney, Department of Justice

/s/ MORTON M. FINE
Morton M. Fine

/s/ GORDON B. SPIVACK
Gordon B. Spivack

/s/ WALTER E. ALESSANDRONI
Walter E. Alessandroni
United States Attorney

/s/ LEWIS J. OTTAVIANI
Lewis J. Ottaviani

Attorneys, Department of Justice
Antitrust Division
Department of Justice
420 Mall Building
Philadelphia 6, Pennsylvania

APPENDIX 2

PHILADELPHIA ELECTRICAL CASES

Case and Defendants	Pleas	Sentences (Fine and/or Imprisonment)
U.S. v. *Westinghouse Electric Corporation, et al.* Criminal No. 20361, Filed: May 25, 1960 (Power Transformers)		
Westinghouse Electric Corporation	Guilty	$40,000
Allis-Chalmers Manufacturing Company	Guilty (6-14-60)	25,000
General Electric Company	Guilty	40,000
McGraw, Edison Company	Guilty	20,000
Moloney Electric Company	Guilty	15,000
Wagner Electric Corporation	Guilty	10,000
J. H. Chiles, Jr.	Guilty	2,000 and 30 days.
W. S. Ginn	Guilty	5,000 and 30 days.
R. N. McCollom	Guilty	2,000 and 30 days, suspended.
J. W. McMullen	Guilty (6-14-60)	3,000 and 30 days, suspended.
J. W. Seaman	Guilty	2,500 and 30 days, suspended.
R. W. Smith	Guilty	3,000 and 30 days, suspended.
W. R. Swoish	Guilty	5,000 and 1 mth., suspended.
U.S. v. *Westinghouse Electric Corporation, et al.* Criminal No. 20399, Filed: June 22, 1960 (Power Switchgear Assemblies)		
Westinghouse Electric Corporation	Guilty	$20,000
Allis-Chalmers Manufacturing Company	Guilty (7-11-60)	10,000
Federal Pacific Electric Company	Guilty (8-16-60)	10,000
General Electric Company	Guilty	30,000
I-T-E Circuit Breaker Company	Guilty (8-16-60)	10,000
Lewis J. Burger	Guilty	2,000 and 30 days.

George E. Burens	Guilty	4,000 and 30 days.
Landon Fuller	Guilty (8-22-60)	3,000 and 1 mth., suspended.
H. F. Hentschel	Guilty	2,000 and 1 mth., suspended.
Houston Jones	Nolo Contendere	1,500
L. W. Long	Guilty (7-11-60)	2,000 and 30 days, suspended.
Frank M. Nolan	Guilty (7-11-60)	1,000
A. W. Payne	Guilty (8-22-60)	1,000
Frank E. Stehlik	Guilty	3,000 and 1 mth., suspended.
J. T. Thompson	Guilty (8-22-60)	2,000
David W. Webb	Guilty (7-11-60)	1,000

U.S. v. *General Electric Company, et al.*
Criminal No. 20401, Filed: June 29, 1960
(Turbine-Generator Units)

General Electric Company	Guilty	$50,000
Allis-Chalmers Manufacturing Company	Guilty (7-11-60)	25,000
Westinghouse Electric Corporation	Guilty	35,000
W. S. Ginn	Nolo Contendere	7,500
C. I. Mauntel	Nolo Contendere	1,000 and 30 days.
W. C. Rowland	Nolo Contendere (1-6-61)	4,000 and 1 mth., suspended.
W. E. Saupe	Nolo Contendere	5,500 and 1 mth., suspended.

U.S. v. *Allen-Bradley Company, et al.*
Criminal No. 20398, Filed: June 22, 1960
(Industrial Control Equipment)

Allen-Bradley Company	Guilty	$40,000
The Clark Controller Company	Guilty	25,000
Cutler-Hammer, Inc.	Guilty	35,000
General Electric Company	Guilty	35,000

Case and Defendants	Pleas	Sentences (Fine and/or Imprisonment)
Square D Company	Guilty	35,000
Westinghouse Electric Corporation	Guilty	40,000
J. M. Cook	Guilty	2,000 and 30 days.
T. C. Finnell	Guilty	1,500
E. R. Jung	Guilty	2,000 and 30 days.
F. F. Loock	Guilty	7,500
W. F. Oswalt	Guilty	4,000 and 30 days, suspended.
U.S. v. *Federal Pacific Electric Company, et al.* Criminal No. 20348, Filed: May 19, 1960 (Power Switching Equipment)		
Federal Pacific Electric Company	Guilty	$15,000
General Electric Company	Guilty	30,000
I-T-E Circuit Breaker Company	Guilty	15,000
Joslyn Mfg. and Supply Co.	Nolo Contendere	10,000
H. K. Porter Company, Inc.	Guilty	25,000
Schwager-Wood Corporation	Nolo Contendere (2-6-61)	15,000
Southern States Equipment Corporation	Guilty	20,000
Westinghouse Electric Corporation	Guilty	20,000
J. E. Cordell	Guilty	1,500 and 1 mth., suspended.
W. T. Pyle	Guilty	1,000
G. L. Roark	Guilty	1,500
John Romano	Guilty	1,500 and 1 mth., suspended.
H. K. Wilcox	Guilty	1,500 and 1 mth., suspended.
W. Maxwell Wood	Guilty	7,500 and 1 mth., suspended.

U.S. v. *Foster Wheeler Corporation, et al.*
Criminal No. 20402, Filed: June 29, 1960
(Condensers)

Foster Wheeler Corporation	Guilty	$20,000
Allis-Chalmers Manufacturing Company	Guilty (7-11-60)	10,000
Carrier Corporation	Nolo Contendere	7,500
Ingersoll-Rand Company	Guilty	20,000
Westinghouse Electric Corporation	Guilty	25,000
C. H. Wheeler Manufacturing Company	Guilty	20,000
Worthington Corporation	Guilty	20,000
H. G. Conkey	Guilty	4,000 and 30 days, suspended.
M. H. Howard	Guilty	2,000
C. I. Mauntel	Guilty	1,500
L. G. L. Thomas	Guilty	4,000 and 1 mth., suspended.
A. M. Tullo	Guilty	3,000 and 30 days, suspended.

U.S. v. *General Electric Company, et al.*
Criminal No. 20235, Filed: February 16, 1960
(Oil Circuit Breakers)

General Electric Company	Guilty	$40,000
Allis-Chalmers Manufacturing Company	Guilty (4-8-60)	20,000
Federal Pacific Electric Company	Nolo Contendere	15,000
I-T-E Circuit Breaker Company	Nolo Contendere	10,000
Westinghouse Electric Corporation	Guilty	30,000
Clarence E. Burke	Guilty	3,500 and 1 mth., suspended.
Royce C. Crawford	Nolo Contendere	2,000
L. W. Long	Nolo Contendere	1,500 and 1 mth., suspended.
William H. Schiek	Nolo Contendere	Not Sentenced.
J. W. Stirling	Guilty	1,500 and 1 mth., suspended.

In the other thirteen proceedings, all pleas were *nolo contendere* and only fines were imposed, except that in distribution transformers two individuals were given suspended sentences. The other proceedings and defendants were:

U.S. v. *I-T-E Circuit Breaker Company et al.*
Criminal No. 20236, Filed: February 16, 1960
(Low Voltage Power Circuit Breakers)

I-T-E Circuit Breaker Company
General Electric Company
Westinghouse Electric Corporation
R. W. Ayres, Jr.
W. T. Pyle
Frank E. Stehlik
J. T. Thompson

U.S. v. *Cutler-Hammer, Inc. et al.*
Criminal No. 20400, Filed: June 23, 1960
(Low Voltage Distribution Equipment)

Cutler-Hammer, Inc.
Federal Pacific Electric Company
General Electric Company
I-T-E Circuit Breaker Company
Square D Company
Westinghouse Electric Corporation

U.S. v. *Sangamo Electric Company et al.*
Criminal No. 20508, Filed: October 20, 1960
(Watthour Meters)

Sangamo Electric Company
General Electric Company
Westinghouse Electric Corporation

U.S. v. *Ohio Brass Company et al.*
Criminal No. 20238, Filed: February 17, 1960
(Insulators)

Ohio Brass Company
General Electric Company
Lapp Insulator Company, Inc.
The Porcelain Insulator Corporation
I-T-E Circuit Breaker Company
A. B. Chance Company
McGraw-Edison Company
H. K. Porter Company, Inc.

U.S. v. *Cornell-Dubilier Electric Corporation et al.*
Criminal No. 20488, Filed: September 15, 1960
(Power Capacitors)

Cornell-Dubilier Electric Corporation
McGraw-Edison Company
General Electric Company
Ohio Brass Company
Sangamo Electric Company
Westinghouse Electric Corporation

U.S. v. *A. B. Chance Company et al.*
Criminal No. 20240, Filed: February 17, 1960
(Open Fuse Cutouts)

A. B. Chance Company
General Electric Company
Hubbard and Company
I-T-E Circuit Breaker Company
Joslyn Mfg. and Supply Co.
McGraw-Edison Company
Southern States Equipment Corporation
Westinghouse Electric Corporation

U.S. v. *McGraw-Edison Company et al.*
Criminal No. 20239, Filed: February 17, 1960
(Lightning Arresters)

McGraw-Edison Company
General Electric Company
Hubbard and Company
Joslyn Mfg. and Supply Co.
Ohio Brass Company
H. K. Porter Company, Inc.
Westinghouse Electric Corporation

U.S. v. *Allis-Chalmers Manufacturing Company et al.*
Criminal No. 20364, Filed: May 25, 1960
(Instrument Transformers)

Allis-Chalmers Manufacturing Company
General Electric Company
Westinghouse Electric Company

U.S. v. *McGraw-Edison Company et al.*
Criminal No. 20363, Filed: May 25, 1960
(Network Transformers)

McGraw-Edison Company
Allis-Chalmers Manufacturing Company
General Electric Company
Moloney Electric Company
Wagner Electric Corporation
Westinghouse Electric Corporation

U.S. v. *Lapp Insulator Company, Inc. et al.*
Criminal No. 20241, Filed: February 17, 1960
(Bushings)

Lapp Insulator Company, Inc.
General Electric Company
Ohio Brass Company
Westinghouse Electric Corporation

U.S. v. *H. K. Porter Company, Inc. et al.*
Criminal No. 20349, Filed: May 19, 1960
(Isolated Phase Bus)

H. K. Porter Company, Inc.
General Electric Company
I-T-E Circuit Breaker Company
Westinghouse Electric Corporation

U.S. v. *General Electric Company et al.*
Criminal No. 20362, Filed: May 25, 1960
(Distribution Transformers)

General Electric Company
Allis-Chalmers Manufacturing Company
Kuhlman Electric Company
McGraw-Edison Company
Moloney Electric Company
Wagner Electric Corporation
Westinghouse Electric Corporation
M. A. deFerranti
Gordon C. Hurlbert
W. R. Swoish
A. R. Waehner
Joel Watkins

U.S. v. *I-T-E Circuit Breaker Company et al.*
Criminal No. 20350, Filed: May 19, 1960
(Navy and Marine Switchgear)

I-T-E Circuit Breaker Company
General Electric Company
Westinghouse Electric Corporation

APPENDIX 3a

J. O. No. 10567

June 19, 1961

INSTRUCTIONS
CLARIFYING INFORMATION
TURBINE GENERATORS
PRICE STUDY
ELECTRICAL EQUIPMENT

The object of this survey is to arrive at the price paid for the basic standard unit of the rating involved, as indicated in the original proposal and contract documents. This means that as complete a list as possible of all original modifications and accessories is required in order to determine the portion of total price which is represented by the basic unit. The questionnaire sheets should be marked only for modifications and accessories which were included in the original order price. If the turbine generator has been purchased at some known discount from net book price, this information will prove very valuable. If not, any information available on individual modification or accessory prices will be helpful and may be added in the right hand margin of the sheets.

If the information on original modifications and accessories is not available but the information on the unit as shipped is available, then furnish this and so state on the questionnaire. In this case, the shipping date and final invoiced price with amount of escalation stated separately, must be given along with other applicable information on Sheet 1 of the Questionnaire under "Changes to Original Order."

J. O. No. 10567 **Sheet 1**

Code ....

P. O. No. ....

Manufacturer ....

PRICE STUDY

ELECTRICAL EQUIPMENT

TURBINE GENERATORS

P

1. *Negotiation Data*

Method of Negotiation	Check Method	Method of Authorization	Date Author-ized
Selective Competitive Bidding....................................	....	Oral	....
Direct Negotiation (Price obtained through negotiation with one supplier)..	....	Letter of Intent a. Company	....
		b. Vendor	....
Combination of Above (Selective competitive bidding followed by negotiation)..	....	Purchase Order	....
		Contract	....

Conditions

Terms of Payment

a. Net .... 30 .... 60 .... 90 .... Other ....

b. Other (Explain, including cancellation clauses, if any)

Were there any conditions of agreement which would influence placing of contract, viz: in package with other equipment, quantity discount, schedule of delivery, or other: ....

....

2. *Price*

Book Price: Per Cent ...., Date of Price Sheet ....

Purchase Order or Contract Price:

Original Order	Net Cost
Original price for basic standard unit of equipment..................................	$..................
Modifications and accessories..................................	....
Direct taxes: State type	....
Freight	....
Amount for supervision of erection..................................	....
Total, Original Price of Order or Contract..................................	$..................
Date stated in quotation or other effective date for order or contract prices: Date	
Changes to Original Order	
Modifications and accessories..................................	$..................
Direct taxes: State type..................................	....
Freight	....
Amount of escalation (attach supplemental sheet to explain terms)..........	....
Amount for supervision of erection or labor for erection..........................	....
Total, Final Price of Completed Order..................................	$ ....

Shipping Terms: Fob factory ...., Fob factory with freight allowed to destination ...., Fob destination ....

Dates of Shipment: Initial .... Final ....

Sheet 2

J. O. No. 10567
Code ....
P. O. No. ....

TURBINE GENERATORS (Continued)

Manufacturer ....
Turbine Design .... Handbook .... Pref. Std ....
Maximum guaranteed capability, kw ....
Type
TCTF ....
TCDF ....
Other ....
Speed of shafts, rpm ....
Exhaust blades, length, in. ....
Generator Design .... Handbook .... Pref. Std ....
Kva ....
H_2 pressure, lb ....
Initial Steam Conditions
Pressure, psi gauge ....
Temperature, F ....
Reheat temperature, F ....
Throttle steam flow, maximum guarantee, lb per hr ....
Number of extraction points ....
Feed water temperature, F ....
Exhaust pressure, in. Hg ....
Auxiliary steam use, lb per hr ....
Extraction point from which taken (from top of cycle) ....
Boiler Feed Pump Drive
(Size of pumps, half size to full .... or less than half size ....)
Type
Main shaft ....
Motor ....
Separate turbine
Rpm ...., Bhp ....
Initial steam pressure and temperature ....
Condensing or noncondensing ....
No. of extractions on boiler feed pump turbine ....
Indoor or outdoor ....

Any special provision for testing of turbine generator unit:

144

Sheet 3

J. O. No. 10567
Code ....
P. O. No. ....

TURBINE GENERATORS (Continued)

Give information only on accessories and modifications included in *Original Contract*.	Provided Yes	Provided No	Price
Initial pressure regulator equipped for motor operation	....	....	....
Load limit device equipped for motor operation	....	....	....
Underspeed release device	....	....	....
Turning gear assembly equipped for solenoid operation	....	....	....
Shaft rotation indicator (cross compound only)	....	....	....
Zero speed sensing device	....	....	....
Automatic turning gear engagement	....	....	....
2nd gland steam condenser	....	....	....
30 per cent oversize gland steam condenser	....	....	....
Quick start features	....	....	....
Vibration trip device	....	....	....
Turbine motors, all totally enclosed type	....	....	....
Automatic load dispatching devices	....	....	....
Provision for operating at 5 per cent overpressure	....	....	....
Provision for gaining capacity by taking heaters out of service	....	....	....
Boiler Feed Pump Drive			
Main shaft	....	....	....
Separate turbine	....	....	....
Provision for testing turbine generator unit	....	....	....

Sheet 4

J. O. No. 10567
Code ....
P. O. No. ....

TURBINE GENERATORS (Continued)

Generator

Manufacturer	....		
Type	Yes		No
Conventional-cooled	....		....
Inner-cooled	....		....
Indoor or outdoor	....		....
Exciter			
Shaft driven	....		....
Motor generator set	....		....
Kv	....		
H_2 pressure, lb	30	45	60
Kva	....	....	....
Power factor	....	....	....
Short circuit ratio	....	....	....

Give information only on modifications and accessories included in Original Contract:

Item	Description or Quantity	Provided Yes	Provided No	Item Price
Bushing current transformers	....	....	....	....
Voltage regulator		....	....	....
Type	....			
Excitation switchgear		....	....	....
Number breakers	....			
Current rating	....			
Enclosure	....			
Spare motor generator exciter		....	....	....
Kw	....			
Enclosure	....			
Outdoor turbine generator only				
Weatherproof complete unit normal temperature		....	....	....
Weatherproofed motor generator set		....	....	....
Turbine walk-in housing		....	....	....

State nature of any special requirements of sufficient significance to appreciably affect price of original contract and give price if available.

146

STG TEXT TABLE 2

WORKSHEET

Code XXX
P. O. (Order No.) — Pref. Std.

Item—Turbine Generator
Type TCTF Speed 3,600
Press. 1,800 Temp 1,000/1,000 Exh. Blades, In. 23
Max Guar. Turbine Capability, Kw 150,000
Rated Generator, Kva 200,535 at 30 lb H_2
Manufacturer: General Electric Co.

Effective Date
Price Agreement 1-25-55 Price $3,204,000
Book Price Section 4716 Page 11 Date Issued
Date Effective 1-3-55

		Book Price
1.	†Basic Price with Standard Accessories	$3,510,000
Price Additions for:		
2.	Next Larger Generator	
3.	Extra Throttle Steam Flow	
4.	Automatic Turning Gear Engagement	
5.	Boiler Feed Pump Drive	
6.	Quick Starting Features	
7.	Weatherproofing	
8.	Bushing Type Current Transformer	8,470
9.	Excitation Switchgear	
10.	Spare MG Exciter	
11.	Turbine Tests in Field	
Miscellaneous Accessory Equipment as follows:		
12.	Amplidyne	8,000
13.	Underspeed Release Device	3,100
14.	Motor Operated Load Limit Device	1,650
15.	Recorders	18,370
16.	Total Net Book Price	$3,549,590
17.	Total Price Paid	$3,204,000

18. Ratio $\frac{17}{16}$ = Calculated Book Multiplier = .903

18a. Book Multiplier Stated by Purchaser Not Stated

19. Ratio .903 x Item 1 $3,510,000 = Est. Actual Base Price Paid $3,169,530

20. Reference Book Price $5,403,100 Date Eff. 4-28-58

21. $\frac{\text{Item 1}}{\text{Item 20}} = \frac{\$3,510,000}{5,403,100} = .650$

22. Item 18 .903 x Item 21 .650 = Ratio of Est. Actual Base Price Paid to Reference Book Price = .587

† Including all standard accessories.

7

HYPOTHETICAL EXAMPLE

(Based upon the worksheet in Text Table 2, p. 7)

Step 1. The unit in question is a reheat unit, preferred standard tandem compound triple flow. The approximate base price given in Text Table 24 (January, 1955) is 56.3 per cent of 1958.

Step 2. The appropriate reciprocal from Text Table 15 is .9655.

56.3 x .9655 = 54.3

Therefore the specific base price is 54.3 per cent of 1958. (Since this case happened to fall in a reference period, there was no need for prorating between the reciprocals for two such periods, the more usual case.)

Step 3. The order price is given in Appendix C, Column 15, as 58.7 per cent of 1958.

Step 4. The percent which the specific base price is of the order price is

54.3 divided by 58.7 = 92.5.

Step 5. The contract price of the order, excluding escalation, was $3,204,000.

Step 6. The specific base dollar price is

$3,204,000 x 92.5 = $2,963,700.

Step 7. ATIG Change in Cost Index, order date (three months' average December 1954 through February 1955) = 118.1.

ATIG Change in Cost Index, eighteen months before shipment (average of February 1955 through July 1956) = 122.6.

122.6 divided by 118.1 equals 103.81, the percentage difference (3.81) between price after allowance for escalation and price before any allowance is made for escalation.

Step 8. The specific base price including escalation is

$2,963,700 x 103.81 = $3,076,617.

Step 9. The total price paid including escalation* was $3,844,800.

Step 10. The overcharge was $3,844,800 — $3,076,617 = $768,183.

---

* Escalation amounted to 20%.

APPENDIX 4

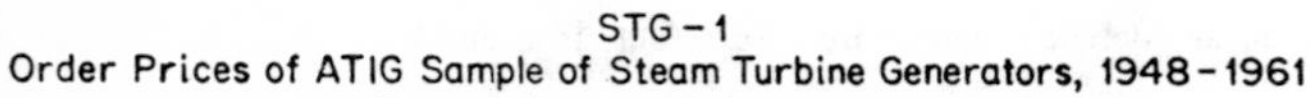

STG – 1

Order Prices of ATIG Sample of Steam Turbine Generators, 1948 – 1961

(Expressed as percent of 1958 peak book)

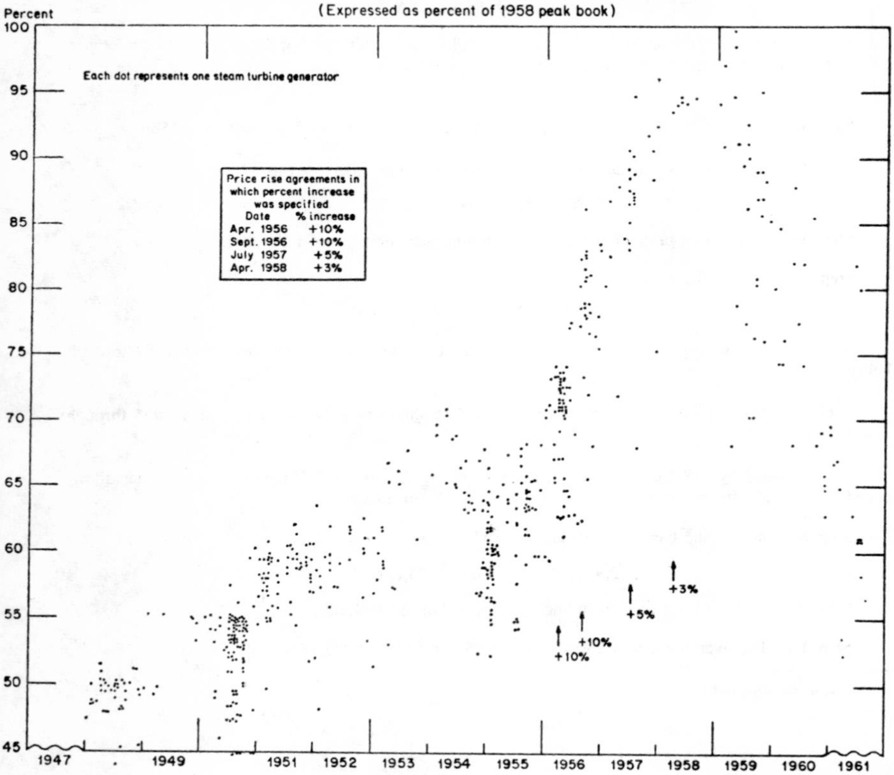

Source: Stone and Webster

PRELIMINARY AND TENTATIVE
6/1/62

APPENDIX 5

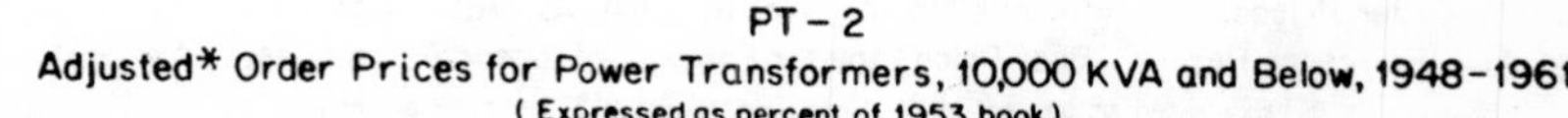

PT – 2

Adjusted* Order Prices for Power Transformers, 10,000 KVA and Below, 1948–1961

(Expressed as percent of 1953 book)

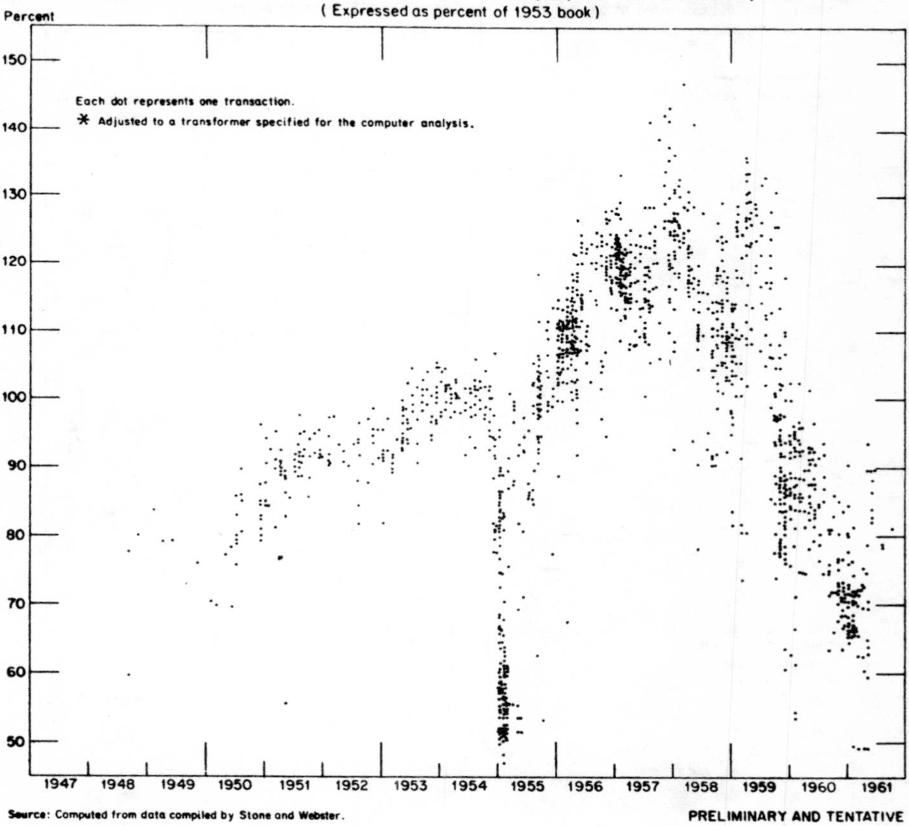

Percent

150
140
130
120
110
100
90
80
70
60
50

Each dot represents one transaction.

* Adjusted to a transformer specified for the computer analysis.

1947 1948 1949 1950 1951 1952 1953 1954 1955 1956 1957 1958 1959 1960 1961

Source: Computed from data compiled by Stone and Webster.

PRELIMINARY AND TENTATIVE
9/1/62

APPENDIX 6

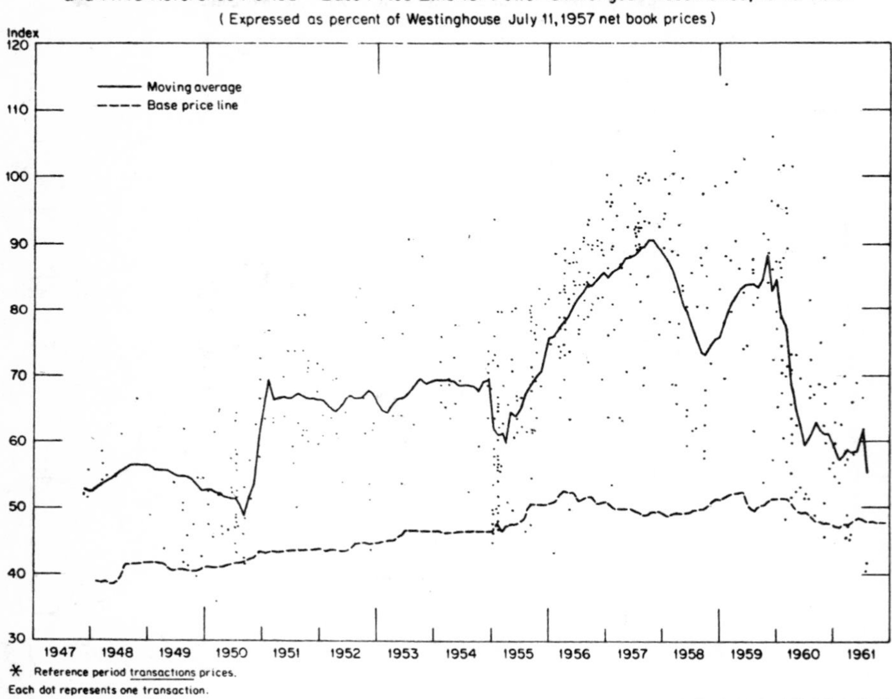

* Reference period transactions prices.
Each dot represents one transaction.
Source: Computed from ATIG data

PRELIMINARY AND TENTATIVE
3/1/63

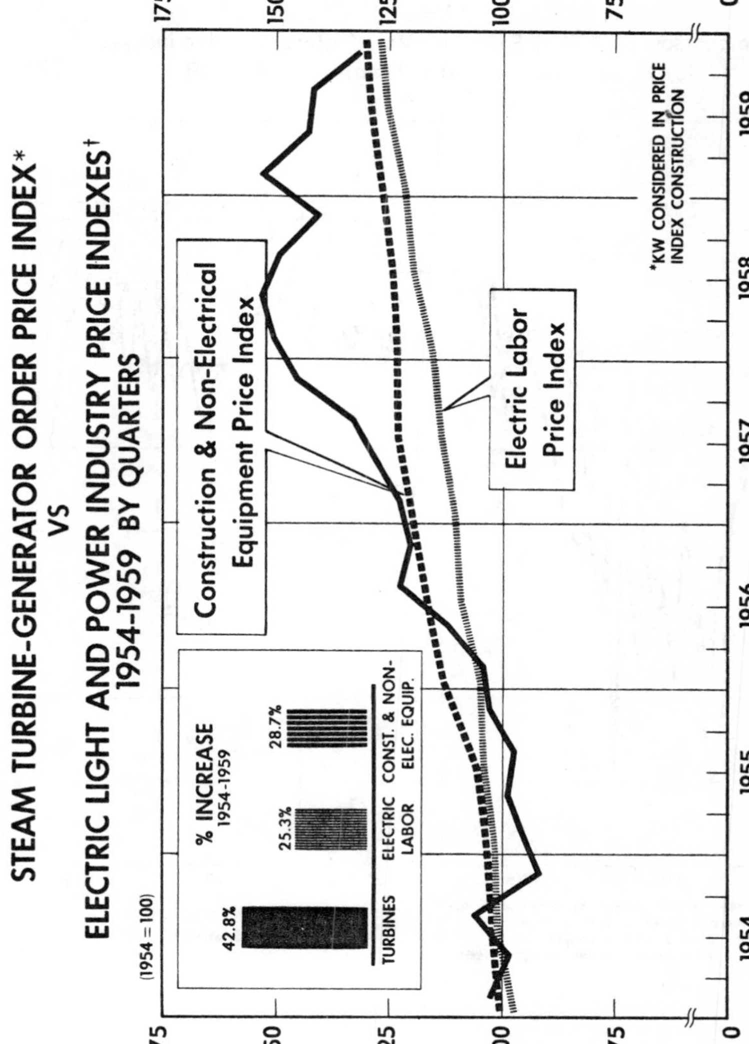

FIG. 47

Source: Electrical Equipment Price Study
† Derived from Whitman, Requardt and Associates Handy-Whitman data

PT – 6
Comparison of ATIG, BLS and Manufacturers' Price Indexes
for Power Transformers, Monthly, 1954-1959
(1954 = 100)

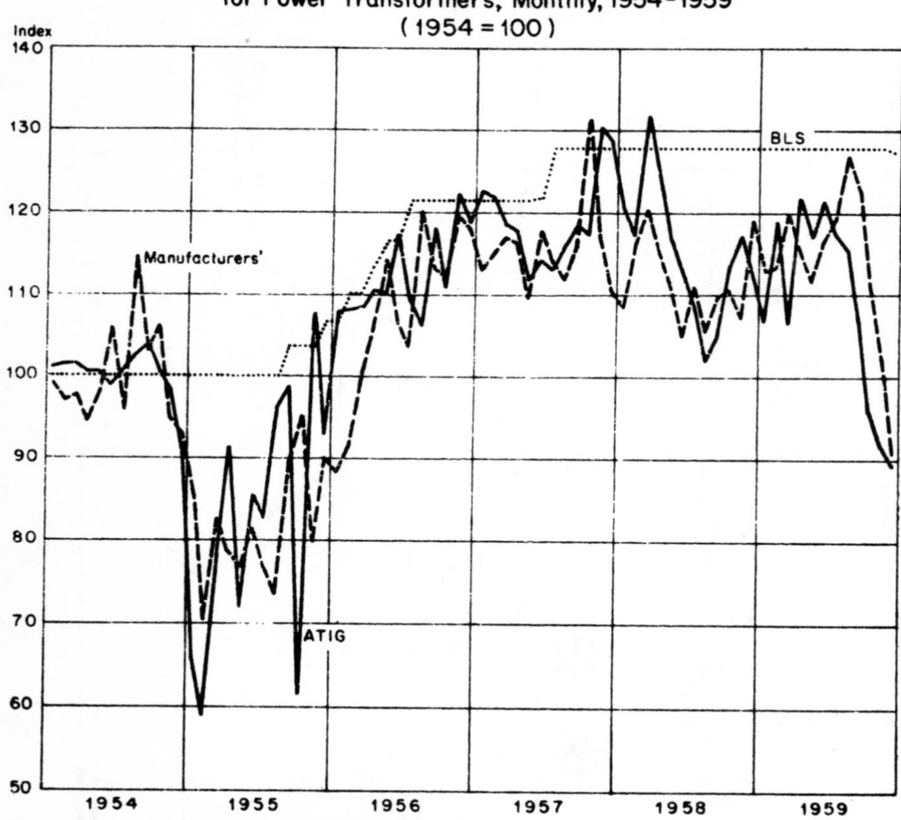

Sources: ATIG – Computed from data compiled by Stone and Webster.
BLS – Wholesale price index for power transformers.
Manufacturers' – Dean & De Podwin paper, American Statistical Assoc., Dec. 1961.

PRELIMINARY AND TENTATIVE
9/1/62

APPENDIX 8b

CB - 16
Price Indexes for Circuit Breakers, 1954-1959
ATIG, Grant Report and BLS
(1954 = 100)

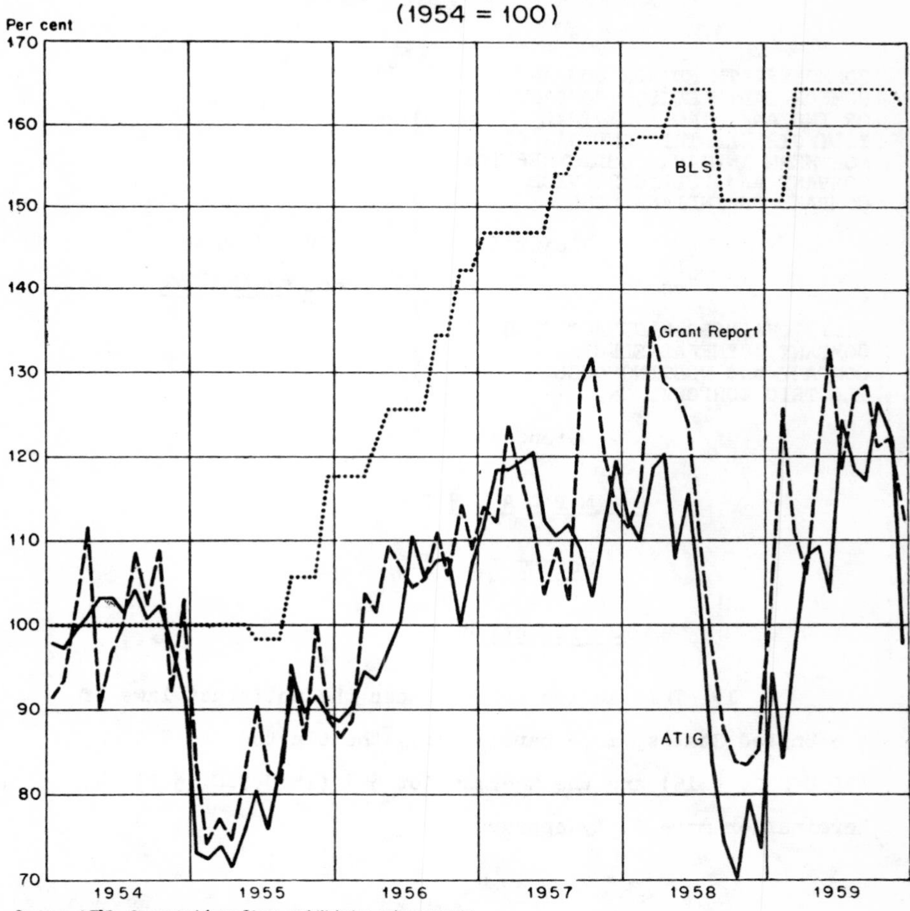

Source: ATIG - Computed from Stone and Webster price reports.
Grant Report - "Product Variation and Price Indexes" by Dean and DePodwin; Dec. 29, 1961; p. 34.
BLS - BLS Wholesale Price Index converted to 1954 base.

PRELIMINARY AND TENTATIVE
2/1/62

APPENDIX 9

TURBINE-GENERATOR UNITS

UNITED STATES DISTRICT COURT
NORTHERN DISTRICT OF ILLINOIS
EASTERN DIVISION

COMMONWEALTH EDISON COMPANY, COMMONWEALTH EDISON COMPANY OF INDIANA, INC., CENTRAL ILLINOIS ELECTRIC AND GAS CO., NORTHERN INDIANA PUBLIC SERVICE COMPANY and PUBLIC SERVICE COMPANY OF INDIANA, INC.,

Plaintiffs,

vs.

ALLIS-CHALMERS MANUFACTURING COMPANY, GENERAL ELECTRIC COMPANY and WESTINGHOUSE ELECTRIC CORPORATION,

Defendants.

CIVIL ACTION
NO. 61 C 1284

COMPLAINT

COUNT I

Jurisdiction

1. This action arises under the antitrust laws of the United States, more particularly the Clayton Act § 4 (15 U.S.C. § 15) and the Sherman Act § 1 (15 U.S.C. § 1), as hereinafter more fully appears.

Venue

2. Each of the defendants maintains an office and transacts business in the Northern District of Illinois.

Plaintiffs

3. (a) Plaintiff, COMMONWEALTH EDISON COMPANY, a corporation duly organized and existing under the laws of the State of Illinois, is now, and was at all times mentioned herein, engaged in the business of furnishing electric service to the public in the City of Chicago and elsewhere in the northern part of Illinois.

(b) Plaintiff, COMMONWEALTH EDISON COMPANY OF INDIANA, INC., a corporation duly organized and existing under the laws of the State of Indiana, is now, and was at all times mentioned herein, principally engaged in the business of furnishing electricity to plaintiffs, Commonwealth Edison Company and Northern Indiana Public Service Company.

(c) Plaintiff, CENTRAL ILLINOIS ELECTRIC AND GAS CO., a corporation duly organized and existing under the laws of the State of Illinois, is now, and was at all times mentioned herein, engaged in the business of, among other things, furnishing electric service to the public in the north-central, central, east-central and southeastern parts of Illinois.

(d) Plaintiff, NORTHERN INDIANA PUBLIC SERVICE COMPANY, a corporation duly organized and existing under the laws of the State of Indiana, is now, and was at all times mentioned herein, engaged in the business of, among other

-3-

things, furnishing electric service to the public in northern Indiana.

(e) Plaintiff, PUBLIC SERVICE COMPANY OF INDIANA, INC., a corporation duly organized and existing under the laws of the State of Indiana, is now, and was at all times mentioned herein, engaged in the business of furnishing electric service to the public in the north-central, central and southern parts of Indiana.

Defendants

4. Defendant, ALLIS-CHALMERS MANUFACTURING COMPANY ("Allis-Chalmers"), is a corporation organized and existing under the laws of the State of Delaware; defendant, GENERAL ELECTRIC COMPANY ("General Electric"), is a corporation organized and existing under the laws of the State of New York; and defendant, WESTINGHOUSE ELECTRIC CORPORATION ("Westinghouse"), is a corporation organized and existing under the laws of the State of Pennsylvania.

Co-Conspirators

5. CARRIER CORPORATION, DeLAVAL STEAM TURBINE COMPANY and WORTHINGTON CORPORATION participated in the combination and conspiracy hereinafter alleged and are hereby named as co-conspirators. Carrier Corporation and Worthington

Corporation are corporations organized and existing under the laws of the State of Delaware; DeLaval Steam Turbine Company is a corporation organized and existing under the laws of the State of New Jersey. In addition, the individuals listed below, in the course of their employment with the indicated companies and, during at least a part of the conspiracy period, in the indicated capacities, and other persons unknown to the plaintiffs, participated in the combination and conspiracy hereinafter alleged and are hereby named as co-conspirators.

Name	Capacity	Company
W. S. Ginn	Vice-President and General Manager, Turbine Division	General Electric
C. I. Mauntel	Sales Manager, Steam Division	Westinghouse
W. C. Rowland	Vice-President, Steam Division	Westinghouse
W. E. Saupe	General Manager, Large Steam Turbine-Generator Department	General Electric

Definition

6. The term "turbine-generator unit," as used herein, means an assembly of a turbine and a generator used in the production or generation of electricity on land by the use of steam, including spare parts therefor.

-5-

Interstate Trade and Commerce Affected

7. The defendants and the co-conspirator companies are the principal manufacturers of turbine-generator units in the United States, with plants located in California, Massachusetts, New Jersey, New York, Pennsylvania and Wisconsin. They sell and ship such units in interstate commerce to purchasers, including plaintiffs, throughout the United States.

Violations Alleged

8. Beginning at least as early as January 1, 1948, and continuing thereafter at least until sometime in 1960, the exact dates being unknown to plaintiffs, the defendants and the co-conspirator companies engaged in a combination and conspiracy in unreasonable restraint of the aforesaid interstate trade and commerce in turbine-generator units in violation of Section 1 of the Sherman Act (15 U.S.C. § 1).

9. Such combination and conspiracy consisted of a continuing agreement, understanding and concert of action among the defendants and the co-conspirator companies, among other things:

(a) To fix and maintain prices, terms and conditions for the sale of turbine-generator units, including the prices, terms and conditions for sales of such units made to plaintiffs; and

(b) To submit noncompetitive, collusive and rigged bids and price quotations for supplying turbine-generator units to electric utility companies, including plaintiffs, and to other purchasers.

10. In furtherance of such combination and conspiracy, representatives of the defendants and the co-conspirator companies met from time to time to discuss the prices, terms and conditions for the sale of turbine-generator units.

11. At some of such meetings, or as a result thereof, it was agreed that the defendants and the co-conspirator companies would change the prices, terms and conditions for the sale of turbine-generator units.

12. Pursuant to such agreements, the defendants and the co-conspirator companies changed the prices of turbine-generator units offered to and purchased by the plaintiffs and changed the terms and conditions for the sale of such units to plaintiffs.

-7-

13. Such price agreements included, among others:

(a) An agreement to adjustments of the price of certain types of turbine-generator units, such adjustments becoming effective in the first half of 1957;

(b) An agreement to an increase of the price of turbine-generator units of approximately 5%, such increase becoming effective in the middle of 1957;

(c) An agreement to an increase of the price of turbine-generator units of approximately 3%, such increase becoming effective in the second quarter of 1958; and

(d) An agreement, which became effective in the last quarter of 1958, that, in respect to sealed bids, prices of turbine-generator units would not be lower than approximately 3% off published book prices and, in respect to negotiated transactions, prices of such units would not be lower than approximately 5% off published book prices.

-8-

14. During the period covered by this Count, meetings among representatives of the defendants and the co-conspirator companies took place from time to time in furtherance of such combination and conspiracy at which bids and quotations to be made to particular prospective customers were discussed.

15. At some such meetings, or as a result thereof, it was agreed that one of the defendant or co-conspirator companies would be given what was designated as "position" in regard to the sale of a turbine-generator unit or units to a given prospective customer and that the other defendant and co-conspirator companies making bids or quotations on the unit or units would bid or quote higher prices than the defendant or co-conspirator company having "position."

16. The "low" bids or quotations with respect to a substantial number of sales of turbine-generator units, including sales to plaintiffs, during the period covered by this Count, were determined not by free and open competition but by such agreements that one of the defendant or co-conspirator companies would have "position" and such "low" bids or quotations were in fact artificially high.

-9-

17. The aforesaid combination and conspiracy necessitated frequent communication among representatives of the defendant and co-conspirator companies. In the course of this communication various procedures were adopted by the defendants for the purpose of avoiding detection. These included telephone calls to and from residences rather than offices of company representatives, the use of public telephone pay stations instead of company telephones and concealment and destruction of written records. Defendants and the co-conspirator companies further actively conspired to rig bids and quotations in such a way as to create the illusion that bids and quotations were competitive. As a result of these and other acts done by defendants and the co-conspirator companies for the purpose of actively and fraudulently concealing the existence of the aforesaid combination and conspiracy, plaintiffs neither had knowledge, nor by the exercise of reasonable diligence could they have learned, of the existence of such combination and conspiracy until they first became aware of the grand jury proceedings which resulted in the indictment of the defendants in June, 1960.

18. On June 29, 1960, the United States of America instituted Criminal Action No. 20401 in the

United States District Court for the Eastern District of Pennsylvania against, among others, all of the defendants named herein. The indictment therein charged that during a period beginning at least as early as November, 1955 and continuing until sometime in 1960, the defendants named in this Complaint, in violation of Section 1 of the Sherman Act, engaged in an unlawful combination and conspiracy in restraint of interstate trade and commerce in turbine-generator units. The indictment further charged that such unlawful combination and conspiracy consisted of a continuing agreement, understanding and concert of action, the substantial terms of which were to fix and maintain prices, terms and conditions for the sale of turbine-generator units, to allocate business, and to submit non-competitive, collusive and rigged bids and price quotations for supplying turbine-generator units to electric utility companies and other purchasers. The indictment also charged that the defendants and co-conspirator companies, for the purpose of forming and effectuating such combination and conspiracy, did, among other things, the acts alleged in paragraph 13 hereof. Allis-Chalmers pleaded guilty to the indictment on July 11, 1960; General Electric and Westinghouse pleaded guilty to the indictment on December 8, 1960; and W. S. Ginn, W. C. Saupe, W. C. Rowland and

-11

C. I. Mauntel pleaded nolo contendere on December 8, 1960. Judgment of guilty was entered on all of those pleas, and sentences were imposed by the Court on February 6, 1961.

19. The effects of the aforesaid combination and conspiracy were that:

(a) Prices of turbine-generator units throughout the United States, including the prices charged plaintiffs, were raised to, fixed and maintained at high and artificial levels;

(b) Price competition in the sale of turbine-generator units throughout the United States, including sales to plaintiffs, was restrained, suppressed and eliminated;

(c) Purchasers of turbine-generator units throughout the United States, including plaintiffs, were deprived of the benefits of free competition in the purchase of these products;

(d) Purchasers of turbine-generator units throughout the United States, including plaintiffs, did not receive competitive bids and quotations; and

(e) Purchasers of turbine generator units throughout the United States, including plaintiffs, were forced to pay artificially fixed prices for turbine-generator units which were higher than the prices they would have paid had no such combination and conspiracy existed.

Plaintiffs' Damages

20. From at least as early as January 1, 1948, and continuing at least until sometime in 1960, a period during which the aforesaid combination and conspiracy existed, each plaintiff purchased turbine-generator units from one or more of the defendant and co-conspirator companies.

21. By reason of the aforesaid combination and conspiracy, each plaintiff has been injured in its business and property, sustaining damages in an amount equal to the difference between the prices charged each plaintiff for turbine-generator units and the prices which would have been established by the operation of free and open competition had no such combination and conspiracy existed, plus the difference between the use taxes, if any, paid and for which plaintiffs will become liable and the use taxes they

-13-

would have paid and for which they would become liable had prices been established by the operation of free and open competition.

22. Pursuant to Section 4 of the Clayton Act (15 U.S.C. § 15), each plaintiff is entitled to recover from the defendants threefold the damages sustained by it and its costs of suit, including reasonable attorneys' fees.

WHEREFORE,

The plaintiffs pray that the combination and conspiracy among the defendants and co-conspirators alleged in this Count I, be adjudged and decreed to be in unreasonable restraint of interstate trade and commerce and in violation of Section 1 of the Sherman Act (15 U.S.C. § 1);

Each of the plaintiffs prays that a joint and several judgment be entered in its favor against the defendants in the amount of threefold the damages sustained by it as a result of the defendants' violations of the antitrust laws alleged in this Count I, together with such interest thereon as is permitted by law, and its costs of suit, including reasonable attorneys' fees;

Each plaintiff prays that the Court grant it such other and further relief as the Court shall deem just.

COUNT II

23. As an alternative cause of action, plaintiffs reallege herein, as though repeated in full, each allegation contained in paragraphs 1 through 7 of Count I hereof.

24. Beginning at least as early as November, 1955 and continuing thereafter at least until sometime in 1960, the exact dates being unknown to plaintiffs, the defendants and co-conspirator companies engaged in a combination and conspiracy in unreasonable restraint of the aforesaid interstate trade and commerce in turbine-generator units in violation of Section 1 of the Sherman Act (15 U.S.C. § 1).

25. Plaintiffs reallege herein, as though repeated in full, each allegation contained in paragraphs 9 through 19 of Count I hereof.

Plaintiffs' Damages

26. From at least as early as November, 1955 and continuing at least until sometime in 1960, a period

during which the aforesaid combination and conspiracy existed, each plaintiff purchased turbine-generator units from one or more of the defendant and co-conspirator companies.

27. By reason of the aforesaid combination and conspiracy, each plaintiff has been injured in its business and property, sustaining damages in an amount equal to the difference between the prices charged each plaintiff for turbine-generator units and the prices which would have been established by the operation of free and open competition had no such combination and conspiracy existed, plus the difference between the use taxes, if any, paid and for which plaintiffs will become liable and the use taxes they would have paid and for which they would become liable had prices been established by the operation of free and open competition.

28. Pursuant to Section 4 of the Clayton Act (15 U.S.C. § 15), each plaintiff is entitled to recover from the defendants threefold the damages sustained by it and its costs of suit, including reasonable attorneys' fees.

WHEREFORE,

The plaintiffs pray that the combination and conspiracy among the defendants and co-conspirators alleged in this Count II, be adjudged and decreed to be in unreasonable restraint of interstate trade and commerce and in violation of Section 1 of the Sherman Act (15 U.S.C. § 1);

Each of the plaintiffs prays that a joint and several judgment be entered in its favor against the defendants in the amount of threefold the damages sustained by it as a result of the defendants' violations of the antitrust laws alleged in this Count II, together with such interest thereon as is permitted by law, and its costs of suit, including reasonable attorneys' fees;

Each plaintiff prays that the Court grant it such other and further relief as the Court shall deem just.

-17-

Attorneys for Plaintiffs

Max Swiren
208 South La Salle Street
Chicago 4, Illinois
FInancial 6-2200

Neil Flanagin
208 South La Salle Street
Chicago 4, Illinois
FInancial 6-2200

Charles A. Bane

Robert F. Hanley

Thomas L. Nicholson

Richard E. Powell

OF COUNSEL:
Isham, Lincoln & Beale
72 West Adams Street
Chicago 3, Illinois
RAndolph 6-0425

John C. Lawyer
Attorney for Northern Indiana Public Service Company

OF COUNSEL:
Lawyer, Friedrich, Petrie & Tweedle
5217 Hohman Avenue
Hammond, Indiana
WEstmore 3-0118

George H. Jirgal
Attorney for Central Illinois Electric and Gas Co.

OF COUNSEL:
Chapman and Cutler
111 W. Monroe Street
Chicago 3, Illinois
RAndolph 6-6130

Paul G. Jasper
Attorney for Public Service Company of Indiana, Inc.
1000 East Main Street
Plainfield, Indiana
TErrace 9-6511

APPENDIX 10

Treble Damage Suits Filed—by Product Line and District

NUMBER OF ELECTRICAL CASES IN SELECTED PRODUCT LINES

Product Line	*Cases*
Distribution transformers	191
Power transformers	158
Power switchgear assemblies	151
Meters	144
Circuit breakers	140
Steam turbine-generator units	125
Power switching equipment	110
Instrument transformers	101
Insulators	96
Lightning arresters	92
Condensers	92
Power capacitors	85
Open fuse cutouts	65
Industrial controls equipment	60
Network transformers	51
Low-volt distribution equipment	50
Isolated phase bus	40
Low-volt circuit breakers	39
Bushings	24
Hydrogenerators	19
Other suits and unaccounted	47
Total	1,880

NUMBER OF ELECTRICAL CASES BY DISTRICTS

District	*Cases*
District of Columbia	47
District of Massachusetts	22
Southern District of New York	427
District of New Jersey	21
Eastern District of Pennsylvania	182
Eastern and Western Districts of South Carolina	7
Middle and Southern Districts of Florida	49
Eastern and Western Districts of Louisiana	9
Northern District of Texas	2
Southern District of Texas	72
Western District of Texas	73
Eastern and Western Districts of Kentucky	37
Northern District of Ohio	58
Southern District of Ohio	20
Middle District of Tennessee	16
Western District of Tennessee	62
Eastern District of Wisconsin	2
Northern District of Illinois	226
Southern District of Iowa	4
Eastern District of Missouri	34
Western District of Missouri	73
District of Nebraska	10
District of Arizona	31
Northern District of California	21
Southern District of California	128
District of Oregon	1
Western District of Washington	141
District of Colorado	40
District of Kansas	23
District of New Mexico	28
District of Utah	14
Total	1,880

Source: Neal and Goldberg, *The Electrical Equipment Antitrust Cases: Novel Judicial Administration*, 50 American Bar Association Journal 621, 622 (July 1964).

APPENDIX 11

"Passing on" Interrogatories on Behalf of Defendants

Definitions

When used in this set of interrogatories, the terms listed below shall have the meanings set forth below:

A) "Complaint Period": The period during which the complaint alleges that a conspiracy existed.

B) "Contested Purchase": Any purchase or contract to purchase with respect to which damages are sought in this action. If the answer to any part of any interrogatory would vary with respect to separate items of a "contested purchase," then plaintiff is requested to answer separately with respect to each such item.

C) "Document": Any letter, report, memorandum, record, study, working paper, data sheet, data processing card or tape, or any sheet or group of sheets.

D) "Plaintiff": The plaintiff separately answering these interrogatories, its domestically domiciled subsidiaries and its merged or acquired predecessors, its present and former officers, agents and all other persons acting on behalf of plaintiff or such subsidiaries or such predecessors, including all past or present employees exercising discretion, making policy and making decisions or participating in any of the foregoing functions with respect to any of the matters which are the subject of these interrogatories, and further includes consultants, past and present (with respect to these matters), or any other person or organization acting in such a consulting or advisory capacity.

E) "Rates": Any charge made to customers for the sale of electricity or rendering of electric service, including minimum bills, penalties for delayed payment, connection or disconnection charges, and also including any adjustment by means of refunds or otherwise to the amounts paid by customers in the past.

F) "Regulatory Agency": Any federal, state, municipal, or other body which regulates or has power to regulate, or did so at any time during the "complaint period" and one year prior thereto, the "rates" of "plaintiff," or any court before which, within such time, "plaintiff" presented evidence of a measure of value of its property used in rendering electric service.

Instruction

These interrogatories shall be deemed continuing, so as to require,

(a) additional answers if "plaintiff" obtains further information between the time answers are served and the time of trial. Such additional answers shall be served from time to time, but not later than thirty days after such further information is received; and

(b) supplemental answers as additional facts, information, or documents come into existence or become available between the time answers are served and the time of trial. Such supplemental answers shall be served quarterly (correspond with the quarters of "plaintiff's" fiscal year).

INTERROGATORIES

1. Specify the laws under which "plaintiff" is organized, and the date of incorporation.

2. Identify any predecessor in interest which made any "contested purchase," the laws under which it was organized, and when and in what manner "plaintiff" became its successor in interest.

3. List each State and County in which "plaintiff" produces, transmits or sells electric energy, or furnishes electric service.

4. State whether there has been in effect at any time after the beginning of the "complaint period" any contract or agreement concerning the rendering of electric service by "Plaintiff" to any person (a) at "rates" based in whole or in part on a cost-of-service formula (excluding rates including a fuel adjustment but not otherwise on a cost-of-service formula), or (b) for exchange, interchange, or pooling of electric power or energy. If so, state the date of each such contract or agreement, the name and address of each party thereto, and the name and address of each person who, on behalf of "plaintiff," participated in the making or negotiation thereof.

5. Has there been at any time an extension or installation for which a contribution was made by or on behalf of any customer or prospective customer, or group of customers (including real estate developers, governmental bodies and other persons who, though not themselves customers or prospective customers, have an interest in the availability of electric service), in the determination of the amount of which contribution the cost of all or part of any "contested purchase" was considered? If so, state separately for each such extension or installation a description of the transaction, the title, date, and other details sufficient to identify each "document" included in the records supporting the transaction and the accounting entries related thereto, and the name and address of the present custodian thereof, or of any copy thereof.

6. With reference to each change in "rates" of "plaintiff" for electric service, beginning with the last such change before the "complaint period," except changes resulting from application of a cost-of-service formula or fuel adjustment formula,

(a) Furnish a description of each tariff (whether designated as Tariff, Rate Schedule, special contract or otherwise), whether or not filed with a "regulatory agency," including identifying numbers and titles of service classifications, and identifying numbers of leaves contained therein, both original and superseding, and the effective date of each such schedule and of each such leaf or group of leaves for a single effective date, in which the change was made;

(b) State the effective date of such change; and

(c) State the amount of the annual net increase or decrease in gross revenues resulting or estimated to result (at the time the change was made) from such changes, and the year for which such calculation or estimate was applicable.

7. As to each "contested purchase," state separately:

(a) The month and year as of which its cost was recorded in the Construction Work in Progress, Electric Plant, plant account in another utility department, or other account of "plaintiff"; the title of each such account and each detailed plant account in which its cost was recorded, the total amount included therefor, and the portion thereof represented by the purchase price (including any escalation or adjustment); the month and year of each transfer between any two accounts; and the state in which its cost was included;

(b) To the extent shown in the books of account, including subsidiary ledgers and continuing property records (whether so entitled or called plant records, perpetual inventory or otherwise) showing physical quantities of plant, whether it or any part thereof has been retired from service, and, if so, the date when it or any part thereof was eliminated from the plant account, and what accounting entries were placed upon the books to reflect such retirement and its disposition (indicating whether held for reuse), including entries for salvage and cost of removal;

(c) The rate of annual depreciation and amortization applicable to the cost thereof shown on the books of account for each year during which it has been included in a plant account on which depreciation or amortization was accrued, together with the method used in determining each such rate, whether straight line or otherwise;

(d) The amounts of depreciation and amortization applicable to the total amount included therefor and to the purchase price thereof, from the date of inclusion in plant in service for each year by accounts (depreciation, amortization, clearing or other) as recorded or reflected on the books and supporting records. If such amounts were not determined by use of rates requested in sub-paragraph (c), above, then specify how such amounts were determined;

(e) If the cost thereof was included in an account or subaccount, for which the cost or the return, taxes or depreciation and amortization applicable thereto has been allocated among states in any evidence submitted to a "regulatory agency" by "plaintiff," or in any negotiation, discussion or other communication to a "regulatory agency" or its staff or consultants, or in any document maintained or prepared by "plaintiff," specify the percentage of the cost, or of the return, taxes and depreciation and amortization (separately, if different) applicable thereto for each state, as reflected in each such allocation for each period for which any such allocation was made.

(f) Whether it has been leased by "plaintiff" and, if so, specify:

(i) the lessee thereof;

(ii) the date of such lease;

(iii) the terms and conditions of such lease; and

(iv) the title, date, author and description of the contents of each "document" used or prepared by or for any person in the preparation of such lease, or in explaining or commenting on the provisions of such lease, and the name and address of the present custodian thereof, or any copy thereof.

8. Specify separately for each sub-paragraph of this interrogatory each annual depreciation and amortization rate (and the account, subdivision, or group thereof to which it was applied), and the average life and average net salvage value (if any) used in determining each such depreciation and amortization rate, which was in any manner related to Electric Plant Account or Common Plant Account or any detailed plant account included in Electric Plant Account or Common Plant Account or any subdivision of such detailed plant account of "plaintiff," and which has been computed or used at any time;

(a) In making an allocation among the functional classifications required to be reported by the Federal Power Commission of any lump sum provision for depreciation or amortization entered in the books of account in which there is included provision for depreciation or amortization upon any "contested purchase";

(b) In making an allocation among two or more detailed plant accounts or subdivisions thereof to meet the requirements of any state, municipal or other regulatory agency, of any lump sum provision for depreciation or amortization or total amount applicable to such functional classification or other group of accounts in which there is included provision for depreciation or amortization upon any "contested purchase";

(c) In determining depreciation and amortization to be included in any federal income tax return or any amendment thereto or any state tax return or any amendment thereto in which there is included provision for depreciation or amortization upon any "contested purchase"; and

(d) In determining the amount of accrued or accumulated depreciation associated with a retirement of any "contested purchase" brought about by a sale or otherwise.

9. With respect to each allocation, determination and study referred to in answer to Interrogatory No. 8, specify the title, date, author (if known) (and his present address and principal occupation) of each "document" submitted to or prepared by "plaintiff" reflecting the result thereof, and the name and address of the present custodian thereof, or any copy thereof.

10. State the name and address of each "regulatory agency," and specify each statute, franchise, ordinance, or other governmental regulation by which any regulation of "rates" has been effectuated at any time during the "complaint period".

11. Specify the "regulatory agency," docket number, name and date of order instituting each proceeding involving the "rates" of "plaintiff," at any time beginning with the last such proceeding immediately preceding the "complaint period," and as to each such proceeding state the date of each decision (opinion, order, or other designation), and whether the determination of the "regulatory agency" was reviewed in any respect by any governmental agency or court, and identify each such agency or court and specify the docket number and date of each Order or Opinion issued by each such agency or court in each such proceeding.

12. State whether "plaintiff" has, at any time during the "complaint period"

(a) Filed periodic reports with any "regulatory agency." If so, identify each such type of report and the agency with which it was filed, and specify whether it was filed on an annual, quarterly, or monthly basis, or other specified time basis, or

(b) Compiled or prepared periodic reports (statements or other designation) to be furnished or made available to trustees, directors, officers or employees of "plaintiff," or for other distribution, concerning construction or operation of electric plant of "plaintiff," or results of operations of electric utility of "plaintiff," and, if so, identify each such type of report and the body or person or persons to whom it was furnished or made available, and specify whether it was prepared on an annual, quarterly, or monthly basis, or other specified time basis.

13. Excluding reports specified in answer to Interrogatory No. 12, and excluding communications filed as a part of the formal rate proceedings specified in answer to Interrogatory No. 11, state whether there has been any negotiation, discussion, or other communication (oral or written) between any such "regulatory agency" and "plaintiff," concerning "rates," or concerning depreciation or valuation of Electric Plant, at any time since the beginning of the "complaint period"; if so, specify

thereof as disclosed in any corporate or internal record, a description of each "document" relating thereto, and the name and address of the author and the present custodian thereof, or any copy thereof; and

(b) The title, date, author (if known), addressee (if any), other details sufficient for identification, and a description of the contents of each "document" received from the "regulatory agency" or its staff, and of each "document" furnished to the "regulatory agency" or its staff or its consultants in connection with each such written negotiation, discussion, or other communication, and of each "document" used in the preparation thereof, and the name and present address of the person who was in charge of its preparation, and of the present custodian thereof, or of any copy thereof.

14. With respect to each formal rate proceeding specified in your answer to Interrogatory No. 11 and each negotiation, discussion, or other communication specified in your answer to Interrogatory No. 13, in which there was furnished by or on behalf of "plaintiff" to the "regulatory agency" or its staff or consultants a measure of value (original cost new, trended original cost new, reproduction-cost-new, or other basis of cost new, whether undepreciated or less depreciation) of its property used in rendering electric service in the state involved, or used in rendering electric service to customers whose "rates" were under consideration, state the date or dates at which each such measure of value was computed, identify each "contested purchase" included in each such measure of value, and as to each such "contested purchase" specify separately with respect to each such measure of value:

(a) The total amount for cost new, and the portion thereof represented by the purchase price, at which it was included in each such measure of value (at each date, if more than one is shown, and average if computed), and the amounts at which it was included in each rate base determined by or for "plaintiff" or the "regulatory agency";

(b) The accumulated depreciation and amortization applicable to such amounts, included in each such measure of value and each rate base;

(c) The amounts of depreciation and amortization charges applicable to such amounts for each test year or other period for which operating revenue deductions (or operating expenses) were presented, computed or tabulated;

(d) The rates of annual depreciation and amortization applicable to it for each test year or other period for which operating revenue deductions (or operating expenses) were presented, computed or tabulated, together with the method used in determining each such rate, whether straight line or otherwise;

(e) Whether any adjustment to the cost new thereof or to the accumulated depreciation or amortization applicable thereto was proposed under any such measure of value, and state whether any other measure of value was proposed, and, if so, identify each such adjustment and measure of value, and the proponent thereof; and

(f) Whether any adjustment was made by the "regulatory agency" affecting any rate or amount inquired about in this interrogatory, and, if so, state the nature and amount of each such adjustment.

15. With respect to each such formal rate proceeding and each such negotiation, discussion or other communication in which there was furnished by or on behalf of "plaintiff" to the "regulatory agency" or its staff or its consultants a measure of value of its property used in rendering electric service in the state involved, or used in rendering electric service to customers whose "rates" were under consideration, which measure of value was based wholly or in part on

(a) trended original cost less depreciation, specify

(i) the name, compiler, publisher, date of publication and other identifying information of each price index, trend or other guide used, which was (1) based wholly or in part on the price of electrical equipment of the category described in the complaint, or (2) applied to an account in which was included the cost of any item of electrical equipment of the category described in the complaint;

(ii) each account, subaccount or property group to which each such index, trend or other guide was applied directly or indirectly, and the depreciated trended original cost and depreciated original cost of each such account (specifying the amount, if any, included in depreciation representing deferred income taxes);

(iii) the total depreciated trended original cost measure of value and the total depreciated original cost measure of value (specifying the amount, if any, included in depreciation representing deferred income taxes);

(iv) each classification (size, type, material, manufacturer or other differentiation) of electrical equipment of the category described in the complaint used as a component in the construction of each price index, trend or other guide listed in answer to (i) above, and the weight given thereto in constructing such price index, trend or other guide at the date or period to which the cost was trended;

(v) separately for each such classification, the percentage change in the price index, trend or other guide at the date or period to which the cost was trended for each change of one percent of the price of electrical equipment in such classification at the date or period; and

(vi) separately for each such price index, trend, or other guide, the dollar amount of change in the total depreciated trended original cost for each change of one percent in each such guide at that date or period.

(b) reproduction cost new less depreciation, specify

(i) each unit cost of any item of electrical equipment of the category described in the complaint used in the reproduction cost study together with a description of the type of equipment to which such unit cost applied and the number of items to which such unit cost was applied in determining reproduction cost new;

(ii) the total depreciated reproduction cost new measure of value and the total depreciated original cost (specifying the amount, if any, included in depreciation representing deferred income taxes);

(iii) separately for each unit cost applied to any item of electrical equipment of the category described in the complaint, the percentage by which it would change for each change of one percent of the price of electrical equipment of the category described in the complaint at the date or period to which that unit cost applies; and

(iv) separately for each unit cost applied to any item of electrical equipment of the category described in the complaint, the dollar amount of change of the total depreciated reproduction cost new for each change of one percent of that unit cost at the date or period to which that unit cost applies,

(c) any basis other than trended original cost less depreciation, reproduction cost new less depreciation or original cost less depreciation, describe in detail each method of valuation applied to each account in which was included any part of a "contested purchase" and specify

(i) the total depreciated measure of value arrived at using such basis and the total depreciated original cost (specifying the amount, if any, included in depreciation representing deferred income taxes); and

(ii) separately for each item of electrical equipment of the category described in the complaint the dollar amount of change of the total depreciated present-day cost measure of value for each change of one percent in the purchase price of that item at the date or period of valuation;

(d) original cost less depreciation or any measure of value specified in sub-paragraphs (a), (b), or (c) above, indicate

(i) whether the "regulatory agency" made any adjustments to the measure of value and, if so, what adjustments, stating separately gross amounts of increases and decreases. If the "regulatory agency" or any member of its staff or any of its consultants stated that it or he gave weight to such measure of value, indicate what weight was stated to have been given to each of the measures specified,

(e) any measure of value inquired about in paragraphs (a) through (d) above, furnish a description of each "document" provided by any person to, or reviewed by, such "regulatory agency" or its staff or its consultants concerning the matters inquired about in paragraphs (a) through (d) above, together with the name and present address of the person who was in charge of its preparation, and the present custodian thereof, or a copy thereof.

16. State whether at any time after a date one year prior to the "complaint period" there were maintained or prepared by or on behalf of "plaintiff" any "documents" which purported to reflect in whole or in part a measure of value of "plaintiff's" property used in electric service (except those used solely for tax assessment or insurance purposes, and those already identified in answer to these interrogatories), or which reflected a rate base, on the basis of original cost less depreciation, reproduction-cost-new less depreciation, or trended original cost less depreciation, or any combination thereof, or any other basis, or which brought up to date from time to time the rate base fixed by any "regulatory agency," or any element included therein. Describe each such "document" and state the period for which it was maintained or prepared, and the name and address of its present custodian.

17. For each date or period for which a measure of value of "plaintiff's" property or a rate base was determined, in whole or in part, in any "documents" referred to in Interrogatory No. 16, to the extent shown therein specify

(a) The amount shown therein of cost new, in total, and separately for plant in service, plant held for future use, and construction work in progress, and separately under each such category for (i) original cost, (ii) reproduction cost new, (iii) trended original cost, and (iv) any other basis with description of such basis, and a statement of the method by which the amount was computed;

(b) The amount of depreciation deducted (whether designated accumulated provision for depreciation, depreciation reserve, accrued depreciation, existing depreciation, or other designation with similar meaning), separately for each such category for each such basis (specifying the amount, if any, included in depreciation representing deferred income taxes);

(c) The working capital shown therein, specifying the variations, if any, in the working capital added to each such basis listed in paragraph (a) above;

(d) The total of each such measure of value and rate base;

(e) The operating income related to each measure of value or rate base, showing the period covered, and the operating income per books and any adjustments made thereto; and

(f) The percentage rate of return on each measure of value or rate base and, if more than one such basis was used, the percentage rate of return upon the final weighted average rate base.

18. As to each "contested purchase" which was included in Electric Plant, state separately whether interest during construction was accrued upon it while in Construction Work in Progress or in another plant account (state title of account), and, if so, specify:

(a) The rates or rate of interest during construction used and the period during which each rate was used;

(b) The amount of interest during construction applicable to the purchase price included in the accounts at the time it was transferred from Construction Work in Progress to Electric Plant in Service or any other plant account (state title of the detailed plant account);

(c) The amount of interest during construction applicable to the purchase price included in each measure of value submitted to any "regulatory agency" in each formal or informal rate proceeding, together with the date as of which such cost new and interest during construction included in each such measure of value was determined, and identification of each such measure of value and each such rate proceeding; and

(d) The percent of total interest during construction which was represented by interest actually paid out in each fiscal year ending on or after the beginning of the "complaint period," describing the method of computation.

19. As to each "contested purchase," the purchase price of which has been amortized, in whole or in part, under Section 168 of the Internal Revenue Code (or under Section 124A of the Revenue Act of 1950 or Section 124 of the Revenue Act of 1939), or depreciated, in whole or in part, under Section 167 of the Internal Revenue Code, or both, state separately

(a) Which of the foregoing Sections of the Internal Revenue Code was used;

(b) The dates when such amortization commenced and ended, and when such depreciation commenced;

(c) The percentage of the purchase price, and the amount thereof, to which such depreciation or amortization was applicable;

(d) The annual percentage rate and the amount of depreciation which would have been deducted for income tax purposes in each year to the present date in the absence of any such accelerated depreciation or amortization;

(e) The rate and amount of depreciation or amortization actually deducted for federal income tax purposes in each year to date;

(f) The amount by which federal income taxes payable for each year were less or more as a result of the difference in the amounts of depreciation or amortization deducted as specified in sub-paragraphs (d) and (e) above;

(g) With respect to such difference in federal income taxes payable,

(i) The entries made in the accounts and the treatment in the financial statements;

(ii) Whether each regulatory agency, in regulating rates of "plaintiff," treated such difference as deferred taxes to be added to taxes payable, and deducted as a cost of doing business for the year, or allowed the difference to "flow through" to net income (if not uniform for the entire period to date of answer, specify dates between which each treatment was in force); and

(h) If the annual depreciation shown in sub-paragraph (d) or the annual depreciation or amortization shown in sub-paragraph (e), or both, was applicable to more than one state for accounting or rate purposes, the percentage thereof applicable to each state, estimated if not exactly known, for each year.

20. Specify separately for each state, for each fiscal year, beginning with the last fiscal year ending before the "complaint period," to the extent not previously specified in the answer to preceding interrogatories,

(a) the rate of return earned upon a measure of value per the books of account of "plaintiff" for the electric operations during such period;

(b) whether such measure of value contains any elements for electric plant other than Electric Plant in Service less accumulated depreciation and amortization applicable thereto, and if so, what elements and the amount attributable to each;

(c) the basis upon which working capital, if any, is included in such measure of value;

(d) what adjustments, if any, to the operating revenues and operating revenue deductions, as shown by the books of account, have been made in computing the rate of return; and

(e) a description of each "document" used or prepared by or for any person in the calculation of each such rate of return, measure of value, operating revenues and operating revenue deductions, together with the name and address of the present custodian of each such "document" or any copy thereof.

21. State whether "plaintiff" has received from any "regulatory agency" at any time after January 1, 1960 any communication (either oral or written) relating to the alleged conspiracy charged in the complaint, or any other alleged or possible conspiracy among any electrical equipment manufacturers allegedly or possibly in violation of the anti-trust laws of the United States, or relating to the possibility that "plaintiff" might recover any damages for any alleged violation of the anti-trust laws, or relating to the disposition of any such damages which might be recov-

ered, and state separately whether "plaintiff" has directed any such communication to any such "regulatory agency" or to any other person. If so, specify

(a) the date of each such oral communication, the name and address of each participant therein, the content thereof as disclosed in any corporate or internal record, a description of each "document" relating thereto, and the name and address of the author and the present custodian thereof; or of any copy thereof; and

(b) the title, author (if known), date, addressee (if any), other details sufficient for identification, and a description of the contents of each such written communication, and the name and address of the present custodian thereof, or of any copy thereof.

22. With respect to each of the foregoing interrogatories, state the name and address of each person whom "plaintiff" has consulted or who has assisted "plaintiff" in preparing the answers to each of these interrogatories.

23. List separately with respect to each of the foregoing interrogatories, to the extent not previously answered in response to these interrogatories, the author, date, addressee (if any), and title (if any), of each document relied upon in answering the interrogatory, and state the name and address of each person who now has custody or control thereof, or of any copy thereof.

APPENDIX 12

All defendants join in submitting the following interrogatories:

DEFENDANTS' FIRST SET OF INTERROGATORIES

Defendants request that each plaintiff, by an officer or managing agent, separately answer under oath, in accordance with Rule 33 of the Federal Rules of Civil Procedure, the following interrogatories:

1. State separately, as to each purchase or contract to purchase with respect to which damages are sought in this action by the plaintiff answering these interrogatories, each of the following:

(a) The date or dates of (i) the bid invitation, if any, (ii) receipt of the bid or quotation, if any (designating the company or person submitting the bid or quotation), (iii) the purchase order, or the formal written sales contract, or the award of the bid, (iv) any letter of intent, or other commitment to purchase or pay a stated price, either verbal or written, given to the seller by the purchaser, and (v) the invoice or invoices.

(b) The name and address of the purchaser and, if the purchaser was not such plaintiff, the nature of the relationship between such plaintiff and such purchaser and of the interest which such plaintiff claims entitles it to damages on orders placed by such purchaser.

(c) The name and address of the person from whom the purchase was made and, if shown on any of the documents referred to in 1(a), the name and address of the manufacturer if other than the seller (including designation of the regional, district or other office of the seller involved).

(d) The file and each other number and symbol assigned to the purchase by the purchaser for purposes of identification of the transaction.

(e) The file, invoice, requisition, order and each other number and symbol assigned to the purchase by the seller, if shown on any of the documents referred to in 1(a).

(f) The product or products and the quantity of each ordered or purchased, the electrical rating, the catalog number, specifications sufficient with other information given adequately to identify the product or products ordered or purchased, and as applicable where the seller was other than a defendant, and if shown on any of the documents referred to in 1(a), the code number, factory number, and serial number.

(g) The order price and the price actually paid for each product ordered or purchased if different from the order price, and the date of the final payment.

(h) The date or dates of final shipment of each product ordered or purchased to the extent that such information is reflected in any of the documents referred to in 1(a).

APPENDIX 13

Set No. 2 of Interrogatories on Behalf of Certain Signatory Defendants

With respect to the products defined in the complaints in the causes in which a signatory defendant is a party: (1) state whether as a general practice each signatory defendant was invited by you to bid or negotiate for the purchases for which you are seeking damages; (2) state whether during the period 1956-1960 you had one or more lists of preferred or qualified suppliers who would be invited to bid or negotiate on purchases of such products, and if so, state with respect to each such list:

(a) the dates of each such list and of any changes therein;

(b) the names of the suppliers on each such list on each of the dates identified in (a) above;

or, in the alternative, produce for inspection a copy of each written list reflecting the information called for in subparagraphs (a) and (b).

Signatory Defendants:

Federal Pacific Electric Company
Cornell-Dubilier Electric Corporation
Wagner Electric Corporation
Moloney Electric Company
Carrier Corporation
H. K. Porter Company, Inc.
Southern States, Inc.
Kuhlman Electric Company
A. B. Chance Company
Foster Wheeler Corporation
Allen Bradley Company
The Clark Controller Company
Cutler-Hammer, Inc.
Lapp Insulator Company, Inc.
McGraw-Edison Company
Ohio Brass Company
Joslyn Mfg. & Supply Co.
The Porcelain Insulator Corporation
Square D Company
C. H. Wheeler Manufacturing Company
Hubbard and Company
Worthington Corporation

Set No. 1 of Interrogatories on Behalf of Plaintiffs

Definitions

A. "You" or "your" means the defendant corporation separately answering these interrogatories, its domestically domiciled subsidiaries and its merged or acquired predecessors, its present and former officers, agents and all other persons acting on behalf of the defendant corporation or such subsidiaries or such predecessors.

B. "Document" means any written, recorded or graphic matter however produced or reproduced.

C. "Identify" or "identification" when used in reference to an individual person means to state his full name if known and his present or last known position and business affiliation. "Identify" or "identification" when used in reference to a document means to state the type of document (e.g. letter, memorandum, telegram, chart, etc.), or some other means of identifying it, and its present location or custodian. If any such document was but is no longer in your possession or subject to your control, state what disposition was made of it.

D. Except where otherwise stated, each interrogatory requests information for the period from January 1, 1955 to April 1, 1961.

I. Existence and Knowledge of Meetings Among Defendants

1. State whether you communicated orally during the period from January 1, 1953, to April 1, 1961, with any officer, agent, employee or person acting or purporting to act on behalf of any other defendant named in the complaint or any other corporation engaged in the manufacture and sale of the product defined in the complaint, or with any intermediary, through statements referring or relating in any way to inquiries from, or efforts made to offer or sell the product defined in the complaint on a specific job, contract or purchase to, third persons, or prices, terms and conditions of sale of the product defined in the complaint to third persons (other than credit data), or to your or such corporation's pricing or selling policy applicable to such product with respect to third persons; except that with respect to any product which was not the subject of a prior government proceeding against you, the date of commencement for this interrogatory shall be January 1, 1955.

2. As to each defendant answering Interrogatory 1 affirmatively state as to each communication:

(a) whether made in person or by telephone;

(b) the date and place;

(c) the content of the communication as disclosed in any corporate or internal record;

(d) an identification of each person who participated in the communication or who had knowledge thereof;

(e) an identification of each document referring or relating to the subject matter of subparagraph (c).

3. Identify each document passing between you and any officer, agent, employee or other person acting or purporting to act on behalf of any other defendant named in the complaint or any other corporation engaged in the manufacture and sale of the product defined in the complaint during the period from January 1, 1953 to April 1, 1961, referring or relating in any way to inquiries from, or efforts made to offer or sell the product defined in the complaint on a specific job, contract or purchase to, third persons, or prices, terms and conditions of sale of the product defined in the complaint to third persons (other than credit data), or to your or such corporation's pricing or selling policy applicable to such product with respect to third persons; except that with respect to any product which was not the subject of a prior government proceeding against you, the date of commencement for this interrogatory shall be January 1, 1955.

4. State whether you were advised as to any oral or written communication, or of the substance or content thereof, at or about either prior to or subsequent to the time such communication was made during the period from January 1, 1953 to April 1, 1961 between any other defendants named in the complaint or between any other corporations engaged in the manufacture and sale of the product defined in the complaint or between any such defendants and corporations referring or relating in any way to inquiries from, or efforts made to offer or sell the product defined in the complaint on a specific job, contract or purchase to, third persons, or prices, terms and conditions of sale of the product defined in the complaint to third persons (other than credit data), or to your or such corporations' pricing or selling policy applicable to such product with respect to third persons; except that with respect to any product which was not the subject of a prior government proceeding against you, the date of commencement for this interrogatory shall be January 1, 1955.

5. Identify each person employed by or who acted for you who testified before any agent, agency or committee of the executive or legislative branch of the United States or of any state or who submitted any written document or statement, data or report to such agent, agency or committee in connection with any investigation of alleged unlawful pricing or alleged

unlawful marketing agreements affecting electrical equipment and affecting the product defined in the complaint.

6. As to each person identified in the answer to Interrogatory 5:

(a) state the date and place such information or testimony was given;

(b) identify the person, agency or committee receiving such information or testimony; and

(c) identify such statement, data or report.

7. Identify each person employed by you or who acted for you who was a witness before the grand jury of the United States District Court for the Eastern District of Pennsylvania which in 1960 returned an indictment charging a combination and conspiracy in violation of Section 1 of the Sherman Act with respect to the product defined in the complaint.

8. State whether or not your company had any policy directed to compliance with the anti-trust laws and, if so, describe the policy and identify any directive or other writing which sets forth such policy.

9. As to each defendant which answers Interrogatory 8 affirmatively, identify each person who, in connection with the product defined in the complaint, was discharged, reprimanded or otherwise disciplined for what was believed to be or found by you to be a violation of such policy.

II. Organization of Defendant

10. If you are or were organized by divisions, departments or other units other than subsidiaries state for each year in the period defined in Interrogatory 1 the name of each such division, department or unit engaged in each of the following activities with respect to the product here in suit:

(a) sales or marketing of such product;

(b) pricing or negotiation with respect to price.

11. As to each division or other unit identified in the answer to Interrogatory 10, identify each person in charge of the activities enumerated in subparagraphs (a) and (b) therein and his immediate assistant.

12. If available and in existence, give an organization chart of each such division, department or other subdivision identified in response to Interrogatories 10 and 11.

13. Identify by name and by date and place of incorporation for each year in the period defined in Interrogatory 1 each present or former

domestic subsidiary of your company which was engaged in any of the activities enumerated in subparagraphs (a) and (b) in Interrogatory 10.

14. As to each subsidiary of your company identified in the answer to Interrogatory 13, state the name of each other manufacturer whose identical or similar product to that here in suit was sold or shipped by such subsidiary and identify which such products were so sold or shipped in each year in the period defined therein.

15. As to each domestic subsidiary identified in the answer to Interrogatory 13, identify the person having the principal and main responsibility for each of the activities enumerated in subparagraphs (a) and (b) in Interrogatory 10 and his immediate assistant.

16. As to any subsidiary identified in the answer to Interrogatory 13 which was acquired by your company as a going concern during the period defined in Interrogatory 1 state the name of such subsidiary prior to such acquisition and the date it was acquired by your company.

17. With respect to the product here in suit, identify by name and by date and place of incorporation any company, the product business of which was acquired by your company during the period defined in Interrogatory 1, giving in each case the date of such acquisition and the disposition of such business.

III. Pricing

18. Identify for the period defined in Interrogatory 1 each person who had authority to or was permitted to make or approve decisions with respect to prices and terms and conditions of sale for the product classifications described in the complaint, including the product here in suit, on the basis of which defendants maintain their records, particularly as to each of the following matters:

(a) establishing or changing list prices, multipliers, net book prices, discounts or other price formulae;

(b) determining whether or not established list prices, multipliers, net book prices, discounts or price formulae and established terms and conditions of sale would be applied;

(c) determining the customers or classes of customer to whom quotations or sales would be made or to whom different price schedules would be applicable.

19. Identify each document stating your export or domestic price policy or the final making and approval of your published prices for the product classifications described in the complaint, including the product

here in suit, on the basis of which defendants maintain their records, for the period defined in Interrogatory 1 as well as such documents embodying intermediate recommendations prior to such final approval by the person or persons having authority to give such final approval.

20. For the period defined in Interrogatory 1 state your cost accounting policy and method of pricing of parts or materials transferred from within your own company for use in the production of the product classifications described in the complaint, including the product here in suit, on the basis of which defendants maintain their records.

21. Identify for the period defined in Interrogatory 1 by number or date and effective period each price list or catalogue, including additions, insertions, supplements and changes therein, issued by your company in connection with pricing the product classifications described in the complaint, including the product here in suit, on the basis of which defendants maintain their records.

22. If at any time you did not have in effect or use a price list, sheet or book in connection with pricing the product classifications described in the complaint, including the product here in suit, on the basis of which defendants maintain their records:

(a) state the period of time during which no price list, sheet or book was in effect or used;

(b) state how prices and price quotations were determined during such period.

23. State whether during the period defined in Interrogatory 1 you ever issued, quoted or used any discount, multiplier or pricing formula in conjunction with a price list, sheet or book in order to determine the price of the product classifications described in the complaint, including the product here in suit, on the basis of which defendants maintain their records.

24. As to each defendant which answers Interrogatory 23 affirmatively:

(a) state the dates of issue, or, if not available, other identifying number or symbol of any document promulgating or stating such formulae;

(b) if any such discount, multiplier or pricing formula applied only under certain conditions including but not being limited to class of purchaser, quantity purchased, or geographical location of the purchaser not disclosed or stated in such document, state each such condition and the discount, multiplier or pricing formula to which it applied;

(c) state the period during which each such discount, multiplier or pricing formula was issued, quoted or used unless it is stated and set forth in the documents listed in subparagraph (a) herein.

25. State whether you ever used a price adjustment clause in connection with pricing the product classifications described in the complaint, including the product here in suit, on the basis of which defendants maintain their records.

26. As to each defendant which answers Interrogatory 25 affirmatively:

(a) state or permit inspection and copying of the terms of each such clause which was in use as an ordinary or standard clause and the period of time during which it was used;

(b) identify as to each ordinary or standard contract price adjustment clause the person or persons who directed the derivation or development thereof;

(c) as to each such ordinary or standard price adjustment clause or provision which was based in whole or in part on any labor or material index or indices, state such index or indices.

27. If any escalation formula was applicable to the product here in suit, list by date or other means of identification whatever studies or reports you have which would reflect the proportion to the total cost of manufacturing such product of the cost of labor, materials, and other cost items, excluding management and overhead, for each calendar quarter during the period from January 1, 1955 to April 1, 1961.

28. List each study or report, if any, concerning the productivity of labor prepared or used by you during the period defined herein, including but not being limited to those used in any labor, wage or salary negotiation affecting employees engaged in the production of the product classifications described in the complaint, including the product here in suit, on the basis of which defendants maintain their records.

29. Identify each study, report or other memorandum prepared or used by you during the period defined in Interrogatory 1 relating to any one or more of the following with respect to the product classifications described in the complaint, including the product here in suit, on the basis of which defendants maintain their records:

(a) new entrants, either foreign or domestic, into the market;

(b) production capacity or overcapacity of any manufacturer;

(c) price structure of any other manufacturer.

30. State, if available, your gross and net sales by quarter and year of your total products, and the product classifications described in the complaint, including the product here in suit, on the basis of which defendants maintain their records broken down according to:

(a) all domestic sales; and

(b) all foreign sales.

If annual sales were reported on a fiscal year basis, state when such fiscal year began.

31. Identify for the period defined in Interrogatory 1 each report, statistical bulletin or memorandum which you have submitted to or received from any trade association relating to the product defined in the complaint with respect to each of the following:

(a) production;
(b) prices;
(c) sales;
(d) costs;
(e) profits;
(f) unfilled orders;
(g) inventories;
(h) shipments;
(i) exports;
(j) imports.

32. Identify each report, statistical bulletin or memorandum submitted by you during the period defined in Interrogatory 1 to the Department of Commerce and to the United States Department of Labor with respect to the product classifications described in the complaint, including the product here in suit, on the basis of which defendants maintain their records, relating to each of the matters referred to in subparagraphs (a) through (j) of Interrogatory 31.

33. State what other companies manufactured or assembled the product defined in the complaint, if, to your knowledge or information, the number is less than 20.

IV. Record Retention

34. State annually for the period defined in Interrogatory 1 the policy of your company with respect to the retention of records and identify any directive or other writing which sets forth such policy.

APPENDIX 15

EXHIBIT "A"

DOCUMENTS TO BE PRODUCED PURSUANT TO RULE 34

DEFINITIONS

(a) Except where otherwise stated, "document" means any written, recorded or graphic matter, however produced or reproduced, prepared during the period from January 1, 1948 through December 31, 1961; or prepared thereafter until July 1, 1962, but relating or referring to the said period (excepting those documents prepared solely for the purposes of this litigation). The term "document" shall include only such matter relating to the product defined in the complaint, and it shall not include any document heretofore produced in any national depository or contained only in any individual transaction file, but the latter exclusion is without prejudice to a further application to the Court by plaintiffs to require search of individual transaction files on the ground that any defendant's production is insufficient.

(b) Except where otherwise stated, "prices" includes both the amount of money for which the product was actually sold or offered for sale in particular transactions and also the amount stated in any defendant's published catalogues or other general pricing documents.

DOCUMENTS TO BE PRODUCED

1. A copy of each price list, price catalogue, discount sheet, multiplier sheet or pricing formula or catalogue, including additions, insertions, supplements and changes therein, issued by you showing either domestic or export prices or terms and conditions of sale, but excluding those heretofore produced in any national depository.

2. Each document evaluating or analyzing prevailing prices or terms and conditions of sale.

3. Each document setting forth, announcing, proposing, recommending or referring or relating to the establishment or maintenance of or changes in prices or terms and conditions of sale instituted or to be instituted by you or by any of your competitors, other than published price catalogues, price sheets, or price lists.

4. Each work sheet or other document prepared in connection with any evaluation or analysis of existing prices or terms and conditions of sale or the establishment or maintenance of actual, proposed or recommended changes in prices or terms and conditions of sale instituted or to be instituted by you or by any of your competitors, other than published price catalogues, price sheets, or price lists.

5. Each document referring or relating to the effect of changes in published or list prices on market shares, bids or actual transaction prices or sales volume, or to the effect of market shares, market prices or sales volume on published or list prices and changes therein.

6. Each document referring or relating to the effect on costs, prices, terms and conditions of sale, sales volume, market shares or other market conditions of actual or proposed substantial changes in production techniques, capital investment or productive capacity.

7. Each document referring or relating to actual transaction price levels or to any changes in or deviations from such levels as to either domestic or export prices.

8. Each document referring or relating to or reflecting the specific circumstances under which you obtained notification of actual or proposed price changes of your competitors or obtained possession of price catalogues, price sheets, price lists or other documents setting forth prices or terms and conditions of sale of your competitors.

9. Each document referring or relating to the effect on prices, terms and conditions of sale, sales volume, market shares or other market conditions of any bid, proposal or sale in the United States of any foreign manufacturer.

10. Each document referring or relating to the competitive situation, to prices or to market shares prepared in connection with the activities or meetings of any corporate committee or body, formal or informal, including but not being limited to Code Committee Reports.

11. Each document referring or relating to the market position or share of the market of any domestic or foreign seller or to the capacity, costs, profit margins or competitive potential of any other domestic or foreign seller, provided that where such information concerning the defendant company producing any such document is contained in the same document, said information shall not be deleted or masked.

12. Each document which shows or refers to order backlogs, period between order date and delivery (lead-time) or percent of capacity utilized by you or your competitors, and each report, summary or analysis thereof.

13. Each document referring or relating to the relationship between costs, profits or prices and any product improvement or technical or quality change.

14. Each document referring or relating to any cost reduction program of you or your competitors.

15. Each document referring or relating to changes in costs or prices as compared with any Bureau of Labor Statistics index or indices or any other index of that type, and each such index prepared by you.

16. Each document referring or relating to the productivity of domestic or foreign labor.

17. Each document referring or relating to the adoption, evaluation or use of any escalation or other price adjustment clause or provision.

18. Each study, report or analysis showing the relative proportion of any material used in the manufacture of each product subject at any time to an index price adjustment clause or provision.

19. Each study made with respect to any product subject at any time to an index price adjustment clause or provision which shows, either with respect to a particular unit of equipment or otherwise, the time during the period of manufacture at which any costs were incurred.

20. Each document showing the proportion to the total cost of manufacturing each product subject at any time to an index price adjustment clause or provision of the cost of (a) labor, (b) materials or (c) other costs.

21. Each document referring or relating to the adoption, evaluation or use of progress payment provisions.

22. Each document stating, summarizing or analyzing bids or quotations submitted by you or any competitor.

23. Each document stating, summarizing or analyzing business received or lost by you or any competitor.

24. Each worksheet, summary or compilation prepared on the basis of raw material submitted for analysis in connection with any order price index or other order or transaction price study, or analysis, including but not being limited to those entitled "Prices and Values in the Electrical Industry" and "Electrical Equipment Price Study" certified by Alexander Grant & Company; and a copy of each such study or analysis.

25. Each compilation of sales data and any explanatory material prepared by you or on your behalf and transmitted to William H. Ferguson, Esq., or Charles S. Burdell, Esq.

26. Minutes of the National Electrical Manufacturers Association (NEMA), its governing body, committees, subcommittees or sections,

without prejudice to a further application by plaintiffs for copies of reports and studies referred to in said minutes.

27. All profit and loss or income statements, long form audit reports, or other similar statements, whether on an actual or estimated basis and whether prepared monthly, quarterly or at other intervals, of each plant, department or division which manufactured or sold the product defined in the complaint and any such statements prepared with respect to any product line which is or includes a product defined in the complaint and such schedules or other summaries, whether on an actual or estimated basis and whether prepared monthly, quarterly or at other intervals, as show the most detailed breakdown of income and expenses, profits and profit margins available.

28. [Paragraph stricken.]

29. All annual plant, department, division and company-wide balance sheets.

30. All annual company-wide profit and loss statements.

31. Records which show, whether on an actual or estimated basis, with respect to each unit of equipment, cost, profit or profit margin.

32. Each document referring or relating to profit goals or to anticipated or budgeted sales, production, profits or profit margins on a company-wide, departmental or divisional basis or with respect to particular units of equipment.

33. Each report, statistical bulletin or other document which you have submitted to or received from any trade association with respect to production, prices, sales, costs, profits, unfilled orders, inventories, shipments, exports or imports, but excluding any document heretofore produced in any national depository.

34. Each report, statistical bulletin or other document submitted by you to the United States Department of Commerce or Department of Labor with respect to production, prices, sales, costs, profits, unfilled orders, inventories, shipments, exports or imports, but excluding any document heretofore produced in any national depository, provided, however, that census reports rendered immune from legal process by 13 U.S.C.A. §9(a) need not be produced or identified.

35. Each document taken to, received at, or prepared during any meeting (at which meeting there was any discussion or mention whatsoever relating to prices, costs, multipliers, discounts, lost business, future business, allocation of business, market conditions, market activities, terms

and conditions of sale, or other competitive activity) attended by any of your employees and by any person employed by any competitor.

36. Each document reflecting the subject matter of, or referring or relating in any way to any meeting described in paragraph 35.

37. Each document containing, reflecting the subject matter of, or referring or relating to any communication, whether written or oral, between any of your employees and any person employed by any competitor which communication concerned in any way prices, costs, multipliers, discounts, lost business, future business, allocation of business, market conditions, market activities, terms and conditions of sale, or other competitive activities.

38. Each document referring or relating to any absence of or limitation on price competition or other types of competition or to the allocation of customers or business.

39. Each document referring or relating to efforts by persons engaging in activities of the type described in paragraphs 35 and 37 to conceal such activities or withhold information concerning them.

40. Each document referring or relating to disciplinary action imposed on or any investigation made of any of your employees with respect to compliance with or violation of the antitrust laws or of any company policy relating to contact with competitors.

41. All minutes of the board of directors or executive or other corporate committee, annual statements, proxy statements and each document referring or relating to Federal Governmental investigations or civil or criminal actions by the United States with respect to possible violations of the antitrust laws of the United States.

42. [Paragraph stricken.]

43. [Paragraph stricken.]

44. The purchase agreement between the Midvale Company and the Midvale-Heppenstall Company dated on or about December 2, 1955, stock subscriptions relating to Midvale-Heppenstall stock, correspondence arranging meetings between Midvale-Heppenstall officers or employees and any defendant herein, documents taken to, prepared during, discussed at or received at any meeting attended by any defendant at which an officer or employee of the Midvale-Heppenstall Company was present, and each study, report or analysis referring or relating to the quality of the Midvale-Heppenstall Company's forgings and the equipment used in their production. Material confidential to the Midvale-Heppenstall Company need not be produced but will be identified.

APPENDIX 16a

Defendants' Set No. 1 of Interrogatories in the Second Priority Product Lines

The undersigned defendants hereby request that each plaintiff answer separately under oath, in accordance with Rule 33 of the Federal Rules of Civil Procedure, the following interrogatories for the period unless otherwise specified, commencing with the date of the earliest commitment or order for a purchase of these products in respect of which plaintiff seeks to recover damages in this action, and ending April 1, 1961.

Definition "A"

"You" or "your" means the plaintiff separately answering these interrogatories, its domestically domiciled subsidiaries and its merged or acquired predecessors, its present and former officers, agents and all other persons acting on behalf of the plaintiff or such subsidiaries or such predecessors, including all past or present employees exercising discretion, making policy and making decisions or participating in any of the foregoing functions with respect to the purchase of these products and further includes consultants, past and present (with respect to these products), or any other persons or organizations acting in such a consulting or an advisory capacity, but only for the purpose of furnishing the name, address, and specialty of such consultants, persons or organizations and for the purpose of identifying but not giving the contents of documents prepared by them.

Definition "C"

As used herein, the term "products" shall mean the products described in the complaint taken as a whole, one or more sizes, ratings, models or types thereof, or one or more items of a particular size, rating, model or type thereof, but shall not include any such products which are not regarded by the plaintiff as falling within the categories large circuit breakers, power switching equipment or power switchgear assemblies.

Definition "F"

As used herein, the term "purchase" shall mean, unless otherwise specified, each purchase of these products made by you from a supplier or contractor during the period of time covered by these interrogatories, whether or not damages are sought to be recovered in respect thereof.

Definition "G"

As used herein, the term "document" refers to any book, pamphlet, periodical, letter, report, memorandum, record, study, working paper, chart, paper, graph, index, data sheet, data processing card or tape, or any other writing, however produced or reproduced (excepting those documents prepared solely for the purpose of this litigation). The term "document" does not include any document contained only in an individual transaction file, but the latter exception is without prejudice to a further application to the Court by defendants to require search of individual transaction files on the ground that any plaintiff's answer is insufficient and to the defendants' right to apply during Local Discovery for the inspection of individual transaction files.

Definition "H"

As used herein, the term "bid" shall mean, unless otherwise specified, any price for these products submitted to you by any supplier or contractor pursuant to any procedure which you considered to be a sealed bid procedure.

Definition "I"

As used herein, the term "quotation" shall mean, unless otherwise specified, any price for these products submitted to you by any supplier or contractor, other than a bid.

Definition "J"

"Identify" or "identification" when used in reference to an individual person means to state his full name and present address if known and his present or last known position and business affiliation. Consultants or experts retained solely for the purpose of the preparation of these cases for trial need not be identified. "Identify" or "identification" when used in reference to a document means to state the date and author, type of document (e.g., letter, memorandum, telegram, chart, etc.), or some other means of identifying it, and its present location or custodian. If any such document was but is no longer in your possession or subject to your control, state what disposition was made of it.

With respect to any of these interrogatories which call for the listing, identification, content or description of documents, any of the plaintiffs may, in lieu of such identification or description, make such documents or copies thereof available for inspection and copying.

Instruction

With respect to each of the following interrogatories which request information concerning particular purchases, identify in your answer each such purchase by the supplier's requisition or general order number, if available, or otherwise by invoice number or other identification.

Interrogatories

1. (a) State whether you acquired or had any information (whether it be actual knowledge, hearsay or rumor; or assumption or surmise embodied in any document), that any officer, agent, employee, or person acting or purporting to act on behalf of any manufacturer of electrical equipment

communicated in any way at any time with any officer, agent, employee, or person acting or purporting to act on behalf of any other manufacturer of electrical equipment with respect to prices, pricing rules, terms or conditions of sale of any type of electrical equipment or the classification of items of any types of electrical equipment as standard or non-standard. (Exclude from consideration in answering this interrogatory all information received or learned solely from any civil or criminal proceedings brought since January 1, 1960 concerning alleged antitrust violations by electrical equipment manufacturers, with respect to these products or other electrical equipment, or any accounts, reports or statements with respect thereto appearing in any newspaper, record of a congressional hearing, or other public record and exclude all information which relates solely to electrical equipment other than these products.)

(b) If the answer to (a) above is affirmative, with respect to each item of such information,

(i) identify each person acquiring or having knowledge thereof and (if different) the person upon whose recollection your answer is based,

(ii) identify the source thereof, including an identification of each person who communicated or through whom such information was communicated,

(iii) if oral, give the content thereof as disclosed in any corporate or internal record,

(iv) give the date you acquired the information, or your best approximation thereof, the place, and the circumstances under which it was acquired.

(c) Identify each document that contains any reference to or reflects any of the matters referred to in (b) above, or your answer thereto.

2. (a) State whether you have received, transmitted or had knowledge of any communication, written or oral, or prepared any document, which commented upon, or recommended action because of, the lack of difference between prices quoted or bid by different suppliers for any purchase or series of purchases by you or any other purchaser of these products or electrical equipment including these products, or which commented upon or recommended action because of uniformity of suppliers' pricing practices or terms or conditions of sale with respect to any such purchase or series of purchases. (Exclude from consideration in answering this interrogatory all information received or learned solely from any civil or criminal proceedings brought since January 1, 1960, concerning alleged antitrust violations by electrical equipment manufacturers, with respect to these products or other electrical equipment, or any accounts, reports or statements with respect thereto appearing in any newspaper, record of a congressional hearing, or other public record.)

(b) If the answer to (a) above is affirmative, with respect to each such communication,

(i) If oral, give the content thereof as disclosed in any corporate or internal record,

(ii) Identify each party thereto, each person having knowledge thereof, and (if different), the person upon whose recollection your answer is based,

(iii) Give the date of the communication or your best approximation thereof, the place, and whether in person or by telephone.

(c) Identify each document that contains any reference to or reflects any of the matters referred to in (a) or (b) above, or your answer thereto.

3. State whether you or any person, association, group, or organization acting on your behalf has conducted, or has authorized any other person to conduct, an investigation or study of the combinations or conspiracies alleged in the complaint, or of the effect of such alleged combinations or conspiracies on purchases in respect of which damages are sought to be recovered in this action, or of the prices which would have been paid for such purchases but for such alleged conspiracy, or any other related matter involved in the so-called electrical equipment antitrust actions, and if so, identify:

(a) Each association, group, or organization with which you have collaborated or in any way cooperated in authorizing or conducting such investigation or study,

(b) Each member thereof,

(c) Each person employed by you or by any such association, group, or organization, who was in charge of conducting any such study or investigation,

(d) Each person employed by you who has knowledge of or who had access to the contents of such study or investigation, and each person not employed by you to whom you transmitted knowledge of or gave access to the contents of such study or investigation,

(e) Each document submitted by any such person, association, group, or organization to you, concerning any such investigation or study,

(f) Each document furnished by you to any such person or to any such association, group, or organization for use in such study or investigation, present custodian thereof, or copy or copies thereof, and the person or persons who were in charge of the preparation thereof.

4. (a) Give the name and address of each consultant rendering services or advice of any kind to you with respect to purchasing or planning for the purchase of these products alone or electrical equipment including these products,

(b) Describe the service or advice rendered by each such consultant with respect to these products alone or electrical equipment including these products, identify each representative of such consultant and your employee who was the person in charge of receiving such service or advice with respect thereto, and identify the purchases, if any, with respect to which such service or advice was rendered, and

(c) Identify each document that indicates the duties, authority or responsibility of each consultant identified in your answer to (a) above.

5. (a) State whether you systematically, regularly or repeatedly have made, participated in, carried out, used in any way, or derived any information from any agreement, understanding, system, plan, arrangement, or method by which, or in connection with which, you or any other purchaser or purchasers received or gave information with respect to these products or electrical equipment including these products, concerning:

(i) Evaluation of price,

(ii) Evaluation of performance,

(iii) Purchasers' purchasing practices,

(iv) Market or book price levels,

(v) Prices quoted or bid,

(vi) Prices paid or to be paid,

(vii) Price rules, or

(viii) Terms or conditions of sale, including, but not limited to, escalation, price adjustment policies and progress payments.

(b) If the answer to (a) above is affirmative, with respect to each such agreement, understanding, system, plan, arrangement, or method:

(i) Give a description thereof,

(ii) Identify each person acting on your behalf, each person acting or purporting to act on behalf of any other purchaser, and each other person who was in any way involved in the making or execution thereof, and

(iii) Set forth the content of all such information orally received or given pursuant thereto as disclosed in any corporate or internal record.

(c) State whether you have communicated in writing with respect to these products or electrical equipment including these products with any person acting or purporting to act for any other purchaser concerning:

(i) Evaluation of price,

(ii) Evaluation of performance,

(iii) Purchasers' purchasing practices,

(iv) Market or book price levels,

(v) Prices quoted or bid,

(vi) Prices paid or to be paid,

(vii) Price rules, or

(viii) Terms or conditions of sale including, but not limited to, escalation, price adjustment policies and progress payments.

(d) If your answer to (c) above is affirmative, identify each document to which you have access, or have had access, which contains any reference to or reflects any of the matters referred to in (c) above, and with respect to each such document, identify each person not employed by you to whom it was sent or from whom it was received.

(e) Identify each document to which you have access, or have had access, which contains any reference to or reflects any of the matters referred to in (a) and (b) above, or your answer thereto.

6. (a) Identify and describe the nature of each questionnaire and survey and each inquiry in connection with any study which you have received which requested information or opinion as to prices, price rules, terms or conditions of sale (including, but not limited to, progress payments, price adjustment policies and escalation), quality, acceptability or other characteristics of these products, and set forth the content of each oral response thereto as disclosed in any corporate or internal record, and identify each document to which you have access, or have had access, which contains any reference to or reflects any response, whether written or oral.

(b) Identify and describe the nature of each questionnaire and survey and each inquiry in connection with any study which you have received which requested information as to your preference for or evaluation of the products of different suppliers and set forth the content of each oral response thereto as disclosed in any corporate or internal record, and identify each document to which you have access, or have had access, which contains any reference to or reflects any response, whether written or oral.

(c) With respect to each questionnaire, survey or inquiry referred to in your answer to (a) or (b) above, identify each written response made by any other purchaser to which you have access, or have had access.

7. (a) State whether you have communicated with any person acting or purporting to act on behalf of any other purchaser of these products, or on behalf of any supplier, or on behalf of any purchasing, trade, professional, municipal or governmental organization, with respect to stand-

ards, standardization or popular ratings of these products, or the effect of any of them on suppliers' prices or pricing rules for these products.

(b) If the answer to (a) above is affirmative, identify each document to which you have access or have had access, which contains any reference to or reflects any of the matters referred to in (a) above, and with respect to each such document, identify each person not employed by you to whom it was sent or from whom it was received.

(c) With respect to each organization or group, section, committee or subcommittee thereof, of which you were a member which was concerned with standards of or for these products, standardization or attempts to standardize these products, or which discussed said subject:

(i) Identify each such organization and group, section, committee or subcommittee thereof,

(ii) Give the date and place of and identify each participant for you at each meeting of such organization, group, section, committee or subcommittee, which was attended by any person on your behalf, at which any of the matters referred to in (a) above were discussed.

(d) Identify each document to which you have access, or have had access, which contains any reference to or reflects any of the matters discussed at any meeting identified in your answer to (c) above.

8. With respect to each communication (except reports made regularly in the ordinary course of business) made at any time up to and including the date of entry of Pretrial Order No. 37, between you or any purchasing, trade, professional, municipal or governmental organization with which you or your employees are associated, and of which, if written, a copy is contained in your files, on the one hand, and Mr. Fisher Black, Mr. Warren Shew or Electrical World on the other hand, in any way concerning prices, price rules, price movements or price levels or terms or conditions of sale (including but not limited to, progress payments, price adjustment policies and escalation) but not including communications solely regarding prices paid for these products alone or electrical equipment including these products.

(a) Identify each person making and receiving such communication and each person having knowledge thereof.

(b) If oral set forth the content thereof as disclosed in any corporate or internal record.

(c) Identify each document in your file that contains any reference to or reflects any of the matters referred to in this interrogatory or your answer thereto.

9. (a) Give the date and place of each formal meeting of any purchasing, trade, professional, municipal or governmental organization,

or any group, section, committee or subcommittee thereof and of each informal gathering in connection therewith which was attended by any of your past or present officers or agents or employees engaged in engineering, purchasing or evaluation of electrical equipment, at which any of the following matters (but excluding matters solely relating to parties or the business of parties other than the plaintiff separately answering these interrogatories) was discussed:

(i) Evaluation of price, performance or other characteristics of these products,

(ii) Purchasers' purchasing practices,

(iii) Market or book price levels of these products,

(iv) Prices quoted or bid for these products,

(v) Prices paid or to be paid for these products,

(vi) Price rules for these products, or

(vii) Terms and conditions of sale for these products including, but not limited to, escalation, price adjustment policies and progress payments,

identifying with respect to each such meeting the organization, or group, section, committee or subcommittee thereof, and the past or present officers or agents or employees engaged in engineering, purchasing, or evaluation of electrical equipment who attended the meeting.

(b) Identify the officers of each such organization, association, society, group, section, committee or subcommittee.

(c) Identify the person having custody or control of the minutes or summary of every meeting listed in your answer to (a) above.

(d) Identify each document that contains any reference to or reflects any of the matters referred to in (a) above or your answer thereto.

10. (a) Identify each summary, study, report or memorandum (but not omit material submitted for rate-making purposes) relating to these products alone or any group or category of electrical equipment including these products to which you have access, or have had access (but excluding matters solely relating to parties or the business of parties other than the plaintiff separately answering these interrogatories), concerning:

(i) Your projected or estimated requirements for these products,

(ii) Quality, efficiency or performance of these products, or electrical equipment including these products,

(iii) Past, present or future purchase price or purchase price trend of these products, or electrical equipment including these products, whether relating to your purchases alone, to the purchases of others, or a combination thereof (excluding documents which relate only to a single purchase),

(iv) Past, present or future book price or book price trend of these products, or electrical equipment including these products, whether relating to your purchases alone, to the purchases of others, or a combination thereof (excluding documents which relate only to a single purchase),

(v) Cost of electrical system expansion, including but not limited to construction and equipment costs,

(vi) Cost or cost trends of maintenance or operation of these products, or electrical equipment including these products,

(vii) Cost per unit of performance or capacity of these products, or electrical equipment including these products,

(viii) The comparative value or utility of these products in relation to cost or some other objective factor,

(ix) Your customers' present or future need for electricity,

(x) Your present or future capacity to generate, transmit or distribute electricity, and

(xi) Your requirements for construction and electrical equipment to provide for the capacity to meet your customers' needs.

(b) State as to each such document whether it has been filed with or made available to:

(i) Any purchasing, trade or professional organization, or group, section, committee or subcommittee thereof,

(ii) Federal Power Commission,

(iii) U. S. Department of Labor,

(iv) U. S. Department of Commerce,

(v) A Public Utility Commission or similar regulatory agency,

(vi) Publishers of the Handy Index or the Handy-Whitman Index,

(vii) Electrical World or other trade publication, and identify in each case such organization or association and the person affiliated therewith with whom the document was filed or to whom it was made available.

11. Identify each of your officers, agents, representatives or employees who is or was employed in a managerial, engineering, purchasing, selling

or marketing capacity by you and who was employed in any such capacity in a priority product line or lines by any corporation named as a defendant or co-conspirator in the Philadelphia electrical equipment criminal proceedings and for each give the name and address of the former employer, the capacity in which the employee was so employed, and the approximate dates of such employment, as shown in your existing employment records or as obtained by a questionnaire.

12. (a) State whether you or anyone acting on your behalf communicated with any state or federal agency charged with enforcing antitrust laws or with any legislative committee or subcommittee concerned with such laws with respect to prices of these products or electrical equipment including these products.

(b) If so, identify each person who did so communicate, the agency or committee concerned, and the approximate date thereof.

(c) Identify each document which formed the basis, wholly or in part, of your response to (a) or (b) above.

APPENDIX 16b

Defendants' Motion No. 1 for Production of Documents in the Second Priority Product Lines

The undersigned defendants hereby move this Court for an order pursuant to Rule 34 of the Federal Rules of Civil Procedure requiring each plaintiff in each of the above actions separately to produce and to permit the defendants to inspect and copy or cause to be copied the following documents now in its possession, custody or control. It is requested that for each document the paragraph of the motion in response to which it is produced should be indicated. Each of the documents requested contains evidence relevant to a matter involved in one or more of the above-captioned actions or is reasonably calculated to lead to the discovery of evidence relevant to such matter.

Definitions

A. "You" or "your" means the plaintiff separately producing these documents, its domestically domiciled subsidiaries and its merged or acquired predecessors, its present and former officers, agents and all other persons acting on behalf of the plaintiff or such subsidiaries or such predecessors, including all past or present employees exercising discretion, making policy and making decisions or participating in any of the foregoing functions with respect to the purchase of these products and further includes consultants, past and present (with respect to these products), or any other persons or organizations acting in such a consulting or an advisory capacity, but only for the purpose of furnishing the name, address, and specialty of such consultants, persons or organizations and for the purpose of identifying but not giving the contents of documents prepared by them.

C. As used herein, the term "products" shall mean the products described in the complaint taken as a whole, one or more sizes, ratings, models or types thereof, or one or more items of a particular size rating, model or type thereof but shall not include any such products which are not regarded by the plaintiff as falling within the categories large circuit breakers, power switching equipment or power switchgear assemblies.

F. As used herein, the term "purchase" shall mean, unless otherwise specified, each purchase of these products made by you from a supplier or contractor during the period of time covered by this motion, whether or not damages are sought to be recovered in respect thereof.

G. As used herein, the term "document" refers to any book, pamphlet, periodical, letter, report memorandum record study working paper, chart, paper, graph, index, data sheet, data processing card or tape, or any other writing, however produced or reproduced, prepared during the period commencing with the date of the earliest commitment or order for a purchase of these products in respect of which the plaintiff making production seeks to recover damages in such action, and ending December 31, 1961, or prepared thereafter until July 1, 1962, but relating or referring to the said period (except those documents prepared solely for the purposes of this litigation). The term "document" does not include any document contained only in an individual transaction file but the latter exception is without prejudice to a further application to the Court by defendants to require search of individual transaction files on the ground that any plaintiff's production is insufficient and to the defendants' right to apply during Local Discovery for the inspection of individual transaction files.

H. As used herein, the term "bid" shall mean, unless otherwise specified, any price for these products submitted to you by any supplier or contractor pursuant to any procedure which you considered to be a sealed bid procedure.

I. As used herein, the term "quotation" shall mean, unless otherwise specified, any price for these products submitted to you by any supplier or contractor, other than a bid.

Documents to Be Produced

1. Each document that contains any reference to or reflects the acquisition or possession by you of any information (whether it be actual knowledge, hearsay, rumor, assumption or surmise) that any officer, agent, employee, or person acting or purporting to act on behalf of any manufacturer of electrical equipment communicated in any way at any time with any officer, agent, employee, or person acting or purporting to act on behalf of any other manufacturer of electrical equipment with respect to prices, pricing rules, terms or conditions of sale of any type of electrical equipment or the classification of items of any type of electrical equipment as standard or non-standard or that contains any reference to or reflects the source of such information, the person through whom it was communicated to or received by you, the person who acquired the information, the content of the information, or the date, place or circumstances under which it was acquired. (Exclude all documents dealing solely with or solely containing or reflecting information received or learned from any civil or criminal proceedings brought since January 1, 1960, concerning alleged antitrust violations by electrical equipment manufacturers, with respect to these products or other electrical equipment, or any accounts, reports or statements with respect thereto appearing in any newspaper, record of a congressional hearing, or other public record and exclude all information which relates solely to electrical equipment other than these products.)

2. Each document that contains any reference to or reflects your receipt, transmission or knowledge of any communication, written or oral, and each document you prepared, which commented upon, or recom-

mended action because of the lack of difference between prices quoted or bid by different suppliers for any purchase or series of purchases by you or any other purchaser of these products or electrical equipment including these products, or which commented upon, or recommended action because of uniformity of suppliers' pricing practices or terms or conditions of sale with respect to any such purchase or series of purchases and each document that contains any reference or relates to the content of any such communication, the identity of any person who was a party thereto or had knowledge thereof, or the date, place or whether such communication was in person or by telephone. (Exclude all documents dealing solely with or solely containing or reflecting information received or learned from any civil or criminal proceedings brought since January 1, 1960, concerning alleged antitrust violations by electrical equipment manufacturers, with respect to these products or other electrical equipment, or any accounts, reports or statements with respect thereto appearing in any newspaper, record of a congressional hearing, or other public record.)

3. Records which show whether you or any person, association, group, or organization acting on your behalf has conducted, or has authorized any other person to conduct an investigation or study of the combinations or conspiracies alleged in the complaint, or of the effect of such alleged combinations or conspiracies on purchases in respect of which damages are sought to be recovered in this action, or of the prices which would have been paid for such purchases but for such alleged conspiracies, or any other related matter involved in the so-called electrical equipment antitrust actions, and each document submitted by any such person, association, group, or organization to you, concerning any such investigation or study and each document furnished by you to any such person or to any such association, group, or organization for use in such study or investigation.

4. Each document that indicates the duties, authority or responsibility of each consultant rendering service or advice of any kind to you with respect to purchasing or planning for the purchase of these products alone or electrical equipment including these products.

5. (a) Each document that contains any reference to or reflects any agreement, understanding, system, plan, arrangement or method you systematically, regularly or repeatedly have made, participated in, carried out, used in any way or derived any information from by which or in connection with which, you or any other purchaser or purchasers received or gave information with respect to these products or electrical equipment including these products concerning:

(i) Evaluation of price,

(ii) Evaluation of performance,

(iii) Purchasers' purchasing practices,

(iv) Market or book price levels,

(v) Prices quoted or bid,

(vi) Prices paid or to be paid,

(vii) Price rules, or

(viii) Terms or conditions of sale including, but not limited to, escalation, price adjustment policies and progress payments.

(b) Each document that sets forth, contains any reference to or reflects any communication by you with any person acting or purporting to act for any other purchaser with respect to these products or any electrical equipment including these products, concerning any category mentioned above.

6. (a) Each questionnaire, survey or inquiry in connection with any study which you have received which requested information or opinion as to prices, price rules, terms or conditions of sale (including, but not limited to, progress payments, price adjustment policies, and escalation), quality acceptability or other characteristics of these products and each document containing any reference to or reflecting any response thereto, whether written or oral.

(b) Each questionnaire, survey or inquiry in connection with any study which you have received which requested information as to your preference for or evaluation of the products of different suppliers, and each document containing any reference to or reflecting any response thereto, whether written or oral.

(c) Each response made by any other purchaser to any questionnaire, survey or inquiry in connection with any study received relating to any of the subjects referred to in (a) or (b) above.

7. (a) Each document that sets forth, contains any reference to or reflects any communication by you with any person acting or purporting to act on behalf of any other purchaser of these products, or on behalf of any supplier, or on behalf of any purchasing, trade, professional, municipal or governmental organization with respect to standards, standardization or popular ratings of these products, or the effect of any of them on suppliers' prices or pricing rules for these products.

(b) Each document that contains any reference to or reflects any of the matters discussed at any meeting during which there was a discussion of standards, standardization or popular ratings of these products or the effect of any of them on suppliers' prices or pricing rules for these products, of any organization or group, section, committee or subcommittee thereof, of which you were a member which was concerned with standards of or for these products, standardization or attempts to standardize these products, or which discussed said subject.

8. Each document that sets forth, contains any reference to or reflects the substance of any communication (except reports made regularly in the ordinary course of business) made at any time up to and including the date of entry of Pretrial Order No. 37 were filed, between you or any purchasing, trade, professional, municipal or governmental organization with which you or your employees are associated, on the one hand, and Mr. Fisher Black, Mr. Warren Shew, or Electrical World, on the other hand, in any way concerning prices, price rules, price movements or price levels or terms or conditions of sale (including but not limited to, progress payments, price adjustment policies and escalation) but not including communications solely regarding prices paid for these products alone or electrical equipment including these products.

9. Each document that contains any reference to or reflects:

(a) the date or place of any formal meeting of any purchasing, trade, professional, municipal or governmental organization, or any group, section, committee or sub-committee, or of any informal gathering in connection therewith which was attended by any of your past or present officers or agents or employees engaged in engineering, purchasing or evaluation of electrical equipment at which any of the following matters (but excluding matters solely relating to parties or the business of parties other than the plaintiff separately producing these documents) were discussed:

(i) Evaluation of price, performance or other characteristics of these products,

(ii) Purchasers' purchasing practices,

(iii) Market or book price levels of these products,

(iv) Prices quoted or bid for these products,

(v) Prices paid or to be paid for these products,

(vi) Price rules for these products, or

(vii) Terms or conditions of sale for these products including, but not limited to, escalation, price adjustment policies and progress payments, or

(b) any of the matters referred to in (a) above.

10. Each summary, study, report or memorandum (but excluding documents submitted for rate-making purposes) relating to these products alone or any group or category of electrical equipment including these products (but excluding matters solely relating to parties or the business of parties other than the plaintiff separately producing these documents), concerning:

(i) Your projected or estimated requirements for these products,

(ii) Quality, efficiency or performance of these products, or electrical equipment including these products,

(iii) Past, present or future purchase price or purchase price trend of these products, or electrical equipment including these products, whether relating to your purchases alone, to the purchases of others, or a combination thereof (excluding documents which relate only to a single purchase),

(iv) Past, present, or future book price of book price trend of these products or electrical equipment including these products, whether relating to your purchases alone, to the purchase of others, or a combination thereof (excluding documents which relate only to a single purchase),

(v) Cost of electrical system expansion, including but not limited to construction and equipment costs,

(vi) Cost or cost trends of maintenance or operation of these products, or electrical equipment including these products,

(vii) Cost per unit of performance or capacity of these products, or electrical equipment including these products,

(viii) The comparative value or utility of these products in relation to cost or some other objective factor,

(ix) Your customers' present or future need for electricity,

(x) Your present or future capacity to generate, transmit or distribute electricity, or

(xi) Your requirements for construction of electrical equipment to provide for the capacity to meet your customers' needs.

11. Each document which formed the basis, wholly or in part, of your response to Interrogatory 12(a) and (b) attached as Schedule A to this Pre-Trial Order.

Schedule I

TO

National Pretrial Order No. 37

(Defendants' Set No. 2 of Second Priority Product Line Interrogatories)

Defendants hereby request that each plaintiff answer separately under oath, in accordance with Rule 33 of the Federal Rules of Civil Procedure, the following interrogatories for the period, unless otherwise specified, commencing with the date of the earliest commitment or order for a purchase of these products in respect of which plaintiff seeks to recover damages in this action, and ending April 1, 1961.

Definition "A"

"You" or "your" means the plaintiff separately answering these interrogatories, its domestically domiciled subsidiaries and its merged or acquired predecessors, its present and former officers, agents and all other persons acting on behalf of the plaintiff or such subsidiaries or such predecessors, including all past or present employees exercising discretion, making policy and making decisions or participating in any of the foregoing functions with respect to the purchase of these products and further includes consultants, past and present (with respect to these products), or any other persons or organizations acting in such a consulting or advisory capacity, but only for the purpose of furnishing the name, address, and specialty of such consultants, persons or organizations and for the purpose of identifying but not giving the contents of documents prepared by them.

Definition "B"

As used herein, the term "practice" or "policy" shall mean each rule, procedure, or directive, formal or informal, and each common understanding or course of conduct which was recognized as such by your employees or other persons acting on your behalf, which was in effect at any time during the period covered by these interrogatories and which were embodied in a written document.

Definition "C"

As used herein, the term "products" shall mean the products described in the complaint taken as a whole, one or more sizes, ratings, models or types thereof, or one or more items of a particular size, rating, model or type thereof, but shall not include any such products which are not regarded by the plaintiff as falling within the categories large circuit breakers, power switching equipment and power switchgear assemblies.

Definition "D"

As used herein, the term "supplier" shall mean, unless otherwise specified, any manufacturer, assembler, distributor or other supplier of products (whether or not a defendant in this case and whether or not located within the United States), or any agent thereof, but excluding all contractors.

Definition "E"

As used herein, the term "contractor" shall mean any person or business organization of any kind, whenever, in connection with a particular transaction or series of transactions involving the purchase by you of these products, such person or business organization (1) purchased these products or negotiated on your behalf for the purchase of these products, and (2) installed these products alone or as a part of any other construction.

Definition "F"

As used herein, the term "purchase" shall mean, unless otherwise specified, each purchase of these products made by you from a supplier or contractor during the period of time covered by this motion, whether or not damages are sought to be recovered in respect thereof.

Definition "G"

As used herein, the term "document" shall mean any book, pamphlet, periodical, letter, report, memorandum, record, study, working paper, chart, paper, graph, index, data sheet, data processing card or tape, or any other writing, however produced or reproduced, excepting those documents prepared solely for the purposes of this litigation, prepared during the period commencing with the date of the earliest commitment or order for a purchase of these products in respect of which the plaintiff making production seeks to recover damages in such action, and ending December 31, 1961, or prepared thereafter until July 1, 1962, but relating or referring to the said period. The term "document" shall not include any document contained only in any individual transaction file, but the latter exception is without prejudice to a further application to the Court by defendants to require search of individual transaction files on the ground that any plaintiff's production is insufficient and to the defendants' right to apply during Local Discovery for the inspection of individual transaction files.

Definition "H"

As used herein, the term "bid" shall mean, unless otherwise specified, any price for these products submitted to you by any supplier or contractor pursuant to any procedure which you considered to be a sealed bid procedure.

Definition "I"

As used herein, the term "quotation" shall mean, unless otherwise specified, any price for these products submitted to you by any supplier or contractor, other than a bid.

Definition "J"

"Identify" or "identification" when used in reference to an individual person means to state his full name and present address if known and his present or last known position and business affiliation. Consultants or experts retained solely for the purpose of the preparation of these cases for trial need not be identified. "Identify" or "identification" when used in reference to a document means to state the date and author, type of document (e.g., letter, memorandum, telegram, chart, etc.), or some other means of identifying it, and its present location or custodian. If any such document was but is no longer in your possession or subject to your control, state what disposition was made of it.

With respect to any of these interrogatories which call for the listing, identification, content or description of documents, any of the plaintiffs may, in lieu of such identification or description, make such documents or copies thereof available for inspection and copying.

The production of a document containing the information sought in an interrogatory will satisfy the interrogatory provided there is an appropriate reference to the document or documents containing the information.

Instruction 1

With respect to each of the following interrogatories which requests information concerning particular purchases, identify in your answer each such purchase by the supplier's requisition or general order number, if available, or otherwise by invoice number or other identification.

Instruction 2

With respect to each of the following interrogatories which requests information concerning any practice or policy, state in your answer the period of time during which each such practice or policy was in effect, if less than the entire period covered by these interrogatories.

1. (a) Identify each of your departments, divisions, bureaus, offices, or other units that has had responsibility for the purchase of these products or electrical equipment including these products.

(b) Identify each past or present employee exercising discretion, making policy and making decisions or participating in any of the foregoing functions in each such department, division, bureau, office, or other designation of your company together with the dates during which such person held such position.

(c) Set forth the duties and responsibilities of each person identified in your answer to (b) above, with respect to the purchase of these products or electrical equipment including these products.

(d) Identify your officers and principal managing agents.

(e) Identify each organization, chart or diagram reflecting the matters referred to in (a) or (b) above.

2. (a) Set forth the powers, duties and responsibilities assigned to your engineering or technical employees in the process of deciding for you which of these products or electrical equipment including these products to purchase, when to purchase it, and from whom to purchase it.

(b) Set forth the manner of resolution of conflicting recommendations from your purchasing employees, and your engineering or technical employees, and your consultants as to which of these products or electrical equipment including these products to purchase, the supplier or contractor from whom to purchase, and when to purchase it.

(c) Identify each document, if any, which forms the basis, wholly or in part, of your response to (a) or (b) above.

3. (a) State whether you have systematically, regularly or repeatedly revealed to or discussed with suppliers or contractors who had then submitted or subsequently submitted a bid or quotation for these products, the price contained in any bid or quotation for the same products submitted by any other supplier or contractor.

(b) If so, with respect to each communication (as disclosed in any corporate or internal record) in which any such price was so revealed or discussed:

(i) Give the date thereof and identify the parties thereto.

(ii) Identify the supplier or contractor whose price was revealed or discussed.

(iii) Identify the bid or quotation or the purchase which was the subject of such communication.

(c) Identify each document, if any, which forms the basis, wholly or in part, of your answer to (b) above.

4. (a) Identify by supplier and date each price book or other document to which you have had access containing prices or discounts, or both, of any supplier for these products, and as to each such price book or other document, state the time period during which you had such access.

(b) State whether your practice was to compute the book or catalogue price and discount (if any) of these products, or any electrical equipment including these products.

(c) Identify each document, if any, which forms the basis, wholly or in part, of your responses to (b) above.

5. If you or your attorneys have interviewed any present or past employee of any supplier or contractor concerning any alleged, rumored or

actual price fixing, allocation, collusion, or discussions of prices, terms or conditions of sale of these products or electrical equipment including these products among any employees of suppliers, with respect to each such interview:

(a) Identify the person so interviewed, the person or persons conducting the interview, the persons present when the interview was taken, the persons having knowledge of the substance thereof, and the persons having custody or control of the recordation of the interview or any summary or evaluation thereof.

(b) State the date and place thereof.

6. If you have any policy concerning the solicitation or acceptance by your employees of gratuities, entertainment or the like from representatives of suppliers:

(a) Set forth the substance of the policy and state whether it has been reduced to writing.

(b) State whether any of your past or present employees exercising discretion, making policy and making decisions or participating in any of the foregoing functions with respect to the purchase of these products from any defendant supplier violated the policy and, if so,

(i) Describe the circumstances of such violation.

(ii) Describe the nature of the gratuities, entertainment or the like solicited or accepted.

(c) Identify each document, if any, which sets forth each policy referred to in your answer to (a) above, and each document, if any, which forms the basis, wholly or in part, of your response to (b) above.

7. (a) Have you adopted or systematically followed any criteria, other than price, terms and conditions of sale, in selecting the suppliers or contractors from whom you would solicit bids or quotations or purchase these products, including, but not exclusively, preferred bidders lists or specifications in terms of a particular manufacturer's products or their equivalent?

(b) If the answer to subparagraph (a) hereof is affirmative, state and describe:

(i) The criteria adopted or systematically followed by you.

(ii) Each instance of deviation from such criteria in the solicitation of bids or quotations or in the purchase of these products, giving, in each case, a description of the product for which bids or quotations were solicited or which was purchased, the identity of your employees responsible for the decision not to apply such criteria, the bids or quotations submitted or purchase price and the respective dates of such submissions or purchase, and the manner in which the solicitations or purchase constituted a deviation from such criteria (failure to include a solicitation of bids or quotations or a purchase in answer hereto shall be deemed to constitute an affirmative statement that such solicitation or purchase was made in accordance with the criteria described in answer to subparagraph (b) (i) hereof).

(c) Identify each document, if any, which forms the basis, wholly or in part, of your responses to subparagraphs (a) and (b).

8. To the extent that the information has not been given in response to any previous interrogatory:

(a) Have you adopted or systematically followed a practice or policy (defined for this interrogatory only as written or unwritten) of rotating, dividing, spreading or allocating your purchases of electrical equipment among any suppliers or contractors?

(b) If the answer to subparagraph (a) hereof is affirmative, state and describe:

(i) The practice or policy adopted or systematically followed by you.

(ii) Each instance of deviation from such practice or policy in the solicitation of bids or quotations or in the purchase of electrical equipment, giving, in each case, a description of the product for which bids or quotations were solicited or which was purchased, the identity of your employees responsible for the decision not to apply such practice or policy, the bids and quotations submitted or purchase price and respective dates of such submissions or purchase, and the manner in which the solicitations or purchase constituted a deviation from such practice or policy (failure to include a solicitation of bids or quotations or a purchase in answer hereto shall be deemed to constitute an affirmative statement that such solicitation or purchase was made in accordance with the practice or policy described in answer to subparagraph (b) (i) hereof).

(c) Identify each document, if any, which forms the basis, wholly or in part, of your responses to subparagraphs (a) and (b).

9. (a) If (as disclosed in any corporate or internal record) you evaluated or recalculated bids or quotations for these products either alone or together with other electrical equipment by taking into account the performance, efficiency, serviceability, productivity or any other characteristic thereof, describe each policy with respect thereto, state the method or methods by which such evaluation or recalculation was made, and specify the formula employed, or the value assigned, to each such characteristic.

(b) Identify each person who participated in or had responsibility for the formulation of each such policy, method and formula.

(c) Identify each study, memorandum or report, if any, which forms the basis, wholly or in part, of your response to (a) above.

10. With respect to each purchase disclosed in response to Interrogatory No. 12:

(a) Identify each instance in which any bid or quotation was evaluated or recalculated, give the amount of each unadjusted bid or quotation, and the amount of the bid or quotation as adjusted by the evaluation or recalculation.

(b) Identify each document, if any, which forms the basis, wholly or in part, of your response to (a) above.

11. (a) Identify each document which refers to or reflects your policy or practice with respect to soliciting bids or quotations for these products or electrical equipment including these products from a supplier whose principal place of business is outside the United States.

(b) Identify the suppliers considered.

(c) Identify each study, report, or other document prepared by or for you alone or in conjunction with any other purchaser concerning the price, quality or availability of such products manufactured by such supplier.

(d) Identify (as disclosed in any corporate or internal record) each person who participated in the decision to solicit or purchase or not to solicit or purchase from such a supplier.

(e) Describe any action taken by you to prohibit, discourage or avoid the receipt of bids or quotations on or the purchase of these products from such a supplier.

(f) Identify each document, if any, which forms the basis, wholly or in part, of your response to (e) above.

12. (a) If you have purchased these products by what you consider to be a sealed bid procedure, describe that procedure in detail, and state the reasons why you selected or used such method of purchase, and identify any statute or governmental regulation pursuant to which such procedure was used.

(b) If you have purchased these products by the quotation method of purchase, state the reasons why you selected or used such method of purchase.

(c) If you have purchased these products without having a quotation or bid submitted by any supplier or contractor, state the reasons why you elected not to receive or did not receive a bid or quotation.

(d) If you have purchased these products by any method not described in (a) through (c) above, describe such method and state the reasons why you selected or used that method of purchase.

(e) Identify each document that contains any reference to or reflects any of the matters referred to in (a) through (d) above (except that, as to any statute referred to in your answer to (a) above, only the statute need be identified).

13. (a) Have you for any period adopted or followed a policy or practice of purchasing these products from a contractor rather than from a supplier?

(b) If so, define the period or periods in which such policy or practice was in effect.

(c) If so, state whether pursuant to such policy or practice

(i) You regularly, systematically or repeatedly specified that the contractors submit bids or quotations for products manufactured by a particular supplier, or whether in your specifications or request for bids, you described the required electrical equipment in terms of a particular manufacturer's products or its equivalent, and if so, identify the supplier of the products so specified.

(ii) You regularly, systematically or repeatedly required or requested contractors to break down in any way the bids or quotations submitted to you, and if so, the categories required or requested to be used in such breakdowns.

(iii) The bids or quotations received from the contractors from whom you made purchases regularly, systematically or repeatedly allocated a portion thereof to the price of the products; and if so, in this connection, state whether the portion so allocated represented the price of these products paid by the contractor; if not, state how you determined the price of these products to you in your answers to defendants' interrogatories.

(d) If so, describe generally the arrangements, agreements, or understandings you had with the contractor or contractors from whom you purchased these products whereby the contractor was paid a fixed percentage over the cost to him of these products or other electrical equipment supplied with these products, or the total construction or installation cost, and identify by title or other description the persons who made or negotiated any such arrangement or understanding.

(e) If so, identify the documents, if any, which, wholly or in part, form the basis of your answer to paragraph (c) above.

14. (a) To the extent not stated in answer to prior interrogatories, state whether you regularly, systematically or repeatedly conducted negotiations with suppliers or contractors,

(i) prior to receipt of bid.

(ii) prior to receipt of any quotation.

(iii) subsequent to your receipt of one or more bids, but before award.

(iv) subsequent to your receipt of one or more quotations, but before placement of the order.

(v) without receipt of any bid or quotation.

(b) To the extent not stated in answer to prior interrogatories, with respect to purchases for which you conducted negotiations,

(i) State whether you regularly, systematically or repeatedly notified other suppliers or contractors from whom bids or quotations had been or were later received that you were or had been negotiating with other suppliers or contractors.

(ii) Describe generally each of the matters which were the subject of the negotiations.

(iii) Identify the documents, if any, which form the basis, wholly or in part, of your response to this interrogatory.

15. Identify each document to which you have access or have had access that contains any reference to or reflects any study or analysis of, or policy or proposal with respect to any price adjustment clause, escalation clause, or other similar provision or price rule to which your purchase of these products alone or electrical equipment including these products were subject or proposed to be made subject.

16. Set forth each of your policies with respect to the retention of records called for by these interrogatories and identify any directive or other document which sets forth such policy.

APPENDIX **17b**

Schedule J

to

National Pretrial Order No. 37

(Defendants' Motion No. 2 for Production of Documents in the Second Priority Product Lines)

Defendants hereby move this Court for an order pursuant to Rule 34 of the Federal Rules of Civil Procedure requiring each plaintiff in each of the above actions separately to produce and to permit the defendants to inspect and copy or cause to be copied the following documents now in its possession, custody or control. It is requested that for each document the paragraph of this motion in response to which it is produced should be indicated. Each of the documents requested contains evidence relevant to a matter involved in one or more of the above-captioned actions or is reasonably calculated to lead to the discovery of evidence relevant to such matter.

Definition "A"

As used herein, "you" or "your" means the plaintiff separately producing these documents, its domestically domiciled subsidiaries and its merged or acquired predecessors, its present and former officers, agents and all other persons acting on behalf of the plaintiff or such subsidiaries or such predecessors, including all past or present employees exercising discretion, making policy and making decisions or participating in any of the foregoing functions with respect to the purchase of these products and further includes consultants, past and present (with respect to these products), or any other persons or organizations acting in such a consulting or advisory capacity, but only for the purpose of furnishing the name, address and specialty of such consultants, persons or organizations and for the purpose of producing documents prepared by them.

Definition "B"

As used herein, the terms "practice" or "policy" shall mean each rule, procedure, or directive, formal or informal, and each common understanding or course of conduct which was recognized as such by your employees or other persons acting on your behalf, which was in effect at any time during the period covered by this motion.

Definition "C"

As used herein, the term "products" shall mean the products described in the complaint taken as a whole, one or more sizes, ratings, models or types thereof, or one or more items of a particular size, rating, model or type thereof, but shall not include any such products which are not regarded by the plaintiff as falling within the categories large circuit breakers, power switching equipment and power switchgear assemblies.

Definition "D"

As used herein, the term "supplier" shall mean, unless otherwise specified, any manufacturer, assembler, distributor or other supplier of products (whether or not a defendant in this case and whether or not located within the United States), or any agent thereof, but excluding all contractors.

Definition "E"

As used herein, the term "contractor" shall mean any person or business organization of any kind, whenever, in connection with a particular transaction or series of transactions involving the purchase by you of these products, such person or business organization (1) purchased these products or negotiated on your behalf for the purchase of these products, and (2) installed these products alone or as a part of any other construction.

Definition "F"

As used herein, the term "purchase" shall mean, unless otherwise specified, each purchase of these products made by you from a supplier or contractor during the period of time covered by this motion, whether or not damages are sought to be recovered in respect thereof.

Definition "G"

As used herein, the term "document" shall mean any book, pamphlet, periodical, letter, report, memorandum, record, study, working paper, chart, paper, graph, index, data sheet, data processing card or tape, or any other writing, however produced or reproduced, excepting those documents prepared solely for the purposes of this litigation, prepared during the period commencing with the date of the earliest commitment or order for a purchase of these products in respect of which the plaintiff making production seeks to recover damages in such action, and ending December 31, 1961, or prepared thereafter until July 1, 1962, but relating or referring to the said period. The term "document" shall not include any document contained only in any individual transaction file, but the latter exception is without prejudice to a further application to the Court by defendants to require search of individual transaction files on the ground that any plaintiff's production is insufficient and to the defendants' right to apply during Local Discovery for the inspection of individual transaction files.

Definition "H"

As used herein, the term "bid" shall mean, unless otherwise specified, any price for these products submitted to you by any supplier or contractor pursuant to any procedure which you considered to be a sealed bid procedure.

Definition "I"

As used herein, the term "quotation" shall mean, unless otherwise specified, any price for these products submitted to you by any supplier or contractor, other than a bid.

Documents to Be Produced

1. (a) Each document in the possession of or obtainable by any plaintiff which was produced by such plaintiff before any Grand Jury in the Eastern District of Pennsylvania in the course of investigations leading to the return of indictments involving these products in that Court in 1960.

(b) Each document which sets forth, contains any reference to or relates to any communication by any plaintiff to any government agency charged in any way with the enforcement of the antitrust laws with respect to prices of these products or electrical equipment including these products.

(c) Each document constituting the personal or company copy of each expense account, travel voucher and supporting documents for each officer, employee, agent or consultant of plaintiff identified in answer to interrogatories attached as Schedule I to National Pretrial Order No. 37.

(d) Each document constituting any diary, appointment note, appointment book, calendar pad, letter book and telephone call memorandum of each officer of plaintiff identified in answer to interrogatories attached as Schedule I to National Pretrial Order No. 37.

(e) All documents in the nature of existing lists or other identifying descriptions, prepared by any plaintiff of documents furnished to any officers, court or agency of the United States or of any state or municipal government in connection with any legislative, administrative or judicial investigation, hearing or proceeding involving the pricing or marketing of these products and copies of each subpoena and other written requests pursuant to which such documents were furnished.

2. Each organization chart or diagram of each of your departments, divisions, bureaus, offices or other units responsible for the purchase of these products or electrical equipment including these products or any past or present employees exercising discretion, making policy or making decisions or participating in any of the foregoing functions.

3. Each document, if any, which formed the basis, wholly or in part, of your response to Set No. 2 of Defendants' Interrogatories, Nos. 2(a), 2(b), 3(b), 4(b), 6(b), 7(a), 7(b), 8(a), 8(b), 9(a), 10(a), 11(e), 12(a) through (d), 13(c) and 14.

4. Each document that contains any reference to or reflects any evaluation, study or analysis of, or policy or proposal with respect to any price adjustment clause or other similar provision or price rule to which your purchases of these products alone or electrical equipment including these products were subject or proposed to be made subject.

Schedule G

to

National Pretrial Order No. 37

(Plaintiffs' Interrogatories in the Second Priority Product Lines)

1. Plaintiffs hereby request that each defendant answer separately under oath, in accordance with Rule 33 of the Federal Rules of Civil Procedure, each of the Interrogatories in National Set No. 1 of Interrogatories on Behalf of Plaintiffs from the period previously provided back to January 1, 1948.

2. Plaintiffs further request that each defendant answer separately under oath the interrogatories set out below for the periods specified therein.

Definition "A"

Interrogatories 1, 2, 3, 4, 5, 6, 12, 13, 14, 15 and 16 request information for the period from January 1, 1946 through December 31, 1963, and interrogatories 7, 8, 9, 10 and 11 request information for the period from January 1, 1946 through April 1, 1961, (unless otherwise specified in any interrogatory) without prejudice to the right of plaintiffs to move in the future for additional information covering a later period if necessary.

Definition "B"

"You" or "your" means the defendant corporation separately answering these interrogatories, its domestically domiciled subsidiaries and its merged or acquired predecessors, its present and former officers, agents and all other persons acting on behalf of the defendant corporation or such subsidiaries or such predecessors, including all past or present employees exercising discretion, making policy and making decisions or participating in any of the foregoing functions with respect to the sale of these products.

Definition "C"

As used herein, the term "products" shall mean the products defined or described in the complaints, in the above-numbered actions, taken as a whole, one or more sizes, ratings, models or types thereof, or one or more items of particular size, rating, model or type thereof.

Definition "D"

"Document" means any written or graphic matter, however produced or reproduced. The term "document" shall not include any document contained only in any individual transaction file, but the latter exclusion is without prejudice to a further application to the Court by plaintiffs to require search of individual transaction files on the ground that any defendant's answer is insufficient and to the plaintiffs' right to apply during Local Discovery for the inspection of individual transaction files.

Definition "E"

"Identify" or "identification" when used in reference to an individual person means to state his full name and present address if known and his present or last known position and business affiliation. "Identify" or "identification" when used in reference to a document means to state the date and author, type of document (e.g., letter, memorandum, telegram, chart, etc.), or some other means of identifying it, and its present location or custodian. If any such document was but is no longer in your possession or subject to your control, state what disposition was made of it.

With respect to any of these interrogatories which call for the listing, identification, content or description of documents, any of the defendants may, in lieu of such identification or description, make such documents or copies thereof available for inspection and copying. The production of a document containing the information sought in an interrogatory will satisfy the interrogatory provided there is an appropriate reference to the document or documents containing the information.

Interrogatories

1. (a) State the quantity of new orders placed with you by domestic purchasers for each of these products during each calendar quarter of the period defined herein, in terms of:

(i) dollars; and

(ii) units, except that subsection (ii) need not be answered as to power switching equipment, unless otherwise ordered by the Court.

(b) State the quantity of new orders placed with you by foreign purchasers for each of these products during each calendar quarter of the period defined herein, in terms of:

(i) dollars; and

(ii) units, except that subsection (ii) need not be answered as to power switching equipment, unless otherwise ordered by the Court.

2. (a) Describe each method or technique and each change or variation therein used by you during the period defined herein to measure your capacity as it relates to the manufacture of each of these products, including, but not being limited to:

(i) normal or standard capacity;

(ii) total capacity;

(iii) total manufacturer capacity;

(iv) general manufacturer capacity; and

(v) total capacity scheduled;

and for each such method or technique, state the period during which it was utilized.

(b) State whether you differentiate production capacity in terms of its comparative efficiency in use, e.g., efficient baseload operations and less efficient peakload operations. If so, with respect to each plant or other unit of your company engaged in the manufacture of each of these products, or any major part thereof, for which you maintained records making such a differentiation on a quarterly, semi-annual, annual or other periodic basis during the period defined herein, state the approximate proportion of your productive capacity classified as efficient as reflected in those records for each calendar quarter (or for each six-month, twelve-month or other period, if your records are not maintained quarterly).

(c) As to each plant or other unit of your company engaged in the manufacture of each of these products, or any major part thereof, for which you maintained records of its capacity on a quarterly, semi-annual, annual or other periodic basis during the period defined herein, state its capacity as measured by each of the methods or techniques, if any, described in (a) above, as reflected in those records, for each calendar quarter (or for each six-month, twelve-month or other period, if your records are not maintained quarterly).

3. Describe the operation of your "order boards" and, as of the end of each calendar quarter of the period defined herein, state their status and the results of their operation as they relate to each of these products.

4. (a) Describe each method or technique and each change or variation therein used by you during the period defined herein to measure your productivity concerning each of these products, including, but not being limited to, the following:

(i) labor productivity; and

(ii) total factor productivity.

(b) With regard to the production of each of these products for which you maintained records measuring your productivity annually or on any other periodic basis during the period defined herein, state your productivity as measured by each of the methods or techniques, if any, described in (a) above, as reflected in those records, for each year or other period, and state the method, theory or formula by which the figures for each year or period were derived.

5. (a) Give a full description of each characteristic including, but not being limited to, modifications, accessories or other variations generally offered in connection with each of these products, which was not included in your price list, sheet or book.

(b) As to each characteristic identified in the answer to (a) above, state:

(i) the period during which it was offered for sale; and

(ii) whether its inclusion in the product resulted in an increase or decrease in the price of each of these products and, if so, the amount thereof and the date, if any, on which such separate charge was discontinued.

6. (a) Give a full description of each significant technical, technological or quality change applied by you to each of these products.

(b) As to each change identified in the answer to 6(a) above, state whether or not it resulted in a price variation, and if so, state whether or not the price variation was reflected in your price list, sheet or book.

(c) As to each change identified in the answer to interrogatory 6(a) above which did result in a price variation which was reflected in your price list, sheet or book, state:

(i) the date of your price list, sheet, or book and the page and item therein in which each of these products containing such change first appeared;

(ii) the period during which each of these products containing such change was first offered for sale; and

(iii) whether its inclusion resulted in an increase or decrease in the published price of each of these products and state the amount of such price change.

(d) As to each change identified in the answer to interrogatory 6(a) above which did not result in a price variation which was reflected in your price list, sheet or book, state whether or not it resulted in a market or other price variation and if so, state the amount, initial date and period of such market price variation.

(e) With respect to each change identified in the answer to interrogatory 6(a) above, state the annual net cost savings, if any, to you as a result of such change.

(f) As to each change identified in the answer to interrogatory 6(a) above which did not result in any price variation, give the information requested in subparagraphs (i) through (ii) of (c) above.

(g) Identify each document which forms the basis of your answer to or which reflects any of the matters referred to in your response to interrogatory 6(a)-(e).

7. (a) State whether you communicated any information to any officer, agent, employee or person acting or purporting to act on behalf of any purchaser of these products, reflecting whether or not any officer, agent, employee or person acting or purporting to act on behalf of any manufacturer of electrical equipment communicated in any way at any time with any officer, agent, employee or person acting or purporting to act on behalf of any one or more other manufacturers of electrical equipment

with respect to prices, bids, quotations, pricing rules or terms or conditions of sale of any type of electrical equipment. (Exclude from consideration in answering this interrogatory all communications of information relating solely to any civil or criminal proceedings brought since January 1, 1960 concerning alleged antitrust violations by electrical equipment manufacturers, with respect to these products or other electrical equipment, or any accounts, reports or statements with respect thereto appearing in any newspaper, record of a Congressional hearing, or other public record, and exclude all information which relates solely to electrical equipment other than these products.)

(b) If the answer to (a) above is affirmative, with respect to each communication of such information:

(i) identify each party thereto, each person having knowledge thereof, and (if different) the person upon whose recollection your answer is based;

(ii) if oral, give the content thereof, as disclosed in any corporate or internal record;

(iii) state the date of the communication or your best approximation thereof, the place, whether in person, by telephone, correspondence or otherwise, and the circumstances.

(c) Identify each document that contains any reference to or reflects any of the matters referred to in (a) or (b) above, or your answer thereto.

8. (a) State whether at any time up to the date of the filing of the answer to this interrogatory you acquired or had any information that any officer, agent, employee or person acting or purporting to act on behalf of any purchaser of these products acquired or had any information that any officer, agent, employee or person acting or purporting to act on behalf of any manufacturer of electrical equipment communicated in any way at any time with any officer, agent, employee or person acting or purporting to act on behalf of any one or more other manufacturers of electrical equipment with respect to prices, pricing rules, bids, quotations, or terms or conditions of sale of any type of electrical equipment. (Exclude from consideration in answering this interrogatory all information received or learned by said purchaser solely from any civil or criminal proceedings brought since January 1, 1960 concerning alleged antitrust violations by electrical equipment manufacturers, with respect to these products or other electrical equipment, or any accounts, reports or statements with respect thereto appearing in any newspaper, record of a Congressional hearing, or other public record, and exclude all information which relates solely to electrical equipment other than these products.)

(b) If the answer to (a) above is affirmative with respect to each item of such information:

(i) identify each person acquiring or having knowledge thereof and (if different) the person upon whose recollection your answer is based;

(ii) identify the source thereof, including an identification of each person who communicated or through whom such information was communicated;

(iii) if oral, give the content thereof as disclosed in any corporate or internal record; and

(iv) give the date you acquired the information, or your best approximation thereof, the place, and the circumstances under which it was acquired.

(c) Identify each document that contains any reference to or reflects any of the matters referred to in (a) or (b) above, or your answer thereto.

9. (a) State whether you have communicated with any purchaser of these products in response or with respect to any communication, oral or written received by you, or of which you had knowledge, which commented upon or recommended action because of the lack of difference between prices quoted or bid by different suppliers for any sale or series of sales by you or by any other manufacturer of these products or electrical equipment including these products, or which commented upon or recommended action because of uniformity of suppliers' pricing practices or terms or conditions of sale with respect to any such sale or series of sales. (Exclude from consideration in answering this interrogatory all communications relating solely to any civil or criminal proceedings brought since January 1, 1960, concerning alleged antitrust violations by electrical equipment manufacturers with respect to these products or other electrical equipment, or any accounts, reports or statements with respect thereto appearing in any newspaper, record of a Congressional hearing, or other public record.)

(b) If the answer to (a) above is affirmative, with respect to each such communication:

(i) if oral, give the content thereof, as disclosed in any corporate or internal record;

(ii) identify each party thereto, each person having knowledge thereof, and (if different) the person upon whose recollection your answer is based; and

(iii) state the date of the communication or your best approximation thereof, the place, and whether in person, by telephone, by correspondence or otherwise, and the circumstances under which it was made or received.

(c) Identify each document that contains any reference to or reflects any of the matters referred to in (a) or (b) above, or your answer thereto.

10. (a) State whether or not you instructed your commercial or sales personnel to withdraw from membership in the National Electrical Manufacturers Association, or any activities thereof.

(b) If the answer to (a) above is affirmative state whether you subsequently instructed such personnel that they could resume such membership or such activities.

(c) If the answer to (a) or (b) above is affirmative, with respect to each such instruction:

(i) state the date it was issued;

(ii) if oral, give the content thereof as disclosed in any corporate or internal record, and identify any directive or other writing that sets forth such instruction; and

(iii) state the reasons for such instruction as disclosed in any corporate or internal record.

11. State the dates in 1959 and 1960 on which each of your past or present officers, agents or employees were served with grand jury subpoenas relating to these products or electrical equipment, including these products, and identify each such officer, agent or employee in relation to each such date.

(With respect to interrogatories 12 to 16 following, the answers are to be given to the extent that the information sought is not otherwise disclosed in other interrogatories or documents produced under the National Discovery Program; provided that the answer shall make appropriate reference to the prior disclosures.)

12. Was your capacity to produce this product increased and, if so, set forth the factors resulting in such an increase in capacity and, as to each such factor, the resultant amount of such increase in capacity each year measured in each way that figures are available, including but not limited to book dollars and KVA ratings.

13. Set forth each new factor or development which resulted in a cost saving to you with respect to the design, engineering, manufacture or sale of this product, and the net dollar amount you saved annually as a result of each such cost saving.

14. Identify each study made by each defendant separately, by one or more defendants, or by any agent or consultant acting for or on behalf of any defendant or its attorneys which refers to or relates to the economic forces of supply and demand (e.g., orders received, backlog of unfilled orders, productive capacity) and state when each such study was prepared, what it purports to cover, and who prepared it.

15. State what data in your possession shows as to each defendant's market share for each year, giving the total for each year for each second priority product.

16. (a) State which of your facilities, if any, was a "bottleneck" with respect to the production of each secondary priority product.

(b) Identify each document, study or report which refers to any facility identified in the answer to interrogatory 16(a) above as a "bottleneck."

(c) Set forth the method which you have used to measure each "bottleneck" identified in the answer to interrogatory 16(a) above.

Schedule H

to

National Pretrial Order No. 37

(Plaintiffs' Motion No. 1 for Production of Documents in the Second Priority Product Lines)

Plaintiffs hereby move this Court for an Order pursuant to Rule 34 of the Federal Rules of Civil Procedure requiring each defendant in each of the above actions separately to produce and to permit the plaintiffs to inspect and copy or cause to be copied the following documents now in its possession, custody, or control. It is requested that for each document the paragraph of the motion in response to which it is produced should be indicated. Each of the documents requested contains evidence relevant to a matter involving one or more of the above actions or is reasonably calculated to lead to the discovery of evidence relevant to such matter.

Definition "A"

Except where otherwise stated, "document" means any written, recorded or graphic matter, however produced or reproduced which was: (1) with respect to paragraphs 21, 26, 34 through 36, 38, 39 and 40, prepared during the period from January 1, 1948 through April 30, 1961, or prepared thereafter, but relating or referring to the said period; and (ii) with respect to all remaining paragraphs, prepared during the period January 1, 1948 through December 31, 1963; provided, that, documents to be produced under paragraphs 6, 11, 13, 14, 19, 20, 27 through 33 and 37 will be produced for each second priority product line ninety (90) days before a case is set for trial in that second priority product line, unless otherwise ordered by the Court; and provided further that documents prepared solely for the purposes of this litigation need not be produced unless otherwise ordered by the Court. The term "document" shall include only such matter relating to the product defined in the complaint, and it shall not include any document heretofore produced in any national depository or contained only in any individual transaction file, but the latter exclusion is without prejudice to a further application to the Court by plaintiffs to require search of individual transaction files on the ground that any defendant's production is insufficient.

Definition "B"

Except where otherwise stated, "prices" includes both the amount of money for which the product was actually sold or offered for sale in particular transactions and also the amount stated in any defendant's published catalogues or other general pricing documents.

Documents to Be Produced

1. A copy of each price list, price catalogue, discount sheet, multiplier sheet or pricing formula or catalogue, including additions, insertions, supplements and changes therein, issued by you showing either domestic or export prices or terms and conditions of sale, but excluding those heretofore produced in any national depository.

2. Each document evaluating or analyzing prevailing prices or terms and conditions of sale.

3. Each document setting forth, announcing, proposing, recommending or referring or relating to the establishment or maintenance of or changes in prices or terms and conditions of sale instituted or to be instituted by you or by any of your competitors, other than published price catalogues, price sheets, or price lists.

4. Each work sheet or other document prepared in connection with any evaluation or analysis of existing prices or terms and conditions of sale or the establishment or maintenance of actual, proposed or recommended changes in prices or terms and conditions of sale instituted or to be instituted by you or by any of your competitors, other than published price catalogues, price sheets, or price lists.

5. Each document referring or relating to the effect of changes in published or list prices on market shares, bids or actual transaction prices or sales volume, or to the effect of market shares, market prices or sales volume on published or list prices and changes therein.

6. Each document referring or relating to the effect on costs, prices, terms and conditions of sale, sales volume, market shares or other market conditions of actual or proposed substantial changes in production techniques, capital investment or productive capacity.

7. Each document referring or relating to actual transaction price levels or to any changes in or deviations from such levels as to either domestic or export prices.

8. Each document referring or relating to or reflecting the specific circumstances under which you obtained notification of actual or proposed price changes of your competitors or obtained possession of price catalogues, price sheets, price lists or other documents setting forth prices or terms and conditions of sale of your competitors.

9. Each document referring or relating to the effect on prices, terms and conditions of sale, sales volume, market shares or other market conditions of any bid, proposal or sale in the United States of any foreign manufacturer.

10. Each document referring or relating to the competitive situation, to prices or to market shares prepared in connection with the activities

or meetings of any corporate committee or body, formal or informal, including but not being limited to Code Committee Reports.

11. Each document referring or relating to the market position or share of the market of any domestic or foreign seller or to the capacity, costs, profit margins or competitive potential of any other domestic or foreign seller, provided that where such information concerning the defendant company producing any such document is contained in the same document, said information shall not be deleted or masked.

12. Each document which shows or refers to order backlogs, period between order date and delivery (lead-time) or percent of capacity utilized by you or your competitors, and each report, summary or analysis thereof.

13. Each document referring or relating to the relationship between costs, profits or prices and any product improvement or technical or quality change.

14. Each document referring or relating to any cost reduction program of you or your competitors.

15. Each document referring or relating to changes in costs or prices as compared with any Bureau of Labor Statistics index or indices or any other index of that type, and each such index prepared by you.

16. Each document referring or relating to the productivity of domestic or foreign labor.

17. Each document referring or relating to the adoption, evaluation or use of any escalation or other price adjustment clause or provision.

18. Each study, report or analysis showing the relative proportion of any material used in the manufacture of each product subject at any time to an index price adjustment clause or provision.

19. Each study made with respect to any product subject at any time to an index price adjustment clause or provision which shows, either with respect to a particular unit of equipment or otherwise, the time during the period of manufacture at which any costs were incurred.

20. Each document showing the proportion to the total cost of manufacturing each product subject at any time to an index price adjustment clause or provision of the cost of (a) labor, (b) materials or (c) other costs.

21. Each document referring or relating to the adoption, evaluation or use of progress payment provisions.

22. Each document stating, summarizing or analyzing bids or quotations submitted by you or any competitor.

23. Each document stating, summarizing or analyzing business received or lost by you or any competitor.

24. Each worksheet, summary or compilation prepared on the basis of raw material submitted for analysis in connection with any order price index or other order or transaction price study, or analysis, including but not being limited to those entitled "Prices and Values in the Electrical Industry" and "Electrical Equipment Price Study" certified by Alexander Grant & Company; and a copy of each such study or analysis.

25. Each compilation of sales data and any explanatory material prepared by you or on your behalf and transmitted to William H. Ferguson, Esq., or Charles S. Burdell, Esq.

26. Minutes of the National Electrical Manufacturers Association (NEMA), its governing body, committees, subcommittees or sections, without prejudice to a further application by plaintiffs for copies of reports and studies referred to in said minutes.

27. All profit and loss or income statements, long form audit reports, or other similar statements, whether on an actual or estimated basis and whether prepared monthly, quarterly or at other intervals, of each plant, department or division which manufactured or sold the product defined in the complaint and any such statements prepared with respect to any product line which is or includes a product defined in the complaint and such schedules or other summaries, whether on an actual or estimated basis and whether prepared monthly, quarterly or at other intervals as show the most detailed breakdown of income and expenses, profits and profit margins available.

28. All annual plant, department, division and company-wide balance sheets.

29. All annual company-wide profit and loss statements.

30. Records which show, whether on an actual or estimated basis, with respect to each unit of equipment, cost, profit or profit margin.

31. Each document referring or relating to profit goals or to anticipated or budgeted sales, production, profits or profit margins on a company-wide, departmental or divisional basis or with respect to particular units of equipment.

32. Each report, statistical bulletin or other document which you have submitted to or received from any trade association with respect to production, prices, sales, costs, profits, unfilled orders, inventories, shipments, exports or imports, but excluding any document heretofore produced in any national depository.

33. Each report, statistical bulletin or other document submitted by you to the United States Department of Commerce or Department of Labor with respect to production, prices, sales, costs, profits, unfilled orders, inventories, shipments, exports or imports, but excluding any document heretofore produced in any national depository; provided, however, that

census reports rendered immune from legal process by 13 U.S.C.A. § 9(a) need not be produced or identified.

34. Each document taken to, received at, or prepared during any meeting (at which meeting there was any discussion or mention whatsoever relating to prices, costs, multipliers, discounts, lost business, future business, allocation of business, market conditions, market activities, terms and conditions of sale, or other competitive activity) attended by any of your employees and by any person employed by any competitor.

35. Each document reflecting the subject matter of, or referring or relating in any way to any meeting described in paragraph 34.

36. Each document containing, reflecting the subject matter of, or referring or relating to any communication, whether written or oral, between any of your employees and any person employed by any competitor which communication concerned in any way prices, costs, multipliers, discounts, lost business, future business, allocation of business, market conditions, market activities, terms and conditions of sale, or other competitive activities.

37. Each document referring or relating to any absence of or limitation on price competition or other types of competition or to the allocation of customers or business.

38. Each document referring or relating to efforts by persons engaging in activities of the type described in paragraphs 34 and 36 to conceal such activities or withhold information concerning them.

39. Each document referring or relating to disciplinary action imposed on or any investigation made of any of your employees with respect to compliance with or violation of the antitrust laws or of any company policy relating to contact with competitors.

40. All minutes of the board of directors or executive or other corporate committee, annual statements, proxy statements and each document referring or relating to Federal Governmental investigations or civil or criminal actions by the United States with respect to possible violations of the antitrust laws of the United States.

41. All studies of prices of these products and of factors which have influenced or affected these prices, provided that no studies need be produced which were prepared in anticipation of litigation, unless otherwise ordered by the Court.

42. Copies of all figures relating to capacity for these products or for electrical equipment including these products which you have submitted to EEI or any other group, organization or agency.

APPENDIX 19

National Exhibit NX247

Page No. 1 84 1956	General Electric		Westinghouse			Wagner Electric		McGraw-Edison		Allis-Chalmers
	Ginn	Ray Smith	Rissinger	Chiles	McCollum	A.C. Allen	McKinley	Plank	Swoish	Long
Jan. 29–Feb. 3 New York	2/1–2/2			1/31–2/3	1/31–2/2	1/29–2/2				
March 12–13 Chicago			X				X			
March 27–29 Pittsburgh			3/28–3/29		3/23–3/29		3/27–3/29			
May 19–23 Hot Springs (NEMA)	X			X	X	X	X			
June 4–6 Atlantic City (EEI)	X		6/3–6/5	X	X		X			
June 11–12 Washington, D.C.	X						X			
June 28 New York					X	X				
July 25 Pittsburgh			X				X			
August 15 Pittsburgh					X		X			
September 10–12 Pittsburgh	9/11–9/12			9/10–9/11	X	X				
September 14–15 Detroit				X	X					
September 28 Cleveland				X		X				
November 11–14 Atlantic City			X	X	X	X	X			X

Page No. 2 1956	GENERAL ELECTRIC		WESTINGHOUSE			WAGNER ELECTRIC		MC GRAW-EDISON		ALLIS-CHALMERS
	Ginn	Ray Smith	Rissinger	Chiles	McCollum	A.C. Allen	Mckinley	Plank	Swish	Long
November 29 Cincinnati				X	X					
December 4 Pittsburgh			X				X			
December 4-6 New York	X			X	X					
December 12-13 New York	X		X							
December 18-19 Chicago			X				X			

APPENDIX 20

NATIONAL EXHIBIT NX248: MULTIPLIERS—LARGER NONSTANDARD TRANSFORMERS

General Electric		Westinghouse		Allis-Chalmers	
Effective Date	Multiplier	Effective Date	Multiplier	Effective Date	Multiplier
9/12/48	.782	9/19/48	.782	9/21/48	1.564
7/26/50	.84	7/28/50	.84	7/24/50	1.68
12/8/50	.90	12/7/50	.90	12/11/50	1.80
				3/28/51	.90
9/28/52	.911	9/29/52	.911	10/6/52	.911
5/10/53	.98	5/18/53	.98	5/18/53	.98
9/14/55	1.08	9/26/55	1.08	9/12/55	1.08
4/5/56	1.19	4/16/55	1.19	4/7/56	1.19
5/1/57	.60	4/26/57	.60		
7/8/57	.625	7/10/57	.625	7/8/57	.625

APPENDIX 21

Chart 3A

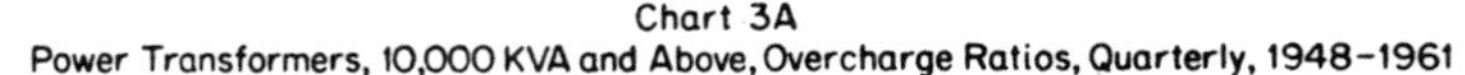
Power Transformers, 10,000 KVA and Above, Overcharge Ratios, Quarterly, 1948–1961

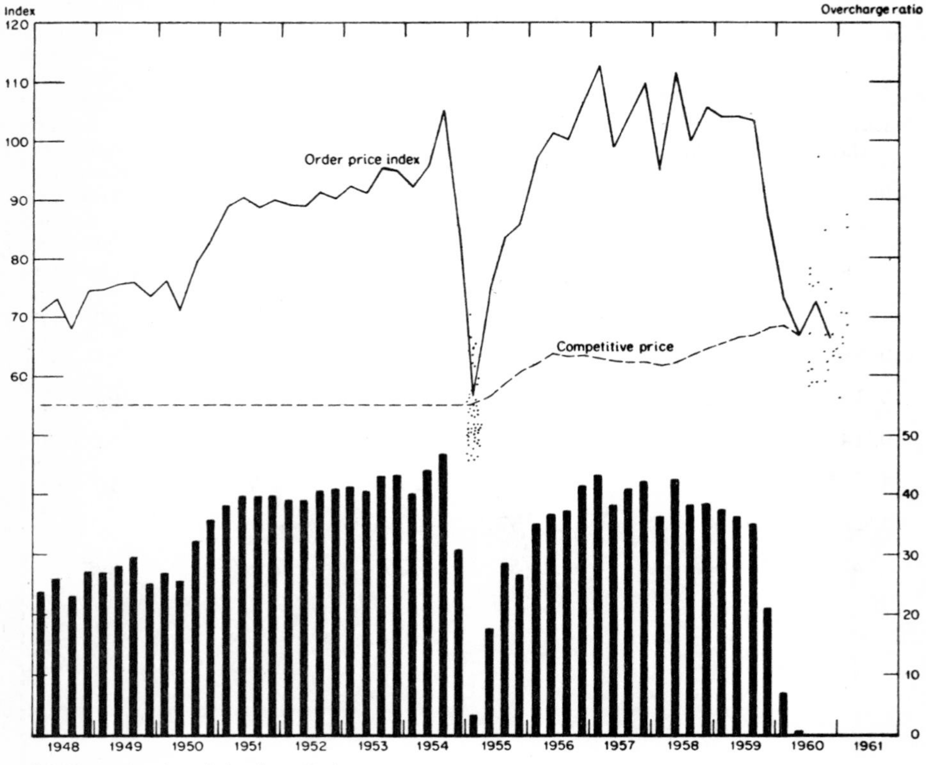

Each dot represents one transaction in a reference period.

APPENDIX 22

Chart 8
Watt-Hour Meters, Overcharge Ratios, Quarterly, 1952-1960

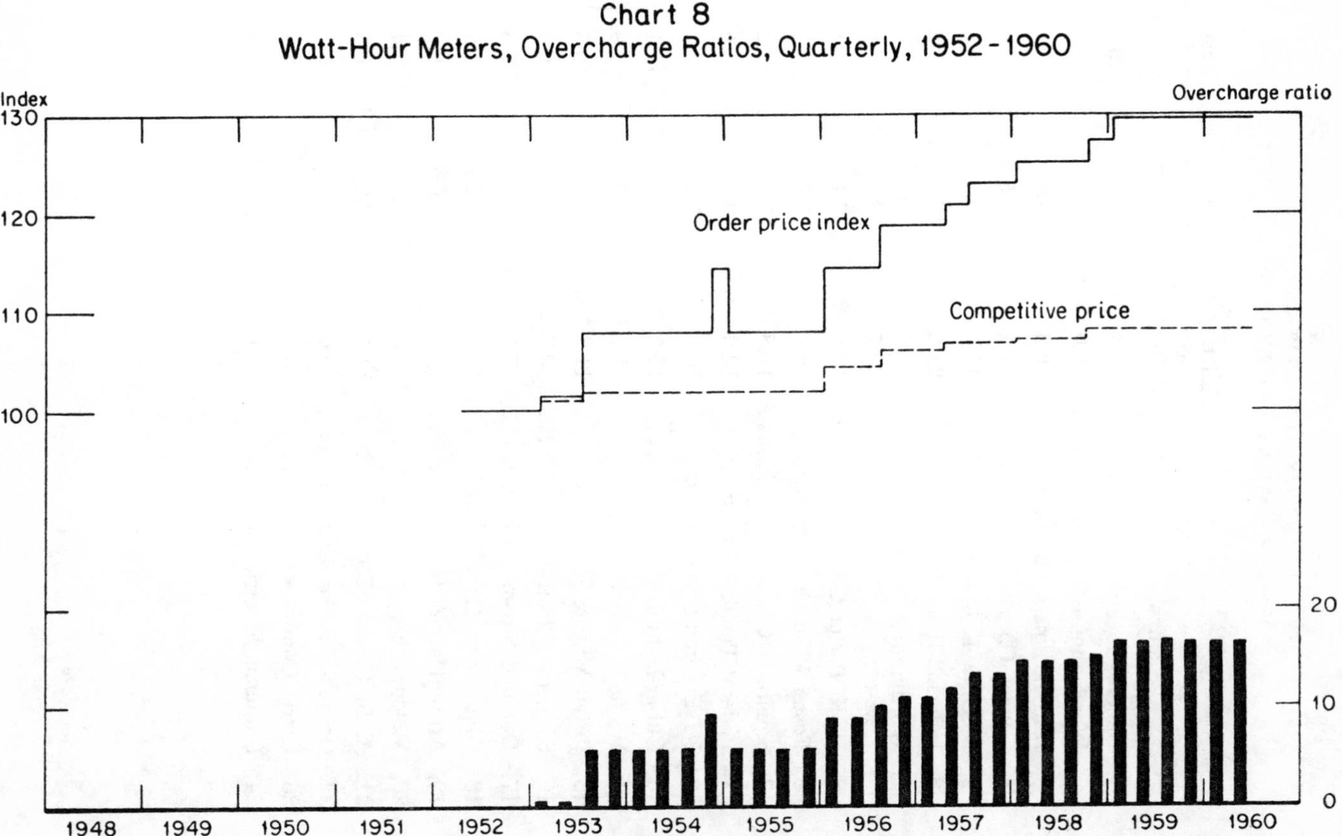

APPENDIX 23

TABLE 10

**TWENTY-FOUR DEFENDANTS—
AVERAGE RATE OF RETURN ON NET WORTH**

Company	Indictment Years 1956-59	Last Five Years 1957-61	Last Three Years 1959-61
1. General Electric Co.	19.4	17.3	16.1
2. Westinghouse Electric Corp.	7.0	7.9	7.4
3. Allis-Chalmers Mfg. Co.	6.4	4.7	3.8
4. Carrier Corp.	7.1	5.6	5.3
5. McGraw-Edison Electric Co.	12.1	9.5	8.9
6. Ingersoll-Rand Corp.	21.2	18.2	16.2
7. Worthington Pump & Machinery Corp.	9.7	7.9	6.8
8. H. K. Porter Co., Inc.	10.6	7.1	6.1
9. Foster Wheeler Corp.	6.7	7.3	9.5
10. Square-D Co.	16.8	15.9	17.2
11. Federal Pacific Electric Co.	12.9	4.6	.6
12. I-T-E Circuit Breaker Co.	10.2	5.9	2.4
13. Cutler-Hammer, Inc.	15.5	12.7	12.1
14. Wagner Electric Corp.	11.2	8.6	7.9
15. Joslyn Mfg. & Supply Co.	11.8	10.0	9.5
16. Sangamo Electric Co.	10.7	7.7	6.2
17. DeLaval Steam Turbine Co.	7.7	7.7	7.6
18. Ohio Brass Co.	12.5	9.7	7.8
19. Arrow-Hart & Hegeman	19.2	17.0	16.6
20. Moloney Electric Co.	5.3	1.3	− 3.4
21. A. B. Chance Co.	14.1	7.9	6.5
22. Cornell-Dubilier Electric Corp.	9.6	− 4.0	−10.7
23. Clark Controller	9.6	6.1	5.8
24. Kuhlman Electric Corp.	11.1	8.9	8.5

APPENDIX 24

TABLE 12

ESTIMATED ANNUAL DAMAGE PAYMENTS IF DAMAGES WERE FIFTY PERCENT OF NET INCOME BEFORE TAXES AND FUTURE PRE-TAX INCOME WERE AT THE:—

(THOUSANDS OF DOLLARS)

Company	1961 Level	Highest Level of 1959-61	Lowest Level of 1959-61	Average Level of 1959-61
1. General Electric Co. . .	$242,079	$280,242	$200,072	$240,798
2. Westinghouse Electric Corp.	45,447	85,947	45,447	70,151
3. Allis-Chalmers Mfg. . . .	5,598	22,865	5,598	13,015
4. Carrier Corp.	7,433	8,266	5,008	6,902
5. McGraw-Edison Electric Co.	13,465	15,049	13,465	14,117
6. Ingersoll-Rand Corp. . .	27,784	24,797	23,784	24,403
7. Worthington Pump & Machinery Corp.	6,000	8,369	6,000	7,361
8. H. K. Porter Co., Inc. .	3,458	6,732	3,458	4,761
9. Foster Wheeler Corp. . .	2,924	5,907	2,833	3,888
10. Square-D Co.	11,656	11,656	10,437	11,224
11. Federal Pacific Electric Co.	None	2,768	None	206
12. I-T-E Circuit Breaker Co.	821	2,748	None	1,094
13. Cutler-Hammer, Inc. . .	5,492	6,648	4,901	5,674
14. Wagner Electric Corp. .	3,396	6,547	3,396	4,725
15. Joslyn Mfg. & Supply . .	3,424	4,631	3,317	3,787
16. Sangamo Electric Co. . .	1,745	3,027	689	1,819
17. DeLaval Steam Turbine Co.	1,435	1,657	1,120	1,403
18. Ohio Brass Co.	1,718	1,728	1,638	1,693
19. Arrow-Hart & Hegeman Electric Co.	3,013	3,448	3,012	3,155
20. Moloney Electric Co. . .	None	None	None	None
21. A. B. Chance Co.	399	827	399	670
22. Cornell-Dubilier Electric	None	729	None	None
23. Clark Controller	380	938	380	613
24. Kuhlman Electric Corp.	431	431	305	378

General Electric Settlement Agreement

Proposed Appendix I.

Purpose

This Appendix to the letter proposal of the General Electric Company dated , 1963 sets forth the alternative methods of price adjustments to be offered electric utility customers by the General Electric Company in voluntary settlement of possible claims arising out of the Philadelphia Electrical Equipment Cases.

General Electric Company will offer to its customers a price adjustment on a product line by product line basis in an amount equal to the higher of application of the formulas on each of nine product lines as described in Section I of this Appendix or 2½% of its purchases of each of fifteen product lines during the years 1956-1959. The fifteen product lines include the nine product lines described in Section I and six additional product lines described in Section II of this Appendix.

Reimbursement of Out-of-Pocket Expenses

In addition to the price adjustments described in this Appendix, General Electric Company will pay an amount for reimbursement of out-of-pocket expenses incurred by the customer before September 10, 1963, and directly related to investigation or litigation matters arising out of the Philadelphia Electrical Equipment Cases.

Such amount shall be calculated on the basis of General Electric's share of such expenses up to a maximum payment of 10% of the aggregate price adjustment produced by application of the formulas described in this Appendix. General Electric's share is deemed to be the ratio of purchases of General Electric products during the period 1956-1959 claimed upon in suits pending by the customer to the total purchases from all manufacturers of products during the period 1956-1959 claimed in suits pending by the customer. Out-of-pocket expenditures subject to reimbursement under this alternative calculation shall include payments to lawyers, economists, statisticians and other specialists and their assistants for work performed in connection with matters arising out of the Philadelphia Electrical Equipment Cases.

Substantiation necessary to obtain reimbursement of expenses shall include but not be limited to copies of receipted invoices or invoice copies plus copies of paid checks covering such invoices together with an affidavit by an officer of the customer attesting to the fact that such expenditures were incurred directly in connection with investigation and litigation matters arising out of the Philadelphia Electrical Equipment Cases.

In agreeing to accept reimbursement under this arrangement, the customer shall also agree that General Electric may, if it desires to do so, arrange for an audit to be performed at the customer's place of business in order to verify the expenditures for which reimbursement is claimed under a proposed settlement on this basis.

The identity of any product has been determined in accordance with the definitions stated in the respective indictments returned against the General Electric Company in the United States District Court for the Eastern District of Pennsylvania during the year 1960.

Purchases made by customers via third parties such as contractors and independent distributors shall not be included.

Section I

Formulas to determine price adjustments have been devised for the nine product lines in which electric utilities are most interested. These nine product lines are as follows:

Turbine-Generator Units
Large Outdoor Oil and Air Circuit Breakers
Power Switchgear Assemblies
Power Transformers
Distribution Transformers
Watthour and Demand Meters
Insulators
Isolated Phase Bus
Power Switching Equipment

Except as noted in the formula descriptions contained in this Appendix, price adjustment calculations have been made on transactions dated during the calendar years 1956, 1957, 1958 and 1959.

The date of a transaction has been deemed to be the month in which a commitment to sell was made to the customer.

Prices paid in connection with any transaction shall be deemed to include escalation paid.

Specific Application of Formulas

1. *Turbine-Generator Units*

The price adjustment to be paid by General Electric on each transaction involving turbine-generators for which a commitment was made during the years 1956 through 1959 is based upon adjusting the billing price (including escalation) to the lowest of either (1) the Handbook price in effect at time of shipment, (2) the September 12, 1955 Handbook price adjusted by application of a Bureau of Labor Statistics Steel Mill Products Index and Electrical Generating, Transmission, Distribution, and Industrial Apparatus Labor Index weighted 39% for material and 61% for labor, or (3) 2½% of the final selling price or (4) a reconstructed price calculated on the basis of a straight line drawn from the September 12, 1955 Handbook price to the March 27, 1961 Handbook price for the size turbine purchased in order to arrive at the reconstructed price at date of shipment. In addition, for turbines purchased prior to 1956 and shipped in the 1956-1959 period, a price adjustment of 2½% of the final selling price of such turbines will be paid. Handbook prices are determined for turbine-generators of equal size and capacity and of similar type and performance and designed for operation under conditions equal to the turbine-generator covered by the transaction in question.

2. *Large Outdoor Oil and Air Circuit Breakers*

Within the four calendar years 1956 through 1959, the continuous period from March 1, 1957 through November 30, 1958 is considered a suitable yardstick period. Review of General Electric power circuit breaker transactions with all customers during this yardstick period produces an estimated average of prices paid for such equipment during the period. This average is expressed as a ratio of the General Electric Handbook prices for circuit breakers in effect during 1954. In calculating price adjustments, final prices paid on each transaction are compared with calculated prices which are obtained by applying the appropriate ratio to the General Electric 1954 Handbook price applicable to the transaction in question. In those instances in which the calculated price is lower than the price paid, an adjustment is made equal to the amount by which the price paid exceeds the calculated price. If a calculated price is higher than the price paid, no price adjustment is made. No price adjustments are paid on transactions occurring within the yardstick period and during January and February 1956. For large outdoor oil and air circuit breakers ordered during the second six months of 1955, an additional price adjustment of 2½% of such purchases will be paid.

3. *Power Switchgear Assemblies*

Within the four years 1956 through 1959, the continuous period from January 1, 1957 through November 30, 1958 is considered a suitable yardstick period. Review of General Electric power switchgear assembly transactions during this yardstick period produces an estimated average of prices paid for such equipment during the period. This average is expressed as a ratio of the General Electric Handbook prices for power switchgear assemblies in effect during 1958. (The power transformer portion of substations is expressed as a ratio of Handbook prices in effect during 1954.) In calculating the price adjustment, final prices paid on each transaction are compared with calculated prices which are obtained by applying the appropriate ratio to a base period General Electric Handbook price of the transaction in question. In those instances in which the calculated price is lower than the price paid, an adjustment is made equal to the amount by which the price paid exceeds the calculated price. If a calculated price is higher than the price paid, no price adjustment is made. No price adjustments are paid on transaction occurring within the yardstick period. For power switchgear assemblies ordered during the second six months of 1955, an additional price adjustment of 2½% of such purchases will be paid.

4. *Power Transformers*

Price adjustments on power transformer transactions are calculated by comparing the final prices paid on each transaction occurring during the four years 1956 through 1959 with the applicable power transformer Handbook prices in effect during the year 1954. The price adjustment to be paid on any transaction is equal to the difference between the price paid and the 1954 General Electric Handbook price for a power transformer of equal size, capacity and performance. If such a comparison indicates that the price paid was lower than the equivalent 1954 Handbook price, then no price adjustment is made. For power transformers ordered during the second six months of 1955, an additional price adjustment of 2½% of such purchases will be paid.

5. *Distribution Transformers*

Price adjustments on distribution transformer transactions are calculated by comparing the indexes of prices paid on purchases occurring within the four calendar years 1956 through 1959 with the General Electric Handbook prices in effect during the last quarter of 1955. To the extent that prices paid are higher than the 1955 prices, a price adjustment is made which is equal to one-half the difference between the two price levels.

6. *Watthour and Demand Meters*

Price adjustments on watthour and demand meters are based upon a comparison of an index of prices paid during the 1956-1959 period with a calculated price level which is equal to prices in effect during the last quarter of 1955 increased in proportion to the annual change in the Bureau of Labor Statistics Wholesale Price Index for Durable Goods. Price adjustments are offered on the basis of the average annual difference between the two price levels and amount to 0.7% of purchases made during 1957, 2.5% of purchases made during 1958, and 4.4% of purchases made during 1959. No adjustment will be made on purchases made during 1956.

7. *Insulators*

Price adjustments for insulators are based upon a comparison of prices paid with applicable 1954 Handbook prices adjusted by the annual change in the Bureau of Labor Statistics Wholesale Price Index for Durable Goods. Price adjustments are offered in the amounts that prices paid by customers during the 1956-1959 period exceed the adjusted 1954 prices.

8. *Isolated Phase Bus and Power Switching Equipment*

Price adjustments on isolated phase bus and power switching equipment are calculated on transactions occurring within the period December 1958 through December 1959. The price adjustments are determined by comparison of the prices paid for each transaction within this period with the average of prices paid during a yardstick period extending from January 1, 1957 through November 30, 1958. Review of General

Electric transactions during this yardstick period produces estimated averages of prices paid for each of these two lines of equipment. The averages are expressed as ratios of the 1954 General Electric Handbook prices for isolated phase bus and power switching equipment. In calculating the price adjustment, prices paid on each transaction are compared with calculated prices which are obtained by applying the appropriate ratio to the 1954 General Electric Handbook price of the transaction in question. In those instances in which the calculated price is lower than the price paid, an adjustment is made equal to the amount by which the price paid exceeds the calculated price. If a calculated price is higher than the price paid, no price adjustment is made. No price adjustments are paid on transactions occurring within the yardstick period or during 1956.

Section II

The price adjustment offered to the customer also includes 2½% of its aggregate purchases of the six product lines listed below:

Power capacitors
Lightning arresters
Open fuse cutouts
Bushings
Network transformers and network protectors
Instrument transformers

Purchases shall represent final billing prices of orders received during the calendar years 1956-1959. A date of an order is deemed to be the month in which a commitment to sell was made to the customer.

Acceptance of Price Adjustments

In those instances in which the Company can effect settlement with electric utility customers, the formal Agreement of Compromise and Settlement will provide the following:

1. General Electric will pay the specific amounts produced as a result of the application of the price adjustment formulas described in this Appendix.

2. The customer will agree to dismiss General Electric from all damage suits which they might have instituted claiming damages on any or all of the products named in the Philadelphia Electrical Equipment Cases.

3. The customer will execute a covenant not to institute or reinstitute suits against General Electric on any claims arising out of any of the Philadelphia Electrical Equipment Cases.

4. The customer will execute a covenant not to sue any other electrical manufacturer on claims for damages arising out of purchases of General Electric products covered by any of the 19 Philadelphia Electrical Equipment Cases.

September 10, 1963

APPENDIX **26**

Agreement of Compromise and Settlement

between

and

General Electric Company

This Agreement, made and entered into this day of 1963 by:

(hereinafter referred to as Claimant) with the General Electric Company (hereinafter referred to as "GE"):

Witnesseth:

A. Whereas, there are pending certain civil actions brought by the Claimant against GE and other defendants which seek recovery under the Clayton Act on account of purchases by the Claimant of certain products, said actions and the products to which they relate being listed below:

B. Whereas, the following products were the subject of certain indictments returned against GE and others during the year 1960 in the United States District Court for the Eastern District of Pennsylvania, and the Claimant may have claims against GE and/or others by reason of purchases of some or all of such products:

(1) Large outdoor oil and air circuit breakers
(2) Power switchgear assemblies
(3) Power transformers
(4) Turbine-generator units
(5) Insulators
(6) Distribution transformers
(7) Low voltage distribution equipment
(8) Low voltage power circuit breakers
(9) Watthour and demand meters
(10) Industrial control equipment
(11) Instrument transformers
(12) Network transformers
(13) Power capacitors
(14) Power switching equipment
(15) Lightning arresters and lightning arrester accessories

(16) Isolated phase bus and isolated phase bus structures
(17) Bushings and bushing accessories
(18) Navy and marine switchgear
(19) Open fuse cutouts and open fuse cutout accessories.

C. Whereas, the parties hereto desire to enter into this Agreement of Compromise and Settlement with reference to all claims which have been or might be asserted by Claimant under the Clayton Act or otherwise, all as hereinafter more fully set forth.

Now, THEREFORE, in consideration of the premises and the mutual undertakings and promises of the parties as hereinafter set forth, it is agreed as follows:

1. The following definitions of terms shall be applicable to this Agreement:

(a) "General Electric Company" or "GE" shall mean the General Electric Company and all of its subsidiaries, affiliated companies and agents.

(b) "Claimant" shall mean the
and all of its subsidiary or associated or affiliated companies and agents.

(c) "Product" shall mean any product mentioned in the preambles of this Agreement.

(d) "Product of GE Origin" shall mean a product manufactured by the General Electric Company or sold under the General Electric trademark.

(e) "Purchase" when used as a noun shall mean a contract to purchase and when used as a verb shall mean entry into a contract to purchase, in either case without regard to whether delivery of the product has been accomplished.

(f) "Claim" shall mean any claim for recovery of excessive prices paid or of damage which is based upon allegations of fraud, overcharges, collusion, conspiracy, or false claim, which has been or might be asserted under the Clayton Act or otherwise, and which arises out of any purchase of any product on or before December 31, 1960.

2. GE will within ten (10) days after the final execution of this Agreement, pay the Claimant the following several sums as voluntary price adjustments, the product and the civil action (if any) to which such price adjustments relate being set out opposite it:

Product Line	Civ. No.	Price Adjustment
Turbine-generators	....	$...........
Oil and air circuit breakers ..	....	....
Power transformers	....	....
Power switchgear assemblies .	....	....
Distribution transformers	....	....
Watthour and demand meters	....	....
Insulators	....	....
Isolated phase bus	....	....
Power switching equipment ..	....	....
Lightning arresters	....	....
Open fuse cutouts	....	....
Bushings	....	....
Network transformers	....	....
Instrument transformers	....	....
Power capacitors	....	....
TOTAL		$...........

3. Within thirty (30) days after the execution of this Agreement, Claimant will move the Court for an order (1) dismissing, as against GE, each civil action heretofore brought by Claimant against GE in respect of any claim as herein defined and (2) dismissing, as against all defendants so much of each civil action as asserts claims for damages based upon purchases by Claimant of products of GE origin.

4. Upon receipt of amounts payable by GE under this Agreement, Claimant will execute a covenant, in the form attached hereto as Exhibit I with respect to all claims being settled pursuant to this Agreement.

5. It is expressly understood and agreed that this Agreement shall not be construed as a release of GE or anyone else as to any claim or cause of action and, except as otherwise expressly provided herein, Claimant reserves all rights against all co-defendants and alleged co-conspirators of GE except as otherwise expressly provided herein.

6. It is expressly understood and agreed that GE does not concede any liability of GE to Claimant and that this settlement is made as a compromise and voluntary adjustment in order to dispose of a matter of possible contention between the parties. GE expressly denies that any liability exists with respect to its sales to the Claimant.

7. This Agreement cannot be changed or terminated orally and merges all prior understandings, representations and undertakings between the parties hereto.

8. Attached hereto and made a part hereof is a certified copy of a board resolution or other certificate verifying that the governing body of Claimant and each of its subsidiaries has authorized the settlement of these claims by the officer signing this agreement and covenant on behalf of Claimant and/or each subsidiary.

IN WITNESS WHEREOF, the parties hereto have caused this Agreement to be executed by their duly authorized representatives as of the day and year first above written.

....

By ....

Title ....

Attest:

....

[CORPORATE SEAL]

GENERAL ELECTRIC COMPANY

By ....

Title ....

Attest:

....

[CORPORATE SEAL]

(Execution of this Agreement by duly authorized representatives of each subsidiary of Claimant appears on the next following page.)

EXHIBIT I

COVENANT

WITNESSETH, that for and in consideration of the payment by the GENERAL ELECTRIC COMPANY of the sum of:

as a voluntary price adjustment to:

(hereinafter referred to as Claimant), the receipt of which is hereby acknowledged, Claimant hereby covenants and agrees that it will forever refrain from instituting, prosecuting, maintaining, pressing, collecting, or proceeding against the General Electric Company, or any of its subsidiary companies or affiliated companies or agents, upon any claims, controversies, actions, causes of action, obligations and liabilities of any nature whatsoever whether or not now or hereafter known, suspected or claimed which Claimant, or any of its subsidiaries or affiliated companies or agents ever had, now has, or hereafter can, shall or may have or alleged against the General Electric Company or its subsidiary companies or affiliated companies or agents based upon allegations of fraud, collusion, conspiracy or false claims which might be asserted under the Clayton Act or otherwise, with respect to or in connection with any purchases made or contracted for by Claimant at any time not later than December 31, 1960, of any of the following products:

Large outdoor oil and air circuit breakers

Power switchgear assemblies

Power transformers

Turbine-generator units

Insulators

Distribution transformers

Low voltage distribution equipment

Low voltage power circuit breakers

Watthour and demand meters

Industrial control equipment

Instrument transformers

Network transformers

Power capacitors

Power switching equipment

Lightning arresters and lightning arrester accessories

Isolated phase bus and isolated phase bus structures

Bushings and bushing accessories

Navy and marine switchgear

Open fuse cutouts and open fuse cutout accessories

And Claimant hereby further covenants and agrees that it will forever refrain from instituting, permitting, maintaining, pressing, collecting or proceeding against any other person, firm or corporation upon any claims, controversies, actions, causes of action, obligations and liabilities of any nature whatsoever, whether or not now or hereafter known, suspected or claimed, which claimant, or any of its subsidiaries or affiliated companies, ever had, now has or hereafter can, shall or may have or alleged based upon allegations of fraud, collusion, conspiracy or false claims which might be asserted under the Clayton Act, or otherwise, with respect to or in connection with any purchases made or contracted for by it at any time not later than December 31, 1960 of any of the aforesaid products which were manufactured by the General Electric Company, or its subsidiaries, or affiliated companies, or agents, or sold by the General Electric Company or any of its subsidiaries or affiliated companies or agents under the General Electric trademark.

It is expressly understood that this instrument shall not be construed as a release of the General Electric Company or anyone else as to any claim or cause of action; that the sum paid by the General Electric Company, as hereinabove stated, does not represent and shall not be construed as compensation for the damages claimed to have been suffered by Claimant with respect to purchases or contracts for the purchase of the products and for the period hereinabove enumerated and that Claimant does not in any manner or respect waive or relinquish its right to proceed against any person, firm or corporation, other than the General Electric Company and all of its subsidiaries and affiliated companies or agents, in respect to claims arising out of purchases of the aforesaid products, except to the extent expressly set forth herein.

In Witness Whereof,
has caused this Covenant to be executed this day of , 1963.

....

By ....

Title ....

Attest:

.. ..

[Corporate Seal]

(Execution of this Agreement by duly authorized representatives of each subsidiary of Claimant appears on the next following page.)

TURBINES

UNITED STATES DISTRICT COURT
NORTHERN DISTRICT OF ILLINOIS
EASTERN DIVISION

COMMONWEALTH EDISON COMPANY, et al., Plaintiffs, v. ALLIS-CHALMERS MANUFACTURING COMPANY, et al., Defendants.	NO. 61 C 1284

ANSWER OF DEFENDANT
GENERAL ELECTRIC COMPANY

Defendant General Electric Company (hereinafter referred to as "General Electric"), answers the complaint as follows:

FIRST DEFENSE

Count I

1. With respect to Paragraph 1 of the Complaint admits that these proceedings are instituted under Section 4 of the Clayton Act (15 U.S.C. §15) and Section 1 of the Sherman Act (15 U.S.C. §1).

2. With respect to Paragraph 2 of the Complaint admits that it maintains an office and transacts business in the Northern District of Illinois; except as so admitted

denies it has knowledge or information sufficient to form a belief as to the truth or falsity of the allegations of Paragraph 2.

3. With respect to Paragraph 3 of the Complaint admits that each of the plaintiffs is engaged in the business of furnishing electric service to the public; except as so admitted denies it has knowledge or information sufficient to form a belief as to the truth or falsity of the allegations of Paragraph 3.

4. With respect to Paragraph 4 of the Complaint, admits it is a corporation organized and existing under the laws of the State of New York; except as so admitted denies it has knowledge or information sufficient to form a belief as to the truth or falsity of the allegations of Paragraph 4.

5. With respect to Paragraph 5 of the Complaint, denies each and every allegation as to the existence of an alleged combination or conspiracy; denies it has participated in any combination or conspiracies alleged in the complaint with any of the individuals or corporations named as alleged co-conspirators or with any other individual or corporation; admits that during the period of time from about January 1957 to about March 1961 W. S. Ginn was a Vice President of General Electric and General Manager of its Turbine Division; admits

- 3 -

that during the period of time from about September 1951 to November 1960 W. E. Saupe was General Manager of the Large Steam Turbine Generator Department of General Electric; except as denied and admitted herein, denies it has knowledge or information sufficient to form a belief as to the truth or falsity of the allegations of Paragraph 5.

6. With respect to Paragraph 6 of the Complaint, no responsive pleading is required.

7. With respect to Paragraph 7 of the Complaint, admits that the defendants and the corporations alleged by plaintiff to be co-conspirator companies are the principal manufacturers in the United States of Turbine-generator units; admits that it has plants located in Massachusetts and New York; admits that it has sold and shipped such units in interstate commerce to purchasers throughout the United States and that in the past it has sold such units to plaintiffs; except as so admitted denies it has knowledge or information sufficient to form a belief as to the truth or falsity of the allegations of Paragraph 7.

8. With respect to Paragraph 8 of the Complaint, denies each and every allegation of said paragraph.

9. With respect to Paragraph 9 of the Complaint,

denies each and every allegation of said paragraph.

10. With respect to Paragraph 10 of the complaint, admits that an employee or employees of General Electric met from time to time with an employee or employees of one or more co-defendants and discussed prices or terms and conditions for the sale of turbine-generator units; except as admitted herein denies each and every allegation of said paragraph.

11. With respect to Paragraph 11 of the Complaint, denies each and every allegation of said paragraph.

12. With respect to Paragraph 12 of the Complaint, denies each and every allegation of said paragraph.

13. With respect to Paragraph 13 (a) of the Complaint, admits that at sometime prior to April 1957 an employee or employees of General Electric discussed with an employee or employees of one or more co-defendants, adjustment of the price of certain types of turbine-generator units, and further avers that it put into effect on or about April 15, 1957 certain price adjustments different from those which were the subject of such discussions.

With respect to Paragraph 13 (b) of the Complaint, admits that at some time prior to June 1957 an employee or employees of General Electric discussed with an employee or employees of one or more co-defendants a price increase and further admits that on or about June 20, 1957 it announced a price increase of approximately 5% for certain types of turbine-generator units, effective July 1, 1957.

With respect to Paragraph 13 (c) of the Complaint, admits that at some time prior to April 28, 1958 an employee or employees of General Electric discussed a price increase with an employee or employees of one or more co-defendants and further admits that it announced a price increase of approximately 3% effective April 28, 1958;

Except as admitted herein denies each and every allegation of Paragraph 13.

14. With respect to paragraph 14 of the Complaint, admits that one or more employees of General Electric met on occasion with one or more employees of one or more co-defendants or alleged co-conspirators and discussed bids and quotations to customers; except as admitted herein denies each and every allegation of Paragraph 14.

15. With respect to Paragraph 15 of the Complaint, admits that one or more employees of General Electric,

- 6 -

met on occasion with one or more employees of one or more co-defendants or alleged co-conspirator companies and that occasionally one of the defendants or alleged co-conspirator companies was given what was designated as "position" and that on occasion the bids or quotations submitted by the defendants or co-conspirator companies were higher than the bid or quotation submitted by the defendant or co-conspirator company with position; except as admitted herein denies each and every allegation of paragraph 15.

16. With respect to Paragraph 16 of the Complaint, denies each and every allegation of said paragraph.

17. With respect to Paragraph 17 of the Complaint, admits that employees of General Electric communicated by telephone with employees of one or more competitors in such a way as to avoid detection by General Electric; except as admitted herein denies each and every allegation of Paragraph 17.

18. With respect to Paragraph 18 of the Complaint, admits that on June 29, 1960 the United States of America instituted Criminal Action No. 20401 in the United States District Court, Eastern District, Pennsylvania, against, among others, all of the defendants named herein.

- 7 -

19. With respect to Paragraph 19 of the Complaint, denies each and every allegation of said paragraph.

20. With respect to Paragraph 20 of the Complaint, admits that during the period alleged it sold one or more turbine-generator units to each of the plaintiffs. With respect to the allegations concerning plaintiffs' purchases of turbine-generator units from other defendants and alleged co-conspirators, denies it has knowledge and information sufficient to form a belief as to the truth or falsity of the allegations of Paragraph 20; denies each and every remaining allegation of paragraph 20.

21. With respect to Paragraph 21 of the Complaint, denies each and every allegation of said paragraph.

22. With respect to Paragraph 22 of the Complaint, denies each and every allegation of said paragraph.

COUNT II

23. With respect to paragraph 23 of the Complaint, insofar as this paragraph realleges the allegations of Paragraphs 1 through 7 of the Complaint, General Electric's answers to those paragraphs are incorporated herein by reference as its answers to said Paragraph 23.

- 8 -

24. With respect to Paragraph 24 of the Complaint, denies each and every allegation of said paragraph.

25. With respect to Paragraph 25 of the Complaint, insofar as this paragraph realleges the allegations of Paragraph 9 through 19 of the Complaint, General Electric's answers to those paragraphs are incorporated herein by reference as its answers to said Paragraph 25.

26. With respect to Paragraph 26 of the Complaint, admits that during the period alleged it sold one or more turbine-generator units to Commonwealth Edison Company and Northern Indiana Public Service Company. With respect to the allegations concerning plaintiffs' purchases of turbine-generator units from other defendants and alleged co-conspirators denies it has any knowledge or information sufficient to form a belief as to the truth or falsity of the allegations of Paragraph 26; denies each and every remaining allegation of Paragraph 26.

27. With respect to Paragraph 27 of the Complaint, denies each and every allegation of said paragraph.

28. With respect to Paragraph 28 of the Complaint, denies each and every allegation of said paragraph.

- 9 -

SECOND DEFENSE

The complaint fails to state a claim upon which relief can be granted.

THIRD DEFENSE

Any claims stated in the Complaint which are based on the matters complained of in the action instituted by the United States referred to in paragraph 18 of the complaint and which accrued prior to June 29, 1956 are barred by the provisions of Section 5 (b) of the Clayton Act, 69 Stat. 283 (1955), 15 U.S.C.A. §16(b). All other claims stated in the complaint which accured more than four years prior to the commencement of this action are barred by the provisions of §4B of the Clayton Act, 69 Stat. 283 (1955), 15 U.S.C.A. §15b.

JURY DEMAND

Please take notice that the defendant General Electric Company demands trial by jury of all issues in this action.

John T. Chadwell

Richard M. Keck
Attorneys for General Electric Company

Of Counsel:

CHADWELL, KECK, KAYSER
RUGGLES & MC LAREN
135 South LaSalle Street
Chicago 3, Illinois
RAndolph 6-2545

APPENDIX 28

THE CODE OF THE LAWS OF THE UNITED STATES OF AMERICA

TITLE 15

COMMERCE AND TRADE

§ 1. *Trusts, etc., in restraint of trade illegal; exception of resale price agreements; penalty*

Every contract, combination in the form of trust or otherwise, or conspiracy, in restraint of trade or commerce among the several States, or with foreign nations, is declared to be illegal: *Provided,* That nothing contained in sections 1–7 of this title shall render illegal, contracts or agreements prescribing minimum prices for the resale of a commodity which bears, or the label or container of which bears, the trademark, brand, or name of the producer or distributor of such commodity and which is in free and open competition with commodities of the same general class produced or distributed by others, when contracts or agreements of that description are lawful as applied to intrastate transactions, under any statute, law, or public policy now or hereafter in effect in any State, Territory, or the District of Columbia in which such resale is to be made, or to which the commodity is to be transported for such resale, and the making of such contracts or agreements shall not be an unfair method of competition under section 45 of this title: *Provided further,* That the preceding proviso shall not make lawful any contract or agreement, providing for the establishment or maintenance of minimum resale prices on any commodity herein involved, between manufacturers, or between producers, or between wholesalers, or between brokers, or between factors, or between retailers, or between persons, firms, or corporations in competition with each other. Every person who shall make any contract or engage in any combination or conspiracy declared by sections 1–7 of this title to be illegal shall be deemed guilty of a misdemeanor, and, on conviction thereof, shall be punished by fine not exceeding fifty thousand dollars, or by imprisonment not exceeding one year, or by both said punishments, in the discretion of the court. July 2, 1890, c. 647, § 1, 26 Stat. 209; Aug. 17, 1937, c. 690, Title VIII, 50 Stat. 693; July 7, 1955, c. 281, 69 Stat. 282.

§ 2. *Monopolizing trade a misdemeanor; penalty*

Every person who shall monopolize, or attempt to monopolize, or combine or conspire with any other person or persons, to monopolize any part of the trade or commerce among the several States, or with foreign nations, shall be deemed guilty of a misdemeanor, and, on conviction thereof, shall be punished by fine not exceeding fifty thousand dollars, or by imprisonment not exceeding one year, or by both said punishments, in the discretion of the court. July 2, 1890, c. 647, § 2, 26 Stat. 209; July 7, 1955, c. 281, 69 Stat. 282.

§ 7. *"Person" defined*

The word "person", or "persons", wherever used in sections 1–7 of this title shall be deemed to include corporations and associations existing under or authorized by the laws of either the United States, the laws of any of the Territories, the laws of any State, or the laws of any foreign country. July 2, 1890, c. 647, § 8, 26 Stat. 210.

§ 12. *Words defined*

"Antitrust laws," as used herein, includes the Act entitled "An Act to protect trade and commerce against unlawful restraints and monopolies," approved July second, eighteen hundred and ninety; sections seventy-three to seventy-seven, inclusive, of an Act entitled "An Act to reduce taxation, to provide revenue for the Government, and for other purposes," of August twenty-seventh, eighteen hundred and ninety-four; an Act entitled "An Act to amend sections seventy-three and seventy-six of the Act of August twenty-seventh, eighteen hundred and ninety-four, entitled 'An Act to reduce taxation, to provide revenue for the Government, and for other purposes,'" approved February twelfth, nineteen hundred and thirteen; and also this Act.

"Commerce," as used herein, means trade or commerce among the several States and with foreign nations, or between the District of Columbia or any Territory of the United States and any State, Territory, or foreign nation, or between any insular possessions or other places under the jurisdiction of the United States, or between any such possession or place and any State or Territory of the United States or the District of Columbia or any foreign nation, or within the District of Columbia or any Territory or any insular possession or other place under the jurisdiction of the United States: *Provided,* That nothing in this Act contained shall apply to the Philippine Islands.

The word "person" or "persons" wherever used in this Act shall be deemed to include corporations and associations existing under or authorized by the laws of either the United States, the laws of any of the Territories, the laws of any State, or the laws of any foreign country. Oct. 15, 1914, c. 323, § 1, 38 Stat. 730.

§ 15. *Suits by persons injured; amount of recovery*

Any person who shall be injured in his business or property by reason of anything forbidden in the antitrust laws may sue therefor in any district court of the United States in the district in which the defendant resides or is found or has an agent, without respect to the amount in controversy, and shall recover threefold the damages by him sustained, and the cost of suit, including a reasonable attorney's fee. Oct. 15, 1914, c. 323, § 4, 38 Stat. 731.

§ 15a. *Suits by United States; amount of recovery*

Whenever the United States is hereafter injured in its business or property by reason of anything forbidden in the antitrust laws it may sue therefor in the United States district court for the district in which the defendant resides or is found or has an agent, without respect to the amount in controversy, and shall recover actual damages by it sustained and the cost of suit. Oct. 15, 1914, c. 323, § 4A, as added July 7, 1955, c. 283, § 1, 69 Stat. 282.

§ 15b. *Limitation of actions*

Any action to enforce any cause of action under sections 15 or 15a of this title shall be forever barred unless commenced within four years after the cause of action accrued. No cause of action barred under existing law on the effective date of this section and sections 15a and 16 of this title shall be revived by said sections. Oct. 15, 1914, c. 323, § 4B, as added July 7, 1955, c. 283, § 1, 69 Stat. 283.

§ 16. *Judgment in favor of Government as evidence; suspension of limitations*

(a) A final judgment or decree heretofore or hereafter rendered in any civil or criminal proceeding brought by or on behalf of the United States under the antitrust laws to the effect that a defendant has violated said laws shall be prima facie evidence against such defendant in any action or proceeding brought by any other party against such defendant under said laws or by the United States under section 15a of this title, as to all matters respecting which said judgment or decree would be an estoppel as between the parties thereto: *Provided,* That this section shall not apply to consent judgments or decrees entered before any testimony has been taken or to judgments or decrees entered in actions under section 15a of this title.

(b) Whenever any civil or criminal proceeding is instituted by the United States to prevent, restrain, or punish violations of any of the antitrust laws, but not including an action under section 15a of this title, the running of the statute of limitations in respect of every private right of action arising under said laws and based in whole or in part on any matter complained of in said proceeding shall be suspended during the pendency thereof and for one year thereafter: *Provided, however,* That whenever the running of the statute of limitations in respect of a cause of action arising under section 15 of this title is suspended hereunder, any action to enforce such cause of action shall be forever barred unless commenced either within the period of suspension or within four years after the cause of action accrued. Oct. 15, 1914, c. 323, § 5, 38 Stat. 731; July 7, 1955, c. 283, § 2, 69 Stat. 283.

§ 22. *District in which to sue corporation*

Any suit, action, or proceeding under the antitrust laws against a corporation may be brought not only in the judicial district whereof it is an inhabitant, but also in any district wherein it may be found or transacts business; and all process in such cases may be served in the district of which it is an inhabitant, or wherever it may be found. Oct. 15, 1914, c. 323, § 12, 38 Stat. 736.

§ 24. *Liability of directors and agents of corporation*

Whenever a corporation shall violate any of the penal provisions of the antitrust laws, such violation shall be deemed to be also that of the individual directors, officers, or agents of such corporation who shall have authorized, ordered, or done any of the acts constituting in whole or in part such violation, and such violation shall be deemed a misdemeanor, and upon conviction therefor of any such director, officer, or agent he shall be punished by a fine of not exceeding $5,000 or by imprisonment for not exceeding one year, or by both, in the discretion of the court. Oct. 15, 1914, c. 323, § 14, 38 Stat. 736.

[The July 2, 1890 Act is commonly referred to as the "Sherman Act." The October 15, 1914 Act is commonly referred to as the "Clayton Act."]

RULES OF CIVIL PROCEDURE FOR THE UNITED STATES DISTRICT COURTS

V. Depositions and Discovery

Rule 26. Depositions Pending Action.

(a) *When Depositions May Be Taken.* Any party may take the testimony of any person, including a party, by deposition upon oral examination or written interrogatories for the purpose of discovery or for use as evidence in the action or for both purposes. After commencement of the action the deposition may be taken without leave of court, except that leave, granted with or without notice, must be obtained if notice of the taking is served by the plaintiff within 20 days after commencement of the action. The attendance of witnesses may be compelled by the use of subpoena as provided in Rule 45. Depositions shall be taken only in accordance with these rules, except that in admiralty and maritime claims within the meaning of Rule 9 (h) depositions may also be taken under and used in accordance with sections 863, 864, and 865 of the Revised Statutes (see note preceding 28 U.S.C. § 1781). The deposition of a person confined in prison may be taken only by leave of court on such terms as the court prescribes.

(b) *Scope of Examination.* Unless otherwise ordered by the court as provided by Rule 30 (b) or (d), the deponent may be examined regarding any matter, not privileged, which is relevant to the subject matter involved in the pending action, whether it relates to the claim or defense of the examining party or to the claim or defense of any other party, including the existence, description, nature, custody, condition and location of any books, documents, or other tangible things and the identity and location of persons having knowledge of relevant facts. It is not ground for objection that the testimony will be inadmissible at the trial if the testimony sought appears reasonably calculated to lead to the discovery of admissible evidence.

(c) *Examination and Cross-Examination.* Examination and cross-examination of deponents may proceed as permitted at the trial under the provisions of Rule 43 (b).

(d) *Use of Depositions.* At the trial or upon the hearing of a motion or an interlocutory proceeding, any part or all of a deposition, so far as admissible under the rules of evidence, may be used against any party who was present or represented at the taking of the deposition or who had due notice thereof, in accordance with any one of the following provisions:

(1) Any deposition may be used by any party for the purpose of contradicting or impeaching the testimony of deponent as a witness.

(2) The deposition of a party or of any one who at the time of taking the deposition was an officer, director, or managing agent of a public or

private corporation, partnership, or association which is a party may be used by an adverse party for any purpose.

(3) The deposition of a witness, whether or not a party, may be used by any party for any purpose if the court finds: 1, that the witness is dead; or 2, that the witness is at a greater distance than 100 miles from the place of trial or hearing, or is out of the United States, unless it appears that the absence of the witness was procured by the party offering the deposition; or 3, that the witness is unable to attend or testify because of age, sickness, infirmity, or imprisonment; or 4, that the party offering the deposition has been unable to procure the attendance of the witness by subpoena; or 5, upon application and notice, that such exceptional circumstances exist as to make it desirable, in the interest of justice and with due regard to the importance of presenting the testimony of witnesses orally in open court, to allow the deposition to be used.

(4) If only part of a deposition is offered in evidence by a party, an adverse party may require him to introduce all of it which is relevant to the part introduced, and any party may introduce any other parts.

Substitution of parties does not affect the right to use depositions previously taken; and, when an action in any court of the United States or of any state has been dismissed and another action involving the same subject matter is afterward brought between the same parties or their representatives or successors in interest, all depositions lawfully taken and duly filed in the former action may be used in the latter as if originally taken therefor.

(e) *Objections to Admissibility.* Subject to the provisions of Rules 28(b) and 32(c), objection may be made at the trial or hearing to receiving in evidence any deposition or part thereof for any reason which would require the exclusion of the evidence if the witness were then present and testifying. As amended Jan. 21, 1963, eff. July 1, 1963; Feb. 28, 1966, eff. July 1, 1966.

(f) *Effect of Taking or Using Depositions.* A party shall not be deemed to make a person his own witness for any purpose by taking his deposition. The introduction in evidence of the deposition or any part thereof for any purpose other than that of contradicting or impeaching the deponent makes the deponent the witness of the party introducing the deposition, but this shall not apply to the use by an adverse party of a deposition as described in paragraph (2) of subdivision (d) of this rule. At the trial or hearing any party may rebut any relevant evidence contained in a deposition whether introduced by him or by any other party.

Rule 30. Depositions Upon Oral Examination.

(a) *Notice of Examination: Time and Place.* A party desiring to take the deposition of any person upon oral examination shall give reasonable notice in writing to every other party to the action. The notice shall state the time and place for taking the deposition and the name and address of each person to be examined, if known, and, if the name is not known, a general description sufficient to identify him or the particular class or group to which he belongs. On motion of any party upon whom the notice is served, the court may for cause shown enlarge or shorten the time.

(b) *Orders for the Protection of Parties and Deponents.* After notice is served for taking a deposition by oral examination, upon motion seasonably made by any party or by the person to be examined and upon notice and for good cause shown, the court in which the action is pending may make an order that the deposition shall not be taken, or that it may be taken only at some designated place other than that stated in the notice, or that it may be taken only on written interrogatories, or that certain matters shall not be inquired into, or that the scope of the examination shall be limited to certain matters, or that the examination shall be held with no one present except the parties to the action and their officers or counsel, or that after being sealed the deposition shall be opened only by order of the court, or that secret processes, developments, or research need not be disclosed, or that the parties shall simultaneously file specified documents or information enclosed in sealed envelopes to be opened as directed by the court; or the court may make any other order which justice requires to protect the party or witness from annoyance, embarrassment, or oppression.

(c) *Record of Examination; Oath; Objections.* The officer before whom the deposition is to be taken shall put the witness on oath and shall personally, or by some one acting under his direction and in his presence, record the testimony of the witness. The testimony shall be taken stenographically and transcribed unless the parties agree otherwise. All objections made at the time of the examination to the qualifications of the officer taking the deposition, or to the manner of taking it, or to the evidence presented, or to the conduct of any party, and any other objection to the proceedings, shall be noted by the officer upon the deposition. Evidence objected to shall be taken subject to the objections. In lieu of participating in the oral examination, parties served with notice of taking a deposition may transmit written interrogatories to the officer, who shall propound them to the witness and record the answers verbatim.

(d) *Motion to Terminate or Limit Examination.* At any time during the taking of the deposition, on motion of any party or of the deponent and upon a showing that the examination is being conducted in bad faith or in such manner as unreasonably to annoy, embarrass, or oppress the deponent or party, the court in which the action is pending or the court in the district where the deposition is being taken may order the officer conducting the examination to cease forthwith from taking the deposition, or may limit the scope and manner of the taking of the deposition as provided in subdivision (b). If the order made terminates the examination, it shall be resumed thereafter only upon the order of the court in which the action is pending. Upon demand of the objecting party or deponent, the taking of the deposition shall be suspended for the time necessary to make a motion for an order. In granting or refusing such order the court may impose upon either party or upon the witness the requirement to pay such costs or expenses as the court may deem reasonable.

(e) *Submission to Witness; Changes; Signing.* When the testimony is fully transcribed the deposition shall be submitted to the witness for examination and shall be read to or by him, unless such examination and reading are waived by the witness and by the parties. Any changes in form or substance which the witness desires to make shall be entered upon the deposition by the officer with a statement of the reasons given by the witness for making them. The deposition shall then be signed by the witness, unless the parties by stipulation waive the signing, or the witness is ill or cannot be found or refuses to sign. If the deposition is not signed by the witness, the officer shall sign it and state on the record the fact of the waiver or of the illness or absence of the witness or the fact of the refusal to sign together with the reason, if any, given therefor; and the deposition may then be used as fully as though signed, unless on a motion to suppress under Rule 32 (d) the court holds that the reasons given for the refusal to sign require rejection of the deposition in whole or in part.

(f) *Certification and Filing by Officer; Copies; Notice of Filing.*

(1) The officer shall certify on the deposition that the witness was duly sworn by him and that the deposition is a true record of the testimony given by the witness. He shall then securely seal the deposition in an envelope indorsed with the title of the action and marked "Deposition of (here insert name of witness)" and shall promptly file it with the court in which the action is pending or send it by registered or certified mail to the clerk thereof for filing.

(2) Upon payment of reasonable charges therefor, the officer shall furnish a copy of the deposition to any party or to the deponent.

(3) The party taking the deposition shall give prompt notice of its filing to all other parties.

(g) *Failure to Attend or to Serve Subpoena; Expenses.*

(1) If the party giving the notice of the taking of a deposition fails to attend and proceed therewith and another party attends in person or by attorney pursuant to the notice, the court may order the party giving the notice to pay to such other party the amount of the reasonable expenses incurred by him and his attorney in so attending, including reasonable attorney's fees.

(2) If the party giving the notice of the taking of a deposition of a witness fails to serve a subpoena upon him and the witness because of such failure does not attend, and if another party attends in person or by attorney because he expects the deposition of that witness to be taken, the court may order the party giving the notice to pay to such other party the amount of the reasonable expenses incurred by him and his attorney in so attending, including reasonable attorney's fees.

RULE 31. DEPOSITIONS OF WITNESSES UPON WRITTEN INTERROGATORIES.

(a) *Serving Interrogatories; Notice.* A party desiring to take the deposition of any person upon written interrogatories shall serve them upon every other party with a notice stating the name and address of the person who is to answer them and the name or descriptive title and address of the officer before whom the deposition is to be taken. Within 10 days thereafter a party so served may serve cross interrogatories upon the party proposing to take the deposition. Within 5 days thereafter the latter may serve redirect interrogatories upon a party who has served cross interrogatories. Within 3 days after being served with redirect interrogatories, a party may serve recross interrogatories upon the party proposing to take the deposition.

(b) *Officer to Take Responses and Prepare Record.* A copy of the notice and copies of all interrogatories served shall be delivered by the party taking the deposition to the officer designated in the notice, who shall proceed promptly, in the manner provided by Rule 30 (c), (e), and (f), to take the testimony of the witness in response to the interrogatories and to prepare, certify, and file or mail the deposition, attaching thereto the copy of the notice and the interrogatories received by him.

(c) *Notice of Filing.* When the deposition is filed the party taking it shall promptly give notice thereof to all other parties.

(d) *Orders for the Protection of Parties and Deponents.* After the service of interrogatories and prior to the taking of the testimony of the deponent, the court in which the action is pending, on motion promptly made by a party or a deponent, upon notice and good cause shown, may make any order specified in Rule 30 which is appropriate and just or an order that the deposition shall not be taken before the officer designated in the notice or that it shall not be taken except upon oral examination.

RULE 32. EFFECT OF ERRORS AND IRREGULARITIES IN DEPOSITIONS.

(a) *As to Notice.* All errors and irregularities in the notice for taking a deposition are waived unless written objection is promptly served upon the party giving the notice.

(b) *As to Disqualification of Officer.* Objection to taking a deposition because of disqualification of the officer before whom it is to be taken is waived unless made before the taking of the deposition begins or as soon thereafter as the disqualification becomes known or could be discovered with reasonable diligence.

(c) *As to Taking of Deposition.*

(1) Objections to the competency of a witness or to the competency, relevancy, or materiality of testimony are not waived by failure to make them before or during the taking of the deposition, unless the ground of the objection is one which might have been obviated or removed if presented at that time.

(2) Errors and irregularities occurring at the oral examination in the manner of taking the deposition, in the form of the questions or answers, in the oath or affirmation, or in the conduct of parties and errors of any kind which might be obviated, removed, or cured if promptly presented, are waived unless seasonable objection thereto is made at the taking of the deposition.

(3) Objections to the form of written interrogatories submitted under Rule 31 are waived unless served in writing upon the party propounding them within the time allowed for serving the succeeding cross or other interrogatories and within 3 days after service of the last interrogatories authorized.

(d) *As to Completion and Return of Deposition.* Errors and irregularities in the manner in which the testimony is transcribed or the deposition is prepared, signed, certified, sealed, indorsed, transmitted, filed, or otherwise dealt with by the officer under Rules 30 and 31 are waived unless a motion to suppress the deposition or some part thereof is made with reasonable promptness after such defect is, or with due diligence might have been ascertained.

RULE 33. INTERROGATORIES TO PARTIES. Any party may serve upon any adverse party written interrogatories to be answered by the party served or, if the party served is a public or private corporation or a partnership or association, by any officer or agent, who shall furnish such information as is available to the party. Interrogatories may be served after commencement of the action and without leave of court, except that, if service is made by the plaintiff within 10 days after such commencement, leave of court granted with or without notice must first be obtained. The interrogatories shall be answered separately and fully in writing under oath. The answers shall be signed by the person making them; and the party upon whom the interrogatories have been served shall serve a copy of the answers on the party submitting the interrogatories within 15 days after the service of the interrogatories, unless the court, on motion and notice and for good cause shown, enlarges or shortens the time. Within 10 days after service of interrogatories a party may serve written objections thereto together with a notice of hearing the objections at the earliest practicable time. Answers to interrogatories to which objection is made shall be deferred until the objections are determined.

Interrogatories may relate to any matters which can be inquired into under Rule 26 (b), and the answers may be used to the same extent as provided in Rule 26 (d) for the use of the deposition of a party. Interrogatories may be served after a deposition has been taken, and a deposition may be sought after interrogatories have been answered, but the court, on motion of the deponent or the party interrogated, may make such protective order as justice may require. The number of interrogatories or of sets of interrogatories to be served is not limited except as justice requires to protect the party from annoyance, expense, embarrassment, or oppression. The provisions of Rule 30 (b) are applicable for the protection of the party from whom answers to interrogatories are sought under this rule.

RULE 34. DISCOVERY AND PRODUCTION OF DOCUMENTS AND THINGS FOR INSPECTION, COPYING, OR PHOTOGRAPHING. Upon motion of any party showing good cause therefor and upon notice to all other parties, and subject to the provisions of Rule 30 (b), the court in which an action is pending may (1) order any party to produce and permit the inspection and copying or photographing, by or on behalf of the moving party, of any designated documents, papers, books, accounts, letters, photographs, objects, or tangible things, not privileged, which constitute or contain evidence relating to any of the matters within the scope of the examination permitted by Rule 26 (b) and which are in his possession, custody, or control; or (2) order any party to permit entry upon designated land or other property in his possession or control for the purpose of inspecting, measuring, surveying, or photographing the property or any designated object or operation thereon within the scope of the examination permitted by Rule 26 (b). The order shall specify the time, place, and manner of making the inspection and taking the copies and photographs and may prescribe such terms and conditions as are just.

RULE 35. PHYSICAL AND MENTAL EXAMINATION OF PERSONS.

(a) *Order for Examination.* In an action in which the mental or physical condition of a party is in controversy, the court in which the action is pending may order him to submit to a physical or mental examination by a physician. The order may be made only on motion for good cause shown and upon notice to the party to be examined and to all other parties and shall specify the time, place, manner, conditions, and scope of the examination and the person or persons by whom it is to be made.

(b) *Report of Findings.*

(1) If requested by the person examined, the party causing the examination to be made shall deliver to him a copy of a detailed written report of the examining physician setting out his findings and conclusions. After such request and delivery the party causing the examination to be made shall be entitled upon request to receive from the party examined a like report of any examination, previously or thereafter made, of the same mental or physical condition. If the party examined refuses to deliver such report the court on motion and notice may make an order requiring delivery on such terms as are just, and if a physician fails or refuses to make such a report the court may exclude his testimony if offered at the trial.

(2) By requesting and obtaining a report of the examination so ordered or by taking the deposition of the examiner, the party examined waives any privilege he may have in that action or any other involving the same controversy, regarding the testimony of every other person who

has examined or may thereafter examine him in respect of the same mental or physical condition.

RULE 36. ADMISSION OF FACTS AND OF GENUINENESS OF DOCUMENTS.

(a) *Request for Admissions.* After commencement of an action a party may serve upon any other party a written request for the admission by the latter of the genuineness of any relevant documents described in and exhibited with the request or of the truth of any relevant matters of fact set forth in the request. If a plaintiff desires to serve a request within 10 days after commencement of the action leave of court, granted with or without notice, must be obtained. Copies of the documents shall be served with the request unless copies have already been furnished. Each of the matters of which an admission is requested shall be deemed admitted unless, within a period designated in the request, not less than 10 days after service thereof or within such shorter or longer time as the court may allow on motion and notice, the party to whom the request is directed serves upon the party requesting the admission either (1) a sworn statement denying specifically the matters of which an admission is requested or setting forth in detail the reasons why he cannot truthfully admit or deny those matters or (2) written objections on the ground that some or all of the requested admissions are privileged or irrelevant or that the request is otherwise improper in whole or in part, together with a notice of hearing the objections at the earliest practicable time. If written objections to a part of the request are made, the remainder of the request shall be answered within the period designated in the request. A denial shall fairly meet the substance of the requested admission, and when good faith requires that a party deny only a part or a qualification of a matter of which an admission is requested, he shall specify so much of it as is true and deny only the remainder.

(b) *Effect of Admission.* Any admission made by a party pursuant to such request is for the purpose of the pending action only and neither constitutes an admission by him for any other purpose nor may be used against him in any other proceeding.

RULE 37. REFUSAL TO MAKE DISCOVERY: CONSEQUENCES.

(a) *Refusal to Answer.* If a party or other deponent refuses to answer any question propounded upon oral examination, the examination shall be completed on other matters or adjourned, as the proponent of the question may prefer. Thereafter, on reasonable notice to all persons affected thereby, he may apply to the court in the district where the deposition is taken for an order compelling an answer. Upon the refusal of a deponent to answer any interrogatory submitted under Rule 31 or upon the refusal of a party to answer any interrogatory submitted under Rule 33 the proponent of the question may on like notice make like application for such an order. If the motion is granted and if the court finds that the refusal was without substantial justification the court shall require the refusing party or deponent and the party or attorney advising the refusal or either of them to pay to the examining party the amount of the reasonable expenses incurred in obtaining the order, including reasonable attorney's fees. If the motion is denied and if the court finds that the motion was made without substantial justification, the court shall require the examining party or the attorney advising the motion or both of them to pay to the refusing party or witness the amount of the reasonable expenses incurred in opposing the motion, including reasonable attorney's fees.

(b) *Failure to Comply With Order.*

(1) *Contempt.* If a party or other witness refuses to be sworn or refuses to answer any question after being directed to do so by the court in the district in which the deposition is being taken, the refusal may be considered a contempt of that court.

(2) *Other Consequences.* If any party or any officer or managing agent of a party refuses to obey an order made under subdivision (a) of this rule requiring him to answer designated questions, or an order made under Rule 34 to produce any document or other thing for inspection, copying, or photographing or to permit it to be done, or to permit entry upon land or other property, or an order made under Rule 35 requiring him to submit to a physical or mental examination, the court may make such orders in regard to the refusal as are just, and among others the following:

(i) An order that the matters regarding which the questions were asked, or the character or description of the thing or land, or the contents of the paper, or the physical or mental condition of the party, or any other designated facts shall be taken to be established for the purposes of the action in accordance with the claim of the party obtaining the order;

(ii) An order refusing to allow the disobedient party to support or oppose designated claims or defenses, or prohibiting him from introducing in evidence designated documents or things or items of testimony, or from introducing evidence of physical or mental condition;

(iii) An order striking out pleadings or parts thereof, or staying further proceedings until the order is obeyed, or dismissing the action or proceeding or any part thereof, or rendering a judgment by default against the disobedient party;

(iv) In lieu of any of the foregoing orders or in addition thereto, an order directing the arrest of any party or agent of a party for disobeying any of such orders except an order to submit to a physical or mental examination.

(c) *Expenses on Refusal to Admit.* If a party, after being served with a request under Rule 36 to admit the genuineness of any documents of the truth of any matters of fact, serves a sworn denial thereof and if the party requesting the admissions thereafter proves the genuineness of any such document or the truth of any such matter of fact, he may apply to the court for an order requiring the other party to pay him the reasonable expenses incurred in making such proof, including reasonable attorney's fees. Unless the court finds that there were good reasons for the denial or that the admissions sought were of no substantial importance, the order shall be made.

(d) *Failure of Party to Attend or Serve Answers.* If a party or an officer or managing agent of a party wilfully fails to appear before the officer who is to take his deposition, after being served with a proper notice, or fails to serve answers to interrogatories submitted under Rule 33, after proper service of such interrogatories, the court on motion and notice may strike out all or any part of any pleading of that party, or dismiss the action or proceeding or any part thereof, or enter a judgment by default against that party.

Index